HANCOCK ON HANCOCK

Praise for *Hancock on Hancock*

"John Hancock is a great director in both theater and film. The best Shakespeare productions I saw in my life were directed by Peter Brook and by John. His movie *Bang the Drum Slowly* is the best baseball movie ever made and a near-perfect film. John did great work and should have been asked—should have been begged—to do more. In *Hancock on Hancock*, John talks through his life. I've spent many wonderful evenings listening to John talk about art. This book is a chance for you to listen to John, too – a great artist talking over film and theater in the last six decades. No regrets, no gripes, just the stories. You'll love it!"

– **Donald E. Graham**
Former publisher of *The Washington Post*
and member of the Pulitzer Prize board
between 2001 and 2010

"John Hancock's *Let's Scare Jessica to Death* is my favorite horror film and I'm delighted that his entire career in the cinema, theater and TV is now the subject of an in-depth study … it's a rare book about the entertainment industry that's honest about the many films that don't get made, or finished, or are finished by others—Hancock has had films taken away from him, and has come in to finish films taken away from other directors—as well as fascinating about the Hancock projects brought undiluted to fruition."

– **Kim Newman**
Author of *Nightmare Movies: A critical history
of the horror film (1968-1988)*, and critic
for *Sight and Sound* and *Empire*

"*Hancock on Hancock* bears witness to a director's singular struggle to grow and to claim his art within the shifting sands of American entertainment. Between the lines of this intelligent, candid account of a unique career, Hancock's forthright voice—full of grit and wit—rings as true as the big-hearted guy himself."

– **John Lahr**
Author of *Prick Up Your Ears* and
Tennessee Williams: Mad Pilgrimage of the Flesh;
former long-serving Senior Drama Critic of
The New Yorker

HANCOCK ON HANCOCK

By Michael Doyle

BearManor Media
2018

Hancock On Hancock

© 2018 Michael Doyle

All rights reserved.

No portion of this publication may be reproduced, stored, and/or copied electronically (except for academic use as a source), nor transmitted in any form or by any means without the prior written permission of the publisher and/or author.

Published in the United States of America by:

BearManor Media
P. O. Box 71426
Albany, GA 31708

BearManorMedia.com

Printed in the United States.

Typesetting and layout by John Teehan

ISBN—978-1-62933-243-7

This book is dedicated with illimitable love and gratitude to two wonderful wives and mothers: Dorothy Tristan and Siân Doyle

John Hancock on the set of *The Looking Glass*, 2013.

Contents

Acknowledgments ix

Foreword by John Lahr xi

1. Youth (1939-1961) 1
2. Theater (1962-2009) 29
3. *Sticky My Fingers, Fleet My Feet* (1970) 87
4. *Let's Scare Jessica to Death* (1971) 109
5. *Bang the Drum Slowly* (1973) 143
6. *Baby Blue Marine* (1976) 179
7. *Jaws 2* (1977) 229
8. *California Dreaming* (1979) 277
9. *Wolfen* (1981) 309
10. Television (1985-1999) 347
11. *The Twilight Zone* (1985-1986) 385

12.	*8 Million Ways to Die* (1986)	423
13.	*Weeds* (1987)	439
14.	*Steal the Sky* (1988)	509
15.	*Prancer* (1989)	541
16.	*A Piece of Eden* (2000)	577
17.	*Suspended Animation* (2003)	615
18.	*The Looking Glass* (2015)	649
19.	Future Projects	683
	Credits	719
	Bibliography	741
	About the Author	745
	Index	747

Acknowledgments

IT IS ONLY APPROPRIATE that the first words of thanks be extended to John Hancock, who generously submitted himself over a span of five years to the interviews that comprise this volume. Without his unflagging support, good humor and searing honesty, the experience of writing *Hancock on Hancock* would not have been nearly half as enjoyable and enlightening, nor the finished result quite as penetrating.

The first stand alone interview was conducted on September 29, 2012, the subjects of our discussion being the making of *Let's Scare Jessica to Death* and the unmaking of *Jaws 2*. Excerpts from this lengthy exchange were published in the December 2016 issue of *Rue Morgue*, which featured a cover story to mark the forty-fifth anniversary of *Jessica's* release. The bulk of the interviews for the book were carried out by telephone over an intensive four month period between June and October 2015, when Hancock was awaiting the release of *The Looking Glass*. During the transcription and editing of these conversations, Hancock graciously subjected himself to further questioning at various times between June 2016 and September 2017, verifying names, dates and other assorted facts, as well as imparting supplementary details and comments to his already exhaustive reminiscences.

In addition the author would like to express his gratitude to John Lahr for providing his engaging foreword, and to Dale Warner for his industrious efforts in digitizing photographs—all of which are derived from John Hancock's personal collection unless credited otherwise. Furthermore, I would like to convey my appreciation to the following people who facilitated me both directly and indirectly in the creation of *Hancock on Hancock*, either by procuring valuable images, contacts and research materials on my behalf or simply by offering information, advice and encouragement: Dorothy Tristan, Bill Badalato, Andrew Tallackson,

Bob Wellinski, Ben Ohmart, Yoram Ben-Ami, Harry Musselwhite, Jason Jolliff, Michael Wadleigh, Rupert Hitzig, Daniel Pugh, Les Pugh, Dave Alexander and Rob Lynch.

Finally, I am indebted to my wife, Siân, who first suggested that I write this book, and my children Poppy and Milo. Each of them suffered and sacrificed through its realization with unswerving patience and love. I only hope that they can somehow share in the sense of fulfillment I feel, and agree that the endeavor was worth it.

Michael Doyle
September 19, 2017

A note to readers: All of John Hancock's comments will be presented in this typeface, except for the titles of films, plays, television shows, books and other works, which will appear in italics.

> *Conversely, the author's commentary will be presented in italics, except for the titles of films, plays, television shows, books and other works, and will be spaced apart from Hancock's words in this manner.*

Foreword
by John Lahr

HE IS "HANCOCK"; I am "Lahr." We have been friends now for fifty years.

Phosphorescent butterflies in ultra-violet light, cast out over the astounded audience by actors wielding fishing poles, brought us together. The occasion was his thrilling, raunchy 1967 Off-Broadway production of *A Midsummer Night's Dream*; and those glowing insects, intended as fairies, were an unforgettable piece of stage magic which broadcast Hancock's interpretive daring. A few weeks after my admiring review in the *Village Voice*, a note from Hancock invited me and my wife to join him and his first wife, the novelist Ann Arensberg, to lunch at their home in Sneden's Landing just across the George Washington Bridge and overlooking the tawny Hudson.

In those days, Hancock answered to the nickname "Bear"; he was a big man but the heft of his intelligence is what impressed. Hancock's energy and his curiosity were captivating. He played the violin, built furniture, tied flies, landscaped gardens, and kept an apiary. His reading was as wide-ranging as his interests. A good director is necessarily a good critic; and Hancock was forensic in his dissection of a story and its rhythms. He was some kind of *wunderkind*. By 1965, at the age of twenty-six, Hancock was running The San Francisco Actor's Workshop, the youngest ever artistic director of a major American repertory company; he had successfully re-mounted Tennessee Williams's *The Milk Train Doesn't Stop Here Any More* after its initial Broadway failure the previous year. Hancock was, as Williams wrote a decade later in *Memoirs*, "the only director who has ever suggested to me transpositions of material that were artistically effective."

Dreamers find each other. Around the time of our meeting, both of us were at a creative watershed. I was bored by reviewing; in his theater work, Hancock had also hit still water. We percolated with ambition and anxiety. Our faith in each other's talent buoyed us up and gave us heart. He asked if I had any ideas for a short film. I sent him a *New Yorker* short story, Gene Williams's "Sticky My Fingers, Fleet My Feet," about an aging touch football jock and the day he has to hang up his cleats. That was the beginning of our collaboration—an artistic conversation which has continued down the decades. There is nothing in my diary about working on the script; or shooting the film near Central Park's sailboat pond; or about Charles Durning, Marshall Efron, Tom Meehan, or myself playing the hapless linemen; there is not even a note about the film's debut at the Coronet Theatre in New York as the short preceding Woody Allen's *Bananas*. The sole entry is about the film's unexpected celebrity:

> February 22, 1971: Today I learned that *Sticky My Fingers, Fleet My Feet* has been nominated for an Academy Award!! What a riot. My only impulse is to enjoy the outrageousness of it. We have no money to take ads in the *Hollywood Reporter* and *Variety*: "Thank you New York, etc." This ruins my amateur standing since I had to take a film scenario out of the library to figure out what the format was—POV, MLS, etc....

Hollywood was suddenly on our horizon, and no joke. We had a calling card. I had an idea for a story about an autograph hound pursuing the famous around New York; to my way of thinking it was a metaphor about the critic's dilemma of living off the energy of others. *The Autograph Hound* began as a film treatment but soon morphed into a novel. I remember the exhilaration of sitting in Hancock's garden and reading chapters to him: the rumble of his endorsing laughter, his brusque canny notes which sent me immediately back to the typewriter. We were on to something. The grandiose plan was to publish the novel, sell it to the movies, and then Hancock would direct it. The novel *was* published (and dedicated to Hancock); it *was* sold to the movies; but, despite his Academy nomination, John was still too unproven for the Hollywood swamis to accept him as director. Two years later, after the success of his break-through baseball film *Bang the Drum Slowly*, which gave Robert De Niro his first major role, Hancock would have had the requisite clout; by then, however, my Hollywood ship had sunk.

For a while, in 1972 and '73, Hancock and I overlapped in Hollywood. For both of us, for different reasons, it was not a happy time. (I remember

Hancock, who is Harvard-educated, standing on his Malibu patio, distraught at having to watch his vocabulary in production meetings; a rich word horde evidently was a turn-off to movie executives). He gutted it out; I didn't. In my naiveté, I'd thought I would alternate writing novels with writing film scripts. After three drafts, two directors, a green light and then a red one, my fling with Hollywood was over. I revised my literary game plan. I left for London and the solitude of my study; Hancock stayed to embrace the hubbub and the hassle of the Hollywood merry-go-round.

By 1976, he'd divorced and re-married the actress and screenwriter Dorothy Tristan who became his collaborator. They and their cats settled high up in Las Flores Canyon in Malibu where Hancock planted vegetables on the terraced hillside and hustled his film projects. The canyon houses were rustic and picturesque; the canyon itself was wild and dangerous, some kind of metaphor for the deceptive barbarity of the film world below. I remember Dorothy sitting in her sun hat writing beside the pool—a pool in which the previous owner had killed herself—with a loaded .38 beside her typewriter. The real whirling damage to their lives came in 1977 from Universal whose swamis fired Hancock as director and Tristan as writer off *Jaws 2*, a potential gravy train that turned into a train wreck. The collapse of the film made it hard for Hancock to get the quality assignments; nonetheless he and Tristan battled back with a series of films, the best of their collaborations being the moving prison drama *Weeds*, which was released in 1987 and starred Nick Nolte.

In 1993, over three days, a forest fire raged through the canyon. Hancock stayed on the mountain as long as he could in a losing battle to save his house. Finally, with the flames reaching blow torch intensity, he had to slide down the steep slope to the safety of the Pacific Coast Highway. Six weeks later the Northbridge earthquake hit. Even that seismic shock didn't shake Hancock's resolve to stick it out. But, later, standing with Tristan in the Malibu Bank of America, the aftershock was the final straw, the defining moment in which they decided to up sticks and retreat to Hancock's family farm in LaPorte, Indiana. The move proved to be a liberation. In 1999, with his penchant for making things, Hancock made his farm into a studio—FilmAcres—where he and Tristan could continue their own independent filmmaking. Drawing on the professional actors and crews from Los Angeles, New York and Chicago, as well as utilizing the local community, FilmAcres has so far produced three features: *A Piece of Eden*, *Suspended Animation* and *The Looking Glass*.

"You have to gradually shape the tree as you want it to be," Hancock's mother once told her over-eager son about pruning their fruit trees. Hancock seems to have applied the same gardening principle to his creative life. *Hancock on Hancock* bears witness to a director's singular struggle to grow and to claim his art within the shifting sands of American entertainment. Between the lines of this intelligent, candid account of a unique career, Hancock's forthright voice—full of grit and wit—rings as true as the big-hearted guy himself.

John Lahr
September 4, 2017

John Lahr is a British-based author and playwright, and the preeminent American drama critic of his time. His works include two novels, The Autograph Hound *(1973) and* Hot to Trot *(1974), as well as eighteen books on the theater and popular culture. Among these are* Notes on a Cowardly Lion *(1969), a biography of his comedian father Bert Lahr, and* Prick Up Your Ears *(1978), his acclaimed account of the life and death of playwright Joe Orton which was made into a film in 1987. Lahr's 2014 biography* Tennessee Williams: Mad Pilgrimage of the Flesh *won five awards including the prestigious National Book Critics Circle Award. He is the first critic to win The National Arts Club Medal for Achievement in the Theatrical Arts and is a two-time winner of the George Jean Nathan Award for Dramatic Criticism, becoming its youngest ever recipient in 1968. He is also the first drama critic to win a Tony Award for co-creating the one-woman show* Elaine Stritch at Liberty *(2001). In 2013, he stepped down as Senior Drama Critic for* The New Yorker *after twenty-one years, the longest anyone has held that position in the magazine's history.*

"A man without a mask."

– Inscription on the gravestone of
English architectural critic, author and
broadcaster Ian Nairn (1930-1983)

1 Youth (1939 – 1961)

JOHN DAVID HANCOCK WAS BORN in Kansas City, Missouri, on February 12, 1939, the only child of Ralph Hancock, a professional musician, and Ella Mae Hancock, a schoolteacher. He was the largest baby in the Kansas City hospital, the first of many prizes. His family is of English, Scots-Irish and German ancestry, the Hancocks having come to America around 1700 and settled soon after in the Shenandoah Valley in Western Virginia. After farming the land, several of his descendants moved to Ohio, and then on to central Illinois at some point during the 1820s where his great-grandfather dealt in poultry. Hancock's paternal great-grandfather was David Duddleston, who owned the local brickworks and also served for a time as mayor of Stewardson, Illinois. On his mother's side, Hancock's great-grandfather, Frederick Rosenthal, had fled Europe in order to escape the draft in Germany that followed the violent uprisings of the March Revolution of 1848. After farming in Iowa for a time, this branch of the family moved to an area near Lincoln, Illinois, where Rosenthal married a Scots-Irish woman named Kerr who hailed from Bloomington, Indiana.

Both my parents were born in Illinois. My mother was born in 1909, on a farm near Lincoln, which is a small town in Logan County. It's located right in the middle of the state, amid the huge, flat plains of corn-land. It's actually in the middle of the best corn-land in the world, I might add, as the top-soil is something like fifteen feet deep. Her father owned an eighty-acre farm and grew corn and had cows, pigs, sheep and chickens.

My grandfather had been to the second grade, and his wife had been to the fourth grade, but they sent all of their six children to college and each one of them got graduate degrees. Now that I think about it, I don't think my grandparents sent them, but each kid somehow managed to go to college, working their way through, and that was a very big deal for them. That was perfectly understandable if you were a parent who had only been to the second or fourth grade. My grandfather had to leave school to work on the farm when he was only eight years-old, so his learning was severely truncated. But he instilled in his children the benefits and importance of a good education and how it could totally transform one's life.

My father was born in 1906, in Stewardson, Illinois, which like Lincoln is a small town halfway down the state. Most if not all of his family hailed from there. Shortly after my Dad arrived in the world, his parents moved from Stewardson to Chicago as this was the time of Upton Sinclair's controversial book *The Jungle*. Sinclair had exposed the scandalously harsh exploitation of immigrants and the unsanitary conditions of the Chicago meatpacking industry during the early years of the twentieth century. The reaction to *The Jungle* was immediate and caused some big political ripples. I believe Teddy Roosevelt quickly sanctioned a thorough investigation of the meat factories, which ultimately led to laws being passed and the creation of meat inspectors. In the wake of this new legislation my paternal grandfather, John Hancock, whom I am named after, was quickly trained to be a Government Meat Inspector. So, the family duly relocated to Chicago and he worked at the stockyards. My grandfather had an ice-pick—the tool of his trade—which he always carried around with him. He would routinely plunge the ice-pick into a side of beef before smelling it to see if the meat was off or it was still good.

My parents met at the University of Chicago. My mother was getting a Master's Degree and my father was still getting his Bachelor's Degree. They happened to sit next to each other at a course called "Recent Social Trends," struck up a conversation and, thankfully, the rest is history. I think they were twenty-nine and twenty-six respectively when they eventually got married. During those first few years they were together my father was working as a musician, he played the double bass and the tuba. He toured with dance bands, even back when he was in high school. It's my understanding that it took him something like six years to get through college because he always had to take time off to earn money as a musician. So, he might have been a little older than some when he got married. I mean, Dad wasn't twenty-two when he was at college, he was closer to twenty-five, and my mother was slightly younger. After leaving the University of Chicago, my mother worked as a schoolteacher and taught math and science at various Illinois schools in places like DeKalb and Rockford. My father was in the Kansas City Symphony during the symphony season and my parents lived down there for three years. I was born in one of those three years.

I came along the year World War II commenced in Europe and my memories of that conflict are few, but vivid. I remember the Battle of the Bulge, oddly enough. It was pitch black outside, I was up early listening intently to reports on the radio, and the windows were iced-up on the inside as it was the dead of winter. One of my favorite bedtime stories was my mother telling me how the war began: Hitler taking over Alsace-Lorraine, then Austria, then the Sudetenland, invading Czechoslovakia and finally Poland with Britain and France honoring their commitment to declare war. How the Germans went around the Maginot Line into the Lowlands and were cunning and brutal. It climaxed with the heroic evacuation of the trapped British Army from Dunkirk. Pearl Harbor was I guess a kind of ghastly coda. Was hope of eventual victory offered to the tired little boy before he went to sleep? I don't remember. Probably.

I also have strong recollections of the end of the war. I can remember driving into Chicago with my mother where the Outer-Drive goes along the lake and you can see the skyline to your left. Suddenly every window of every building was spewing fluttering torrents of confetti and paper, cascading down to the ground below. It was a magical sight, or it seemed that way to my six year-old eyes. I can remember turning to my mother, and saying, "What is *that*?" She said, "Japan must have surrendered." The whole world seemed to erupt into colorful celebration in that one moment and it has always stayed with me. See, I had thought most soldiers died in a war, it always seemed that way in movies, and windows in the neighborhood were filled with gold and silver stars. So, I can still recall the palpable sense of relief and joy people were feeling, including my own family as I had an uncle named John Crawford who fought during the war. My father did not serve as, aside from being married, he was a little too old. No doubt, to the profound happiness of our family, he was not drafted.

We lived in Berwyn, which is a suburb of Chicago. It's about forty minutes away from The Loop in downtown Chicago, a mere twenty minutes nowadays with the advent of better roads. Berwyn is right next to Cicero, which was the home of Al Capone. Our place was a comfortable two-storey house. My father's older sister, my beloved Aunt Gladys, and her husband, Uncle Arnold, lived on the first floor and my parents and I on the second floor, but we could all come and go as we pleased. I still drive by that house occasionally and, about twenty years ago, I stopped my car, approached the front door and asked the current owners if I could go in and take a look around. They kindly agreed to this and I was immediately struck by how small and compact the rooms were. Obviously, that can sometimes happen when you return as an adult to an environment you inhabited as a child. It was such a curious feeling being back at that house. I believe the family living there were Polish and had placed an inordinate amount of crucifixes around the house.

Back when I was growing up, our neighborhood was entirely White and largely Bohemian—more than half of the residents were from the Bohemian part of Czechoslovakia. There were no Blacks or Mexicans and people seemed ruthlessly intent on keeping it that way. In fact, there were three times in my life when Blacks tried to move into Berwyn or Cicero and on each occasion they had to bring out the tanks because of the race riots that quickly ensued. Locals reacted violently to their presence and burned their houses, that kind of thing. So, I had no Black friends as a child but our family was not racially intolerant as some others were. They were Roosevelt liberals, and my father had sat in many times in Black jazz clubs in Kansas City after the Symphony concerts. When he taught at Roosevelt University, he had an extremely talented Black student on the double bass named Ortiz Montaigne Walton whom he was fond of. Ortiz's father was a charming Pullman porter, with the vaguely Uncle Tom-ish manners that went with that, but Ortiz himself was my first experience of a Black Muslim and, at the age of nineteen, he was already talking about Elijah Muhammad and Malcolm X. Ortiz became the first African-American member of any major American symphony when he played in the Boston Symphony Orchestra, but his career was severely damaged when heroin was discovered in his hotel room. Ortiz claimed it had been planted there, but who knows, maybe he was taking heroin. I suspect the latter as I heard later he had some issues. You can also see how, in an all-White orchestra, certain individuals might want to get rid of the one Black guy. If Ortiz did indeed have a drug problem to begin with, they could have certainly taken advantage of it. But he was an interesting guy and like nobody else I knew as a kid.

The same year I was born, my parents bought a farm near LaPorte, Indiana, which is where I live now. By this time my namesake grandfather, John Hancock, had retired as a Government Meat Inspector and had a pension he was able to access. Aunt Gladys and Uncle Arnold also kicked in some of the money, and together they purchased the property. My grandparents were able to live there, but for me, Mom and Dad, the farm was a place we mostly frequented on weekends and during summers. Uncle Arnold had a good job at a steel company in Chicago and so he and Aunt Gladys were also there at weekends and during summers. As the men worked in the city, the women kind of ran the whole operation: my mother, my grandmother and my aunt. Back then, it was something of a nudist time when people were beginning to think about health and getting some sunshine on their skin. I remember my mother and my aunt embraced this rather liberating trend and would both venture outside in the nude and start thinning peaches. They would be standing there naked, knocking peaches out of a tree with a bamboo pole. The little peaches would rain down on their tits and it was quite a strange and wonderful sight to behold as a child. Our family started doing well in the fruit business and bought a second farm, and then a third, and things were going good for us.

As far as religion goes both my parents were Methodists, but they were not deeply serious about religion. I do recall that for a while we all went to church on a Sunday, but that gradually tapered off. I remember the Methodist Church of Berwyn had a banner over the altar which had huge letters that read: "Fear not for I am with you." I didn't draw much comfort from those words, but they have remained with me for some reason. What I find interesting now is the fact that I'm fond of hymns and have been since childhood. I like the melodies and still find them strangely reassuring. Another memory that has stayed with me is my being confirmed. I didn't really want to be confirmed, but I went ahead and did it anyway. It seemed that it was what certain people wanted and expected of me. Unfortunately, this meant that I had to go to the church every Saturday morning, which made me miss a television series about Custer's Last Stand that all my friends were watching. That caused me great pain and anguish at the time.

Another thing that troubled me was the minister in Berwyn. I was very put off by him. He was not very bright, and was kind of wimpy and wet, as well as utterly insincere. I don't know how you feel about religion, but I've always thought that low-life dim-wits often go into the ministry. Of course, not everyone is of that caliber and I do know some Harvard classmates who have made smart and splendid ministers. All the same, back then, in the suburbs of Chicago, the quality of the people who wanted to be clergymen was low. Even as a child I can recall looking at the guy at our church, and thinking, "Jesus, *this* guy is a minister?!" That's when I really started to question the ineffable things I was being invited to believe in. I mean, there was no evidence being presented to me of the existence of God and, coupled with the fact that I had no desire to be around a character like this, it was enough to deter me from fully embracing religion at a young age. So, I had this growing disbelief within me and would frequently ask my parents if God was real. They would both say that they believed in Him, but, despite their assertions, when I expressed my own doubts as to His existence, my father would occasionally concede, "Yeah, I know what you mean." Those are the moments you have as a kid where the veil is kind of pulled aside and you start to see the world as it really is; you understand that adults don't have all the answers and can often be as confused and bewildered as their children.

My parents' marriage was an extremely happy one except for the fact that my father drank. Despite this, I never heard my mother and father fight. Ever! When you stop and consider that fact it seems quite bizarre and possibly even unhealthy. In a way, that lack of tension and argumentation at home did not prepare me for the high levels of anger and vitriol that I would later encounter in the New York Theater Scene. I just wasn't used to seeing people screaming invectives at each other and becoming wildly confrontational. I found it very hard to deal with at first but then, after some time had passed, I managed to learn how to do it myself. I grew up in a quiet and rational household where, for the most part, the adults were consistent. I suspect that a lot of the tensions and disharmony that may have surfaced from time to time were concealed from me as a child. I don't know. I'm merely speculating here because, again, my parents had such a happy marriage.

I would describe my father as an actor to some degree. He was incredibly smart, but was a very emotional person. He had this self-defeating attitude about certain things and was prone to depressions that were brought on by alcohol. If drinking makes you morose and despondent then my father was definitely susceptible to that. The question I've asked myself from time to time is if drinking makes you feel so terrible and suicidal then *why* do it? Looking back, I was upset and concerned by my father's drinking. I should clarify that when I say my father was an actor, I mean he perhaps had a tendency to be somewhat emotionally manipulative. Well, in that regard, maybe it wasn't entirely acting. Maybe he just couldn't help himself. My father was not a strict disciplinarian and I'd often get away with stuff that I'm sure a lot of other kids would have been severely punished for. A good example would be the time I built a fire in a corner of my parents' bedroom. I made a little campfire of matches and various other flammable materials at hand, and excitedly lit them. Luckily, my mother managed to discover this and put the flames out before the fire consumed the house. My father did not react as strongly to that indiscretion as he perhaps should have, but that was him: unpredictable and vulnerable as he was.

Conversely, my mother was a very sane and steady person. She was a warm and intelligent woman, with emotional integrity and a real fidelity to herself. I loved her and I love her still. There was a calmness and sereneness to her which was fairly unwavering. I remember that when I was eight years-old, she and I were flying from Havana to Key West during the Batista time when the plane suddenly got embroiled in a terrible storm. The other passengers on the flight were terrified and I felt frightened, too. I looked at my mother, and said, "What if we die?" She then gazed down at me and calmly replied, "Well, we've had a good life." That was an extraordinary moment for me because it revealed a lot about who, and what, she was. My mother had grown up during the Depression and she had a kind of practical and fatalistic view of things. Even when it came to my father's drinking, she dealt with it by crying silent tears. She would just wish that he wouldn't drink, but she never threatened to leave him over it. She remained constant. One of my mother's strong beliefs was in steadiness, which has a lot to do with self-sameness. It's like what Erik Erikson, the famous developmental psychologist and psychoanalyst, once said: "Fidelity to your own nature." My mother had a kind of farmer's wisdom, as strange as that may sound, and she lived by it.

When she and I would discuss the other farmers who had failed around us, I'd ask, "What did they do wrong?" She would then explain that some of these farmers had planted grapes and, just three years later, had suddenly decided that they needed to plant soybeans instead. So, after changing their minds, they'd tear out the grapes and, eventually, this uncertainty and indecision led them to the swift conclusion that what they really needed to do was sell their farms. To her, that was wrong. What you had to do was make your choice and stick to it. Nowadays, you can get varieties of apples that bear in maybe four or five years but, back then in the 1940s, it took ten years for them to bear. To plant a big orchard, one from which you are not going to receive any income for eight or ten years, requires a certain sense of patience and fortitude. You had to possess the sturdiness to stick around; the desire to keep doing it for a decade without any immediate rewards. My mother had that. Here's another example: when my father died in 1981, I tried to help her keep the farm going. So, I flew back from Hollywood and did a little pruning. Now, one of the ways you start to prune is you make a huge cut on each apple tree and this is what I proceeded to do. My mother looked at what I was doing, then looked at me, and said, "You know, pruning is very much like teaching a child: you don't want to correct them all in one year. You want to do it with a plan for two or three years. It's the same thing here. You have to gradually shape the tree as you want it to be." To be able to do that took patience, and she had it in abundance.

The kinds of things I enjoyed doing as a boy were collecting butterflies, tying flies and fishing. I also hunted briefly, too, but I didn't like it. I found it distressing to watch the animals looking up at me as they were dying. It was depressing, seeing them bleed out and the lights dim in their eyes. I can still recall an upsetting episode that took place on the Eastern shore of Maryland when I shot a goose. Immediately afterwards I thought, okay, that's enough of *this*! It was the last animal I killed, and I looked for other less destructive things to do. I was a slightly overweight child but, as far as sports went, I was good at football and less good at baseball. I was known as "pus-arm" by some of the kids—not a good name—due to my inaccurate throwing. I could hit the ball and that was about it. I wasn't the most popular kid, but I always had a good friend or two and was a reasonably happy child. Having the name Hancock, my boyhood friends would call me "Handjob" or "Fistprick," or more fondly "Hanny." So, I had several interesting nicknames in my youth.

Needless to say, having to go out to the farm in Indiana every weekend removed me from certain relationships and friendships, and that sometimes got me down. I was very much alone on the farm. There were no friends, nobody my own age to play with; and I sometimes had to rely on my imagination in order to entertain myself. One wonderful thing, though, is that I grew up surrounded by six adoring adults. Aunt Gladys and Uncle Arnold had no children and so I was their little boy, too. I'd go downstairs in the morning and my aunt would say, "Let me make you some waffles and I'll put ice-cream on them." I'd then say, "That would be nice, but my mother doesn't want me to get any fatter." Aunt Gladys would then hug me and whisper, "Oh, it won't hurt you!" She filled me with sweets and the confidence I could do and be whatever I wanted: the descendent, she said, of a signer of The Declaration of Independence, and related to George Washington, and born on Lincoln's birthday. Only the last of these, I think, was true, but I was like this beloved little star at the center of these people's universe.

I attended Morton High School in Cicero, which had 5,600 students and occupied an entire city block. It was four stories and the kind of place where a kid could get lost. Because of the high level of Bohemians who attended there, for twenty-five or thirty years Morton had a prestigious orchestra with a hundred people in it. So, naturally, orchestra was a very big deal there (and so was band) and I kind of lived socially in the music department. Some of the teachers at the school were good, but some were not. As a matter of fact, of all the public schools in Chicago back then, Morton would rank firmly below the middle in terms of its success. I was a fairly accomplished student, strong at some subjects, weaker at others. For instance, I always got A's in English, Spanish and economics, but got a D in geometry. However, on the whole, my grades were good, but my parents never pushed me hard to study at school. They mostly left it to me to motivate myself.

As a child, I had certain fantasies of what I wanted to be when I grew up. One of my first ambitions was to be a concert violinist and I started having violin lessons at the age of four. I enjoyed them, but I did not enjoy practicing. I found it lonely and boring. My fundamental problem as a violinist had to do with an inability to truly commit to practicing. I mean, you need to be able to practice for four or five hours each day in order to excel and I just couldn't do that. I didn't have the dedication. My first violin teacher was an Austrian gentleman named Henry Heyza, whom I would go to once or twice a week in downtown Chicago. Then, in high school, I began studying with a guy named Miller twice a week. I'd take the train in, walk eight or nine blocks to the music lesson, and then take the train back and walk home from the station. Both Heyza and Miller were nice guys. Heyza was very charming and warm. Miller was a little drier and waspier.

I had been concertmaster at grade school, and then again at high school, before taking that same position with the Chicago Youth Orchestra. There was also a summer orchestra at Northwestern University where I was a concertmaster. My job involved being the first chair violinist and so if there were any solos I would play them. As concertmaster, you kind of lead the section and get to shake the conductor's hand. You are the person who asks the oboe-player to play the A, and everybody tunes to that. You are also the one that finally gets up after a performance and it's a signal to everybody to leave. It's things like that. Those experiences made me feel that I could possibly excel at something, but, ultimately, I did not excel enough at music. What was very upsetting for me was the summer I went to a music festival at Tanglewood: I was eighteen at the time and discovered that a thirteen year-old kid there named Bobby Notkoff was already ten times better than I was. I learned I was up against kids who were willing to try harder than me, to put in the hours of practice that were needed. That was a deeply troubling and sobering moment, so much so it made me decide to cast around for something else to do. I wanted to be able to compete better, and really enjoy whatever it was I was doing.

I decided to write a musical comedy. It was based on *Cyrano de Bergerac*. At Tanglewood, I had a met a talented and very strange kind of young genius composer whose name I can never remember. He was fourteen at the time, four years younger than me, but everybody already thought he was fabulous. I felt this kid would be a good fit to do the music and so I approached him about a possible collaboration. Unfortunately, it didn't go too well. I just couldn't get him to think a certain way. I mean, the kind of musician you met at Tanglewood was probably not a likely candidate to write a commercial Broadway score, or even an acceptable Broadway score. They were more into Schoenberg and Stravinsky than Bernstein and Sondheim. They didn't necessarily possess that very particular and easy melodic gift you need to write catchy songs. Where that young genius composer is right now, I have no idea. But the young violinist I was so envious of, Bobby Notkoff, is currently playing avant-garde jazz in Los Angeles. Anyway, despite the musical comedy dying a death, it did eventually lead me to investigate the theater as a platform for creative expression and, in turn, that led me to what it is I do now.

After my experience at Tanglewood, and my eventually going to study at Harvard the following year, I was removed from certain things: from the violin and from my father. I was then able to separate myself from music and began to reassess everything. My father wasn't upset that I didn't follow in his footsteps and pursue a career in music. He didn't want me to be a musician especially and maybe he sensed that I didn't quite have the talent to be a really good one. He thought it was a difficult profession for some people to maintain and possibly not rewarding enough when you considered all the effort that it demanded of you. He was just as happy to see me do something else. I came to understand that although my father had advised me against going into music, on a conscious level I wanted to be like him. On the other hand, I also wanted to defy him. So, it was a very strange contradiction. But at that moment I simply stopped playing the violin and the last of my waning desire for the instrument vanished.

Although music had been my first love I was crazy about movies. There was a theater four blocks away from our home, the Roxy Theatre in Berwyn, and I would go there every Saturday and see a double feature as well as cartoons and newsreels. That was a regular thing for me and I enjoyed it. For a quarter you could spend the entire afternoon looking at movies. I don't remember the first film I saw, but I do remember being taken away screaming from the theater while watching *The Wizard of Oz*. The moment when the trees suddenly started moving and reached out to seize Dorothy and her friends absolutely terrified me! Among the first films I recall seeing were animated features like *Dumbo* and *Snow White and the Seven Dwarves*, several of those early Disney classics. I saw all the pictures starring John Wayne, and most of the pictures made by John Ford. I was rather taken by the look of Ford's *The Long Voyage Home*, which was adapted from four one-act plays by Eugene O'Neill. I appreciated its execution on a technical level, particularly the remarkable photography by Gregg Tolland, but I didn't like that movie as much as I liked some of Ford's more robust pictures like *Stagecoach* and *The Searchers*. I also dearly love *How Green Was My Valley*, but I didn't actually see that movie until much later in life.

One picture I adored as a kid was Allan Dwan's *Sands of Iwo Jima*. Yes, it was an unabashed flag-waving war movie to be sure, and you look at it now and it's bursting at the seams with clichés, but the action sequences are still accomplished. When John Wayne's marine sergeant was killed by a Japanese sniper's bullet, I took that very hard. There were also some really good pictures made by William Wyler that I enjoyed in my youth without being aware the same man had made them. Then there were the films of Howard Hawks such as *The Big Sleep* and *Red River*. I remember a lot of Hawks' pictures from the Forties and Fifties, but I wasn't as conscious of him as a director back then—or of Wyler—as I was of Ford. Truly, the picture I was most desperate to see as a kid was one that was unfortunately adults only. The title was something like *American Women in a Japanese Prison Camp* and I can recall being upset that I couldn't get in to see it. As the story revolved around a female prison camp, I figured there would be assorted acts of cruelty, violence and inhumanity. These were things that my twisted little brain wanted to witness, but I was denied them! It's possible this picture was *Three Came Home*, but I don't think so. *Three Came Home* is a good picture, whereas the one I wanted to see was much more of a B movie, almost a C movie, and had more exploitation; lots of women having their blouses ripped and their breasts slapped. At least, that is what I hoped.

There were other discoveries I made. One of my cap-gun friends (I played a lot of guns as a child) mentioned "Slaughter on Tenth Avenue," I guess in reference to the mayhem we imagined we were creating in the neighborhood with our cap-guns. I asked what that was, and he said he'd just seen this great thing at the movies. So, I went to see it. It was a dance sequence in a 1948 film directed by Norman Taurog called *Words and Music*—Gene Kelly and Vera-Ellen in a tragic ballet to a great Richard Rodgers melody. It was so different than boring Busby Berkeley patterns, this was vital, sexy, colorful. It was *street* really, although we didn't know there was such a thing then. And there was something about how perfectly the feeling of the beautiful melody worked against the violent movement that I realize now, looking back, is a thing I've sometimes tried to emulate in my work. I immediately became a Gene Kelly fan and followed him through *Singing in the Rain* and with even greater enthusiasm, *Lili*. I responded more to Gene Kelly than Fred Astaire.

It wasn't until I saw Carol Reed's *The Third Man* that I first began to seriously consider what a film director was and what they did. I was about fifteen or sixteen at the time. There was something in that movie that aroused my curiosity about the whole mysterious process of filmmaking. I thought the expressionistic photography, the angles, the whole atmosphere of the post-World War II milieu of Vienna was just wonderful. I also remember that my father had seen it before me and was particularly taken with Anton Karas' zither score. He urged me to see *The Third Man* and it had such an interesting look I was suddenly conscious that there was a guiding intelligence behind movies that was called The Director. I then started looking at cinema differently and was more conscious of the artifice, of the wheels turning around, in terms of lighting, cinematography, performance, set design, props, music, how all of these things were being deployed in order to create a specific experience and presentation. If *The Third Man* had made me think about movies more profoundly, it wasn't until I saw the films of David Lean—such as *The Bridge over the River Kwai* and *Lawrence of Arabia*—that I really wanted to be a director and do it myself. I know that a lot of directors of my generation adore *Citizen Kane*, and that was the movie which really demanded that they start examining the process. But I didn't love that picture as much as some of the other films I've mentioned.

The activities we did as a family often reflected my parents' interests in the arts and so I guess I had a very cultured upbringing. When they weren't working on the farm, Mom and Dad would take me to various concerts and performances. I saw everything from the Budapest String Quartet to Segovia to Robert Frost reading his poetry, and it was all wonderful. There were a lot of visits to auditoriums in downtown Chicago or the University of Chicago to see various things. My father had the highest-paying job for a bass player in the city, which was at the NBC Orchestra, but he could play chamber music on the side. Like when the Budapest String Quartet would come and they wanted to play Schubert's *Trout Quintet*, he would play with them or with the violinist and conductor Alexander Schneider. So, there were a lot of evenings spent hearing my father perform chamber music. At home I was introduced to several other great works of music and literature—some I responded to strongly, others less so.

My own tastes and interests as a child ranged from the high-brow to the low-brow. I not only loved the movies, I was a great radio listener too. My favorite shows were *Jack Armstrong*, *The Lone Ranger*, *Tennessee Jed*, all the celebrated favorites of the age. I also liked *The Jack Benny Program*, along with everybody else it seemed. I read comic books such as *Superman*, *Donald Duck*, and *The Three Little Pigs*, and I also enjoyed *Li'l Abner*. I didn't especially like *Dick Tracy* as some other kids did. I preferred a certain comic book that was very much like the movies they make now: it was about six people from different countries that are fighting international crime and they all wear these kinds of fascist outfits. I was very taken with them and read the issues religiously. I forget the name of it now, but I would be very interested to see those comics again—if only for the sake of nostalgia. I enjoyed reading as a child and devoured certain books. When I was eight my father gave me a copy of *Hamlet*, and I must admit that I read *at* it. I didn't quite appreciate that gift until I got a little older.

Then, between eighth grade and my being a freshman, or somewhere early in high school, my father gave me a copy of James Joyce's *Ulysses*. That book soon became incredibly inspirational and important to me. I loved it dearly. What captured my imagination was the incredible Nighttown, Dublin's red light district; the hallucinatory dreamscape of it, the wildness of it, the filthiness of it. I can remember also adoring the wonderful section where Leopold Bloom returns home late at night with Stephen Dedalus in tow and they chat profoundly about various subjects. Bloom has lost his own son and takes an immediate liking to Dedalus, who offers him some respite from his loneliness. Dedalus has a difficult relationship with his own father, and Joyce makes references to other father and son stories such as the *Odyssey* and *Hamlet*, which was when I came to appreciate Shakespeare's play a little more and understand its implications. The various chapters of *Ulysses* are written in different styles, and this particular one—which is Episode 17—is written in the form of a Catholic catechism. It's so beautiful, such exquisite writing, it made me desperately want to be involved in doing something creative.

We also had a record of Siobhan McKenna reading "Molly Bloom's Soliloquy", which was the eighteenth and final episode of *Ulysses*, and presented that character's thoughts in an uninterrupted stream of consciousness. I was very taken with the dirtiness and earthiness of that passage, and also the unaffected beauty of it. I would invite friends over to my house and play that record for them because it was all about sucking dicks and urinating, that kind of thing. I was, and remain, a huge James Joyce fan and I went on to read everything he ever wrote including *Finnegan's Wake*. Well, the truth is I read *at* it, as nobody really reads *Finnegan's Wake* (although I've heard it said that a few people do). What I admired most about works like *Ulysses* and *Finnegan's Wake*, even from an early age, was Joyce's fearless experimentation; the way he was willing to push the accepted boundaries of the novel in terms of form, structure and language. It was revolutionary and freeing, as well as being hugely influential on the efforts of subsequent writers. Nothing was ever the same again after Joyce. Not for anyone and certainly not for me in terms of my own first fumbling creative ambitions. Inspired by Joyce and other writers, when I was about sixteen I started to write poetry. I had an English teacher named Mrs. Zerwer, who greatly encouraged and believed in me. As a matter of fact, she loved my poems so much she got them published. The students at Morton that were studying printing needed something to print and so Mrs. Zerwer kindly arranged for them to publish a collection of my poems. It was such a thrill to not only see my own work presented that way, but actually see my name in print. It was another small step forward in terms of my developing a creative voice.

When I was sophomore, one of the most important things that happened to me was I started dating a senior named Lillian Svec. Lillian was a beautiful blonde and the kind of student who never got anything less than a straight A. She was valedictorian of her class at Morton and was also valedictorian at Northwestern University where she later went. Meeting her was a very big deal in my life in more ways than one. Clearly, to be with an older girl was quite an achievement for me at that age, particularly one who was not only gorgeous and smart but talented. Lillian played concerto piano with the orchestra and also played the double bass, and I just fell head over heels for her, and she for me. I must have been mature for my age (I've always wanted to be older). Anyway, when Lillian went off to Northwestern, we tried to keep the relationship going. I would attend various events at Northwestern while still a high school student, but it all seemed incredibly sophisticated to me. I felt totally out of it and was dreadfully insecure about who and what I was in comparison with her chic sorority sisters. Then Lillian started going out with Joe, a Hungarian, and broke my heart. For a while I was completely lost.

One of the things I sought solace in was music. I drew comfort from listening to Richard Strauss and Gustav Mahler. Over and over again I would play Mahler's *Das Lied von der Erde* (*The Song of the Earth*) with Kathleen Ferrier singing in Bruno Walter's wonderful recording. The Chicago Symphony was performing a lot of Richard Strauss at that time with Fritz Reiner as the conductor, making fabulous recordings of it. I found myself constantly returning to that music, getting lost in it, finding consolation in it. I was enraptured by *Ein Heldenleben* and *Also Sprach Zarathustra*, too. At one point in high school, when it was slowly ground into me that I was not of the correct caliber to be a concert violinist—and after Lillian Svec went away and I was forced to go out with lesser girls—I would come home from Morton, lie down and take a nap while listening to Strauss. This was a very dark period for me. I was severely depressed and mired in introspection. Then one day my mother said to me, "I never realized how ambitious you were. I didn't know how important it was to you to be the best at something. I thought you just wanted to be happy."

> *In 1957, Hancock was convinced to apply to Harvard University in Cambridge, Massachusetts, the United States' oldest institute of higher learning, where he would study English. With his father earning a good living as a professional musician, finances would not be an insurmountable problem.*

I had originally intended to go to Northwestern, because I'd played in the orchestra there, and that was where Lillian Svec was going and perhaps I thought we could get back together. I told my parents of my intentions and my father said, "Why do you want to go to Northwestern? For the same amount of money I could send you to Harvard." I hadn't even considered Harvard as a possibility, as I don't think any more than one or two students from Morton had ever gone to an Ivy League school. But then I met with the college advisor at high school, and he agreed with my father and suggested that I apply to Harvard. I said, "Well, what happens if I don't get in? Don't I need to apply someplace else as well?" The college advisor replied rather assuredly, "You'll get in, believe me. All you have to do is just apply there." He felt confident I would make it in without any problems as I'd previously taken some tests that I had done extremely well on—a vocabulary test being one of them. So, I started to think seriously about Harvard and gradually understood that it was the best place for me to be. I guess my college boards were good enough and the admissions people sufficiently impressed that I did indeed get into Harvard and spent the next four years of my life there.

I recall that next period of my life with great fondness. I wasn't crazy about Boston as a city, but I was crazy about the people I met at Harvard. I was crazy about my classmates. I mean, there was a vast difference between the people I met there and the people I had gone to high school with. They were just much more interesting and vital and questioning. Really, I felt I learned even more from my classmates than I learned in some of the classes. I hung out with some wonderful people, who later went on to have spectacular careers in various fields. My room-mates included John Casey, who subsequently won the National Book Award for his novel *Spartina*; the composer John Harbison, who won the Pulitzer Prize for Music for his composition *The Flight into Egypt*; and Joel Henning, who became a highly successful lawyer in Chicago. Stephen Truitt was another. The grandson of "The Veep," Alben W. Barkley, he's a lawyer in Washington now and is very involved in representing prisoners at Gitmo. I was also in the same playwriting class as Deric Washbourne, who later wrote *Silent Running* and *The Deer Hunter*, and Arthur Kopit, who wrote a whole bunch of acclaimed plays such as *Indians* and *Wings*, as well as the book for the musical *Nine*.

There were a number of teachers at college that left a lasting impression on me. I remember a teacher named Bates that taught a wonderful course on Milton. My first year there, I also took a Shakespeare course with about five hundred other students that absolutely enthralled me. It was taught by Harry Levin, a celebrated academic and critic. Levin had written a wonderful book called *James Joyce: A Critical Introduction*, which I'd read before I came to Harvard. It gave me a new and better understanding of

Joyce's work, so I immediately approached Levin during his office hours and got his permission to sign up for his Shakespeare course, even though it was not supposed to be for freshmen. The first play we studied in depth was *Henry IV, Part One*, and I was particularly moved by the father/son stuff between Falstaff and Prince Hal as it echoed my relationship with my father, whom I was missing desperately. I was homesick my first year at Harvard. Even now, when I'm directing, I still think back and reflect on different things Harry Levin said during those lectures. He was wonderful at calling your attention to the ways Shakespeare does certain things in his plays—some that are rather obvious, others less so. For example, Levin pointed out that Shakespeare never has any character eavesdrop without hearing something bad being spoken about them in their absence.

There was also an associate professor named Robert Chapman, who taught Modern Drama and playwriting. He lived in the same dorm I did, Eliot House, and we ate together a lot. Chapman had co-authored an adaptation of Herman Melville's *Billy Budd* for Broadway, and had been teaching at Harvard since the early 1950s. Another incredible teacher I had—although the reading list for his classes was just a killer—was Zbigniew Brzezinski, who later served as a counselor to Lyndon B. Johnson and eventually became National Security Advisor during Jimmy Carter's presidency. He taught a course on Eastern European Communism that I found very interesting. I also took a course in Soviet Literature where you read a lot of Stalinist literature: quality stuff from the likes of Mikhail Sholokov and lesser works about, say, the making of a dam or the elimination of an American spy; also Boris Pasternak's *Doctor Zhivago* and the works of Vladimir Mayakovsky and Sergei Yesenin.

And then there was Erik Erikson, who came to teach at Harvard for about two years, and became terribly important to me. In his role as a psychologist and psychoanalyst, Erikson famously invented the concept of "identity crisis" and also formulated his eight stages of psychosocial development that a human being should go through from infancy to adulthood. I really devoured and deliberated his whole system of psychology and still think in those terms. I mean, I've often analyzed the things I'm doing in Eriksonian terms. Erikson himself looked like God! He didn't have a beard, but he had white hair and seemed to be around the same age. In 1950, a few years before I met him, he had written his influential book *Childhood and Society*, in which he introduced his ideas about the human life cycle, the series of conflicts we all face in our lives. *Childhood and Society* also contained a fascinating chapter about Hitler's childhood, which I found revelatory. Indeed, I was so taken with it I was directly inspired to later write a screenplay called *Fire Music* that dealt with Hitler's early life.

While I was at Harvard I still went to see movies all the time and would discuss them with my friends. There was a theater near Harvard Square called the Brattle Street Theatre, where they showed a lot of diverse international pictures. That place seemed to screen everything and I was exposed to European movies in a pretty big way. It was there that I discovered the cinema of Ingmar Bergman and he remains one of my favorite filmmakers. I was astounded by the craftsmanship and the savage delicacy of Bergman's work, as well the sheer scope of the existential questions he posed: questions about family, faith, sex, loneliness, despair, every kind of human emotion and desire. His films were both sensual and intellectual experiences, and they were compassionate, too. I also saw a lot of the Italian neo-realism films of Rossellini and Fellini, as well as the French New Wave films of Truffaut and Godard. This was the time when everybody who was my age in America first fell in love with those pictures. I went over and over again to see Laurence Olivier's *Henry V*. I couldn't get enough of it. I thought Olivier's acting and directing were wonderful. The picture was a feast for the senses with glorious Technicolor cinematography and William Walton's great score. *Henry V* is surely one of the best films ever derived from a play.

I should say that at this point in my life I wasn't thinking about the possibility of my making movies one day. I was entirely focused on directing for the theater. There were no courses in practical directing and acting at Harvard. Absolutely nothing was offered at that point. If you were so inclined, maybe you could take Chapman's playwriting course, which I did twice, but that was as far as it went. There was, however, a very active and vibrant theater scene at Harvard, but that was entirely run by students without the involvement of faculty advisors. I found this freedom and lack of supervision helped me learn how to run things myself. It taught me how to be self-starting and self-reliant, and take responsibility for organizing and motivating various projects and people. Even though I was studying English at Harvard, what I really did was direct theater. I gradually subordinated everything to doing one play after another, and that quickly became my sole focus.

The summer between my freshman and sophomore years, I apprenticed at a dinner theater on the south side of Chicago called Drury Lane. They booked in stars like Jan Sterling and Peggy Wood for two week runs. I was the stage manager, a considerable responsibility. I was proud when a snazzy little visiting director from New York asked my opinion. I liked to watch him move around the house during rehearsals—it was theater in the round—so he could view the action from different sides. I planned to do that if I ever directed. I commuted to Chicago from northwest Indiana on the train, and had plenty of time to read. So, I read all of Eric Bentley's theater books several times, including *The Playwright as Thinker*, his monumental study of drama, as Eric was one of the most important critics and theater thinkers at that point. It was also natural, being in the Chicago area, to call Lillian Svec and see if she was still involved with her Northwestern boyfriend. She wasn't, and we got back together soon after. All seemed right with the world once again.

Back at Harvard that fall, I read for the part of the sad sack violin-playing brother, Andre, in a production of Chekhov's *Three Sisters*. I wanted the part badly, and I think I auditioned well, but I didn't get it. The director instead cast her friend. So, I decided to direct. The first play I directed at Harvard was an adaptation of *Woyzeck* by Georg Büchner, which is a naturalistic working class tragedy about a German soldier who is driven mad by his cheating wife. There's also an opera of Büchner's drama by the Austrian composer Alban Berg, performed under the title *Wozzeck*, but I did a production of the play. As we were working on *Woyzeck* it came to me that I really wanted to do this, to be a director. It felt so natural and creatively empowering. I liked it and felt that I had possibly discovered my purpose in life. Also, I just enjoyed bossing people around so much. That felt *real good!*

Later that fall, Lillian Svec came to visit me at Harvard for a long weekend. It proved to be a defining episode. She came to a rehearsal of a farce I was doing by Cervantes (I did an evening of three farces: one by Cervantes, *The Judge of the Divorce Court*, and one by Ludvig Holberg, *The Healing Spring*. A third farce, *Pierre Patelin*, was directed by my room-mate Bill Gordy. The plays were funny and I was happy with them). Watching the rehearsal one evening, I think Lillian learned the true intensity of my passion for directing theater and the fact that this was something that I might want to possibly do for a living. It came as something of a surprise to her. You see, Lillian came from a family of people who thought very seriously about life, society, and personal responsibility. Her father was a high school principal, her much-loved aunt worked with mentally disabled children, and Lillian herself was striving towards being a speech therapist. With this background, she strongly believed that you should do something important with your life; something that really helped people in a direct and constructive way, like a doctor. I don't think she placed music or the theater in that same category of importance. Lillian believed that those were things you should do as a fabulous hobby, not as a profession.

Anyway, that night, after the rehearsal was over and I was walking her back to her hotel, she said, "I don't know how I would feel about supporting you while you got started in the theater." In that moment, as those words left her lips, my heart *froze*! It had never crossed my mind that she would support me. It wasn't about money, or responsibility, or contributing to society, it was something else entirely. I realized to my horror that Lillian did not respect the arts, she positively didn't, and I couldn't be with someone like that. I think in that moment I stopped loving her. It was the end for us. Six weeks later I was going out with Caroline Cross, the daughter of the President of American Motors. Then, eight months after that, I was living with an actress with a trust fund. It wasn't the money in those cases either, but you know, there it was, and money never hurts.

In August 1959, when I was twenty and between my sophomore and junior years at Harvard, I had another significant romantic entanglement. It began when I attended a children's theater workshop at the Dunes Summer Theatre in Michigan City, that was being run by a wonderful guy from the BBC named John Allen. We met there every day for two or three weeks, a group of around twenty people that came from all over the Midwest but mostly consisted of women who were interested in Children's Theater. We worked on Shakespeare's *The Tempest* and the experience was also a contributing part of what led me to becoming a director. In the discussions we held, I sort of found my voice as a director. John Allen encouraged me, and told me he thought it was something I could do. That experience was memorable enough but this was also the time and place where I fell in love with my first communist girlfriend. Her name was Nina Landau and she came to the workshop with a girlfriend from Madison, Wisconsin. She was twenty-six, had a couple of kids, and was married to Saul Landau who was a grad student and teaching assistant at the University of Wisconsin. Both were from New York, but they'd gone to Wisconsin because there was a history professor there named William Appleman Williams who was critical of America's Imperialist foreign policy (this was part of the early awakening from the McCarthy era).

Nina was a red diaper baby—half-Jewish, half Colombian Indian, with striking cheekbones. Her father had been a Colombian communist and her real name was Lenina. Saul was the editor of *Studies on the Left*, published by some rich guy who had been on the edges of the Rosenberg spy business (he'd been questioned forever but never actually indicted). I don't know about Saul, but Nina was a communist. She'd had her passport taken away because she'd gone to a youth convention in the Soviet Union, followed by a trip to China on the Trans-Siberian Railway. She was quite an important person in my life and we were madly in love for a while. Nina wanted to leave her husband and come live with me at Harvard. When the children's theater workshop was over, we arranged for me to meet her kids in the toy department at Marshall Fields in Milwaukee. I never showed up. My parents wouldn't let me have the car! Shame! But they were only looking out for me. I had to have Nina paged in the toy department. I remember that she said, "Well, this was a long drive for nothing." About a week later, the FBI came and questioned me about her. I told them they had no business investigating American citizens for their political beliefs and sent them on their way.

I went back to Harvard early that fall to direct a production of Tennessee Williams' *The Glass Menagerie*. It's a play I'd first read in high school and loved. My father had given me a record of Williams reading the Gentleman Caller scene, and I'd listened to it over and over. To a substantial degree it's about leaving home, and it tapped into my homesickness. I did a good job directing it and it got rave reviews, both from *The Harvard Crimson* and the Boston papers. My parents came to see it and were impressed. I remember it as a wonderful production. That probably cemented it for me. That was the moment when I knew for certain that this was where my future lay. I can remember watching the audience during the performances, seeing how they reacted at various moments, and it was deeply thrilling. It's easy to forget these kinds of moments when you've enjoyed a long career, but those first few plays were so formative and special. If they hadn't have worked out, things may have been very different for me. Fortunately, they did work out and I got lucky with two of the actors in the cast. The girl who played Laura and the guy who played the Gentleman Caller fell in love during the rehearsal period. This completely transformed everything and somehow made it more authentic and meaningful. So, every night, they just talked the lines back and forth in the most natural way. It sounded absolutely real every time. It truly made that production.

I was less pleased with what I did next: a production of Sean O'Casey's *The Plough and the Stars*. The play deals with the Easter Rising of 1916 and I directed it with a strong anti-war slant. In truth, I didn't have to try too hard to insert that quality into it as it was already inherent in the play. O'Casey was a communist and *The Plough and the Stars* is certainly anti-war. It was very violent, but I suppose I dialed up the bloodiness—so much so that it backfired one night. There was a soldier on stage who was supposed to be shot in the stomach. I'd given him a condom filled with blood to break at the appropriate point, but for *once* a condom held (it must've been made of tougher stuff). The actor was caught with it in his hand, and the condom was clearly visible to the audience. There was a guffaw from a few guys in the front row. We were doing the play at a theater in a jock club at Harvard called Pi Eta, so there was a decent percentage of athletes in the audience. Their ridicule started with the bloody condom and continued until they were hooting towards the end of the act about the sufferings of my leading lady. I was cranked up enough on diet pills that when the lights came on for intermission, I assaulted the most vocal guy in the first row. I pounced on him, punching, and yelling, "You cocksucking son of a bitch!" The next thing I remember is going to the floor with three or four football players on top of me. My ear turned green inside and stayed that way for weeks.

> *While at Harvard, Hancock encountered the works of the Marxist poet, playwright and theater director Bertolt Brecht. Born in Augsburg, Germany, in 1898, Brecht had established the Berliner Ensemble theater company in East Berlin, in 1949, with his wife Helene Weigel, and would eventually become one the most important practitioners in Twentieth Century Theater. Although Hancock rejected some of Brecht's Marxist notions of theater as a vehicle for rational didacticism, he would still seek to "preserve the purity and power" of his plays when transferring them to the stage. Indeed, Brecht would threaten to be an indissoluble influence on Hancock's continued development as a director.*

Discovering Brecht was like finding Joyce, another big deal. Brecht became a source of inspiration and direction for me to such an extent that for much of the next decade he really had me in a headlock. It took me a long time to kind of shake loose and find a new way. I almost had to exorcise Brecht from my soul, which I'm sure is how a lot of creative people feel when they first fall in love with an artist and absorb their influence and ideas. In fact, I only felt I had departed from a Brechtian aesthetic when I later went to San Francisco and did an acclaimed production of *A Midsummer Night's Dream*, and that was in 1966. My early favorites of Brecht's plays were *The Caucasian Chalk Circle* and *Mother Courage and Her Children*. I thought *Chalk Circle* in particular was entertaining and emotional, very strong stuff, but as far as *Mother Courage* was concerned, even back then I can remember wondering if an American audience could sit for that long—and with that much talk—and still engage with the piece. By directing them, I learned that Brecht's plays do a strange thing: in a lot of British and American plays, the first act is very strong and the second act may be less so. But with Brecht it's quite the opposite: the plays kick you at the end! You get an unbearable feeling in the pit of your stomach at the climax of *Mother Courage* or *Edward II*, and, to a lesser extent, *Chalk Circle*, as that play has a rather charming end. All of these works engender great feeling that builds to a finale that is remarkable.

Brecht also explored theater as a forum for political ideas and the creation of critical aesthetics of dialectical materialism. But I feel that, in the middle of his life, he went too far in this direction. He just went a little nuts for politics and anti-bourgeois themes. He wrote teaching plays—or, more accurately, propaganda plays—that were designed to be performed in schools. When you examine his career as a whole, you can identify three distinct phases of it: there is the early expressionist period which consists of plays like *Baal, In the Jungle of Cities, A Man's a Man* and *Edward II*. Then, in the middle of his career, after he had committed to the Communist Party and their ideals, Brecht wrote overtly political plays like *The Exception and the Rule, The Mother* and *The Measures Taken*, the latter being an unrestrained Stalinist tract that is terribly fascinating and a production I've always wanted to do. Despite that desire, I generally find this second phase of Brecht's career to be less interesting than the first. However, when he got around to the third phase of his career and wrote late plays like *Mother Courage, The Caucasian Chalk Circle, Galileo,* and *The Good Woman of Szechwan*, politics became less important to Brecht than character, entertainment and emotion.

During my time at Harvard they built a new theater, the Loeb Drama Center. One of the very first productions scheduled there was *Chalk Circle*, which I was going to direct. So, the summer before, I secured a grant to go to Europe to see the work of Brecht's Berliner Ensemble. This was done through the assistance of Robert Chapman. I spent a wonderful summer looking at theater in Europe, attending performances in Paris by the Berliner Ensemble and Roger Planchon's Théâtre de la Cité in Avignon. I was there with Margery Ziskind, the actress with the trust fund I mentioned earlier. I remember that we flew to Paris and before Margie and I had even checked into a hotel, we headed straight to the Sarah Bernhardt Theatre where the Berliner Ensemble was performing. We got tickets for their opening and were quickly adopted by a Colombian communist named Enrique Buenaventura, who helped us find a hotel and introduced us to several important French communists. These guys eyed us up as potentially good candidates to attend a Moscow youth festival, like the one that had cost Nina Landau her passport. Ultimately, we were deemed to be insufficiently Left for the honor and that opportunity went away. It was not an easy trip. Margie was terribly guilty about her little boy, Ned, who we had left with her despised mother back in Lowell, Massachusetts. She was also guilty about her father, whom Margie felt she'd killed by marrying her first husband. I gather her father had disapproved, and the marriage had been followed by a fatal heart attack. So, there were copious tears in the night—night after night. I wasn't prepared to handle it. As I've said, my mother was so steady and stoical. It seemed bitter and self-defeating to me to be traveling across Europe with someone you love and be so unhappy, but we were linked by the fact I had cast her as the lead in *Chalk Circle*.

That production was a huge undertaking, a cast of fifty or sixty, a big revolving stage and many sets. Eric Bentley, the aforementioned critic, editor, playwright and translator, came to a lot of the rehearsals we held, made excellent suggestions and worked closely with me on the play. Eric was considered the pre-eminent authority in America on Brecht's work, so it was a big deal for me to become friends with him. He was such a warm and giving person. Eric was at Harvard in the fall of 1960 to deliver the Norton Lectures, which is a huge honor. I mean, you had people like Igor Stravinsky, T.S. Eliot and Robert Frost giving those lectures, which gives you an indication of his standing. Eric was destined to become an important mentor for me, probably the most important, and was a big part of making *Chalk Circle* a success. I remember Edmond Wilson, who was America's most important literary critic, wrote in *The New Yorker* that seeing our production had finally made him understand why people appreciated Brecht. That was an incredible accolade.

The story of *Chalk Circle* is of a royal baby who is abandoned by its mother during the terror of the revolution, and is taken care of by a servant girl (played by Margie). The servant grows to love the child, but when the bad time is over and order restored, the royal mother wants her child back. A judge sets up a contest. Whichever woman can pull the child out of a circle he draws on the floor with chalk can have it. The servant girl can't bear to hurt the child, can't pull him in half, so of course she loses. The judge then gives her the child. What there is, he says, should go to whoever is best for it. Interestingly, Brecht had written a kind of framing device or prologue that I felt was remarkably ineffective when you considered the fact that it began such a wonderful play. The prologue involved the meeting of the members of rival collective farms in Soviet Georgia shortly after World War II. It was propagandistic and featured characters called Tractor Driver and Herdsman, and so forth. As the German Army approached, Stalin had relocated certain minorities he considered untrustworthy. He'd sent a valley of goat people east of the Urals, and while they were gone, others had taken the pastures and planted fruit trees. So, now the war is over and the herdsmen are back and you have rival groups contending for the same land. Collective farms collide! A discussion becomes a quarrel that they try to resolve by performing the play which is *Chalk Circle*.

I had first read the play in Eric's translation without the inclusion of the prologue. Then I became aware of it as an addition and thought that maybe Eric should write something that replaced it. I drove down to Wellfleet, Massachusetts, where Eric had a house, and got him to write a poem instead of the prologue. For some critics, I'm sure what we did was considered rather intrusive and presumptuous—I know Robert Chapman felt that way—but I don't think the prologue had existed when Eric first translated the play. I think it was written substantially later, possibly after the war, when Brecht had returned to East Berlin from Hollywood in the late 1940s (where he had been living in exile for six years) and founded the Berliner Ensemble. Whenever it was, I don't know how to successfully convey the full inadequacy of it. The prologue simply didn't work, so I didn't use it.

In 1961, the year I graduated from Harvard, I saw that the Loeb Drama Center was empty and was not going to have anything on that summer. I got the idea that we should have a summer company there and do plays throughout the season. As I've intimated, Chapman and I were close but, surprisingly, when I approached him with the idea, he said, "No, I don't think so." That response shocked and hurt me. Frankly, I didn't understand or expect it. But I was still determined to get something going that summer and thought of a different strategy. So, ignoring Chapman's refusal, Eric Bentley and I went to see McGeorge Bundy, a real powerhouse, who was the Dean of the Faculty of Arts and Sciences at Harvard and would later become the National Security Advisor for John F. Kennedy and Lyndon Johnson. Eric and I managed to talk Bundy into overruling Chapman and I was then allowed to form a summer company during the very first year of this new theater's existence. I later auditioned in New York and around Boston for actors, and we eventually mounted four plays. I directed three of them and they represented my first professional directing.

It was a good company. There was Jane Alexander, who later worked a great deal and became a Tony Award-winning and Academy Award-nominated actress. In the 1990s, Jane was recruited by President Clinton to run The National Endowment for the Arts. Faye Dunaway was also in our company. I thought she was incredibly beautiful and sexy, but not that real, quite stiff actually, and I was shocked when she later went on to enjoy such a big career. I remember shouting at her one afternoon; she was playing a prostitute with one leg up on a chair, and I yelled, "Why are you invariably drawn to the cliché?" She didn't answer back, but we never really liked each other. For the opening play at the Loeb we did Shakespeare's *As You Like It* with Faye playing Phoebe and Jane playing Rosalind. Faye's acting teacher from Boston University, Ted Kazanoff, was a wonderful Jacques. He had such authority; his Seven Ages of Man monologue was usually rewarded with applause. The production was critically successful and provided us with a good start.

For the second production we did Jean Anouilh's *Antigone*, which is derived from the Greek tragedy by Sophocles. Anouilh's play, which is probably his most celebrated and popular work, was originally performed in Paris during World War II when France was occupied by the Nazis. So it depicts an individual, Antigone, up against an authoritarian regime, with obvious parallels to the French Resistance and their struggles against Hitler's Germany. I felt that it was an interesting examination of idealism, morality and fate. Margie Ziskind played Antigone, and Faye Dunaway played her sister. I was proud of that production and Faye was a little better in this one. A friend of Robert Chapman directed George Bernard Shaw's *Misalliance* for our third show, again with Jane and Faye. It was hilarious and I think maybe Faye was better for other directors than she was for me.

For the final production of our summer theater in August 1961, I directed a version of Brecht's *A Man's a Man* in a translation by Eric Bentley. The play follows the story of Galy Gay, an Irish porter who is living with his wife in a fictional British colony in India. Gay is enlisted by three British soldiers to replace Jeriah Jip, the missing member of their machine-gun unit who has disappeared during a raid on a Buddhist pagoda. Through a process of dehumanization where he is kind of taken apart and reconstructed, Gay is gradually transformed from an ordinary and harmless civilian into what is effectively the perfect bloodthirsty soldier. Eric and I devised a little prologue for our version that set it up as a recruiting show performed by the soldiers for the audience. It was effective.

The summer theater at Harvard was an enormous success. The response to *A Man's a Man* was wonderful. It turned out to be even better than *The Caucasian Chalk Circle*, and was probably the best of the plays I did at Harvard, although it's difficult to be objective now, particularly as so many years have passed. The respected theater director and critic Harold Clurman, as well as the director Alan Schneider and several other notables, came up from New York to see *A Man's a Man* and were impressed with it. I was literally floating I was so proud and happy! I was happy for my own success and I was happy that so many great people were acknowledging it, people whose work I had admired. I mean, many times I've been inspired by seeing another director's work on the stage. For instance, I was greatly affected by the work of the directors I had seen at the Berliner Ensemble, particularly that of Peter Palitzsch who had directed *The Resistible Rise of Arturo Ui*. I thought he was brilliant and it was galvanizing for me to see his stuff. It was so fierce and challenging, and it was also true to Brecht's voice which I felt was important. I felt the same way about Alan Schneider's work. I had seen *Who's Afraid of Virginia Woolf?* on Broadway and thought Alan had done a sensational job of directing that play. He had also done a wonderful production of Samuel Beckett's *Endgame* Off-Broadway in 1958, so Alan was a good director. To suddenly know him, and call him a friend, was incredible. Actually, getting to know Schneider and Clurman was how I got started directing theater in New York; it was through those people that saw my work at Harvard. So, this was really a beginning for me.

Theater
(1962 – 2009)

FOLLOWING THE SUCCESS *of his summer company at Harvard, and having befriended such notables as Harold Clurman and Alan Schneider, Hancock expediently made the move to New York in late 1961 to further pursue his career as a theater director. His friend and mentor Eric Bentley, who had established several meaningful connections with various prominent Off-Broadway figures, introduced Hancock to Konrad and Gay Matthaei, owners of the New Repertory Theatre Company. After accepting the position of artistic director there, he hastily began work on a production of Alexander Ostrovsky's 1859 drama of social criticism* The Storm *before turning his attention once again to Bertolt Brecht, the playwright whose works had brought him his first intoxicating taste of acclaim.*

In September 1962, it was announced to a startled press that there would be two simultaneous productions mounted in New York of Brecht's Mann ist Mann *(or to give the play one of its more cumbersome variant titles* Man Is Man: The Transformation of Galy Gay in the Military Barracks of Kilkoa in the Year 1925*). Each presentation would be derived from different translations with Hancock working from the Bentley translation of the original 1925 text (entitled* A Man's a Man*) which he had directed in Boston the previous year. The rival production was being staged by The Living Theatre as* Man Is Man *under the direction and set design of Julian Beck. This version was derived from a translation by Gerhard Nellhaus that was*

> based on Brecht's final revision of the work, which the dramatist had completed in 1953, three years before his death of a heart attack at the age of fifty-eight.

Konrad and Gay Matthaei had initially set-up the New Repertory Theatre Off-Broadway with a female artistic director. Unfortunately, or perhaps fortunately, they weren't happy with the job she was doing. So, the Matthaeis fired her and were then actively looking for a replacement. I had met them briefly on a trip to New York with my Harvard girlfriend Caroline Cross (Konrad was from Detroit automobile money like Caroline's father) so when Eric kindly recommended me for the job, Konrad and Gay agreed to hire me. I duly took over a floundering production of *The Storm* that my predecessor had been working on. They had actually been in previews on *The Storm* when I assumed control, so I only rehearsed the play for eight or ten days. I then made the mistake of putting my name on it, which was an error I never repeated in my career when I took things over both in theater and in film. The production didn't do well at all, and I remember digesting a line in one review that read: "*The Storm* is fumblingly directed by John Hancock." That appraisal was entirely earned on the basis of her work, not mine, but it didn't matter. Even though *The Storm* was not a success, the Matthaeis still wanted to continue doing more productions. So, we next considered doing Ibsen's *The Wild Duck*, which is a play I've always wanted to direct. We talked to Gene Hackman about playing the lead, but then Hackman took another job and the project stuttered to a halt even before it really got started. We looked about for something else to do and eventually settled on the idea of mounting Brecht's *A Man's a Man*. I was happy about this as I was already well-versed with the material.

So, we announced *A Man's a Man* as our next work, but then, almost simultaneously, The Living Theatre announced it as their forthcoming production, too! That was a remarkable coincidence, one I don't think any of us saw coming. It soon transpired that Julian Beck and Judith Malina, the people who ran The Living Theater, had secured the rights directly from the Brecht Estate—namely Helene Weigel and Stefan Brecht, the latter the playwright's son. Incidentally, I had been arrested with Beck and Malina earlier that same year. There had been a big demonstration—not in Times Square but three or four blocks north of there—against the resumption of nuclear testing in the atmosphere. Kennedy was going to detonate bombs in the atmosphere again and I went down there with Michael Ritchie, who later became a film director and made *Downhill*

Racer and *The Bad News Bears*. Mike and I were friends in New York, and we were both incensed about the situation. I remember that during the demonstration something compelled me to sit down in the street, like Lord Russell was doing in London, in peaceful protest. Unhappily for me, the New York Tactical Police Unit did not appreciate the subtleties of civil disobedience and began clubbing us all with their nightsticks. There was a lot of blood—a plethora of broken noses and gaping head-wounds that were gushing copiously. After beating us, the cops dragged us away and threw us into the back of paddy wagons, where we continued to bleed over each other. In the next issue of the *Sunday New York Times*, there was a picture of me sitting in the paddy wagon looking very hardened, as well as another picture of Julian Beck looking crazy. From this experience of being briefly incarcerated with him, I learned that Beck was something of a screamer. I remember him being dragged bleeding to the paddy wagon, shrieking, "They're killing us! They're killing us!" It was quite something. Oddly enough, also present that day was Joseph Chaikin, who was the leading actor of The Living Theatre and was starring as Galy Gay in their production *Man Is Man*. Joe was a good actor and a wonderful guy, and it was a pleasure being beaten and arrested with him.

Getting back to Beck and Malina, I must say they were so emotionally free it was scary. Julian acted scary and he certainly looked scary! He was so liberated and uninhibited there was something decidedly unsettling about him. It was the same with Judith, too. The Living Theatre had traveled all over the world doing experimental theater, appearing nude in some productions and being arrested for indecency, and pushing boundaries to their utmost. But anyone who had seen their productions knew they were good. I can remember when The Living Theatre did *The Connection*, Jack Gelber's play about the dead-end life of junkies, which had opened Off-Broadway in the late 1950s. It was wonderful. Then they did *The Brig*, an anti-authoritarian drama set in a military prison, and that was another fabulous and award-winning production. They also did a version of *Frankenstein*, which was intriguing. I find Judith Malina's film work to be less interesting than her theater work, but she and Beck were very intense, very creative people. They had an open marriage and were these radical and unconstrained Village People at a time when that was not so common.

Of course, certain individuals cried foul when they learned of our production and claimed it was illegal or unauthorized, but Eric was insisting that the work was in the public domain. The Living Theater was doing a translation of the play based on a later revision by Brecht and we were doing Eric's translation of Brecht's original version. This distinction would prove to be all important. I think Eric was excited by the competition and was also intrigued to see how different their version would be in comparison with ours. Knowing there were two productions of *A Man's a Man* being mounted in New York at the same time, obviously, one could argue that The Living Theatre was very important at that point in time and I believe remains the oldest experimental theater group in America. Julian Beck and Judith Malina were the darlings of avant-garde theater and, for this reason and others, some would have perhaps thought it best that we retreat and abandon our plans to compete with them. Not so! Eric and I, and the Matthaeis, all simply said, "Oh, to hell with it. Let's just go ahead and do this!" That proved to be a very wise and profitable decision.

To this day, *A Man's a Man* is rarely done and that's because it's a difficult play. It's pretty hard to figure out. What's important to remember is that Brecht wrote it for himself to direct, so he didn't worry about clear stage directions, and it's sometimes difficult to work out exactly what's happening—what Brecht *meant* to happen. This can be both intimidating and liberating for any director that takes it on. Casting all modesty aside for a moment, I've always been adept at figuring out plays without stage directions. I've always been able to find a workable solution for what a play should be. I find it's merely a matter of careful investigation of what must be taking place in order to give rise to those written lines. Frankly, The Living Theatre's production was ultimately less good at that. They hadn't figured out what was supposed to be happening and they were also hampered in other ways, too. Brecht had revised *A Man's a Man* many times, but I don't think his revisions were as strong as his original draft. Eric felt that Brecht had clearly got it right on the first attempt and his voice had really started to emerge as a playwright.

Again, luckily for us, we were doing his first draft and The Living Theatre was doing his revised version. In my opinion, the reason why the amended versions are weaker is that Brecht had lost some of the craziness in his later drafts. He was in the process of not being so free and expressionistic, and was injecting a little more communist meaning into things. I also think Brecht was embarrassed by some of the sexuality present in his early works, which seemed strangely bisexual and orgiastic. So, he toned down and diluted some of those elements and I feel that was a mistake. *A Man's a Man* has its problems in its early sections, but it's still a very powerful and important play. Despite its deficiencies, it's similar in some ways to the story of *The Godfather*; a parable about how a child of light becomes a child of darkness. It explores how, in the process of growing up and facing the demands and influences of society, people can turn evil. You could also say that it comments on the dehumanizing nature of military life and how it often sucks the sweetness out of people. It takes the child out of them, and hardens them, and in the process reveals how fragile and malleable our identities really are.

I remember that when we started casting *A Man's a Man*, we were seeing actors every ten to fifteen minutes, one after the other. We were looking for somebody to play the role of Sergeant Bloody Five: a hard-ass disciplinarian who, when it rains, turns into a lascivious, permissive mess. And, sure enough, it rains and Bloody Five ends up shooting his dick off. This character was *the* driving force on the plot as the Machine Gun Unit's fear of him is what forces them to turn Galy Gay into their fourth man, Jeriah Jip, who has been lost when they looted a Buddhist pagoda. Among other things, the actor playing Bloody Five would be reciting an admiring, even heroic, poem called "Little Bill." The chorus would run, "And with Bill, Bill, Bill, it was kill, kill, kill!" It was the story of how he executed six Sikhs. During our auditions, in walked the distinctive-looking figure of Michael Conrad. I remember he handed me his resume, and I said, "Okay, tell me what you've done." Mike then proceeded to tell me about his career and, as he was speaking, my secretary quietly handed me a little pink slip of a phone message. My eyes flicked from Mike's face down to this message to see who had called, and this took all of a few seconds. Suddenly, Conrad stood up and barked, "What are you doing? This is my life here! You can't listen to me for one measly fucking second? This is my *life!*" Enraged, he then turned and stomped out of the theater. I said to myself: "Jesus Christ, he's perfect! Isn't that what we really want for Bloody Five—somebody crazy and angry?" So, I quickly chased after Mike, apologized profusely, and we cast him. But then Mike turned out to be a little too crazy and angry. I'll never forget that whenever he got infuriated, his one eye would go off to the side. So, you could literally see when his blood was boiling, and it was a curious and unsettling thing to witness. I knew people like Stefan Gierasch, an excellent actor, who would cross the street whenever he saw Mike coming in his direction. This was because Mike was so fucking crazy! I had terrible fights with him throughout our time on the production. In fact, Mike happily informed me one day that he had killed people with piano wire in Korea and I thought this was something I would do well to keep in mind. He actually came after me on one occasion and aggressively attacked me. He didn't hit me, but he came terribly close to it.

Mike Conrad wasn't the only difficult actor I dealt with on the production. I originally cast Vivian Nathan as Widow Begbick, but eventually fired her and replaced her with Olympia Dukakis shortly before our opening performance. My reasons for dismissing Vivian were her slow pace and lack of sparkle, but it was also the fact that she and Mike were fighting so much. There was a scene where Bloody Five was supposed to pick up the Widow Begbick and carry her off-stage in order to fuck her. Whenever we did this, Mike would physically hurt Vivian quite badly. She came to me and showed me the bruises on her body. I said, "Mike, look at this! Look at what you've done!" He in turn protested his innocence: "No, I'm not like that. I'm a very gentle person." Of course, Mike was indeed being overly aggressive and violent towards Vivian, and the tensions between them continued. It soon became an untenable situation between these actors and I had to figure out some way to resolve it. I mean, here I was—fresh out of Harvard and working Off-Broadway with my suit and shit—and these two people are screaming wildly at each other: "You're no man!" "Well, you're no woman!" It was all that kind of stuff and the aggravation showed no signs of ceasing. I asked myself, "Okay, what can I do here?" I then decided to sit the two of them down and try to mediate. Regrettably, that little meeting I organized erupted into further screaming and shouting, and was followed by Vivian fleeing the theater in tears. It was one of those situations where you think you're going to make something better and you end up making it much worse. Finally, the last course of action available to me was to fire one of them. So, we ended up letting go of the actor who was less effective in their part. That was undoubtedly Vivian. It would be fair to say that we kept the criminal and punished the victim. But it was a difficult situation and I had no other option. I'm certainly not proud of myself for what I did.

Another difficult actor on *A Man's a Man* was Harvey Solin, who played Uriah, one of the soldiers who enlist Galy Gay. Occasionally, you work with somebody who repeatedly fails or refuses to take notice of a certain direction you've given them. On this particular production that somebody was Harvey. At one point during the play, he took a pause that I felt was unconscionably long. I mean, he literally just stood on the stage drinking in the audience's undivided attention. I simply couldn't bear that pause lasting for such an extended time. It was excruciating to behold. I went up to Harvey after one performance, and said, "What the hell are you doing? Would you please not take so long on that pause?" Unfortunately, he refused to take that piece of direction and just continued to do it. So, I fired him. Postscript: ironically, a few years later, when I did a production of *A Man's a Man* in Pittsburgh, I hired Harvey again for the very same part. I reminded him not to pause as agonizingly long as he had done previously in New York and, thankfully, the second time he got it.

Some of the first lessons I learned as a director were the most painful and revealing. Alan Schneider is a good case in point: when Alan had come up to see *A Man's a Man* in Boston, he had been incredibly encouraging and supportive of me. When I first arrived in New York, he had helped me get started and had been my friend. However, when I started getting directing jobs that he wanted, our relationship quickly changed. For instance, I can recall asking Alan for a list of who he thought were the good actors in New York who were working Off-Broadway. He then kindly supplied me with one, which, I later discovered, was a list of some of the most difficult and demanding and disruptive actors I've ever worked with: Mike Conrad, Vivian Nathan and Harvey Solin being just three of them. There's no denying it, he gave me a list of absolute *killers*! Whether this was a deliberate act of sabotage or Alan really got along with those people because he was a different character than me, I may never know. I strongly suspect it was an intentional attempt at subversion on Alan's part that was designed to hinder and obstruct me. I still believe that. Our friendship never really survived these tensions and hadn't repaired itself by the time he died in 1984. Alan was working on a Harold Pinter play in London, when he stepped off the curb and was looking to his left for oncoming traffic. He was then struck and killed by a motorcycle coming from his right. As an American in England, you don't expect—or you momentarily forget—that people drive on the left.

We previewed *A Man's a Man* forever and I must say that was very hard for me. When you do previews for any length of time, all the directors in town come to see the play and they try to get your job. First they attend the previews and then they contact the producers, and say, "Look, this production is not good, but I can fix it for you." There was a rather poisonous and conspiratorial atmosphere back then in the New York theater scene. There were guys like Jerry Robbins, Zero Mostel and my good "pal" Alan Schneider who would all come circling around like sharks, trying to push you out so they could slide right into your seat. Schneider's treachery in particular was a bitter pill to swallow as—

again—he had been my friend. I considered Alan's behavior to be a very painful betrayal. I suddenly thought, "My God, is *this* what happens here? Is this how the business works? This is terrible!" I think one reason why directors like to try out-of-town previews instead of having in-town previews is because at least somebody has to make some effort in order to fuck you over. They have to take a train, or get on a plane, if they really want to steal your job.

> *The Living Theatre's production of* Man Is Man *opened on Tuesday, September 18, 1962, in their home theater located at 530 6th Avenue (Avenue of the Americas). A day later, Hancock and Bentley's* A Man's a Man *opened on Wednesday, September 19, at the Masque Theatre on 42nd Street. It would eventually close on February 17, 1963, after 175 performances. Although* A Man's a Man *would accrue the greater share of favorable critical plaudits, both productions would garner significant awards. Joseph Chaikin won the 1963 Obie Award for "Distinguished Performance by an Actor" for his portrayal of Galy Gay in Beck's production, while Olympia Dukakis claimed the corresponding actress honor for her role as Widow Begbick in Hancock's.*

It's still incredible to think that these rival productions opened on successive nights, but it turned out to be the best thing that could have happened as we triumphed in the reviews. We were able to say that no less than twenty-six critics preferred our version. I'm paraphrasing, but the notices generally said, "The Living Theatre's version is no good, and this is wonderful." So, it was a fairly comprehensive victory for us. The fact that the critics got to see the same play—one right after the other—in quite different interpretations, probably made the distinctions all the more clear. I have this lasting memory of going down to 42nd Street and Broadway at 5:30 AM the morning after we'd opened, so I could get all the newspapers. Seriously, it's truly one of the unforgettable experiences of my life. I can recall buying all these papers, holding them in my trembling hands as I stood on the corner by the newsstand, poring over every sentence of every review. It was exhilarating! The critics had written glorious things like: "John Hancock's appropriately bold signature is writ large." I was deliriously happy and proud.

I went to see The Living Theatre's competing production a couple of weeks after our respective openings and I saw for myself that ours was undeniably superior. Looking back, I think what impressed the critics most about our production was that it was fast, flashy and musical (we had four songs by Eric put to music by Joe Raposo). It was very wild, violent and entertaining. When I had been to the Berliner Ensemble, and attended their production of *The Resistible Rise of Arturo Ui*, I saw how you could do fast and flashy stuff in Kabuki masks and everything. I really understood the Brechtian theatrical aesthetic and I feel the reviews supported that. "Finally, here is somebody who really knows about Epic Theater and Brecht," one critic wrote. I had learned what Brecht was trying to do as a director, what his theater was trying to do, and was humble enough to replicate that same approach. I've had a terrible problem with directors like Jerry Robbins, who later did *Mother Courage* on Broadway, who feel they must "improve" on the work. When there is a production by the playwright that is definitive, how do you then have the ego and audacity to say: "No, forget about that. I'll do my own version!" Why wouldn't you want to examine Brecht's original approach in his productions, look at pictures of them, maybe even have seen the play performed somewhere else, and consciously seek to achieve or approximate the same thing? I think the lack of humility and deference in all that is astounding. And, what's more, nearly all these productions that ignore the originals fail. The plays need the same kind of theatrical gloss that Brecht initially brought to them. He was a flashy, jazzy director who really knew what he was doing.

The reviews for *A Man's a Man* are what set me up as a working professional director. It's that production that got me started on a solid footing. Eric Bentley was as ecstatic about the New York production as he had been about the Cambridge production. We really did *A Man's a Man* together. Eric was there each and every day—from the time we cast the play all the way through to the end—and he always offered me strong support and sound advice. Eric later dedicated the published version of *A Man's a Man* to me and we had a wonderful working relationship. Even the bad stuff that happened with one or two of the actors was an experience I was able to use. Literally, one of the best pieces of advice I ever received about directing for the theater came from Clifton James on *A Man's a Man*. Clifton was one of Elia Kazan's actors and he told me, "You know, John, praise is the key to the actor. You get more flies with honey than you do with vinegar." I've often thought about those words and have endeavored to heed them when dealing with actors of various temperaments and dispositions. I read Faye Dunaway's autobiography as she had also worked with Kazan on his movie *The Arrangement*. During filming, she would repeatedly hear him gush, "Oh, my God! That's so good! That's great! Now, let's try this…" Then they would do the scene an entirely different way. On one occasion, Faye asked Kazan, "Why do you say that the take is great if it isn't great?" He replied, "Well, I've tried telling the truth and it's so much better to lie and praise." I tend to agree with that view. I think you get much more from actors by praising them than you do by giving them the truth. A lot of actors require near-constant assurance. You have to keep stroking them, and telling them how wonderful they are.

After a play opens, I often find it difficult to continue to go back and see the show and meet with the actors and crew in order to discuss new ideas and make changes. They want you to come, but I find it very hard. Why, you might ask? Well, it's basically because as a director I come to a certain point where I've just had it with that particular production. Generally, I've worked so hard on it, and have seemingly explored every conceivable possibility and idea, I just want to put it all behind me and move on to the next project. Sometimes, if I do go back to a play, all I see are the failures or the things I didn't adjust or finesse. There is always a temptation to return and keep working on it and, truth be told, I sometimes find I have to do that. I *have* to go back! *A Man's a Man* ran for six months, and I remember during that time I went off to direct *Galileo*. Then I came back and went to see *A Man's a Man* and it was the same thing that always happens when the director goes backstage afterwards: he says, "Take out the changes and the improvements!" I felt that very strongly, certainly in response to Harvey's excruciating pauses that seemed to have gotten longer in the interim. Actually, it was at this exact point in time that I decided to fire him.

There's no question about it, actors do tend to wander and stray from your direction when you are not around. They make it their own, as any great play is always an evolving and growing thing in that it hopefully keeps getting better and stronger. This occurred when I did *A Man's a Man* again in early 1967, in Pittsburgh. The play had been running for a couple of weeks and I came back and saw that the actors had made several improvements and refinements to it. Again, this is by no means unusual. Inevitably, a couple of weeks into a play's life, the actors have often found their stride, and a lot of their instincts and independent notions ring true. We had some wonderful actors in that subsequent production and they definitely added a lot more texture to their performances. That was assuredly one of those times when I returned, and said, "Thank God for the improvements!" You invariably hope that you have created an environment that helps the actors to grow and contribute, despite the sense of proprietorship you often feel as a director.

> *After the acclaim heaped on* A Man's a Man, *Hancock traveled to Houston, Texas to direct a production of Brecht's* Life of Galileo *at Rice University in early 1963. The play had been hastily written by Brecht during sixteen days of November 1938 (under the title* The Earth Moves*), and had premiered in Germany in September, 1943. It concerns the events leading to the trial and condemnation of the Italian astronomer and philosopher Galileo Galilei by the Roman Catholic Inquisition. Disappointed by the experience, Hancock was compelled to make his first investigations into film, spending the next few years pursuing various literary properties that he could adapt into a feature. Concurrently, he continued to direct for the theater, eagerly accepting an offer from Tony Richardson to steer a production of Tennessee Williams'* The Milk Train Doesn't Stop Here Anymore *at the Royal Court Theatre in London, England, for the English Stage Company. The play had only recently received its Broadway debut in January 1963 at the Morosco Theatre with Hermione Baddeley starring as Flora 'Sissy' Goforth, but had earned poor reviews.*

Galileo is another difficult and challenging play. It's less persuasive than *A Man's a Man*, but it does contain a lot of fascinating themes. What Brecht is saying with it—I don't know that it's necessarily true but it's what he's saying—is there was an exciting time in history, the Italian Renaissance and thereafter. A time when science and information and education had a chance to be widely popular and serve the people, but the powers that be, of reaction and religion, impeded that opportunity and stopped it dead. The playwright argues that they made science and education serve the power elites, and further, that Galileo, in renouncing the truth of his discovery that the earth went around the sun and not vice versa, played an unfortunate part. His betrayal was not unlike, to Brecht I suppose, the knuckling under of German intellectuals to Hitler, or the willingness of Oppenheimer to develop the atom bomb. When Galileo is confronted by the Inquisition, he says, "They showed me the instruments," and betrays himself and abandons his life's work. He ends up a broken man, eating goose with the grease running disgustingly down his chin, still thinking of the sky. He asks his daughter how the stars are tonight, and she says, "Bright." A children's choir sings as the curtain falls: "Guard science's light/ Kindle it and use it right/Lest it be a flame to fall/Downward to consume us all."

Like *A Man's a Man*, I believe *Galileo* is a play that Brecht revised over the course of many years, the third and final revision coming just a few years before his death. I had seen a version of *Galileo* performed in Paris by the Berliner Ensemble and really wanted to do it myself. Lamentably, I found it difficult to duplicate what the Ensemble had done within the strictures at Rice University. It just wasn't possible and I had to compromise on one or two things that I did not want to compromise on. Ultimately, because of that, I wasn't happy with the production and found it lacking. Also, to be completely honest about it, I couldn't properly cast the play. The cast was made up of community actors and student actors, and they simply weren't skilled enough to convey what was needed. In that regard, *Galileo* was a very frustrating experience; particularly as it followed on from the triumph of *A Man's a Man*. My confidence was shaken a little bit, but that didn't last very long. I was determined to keep working, keep building a career, and possibly tackle another of Brecht's works.

One I've always wanted to direct is *Rise and Fall of the City of Mahagonny*, the opera by Brecht and Kurt Weill. Along with *The Wild Duck*, it's genuinely the one production I wish I'd done. I was desperate to get it on and Stefan Brecht and I tried very hard to set it up Off-Broadway after I did *Galileo*. We arranged a meeting with Lotte Lenya, who was Weill's widow (Weill had died in 1950) and was representing his estate. She is also famous for playing Rosa Klebb, the sadistic Soviet agent with retractable blades in her shoes, in the James Bond movie *From Russia with Love*. I can distinctly recall picking Lotte up in Brooklyn Heights to take her to the meeting and she was extremely flirtatious with me. She was quite a lot older than I was at the time, but I still got the feeling she was fuckable.

Anyway, we arrived at Ballato's Restaurant on Houston Street, which is still there I believe, where we were meeting Stefan. Almost immediately after taking our seats, Lotte and Stefan got into a terrible fight. Basically, the cause of the argument was our asking for nine union musicians in the pit instead of seventeen union musicians. This was an important point. I mean, in the theater the weekly nut is the crucial thing. It's not a question of how much you spend on the sets or costumes, or whatever, it's how much does it cost to run every week between the acting salaries, and paying the stagehands and the musicians. Naturally, when considering this, the difference between seventeen union musicians and nine is huge. Shortly after broaching this subject, Lotte and Stefan started screaming at each other and things deteriorated further from there. Stefan said, "I never thought of *you* as an actress!" To which Lotte replied, "I was an actress with your mother in the Schauspielhaus!" And this went on and on, with me sitting between them, trying desperately to smooth things over. That was never going to happen and the evening went badly. So, we were not able to get Lotte to reduce the requirements of union musicians in the pit and the chance to do *Mahagonny* vanished. Nor did I get laid.

I then tried to get a few other things cooking. When I was in New York, in 1962, I had met Brian De Palma. At the time, Brian was trying to screw Margie Ziskind's sister, Ellen, because he was at Sarah Lawrence and Margie's sister was also studying there. Brian and I got to be friends and what's interesting is he was kind of goofy and rabbity back in those days. Obviously, later, he became an extremely skilled director and is generally viewed now as a slightly more dour and serious personality. But, back then, he was a goofy guy and a lot of fun to be around. One day Brian came to me, and said, "I have a great idea! Why don't we gather a bunch of directors together and do something? We'll get you, me, and a couple of other people we know, to each make a short film. Then we'll put all of these shorts together to form an anthology movie and we'll market it as a feature. What do you think?" I said, "That sounds like a terrific idea. Let's do it!"

So, Brian and I organized a whole series of meetings with various interested people. Among those in attendance was Ulu Grosbard, who had at one time been Elia Kazan's assistant and was a good director Off-Broadway. Ulu had done a wonderful production *of A View from the Bridge* with Robert Duval and Susan Anspach, and, years later, directed two excellent films: *Straight Time* and *True Confessions*. Also present was Nell Cox, who had replaced Margie Ziskind as my girlfriend by this point, and would later direct among other things a few episodes of *Hill Street Blues*. Nell had worked with Albert and David Maysles, and D.A. Pennebaker, and all those filmmakers that had shot amazing documentaries on the

Kennedys and Bob Dylan using handheld 16mm cameras. Jill Clayburgh, who was Brian's girlfriend at the time, also came to all the meetings. Then, last and certainly least, there was some guy who had directed porno movies who was hoping this project would allow him to do something that was not porno. I remember this individual would always bring his porno star with him to every meeting.

During our early discussions, each of us talked about our hopes and wishes for the movie. Some people didn't know what story they wanted to do, but I already knew exactly what I wanted to do. I was going to make a short based on a story by Saul Bellow called "The Wrecker." It was about a guy who has been so miserable and despondent in his New York apartment that, when the building is scheduled to be torn down, he willingly stays behind to wreck it himself. The film would have pretty much shown the guy systematically destroying his own home and remembering the different things that happened there. So, after choosing my story, I came out to Chicago and went to see Saul Bellow in his office at the University of Chicago. I talked to him about the project, and about who was involved, and convinced him to give me the rights to "The Wrecker." Despite our noble ambitions, the anthology film eventually evaporated. The truth is nobody else came up with a really good idea. "The Wrecker" was a strong idea for a segment, but none of the other suggestions were especially strong. My fellow directors only had fragments, or an individual scene, and it was all very vague. It's funny, but I remember running into Brian many years later when I was down in Dallas during the American Film Festival. I was there with *Bang the Drum Slowly* and he was there with *Get to Know Your Rabbit*. We had dinner with Richard Schickel, who at that point was the *TIME Magazine* film critic, and we reminisced, albeit very briefly, about our lost anthology movie.

Around this same time, I was contacted by Tony Richardson who had seen *A Man's a Man* Off-Broadway and really liked it. Tony was part of the "British New Wave" of filmmakers, and had already made the movie adaptation of *Look Back in Anger* and had just finished shooting *Tom Jones*, the latter a truly brilliant film for which he won an Academy Award for Best Director. Tony had asked me if I wanted to direct a version of Tennessee Williams' *The Milk Train Doesn't Stop Here Anymore* for the English Stage Company at The Royal Court. I immediately said, yes, and flew over to London feeling incredibly excited about the opportunity to work in the land that had produced Shakespeare, Milton and Marlowe. What I love about the United Kingdom is there are so many theaters and so many smart, verbal people. English people in particular seem to be smarter than Americans. But I do think that can sometimes be a dangerous misapprehension in our country. I mean, you can come over to the States with a British accent and sound authoritative and knowledgeable. People suddenly listen to you and take you very seriously, but you can still be dead wrong about something. Anyway, shortly after arriving in England, I discovered that I was actually "co-directing" *Milk Train* with Tony's partner, George Devine, who ran the company with him. I was not made aware of this fact beforehand when I'd talked to Tony and thought it was rather an odd thing to do. Despite this, I met with George and found that I very much liked him, and we were both happy to proceed together.

Ruth Gordon had already been cast in the lead role of 'Sissy' Goforth, the wealthy old woman who is dying on an island off the coast of Italy as she dictates her memoirs to her secretary. George and I went out to the airport to meet Ruth as she flew in from the States. We both dutifully stroked and feted her, as you often do with actors, before escorting Ruth to a hotel in the city. We then started rehearsals on *Milk Train* and quickly discovered at the very first rehearsal that Ruth had come with all of her lines learned and all of her gestures fixed. She already had the whole performance and it was very mannered and artificial. Ruth was playing this Southern woman in a New York accent and she was not believable in any way. It was entirely fake—fake acting. We let this go on for a while and then, at a certain point, I said, "Ruth, why don't we just slow things down a little and try not to perform yet. Let's just talk the lines back and forth and listen to each other." She then rather scornfully replied, "What is *this*? The Group Theatre? The Actors Studio?" She then stared coldly at me and George, and hissed, "You two make me sick!"

After that remarkable outburst, we just sat back, kept our mouths shut, and Ruth continued to do what she was doing. At the end of the day when the rehearsal was finished, George and I went into his office, which was located way up in the attic of the theater. Without pussyfooting around, I said, "Look, we have to fire her. This is a very important play to Tennessee as it's about the death of his lover. *Milk Train* represents a chance of a rebirth for him—if he can see it done well. I don't think that will happen with *that* woman in the role. She is going to kill it." George just nodded, and said, "I know, she's horrible!" I then asked, "Well, why the hell did you cast her?" He said, "Ruth Gordon is a big star in London. She was a hit here in *The Matchmaker* and I don't know who we can get to replace her." As we went back and forth on the matter, George was looking rather tired and agitated. At one point, he complained that his arm was hurting, but at last he agreed with me: "Yes, I think you're right about this. We should just go ahead and fire her and look for somebody else." And, just like that, it seemed like the decision had been made: Ruth Gordon had to go!

Unfortunately, later that same night, George had a serious heart attack and was in no condition to discuss business any further. As a matter of fact, he died only a year or two afterwards. Looking back now, I realize that the heart attack was starting as George and I was speaking that day, although neither of us realized it at the time. With George now terribly ill, I was stuck with this venomous woman whom I hated and who hated me. As we continued working, I decided that I simply wasn't going to just sit there and be yelled at by her. I was going to yell right back! So, Ruth and I fought furiously for the next four or five days and it was a grim time. There was nobody around who had the authority to close the production as George was incapacitated and Tony was off someplace in America preparing a movie—it might have been *The Loved One*. Finally, in desperation, somebody got the board at the Royal Court together and *Milk Train* was officially cancelled. It was a lamentable and disappointing course of action, but an entirely necessary one. Ruth Gordon was a total harridan and I was happily cursing her name. Then, a decade later, shortly after I had made *Bang the Drum Slowly*, I stepped into an elevator at the William Morris Agency and who did I have the satisfaction of sharing the ride up with? None other than Ruth Gordon! It was the first time we had laid eyes on each other since the big blow-up in London and I was braced for an icy reception. Incredibly, it never came. Ruth was strangely nice to me, greeting me like an old friend. It was as if nothing bad had ever happened between us. If Ruth had only been half as pleasant as she was in that elevator, no doubt *Milk Train* would not have closed.

A few years after my first trip to continental Europe, I returned there for a second visit. This was right after my unfortunate experience at the Royal Court. I had gone to Paris on my Harvard grant but, on this occasion, I left London and went to East and West Germany. I was accompanied by Nell Cox, who I was in a relationship with for a year or so, maybe a couple of years. On this return visit, I stayed for three or four months, traveling to West Berlin and living there. Every day I would then leave West Berlin and go over to East Germany, which was not easy. You had to go through Checkpoint Charlie, which was heavily guarded and always had a palpable air of distrust and threat. I was making the journey through Checkpoint Charlie so often the guards kind of got used to me, but not entirely. They would routinely change them and so you'd be dealing with different guards at different times, but they all had that same somber and mildly sinister look. They were these very careful, very cold East German soldiers that would study you suspiciously with these dead eyes. I never got used to them.

While visiting East Germany, I had an opportunity to study the Berliner Ensemble up close and got to be quite friendly with Brecht's widow, Helene Weigel. Weigel (I never called her Helene, she was "Helli" to her close friends, which I was not, and "Weigel" to everyone else) had been Brecht's second wife and had bore him two children. She was an actress of great distinction, as well as an able administrator having taken over as artistic director after Brecht had died. I remember Weigel would call me "Cicero" because they had staged Brecht's *The Resistible Rise of Arturo Ui*, and a big chunk of that play is set in Cicero, Chicago, and deals with a fictional mobster in the 1930s. At this point in time, I had already successfully done *A Man's a Man* Off-Broadway, and so I was suddenly somebody to Weigel. She knew exactly who I was and was very nice to me. She showed me around, showed me for starters the peephole that enabled the artistic director to spy on what was happening on stage and still do office work—something I came to envy later when I became an artistic director myself.

Because I praised their costumes so lavishly, Weigel gave me samples of the company's fabrics, showed me how they were designing and making their costumes, and taught me new techniques of antiquing (where you make the clothes look old). One thing she showed me that was particularly impressive was a pinstripe suit. They'd needed it for some production right after the war when they couldn't get pinstripe. So, they had taken dark blue fabric and someone had laboriously painted the pinstripes on with "bleichlauge." "What is bleichlauge?" I had asked. "Bleichmittel, bleichmittel!" she insisted. Turns out it's bleach. Naturally, the Berliner Ensemble always had the very best costumes and sets. Everything looked expertly old and worn and patched. They were wonderful technically at ageing things and creating a decidedly impressive stylistic environment. For instance, there was a particular grain to the wood of their sets which, I once observed, they accomplished with the use of blowtorches. Eric Bentley used to joke about the advantages they enjoyed of "slave labor." Weigel also allowed me to attend all the rehearsals, which I thought was especially nice of her. It was particularly fascinating to inspect the work that the Ensemble was doing in comparison with what was being done in American Theater at that time. They not only had different and innovative ways of doing sets and costumes, they had a unique and disciplined way of exploring and presenting the plays. Eventually, we—meaning the Americans and the British—all embraced aspects of the Brechtian approach as well in terms of our application of his staging techniques. I mean, if you look at say *Evita*; that is unquestionably a Brechtian production that lays bare his influence. If you look at the way theater is done now it's much more open and accessible, certainly in terms of our being willing to let the process of changing sets be visible and that kind of thing.

I remember that during my visit, Weigel was playing Mother Courage and I got to see once again just how accomplished she was as an actress. When you are an artistic director you often have directors working for you, and Weigel didn't direct herself. In that regard, she was different to the kind of artistic director I would later become, but she had a deep knowledge and appreciation of the craft as well as a real warmth and generosity. Weigel didn't talk much about the personal aspects of Brecht, and I never picked her brain about him or their relationship. I don't know if that was a mistake or not. Maybe it was. Maybe it would have given me further insights into his work. One thing she did take pains to explain to me was the reasons why the Berlin Wall had been built by the German Democratic Republic just two years before. Weigel talked at length about the "brain drain" and the country's concerns over the exodus of emigrants. East Germany was training their own citizens only for a lot of them to depart to find jobs in West Germany. So, in order to stop them from losing so many people, they built the Wall and effectively cut off West Berlin from the East. Weigel also talked about how East Germany had no glass and the economy was severely depleted and hampered. I'll never forget that she had a picture of Joseph Stalin in her office—and this was in 1963 after Stalin had been denounced by Khrushchev in '56. I mean, you were not supposed to have a picture of Stalin anymore but she had one openly displayed. She was an extremely committed communist and a fascinating woman. I learned a lot from Weigel in that short space of time.

After leaving East Germany, I then went to Paris once again. While there, I looked into the possibility of securing the rights to several interesting French plays I had seen: one was a comedy written by Roland Dubillard called *Naïves hirondelles*, and another was a play by the late Boris Vian. I talked to some playwrights and asked them if they would be willing to let me have the rights if I could set-up some of these productions Off-Broadway in New York. They agreed, but I didn't actually make the contracts. There were also a couple of things I had seen in various Paris theaters—not big theaters, just little ones. I couldn't speak French, but the plays seemed good and the audience reaction was favorable. People were also recommending them to me and saying they would translate well in the States. I then met a French producer over there named Napoleon Murat, whose ancestor had been one of Napoleon's admirals or generals. Murat advocated some of these works, too, and through him I got to meet Louis Malle, who also kindly recommended a couple of plays to me. I was happy to meet Louis and I later became a great admirer of both his French and American films. I particularly like *Damage*, which is one of his final pictures. Malle was very charming, very small and very French; just a really friendly, helpful guy. I can remember feeling sad when I heard that he had died. I was thinking about him again only recently as I've just finished reading the autobiography of his widow, Candice Bergman. I found the section on Malle's death to be quite moving.

> Hancock returned to America from Paris in November, 1963, shortly before the assassination of John F. Kennedy in Dallas, Texas. Frustrated at the delays and lack of interest in setting-up Naïves hirondelles *Off-Broadway*, he once again turned his attention to film. In early 1964, Hancock inquired into the availability of the rights to Dick Francis' recently published second novel, Nerve, *a thriller about a steeplechase jockey who is embroiled in a deadly mystery. After failing to entice anybody into optioning the book on his behalf, Hancock looked for another property (although* Nerve *would be a project that he would pursue more vigorously once he was established as a film director). His next thought was to adapt John Barth's 1958 novel* The End of the Road *as a screenplay that would mark his debut feature.*

I had first read Barth's book when I was eighteen and had been impressed with its irony and honesty. I thought the story itself was fairly straightforward: you have the nihilistic character of Jacob Horner, a hopeless guy who sees no reason to do anything and can't decide what to do with his life or where to go. He is rescued by a crazy doctor who, through a series of bizarre treatments, revitalizes him and sends him off to teach in a little college in Maryland. While there Horner meets a vigorous and decisive existentialist named Joe Morgan who has a very pretty and subdued wife named Rennie. They get to be friends and, to kind of test his wife—or to test his relationship with Horner as he possibly has a secret homosexual desire for him—Joe pushes Rennie to go horseback riding with their new companion in an effort for her to get to know him better. Rennie and Horner then have an affair, which ends disastrously when Rennie gets pregnant and dies in a botched abortion.

The End of the Road is evidently a dark story, but there is some humor in it. The book is partially a satire of radical psychiatry, but that element interested me less than the tragic love triangle. I've always been interested in the profundities of human sexual behavior, desire and experimentation; how these things can be both empowering and destructive. I once co-wrote a screenplay about a White guy who likes to watch his wife fuck Black guys. Admittedly, that script was a comedy, but there was still a lot of truth in it about human relationships. Interestingly, when I first got to New York, Harold Clurman had given me a list of plays to track down. One of them was Robert Lowell's *Endicott and the Red Cross*, which I eventually ended up doing in 1968, and another was a dramatization of Dostoevsky's tragicomedy *The Eternal Husband*, which I found intriguing as it dealt with the complexities of adultery and being a hapless cuckold. It was interesting that Harold should recommend that specific play to me, as he was at one time married to Stella Adler, the famous acting teacher, who would literally fuck anything! I mean, she fucked cops because they had blue underwear. I've often wondered what must have been going through Harold's mind during all of Stella's unfaithfulness; how he dealt with all the terrible pain and embarrassment she must have caused him. To me, those kinds of relationships are fascinating to explore dramatically.

Anyway, on the basis of the wonderful reviews I had received for *A Man's a Man*, I drove out to Central Pennsylvania to meet with John Barth. He was working as a professor at the Pennsylvania State University at the time, and talked and walked with the air of a serious-minded academic. What I recall most about our meeting was Barth telling me that he brewed his own beer. He was very anxious that I should try it, but I didn't drink and so politely declined. Barth was somewhat shattered by my refusal to partake in his beer and it took him a few minutes to recover from the disappointment. Looking back, I should have had the good sense to drink what was offered me as my reluctance could have possibly jeopardized the whole deal. You never know. Now that I think about it, I may have indeed drunk his beer just to keep him happy. Yes, I'm certain that I did. Barth then agreed to give me the rights to *The End of the Road* and the deal was initially for something like five dollars a year, with the right to renew the option for another year for another five dollars.

My next move was to try to get Konrad and Gay Matthaei involved with the project. They were interested in helping out and duly put up some of the front money, and also money for some other people I wanted to bring in. We then commissioned about three or four screenplays of *The End of the Road*. The first draft was done by a writer whose name I can no longer remember. He was Ned something-or-other. Ned was nobody important, and had never written anything before, but he turned in a fairly good draft. I then wrote a couple of subsequent drafts, which improved it even more, and I felt confident we had something great. Of course, there was always a problem with the ending in that the story culminates with this ghastly abortion. I knew people would have a big problem with that scene. Another guy I involved in the project was the pop artist Jim Dine. At the same time I was developing *The End of the Road*, Jim and I were working for the producer Cheryl Crawford, who, along with Harold Clurman and Lee Strasberg, was one of the three people who founded The Group Theatre in New York. Cheryl had wanted to do a version of *Oh! What a Lovely War*, and transpose the story and characters from the First World War to the American Civil War. I was trying to put that together for her, coming up with some ideas about how we could possibly do it. Jim was going to design the costumes and sets for the show, and was doing these wonderful pictures of Abraham Lincoln and Robert E. Lee. Jim and I became friends and I talked to him about *The End of the Road*. He then did a series of storyboards for me that I hoped would help us sell the project. Despite this, and the bunch of different screenplays we did, the film did not move forward.

Ultimately, I think there were a number of reasons why we failed to get the project off the ground—chiefly, because it was hard to raise the necessary money. Considering the fact that I had not done a film before, people hesitated at the prospect of financing the work of a first-time director. I also didn't have access to the kind of actors that would have assisted in getting people to part with their money. I was just a young guy at the time with no credits, only these stupendous reviews I'd received for an Off-Broadway play. It just wasn't enough to get the movie going. Then, in 1965, I got the offer to take over the Actor's Workshop in San

Francisco and *The End of the Road* was further interrupted. Eventually, the project just died away. It was a bitter disappointment because I loved Barth's book and was passionate about bringing it to the screen. Sadly, that responsibility would be placed in the hands of others. Several years later, in 1970, Aram Avakian made his version of *The End of the Road* and that soundly put an end to the whole matter.

If I was invited to critique Aram's film I would firstly say that it's visually fabulous. *The End of the Road* was Gordon Willis' first picture, shortly before he moved on to shoot *Klute* for Alan J. Pakula and *The Godfather* for Francis Coppola, and effectively redefined cinematography. Aram himself was a brilliant still photographer, as well as a wonderful editor, so I'm not surprised it's sumptuous to look at. But I do think that because Aram was a first-time director, he allowed himself to be misled by Stacy Keach and Harris Yulin (who played Jacob and Joe respectively), and, to a larger degree, his screenwriter Terry Southern. At that time Terry was riding on top of the world after writing *Dr. Strangelove* with Stanley Kubrick, and co-writing *Easy Rider* with Peter Fonda and Dennis Hopper. He was hanging out with The Beatles, and that kind of thing, but he was a drunk and a doper. During the making of *The End of the Road*, he insisted on all kinds of strange line readings that he wanted to do. Keach and Yulin happily did them for him, and I think the picture suffered greatly for it. All four of them simply butchered the novel. They ignored Barth's story and just indulged in tired little things that were amusing to them.

Dorothy Tristan, who was Aram's wife at the time and mine now in what one might see as a bizarre twist of fate, is brilliant in the role of Rennie. She chose to ignore Terry and I think her performance benefited from that decision. The controversial abortion scene—which I had found problematic when we were originally developing the project—is absolutely harrowing and earned the picture an X-rating. Dorothy really went all out in depicting the agony of what it is to be brutally scraped on the inside. She was simply astounding in that scene. What's even more remarkable is that was the first scene she ever did—that was on the very first day of shooting! Dorothy really pulled out all the stops. The abortion remains extremely difficult to watch, but I hope I would have done it just the same way as Aram did. I hope I would have pushed it as far as he did. Aram's movie was not a hit when it came out, but it has enjoyed quite a renaissance in recent years. Steven Soderbergh has championed the film as a "lost classic" and even convinced Warner Bros. to release it on Blu-ray. So, it's getting a lot more respect now than it ever has. But I don't mind admitting that I would have made an entirely different movie to the one Aram made.

The notoriously brutal critic John Simon panned *The End of the Road* in the *Sunday New York Times*, but he loved Dorothy. It was worth seeing, he said, just for her "shiningly irrefutable performance." Permit me to quote a little more of him, as I have Simon's review here: "Now she is the prototypical dowdy faculty wife; now a blazing maenad unleashed on our libido; now a china shepherdess so fragile her own breathing might shatter her; now a goddess shooting up high above any mere man in the immensity of her love and wrath." Clearly, he had a crush, as did I. I should probably explain why at this point, since she eventually became a central part of my work and life. See, I knew the subject matter so well, I'd written numerous drafts of the screenplay, but I'd always been puzzled about the wife's motivation: why does she let her husband push her into a relationship with another man? I saw Dorothy in the film and understood why. It was a mysterious blend of anger ("You want me to do this? Okay, I'll show you,") and pride in her sexuality, and darkness, and a million other colors, just like Simon says. It was a magical performance. It worked a kind of alchemy in my soul. I saw that here was an actress, a beautiful actress, who showed *me* something about a work I knew well. What Dorothy did went beyond what an actress usually does. It was a creative act, like writing. Here, I thought, is a creative artist. And she's living up the road in Sneden's Landing, which is on the Hudson River about forty minutes outside New York, with her husband! Yes, as I was with my wife, Ann Arensberg, being ostensibly happy. But there she was.

> *In 1965, when he just twenty-six, Hancock was approached to take over as artistic director of the San Francisco Actor's Workshop. Founded in 1952 by Herbert Blau (1926-2013) and Jules Irving (1925-1979), the company had quickly gained a reputation as "one of the nation's cutting-edge regional theaters," mounting notable productions of Harold Pinter's* The Birthday Party, *Samuel Beckett's* Waiting For Godot, *Jean Genet's* The Balcony *and Arthur Miller's* The Crucible. *Hancock directed several successful productions between 1965 and 1966 including revivals of Bertolt Brecht's* The Life of Edward II of England, *Saul Bellow's* The Last Analysis, *and, in an effort to possibly erase its painful cancellation at the Royal Court two years previously,*

Tennessee Williams' The Milk Train Doesn't Stop Here Anymore.

The Actor's Workshop was *the* big regional theater in San Francisco. At that point in time, it had been around for fourteen years and Herbert Blau and Jules Irving—the latter being Amy Irving's father and Priscilla Pointer's husband—had done a good job of running it. Elia Kazan, Robert Whitehead and Harold Clurman were fired at New York City's Repertory Theatre of Lincoln Center as they'd had a season and a half of theater that the board wasn't particularly happy with. So, this change necessitated them bringing in somebody else and they managed to lure Herb and Jules from the Actor's Workshop. In turn, Herb and Jules brought along with them a big chunk of their acting company from San Francisco after taking over at Lincoln Center. This left a sizable hole and so the question was promptly raised whether they should close down the Actor's Workshop or make some efforts to keep it going in one form or another. Jules and Herb had seen *A Man's a Man* in New York and loved it. They suggested that I go out to San Francisco and meet with the board to see if they would be interested in hiring me, which they were.

My first job as artistic director was to rebuild and replenish the acting company. As I proceeded to do this, I was also carefully choosing the plays and would eventually direct most of them myself. Sometimes I hired other directors to work on certain productions as we had two theaters out there. I had a couple of what you could call associate directors that were working under me. We did a version of Michael McClure's *The Beard*, and also did Rick Cluchey's play *The Cage*, which my partner out there, Kenneth Kitch, directed. However, the very first thing I did in the summer before our subscription season started was get Tennessee Williams to come and work with me on rewriting *The Milk Train Doesn't Stop Here Anymore*. I wrote to Tennessee and told him of my plans for the Actor's Workshop and how much I wanted to mount *Milk Train* there. It turned out that he was more than happy to come out and work on the play with me, and be in San Francisco. I had first met Tennessee several years earlier at The Y in New York, which was over on the Westside, on 63rd Street. This was shortly before I went to England to do the production that blew-up at the Royal Court. I can remember introducing myself to Tennessee in the locker room as he was taking off his rubber swimsuit, which was a horrible thing to behold. It was a nasty, grey, skin-fitting condom-like thing, only thicker! So, I only knew him from that brief meeting.

Getting to know Tennessee a little better on *Milk Train* was wonderful. Aside from doing *The Glass Menagerie* at Harvard, I had of course seen and read so many of his plays. In fact, Richard Brooks' movie of *Cat on a Hot Tin Roof* is one of the reasons I wanted to go into the film business. So, I was a really big fan of Tennessee's work and I know that he felt that. He sensed how great I thought he was. As Tennessee and I were toiling on *Milk Train*, I was flying to New York and holding auditions, trying to assemble a new company for the fall subscriptions season. Although I was working with the leftovers from the previous regime, we put together a very good cast. Winifred Mann, who had been a fabulous remnant from Blau and Irving's incarnation of the company, played 'Sissy' Goforth, and there was another actor around San Francisco named Robert Benson, who I cast as the young man who comes to her villa overlooking the Mediterranean. The first thing I had Tennessee do was read the play to the cast as he was a fabulous actor. I mean, Tennessee was so incredibly subtle, just a tightrope between different colors and textures.

This first collaboration was a truly amazing experience. We never had anything bad happen, not on this one. Later, on other projects we did together such as *The Two-Character Play* and *Stopped Rocking*, I had incredible scenes with Tennessee. I got to witness his tempestuous and difficult side, but *Milk Train* was a picnic in comparison. It turned out to be a very good production. In his book, *Memoirs*, which was published in the mid-1970s, Tennessee wrote that of all the directors he'd ever worked with, I was the most talented for suggesting "transpositions of material that were artistically effective." That compliment arose from our time working on *Milk Train* together. There were scenes between the old lady and the young angel of death figure, and there were scenes between the old lady and the secretary who is typing up her autobiography. By having the actors read it to him, I demonstrated to Tennessee that if the scenes between the old lady and the secretary were between the old lady and the angel of death, they would be far more effective. Tennessee agreed with me and duly incorporated those changes into the play.

I remember that after each preview we held, Tennessee would immediately run off to a place called The Tool Box, which was some kind of terrible S&M gay bar that had opened a few years earlier and was very popular with the homosexual community in San Francisco. Naturally, it was not a terrible place to him as he really loved it there. Tennessee only attended about half or two-thirds of the rehearsals. He always got up late as he'd usually been out living it up at The Tool Box the night before.

But even getting Tennessee involved with the Actor's Workshop proved to be a major publicity coup for us, attracting somebody of his fame and stature. It earned us the unexpected attentions of Herb Caen, who was a celebrated and popular journalist for the *San Francisco Chronicle*. Caen had a very important column where he reported on all the comings and goings and happenings that occurred in the area. I became his pet for a while and that was a valuable position to be in. Suddenly, we were getting noticed and discussed by people. The resulting exposure meant that the company quickly acquired more subscribers than they'd ever had in their entire history. Indeed, we raised much more money than had ever been accrued previously and we had an incredibly successful season up there.

The play that opened our subscription season was a production of *Edward II*, Brecht's adaptation of Marlowe's historical tragedy. I loved that play and Eric Bentley's poetic translation is the best thing he's ever done and serves it perfectly. *Edward II* was an important evolution in terms of my development as a director. Paul Gemignani composed the music, and was in the band for it, and he later became a significant conductor on Broadway musicals for Stephen Sondheim. Barton Heyman played Edward, and was very good, but what distinguished that production for me was our utilizing a big spectacular revolving stage. A considerable part of Brecht's play is consumed by a battle and I started thinking about how we could do the fight in a way that was startling and fresh. I wanted the audience to respond in a different way and thought I could achieve this by using certain filmic techniques. This was the beginning of my thinking *cinematically* in terms of conveying certain ideas and emotions on the stage. It's hard for me to explain, but thinking about the Berliner Ensemble's various productions of Brecht, and all the things I did with the revolving stage, how similar certain techniques I deployed in the theater were to tracking shots in film. I don't know if you can visualize an action like the fight in *Edward II* where I had soldiers battling on a revolving stage, or the chase on a revolving stage that we did later in *A Midsummer Night's Dream*, but I felt those moments were very much like when you move the camera on a dolly.

I discovered that thinking cinematically in theater opened me up to new ideas and new approaches, and was enormously beneficial. I've always thought that some of Brecht's plays, such as *Mother Courage* for instance, were conscious attempts to bring film into the theater in a very direct way. There was an exhilarating moment in *Mother Courage* where Courage is dragging her wagon along and it was performed on a revolving stage. This gave it an uncommon sense of energy and action, and I felt the audience responded accordingly. Granted, if you have a tracking shot in a movie of a woman dragging a wagon along a road it doesn't have that same sense of uniqueness as the tracking shot is a standard technique used in film. The movement of the camera still registers visually and impacts you emotionally, but not in the same way as approximating the same sensory effect in a theatrical experience. *Mother Courage* perhaps wouldn't work half as well as a movie as it does a play. Curiously, Brecht's plays are very much like screenplays in that they don't all take place in one fixed location. Like Shakespeare, they are episodic and, generally speaking, there is a lot of movement contained within them. I came to realize later when I reflected on productions like *Edward II* that it was a logical progression for me to love that kind of theater and then make the transition into doing movies. Doing a Brecht play wasn't the same as doing a play by Shaw or Ibsen. Brecht's work had that distinct filmic quality to it—again, that aspect of movement and action—which I adored.

In some ways, I never made a distinction between directing for the stage and directing movies. I always knew I could do both, even back in 1965, and that's exactly what I did. To me, theater and film was basically the same in terms of their requirements and were only separated by their technical demands. I mean, the job of the theatrical director is to block the play; to inspire and lead a crew of people. You have to deal with actors; be cognizant of story and character, and always make these things clear to the audience; you have to deal with all the visual aspects of set design and costume and lighting; you have to maintain a sense of rhythm and pace— know exactly when to speed things up and slow them down, and make the transitions from contrasting moments of sadness and humor and tension work. In that regard, theater is very similar to film. As a director you are still asking yourself the same questions: what works? What doesn't work? How do you get the most out of a group of people? Obviously, a director has to understand the play he or she is directing. So, there is an element of reading and analysis involved; discovering what the beats are, and what the characters want. What is the event? What is taking place? You try to identify and isolate all of these things in order to re-create the play and bring it to life.

The second play I directed in the subscription season was a production of Saul Bellow's *The Last Analysis*. I'd describe the central character of that play as being like Jackie Gleason if Gleason has read too many psychology books and wanted to psychoanalyze himself as a television spectacular.

Abe Vigoda played the lead in it and was brilliant. He had played some kind of bishop in *Edward II* and, as we were rehearsing that play, Abe had unexpectedly started shouting his lines in this loud grand voice. I said to myself, "Whoa, what have I got *here*?!" I mean, I had been attending readings in New York, selecting a bunch of capable actors before flying them to San Francisco and finding them apartments, but all of a sudden I had this guy who was outrageously funny. I was delighted with that discovery, so I decided to cast Abe in our next production, too. That proved to be a wise decision as he was absolutely hilarious in *The Last Analysis*. Honestly, I've never heard an audience laugh so much during a play. Ever! It was very, very funny.

I'm still very proud of *The Last Analysis*, but I've always wanted to do it again. There was a lost of restless invention in Bellow's play and, despite how well that production turned out, it's one of those works I think I could do even better now. But it wasn't all smooth sailing. There was an old actor around San Francisco at the time that had done quite a lot of work there. The floor of our set was covered with books and this actor kept stumbling over them as he was trying to move about and deliver his lines. Eventually he blew up at me, and shouted, "You don't know what you are doing!" In response to that outburst, I promptly fired him. The only problem about doing that was we were opening the following night! So, what I did was I cut his part. I just excised it totally. Rather than harming the play or rendering it insensible, it made *The Last Analysis* much better. The play was suddenly shorter, tighter, more focused, and it turned out that this guy's character was effectively doing nothing but talking. It was very interesting. Of course, I'm sure that Saul Bellow wasn't particularly happy about what I did, but it worked out great.

Mind you, not everything we did in San Francisco was great. We mounted a production of August Strindberg's *The Father* that I don't feel I did as well on as some of the other plays I directed there. *The Father* is a naturalistic tragedy that concerns a cavalry officer and the family of women who share his household; how his patriarchal authority is challenged when he and his wife disagree over the future of their daughter. The wife then suggests to her husband that he may not be the girl's father and this revelation has terrible consequences that follow. The play takes place over the course of a day and is essentially a study in the battle of the sexes as the parents—who are two very different people—fight for possession of their child. I initially felt that with all that dramatic and thematic meat on it, *The Father* would be a strong choice for us. Not so. The play was maybe not cast as well as it might have been, and some of the performances were a little flat. One thing I do remember about that production was, at the time, I was very interested in Op Art, in devising images and compositions that worked like optical illusions. We created a wallpaper to be used on the set that was in essence a work of Op Art which was designed to encourage the audience to hallucinate lines running through it. We went into previews with that set and it was so effective and so intense, people did begin perceiving all kinds of patterns and shifting movements in the wallpaper. I think it was far too disconcerting and disturbing for them, as well as being extremely distracting. Hence, I had to spray the set down, tone the Op Art down a little, and not make it quite so vivid.

> *Hancock's fruitful tenure at the San Francisco Actor's Workshop came to an end in the summer of 1966. Shortly afterwards, he was appointed artistic director of the Pittsburgh Playhouse, Point Park University's performing arts center, where he had originally intended to spend a further year. Unfortunately, his reign was curtailed abruptly in early 1967, but not before he mounted a stunning production of Shakespeare's* A Midsummer Night's Dream. *Hancock would eventually take the play to New York later that same year, consolidating his growing reputation as one of the best and most adventurous Off-Broadway directors of his generation.*

I don't mind telling you that my time at the Pittsburgh Playhouse was not a happy one. Basically, the reason I went there was because of a huge financial offer that we simply could not refuse: they literally tripled our budget and doubled my salary. It was impossible to turn down such a lucrative deal. So, I moved my entire company from San Francisco to Pittsburgh, and the actors were bitter at me about that as the towns there aren't nearly as nice. Upon my arrival, I discovered that the Board of Directors at the Playhouse were Republicans. It had never occurred to me that the board of a theater could possibly be Republican never mind Conservative. Nonetheless, some of them were, although H. John Heinz III, who was not Conservative and later became a senator, was also on the board. He and I became good friends.

As the very first production, I did *A Man's a Man* again and Charles Durning played the lead. He was absolutely wonderful in it, and it was a solid effort. In 1999, there was an article in the *Pittsburgh Post-Gazette* in which Charlie recalled his experiences with me on the play we'd done more than thirty years earlier. He revealed that he had once thrown his metal make-up case at me in anger after a performance of *A Man's a Man*. What Charlie said is true, but his fury was short-lived. What happened was I was having trouble during previews getting the pace of *A Man's a Man* fast enough. We had silent film exercises in the afternoon where the actors performed at that silly pace. It was great fun, but then, that evening, things were slow again. So, I stopped the preview and they performed it from the top again at a faster pace. It was my way of getting their attention. I then went backstage after the intermission to smooth some ruffled feathers when Charlie came charging out of his dressing room, tearing half the door off its hinges! I don't remember him throwing his make-up case at me as he mentioned in the article, but things were smooth again between us by the next day.

However, it soon became apparent that things were anything but smooth between me and R.K. Mellon of the Mellon family. Despite the play being wonderful, Mellon had heard there was a urinal on the stage and this caused great unrest. In just a single week, the grants from all the Mellon corporations were swiftly cancelled. I'm not kidding. The $50,000 from U.S. Steel, the $50,000 from Alcoa, the $50,000 from the Mellon Bank, Pittsburgh Plate Glass, and monies from other organizations, were angrily withdrawn. We literally lost $300,000 in just seven days, as crazy as that sounds. Let me reiterate: this was all because Mellon had "heard" there was a urinal on the stage. Sure, it was true, we did indeed have a urinal, but Charlie hadn't actually peed in it, he had merely pretended to. That fact did not matter. The money was gone! We later called this event "The $300,000 Leak."

Following this bombshell, we then diligently went about raising the money from the public, but, after all these difficulties, I took what had happened very badly. I took it so badly that I attacked! This was all taking place during the Vietnam War and, befitting such a tumultuous period in our nation's history, *A Man's a Man* is a very strong anti-war, anti-militarism play. I had recently befriended Donald E. Graham, who, after graduating from Harvard, had volunteered to serve in the U.S. Army and later went to Vietnam. In the 1970s, he became the publisher of *The Washington Post*, which is an extremely powerful position in America. But back in 1966, Don was stationed near Pittsburgh and he came to all the productions we held. I spent a lot of time with Donny and got to be very close to him. I wanted to hit back at what I saw as the injustice of what had occurred. I talked to Donny about it, and, since there was some press interest in the story, he was kind of writing my material for me. So, there I was on the front page of the newspapers in Pittsburgh, day after day, saying exactly what Donny told me to say about the Mellons! A result of all this was the board divided in half; half of them wanted to fire me and the other half didn't.

Finally, it was decided that I should be dismissed and John Heinz resigned from the board in protest. It was a messy situation, but was also rather revelatory. I mean, there was a big cultural divide in Pittsburgh at that point and it was becoming apparent to everyone. There were some people that wanted an interesting and vital theater and there were others who wanted a kind of tepid country club theater. Before we came along, the board would have probably been content to have done twenty-five years of *Under the Yum Yum Tree*. There was only one problem with that: the board had decided they wanted to get Rockefeller, and Ford, and National Endowment of the Arts grants, and you can't get those if all you want to do is commercial summer stock fare. So, they wanted to have a new and slightly more daring artistic regime that would enable them to secure these grants that they craved. It was too bad for me that the audience was incurably trained to watch Broadway comedies and the board's ambitions and focus, as well as their own sense of morality and decency, was very fixed and parochial in my opinion.

After the debacle in Pittsburgh, I came back to New York in 1967. I then did a production of *A Midsummer Night's Dream*, which is a play I had mounted both in San Francisco and in Pittsburgh. Ted Mann and his partner Paul Libin produced it Off-Broadway at the Theatre De Lys (now the Lucille Lortel Theatre in Manhattan's West Village), which, back then, was the best Off-Broadway theater. Ted and Paul ran a very important Off-Broadway company called Circle in the Square. They had done a famous production of *Summer and Smoke* in the early 1950s, as well as acclaimed revivals of *The Iceman Cometh* and *Long Day's Journey into Night*, and had discovered a lot of great people like Geraldine Page and Jason Robards. Ted and Paul had come to Pittsburgh and seen my production of *A Midsummer Night's Dream* there. They were apparently impressed enough with it to want me to bring the play to New York and restage it. I was more than happy to do it again, and we got some good people involved with the project. I also had some new ideas I wanted to try out.

When I had originally done *Midsummer* in San Francisco, in 1966, I had taken the cast to the woods at night for what turned out to be one of the best rehearsals I've ever had. Unfortunately, it also resulted in major poison oak for everyone—me above all as I had a particularly nasty allergic reaction to it (I still have faint scars from my persistent scratching during previews). The bulk of Shakespeare's play takes place in the woods at night, and I thought it would be interesting to explore what darkness does, and dew, and "rough uneven way." What is it if you can't clearly see the face of the person you're supposed to love? One of the key tools of the Stanislavski system is getting the actors to make the place real for themselves, and here was a fast way of doing that. I just felt that they would get so much out of it, and they did too. They came back all excited—that was until the poison oak hit—and even with that, I think they were glad we did it. An interesting sidelight on the *Midsummer* rehearsal in the woods: Ted Mann later started directing himself and in his autobiography he mentions how a cast visit to Eugene O'Neill's house made all the difference in his production of *Long Day's Journey into Night*. I can see that: standing in real rooms and making all that seem real.

For me, rehearsals on a play are always a fascinating stage of the process. It's really the time when the focus is placed on the actors and they start to come to the fore in terms of importance and contribution. I don't involve actors in every step of a play's creation as some other directors might do. I'm sure there are some who consult with the actors on everything, but I don't. I think you do have to accommodate their thoughts about costume, for instance, but not about things like lighting or the physical staging of a play. I pretty much block all the stuff myself when directing for the theater. I come in already knowing exactly how I want it to be blocked. If a particular actor doesn't feel comfortable with a piece of blocking, you can always modify it, or simply ignore them and get them to do it your way. Occasionally you have to do just that, you have to be strong, but it's not usually a contentious or confrontational thing. You are always working the details out together, trying to find the best and most effective result, and a lot of that work is done in rehearsal.

The sets and costumes for *Midsummer* were done by Jim Dine, who had remained a friend since our unsuccessful attempts at getting *The End of the Road* on as a movie a few years earlier. Our collaboration on the play was great and Jim was always a lot of fun to work with. In our early discussions I talked to him about creating a kind of dream-like atmosphere that was rich in wonder and magic and sensuality, but was also very funny and wild. I also wanted it to be playful and heartfelt, something that was bursting with life and energy, and have the audience really feel all of those things when they watched it. I had carefully studied Shakespeare's play when we had done the earlier productions and wanted to get back to what I thought he had intended: the transformative interplay between dreams and reality, logic and fantasy. *A Midsummer Night's Dream* is one of those plays people think they know all about. I mean, it's often done a certain way. For a long time, it had been in the domain of fairies in tutus and gauze and glitter, all that stuff, and something was missing from it. I'd always remembered Max Reinhardt's 1935 film version with James Cagney as Bottom and Mickey Rooney as Puck, and I acquired some ideas from that picture. I liked the kind of slapstick energy it had, although it's by no means perfect and some of the parts were perhaps badly cast.

Despite my wanting to return to what Shakespeare did, I also wanted to utilize things that gave the play a new vitality. So, I tried to do it in an overtly sexual way. It had certain communist aspects in terms of the mechanicals that put on the play, but it had a distinct eroticism that felt authentic. For me, *A Midsummer Night's Dream* was about the ambivalence of love; how you can betray your partner just for no reason; for the opportunity presenting itself really. Jim and I talked a lot about this, about the vagaries of lust and love, and we involved a lot of funny and innovative pop art stuff to help us sell some of our ideas. For instance, one of the things we deployed was flashing codpieces whenever certain characters got aroused. It was very amusing. We did some of the fairies using puppets, and had dolls with wings, and big hairy bats and other assorted creatures. Using ultraviolet light, Oberon became a silver lamé shroud that looked like no one was inside it.

We also utilized a lot of slow-motion—the actors literally moved around on stage in slow-motion and it was hysterically funny. Abe Vigoda in particular had been sensational at doing slow-motion in the San Francisco production. Shakespeare does some interesting things with time in the play, there's a timeless, dreamy quality in terms of how long the events go on for. But this was another concerted effort to apply filmic techniques to theater in a forthright way. As I had done on *Edward II*, I once again used a revolving stage when we were having chases through the woods. This time I had real trees positioned on the revolving stage that were fully in bloom and we covered the tubs they stood in with floral oriental rugs. We used a lot of music including Mahler's *The Song of the Earth*, which had been so beloved and reassuring to me in my teenage years. We also used a lot of Mendelssohn—as Reinhardt had done in his movie—and a lot of jukebox music, and tried to create this sensory experience.

In the New York *Midsummer*, we had Alvin Epstein playing Oberon, Gloria Foster playing Titania and Susan Anspach playing Hermia. I also re-hired Barton Heyman and Alan Manson, who had played Puck and Bottom respectively in Pittsburgh, to resume their roles, before bringing in Robert Benson from San Francisco to play Helena. Having the role of Helena done by a big man in drag was a fairly unusual thing to do at that point in time. Of course, it wasn't back in Shakespeare's day as they had men playing all the female parts. The cast were—for the most part—very good and compliant with the notable exception of Susan Anspach. Susan was a wonderful actress, but she made everyone crazy. First of all she wore transparent blouses to rehearsals with her nipples hidden behind nasty little band-aids. Then she fucked the actor playing Demetrius and de-balled the actor playing Lysander whom she was supposed to love. How did she de-ball him? Just by making faces while they were playing scenes together, which conveyed she didn't respect him as an actor or a man. It became such a problem I had to end up switching the Lysander and the Demetrius in their parts—and they were far more suitable the way I first had them. Then, I'm ashamed to say, Susan and I found ourselves kissing at one of those take-the-cast-to-the-woods-at-night rehearsals I'd grown so fond of having for *Midsummer*. It went no further, but it was not a good idea. Don't mess around with your leading lady! And if you do, don't fail to consummate! It puts her in an unpleasantly powerful position. Later, when I realized Susan was casting a sour pall over the production, I got on the phone and begged my Hermias from San Francisco and Pittsburgh to come take over the role, but they were bitter over the fact I hadn't cast them in the New York production to begin with, and were deaf to my pleas. Not my happiest moment, because I felt I'd done it to myself. Susan has earned a legendary reputation as a difficult actress, but fucking anyone in a cast can be incredibly disruptive.

> *A* Midsummer's Night Dream *ran for twenty-eight performances from June 29 to July 23, 1967. Indicative of most notices were the ones featured in the* Village Voice *and* Cue Magazine, *the latter particularly fulsome in its praise: "This brutal, vulgar and erotic production of Shakespeare's sex fantasy is the most original and arresting*

I've ever witnessed. This is the best of all the Dreams *and an important pioneering effort in re-interpreting the play."* As if to confirm its innovation and inventiveness, the production won Hancock the 1968 Obie Award for Distinguished Direction.

I had read John Lahr's incredible rave of *Midsummer* in the *Village Voice*, where he was the drama critic for a while, and was delighted with it. I wrote him a thank you letter and he responded. We then arranged to have lunch together, and Lahr and I became fast friends. He and his first wife, Anthea, would come and stay overnight with me and my first wife, Ann, at our home in Sneden's Landing. Lahr remains a dear friend to this day, and it all began with that wonderful review he wrote of *Midsummer*. I also remember the review in *Cue Magazine* well, and was very pleased with it, but not all the notices were as spectacularly positive as those two. I remember the review in *The New York Times*, for instance, was somewhat mixed. Now, I must tell you something important concerning these kinds of adverse reactions: when you bring in productions from out-of-town, ones that have possibly achieved a degree of success and acclaim elsewhere, it can occasionally attract some negativity from the critics in New York. I mean, there had been a lot of press in the *Times* about the previous productions in San Francisco and in Pittsburgh, and how well they had done and been received. So, when this production came in, I think there was already some pre-conceived prejudice against us that was brewing. Before they saw *Midsummer*, the New York critics came out with comments like, "Oh, I hear this is great. Well, maybe it's not quite as great as all the out-of-town hoopla is suggesting." It was that kind of thing. I felt that attitude probably infected *The New York Times* in their perceptions of and response to the play, which was unfortunate.

But I must also admit that the production was better and more alluring in Pittsburgh. The truth is I think Susan hurt the New York production a little bit. The Pittsburgh production was just more charming and had a different cast—we just had my company of actors out there. There was nobody in it you would have heard of, with the possible exceptions of Barton Heyman and Alan Manson who I later cast in *Let's Scare Jessica to Death* and *Bang the Drum Slowly*. Incidentally, Barton had a tendency to take LSD whenever we were working. His thirst for it sometimes made me feel quite miserable, but he never had any trouble remembering his lines when he was high. To be fair to Barton, he wasn't on LSD quite as much in Pittsburgh, but this was mostly due to the fact that it was much harder to obtain there than it was in San Francisco. By the way, he looked appropriately psychedelic in his role as Puck. I remember we painted him in horizontal rainbow stripes from top to bottom, and he had a little tiny sort of jock-strap swimsuit on him. I insisted on him having a lot of thick pubic hair that was bursting out and hanging halfway down his thighs on the inside. It was quite a sight.

Winning the Obie was the icing on the cake. I suspect that Lahr was really the guy behind my getting the award as he was on the Obie Committee alongside Clive Barnes and Michael Smith. What it did for my career, I don't know. It was good to win a big award as it did give me an added confidence to continue following my own way. I stopped doubting myself, that's for sure. I stopped questioning whether or not I should put certain things I liked in productions simply because I liked them. I learned to trust my own instincts and judgments, and be a little more fearless. That was a good thing, I feel. As for the importance of awards from a more personal perspective, I'm definitely not cynical about them. I'm always very happy to receive an award, or recognition of any kind, as it shows that the work you are doing is accomplished and appreciated. Some people have a very complicated relationship with awards and award ceremonies, but I have a very simple one: I like them! *A Midsummer's Night Dream* acquired a somewhat notorious reputation very quickly as a bawdy production, but it was also beautiful and daring. Truly, it's the thing I'm most proud of in my entire career. There's nothing I've ever done that is as good as that was. I once thought about doing my *Midsummer* as a movie, but it never quite happened. Maybe that was for the best. Maybe it's right that it only existed as a play, as an event, and had a finite existence. I mean, there's something exquisite about the fact that it now only lives in my memory, and the memories of the actors and audience members who saw it, such is the wonderfully terminable nature of theater.

> *If* A Midsummer Night's Dream *had catapulted Hancock to dizzying heights of acclaim, his next production as director would see him temporarily descend into the stygian depths of notoriety. Produced by Cheryl Crawford,* The Freaking Out of Stephanie Blake *was an expensive Broadway comedy about a spinster from Ohio who journeys to New York and discovers that her niece has fallen in with a group of hippies. Boasting a strong cast headlined by Hollywood*

star Jean Arthur (who had only recently made her overdue return to acting), previews of the play had initially been penciled in to commence on October 10, 1967, at the Eugene O'Neill Theatre, with an opening scheduled for October 30. These were abruptly cancelled and Hancock would leave the production in acrimony during rehearsals, replaced by Michael Kahn. The Freaking Out of Stephanie Blake was then rescheduled for a November 4 premiere, but would achieve infamy in the annals of Broadway history for closing before it officially opened at an estimated cost of $250,000.

I'd had a certain amount of positive press in *The New York Times* during my sojourn in regional theater. Judy Stone, who was I.F. Stone's sister, had done a piece about me in San Francisco called "Making A Small Miracle," and Howard Taubman had also interviewed me (I remember driving out to a restaurant overlooking the water in Saucelito for that particular conversation). There was also a snotty piece by Peter Bart, who later achieved fame as an executive at Paramount Pictures, but as they say, perhaps wrongly, there's no such thing as bad publicity—just spell my name right! Maybe the *Times* guys were using my being there to get the paper to pick up the check for their nice visits to San Francisco. Then, when I'd been in Pittsburgh, there was another wonderful article about my work there, I forget by whom. One of the Broadway actors in our Pittsburgh company, the aforementioned Alan Manson, had even said to me with rueful admiration, "Guys work their whole life to get a fraction of what you're getting at twenty-six."

So, everything was going great and people in the business knew of me when I got back to New York. I already knew Cheryl Crawford from before, through Harold Clurman and our failed efforts to put together the Civil War version of *Oh, What a Lovely War*. I was pleased, but not entirely surprised, when she called me asking if I wanted to direct a Broadway show. *A Midsummer Night's Dream* was still running at this point, and I guess her playwright had seen it and liked it well enough. His name was Richard Chandler and he was Cheryl's assistant. Dick was from a wealthy Illinois family that had something to do with Caterpillar, Inc., and *The Freaking Out of Stephanie Blake* was his first play. It was hippie time in Greenwich Village and the work was an attempt to capitalize on it for a Broadway audience. I must admit, I was not wild about it. I thought the play smelled of inauthentic commercial aspirations (you can hear it in the title), but I wanted to do a Broadway show. Ah, the fatal lure of overweening ambition!

Cheryl had a true star lined up for the production, the inimitable Jean Arthur. On the basis of Jean alone, there was already half the money for the production from Paramount, with Chandler's family I gather putting up the other half. They flew me to Big Sur, California, to meet Jean because she had director approval. I had loved her in George Stevens' *Shane*, playing opposite Alan Ladd and Van Heflin as the rancher's beautiful wife. I guess everyone did. I found her small, gay, and still pretty. At our meeting, Jean suggested that we read the play together. I warned her I wasn't an actor, but she didn't care, and we just did it. We liked each other. I had passed the test and, after a long fog delay at the Big Sur airport, I flew back to New York as the official director of *The Freaking Out of Stephanie Blake*.

Shortly afterwards, I had lunch with Harold Clurman at the Russian Tea Room to thank him for recommending me to Cheryl. He warned me, "Whatever you do, don't yell at her." "Cheryl?" I asked. "No," he replied, "*Jean.*" I gather Harold had once cast her in a production of George Bernard Shaw's *Saint Joan* and they were in Philadelphia trying out on their way into New York. He had raised his voice a little while giving notes after a performance. Now, Harold had an odd way of speaking in public. I have never seen anything like it. It was unbelievable, a total transformation. This mild, rational little guy would suddenly become a mad man. Talk about fervent! Still rational, indeed brilliant, but talking so fast he would stumble over himself. There's a story concerning some performance Harold was directing of an Odets play at the Group Theatre, probably *Awake and Sing*, where he was so wound up giving notes he lost his breath and fell at Sandy Meisner's feet. Ever droll, Meisner had remarked, "*This* is why I'm in the theater." Anyway, maybe Harold yelled a little at Jean Arthur for she then *disappeared* from the production. That was it. Gone! They had to close as, plainly, they couldn't come into New York without a Saint Joan. Thus, as Harold explained it to me, my job was always to be nice to Jean; to nurse her along and, above all, get her to open the show. I learned later that *Saint Joan* wasn't the only time she had vanished. There was another show, I forget what it was now, and Jean had simply decided at the last minute that she just couldn't do it. You see, she was afraid of audiences. Films weren't a problem for her, but she was phobic and worried that a live audience might see up her skirt. But, you know, these are things you have to contend with as a director and I thought I was equal to the task.

The first hint of trouble we had with the playwright was over the set. I had one idea in mind and he did not want it. Now, here's the thing about the Dramatist Guild contract: whereas in the film business writers have too little power, in the theater they have too much. That's in my opinion, and I just mean in terms of the minimum agreement. You can't change a line without obtaining their permission, can't stop them from rewriting and changing the play however they want. They have approval of you, the director, as well as approval of the set, the costumes, the casting, a whole long list of things. In the case of someone like Arthur Miller, or Tennessee Williams, or Paddy Chayevsky, or Neil Simon, that's fine, because they've earned it. But for a first time writer? At any rate, I had to alter my design to suit Dick Chandler. What's worse is he waited to raise his objections until we were having a big meeting on the stage of the Eugene O'Neill Theatre with all the prop people, and stage hands, and designers, and everyone else, present. Someone told me afterwards, "You should have resigned right there." I now think they were right. These are public battles that you have to win early on, or the opposition has the whammy on you.

But I loved Jean Arthur, loved working with her. She's one of the best two or three actors I've ever worked with. And she liked me, too. It was a love affair for a long time—without consummation, of course. She told me that I reminded her "so much" of George Stevens. Maybe Jean told all her directors that, but I don't think so. In actuality, *were* there even other directors? I mean, at this point, she hadn't worked for a decade or more. I do recall that she repeatedly did a rather strange thing: Jean had her lady companion/lover with her in New York and, in an effort not to attract attention, they would leave the theater after every rehearsal wearing these grotesque Halloween masks. Well, there was already a crowd—there always was—of autograph seekers waiting for her outside, because she was a big star. This spectacle with the Halloween masks only succeeded in swelling it, doubling it, tripling it! Pretty soon there was a mob of people every day pulling at these two masked women as they ran for their limosine. I'm sure that upset Jean, but who knows? She was the cause of it. Cheryl tried to stop her, but Jean knew better.

Then the rewrites started. As previews approached, Dick Chandler got scared. He was going to be disgraced, he must have thought, by what he had written. So, he tried to fix what needed fixing, yes, but could *not* be fixed by the pages he started churning out—and I mean churning! It was just massive. New lines for the actors to learn every day. New sets and a different running order for me to quickly assimilate. I tried valiantly to stop it. I told Chandler, and Cheryl, that we couldn't possibly absorb that much new material and tech the show at the same time. It was creating chaos and, besides, it was dangerously exhausting Jean. Chandler insisted, he *had* to have these new scenes, and Cheryl could do nothing to stop him. It ended badly between them. And it ended badly for me. I fought too hard and was fired.

Two or three days later, at the first public preview of *The Freaking Out of Stephanie Blake*, Jean Arthur made her entrance. She walked forward to the apron of the stage and then, quite unexpectedly, sank to her knees. She told the audience she was "just too tired" and couldn't do the show. "Yes, you can," bellowed Cheryl in her manly voice from the back of the house. Well, Jean couldn't and she wouldn't. That was it. The show closed without a public performance. I ran into Harold Clurman several weeks later, again at the Russian Tea Room, and he inevitably asked, "What happened?" "I yelled at her," I joked rather humorlessly. "What did you do that for?" "I didn't," I said, and told him the truth of what had occurred.

> *In May 1968, following his onerous experience on* The Freaking Out of Stephanie Blake, *Hancock directed a successful mounting of Robert Lowell's* Endicott and the Red Cross *at the American Place Theatre. An account of the rebellious actions of the zealous Puritan governor John Endicott and the profound disdain he feels for his colony's high living, the cast included Kenneth Haigh, James Brochu, Ralph Canton and Spalding Gray. Although* Endicott *quickly restored his confidence and reputation, Hancock would once again encounter adversity during his strained involvement in the troubled follow-up production,* Boy on the Straight-Back Chair.

I'm not certain how I got involved in *Endicott and the Red Cross*. It might have come about through my lawyer, Alan Schwartz, whom I believe was the President of the Board of the American Place Theatre. The play itself was an adaptation of a short story of Puritan history by Nathaniel Hawthorne. Robert Lowell, who at that point was considered the Great American Poet, had done an evening of three plays that he called *The Old Glory*. Two of them were based on short stories by Hawthorne—the other being "My Kinsman, Major Molineux." The third play was derived from a novella by Herman Melville called *Benito Cereno*, which concerned a revolt on a Spanish slavery ship. Kenneth Haigh, the British actor who had famously played Jimmy Porter in *Look Back in Anger* at the Royal Court, starred as Governor Endicott. I wasn't crazy about Haigh, I never quite believed him as an actor, but it was a good production. *Endicott* did well in a limited run of around six weeks and the critical reception was also favorable. The American Place Theatre often did a season of plays that ran for a couple of weeks, sometimes six to eight weeks.

Interestingly, I do remember suggesting some cuts in the play to Robert Lowell one day. He said, "Oh no, those are my *longueurs!*" I persisted, saying that maybe audiences weren't fond of longueurs, but Lowell had a witty retort: "How much are they charging at American Place? Not much, I imagine. Let's do a cut version like you want, and we'll do it for a couple of performances at twice the price." This was not dissimilar to a moment I had shared with Tennessee Williams a few years earlier. I had suggested some cuts to him in several lengthy passages in *Milk Train* and Tennessee had responded by saying, "Oh baby, we can't expect them to like *that*. I'm talking to them about the end of the world and I want them to hear it." I've always found it profitable to know how to negotiate various moments and situations you encounter as a director. In fact, around this same time, I also taught directing once a week at the Circle in the Square, which I enjoyed. I had some good students, nobody who went on to become big names, but there were some talented people there. Teaching directing is such an interesting thing: you try to arm people in their fight to make and maintain a career, but there are so many variables and anomalies and coincidences and perversions and sacrifices along the way, it's really down to the individual's tenacity and psychological make-up. Can you be and do everything that you need to be and do in order to succeed? When I was teaching students—and even when I teach them now—I just impart to them what I was thinking and feeling at any given time. That's the best you can do.

Anyway, the management at American Place had liked the production of *Endicott and the Red Cross*, as had Lowell. This was really important in New York at that point since "Cal", as he was known, was the aforementioned Great American Poet. So, the American Place asked me if there was something else I wanted to do. Stefan Brecht had turned me on to a wonderful enterprise in the Village, Charles Ludlam's Theatre of the Ridiculous, which had begun as an American movement in the mid-1960s. They were doing things like *The Conquest of the Universe,* or *When Queens Collide,* or Ludlam was playing the female lead in *Camille,* which he also wrote. It was hilarious stuff with an underpinning of sorrow that departed from the naturalistic style. One of the great tragedies of the American Theater is that Charles Ludlam died of AIDS in 1987. He was brilliant. One of his authors was a man named Ronald Tavel. Ronny had also worked with Andy Warhol and The Factory. I sought him out and read his plays. One of them was perfect. It was called *Boy on the Straight-Back Chair.* I took it to the American Place and they loved it as much as I did.

It told the story of a serial killer known as the Pied Piper of Tucson. This killer was a short guy—he'd put crushed beer cans in his motorcycle boots to make himself taller—who would lure girls into the desert before proceeding to beat their heads in with rocks. The play had a lot of songs, Tavel was a good lyricist, and the artistic director at the American Place, Wynn Handman, suggested a young composer who had just come to New York by the name of Orville Stoeber. That began a fruitful creative relationship between Orville and I that continues to this very day. I then got Bob Lavigne to design the show, as he had the costumes for *Endicott,* and a dozen other things for me—he was my designer from San Francisco and Pittsburgh, and had worked on *Midsummer.* We came up with a fabulous scheme to do the play which later won awards. We had a wonderful cast, too, including Doris Roberts, Kevin O'Connor, Gloria LeRoy, and, as I say, it was a great production.

But damned if the same thing didn't happen with the writer as had happened on *The Freaking Out of Stephanie Blake*! Tavel wasn't happy with his perfect play. He began to feel it was too simple, that he would be disgraced in the eyes of his Village friends, Andy Warhol perhaps. I don't know who he was trying to impress, but it suddenly had to be artier and more poetic. So, here come more pages and they were not good pages. They were bad, bad pages, arch stuff that didn't make sense. Really bad! I felt Tavel was ruining his play and told him so. And apart from the quality, he was adding somewhere between thirty to fifty percent to the running time! The subject couldn't take that. And it certainly wasn't the play I had signed on to direct. Again, I suppose I fought too hard, because Ronny decided he wanted to have me fired and replaced with my assistant, Lee Von Rhau, with whom he shared a cab ride home every night. Ah, treachery. Wynn Handman and the management at American Place Theatre objected, but Tavel threatened to go the press. Not good for the American Place which was set up in its charter as a home to nurture playwrights. So, I left the play. It was a terrible time in my life. Both *Boy on the Straight-Back Chair* and *The Freaking Out of Stephanie Blake* are sources of considerable misery for me—especially since my sets and costumes for the Tavel play went on to win the Obie.

> *As the 1970s dawned, and his career as a filmmaker finally began gathering momentum, Hancock's theater output decreased appreciably and was eventually put on hold for several years. Having earned an Academy Award nomination in 1971 for his twenty-minute film* Sticky My Fingers, Fleet My Feet, *the short was already making the rounds of the studio development departments as Hancock busily began preparing his debut feature* Let's Scare Jessica to Death. *After being invited by executives to submit "whatever film ideas he wanted to do," Hancock proposed a biopic of the volatile and highly influential French poet and adventurer Arthur Rimbaud (1854-1891) that was to be scripted by Tennessee Williams. Despite the subsequent failure of the Rimbaud picture to materialize, Hancock and Williams would continue their occasionally fraught working relationship periodically throughout the next decade, discussing assorted projects for theater, film and television. Sadly, none of these enterprises came to fruition—with the notable exception of a revival of Williams'* The Two-Character Play, *which had failed in its London debut in 1967. Rewritten by the playwright in the intervening years (following its American debut as* Out Cry *in July 1971), Hancock's version starred his new wife Dorothy Tristan and was mounted at the Callboard Theatre, Los Angeles, in 1977.*

Tennessee had told me as early as 1971 that he wanted to do a film about the life and death of Arthur Rimbaud. It was something of a passion project for him and it greatly occupied his thoughts for a time. He wanted me to direct the movie, and so I got together with him at the New York apartment where he lived on East 72nd Street and we began discussing it. Tennessee gave me a much-thumbed biography of Rimbaud that he wanted to base the screenplay on. I knew little about the subject before reading it, other than the fact that Brecht had ripped-off (or paid homage to) one of his poems. What was interesting to me about Rimbaud's story was that he "withdrew from art" and went off to be a merchant in Africa. How strange! It was inexplicable really. I'm sure what was interesting to Tennessee was the fact that when Rimbaud got sick and returned from Africa, his sister nursed him until he died—particularly since Tennessee's sister, Rose, was one of the three most important people in his life. In his biography, *Tennessee Williams: Mad Pilgrimage of the Flesh*, John Lahr thinks that in the face of unremittingly bad reviews, Tennessee might have flirted with, or pretended to flirt with, the idea of doing something else (hence his interest in this story) and, of course, the fact that Rimbaud was gay. I tried to get the Rimbaud film on, but I don't think there was much enthusiasm for it from anybody, despite the fact that Tennessee was involved. I remember giving various people at the studios the Rimbaud biography and them *not* being interested in a Tennessee Williams screenplay based on it. There was definitely some resistance to the project for several reasons.

Six years later, just before I went off to do *Jaws 2*, Ken Kitch and I did *The Two-Character Play* with Tennessee in a beautiful little theater on Melrose Place, which, as far as I can see, doesn't exist anymore. Tennessee had written the play after suffering a breakdown and then rewrote it after apparently recovering, but it's rarely performed. Our experience together on *Two-Character Play* was a memorable one for me, occasionally for the wrong reasons. I remember that Tennessee and I were talking about something meaningful in his New York apartment—this was way before we went out to L.A. to do the production. He was on pills and was drinking heavily, and was having some balance problems. At one point Tennessee got up, staggered across the room to procure yet another drink and abruptly fell to the floor. And I didn't pick him up. I just stayed right where I was sitting, looking at him, not moving a muscle to provide any assistance.

About six months passed and I didn't see or hear from Tennessee at all. Then he suddenly reappeared again and suggested that he and I have dinner together. So, we went to Elaine's, an Italian restaurant which, at that point in time, was *the* hot place on the Upper East Side. As we sat there, Tennessee was looking at me rather earnestly and I knew he had something he wanted to say. Finally, he said, "You know, I hated you. I've hated you for these past six months because you did not pick me up off that floor. But now I've come to realize that you were trying to tell me that I could pick myself up." My only response to that was, "Yeah, maybe." The truth is I can remember saying to myself at that moment, "If you and I are talking about your life's work—something that I assume is very important to you—and you decide to get wasted and fall down because you are getting yourself another drink, yeah, you can damn well pick yourself up!" As I was thinking all this, Tennessee continued: "My mother used to fall down in order to seduce my father. Maybe I was trying to seduce you that night." I just chuckle at that now because I don't think I was really Tennessee's type.

I'll never forget the day that Tennessee came out to a dress rehearsal of *The Two-Character Play* with his agent, Bill Barnes. Before we started, I said, "Tennessee, the actors don't feel secure yet with the lines in the second act. So, I thought we would just show you the first act." We then performed it for him and afterwards I approached Tennessee, and asked, "Well, what do you think?" He then hissed at me in his deep Southern accent, "I will denounce *this* with every fiber of my being! You cannot treat a playwright like this! You simply cannot! You have left out the single most important scene, where they go to the market!" I said, "Yes, Tennessee, but that happens in the second act. We're just doing the first act for you, remember?" He suddenly cried, "Nooooo! I'll say it again: you cannot treat a playwright like this!" And he just continued to rave on like that unabated. At one point he even dragged Dorothy into his rant, "And your wife looks like Angie Dickinson on a bad night!" After listening to all this I'd finally had enough, and said, "Okay, this production is cancelled! We are not going to do your play." Inevitably, the argument then reached new levels of vitriol and we started shouting at each other: "Fuck you!" "No, fuck you!" Then Tennessee went stomping out of the theater in a rage and I followed him outside. As he was getting into his limousine, I yelled at him: "You phony cocksucker!" With that Tennessee suddenly stopped, drew himself up haughtily, and exclaimed, "Well, I've certainly never been called *that*!" Then he clambered into his limo and was gone.

After that incredible scene, Dorothy and I went home to Malibu. That same night, around two o'clock in the morning, the phone starts ringing. I pick it up and on the other end of the line is Bill Barnes. Bill says, "Tennessee is absolutely mortified about what occurred, John. He desperately wants to apologize to you. Could you please go to his bungalow at the Beverly Hills Hotel in the morning at eight o'clock?" I said, "Yes, of course." So, I went at the agreed time and there was Tennessee, sitting in his silk bathrobe bright and early. He was busily tapping away on a typewriter with a cup sitting nearby on the table that was about two-thirds brandy and one-third coffee. He greeted me warmly, and said in a soft voice full of remorse, "I'm so very sorry about what happened. I'm just utterly mortified about it." I said, "It's okay, I understand. Let's just forget about it. But maybe you should apologize to Dorothy about what you said." He nodded and readily agreed to this. So, later that afternoon, Tennessee came to the theater as he promised he would. Ken Kitch's wife, Hilary, who, like Dorothy is also blonde, was ironing costumes backstage when Tennessee meekly approached her and began apologizing profusely. He thought it was Dorothy and I don't recall if Hilary had the heart to tell him who she really was.

I have so many stories about Tennessee, so many. I remember that Kitch and I wanted Tennessee to stick around for a while to rewrite *The Two-Character Play* as we thought it needed a lot of work. So, we hired a very attractive driver to ferry him around and Tennessee was utterly entranced by this handsome young man. He took him up to the Fairmont Hotel in San Francisco for a weekend and was all excited about the trip. However, when they arrived back a few days later, Tennessee was suddenly looking all morose. So, I asked him, "What's wrong? What happened?" Tennessee then explained rather glumly, "The boy wouldn't *put!*" What had happened was—and this story is according to Tennessee, so you can't be sure that it's entirely true—but he claimed that they had had a suite with adjoining rooms and this pretty boy wouldn't unlock his door to him. Apparently, as he listened through the wall, Tennessee had heard the boy having sadomasochistic sex next door with somebody else. The kid was being beaten and he wouldn't let Tennessee inside his room to join the fun. So, Tennessee came back all bitter and despondent about this, but he eventually put the whole episode behind him and we continued working.

Tennessee was always subject to some pretty wild and outrageous behavior. I'm sure a very conscious part of him thrived on knowing he was getting a big reaction out of somebody. For instance, I can recall one small incident that took place in the intermission during one of the previews we held on *The Two-Character Play*: Tennessee and I were talking intensely about the production and continued our conversation as we walked into the men's room together. Tennessee was taking a leak and some guy was peeing right next to him at the urinal. Everything seemed rather calm and benign—as it should be in any men's room—but then, suddenly, Tennessee whirled around on him, and cried, "Are you trying to see my *cock*?!" This guy was stunned by the force and nature of the question and I was a little stunned by it, too. It was another of those incredible Tennessee moments that you didn't see coming but, at the same time, you always half expected. I mean, Tennessee had a need for attention and if he couldn't satisfy that craving in good ways he would do it in some other way that was probably bad.

At some point during 1980, three years after we did *The Two-Character Play* together and the Rimbaud biopic was all but a distant memory, Tennessee wanted me to do a second film project with him called *Stopped Rocking*. At this point in his life he was something of a shadow of his former self. His behavior was as unpredictable as it had always been, but there was a darker and more troubling aspect to it. I was rather alarmed at how his mental state had deteriorated in the time since we had last seen each other. He seemed so very different to me. I wonder now if he felt something had changed within him, too. I don't know. I remember that when we met to discuss *Stopped Rocking* one of the first things Tennessee said to me was how disappointed he was in his physical appearance. He was not happy about the way he looked at all. He claimed that he was having some trouble getting laid because his body apparently wasn't as nice and as firm and as attractive as it had once been. Tennessee was clearly preoccupied with his appearance but not with how he appeared, if you take my meaning.

Anyway, *Stopped Rocking* was a screenplay that had never been produced. It was the story of a gym teacher in a St. Louis high school, whose much-loved wife is in a mental institution. He visits her religiously every week and she lives for these visits. The problem is that now he has fallen in love with a young colleague—she also teaches gym at his high school—and she's going to be moving to Denver to take a position there. He desperately wants to go with this young woman and is ridden with guilt about it. So, the husband checks his wife out of the mental facility for a long weekend camping trip in the Ozarks where he intends to break the bad news that he won't be coming to see her anymore. It doesn't go well (things don't, of course, in movies) and there are some grueling, wonderful scenes. The wife is one of those great Tennessee hysterical heroines and at one point she desperately throws herself into a river, only to be rescued and plied with antidepressants by the husband. The script ends with the husband taking her back to the institution and leaving her there. As he drives away in the car, the wife gradually…stops…rocking.

Stopped Rocking has to be about Tennessee and Rose as there was a time when he had to stop visiting his sister. The guilt of that decision is a recurring theme in his work. It's at the end of *The Glass Menagerie* with Tom's rueful, "Oh, Laura…Laura, I tried to put you behind me, but I am more faithful to you than I intended to be." One of things I observed from my many meetings and conversations with Tennessee was the fact that his past was always very much his present. I think he was haunted by his childhood and certain memories remained with him all his life. He was confined by his childhood in some ways—as many people can be stuck in childhood—so I don't think that's unusual. I do find it fascinating and a little sad, because you have to let some of that go. There are people who can never escape the events of their formative years and it can cast an enormous shadow over their lives. Some artists and writers use their youth as inspiration and they mine their childhood for ideas and feelings and stories, but then they have nothing else to offer from a more mature perspective. I'm not saying that Tennessee was like that, he certainly wasn't, but his childhood was always with him and the ghosts of it are present in his work.

Tennessee and I talked about Rose a lot. He'd say how much he loved her, as in, "You know, I *loved* my sister." She came up while we were working together through the preview process on *Two-Character Play*. He wanted the sister in the play to be very much like his: the frailty, the vulnerability. And talk about being trapped in your childhood! The brother and sister in *Two-Character Play* end up literally locked together in a Siberian theater. Now, there he's talking about his fate as an artist—trapped in the theater, with his sister. So, Rimbaud's idea of chucking it all and going off to Africa to be a businessman may have had its momentary appeal as a life not lived. And Rimbaud got to end up with his sister anyway. But Tennessee's guilt is also present in one of his poems, "Cried the Fox." My first contact with that poem was around 1955 on the record of Tennessee reading his poetry and a scene from *The Glass Menagerie*. In it, there's a line where he talks about his "fatal returning to places that failed him before." If I remember correctly, Lahr feels that this line is Tennessee talking about his fate as an artist; not being able to go behind the material of his childhood. But the poem was written so early in his career, when Tennessee wasn't having those kinds of problems. I suspect he's just talking about himself, not as an artist but as a person, and, surely, he's also talking about us.

Tennessee thought that *Stopped Rocking* was the best thing he had done since *Night of the Iguana*, and I was in full agreement with him on that. I thought his script was very strong—a remarkable piece of writing.

Others were also greatly excited about the project such as Hallmark, who really wanted to do it as a Movie of the Week. So, one night, Tennessee and I went out to dinner with a producer from Hallmark to discuss the project and hopefully work something out. We climbed into a limousine and drove to some Italian restaurant in Beverly Hills because Tennessee wanted to have calamari fritti. When we arrived there and got out of the limo, Tennessee was holding onto my arm as he was on liquor and downers. He was having his usual balance problems and we needed to cross the street to get to the restaurant. Now, under some of the streets that lead out of the mountains, there are these huge storm drains that are designed to carry off water during flash-floods. The gutter openings to these waterways are pretty big and, as we walked steadily to the far side of the street and approached one, Tennessee suddenly whirled around with these crazed eyes. He looked utterly terrified of me and took a stuttering step back. I didn't know what was going on. I just stood there as he stared at me with this wild and fearful expression. We eventually entered the restaurant and it came out later during the course of the evening what had prompted this weird behavior. Tennessee said, "I thought you were going to push me down in there." Then he chuckled about it like it didn't mean anything, like it was a joke, but there was something troubling and disconcerting about his manner. I then said to myself: "Whoa, this guy is just too crazy to be around! He's not good enough anymore to be this crazy."

Despite this incident, I decided to persevere with *Stopped Rocking* as it was just so wonderful and I knew it would make a terrific movie. My only problem with it was the middle section of the script, which I felt needed a little more work. Something I wanted to do was have the actors read it aloud for Tennessee and then discuss the finer details afterwards; what worked, what perhaps didn't work. Tennessee was agreeable to this and so I gathered together Richard Jordan, Blair Brown and Harry Hamlin—some well-known and respected actors—in the living room of my house in Malibu. We all assembled beforehand and read through *Stopped Rocking* a couple of times. Then we were ready to read it for Tennessee and made arrangements for him to come to the house. I can still vividly recall seeing Tennessee's car pulling up in the driveway and watching him slowly clambering out of it with Bill Barnes before staggering towards the door. I could immediately see that he was *really* drunk and was also on something. Well, Tennessee was always on something. He was always on booze and downers and speed, but mainly booze and downers.

Tennessee came inside the house and shakily negotiated the three steps that led to our sunken living room. He greeted everybody and then sat down in a chair. As he did so, I noticed that he had a copy of his script with him. I thought that was good because maybe he'd make some notes as we worked. The actors were arranged in a circle, and were waiting for Tennessee to settle himself. But then he unexpectedly proceeded to open up his script and started to read. Richard, Blair and Harry were just sitting there, listening to him as he painfully slurred through his own words. We all exchanged embarrassed glances at each other, not knowing what to say or do. I mean, this wasn't just anybody sitting there, this was *Tennessee Williams*! Nobody wanted to interrupt him, or hurt his feelings, or in any way rock the boat, right? Finally, after he had recited nearly a page and a half, I gently intervened and said, "Forgive me, Tennessee, but we have all these wonderful actors here today. We were thinking that we would read the screenplay to you, not you to us." He looked somewhat groggily at me over his glasses, and said, "Oh, okay, fine." He then closed his copy, removed his glasses and sat back in the chair as we started to read *Stopped Rocking* aloud. Within a few short minutes, I looked over at Tennessee and noticed he had fallen asleep. So, now what do you do? What *can* you do? Almost in soundless agreement, we simply decided to continue plowing through the script as our invited guest stirred occasionally in his slumber. Afterwards, Tennessee awoke, got back up on his unsteady legs; mumbled a few slurred words of thanks and left. Alas, the producer from Hallmark was also present that day. He was so appalled by what happened he quickly lost all interest in the project, and that was it. That was the end. We really did stop rocking.

After that day, I never saw nor heard from Tennessee again. When I learned that he had passed a few years later, in early 1983, and discovered the nature of his demise, my first thought was what a terrible way to die. Tennessee had apparently choked in his suite at the Elysée Hotel in New York on a plastic cap—not the cap from a bottle of alcohol mind you, the cap from a medicinal bottle. I'm not certain that was true, but it was the first report. Some people don't believe that story and suspect something else occurred, but most people accept it. Some say the drugs and alcohol he was ingesting negated his gag reflex, or something, and caused him to choke to death as he inhaled the cap. It's true that Tennessee was always—certainly all through the time that I knew him—mired in serious drug and alcohol dependency, and he also had problems with depression. It was very, very sad. Despite how crazy and tempestuous he could be, I really loved the guy. I always had an enormous amount of affection for him and I felt he had a lot of affection for me, too.

When I reflect on Tennessee's body of work I think his strengths as a playwright rest in his enduring insights into human frailty and brutality, and the dialogue he wrote to evince those things. He was an undoubted master of lyrical dialogue and that's truly a gift. It's not something you can simply acquire, I don't think. There are just some writers who have the ability to compose great dialogue and there are others who struggle desperately with it. Along with Eugene O'Neill and Arthur Miller, Tennessee is regarded as one of the three greatest playwrights of twentieth century American drama, and that is only right. I'm actually not a big fan of O'Neill's work, but I think Miller's *Death of a Salesman* is probably better than anything Tennessee ever wrote. *A Streetcar Named Desire* and *Cat on a Hot Tin Roof* are both monumental achievements, and, in a way, *The Glass Menagerie* is better than anything anybody ever wrote—again, with the sole exception of *Death of a Salesman*. Tennessee's works became quite experimental as his career progressed and I don't like some of his later plays very much. He is one of those playwrights who got worse as he got older, not better, which is something I find hard to understand. His deterioration is also fascinating to me. I mean, why did it happen?

My explanation for it is this: Tennessee wrote so personally and so purely, whatever was troubling him at any given point, whatever he was thinking and feeling in that one moment, he would simply type it directly into the play. He once said as much to me: "I just sit down and whatever is bothering me I put it on the page." When he first started out as a playwright, and was living a tormented but relatively normal existence, people found it easy to relate to his work. For instance, *The Glass Menagerie* is very accessible as everybody has left home, or felt homesick, or experienced family problems of some kind or another. But as Tennessee came to live in an increasingly rarefied atmosphere, and dwelt in a bizarre world of fame, sex and perpetual travel—rent boys, alcohol and drugs, the Divina Costiera, and so forth—he continued to write so personally about these things he experienced that, naturally, a considerable chunk of the audience didn't identify as much. He was so immersed in this exotic gay world I think he lost something as a writer. Each successive play he wrote became ever more progressively removed. No doubt, there is a big difference between a story about a person burdened by his family and is leaving home, than there is a story that details what it's like to be dying in luxury on the Italian coast with a young poet that comes to visit you.

Also what happened, again, because the later plays are not as good as the early plays, is the critics viciously turned on him. They were complaining, "Hey, I came here expecting *The Glass Menagerie* and *A Streetcar Named Desire* and *Cat on a Hot Tin Roof* and *The Rose Tattoo*, and instead you give me *The Two-Character Play*?! What fucking good are you?" And yet, if *Two-Character Play* had been the work of a new writer they would have all unanimously crowed, "My God, this play is fabulous! It's so promising and inventive and rich, it clearly heralds the dawn of a major new talent!" But, back then, Tennessee got the shit mercilessly kicked out of him by the critics time after time after time. He was viewed as this fading glory, his best work far behind him, and some of that was indeed true. Interestingly, some of the later plays that were initially derided are now being revived and reappraised and re-valued. Of course, all of that comes far too late for poor Tennessee.

In the decades that followed The Two-Character Play, *Hancock worked sporadically in theater as his film and television career progressed steadily. In 1984, he directed the American debut of Jonathan Falla's* Topakana Martyrs' Day *at the Los Angeles Actors Theatre. The play had originally been performed the year before at London's Bush Theatre, under the direction of Simon Stokes, and was based on the author's own experiences as an Oxfam-sponsored relief worker during a famine operation in Karamoja (a region of Uganda) in 1981. Then, between the release of his films* Suspended Animation *and* The Looking Glass, *Hancock worked on a further four plays. He steered a lackluster production of Elaine May's musical satire* Adult Entertainment *at the Dunes Summer Theater, Michigan City. This was followed by the thriller* The Brother, *which dramatized the notorious Cold War spy case that resulted in the conviction and execution of Julius and Ethel Rosenberg, as well as a revival of Marsha Norman's Pulitzer Prize-winning* 'night Mother. *Both plays were performed in repertory, in Chicago, from August to November of 2007. Finally, in July 2009, Hancock directed an adaptation of Michael Frayn's* Noises Off *at the Wellfleet Harbor Arts Theatre Julie Harris Stage in Cape Cod, Massachusetts.*

I directed *Topakana Martyrs' Day* shortly before I went off to do *Hill Street Blues* and *The Twilight Zone*, and was preparing *Weeds*. Jonathan Falla was a British playwright and I thought his play was very, very funny. It was set in a field station that stores bulk food and concerned a small group of aid workers in Uganda during the revolution. I understand that it was based on actual events that occurred following the conflicts and droughts that afflicted East Africa. Although the idea of doing a comedy about famine relief in Africa wouldn't seem to be a particularly amusing or tasteful premise, I think that was what was initially so offbeat and interesting about it. *Topakana Martyrs' Day* was a daring approach to take because it was written at a time when famine in countries like Ethiopia was reaching devastating proportions. I mean, it was beyond a crisis, beyond a humanitarian disaster, it was a tragedy that affected and haunted and shamed us all. Somehow Falla found the humanity and feeling in what was a very grim subject matter. The play starred Dorothy Tristan, Peter Noone (Herman of Herman's Hermits), Grand L. Bush and Niche Saboda. Noone was easy to get along with—he kept a bit of a distance like it is with Brits sometimes—but I remember he did help us record the music for the production.

We had great music on *Topakana Martyrs' Day*, actually. Fred Karlin was a big composer at that time and was active in the Academy. By this point, he had already scored *Baby Blue Marine* for me, and I got him to do the music for the play for free—principally a funny version of his Oscar-winning hit song "For All We Know" with an African beat. It was wonderful, the sweetness of the melody played against the strange arrangement. It tore in two ways like I like things to do. Speaking of using a beautiful melody over moments of carnage or sorrow, that's Mahler, isn't it? It's the same approach found in *Oh, What a Lovely War*, and in *Dr. Strangelove* with Vera Lynn singing "We'll Meet Again" as the bombs go off at the end. These are all works that I've loved—again, I adore things that cut two ways. Anyway, Fred was a good friend. Dorothy and I saw quite a bit of him and his wife socially, that was until they experienced a terrible tragedy: their son, Kristopher, opened the door of the house where he was living and found his sister, Wendy, Fred's daughter, standing there with a shotgun. She killed him. That was desperate tragedy enough, but then Fred's wife went a little mad—more than a little maybe but with good reason—as the funeral parlor had somehow *lost* the boy's body! She was there outside the building picketing, as poor Fred tried to hold things together with what was left of his family. We slowly drifted apart after that. I'm not sure why. Probably what happened was way too intense for him to want to see people. I think Fred had written "For All We Know" thinking of his wife, looking back when things were good between them.

I did Elaine May's *Adult Entertainment* in 2005. It's a very funny two-act play about five porno actors who get involved with the making of an art movie. Like *Topakana Martyrs' Day*, it takes a rather difficult and problematic subject (in this instance the porn industry) and tries to fashion a comedy out of it. We mounted it locally here, in Indiana, with local actors. Jeff Puckett was in it, appearing between his performances in my movies *Suspended Animation* and *The Looking Glass*, and he was good, but, ultimately, *Adult Entertainment* was a frustrating experience. I was doing it at a community theater with amateur actors. The tech people, such as they were, never finished the set on time. It had been a long time since I had worked in that kind of situation—if ever! Some of the actors never had the lines memorized well enough for me to get the pace going. I like things to be slick, and this was not. I wouldn't go into something like that again, nor, I suspect, would they want me. I was too just explosive working in a situation where people simply wanted to have a good time being in a play. I've had, oh, I don't know, a number of nuclear moments over the years, but this one may have taken the cake in terms of volume and rage.

More satisfying and successful was a play I wrote and directed in 2007 called *The Brother*. It had a twelve-week run at the Theatre Building Chicago, in repertory with a production of *'night Mother*, which I also directed. *The Brother* is based on Sam Roberts' book, *The Brother: The Untold Story of the Rosenberg Case*. I had heard a review of the book in 2003 on National Public Radio and immediately sent away for it on Amazon as I've always been interested in the Rosenberg case. I devoured *The Brother* and was impressed with how Roberts had detailed the tragic and complex history of David Greenglass, who was an atomic spy for the Soviet Union assigned to The Manhattan Project. Greenglass had a sister named Ethel Rosenberg and, in order to save his wife from indictment, he testified falsely under oath against Ethel and her husband, Julius, implicating them both in the crime of stealing atomic secrets and passing them on to the Soviets. The Rosenbergs ended up being sent to Sing Sing where they were both executed in the electric chair in June 1953. More than sixty years later, the case still causes a lot of conjecture and opinion and emotion as Greenglass only served ten years in prison before disappearing with a new name and a new identity. At first, I wanted to make a movie out of Roberts' book and so I wrote a screenplay. Linda Yellin, who wrote the novels *Such a Lovely Couple* and *What Nora Knew*, was involved in the script for a while. Sadly, I wasn't able to get the project on, but I was so preoccupied with the story I ended up adapting that screenplay and doing *The Brother* as a play. The cast included Robert Breuler, who played Greenglass, Justine Serino, Allison Weiss and Anthony Tournis, and it turned out very well. The play still retained a lot of the intrigue and the raw emotion that charged the screenplay, and I was incredibly proud of that production.

As I said, *The Brother* was running simultaneously on a twelve-week run in the same theater with *'night Mother*. That play is really about insufferable loneliness and despair, and how destructive a sense of isolation and alienation can be to a person, and their own identity and sense of self-worth. It begins with a daughter telling her mother that she plans on killing herself by the morning and this leads to a dark night of the soul. It's very stirring stuff, very suspenseful and intimate, and it ends on a rather depressing but authentic note with the daughter finally taking her own life. There is some humor in it, too, but it's really the story of a person at the end of their ropes. I needed two strong actors to carry that drama off and I got them in Elaine Rivkin and Dorothy Tristan, who played the daughter and mother respectively. They were both wonderful in it. The reviews for *'night Mother* were very good, and both Elaine and Dorothy were rightfully acclaimed for their performances. However, the reviews for *The Brother* were decidedly mixed—much to my huge disappointment. I got a conspicuously mixed review in the *Chicago Tribune*, which is a very important newspaper that you really want on your side. I still feel aggrieved about it, really. I believe they called the play "melodramatic" and claimed that it lost its way towards the end, but I reject that. I think *The Brother* was a terrific production.

Noises Off, which I did two years later, is another funny play. Those who don't know it are often familiar with the terrible movie adaptation Peter Bogdanovich made in 1992 that starred Michael Caine and Carol Burnett. Bogdanovich did not do a good job with the material, which is a shame. We cast actors from Cape Cod for our production and found one wonderfully talented actor named Robert Kropf, who is also an excellent director. Kropf has been very successful at adapting Ibsen and Chekhov in the theater since then, and he was a joy to work with. *Noises Off* is very amusing, but I found it difficult to do as it's so precisely measured. Every line and scene has been carefully plotted by Michael Frayn and any attempt to credibly depart from the way he wanted the play staged ends up not being as funny or as good. I found that rather frustrating as I didn't have as much room to experiment with it as I have done on other plays I've directed. As always, I try to respect the playwright's ideas and intentions, but it's also fun to throw in a few ideas of your own as you can occasionally discover something that is equally or perhaps even more effective than what you've got. I did try a few things in the production, but they simply did not work. So, I meekly crawled back to the way Frayn wanted it done. Basically, you either do *Noises Off* exactly the way he wrote it or you fail. It's insanely exacting for any director to tackle, and I did sometimes feel like I was merely painting by numbers. That said, when I saw that the play worked, it provided me with enough satisfaction.

With carefully constructed things like *Noises Off*, it's always reassuring to know that you're working with material that the playwright knows inside out. All the writers I worked with throughout my career had a firm grasp of the themes and meanings of their plays. I've heard this isn't always the case with every playwright as some can be reluctant to articulate precisely what the play means and is saying. Writing can be a mysterious thing and the process can be different for each person, just as analysis and interpretation can be different for each person. Who is right and who is wrong about something? Nobody is really. The writer may not understand the play as he or she is writing it, but I think many of the best writers do. Of course, meaning can change over time. Also, I happen to think that people like Harold Pinter and Samuel Beckett deliberately did not want to reveal what their plays were about, and for me that was a cheat; it was them adopting an artificial pose. It seems like the playwright should be able to tell the poor director how they see something and what it means, although, again, things are constantly open to interpretation and re-interpretation. I guess the mystery is preserved if you don't explain everything, but I like to be let in on the secret because it helps me to do the play right.

There are those who are afraid that if you impose a particular meaning on something it may always have that meaning and can't be read as anything else. They fear that the play is suddenly locked into one definitive interpretation. I don't know if that is true or not, or even if it's important. I really don't. I always make a lot of notes before and during a play as I strive to understand it, but even my understanding is subject to change over time when you are removed from the experience of doing the play itself. In my experience, I haven't found that actors fail to understand the play or their characters—certainly not after the rehearsal period is over and the performances begin. All the actors I've worked with have had a firm grasp of everything. Some of the best actors I've worked with in the theater—people like Jane Alexander, Charlie Durning, Dorothy Tristan, Jean Arthur and Eileen Atkins—all had an innate understanding of the material we were doing. They could challenge you, inspire you, and even enlighten you on certain aspects of the piece. That's what you want from any actor: a collaborator and, in some ways, a co-conspirator who is willing to go through it all with you and take some chances.

I feel I got better as a director with the more plays I directed, but not enormously better. I was good, I think, from the very beginning. I have improved on certain skills and knowledge over the years, but I always felt confident in my abilities from the first play I did. I have gotten better at dealing with actors, not fighting with them, not getting upset with them, and I undoubtedly became less afraid as time went on. What I enjoyed most about working in the theater was having an acting company where you work with the same people over and over again, and you see each other socially. As the artistic director, you are important in their lives and I miss that high level of warmth and camaraderie and support. I really loved it. As a freelance theater director, or as a film director, you move from one project to another and sometimes you work with the same people but a lot of times you are around perfect strangers. It's much nicer to be working in the kind of family situation that an acting company provides you. It's somewhat reassuring and familiar, and a lot of the best work is done in those environments. One of the ways I make my movies is I hire some of the same people again, in an effort to replicate the same atmosphere and feeling that I had working in the theater.

3

Sticky My Fingers, Fleet My Feet (1970)

AFTER WORKING SUCCESSFULLY in Off-Broadway theater for nearly a decade, Hancock now ardently probed and pressed for that elusive first opportunity to direct his own film. By 1970, a number of intriguing movie projects had already stalled or disintegrated at various stages of their development. Undeterred, Hancock allied himself with a young New York screenwriter named Mark Fine who had conceived a story that was an "ambitious" distillation of the ambience and ideologies of 1960s counter-culture America, and concerned a group of artists and musicians living in Greenwich Village. As with every other filmmaking venture that had preceded it this feature would stutter to another depressing halt, spurring Hancock to once again explore other avenues of financial support that could facilitate his ambitions. One potential resource was the American Film Institute, which had been founded three years earlier in September 1967 with a remit to provide education and support to fledgling filmmakers, as well as striving to honor the work of established artists and preserve the history of motion pictures for posterity. After successfully soliciting the organization for a grant, Hancock would finally get his chance to direct a short film. The resulting work, Sticky My Fingers, Fleet My Feet, *would ultimately gain an Academy Award-nomination for Best Live Action Short and effectively kick-start his filmmaking career in emphatic fashion.*

I don't remember the name of the script that Mark Fine wrote anymore, but it was a good one and I'm sorry the movie never happened. I do recall that it was a love story with an unhappy ending. I think it was probably autobiographical on Mark's part. He was the nephew of Katya and Bert Gilden, who'd written *Hurry Sundown* together under the pen-name of K.B. Gilden, and they had some contacts in the film business. One of them was Carl Foreman, the screenwriter of *High Noon* and *The Guns of Navarone*, who had been blacklisted by Hollywood after appearing before the House Committee of Un-American Activities. Foreman was an impressive man and he helped us attach Michael Douglas to the project. I believe that Michael had not even done the television show *The Streets of San Francisco* with Karl Malden at this point in time. I then brought in Anjanette Comer, who had starred in Tony Richardson's *The Loved One*, to play opposite Mike. Another guy we involved was Dave Golden, an established production manager around New York, who was really the top guy in town. Dave did the schedule and the budget we hawked around for financing, but, like every other movie I tried to get off the ground back then, it just died away.

By this time, I was reasonably desperate to get a picture going. I had heard through the grapevine that the American Film Institute had formed, and thought the whole organization and its objectives was a worthy endeavor. I'd also heard that they were offering grants to new directors, so I decided to apply for one. I had all these good reviews from the various theater productions I'd directed throughout the years and I also had some letters of recommendation from several prominent figures such as Tennessee Williams and Gregory Peck. During all the craziness that had occurred in Pittsburgh with R.K. Mellon, I had gotten Tennessee to write a letter to the board and the local press on my behalf. He wrote a wonderful letter saying, "Wherever John Hancock is, there is dramatic excitement," and so forth. So, I knew I could get a good letter from him again when I was approaching the AFI for a grant, and Tennessee came through, as did Gregory Peck.

My first contact with Peck had come shortly after I had taken over the Pittsburgh Playhouse. I had been there about five weeks and was sitting in my office one day planning the season, when I got a call from him. Peck explained that he had started his career at the La Jolla Playhouse in San Diego, California, which he had co-founded in the 1940s, and is where he first started out as an actor. So, he undoubtedly had great emotional attachment there and was trying to help them in their search for a new artistic director. He asked me if I would consider the job. Well, it was *Gregory Peck*, and he didn't take no for an answer easily! I explained that I was flattered, but I had just arrived in Pittsburgh after a quick year and a half running the theater in San Francisco; and I was afraid I'd look like an idiot even thinking about jumping ship so soon. Peck wasn't convinced. He said they would really make it worth my while, and asked if I would please think about it. But I just couldn't. It was too crazy. I saw a certain amount of him after *Bang the Drum Slowly*, when I was living in Malibu. Peck had a big house in Brentwood and we gardened together a bit. He gave me good advice about compost for the hard clay soils and what to plant, and so forth. He really knew what he was doing. I always wished we had worked together, because I grew up loving his pictures—except for his Captain Ahab in *Moby Dick*.

At the point in which I was trying to secure the grant to make a short film, Peck was President of the AFI's Board of Trustees. I still had his phone number because he'd asked me to call him if I changed my mind about the La Jolla job. He wrote a very nice letter on my behalf and I think that his kind words—and those of Tennessee—went a long way towards establishing my validity and credibility in certain people's eyes. I then went to Washington to meet with George Stevens, Jr., who was chairing the AFI at the time. My good friend Donny Graham, who was already well on his way to becoming a powerful figure in Washington, also talked to George on my behalf. So, I guess you could safely say that I lobbied for the grant, and through my efforts and the efforts of my aforementioned friends, I did indeed get $10,000 to make a short film. However, I got it "conditionally." Basically, the AFI informed me, "Okay, we want to give you the grant but not for the story that you propose to make."

The story I had originally submitted was written by a friend of mine named Jim Guetti and was set during the time of the Vietnam War. It concerned these young boys who venture out on a hot summer day—a special day when dragonflies suddenly fill the air. These kids go around with baseball bats or paddles, sticks of some kind, and start brutally swatting the dragonflies out of the air. I thought it was the kind of story the AFI would go for, something that was perhaps allegorical in the sense that it referred to the war in Vietnam and the human capacity for cruelty, but I was wrong. The guys there were smart enough to realize what I did not, that this was a terrible idea for a short. Not knowing much about film, I hadn't considered the fact that I would have to wait for that special day when the dragonflies finally emerged. I would also have to have the camera equipment and actors ready at that exact time, and how the hell was I going to get these insects to hover still while the actors swatted them? These were not things I had given much thought and, more than that, it was kind of a gloomy subject anyway. The AFI then said, "Why don't you find another story that you want to do; one that is a little more practical and upbeat?"

So, I went to a library and gathered up as many collections of short stories as I possibly could. I pored through all of them in the hope of finding something that really sang to me. I did unearth a wonderful story by John Updike that had been published in *The New Yorker* called "Bech Takes Pot Luck," which was about a famous Pulitzer Prize-winning Jewish writer who starts smoking marijuana. Unfortunately, we couldn't get the rights to Updike's story, but the AFI liked that choice and felt confident that I was on the right track. We then tried to acquire the rights to about three or four other stories, all without success, and I even tried to sell them on the idea of doing "The Wrecker," the Saul Bellow tale I'd initially planned on contributing to the long-deceased anthology film with Brain De Palma. That choice didn't work out either for some reason and I was beginning to feel a little concerned that we might not find something really good.

> *Another short story that was brought to Hancock's attention was* "Sticky My Fingers, Fleet My Feet" *by Gene Williams. First published in* The New Yorker *on September 11, 1965, it concerned a dreamy writer named Norm who has an all-encompassing passion for football. Criticized by his cultivated wife, Marian, who labels him "immature," he departs one afternoon for Central Park to play a game of touch football with his businessmen friends (all of whom have christened him the "sticky-fingered antelope" due to his admirable skills as a wide receiver). Norm's superiority among the flabby coterie of lawyers, analysts and ad men who furnish each of the opposing teams is suddenly challenged when a skinny fifteen year-old kid named Wesley turns up to participate and ends up taking the spoils. His ego bruised and fervor for the sport swiftly diminished, Norm limps home and comes to the painful realization that football is a young man's game and he is too mature for it. Marian puts him in a bathtub to soak his weary body and*

> *reminds Norm that he is the best tennis player on the West Side. This soothing admonition prompts Norm to decide that he will now direct his energies into tennis, and he immediately starts practicing backhand strokes in the tub.*

It was John Lahr who first suggested "Sticky My Fingers, Fleet My Feet" to me, and I'll forever be grateful to him for that. I was immediately intrigued by the poetry of that title and wanted to know more about it. I then read the short story and thought it was terrific. I was captivated by the fact it was about these middle-aged businessmen with pulled muscles and creaking joints and burning ulcers, who meet to play a game of touch football. It was such a simple but potent tale. There were something effortlessly charming and wistful and funny about it, I instantly knew that I had found my story. More importantly the AFI also liked it, too. So, after we got the go-ahead, we acquired the rights to Gene Williams' story without any fuss. Lahr and I then collaborated on the script together and it was an easy process. I believe that Lahr did the first draft and then passed it to me. I then rewrote his draft before passing the script back to Lahr where he prepared the final version. We didn't make any significant changes to Williams' story as we felt it worked perfectly fine as it was.

Incidentally, despite Lahr co-writing the script and our maintaining a strong friendship over the years, John has never written a feature screenplay for me to direct. That's probably because he's been incredibly successful as a critic, novelist and biographer, and has been very busy over the years. The closest we got to doing a movie together, which really wasn't that close at all, was an adaptation of his novel *The Autograph Hound*. The story involves a busboy at a New York restaurant who goes to some incredible lengths to collect the autographs of famous movie stars. Joe Wizan, who later became the head of 20th Century Fox for several years, optioned the book and had the project set-up for a while with Mark Rydell as director. My brief involvement was in 1973, around the time I was editing *Bang the Drum Slowly*. I never got that deeply involved with *The Autograph Hound*, but I believe Lahr thought I might direct it. I really did want to because it's such a fabulous book, but it was optioned for a lot of money and the producers went to a more established director.

Anyway, after receiving $10,000 from the AFI and locking down a shooting script, I began putting together the cast and crew. Since *Sticky My Fingers, Fleet My Feet* was going to be my first film I thought it would advantageous to have as many familiar and friendly faces around as possible. I reasoned it could only be beneficial to be surrounded by people I trusted, who would offer me support and encouragement—as well as doing exactly what I said! Of course, the all-important role in the film was that of Norm the dreamer, the narrator and chief protagonist. I originally cast Barton Heyman as Norm, as I'd worked with him so much in the theater and we were good friends. Sadly, Barton then injured his knee during a production of Arthur Kopit's *Indians* in Washington DC and was limping quite badly. He was in no physical condition to be the "sticky-fingered antelope" that I needed. So, we quickly had to look elsewhere for our lead. As the start-date was looming closer and closer, I decided to replace Barton with someone who now, in hindsight, seems a rather obvious choice: Gene Williams, the author of the short story. Casting Gene was really a moment of desperation on my part as we had suddenly lost Barton, but it made perfect sense. I mean, *Sticky My Fingers* is autobiography, it's Gene's story. It may have been quite a leap for Gene to go from writer to actor, but he wanted to do it and acquitted himself extremely well.

When we were looking for a group of guys to play Norm's businessmen friends, one of the first actors I cast was Charlie Durning, whom I'd worked with in Pittsburgh. Charlie played Gratzwald, the equally-competitive captain of the team that faces off against Norm's team. I then cast Marshall Efron and Al Leberfeld, two guys that had both been in my San Francisco and Pittsburgh companies (Al had played Oberon in my early productions of *A Midsummer Night's Dream*). I also cast Val Bisoglio in the role of Marv, as I had seen him at the Actors Studio and felt he had great qualities. John Lahr had already agreed to play the bespectacled guy with the white mouth-guard. Lahr wanted to do it and I thought he would be wonderful. It was also good to have him on the set with me as I felt he could be another steadying influence. The mustachioed George from BBD&O was played by Thomas Meehan. He was around New York at that point, writing for here and there, but Tom is now by far the most successful writer of musical books working today. I mean, he did productions like *Annie*, *The Producers* and *Hairspray*. He's basically "Mr. Book" for Broadway musicals and I always get a kick out of seeing him in the film. We also needed to find a kid to play Wesley, the scrawny teenager who joins the men in their game of touch football. We found one in Havelock Hewes, who was the son of Henry Hewes, a very important drama critic who wrote for *The Saturday Review of Literature*. Henry had given me several good reviews for my theater productions and so I dutifully paid a debt there. Havelock was also a very nice boy and he did a good job for me.

The character of Norm's wife, Marian, who makes bookend appearances in the film, was originally played by Linda Lavin. Linda is a good actress who has enjoyed a lot of success and won the Tony Award, the Obie and a Golden Globe, but I did not like what she was doing with the role. I thought she was way over the top, working too hard for laughs, and so I fired her. Soon after I recast the part with Carolee Campbell, who had been yet another member of my Pittsburgh company. I had always liked Carolee and had seen her do a wonderful scene with Val Bisoglio at the Actors Studio (I think they were even an item at one point but then she later married Hector Elizondo). Carolee came in and quickly grasped the correct register for the character, and played the wife much straighter. The change in actress necessitated our shooting the interior scenes in Norm and Marian's apartment twice. We had formerly shot the scenes with Linda Lavin as Marian in an office at Bill Wilson's Saturn Pictures, which we tried (and failed) to decorate so that it would look like an apartment. Bill was one of the producers on *Sticky My Fingers* and I'd recruited him in my persistent efforts to get *Nerve* on as a movie. The second time we shot the scenes with Carolee as Marian was in someone's apartment we borrowed on the Upper West Side, I think on West End Avenue.

I can clearly recall the day we first gathered in Central Park to shoot the exteriors. As we started filming I realized there was only one small problem: I did not know how to make a movie! That was an incredible thing to acccpt this far into the process, but I was so caught up in the excitement and delirium of everything I just hadn't thought about it. Rather early on in pre-production I had enlisted the help of a woman named Kit Clarke, who was part of the documentary scene in New York (I believe it was Kit who later got us the use of a friend's apartment to re-shoot our interiors). I was talking with her one day and she mentioned having recently worked with a cameraman named Robert Elfstrom on some civil rights documentaries in the South. Kit felt that Elfstrom would be a good fit for my project as he was a very able guy. It turned out that Bob was excellent at shooting hand-held footage and was also quite athletic. He was capable of running at speed with the camera as the actors were making the various plays and he had considerable endurance. Bob had been an acrobat at one time and he could really move; so light and dexterous on his feet.

Not knowing what the hell it was I was doing, it was great to have somebody like Bob around. He was not so accomplished at lighting, but he had a good eye and was fairly inventive. In fact, a lot of the most effective shots in *Sticky My Fingers* are Bob's framings to some degree. I like the opening shot which shows a hand raised to the sky, and the fingers obscuring the sun as a football sails through the air in slow-motion. That was actually Bob Elfstrom's hand. I decided to commence the film that way because it presented a kind of mystery that was unfolding. There was the uncertainty of where you were and what exactly you were looking at. You hear the cheering roar of an unseen crowd and you wonder if we're at a professional football game. The opening shot sets it up as one thing, but then, when the audience sees this ordinary guy awkwardly catching the ball in a park, it always gets a laugh. I mean, up until that moment, it could be a star performing at the Superbowl, but then it pays off wonderfully.

As we started shooting, the actors mostly just played football and ran about as Bob tried to find some interesting shots and moments we could use. I can remember looking over at Bob this one time and noticed that he was playing catch with the assistant cameraman and shooting at the same time. He literally had the ball in one hand and the camera in the other. I approached him and said, "What are you doing? Film is expensive; we can't afford to be screwing around here." Bob replied, "You are going to need some of these shots, believe me." Boy, was he right about that! Later on, when I was cutting the film, I realized that the image of a ball sailing through the air was the solution to not being able to get something in one shot. It basically gave me something to cut *to*. I quickly learned that by shooting a ball in flight or shooting the actors' feet shuffling and running over the ground, I could solve certain problems and knit disparate elements together.

Another swift lesson came when we were rehearsing the action with the actors: I discovered that if we ran one of the plays it was fine, but if we ran the same play twice or three times in rehearsal the guys were finished! They simply did not have the stamina to keep doing it. The game was not something we could rehearse without physically exhausting the actors to the point where they couldn't go on. As somebody who was coming from the theater and was used to rehearsing extensively this came as quite a shock. I had been able to block some very elaborate action on revolving stages in my plays that involved a lot of movement. I really knew how to block stuff so precisely I was always aware of exactly what was happening and what I needed. I started to shoot *Sticky My Fingers* with this same elaborate approach to blocking in mind and quickly realized that it just wasn't practical. For instance, one actor would throw a wild pass that would go astray, or another would fail to see the ball coming, or would drop it as he was trying to catch it. All kinds of things were happening that would disrupt us. We were always contending with the unpredictable flight of the football and the actors' lack of fitness and technical ball-playing skills.

For all that, it must be said that some of the actors were proficient at football. Val Bisoglio was pretty good and, of course, Gene Williams could really play. A lot of the other guys were not what you would call prime physical specimens, which was part of the point we were making in the film, but Gene was in good condition. He was a very adept wide receiver in Central Park and could run plays a number of times without ever getting exhausted. You can see that in the film, how Gene dances and glides and shimmies about. What's interesting is I recently heard that Charlie Durning was a former dancer and I did know that fact to some degree back in 1970. I'd probably just forgotten it, I guess. Charlie occasionally exhibited some of that grace when we were shooting, but by the time we did *Sticky My Fingers* he was overweight—not badly at this point, but he plainly didn't move as well as he once did. Charlie had also been a soldier at one time and he was a physical guy.

In contending with these unforeseen difficulties, I couldn't get some of the shots that I'd wanted. I would try to get the shot a couple of times, but then the actors would have to rest for half an hour as they were breathless and sweating profusely. This necessitated a rethink on my part to some degree, and I had enough sense to throw aside my original plan for the shoot. Always when you are directing a film, you go into it knowing the way you are going to do it. When that way isn't working out too well, you are faced with an inevitable decision: should I persist with what I'm doing and be true to my initial scheme, or should I throw all of it out the window and try something else? I believe that sometimes you need to have the balls to throw your first approach out, readjust and rethink what it is your doing, and find another way. Obviously, for a first-time director that can be a profoundly alarming and daunting prospect but sometimes it's an entirely necessary one. In this case, I did throw everything away and we just started along a new path. I figured it was the only available course of action to me if I was going to get everything that I needed.

As we were shooting though, I gradually had the disconcerting feeling that I was merely photographing football plays. I wasn't capturing

Norm's dream, I wasn't capturing the emotion and the fantasy; I was simply photographing guys running around with a football. Upon making this realization, I said to Bob Elfstrom, "Look, I'm not getting the appropriate feeling here. There's no magic, no drama, it's just play after play." Thus, I had to reconsider how I was going to invest the film with the qualities I wanted. Then, quite suddenly, I guess by accident really, I learned about backlight. I discovered that if you reposition the actors where you are shooting on the field—because you can't tell which way is which anyway—and you shoot them in backlight, you start to infuse the images with that delirious feeling of glory that Norm is so desperately trying to create or re-create. I then decided to shoot in slow-motion as that was another way of getting inside Norm's head, of visualizing his dream, where every small moment magically comes alive for him. It just added a certain resonance to the shots.

Slow-motion, then, was a way of being subjective and catching the way the characters are experiencing those moments—whether it's through Norm's eyes or their own. It evinced Norm's vision of himself as a pro-athlete. It's also a little like a quote from playback in a televised football game. Effectively, it's the way Norm is seeing himself on television in playback. It's somewhat resonant of the means in which people live out their fantasy, particularly fantasies of competing in professional sports: they do it as if it's being televised, and watched, and commentated on by others. I could have over-emphasized that point by having somebody like Howard Cosell commentating on the action. Actually, while I was preparing *Sticky My Fingers*, I went to CBS and met with the director of all the NFL football games for the network, and asked how they covered football games. He was very nice and helpful and I came away with a couple of ideas. I wanted to bring some of that approach into how we covered this simple football game these guys were playing. At one point, as the game progresses, the music gets slower as the action shifts into slow-motion, and it's a simple but effective way to illustrate that the guys are getting tired and are out of shape. I specifically instructed my composer Orville Stoeber to do that with the music. I think Orville did a very nice job on *Sticky My Fingers*. He came up with a catchy theme that caught the delicate spirit of Norm's dream.

We decided to have Norm narrate the film as it was another more obvious means of getting inside his thought process. That's part of how we know exactly what he is thinking and feeling, and some of that narration is amusing. Gene Williams helped with those lines, as did John Lahr. Both of them were very involved in the editing phase, providing voiceovers and offering constructive comments, and much of the narration is taken directly from Gene's short story. The narration is also a functional thing in that each of the characters in the game is introduced by Norm with a freeze frame. He has a line for each of them and I thought it was important to know the guys' occupations and a little something about them. For instance, the way that Norm describes Big Marshall: he just stops mid-sentence, sighs, and has nothing complimentary to add except for "Nice guy, though." That's really funny and Marshall Efron plays that part so wonderfully. Of course, Norm is also providing a kind of running commentary on the game when he makes observations like, "Lawyers make great broken field runners," and "Analysts make great linebackers."

Thankfully, we didn't have any problems shooting in Central Park from passersby—not so much, really. We would just say "please" and wave them on, and they would continue on their way. To some degree it was okay to have several casual spectators present because people do stop to watch games of football in public places, and there's so much movement in the foreground usually, you don't notice if the backgrounds are different or not there anymore. Speaking of noticing things in the background, there's a shot where Norm is going out endlessly for one of those passes. We filmed it with Gene running in a circle around the camera—if you do that with a long lens it looks like he's running in a straight line. In this case you can see the entire crew standing there with reflectors! But no one has ever noticed that.

> *Perhaps inevitably for a first time filmmaker with a limited awareness of the medium he was working in, Hancock was beset with a number of personal insecurities. Despite his confidence steadily growing throughout the initial weeklong shooting schedule, he was not happy with the results he was producing, as were others connected to the film.*

Bill Wilson had suggested that I hire an editor named Eleanor Hamerow, who had cut a lot of documentaries in New York. So, at his behest, I did. As we were cutting the footage together, I can remember once remarking to Eleanor, "Hey, why don't you use this shot here?" She looked at me rather coldly, and said, "Because I don't want to." I said, "But I think it would be funny." She then hissed, "*You* are going to tell *me* what's funny? Look at what you've shot!" Well, shortly after that exchange I fired her, but Eleanor wasn't the only person who expressed a negative opinion of the assembly. Another of the producers was a guy named Sanford Evans, whom I believe was working for McCann Eriksson, or possibly some other big advertising agency, at the time. He had apparently been on a lot of shoots and was recommended to me as somebody who knew a lot about film and would be helpful to my cause. At one point Sanford came in, looked at the Eleanor Hamerow cut and reacted in a similarly disparaging manner. He basically said, "God, I'm so disappointed! Frankly, I don't want anything more to do with this film."

Naturally, I took his response badly and it was a dark and difficult moment for me. Although I was dying inside, I just said, "Oh, okay. Bye." Later, when *Sticky My Fingers* was nominated for an Academy Award, Sanford suddenly crawled back out of the woodwork and announced that he wanted to accept the award. I couldn't believe my ears and, on the possibility that we did indeed win the Oscar, I actually got the AFI to prevent that from happening. The truth is Sanford could have potentially destroyed me at the point in which he abandoned the film, because that was a time when I really needed some support and a big injection of confidence. It would have been very easy for me to have given up, or just muddled my way through it, but I had no intention of doing either thing. I do have to concede that certain people were entirely justified in their opinions. What Eleanor and Sanford saw that day was not good at all, and I wasn't happy with the film either. But I simply could not afford to have the film fail.

That said, there was now a significant problem I faced: we had basically exhausted the $10,000 the AFI had given us. That was all gone. So, if we were to correct certain problems, we needed some additional money from other sources. I understood that I was in the middle of the difficult process of learning how to direct a film. It hadn't gone as well as I'd hoped and I really felt that we needed to shoot some more stuff in order to make it better. I eventually approached Kit Clarke and secured an added $13,000 from her. Kit had money from her family, a trust fund of some sort, which enabled us to shoot some more footage. We then summoned the actors back together maybe four or five more times, and they were all willing to come. I believe the first shoot had consisted of something like six or seven days and the re-shoot was a further six or seven days. Altogether, this took place over the period of a month. But I must tell you, raising that extra money from Kit was not easy. If I hadn't have secured those funds and shot more scenes, it's certainly conceivable that my career could have been very different.

> *Some of the aspects that had initially appealed to Hancock about Gene Williams' short story were its playful treatise on faltering masculinity and the encroaching acceptance of one's own mortality. These would be themes the filmmaker would return to and explore further in a few of his subsequent pictures.*

Sticky My Fingers taps into the idea that men often savor the small and trivial triumphs amateur sports provide them with among their peers. These victories mean very little in the grand scheme of things, and are sometimes quickly forgotten, but that fleeting moment of glory becomes all important to them. It's a childish thing, really, like Norm making a record in his notebook about the number of passes he catches is a way of his keeping the memories and fantasies alive. It's like a serial killer gathering trophies of his victims, only it's less gruesome! Then Norm's wife questions his maturity and he replies, "I'm a very mature pass receiver." But you can clearly see the competitiveness among men when they are playing sports; how it becomes everything for them, how it brings out their aggressive natures and instincts. It's just a game, but there is always that element of one-up-man-ship to it; of getting ahead, of being a winner, which is the American way. Also, the very subject matter of this film was redolent of a time in the movie business when for some reason the majors were being run by the kind of men who played touch football and wanted to be like the Kennedys. After it was made, *Sticky My Fingers* made the rounds of all the executives' offices and it really spoke to them, because it was *about* them. So, that was a very lucky choice of material on my part and it led to further opportunities for me down the line.

A scene that encapsulates the sense of the schoolyard reborn is when Norm and Gratzwald are picking their respective teams from among the guys. I think that's something a lot of people can relate to from their own youth. I can definitely remember those kinds of situations; how painful it is for any kid to be picked third from last, or second to last, or, heaven forbid, last of all! I can vividly recall the discernible tension of waiting for the kids to make their next choice and for my name to be called. As I believe I already told you, I was known as "pus-arm." So, typically, I was never going to be among the first to get picked. In those kinds of situations, it can sometimes be your age and social standing as well as your athletic ability that ultimately determines any decision. There is no room for feeling or for sentiment in these things. That's also true of the moment when the little girl picks the ball up off the ground just as the men are about to start the game, and her mother says, "Give the gentlemen their ball." There is no room for cuteness or feeling at that moment either; it's all about the importance of the game and nothing else. They don't find this child amusing or sweet at all. While we're on the subject, I don't know who that little girl was but I do know that the mother was played Rhoda Gemignani, who was also from my San Francisco and Pittsburgh companies and had at one time been the wife of Paul Gemignani.

This lack of sentiment I'm talking about also applies to the character of Wesley. It almost goes without saying that he is a cold dose of reality and a reminder to Norm that he is getting old. When the kid first appears onscreen it's quite obvious from the look Norm gives him, and the narration that plays over the shot ("I'm not that much older than he is"), that he resents his presence right off the bat. This is because the kid is a different age, he's young, and is not part of that same macho mindset. He doesn't have as much to lose or as much to gain by playing. In a way, the kid forecasts Norm's failure as Wesley is really the agent of doom for him. There's a funny moment when Marv comments, "That kid looks tough," and we cut to a shot of Wesley sitting on the grass, absently plucking grass out of the ground. I mean, the kid is not a monster or anything, he's just a kid, but they are still threatened by him. Finally, there's one final irony when it's revealed that Wesley doesn't even play football and is merely the manager of his high school team.

There's also that pertinent line you hear where Marv screams to Norm during the game, "Shake that kid loose! Shake him loose!" And Norm just can't shake Wesley loose. The kid is always near him and he will catch up with him eventually. That's another little metaphor for the cold, damp hand of middle-age settling on one's shoulder. I love all those shots, by the way, the speed and motion of them; the way Norm dances about desperately trying to elude Wesley. The winning of the game is so important for him. It's everything! I like Norm's mantra that is heard repeatedly throughout the film: "When the going gets rough, the rough get going." There's something quite sad and pathetic about hearing those words spoken by this guy who is not quite in touch with reality. I think that quote—which has been regurgitated many times over the years in playing fields and offices and boardrooms and bedrooms across the world—may have originated with Bobby Kennedy. It certainly feels like it came from somebody like that. I think it's another distinctly robust American phrase; a true Americanism.

There's a fantastic series of shots in *Sticky My Fingers* that take place when Norm is trying to shake the kid loose, in which a squirrel is briefly glimpsed. I'm so glad when people notice and comment on that moment because it's exactly where I learned how to edit; that's how I discovered that cutaways work. We were trying to finish the film and, by this time, I had already replaced Eleanor Hamerow with a girl named Toni Mendell. Toni had a history of heroin addiction and she would sometimes disappear when we were working, leaving me alone. I remember being on my own in the editing room, in the middle of the night, learning how to cut film myself. I put the shots of the startled squirrel together with shots of Norm's feet running, and suddenly exclaimed, "My God! Cuts work! They really do!" It was like unearthing some secret knowledge or something, it was a revelatory moment for me. I love the shots of the squirrel, actually. It's almost like the squirrel is reacting to Norm as he runs on the field. It's as if nature itself is enraptured with the outcome of the game. So, nature is doing its bit in perpetuating the fantasy. The importance Norm places on the game is obvious but now it seems like the whole world is aware of it, too.

Then the rainstorm arrives and threatens to disrupt the game. That was a fortunate addition as we could never have afforded a rain machine. The rainstorm is not featured in the short story, it just happened and we took full advantage of it. We simply incorporated it into the narrative. I then had Gene improvise that line where Norm announces, "It's not rain; it's a summer shower!" As I recall, it rained for about three hours that day, and we just kept on shooting to ensure that I could get as much coverage as I possibly could and fashion a good sequence out of it. If it had abruptly stopped raining any sooner than it did, we would've probably had to throw that section of film away. When we were editing I realized that the rainstorm steers the story towards its conclusion; the game seems to descend to a more wild and primal level. I love Marshall Efron's improvised line, where he cries, "The rain is come! The rain is come! This desert will be converted into a valley; a fertile plain, a cornucopia of blah-blah-blah." It's like all social bonds are suddenly loosed and you can say anything, and you don't care about the game anymore. Everybody cracks up during that scene which is always a good sign that something works.

At the end of the game, in defeat, Norm reasons that you have to face life at some point. Like when he says, "If you live long enough, you get old. It happens to everybody." Norm is finally facing his own mortality there, I think, rather than being lost in the reverie. He's been sent flying face-first into the mud and he picks himself up, and groans, "God, my wife is going to be so childish about this." That is until the end, when hope returns to him and the dream is suddenly reawakened. The principal theme of *Sticky My Fingers* as I saw it was the indestructibility of hope. Few things are as impervious to time and misfortune and disillusionment as faith. It makes us blind to all that stuff, don't you think? Whatever happens to us as human beings, however bad things get and whatever fate befalls us, there is always one ember of hope that continues to burn inside us; and from that one ember a wildfire can rage. I think it's just the way we are programmed and it has something to do with the idea that where there is life there's hope. In the context of this story I feel it's true.

That feeling is reinforced at the end when, in his misery, Norm decides that he will now give up football and will instead become a tennis star. Incidentally, the sound effect of a racket hitting a tennis ball as Norm practices his forehand and backhand in the bathtub was not written into the script; that was an idea I had during the editing process. I think Gene appreciated that small addition. I believe we are led to think by that conclusion it's the end of the touch football games in Central Park—at least for Norm it is. In being a film about ageing and having the shit kicked out of you by a high school kid, *Sticky My Fingers* is also about a man's dream of being *somebody* and the difficulty we often have in surrendering our dreams; how one strives to keep the dream alive and how horrible it is when reality intrudes on our fantasies. So, the film is ultimately about the destruction of the dream and the rebirth of the dream.

When I think about *Sticky My Fingers* now I occasionally shudder at how close it came to going wrong for me; how difficult it was to raise the extra money to finish it and how it looked like ending in failure. But I'm incredibly proud of the film. I still think it's funny and I love all the movement and energy it has. The only thing that bothers me now about it is the synch in a couple of places. The first thing the negative cutter—whose name I've long forgotten or suppressed—did when I got there, was cut off the Academy leaders and throw them away. Why he did that, I have not a clue. It was total incompetence. An Academy leader is the length of film attached to the head and/or tail of a reel for editorial purposes, or for exhibition, and features a countdown from eleven to three. On the number three there's a *pop*. You synch up that pop with the pop on the soundtrack and you're in synch for the whole movie. But this guy took those and threw them away! Maybe he thought they were too worn or something, but this meant that he lost synch, in essence forever, on the picture. So, how do you fix that problem? You start looking on the picture track for something like a handclap, and then you slide the sound track until its handclap synchs up with the picture.

But if, let's say, in the original synching up of the dailies, a shot or two was synched up a frame off (this happens occasionally) perhaps the sound on those shots is a frame late; and maybe elsewhere in the picture you have a frame or two where the sound was synched up a frame early, then by using that handclap as a synch point you've thrown some of the picture back into perfect synch. But elsewhere you can now be two or three frames out of synch, which starts to become really noticeable. So, then you strive to correct that. Okay, in an attempt to correct that type of thing, I watched this guy take a splicer and cut in the *middle* of a shot on the negative! On the *negative*! I said, "What the hell are you doing?" He replied rather guiltily, "Well, it will give it energy." Christ, I've dealt with some pretty lame people, but he truly was among the lamest of the lame. There's also the problem of the magnetic track for 16mm not being one hundred percent stable. It can stretch a little. So, things didn't have to be properly synched to begin with in order to be a frame or two off. The center of it is once those Academy leaders were gone we were in a world of shit. And chopping a frame out in the middle of shots only made it worse.

> *As specified in the contract he signed with the AFI,* Sticky My Fingers, Fleet My Feet *concludes with a card that openly states: "The Filmmaker John Hancock received a production grant from the American Film Institute." Following a screening for the Board of Trustees, the short was later broadcast by CBS during halftime of their annual Thanksgiving football game on November 26, 1970. Thereafter it was released nationally and accompanied screenings of the Woody Allen comedy* Bananas *(1971). The film was then nominated for Best Live Action Short at the 43rd Academy Awards ceremony on April 15, 1971, which was held at the Dorothy Chandler Pavilion. The other two shorts recognized that evening were Robert Seigler's* Shut Up…I'm Crying *and James R. Rokos'* The Resurrection of Broncho Billy—*the latter co-written, scored and edited by John Carpenter who would later achieve fame for such movies as* Assault on Precinct 13 *(1976),* Halloween *(1978) and* The Thing *(1982).*

The AFI was delighted with the film and the Academy Award nomination. They were more or less in their infancy back then and *Sticky My Fingers* was viewed as being the first really good thing that had happened to them. So, it was an important development for the organization. We held an extremely successful screening for the Board of Trustees—Jack Valenti, Charlton Heston, all those people were in attendance. They were all very proud of it and were congratulating me. They were thrilled to have something to show people to demonstrate that the AFI was a good thing; that it had purpose and direction. By this time, Heston was the Chairman of the Board having recently replaced Gregory Peck and everybody was feeling very positive about stuff. That feeling only grew when the film was screened during the big Thanksgiving football game by CBS. I watched that with my wife, Ann, in Sneden's Landing, and it was a big deal for me. Certainly, a lot of people saw that particular screening and it was really the perfect place to show *Sticky My Fingers* for obvious reasons. The short being paired up with *Bananas* in theaters was also a pretty big deal, and both things got me a lot of attention. Regrettably, we did have to trim the film a little for CBS for reasons of time and had to omit the credits. So, aside from the incredible pride I felt at it being shown so prominently, I was concerned about what might have been lost and what people who worked on it would think when they didn't see their names.

I've preserved some fairly vivid memories of what I felt the day of the Academy Awards ceremony, and in the days leading up to it: excitement, dread, pride; lots of contrasting emotions. Everybody I spoke to who had seen all three films nominated that year insisted that I would win. *Everybody*! Indeed, so often was I told this by people I began to perhaps believe it myself, and that was a dangerous thing. I went to the ceremony that night feeling quietly confident, but still somewhat apprehensive. I was accompanied by Ann, and George Stevens, Jr. and his gorgeous wife, Liz, and had prepared myself to deliver a thank you speech upon accepting the award. I knew what I wanted to say and probably imagined my walking up on stage and taking the statuette in my trembling hands, all that wonderful stuff. But I must admit that I found the prospect of delivering a speech very scary and I did have considerable anxiety about it. When another name was then read aloud by the presenters I had this terrible sense of the bottom falling out of my world; an ejaculation of remorse and relief. I felt remorse for the fact I'd lost, but also relief that I didn't have to get up on stage and struggle through a speech. So, it was a peculiar mixture of crushing disappointment and this sudden sensation of calm flooding my entire body.

What was interesting is that during the course of the evening all the winners were taken out of the audience and the mood steadily darkened, and turned quite depressed and grim. The crowd was gradually made up of the losers, who were all sitting there alone with their regrets and bitterness. It was a weird thing to experience, actually, to reflect on your own misfortune in the harsh glare of another's triumph. It made the loss feel all the more acutely painful. I also remember the party we attended after the ceremony was over. Richard Zanuck was one of the first people who congratulated and commiserated with me. I never met my fellow nominees, nor, frankly, did I want to. Gradually, as the hours ticked by, my mood did get a little brighter and I put certain things into perspective. I realized that it was great just to be nominated, particularly when I reflected on some of the dark moments I'd experienced while making *Sticky My Fingers*. Also, I'm very fond of George and Liz, and we had a really good time that night—obviously not as good a time as if I had won, but we had fun. That occasion in 1971 remains the only time I've ever attended the Academy Awards. It is too painful to endure if you are nominated and lose, but I suppose it's far more painful if you are not nominated at all.

I do feel compelled to add that this was a time in the Academy's history when you could vote without seeing the picture. As ridiculous as this might sound, people actually voted on titles. You didn't have to provide any record that you had viewed the films in the theaters, and, back then, there were no video tapes or DVDs or Blu-rays sent out to voters. Again, for those who hadn't taken the time and effort, the decisions were made entirely on how the titles sounded. I hope I don't come across as too impudent, but I do feel that I would have won the Oscar if more people had in fact seen each of the three films. I honestly believe that. I want to be generous about the other two films that were nominated that year, but the truth is I did not like either of them. I saw both *The Resurrection of Broncho Billy* and *Shut Up...I'm Crying* and I genuinely thought—I still do—that *Sticky My Fingers* was by far the superior work. That's not sour grapes on my part or anything. I'm just being honest with you. I was very proud of my film and the many positive reactions it was getting told me I had something good. Of course, my perfectly biased opinion alone wasn't going to win me the Oscar! While on the subject, I should add that I did not know until recently that John Carpenter was in any way involved with *The Resurrection of Broncho Billy*. I was very interested to hear it. Carpenter is a filmmaker I admire and he's gone on to have a great career.

I believe the guy who went up on stage to accept the Academy Award that night was the son of an agent or something.

> *After profiting from their assistance in getting his film career activated, Hancock showed his gratitude by serving on the Board of Trustees for the American Film Institute for four years between 1973 and 1977.*

Those early days at the AFI were very interesting, and I learned a lot about the industry and some of the powerful personalities who operated within it. I basically met *everybody*! Meetings were these wonderful luncheons at the Greystone Mansion above Beverly Hills. Charlton Heston presided in his Moses-like way—actually, he had a bit of imp in him as well. It really helped my career; it didn't hinder it in any way. I believe that part of the reason I later got the opportunity to direct *Jaws 2* was from my knowing David Brown from the Trustees. I came to be on the Board through George Stevens, Jr. The AFI thought it would be good to have filmmakers serving as well as people like Ted Ashley, who was running Warner Bros. at the time, and various other heads of the studios. Ashley was very impressive—the most impressive man in the room. William Friedkin was also there, as was Mervyn LeRoy of *I Am a Fugitive from a Chain Gang* fame and George Seaton, the writer/director of *Miracle on 34th Street*. Now that I think about it, I believe that Billy, Mervyn, George and I were the only film directors serving. So, it was just the four of us. Also present was the journalist Shana Alexander (whom I got to flirt with) and the poet and activist Maya Angelou (I didn't flirt with her). Our role as Trustees involved several duties, such as deciding certain things about the school that the AFI had set up there in Hollywood. Another obligation entrusted to us was selecting who would be the recipient of the yearly Lifetime Achievement Award. That was always a lot of fun and would occasionally provoke some lively and fierce debates.

For instance, I can remember a fight I had with Barry Diller, who later went on to be the head of Paramount and 20th Century Fox, and was Jeffrey Katzenberg's boss at one point. Diller and I were arguing over whether or not the award should go to Frank Capra. Diller aggressively felt that Capra was deserving of the accolade as he was a multiple Academy Award-winner and had directed many "classic" films. I'm not a big Frank Capra fan and never have been. Some people would probably imagine I was, as I occasionally have a weakness for sentimentality in my movies as Capra did, but that is not the case. I was strongly advocating Cary Grant as I thought it would be advantageous to the ratings as well when the ceremony was telecast—unaccustomed as I am to thinking about those kinds of things. As a matter of fact, some people now feel that one of the problems with the award is that some candidates are rejected because they would not make good television. But I thought that Grant was a good choice for most other reasons, too. Diller thought otherwise and we had a little blow-up at the Trustees' meeting over it. It didn't matter anyway as I think the honor was eventually given to James Cagney that year, somebody whom I also felt was worthy of recognition. I don't believe Grant ever received the award, although in subsequent years he had what amounted to a standing offer to do so (which he always declined), but Capra eventually did. Of course, there are a lot of notable people who never got it, so Grant resides in some rather esteemed company.

> *In 1974, a festival called "Hollywood's New Directors: Early Works" was held at the Whitney Museum of American Art in Manhattan. The program consisted of five shorts by five emerging filmmakers: Martin Scorsese's* It's Not Just You, Murray; *George Lucas'* Electronic Labyrinth; *Brian De Palma's* Woton's Wake; *Terence Malick's* Lanton Mills *and John Hancock's* Sticky My Fingers, Fleet My Feet.

I do remember the "Hollywood's New Directors" festival taking place. I was among some quite prestigious guys there: Scorsese, De Palma, Lucas and Malick. Quite incredible! I remember being told by someone that was a good screening and *Sticky My Fingers* had been very well received. That pleased me a great deal. I didn't attend the festival but I did read the press, which was all just fabulous. I remember there was a caption in one of the articles that read: "Who's the New John Ford?" They were speaking about all of us: "Which of these five young directors will go on to become the next John Ford?" I don't know if that really happened to any of us as Ford is Ford. There is only one and there can never be another. But it was all a heady time, and I think the 1970s was a glorious era in American cinema. So many great movies were made and so many great directors arrived. I felt in those early years that the future was bright for all of us and that anything was possible. There was a real sense of anticipation and excitement about what we could possibly achieve in the industry in the coming years. Looking back now, it's wonderful to think that I was included among some of the most important American directors of that time. I'm very proud of that.

Let's Scare Jessica To Death (1971)

AROUND THE SAME TIME *that interest in the prospective Arthur Rimbaud biopic was evaporating (and shortly before the successful Thanksgiving telecast of* Sticky My Fingers, Fleet My Feet*), Hancock was contacted by Charlie Moss, Jr., a recent law school graduate and exhibitor who shared his ambitions of breaking into the movie business. Aided in his efforts by William Badalato, another budding producer, Moss had already began interviewing several promising New York filmmakers in an attempt to find one that could helm a screenplay he had latterly commissioned from a Connecticut writer named Lee Kalcheim. Lumbered with the title* It Drinks Hippie Blood, *Kalcheim's story was a coarse horror-comedy about a group of dropouts who arrive at a secluded New England house and are stalked by a sanguineous "gay monster" that dwells in a nearby cove. This creature periodically reaches out of the water to seize its unsuspecting victims, and is finally destroyed during a climactic sequence in which the hero rides his motorcycle towards the monster and impales it—with priapic precision—on the sharp end of a pole attached to the American flag. Despite being amenable to tackling any genre of commercial cinema as a useful route into the industry, Hancock was still eager to make a picture of distinguishable quality and personality; one that would not insult an audiences' intelligence and would likewise firmly announce his arrival as a bona fide film director.*

Before one's career as a director has started, I'm sure there are some who have a rigid idea or fixed strategy in their head about what the business is and what they intend the course of their career to take. You might imagine how it will unfold, the movies you'll one day make, what Hollywood is, and all these supposed eventualities. That's an unrealistic and immature expectation to have. It's a dream, really. There's too much volatility and too many obstacles in filmmaking for one to have any indefatigable certainties about the industry. So, it's just not possible to *plan* a career. If I'd had any such thoughts back in 1970, I'm sure they were quickly beaten out of me by the realities of the business within a short time. Be that as it may, after *Sticky My Fingers*, when I was trying to work my way into movies, I don't think I could have accepted just any kind of picture that was being offered me. Sure, I wanted to get ahead, to keep moving forward, and it was a natural progression to make a feature after doing a short film, but I also wanted to make a movie that meant something to me; something that was good. That was the important consideration, it had to be *good*. If by chance or circumstance it wasn't, I wanted the freedom to make it so.

One thing I've always found interesting are the subjects directors choose, both at the beginning of their careers and when they are more established. What makes an artist attracted to a particular idea, theme or story? Is it appetite, experience or necessity? I have this theory that most filmmakers approach these decisions from a decidedly pragmatic and self-serving perspective. That is to say, for most of us it's more about maintaining and preserving a career than it is about consistently finding material that accurately expresses our personality and politics (you try but you don't always succeed). What I'm trying to tell you is the choices directors make at various stages of their career are determined by many things: success and failure primarily, but also the demands of the audience, popular trends, and so forth, and where you are exactly. I mean, are you a young director just starting out or are you experienced? You know, most directors just want a job; they just want to keep on working, even though they may see something specific in a script or an idea that expresses one aspect of themselves or their interests. Many critics perceive a director's films to be an expression of their personal preferences and ideologies, but that isn't always the case. It's feasible that a filmmaker can go through their entire career and make films that express none of his or her actual views, tastes, background, or indeed anything that reflects the truth of who or what they are.

The first iteration of *Let's Scare Jessica to Death* threatened to fall into that category. It didn't speak directly to my tastes, but I fashioned it into something that did become a part of me. I made it my own. How the project came my way was through William Wyler's daughter, Catherine Wyler, who was working as a development executive for Joseph E. Levine at the time. When *Sticky My Fingers* was being passed around between the script readers and acquisitions people in the studios, Cathy saw it, liked it, and then recommended me to the producers of *It Drinks Hippie Blood*—a truly awful title—who were looking for a director. There was a very important chain of exhibitors known as B.S. Moss Enterprises that were run by a father and son team who were both named Charlie Moss. I guess Benjamin S. Moss was the grandfather who'd started it all, but Charlie Sr. and Charlie Jr. owned the Criterion Theatre as well as a number of other theaters on the East Coast (around nine or ten I believe). Back then, the Criterion was probably the best theater in New York. It was something like a 2,000-seat auditorium and was located right on Broadway, just north of 42nd Street. I remember its entrance was wide, took up a chunk of the block, and was the theater where *Lawrence of Arabia*, *Doctor Zhivago*, and several other major pictures had opened. Basically, the Mosses wanted to make a movie—a scary movie—that they could exhibit and had initially hired Lee Kalcheim to write it.

Kalcheim later wrote episodes for comedies like *M*A*S*H* and *All in the Family*, and he specialized more in humor than horror. Naturally, he delivered a script that read like a parody of a scary movie. It was a playful send-up of the horror genre and didn't take itself seriously at all. From what I remember, it still had some hippies moving out to an isolated house in the country who encounter a blood-drinking monster that lives in the water. That was the nugget of a good idea but Kalcheim's whole approach to the story, the characters and the monster did not interest me very much beyond that. Following Cathy's generous endorsement, the Mosses then asked me if I wanted to do it, and I said, "Sure, but only if I can re-write the script." I made it eminently clear to them that I did not want to do a satire of a horror picture. I wanted to do a movie that was legitimately terrifying.

> Although he now admits to being "quietly desperate" to direct a feature, Hancock's less than enthusiastic response to Kalcheim's draft meant he would only accept the assignment if he could comprehensively rewrite the screenplay. After

> this proviso was deemed unobjectionable by the producers, Hancock proceeded with his revisions, investing the narrative with a determinedly somber tone and serious intent, as well as various aspects of his own intimate history. This, he readily confesses, was a conscious effort to "appropriate" the project and "make it something unique to me." Jettisoning all the farcical and satirical elements from the story, the filmmaker also transposed the events and action to an isolated fruit farm. Subsequently, both he and Kalcheim would adopt pseudonyms on the script: Kalcheim using the moniker Norman Jonas and Hancock following suit with Ralph Rose.

I believe Kalcheim used his father's first name for his credit, as I did with mine, but, in retrospect, I probably made a mistake in using the pseudonym. The producers wanted certain things in the script like a séance and this mysterious girl dressed in white who appears to Jessica. These additions didn't make much sense to me, but the Mosses felt they would be particularly enjoyable and scary. I trusted their instincts because they had a concrete experience of audiences; they knew what people liked and what they didn't like and in that regard they certainly had an advantage over most studio executives. If you are a seasoned exhibitor, you know what kinds of sequences will make audiences get up and go buy candy and what sequences will keep them glued firmly to their seats. So I inserted the things they asked for into the screenplay, thinking, "Well, they are probably smart so I'll do as they ask." But, again, not all of their ideas and suggestions were entirely logical to me. That's why I didn't feel comfortable taking credit for them myself. It wasn't that I lacked confidence in the project; I merely felt there were some cheap and exploitative elements in it. I didn't want to be deemed responsible for these things as a writer, but I was certainly willing to be held accountable for them as a director. I can only presume that Kalcheim felt the same way from his perspective, since he is also credited under a different name. By the way, I've never met Lee Kalcheim to confirm any of this. I'm merely assuming that, like me, he wasn't particularly proud of the script either.

> Hancock's amended story concerns Jessica, a gauchely vulnerable woman who has recently released from a sanatorium after suffering a breakdown. Together with her

husband Duncan and their friend Woody, they travel to a remote Gothic farmhouse to start life over. Accessible only via ferryboat, the three arrive at their new home—known locally as the Old Bishop Place—and quickly discover a hippie named Emily squatting inside. Jessica and her friends invite her to stay and, later that night, Emily suggests they hold a séance. Disturbed by the ritual and struggling to preserve the veneer of normalcy, Jessica begins hearing voices whispering to her. In the days that follow, the most benign of activities (a trawl through a luminous attic for antiques, an afternoon swim in the nearby cove) suddenly become disturbing.

Visiting the local town with Duncan in order to sell the items they have collected, Jessica discovers it consists exclusively of creepy old men wearing bandages over strange wounds. She then learns from Dorker, an antique dealer, that their farmhouse was once home to Abigail Bishop, a Victorian woman who drowned in the cove on the eve of her wedding and is now said to wander the region as a vampiric spirit. Unnerved by the story, Jessica is later terrified when she stumbles across Dorker's bloody corpse in a creek and encounters a mute girl in white who warns her away. Fearing that her sanity is collapsing, Jessica soon begins fearing for her life when she regards an old family portrait and notices an unerring resemblance between Abigail Bishop and her newfound friend Emily.

My initial approach to re-writing *Jessica* was to introduce as much personal and autobiographical material into the film as I possibly could. So the location of the fruit farm, an apple farm, and the image of the crop sprayer spewing pesticide is very much a scene out of my own childhood. I have very strong memories of my father arriving back home coated white with poison and I did a lot of spraying myself, so that cozy rural milieu was incredibly familiar to me. My father also played the double bass like Jessica's husband does in the film. As a child that big, black, coffin-like bass case was very much a fixture of my youth. It was something that traveled back and forth with us from our house in Chicago out to our farm in Indiana because, being a musician, Dad would take his bass along so he could practice. I do think the feeling of being alone on the farm as a child filtered into both the script and the film. I don't know to what extent I specifically set out to do that, but it did make its presence felt. *Jessica* is a little like a child's view of moving out to a farm: that feeling of wonder, curiosity and fear. I was very fond of our farm but the pesticides, the loneliness, the graves, and the idea that a lot of other people had actually died in the house where we were living, all of those things crawled out from my conscious and subconscious mind, and informed the movie. I also had the idea that a farm can be a dangerous place. There is equipment there that can harm and kill you; a crop sprayer can poison you, all of these things. I thought a farm would also be a far more interesting location for a scary movie than some cobwebbed castle in Transylvania; terrible things happening in an area of beauty and apparent tranquility.

I've always liked horror films, but I was motivated to make *Jessica* the kind of horror film that I wanted to see, something that spoke to my fears. I was alarmed by the notion that you can't defuse or defeat evil—it forever lives inside and all around us—so I worked that fear into the story. I actually scared myself one night when I was writing the script and that experience was revelatory to me. I didn't think it would ever be possible to scare myself during the act of writing and concentrating, but it did induce the shivers in me. I was writing the script at night and, at that time, I was still living in Sneden's Landing, which is an old Tory place. That house and the surrounding neighborhood had a peculiar atmosphere to it and the shadows always seemed very thick and threatening. The air was almost pungent with a Revolutionary War feeling and you really found it easy to believe that ghosts were wandering around that area at night. It was perfect, as I found that unnerving atmosphere assisted in getting me into the proper frame of mind to create a horror movie.

> *With its delicately constructed air of growing unease and oppressive narrative that spotlights an emotionally vulnerable female protagonist,* Let's Scare Jessica to Death *has drawn commodious comparisons with Herk Harvey's* Carnival of Souls (1962) *and George A. Romero's* Night of the Living Dead (1968), *two seminal horror movies. Hancock insists that neither of these works were a formative influence on his production and any similarities are both unintentional and coincidental.*

It's true that *Carnival of Souls* and *Night of the Living Dead* sometimes get mentioned in relation to *Jessica*, but I had not seen either film before making my picture. As a matter of fact, when I eventually saw *Night of the Living Dead* a few years later, I didn't like it at all. Frankly, I found it crude and heavy-handed and I'm still not a fan of it. I don't wish to offend or dismay anybody by saying that. I certainly appreciate the fact that a lot of people consider that picture to be important and influential; I'm merely stating it was neither of those things for me. However, one film I did very much like—and I had seen it before making *Jessica*—was Robert Wise's *The Haunting*. I thought that was a stunning movie and the idea of having a neurotic female as the lead character was an incredibly useful thing. It invited all kinds of underlying textures, subtleties and developments to our story.

There is a recurring tradition in literature, in ghost stories and horror stories, of the unreliable narrator. You don't know if you can trust the observations and perceptions of the main protagonist and you begin to question everything you've come to learn about them. Is this really happening or is it all just a by-product of madness and delusion? I loved *The Turn of the Screw*, the way that novel makes you question whether or not the supernatural events are actually occurring or the heroine is crazy. I thought it would be interesting to have a central female character in *Jessica* that is recovering from the effects of a nervous breakdown. This fragile and possibly dangerous woman is struggling to hold it all together and her slack grip on reality is loosening further. So, there's an apparent threat that she will relapse and be totally consumed by her illness and I thought that would be a fascinating element to play with. I had this idea that if she snapped again, this time she wouldn't be able to make it back and that would be *that*! I felt this not only gave the film an interesting tension in terms of her wellbeing and relationships, it also gave it an unmistakable quality of sadness, too. So much so, I think *Jessica* can be considered a tragedy.

I must say that another influence on the movie was Alfred Hitchcock. Before I made *Jessica*, I screened any Hitchcock picture I could get a 16mm print of. I bought a projector, rented the prints, and just sat in my living room watching them over and over again; stopping and starting the films, making copious notes. I marveled at how Hitchcock was able to achieve the effects he did in his movies: the camera angles, the camera movement, the editing, sound and music; the way he used all of these elements to carefully construct suspense just seemed remarkable to me. Hitchcock is a great stylist and his films are often considered to be exercises in style, but they are so much more than that. He pretty much formulated the vocabulary for the thriller and horror genres, and discovered new ways to create suspense and scares. He invented a new language for this kind of cinema and to this day I don't think anybody can speak that language better than him. Nobody has ever approached Hitchcock's ability to unsettle an audience quite like he did. The rhythms are all very precisely measured and the mechanics of what he is doing may not be spontaneous, and are often very self-conscious, but the overall effect is undeniable. *Jessica* is perhaps not Hitchcockian in the strictest definition, but the way Hitchcock retarded the pace in his pictures was something I definitely wanted to replicate in my film.

Ironically, one of the most difficult aspects of *Jessica* for a modern audience to accept is it's deliberately measured pace, but that's probably true of most pictures made before 1980. The characters are allowed to behave and develop, and the atmosphere slowly thickens and escalates over time, before the final section just pummels you with an onslaught of terrors. When you look at the majority of films made in the commercial cinema today, they have a lot of quick cuts and it's somewhat unfashionable to allow a scene to simply play out. That's probably the influence of music videos, TV commercials and the Internet on movies, and the fact that a lot of people simply don't have the patience for that kind of filmmaking anymore. But back then, after bingeing on a lot of Hitchcock, I tended to retard the pace in *Jessica* as a means of developing and sustaining tension at certain moments. I mean, how you move time is one of the most crucial things you can do as both a writer and a director. And to build suspense by impeding and slowing down the action is, again, something I saw Hitchcock do repeatedly and expertly in his pictures. By consciously emulating that approach, I had sort of discovered a key into making *Jessica* something that would contain a lot more power and effectiveness than it might have otherwise done.

> *Now officially awarded the more subdued title of* Jessica, *Hancock and his producers began holding casting sessions for the film at the B.S. Moss offices located on Broadway. The six principal roles would each go to actors whom the director had worked with previously in the theater—the exceptions being Gretchen Corbett, who was cast as "The Girl" in white, and Zohra Lampert, who would essay the titular role. A respected New York actress who had attended*

> the High School of Music & Arts and earned two Tony Award nominations, Lampert's film credits had included Pay or Die *(1962),* Splendor in the Grass *(1963) and* Bye Bye Braverman *(1968).*

I had seen Zohra Lampert in several plays and had also dated her briefly. In some ways, she was as delicate as the character of Jessica in real life. She had that same vulnerability and gentleness about her. The first time I saw Zohra perform was when she was playing this brassy, daffy girl in the Broadway comedy *Look: We've Come Through*, which was directed by Jose Quintero. She was just hilarious in it and was obviously a gifted actress. Zohra exuded some of the same qualities in that play Joan Cusack later exhibited, particularly the nutty radiographer that Cusack played in *Men Don't Leave*. I then saw Zohra play Anne Bancroft's daughter, Kattrin, in a terrible production of *Mother Courage and Her Children* that Jerome Robbins directed at Broadway's Martin Beck Theatre. It wasn't good at all, but Zohra was fabulous in it, the one shining light. That's when I really got to know her and appreciate her talents. She was somebody I very much wanted to work with and when we finally got *Jessica* together, I knew she would be perfect for the lead role. Zohra could play the fragility of the character, but she could also authentically convey the fear and the terror, which was of equal importance. Most of all she was a good *screamer!* That appears to be a prerequisite for women in horror films.

The rest of the actors were all people I knew from New York. Mariclare Costello had helped me cast *The Freaking Out of Stephanie Blake*, the play with Jean Arthur that famously never opened. Mariclare had been a reader, she read with other actors. I thought with her pale, freckled skin and flaming red hair, she would be a wonderful choice for the role of the ghost girl. I then hired Kevin O'Connor to play Woody, Jessica and Duncan's hippie friend. Kevin had played the lead in *Boy on the Straight-Back Chair*, that other ill-fated experience for me. Both of those productions had been negative things in my life, but that didn't prevent me from wanting to work with Mariclare and Kevin again. As you know, I'd done a whole bunch of plays with Barton Heyman, and he was probably my first choice to play the role of Duncan. I'd also done about three or four plays with Alan Manson, who played the antique dealer that Jessica and her husband encounter. So, these were all people that I had worked with previously and, looking back, it was basically the same situation I'd aimed for on *Sticky My Fingers*: that instant familiarity you get from working with actors you know probably helped to put me a little more at ease. Since this was my first feature, I already had a multiplicity of things occupying my mind, so I wanted actors who could give me something good and wouldn't require too much attention.

Originally, I had planned for the four principal actors to appear naked in the film at some point as they were meant to be these hippies and free spirits, people in tune with nature. We had several scenes in the screenplay of Jessica and her friends frolicking about in the cove and I felt that they should all be swimming and bathing in the nude. Maybe it was the time. I don't know. *Oh, Calcutta*, a nude show, was on Broadway, and there was also *Hair* and several other plays that featured extensive nudity. Actresses from these productions came in and whipped off their clothes like it was completely natural. I held auditions at the B.S. Moss offices in order to find actors who would be comfortable appearing naked onscreen but, by the time we finished the casting process, Charlie Moss, Jr. and I had come to the conclusion that we needed to go for acting over nudity.

> *Filmed over twenty-six days on a budget of just $250,000, principal photography on* Let's Scare Jessica to Death *took place in the October and November of 1970, in and around towns in southeastern Connecticut—namely Chester, East Haddam, Essex, and Old Saybrook. The exterior of the home that Jessica and her friends purchase, with its distinctive tower, was a nineteenth century farmhouse in Old Saybrook that had been discovered during a preliminary scout undertaken by Hancock, Moss, and Badalato. The farmhouse interiors were filmed three miles away inside the E.E. Dickinson House located on 34 North Main Street, Essex. Other locations utilized by the filmmakers included the First Church Cemetery in East Haddam (where Jessica finds her doomed pet mole) and the Hadlyme Ferry in Chester, which proved another serendipitous find that would feature prominently in the movie.*

In scouting the film, I found several spooky locations that certainly scared me—interiors as well as exteriors. Finding the farmhouse in Old Saybrook was extremely fortunate. It was such a scary place to be and was unnervingly quiet. That was one of the first things I noticed about it—the silence, the mood. It was also such a visually striking property with the tower and everything; it was just perfect for our needs. I got that same uneasy feeling when I first went to the old Dickinson House in Essex to inspect where we shot the interiors. I can distinctly recall looking around the place, moving from room to room before going upstairs, and a chill went right *through* me! It had a weird air of dread about it. Not something you can articulate exactly. When I was inspecting the property I can remember saying to myself, "If this house scares me and I'm just scouting the place, what will it look like on film when we really spook it up a little?" I used an upstairs hallway in the house where Jessica and her companions are staying that had so many doors there was something quite disturbing about it: the idea that someone—or some *thing*—could suddenly come lurching out of the shadows at any moment and grab you. It was very unsettling. I think a couple of the most effective scenes in *Jessica* are filmed in that hallway.

My theater designer Bob Lavigne and I had always wanted to try something in the style of the Austrian painter Gustav Klimt with regard to the film's interiors. *Jessica* felt like a chance to do the kind of highly patterned wallpapers there would be in an old house as well as the bold patterns of some flower-children clothing; it seemed like you could get the two vibrating against each other in interesting Klimtian ways. In the end, we just did it with the wallpapers, which I chose carefully, but didn't do it with the clothes. Did I chicken out when it came to the costumes? Maybe, but it just seemed more important at the time that the actors look nice in them. Also, would it have been too artificial? I don't think so. But it's just something we weren't able to bring off within the practicality of the budget and the constraints of time. However, the main reason that I relented on the costumes is I didn't want the actors to look clownish. Wearing that much extravagant pattern says something about you, doesn't it? And I didn't want to say that. There were also some period costumes like the wedding dress that Abigail/Emily wears, and the apparel that is worn and briefly glimpsed in the old Bishop family portrait that Jessica discovers in the attic. Incidentally, I don't recall exactly who the two creepy people posing with Mariclare in that photograph are, or for that matter who took the portrait for the film.

Places and things are so important in creating the right atmosphere. The movie is intentionally littered with images, objects and emblems of death: Jessica taking walks through cemeteries, doing the charcoal grave-rubbings and hanging them on the Klimtian bedroom wall. One of the opening shots of the picture sees Duncan's big, black bass-case being loaded into the hearse and it resembles an undertaker loading a coffin. I wanted to get that feeling across right from the first few frames, that death was everywhere, it was always present. I think Jessica is a character who is both fascinated and haunted by the specter of death; of decay; of darkness; of the abyss. It's easy for the audience to look at somebody like her and their first response is one of pity or sadness, perhaps even anger and intolerance. But I do think there is an eventual realization that we have all felt what Jessica feels at one time or another. In our lives we've all experienced moments of loneliness, isolation, anguish, terror; a feeling that we are no longer in control of our own lives and destiny. We are all vulnerable to some degree. Jessica could be us and we could be her, and that's one of the things that gives the movie its power.

> *With the abundance of evocative imagery in* Let's Scare Jessica to Death—*mist hovering over the still surface of a cove at dusk; autumnal orchards and creeks spread with ominous shadows; grave-etchings on a bedroom wall stirred by the wind—one could be forgiven for thinking that Hancock was determined to deliver a picture that would not register with audiences as stage-bound or passively theatrical.*

Honestly, I don't think there was ever the danger of my making a film that was in any way stage-bound. After directing so many plays, I probably wanted to be unbridled and venture off in a certain direction; deliver a work that was more about images and visuals, and try to get some of the emotion and tension from that rather than making static scenes of people talking in a room—although that's in there, too. I don't have a problem with films that are stage-bound or theatrical (just as I don't have a problem with plays that are filmic and mobile), but if you are making a movie I think you should explore everything that cinema offers you as a director. I mean, *Jessica* was a horror film and horror films rely on certain effects and atmospherics in order to be successful as you have to construct moments of fear and suspense. But the way I directed *Jessica* was not a conscious reaction to my having worked extensively in the theater. I wasn't always anxious for achieving an expressive or poetic image, or making unmotivated camera movements, just for the sake of it. It was simply the demands of dealing with this new medium and all the budgetary limitations we faced. So, I was mostly conscious of trying to learn as much about the craft of filmmaking as I could and just rode through all the trials and errors.

    I was focused on trying to create a distinctive look and feel to the film, and did my best to communicate my ideas and instructions to the crew. True, because it was my debut picture, *Jessica* was this profoundly revealing experience for me. It was sometimes difficult to get any sense of whether or not the movie was going to be good. I'd shoot something and maybe it wasn't quite what I wanted or expected, and then I'd shoot something else and a particular shot or a performance by one of the actors would suddenly energize me again and fill me with this barely contained excitement. So, there were moments of doubt and despair, and there were moments of triumph and exhilaration. It was a real heady mixture. There were also days when I felt that luck was really with me. One was the very first day we were filming exteriors outside the old house: this eerie fog suddenly appeared as if from nowhere and enveloped the place. We were all just standing there with the camera ready, staring at the fog which almost seemed to materialize on cue. We all cried, "Look at *that*! Look at the production value!" We then started rolling and those creepily evocative shots were used throughout the picture. It was an incredible moment of good fortune, that it should arrive as we were about to shoot, but it gave the whole area an even more tangible sense of mystery and dread.

    The making of the picture was extremely fast and hard. We worked long, tiring hours. I mean, twenty-six days is not an especially long time to make a movie. As a result of feeling this weight of nervous tension, I developed the long-term habit on *Jessica* of taking my pulse during shooting. I don't know why, but I've done it for years. I'm just neurotic I guess. I had to make sure I was still alive! But the simple fact of the matter is I didn't really know how to direct a film back then. I was still new to the medium. I had made *Sticky My Fingers, Fleet My Feet*, but I still didn't feel entirely confident about what it was a film director actually did; or how I was going to be able to accomplish what I wanted to accomplish with the movie and bring the written words and pages to life. I didn't seem to have a command of space and spatial movement, and how to physically shape a scene, something that had always come easily to me on a theater stage. So, the first valuable lesson I learned on *Jessica* was about how to block for the camera. When we were out on location I can remember not knowing exactly where to position the camera, which angles to use, and what direction the actors should be moving in, or if they should remain static. The choices seemed limitless and limited at the same time.

It took me about a week before I realized how important it was to set marks for the actors. My first cameraman on *Jessica* was a guy named Bob Bailin. He kept stressing to me the consequences of not having actors hit their marks, but I wasn't really listening to him. I felt strongly that by forcing an actor to hit a mark, we would somehow kill their spontaneity and aliveness, and restrict their energies in some way. I had worked quite openly with actors in the theater and was always fastidious about allowing them to fully express themselves. I wanted actors to be real, and *in* the moment. I found the prospect of limiting and confining those qualities to what the camera sees extremely frustrating. I would ask questions like, "Okay, tell me again why we can't just photograph this performance happening and the scene will not be as good?" Bailin kept insisting that he needed the actors to have marks in order for him to keep the performers in focus during a shot, as well as keeping them firmly in the frame when the camera was moving or panning. I wasn't getting along with him for this and several other reasons. But then it suddenly occurred to me one day that, yes, he was right! You do have to block scenes very precisely through the lens, and actors can hit a designated mark and still be very much alive in a scene. So, I quickly learned to recognize and respect the technical demands and requirements of filmmaking. However, there are cameramen out there who know how to free the actors up in a scene without killing the spontaneity.

Most of the crew on *Jessica* was a little green, but what we lacked in experience we more than compensated for with passion, enthusiasm and determination. We all really wanted to work hard to make the best movie we possibly could. That said, for some reason, the fact I was learning how to make a movie as we going along seemed to unsettle and annoy Bob Bailin. The guy appeared to have nothing but seething contempt for me. He thought I was operating *way* out of my depth and didn't mind sharing that opinion with me and one or two others. So, I fired him after the first week and found somebody else in Robert Baldwin who was willing to work more harmoniously with me. Baldwin didn't consider me a complete incompetent, and neither did he look at me with the unrestrained antipathy that his predecessor had. I thought that was a good start to our working relationship. Baldwin had shot a couple of movies before *Jessica* and was a capable DP who brought a lot of energy and good ideas. For instance, I remember he had a great idea for the ghostly apparition of

Abigail Bishop appearing and disappearing in the lake. Baldwin said he had filters that worked sort of like Venetian blinds and he showed me how if it was rotated one way, you could see the ghostly figure under the water, but when it was turned another way, only the reflecting water was visible. I thought it was a great in-camera effect, and just what we needed.

Aside from my difficulties with Bob Bailin, we had a fairly happy set. I must say that Charlie Moss, Jr. and Charlie Moss, Sr., were terrific producers to work with. The father was something of an absent figure on the set, although he does play one of the weird and wounded old guys Jessica meets in town (he's briefly seen on the porch during one scene wearing a bandage around his neck). Despite his absence, Charlie, Sr. was clearly the guy in charge of things. We all knew that. However, the son was present for every day of the shoot and Charlie, Jr. was a delight. Despite our relative inexperience, we always strived to approach the work professionally and I made a concerted effort to get along with him. I felt it was important to maintain a good relationship with my producers and, at the end of every day, I always made sure to find Charlie, Jr. and discuss the day's work with him: what we had done, what we planned to do the following day, and so forth. I think he appreciated that, as did Bill Badalato, my co-producer. After our experiences on *Jessica*, Bill would become my best friend and would go on to have a great career, producing huge Hollywood movies like *Top Gun*, *Alien Resurrection* and *About Schmidt*. He would also work for me on my next picture, *Bang the Drum Slowly*, as well as on *Jaws 2*, *Weeds*, *Prancer*, and other projects.

Another valuable lesson for me during the making of *Jessica* (one that did not strictly require any technical proficiency) was to trust in the knowledge that what scares me will also scare an audience. If I saw a creepy hallway, or a shadowy orchard, and if I had an instinct about how a certain unnerving moment should play, I knew it would translate effectively for people. In that sense I really opened myself up to the darkness, so to speak, and let it in. A lot of the time fear is a ubiquitous thing in terms of what inspires that emotion in people. We all know there are a great many frightening things out there in the world. Of course, fear can also come from something specific and personal, but I truly believe that most of us are afraid of the same things. What scares somebody in America will also scare somebody in Bangladesh, and China, and South Africa, and Wales, if you can strike that collective note as a filmmaker. The fear of death, of violence, of madness, all these things are prevalent and each can make you afraid. In regard to this movie, it seems to me that madness is a particularly terrifying thing for people to deal with because at least death can bring an end to things. To live with madness—not only the prospect of a person losing their mind but the thought of becoming a victim of someone that has lost their mind—is very scary. I learned that on *Jessica* as, oddly enough, maybe it was something I'd never seriously considered before.

Aside from taking my own pulse, I formed several other habits on *Jessica* that have remained with me to this day. As a director, I always tend to get up a couple of hours before I have to go shoot. I like to prepare myself both mentally and physically, and carefully plan my shots for the day. After I make the shot-list, I then hand it to the assistant director and he can always keep everybody a step or two ahead of us. I like people to know exactly what it is we are going to be doing next, so that the work can proceed in an organized and efficient manner. During the shooting of *Jessica*, I do remember that I couldn't get breakfast at the motel where we were staying right out on the peninsula in Old Saybrook. It was a wonderful motel as the Mosses made sure the cast and crew had a comfortable place to stay, but the kitchen did not open until around the time of the call. This meant I had to regularly contend with the unhappiness and unhelpfulness of that. You see, it's very hard for me to plan my shots and concentrate fully without a certain amount of coffee in my system. It just seems to act as a boost for my whole day. There were small things like that which troubled me—little grievances and light disturbances—that nonetheless still conspired to distract me at times when I was tackling all the big things. Looking back now, maybe I was searching for reasons or explanations as to why I was finding certain tasks difficult to deal with. It wasn't my inexperience at filmmaking, or my own fears and insecurities coming to the surface. It was merely the fact I had *no* coffee in me!

> *Hancock's instinct for creating "quiet scares" is powerfully in evidence during the film's most justifiably celebrated and chilling moment, which occurs during an afternoon swim Jessica and Emily undertake in the nearby cove. Lensed in the picturesque Pattaconk Reservoir in Chester, this alarming passage details Emily silently sinking beneath the still water in a contemporary bathing costume only to sullenly re-emerge moments later in a sodden nineteenth century wedding dress.*

God, I don't know where that idea came from. I do know that over the years a lot of people have told me they find that scene incredibly unsettling. That image just came to me suddenly one night as I was writing. Actually, that was the same night I told you about earlier when I got scared working on the script. It was that very sequence, and the one that directly follows it where Jessica runs inside the house, barricades herself in the bedroom and hears the voices whispering to her in the darkness, saying, "I'm still here" and that kind of thing. Again, it really gave me the chills when I was writing that stuff. I can remember stopping writing at one point and looking nervously around the room, half expecting to see a dark figure silently watching me from some shadowy corner. It was very peculiar as I had always considered myself to be a fairly rational and steady person. I still do. But this terrible dread really took hold of me that night and *squeezed*. It's strange how your mind can become affected like that; when it's dark and you're alone and you're dreaming up these morbid scenarios. I don't know. Perhaps you are somehow leaving yourself open to these fears merely by entertaining such terrible thoughts in your imagination. But the sight of Emily rising out of the water as this dripping apparition in a wedding dress seemed a disturbing one to me for some reason. It's just so unexpected and weird and potent. I immediately knew it would be very scary if I executed it right.

    The scenes we shot in the lake were very difficult to do. It was a beautiful location but it was the fall and the temperatures were incredibly cold. Of course, then we had to go into the icy lake with the camera and shoot the scenes—and the water was absolutely *freezing*! That was extremely uncomfortable. Being cold is one thing; being cold and wet is quite another. Most of my lower body was rendered numb by the water but I could still feel the disagreeable sensation of fish nibbling on my legs. They'd brazenly swim up to you, taste you a little, and then dart away. It wasn't the most pleasant of experiences. I can distinctly remember feeling glad that I was safely on the shore with the camera shooting Mariclare Costello emerging from the lake. I'd spent a lot of time filming with the actors in the cold November water and, frankly, I was thankful to be out of there. But all the actors were real troupers. They are supposed to look like they're frolicking about and having a fun time when in reality they could hardly breathe. Mariclare had to slowly, mournfully, walk out of the icy water in all that pale make-up and look scary, and that wasn't easy. It was well worth it though, because we got a disturbing moment out of it—one that people still remember and are affected by.

We also had to realize this creature that Jessica sees moving below the surface, and this was before animatronics and mechanical effects were common tools. We didn't have the time or money to do anything complex. So, the morning before we shot that stuff, Charlie Moss and I worked this thing out in the swimming pool at our motel using a dummy with cement blocks at the bottom attached to various pulleys. We used the buoyancy of the puppet, pulling it up and down with a cable, and allowed the movement of the water to emphasize the swirling motion of the hair and the dress. It was strangely disturbing to behold, actually. As far as special effects go, I learned on later pictures like *Jaws 2* and *Prancer* that you don't always need twelve guys operating animatronics, making eyes blink and mouths open, to do good stuff. The most effective things are often the most simple to realize. It also helps that when we cut from the mechanical revenant to Mariclare rising out of the water, the way she plays those moments are so chilling it really helps to sell the sequence.

We also had to do the various wounds that Mariclare's character inflicts on her victims as she's cutting them with a knife and feeding on their blood. When you are dealing with special make-up it's another technical consideration. So, you have to light it properly, make sure it looks good and works. That took time and I had to be patient and understanding. One other thing I had to be patient about was the mole that Jessica finds in the cemetery and adopts as a pet. Somebody on the crew brought me a mole and it was great. Then this creature had obviously reached the end of its lifespan and quietly died. This fact was hidden from me for a time. I can remember asking Bill Badalato, "Hey, how's our mole doing? Is he well?" Bill would say, "Yeah, he's fine. He's just sleeping." Well, the mole would sleep day after day, and it never once stirred in its slumber. "It must be hibernating," somebody offered, but I've learned that moles do not in fact hibernate—contrary to popular opinion. No, our mole wasn't sleeping. It was quite dead. This necessitated us finding a replacement mole, but one was not readily available. So, we used a different animal instead that did not look like a mole at all. I believe we ended up using a mouse. It was a terrible betrayal, but you have a lot on your mind when you're directing a movie. So, I disguised my bitterness and tried my best to go on.

Something else I did find strangely amusing, and this hasn't got much to do with *Jessica* but it's something you may find interesting: shortly after we filmed the movie, Mariclare Costello married the actor Allan Arbus. Arbus had once been a photographer, but later became an actor who specialized in playing ghoulish parts—namely villains and other unsavory characters. His first wife happened to be Diane Arbus, herself a famous photographer who was known for her ghoulish images and portraits of freaks, circus performers and other highly unusual people. I found it interesting that after making our ghoulish little film, Mariclare was then betrothed to the ghoulish ex-husband of this ghoulish female photographer. And I don't repeatedly use the word *ghoulish* without good reason, too, as my second wife, Dorothy, had some firsthand experience of both the Arbus'. When Allan Arbus was a photographer, Diane Arbus worked as his stylist. Back then, Dorothy was a model but she never liked to work with them as they were always both absolutely silent and rather unnerving to be around. As they would be preparing to shoot, Diane Arbus would be pinning the clothes on Dorothy in order to make the costume they were photographing more form-fitting or whatever. Diane would do this without ever once uttering a single word. She would make no effort to lighten the mood or pass the time, or indeed offer any small gesture to relax the model. Can you imagine what it must have felt like to be alone in a room with those two people for an extended period of time? But that's the peculiar atmosphere they both preferred to work in: this empty, morbid silence. I mean, forget about *Jessica*, now that is *really* fucking creepy!

> Let's Scare Jessica to Death *is imbued with a palpable foreboding and sadness that ripples through its running time. Whether its terrors are the corollary of a crumbling psyche or the torments inflicted by a bloodthirsty revenant, Hancock's lyrical visuals and Zohra Lampert's tour-de-force starring turn combine to create one of the most harrowing portraits of female neuroses and mental disintegration in genre history. They are aided in no small part by an innovative score (one of the first horror films to feature a synthesizer in its cues) and imaginative sound design. Indeed, one of the most quietly devastating things in the film that assists in illustrating Jessica's torturous descent into madness is the use of whispering voices and an internal monologue on the soundtrack.*

After working with him briefly on *Boy on the Straight-Back Chair*, and having him score *Sticky My Fingers* for me, it was a logical development for Orville Stoeber to compose the music for *Jessica*. I had certain ideas, certain moods I wanted to convey in the picture, and he came up with these mournful melodies on piano and guitar that worked very well. But we also needed something that carried a little more obvious threat, a more intense element of dread, and one way to achieve that was to incorporate synthesizers into the score, which was a fairly radical idea for a horror film back in 1971. I had a little familiarity with electronic music from my time in San Francisco, where the composer Morton Subotnick was one of the guys hanging around the Actor's Workshop. I never used him for anything because I didn't really like electronic music, and it was not what I needed. But now, as I worked on the score for *Jessica* with Orville, I came to feel Orville's talent was not for evil.

At one point, Orville told me that he had thought he was an angel when he was a kid—angel voice, sweet face, blond hair, a religious family. Being a child of light, I saw he was having difficulty accompanying his wonderful melodies with something ghastly and dark. I played a little of Stravinsky's *Petrushka* for him, as there's a place where the ballerina is dancing to a sweet melody with a Moor and you hear the clashing surge of his dark phallic power in the bass undercutting the sweetness (not politically correct today, but there it was, an evil Moor in musical form). Orville liked the effect but had trouble replicating it. It just wasn't his thing. So, we agreed to seek out someone like Walter Sear, who, like Subotnick, was a veritable pioneer in the use of synthesizers. He had a little studio in the bowels of a building on 57th Street, between the DGA and the Russian Tea Room. Walter was delighted to help us and we enjoyed working with him. He added some of the droning, threatening-sounding electronica to Orville's more melodic compositions. I was very happy with his stuff, because it did its job. It unsettles you, agitates you.

In the big time, scores are recorded to picture. We weren't big time. We had to record music to a click track in order to get the cue to last just long enough to cover the piece of film you wanted it to accompany and no longer. But how to get the clicks at the right rate to accomplish that took some doing. It required some math from guys who didn't think that math was their strong suit, but we finally succeeded. I found out later with some bitterness, when I worked with Fred Karlin on *Baby Blue Marine*, that there was a book that did these calculations for you. As I think about it now, I'm not sure if we married Sear's synthesizer tracks with Orville's tracks at Sear's studio or we went into the mix with them separate so that our sound engineer Dick Vorisek could control the balance. That would have been the best way, even though it might have meant more time at a higher priced facility and mix stages are expensive. But I suspect that we mixed them down at Walter's place, just so we could be sure what we had.

People often think of film as essentially a visual medium, which it is, but sound is also of crucial importance to the success of any picture. On *Jessica*, I discovered that a rich and subtle sound design and an evocative score could give the audience so much more in terms of information and emotion and rhythm and texture. The two things, sound effects and music, can be interchangeable in terms of conveying that information and emotion to the viewer. They are sometimes the same thing. Interestingly, early on in the picture, as Jessica and her friends are on the ferry and it approaches the dock, we briefly hear the sound of what appears to be a female screaming. This is rather curious and is not part of the score as one might think. It could easily be construed as a sound effect of a creaking cable, or the gangway lowering, or the boat skidding against the wharf, but it's none of those things. It was the cry of an eagle or hawk that we put in, which assisted in building an effectively disconcerting atmosphere as swiftly as possible.

I first had the idea for the whispering voices that Jessica hears when I was writing the script, but that approach became far more elaborate during post-production. Since this brittle woman has only just been released from an asylum, I felt there was always the possibility that she might hear voices; that this veiled madness could somehow be roused and accelerated by her surroundings and the people she meets. Of course, it may all be happening to Jessica for real and this evil entity is indeed out to get her. The auditory elements helped to embellish that uncertainty. So, the whisperings and mutterings on the soundtrack gradually evolved and got thicker and denser. They became this cacophony that is always questioning and disturbing and pleading with Jessica. I can remember sitting down and writing dialogue for the voices while we were in the editing room cutting the film. I had to figure out exactly what they were going to say; when they should speak and how they could contribute to the character and the narrative. It was important that the voices gave the ambiguous impression that this woman may be losing her sanity again. Is she being haunted by something supernatural or is she continuing to experience the same psychological and emotional problems?

There are several things in the movie that might be real or might not: is Emily really this deathless vampiric ghost who is drinking the blood of the townspeople? Is the fidelity of Jessica's husband in question? Is there really something living under the water in the cove? I didn't feel it was important to answer all of those questions as in real life we don't always get the answers to the questions we ponder. There is much we will never know, even about those who are close to us, and mystery and ambiguity make good drama. Regardless of whether you think the visual and auditory presences are hallucinations, whatever Jessica believes to be true *is* true as the film is entirely subjective. We are seeing and hearing this stuff through her eyes and ears, and the events are colored by that subjectivity. However, a good example of playing with and subverting that idea is an early scene in the film when Jessica, Duncan and Woody first arrive at the Old Bishop Place. As they enter the house, Jessica looks upstairs and sees a dark figure standing there that suddenly darts into the shadows. I've already placed an element of doubt in the audience's mind—through the voiceover, and through an early appearance by the girl in white—that these things may not be real. But then Duncan confirms it for us when he says, "It's okay, Jess. I saw it, too." He then chases after the dark figure and Jessica turns to Woody and excitedly says, "I really did see something!" I find that a strangely touching moment. I love the way Zohra delivers that line almost with relief. It's like Jessica desperately wants it confirmed that she isn't crazy anymore.

The big scare that eventually follows, when Emily suddenly leaps out of the darkened doorway, is one of those rare instances in movies when the "normal" people get to see what the "crazy" person sees. That's when the confirmation comes that the thing lurking in the shadows is real. I mean, Jessica is so happy that it's actually *there*! It's the most frightening moment in the film in terms of giving the viewer a serious jolt. Sitting with an audience in the theater, and watching them watching that scene, I saw just how truly hair-raising it was. It may be hard for younger people to believe, but the audience was literally leaping out of their seats and screaming. Big jump-scares like that did not seem to be as prevalent back then as they are today. They were still fairly novel. Nowadays, filmmakers like to assault the viewer every five minutes or so with one aggressive jump-scare after another, until their effectiveness is blunted. Incidentally, when Richard Zanuck later hired me to direct *Jaws 2*, he singled-out that particular moment in *Jessica* as the thing that got me the job. That scene really terrified Dick and he witnessed the big reaction it got from audiences, too. People have sometimes speculated that the scary swimming sequences in *Jessica* are what got me *Jaws 2*, but that's not true. It was *that* scene.

In the case of *Jessica*, I think the autumnal landscape can be read as a reflection of the lead character's psychology, or pathology, whatever you want to call it. The fall is a time of death and decay in some ways, of natural change and disintegration, and there is a terrible beauty about all that. It helps us to understand that everything is finite. "Frail as the leaves that shiver on a spray, like them we flourish, like them, decay," which is the poem on the grave rubbing that Jessica recites to Duncan and Woody in the car. It was interesting to be shooting in that environment, at that time of year, where the days are bright and cold, and the nights arrive swiftly and are very dark and *very* cold. The fall is like no other season. Old Saybrook and Essex were just gorgeous places to visit, and I'm fond of apple orchards and fields and trees, things like that. But there is something melancholy about those things during the fall that was in keeping with our story. The fall is kind of like summer's final flourish before it dies away. The different colors are so vivid and beautiful—reds, browns and golds—and I think the moods complemented and enriched the movie. Of course, there's also something quite threatening and unsettling about the fall in that it seems like the good times are over.

Like Jessica, some people are ill-equipped to deal with life in the country. It clearly isn't for everyone. Moving from the city to the country, there is this sense that you are retiring from reality in some ways, or experiencing a different kind of reality, in that you're settling for life at a much slower pace. You do get the sense that you're giving something up in a way and that this rural paradise can suddenly take on a disquieting and isolating quality. There's an incident in Willa Cather's novel *My Ántonia* where a farmer named Shimerda, who is rather lonely and depressed, goes into a barn in the middle of winter, puts a shotgun in his mouth and blows his brains out. I've never forgotten that, how the country is not always a realm of peace and contentment. It can be a place of misery and death that merely provides you with a whole new set of problems. I mean, there is something about vast open spaces and huge fields, of being far from the barn and the house—way back in a field on a piece of machinery, or with a hoe, or some other tool—that to me is very scary. There is a word for the fear of open spaces and deserted flat fields. The area where I live in Indiana is rolling, but I do still have that unsettling feeling sometimes of the vastness and emptiness of space that fills me with dread; the unnamed terror of finding yourself way, way back in a field with no one else around, and the sky and the ground seem almost endless. I've tried to come to some sort of accord with that fear, but it's a very peculiar and powerful thing.

Zohra was so great at capturing that quality of terror and sadness in her performance. Over the years people have said to me, "You must have known as you were shooting that Zohra Lampert was giving you something extraordinary." Well, yeah, sure, but I always believed in her abilities as an actor. I knew Zohra would do a wonderful job as Jessica and, of course, the casting of that part was crucial. It goes without saying that the picture would not have worked half as well as it did were it not for Zohra making that character seem so totally real and three-dimensional. You believe that this fractured woman has had a troubled history, even though we are really only seeing her during the final demise of her sanity. There is a terrible sense of inevitably about the story and the character: you know from the start that things are not going to end well and it's just of matter of how and when. That was something I very much had in mind from the outset. I talked to Zohra about it and she understood how important that was. If we had hired an actress who was incapable of evincing all of those things—the terror, the vulnerability and the confusion—we would have been dead in the water (no pun intended). There's no denying that a lot of what makes *Jessica* so compelling and affecting is the strength and subtlety of Zohra's performance.

> *Hancock's picture ends as it began, with Jessica sitting alone in a rowboat at dusk on a secluded lake. This is not before a sustained sequence of dread in which Jessica is terrorized by Emily/Abigail and the bandaged townsfolk, and discovers the exsanguinated remains of the mute girl in white and Woody. After clambering in the rowboat and paddling out into the cove, a ghostly hand reaches out of the water to seize Jessica. She repeatedly stabs the apparition in the back and, as the bleeding body floats away, Jessica sees that it is Duncan. "I sit here and I can't believe that it happened, and yet I have to believe it," she ponders in a voiceover. "Nightmares or dreams? Madness or sanity? I don't know which is which."*

The decision to bookend the picture with the image of Jessica sitting in the rowboat at dusk was made in post-production. That was not written in the original script. It essentially makes the film one long flashback, so there is a terrible sense of entrapment to the proceedings. The ambiguity of the ending was really an experiment I conducted. It was meant to reaffirm the fact that evil continues to exist in the world. It's still out there, it's not defused, it's not defeated, and everything is not going to be alright. That was the influence of Hitchcock again there in some small way. In my delving wholeheartedly into Hitchcock's filmography, I had noticed that in some of his movies—like *The Birds* for instance—the evil was not always conquered. Sometimes the good guys triumph, but other times the evil survives in some form or another. That was something I wanted to have in *Jessica*: the idea that there is a persuasive sense of the ominous in the world that isn't going away.

In that regard, I think the ending of my movie is truthful. The climax may not be entirely acceptable to all viewers, but it is authentic; it's authentic to the character of Jessica and her perceptions, her reality. It's also a brave ending, I feel. When you are a younger director, perhaps starting out and doing your first few independent films, you are often much bolder in your approach to things. I definitely was. Sometimes that's because you don't know enough and other times it's because you're not afraid to try things. I think on *Jessica* it was really a combination of both those factors—ignorance and bravery. Later, on some of the other pictures I made, maybe I was a little more conservative and restrained and not so willing to take really *big* chances. On other occasions I'm sure the opportunity was taken out of my hands, or I didn't think there was a clear opportunity to even try, or I was politely discouraged from doing so.

This gets back to what I mentioned earlier, about the wrong ideas and expectations directors sometimes get about things. Generally speaking, when a filmmaker tastes some success, it's more about maintaining your position and not rocking the boat too much. A lot of filmmakers don't want to take big chances and possibly lose their newfound position. But on *Jessica* it was different because I was operating under the vigor of youth and purity. I do think that the uncertainty of the climax gives the film a lasting power. Ending the picture as it began, with Jessica sitting alone in a boat trying to make some sense of the events she has—or possibly has not—experienced, was an interesting and unusual way to go. Aside from being circular, which in a sense is like being stuck in a bad trip, I thought it was also haunting. Unfortunately, I don't think everyone felt the same way and agreed with my approach. If you read some of the reviews back then, it's pretty clear that some critics were very confused and unsure about the climax. I believe that the passage of time has revealed the ending to be one of the strongest aspects of the movie. People are perhaps more accepting of that kind of ambiguity and uncertainty today.

> *Filmed without a distributor,* Jessica *was picked up by Paramount Pictures. After apparently considering* The Satanists *as a possible if entirely inappropriate title, the studio rechristened Hancock's movie* Let's Scare Jessica to Death, *playing into the feelings of paranoia and anxiety the filmmaker had sought to cultivate.*

Paramount demonstrated great faith in the film. They gave it a wide release—just a sensational release. That title, *Let's Scare Jessica to Death*, was Paramount's title as we originally called it simply *Jessica* (I have no memory of Paramount ever seriously considering *The Satanists* as a title). Frank Yablans, who was running Paramount at that point, came in with his team and gave the movie a more commercial-sounding title. I think the studio was right to do that as they really knew how to sell it. They knew how to generate the right heat and it was fascinating to observe them working to create the moody ad campaign for my movie. They did a great poster for it and wanted to emphasize certain aspects more prominently. It was like, "Okay, this is a horror film, so let's make that fact clear to the audience. Let's not be hesitant about this. Let's eagerly embrace it and see how they respond." It was an interesting period in Paramount's history—this was just after *Love Story* and just before *The Godfather*—and they were very excited about *Jessica*. Frank Yablans didn't think it was a risk to acquire the picture, nor did he ever consider it to be too low-brow for his studio. It was quite the reverse. He really believed in the quality of the film and was delighted to have bought it. I drew a lot of confidence from Frank's enthusiasm. I said to myself, "Well, if he really likes my movie this much maybe I have something good here. We have obviously done something right."

When the picture was first screened at the Criterion, they used all the old kind of ballyhoo: outside the theater they had a horse-drawn hearse and coffins, and really created this wonderful, celebratory atmosphere. That energy was then carried inside the theater when the audience sat down to watch the movie and they really had a great time with it. Seeing the picture play as well as it did that night was terrific. It was a packed house with *the* most vocal crowd I've ever been a part of. They were about seventy percent Black and were constantly yelling at the screen: "No, don't go in there! Oh God, get away from there! What are you *doing*?!" It was a remarkable opening, actually. I mean, it was such an exhilarating and satisfying experience for me to personally witness that kind of reaction to my first film. I can't tell you. *Jessica* then played all over the country and made a lot of money, which made everybody happy.

Here is another amusing aside: as I said, our producers, the Mosses, owned these theaters which happened to have extremely ghoulish-looking ushers working in them that were on minimum wage. The employees at the Criterion were required to wear old-fashioned usher costumes and the management often used them as messengers. So, if you were working in the editing room, you would look up and suddenly see this weird guy who looked like Frankenstein in an antiquated usher's uniform standing silently before you. These ushers would seemingly appear from nowhere, either bringing your opticals back from the optical house or delivering a memo from the office. It was amusing but, occasionally, also a little unnerving—just suddenly seeing them hovering there. Despite that, I must say, they also seemed perversely appropriate for the subject of our film.

> *In keeping with the critical reaction allocated to most low-budget independent horror films of the age,* Let's Scare Jessica to Death *reaped unfairly mixed reviews following its release on August 27, 1971. After beginning his notice rather promisingly by labeling Hancock's ambitious chiller "The thinking man's vampire film," Roger Greenspun of* The New York Times *swiftly bared his fangs in claiming the film made no sense; "sacrificing some of its best ideas to trivial shock effect [and] relinquishing even the slightest claim to suspension of disbelief." Despite highlighting its pleasingly picturesque settings and eerie score, the review in the* Los Angeles Times *similarly denigrated* Jessica *for its "poorly resolved" screenplay, stating: "As it turns out, the picture builds and builds only to let us down. In short, Hancock has created an intriguing, realistic psychological drama so effectively that it's unfortunate that vampires are brought in to resolve it." Released in Great Britain on November 26, 1971, the response was no less charitable.* Monthly Film Bulletin *wrote: "Apart from the striking novelty of a vampire who thrives in water and wields a knife to gash her victims,* Let's Scare Jessica to Death *generally treads well-mapped ground ... The most potent moments are fairly*

> conventional mainstream horror; the weakest are those where Hancock succumbs to the temptation to make every shot 'a work of art.'"

I think there is always the temptation to read every review, particularly at the beginning of your career when you are new to filmmaking or the theater. Admittedly, I've done that more than once; hunted down every review of my work I could find and dissected every sentence. That's not always healthy, of course, as there is a dangerous tendency in some artists to believe everything that the critics write and say about you. That can be destructive and misleading, I feel, because the critics can often be very wrong and very stupid. Not all of them, but undoubtedly some of them. They spend a couple of hours writing a review that destroys a piece of work which might have taken years to bring to fruition. Sometimes they can even wreck a whole career. That's a fascinating kind of power, isn't it? It really is. Occasionally the reviews I read are valid, fair and well thought-out; other times a review reads like they are talking about some entirely different movie. But I do think that *Jessica* confused and confounded some critics. As it was my first film I felt some of those shots rather acutely, but I also believed that I had made a pretty good movie. I do recall that my father *loved* it! That was good enough for me. That he liked it so much.

Oddly enough, *Jessica* was awarded an X upon its release in England. I have no idea exactly what moments in the movie could have possibly warranted such a rating. In truth, we were all greatly puzzled by it. The British censors were ruthlessly puritanical at that point in time and were apparently tough to deal with. I believe several horror films that came after *Jessica*, such as *The Exorcist* and *The Texas Chainsaw Massacre*, also ran into problems in the United Kingdom. I take a few crumbs of comfort in knowing that my picture was in some rather esteemed (and notorious) company. Look, I can see where the censors may have had a problem with a teenage girl repeatedly impaling her vagina with a crucifix, but I couldn't see how *Jessica* could be the target of their attentions. It was bewildering to me, I must say, as the violence and gore in the film is hardly excessive. The only disturbing and oppressive elements are the tone, mood and atmosphere. Maybe that's what they initially objected to—either that or possibly the murdered mole. I really couldn't say. Yeah, it must have been the mole!

> *Some observers have commented in retrospect that* Let's Scare Jessica to Death *serves as a haunting elegy for the "bitter disappointments of the Love Generation." Whether by accident or conscious design, the film does effectively isolate and illuminate the death and corruption of counterculture values during the early years of the post-1960s hangover. It also anticipates the festering paranoia that was to manifest strongly throughout the 1970s in the wake of such events as the Watergate scandal, the assassinations of Harvey Milk and George Moscone, and the Jonestown Massacre.*

I was a little too old to be a hippie. Well, I was a hippie in a way I guess, but maybe I considered myself to be something of an observer rather than an active participant in the whole *Love* thing. I don't know. Among many considerations there is the work that you do and there are your thoughts and observations on the world around you, and then there are the people you associate with. I mean, back then, politics was also a way to socialize and discuss what was happening in America and elsewhere. But I think the 1960s has been mythologized and aggrandized in some ways in terms of this idea that love was an unstoppable and self-organizing force that was positively changing the world. In reality there were many social, cultural and political factors that were changing society and not all of them were for the better. I'm sure the cynics among us will argue that the counterculture was a phenomenon that simply emerged at a point in our history when people retreated from responsibility—and, in some cases, reality—grew their hair long, took a lot of drugs and talked bullshit. But what did it all really mean? Why did it come to an end? And what came afterwards?

Back then, half of my friends were on LSD most of the time—especially Barton Heyman. I'd spent a great deal of time watching him in the theater on LSD, which was quite an experience. As I believe I told you, Barton could make me feel despondent sometimes with his routinely being high. He enthusiastically embraced that drug and I just couldn't. Maybe there was some small resentment on my part about that, but I don't think so. Work is work and play is play, and the two don't always make for a positive mix. As I remember it, Barton was not at all high during the making of *Jessica*. As a matter of fact, by that time, I don't think he was doing that much LSD anymore—possibly another indication that the Sixties were over, at least for us. Personally, I was more interested in amphetamines than hallucinogens and other supposedly mind-expanding drugs. I don't think I had the temperament or the inclination to do LSD, certainly not with the relish that some of my friends exhibited.

This is why I was always a little cynical about Love, not about the reality of love and the profound feelings you have for those close to you, but about the Love Generation itself. I knew a lot of hippies back then and I can remember thinking, "This is all just a fad. It will eventually pass and be replaced by cynicism, suspicion and despair. Just you wait and see!" And that pretty much came to pass throughout the 1970s. I think as a society and a nation, we did become more suspicious and cynical and despairing as that decade wore on. You could already feel that negativity brewing when we were making *Jessica*; that things weren't working out the way some of us had hoped and dreamed they would in the late 1960s. There was Vietnam, all the civil unrest, the assassinations of Martin Luther King and Bobby Kennedy, and the dream was already over. So, I was aware that the ideals of the Love Generation were perishing. Maybe that was the significance of Jessica and her friends riding around in a hearse with the word "Love" painted on it. It may have symbolized that those hippie values were now dying or dead. But there was also something weirdly cosmic to me about the contrast present in that image which spoke to the eternal mysteries of life and death. To what extent my own cynicism is reflected in *Jessica*, I think it unquestionably made its present felt whether that was consciously or subconsciously.

Some people have read all kinds of meanings and symbols into the movie. I do enjoy that level of scrutiny, because it's always interesting to hear various observations of your work. For instance, certain critics have suggested that the old man on the ferry at the beginning represents the Ferryman of Hades as depicted in Greek mythology, transporting souls of the recently deceased across the river Styx from the land of the living to the ancient Underworld. Somebody else recently talked about Jessica in fact being dead—an unfortunate victim of suicide—and the film merely details her existence in a kind of purgatory for which she must atone for her terrible sin. That was not my intention. But I like things that can be perceived in contrasting ways, and that also extends to what people see in a movie and *believe* you have intended. Interestingly, shortly after *Jessica* came out, my old college room-mate John Casey told me that he thought the ghost in the film was "clearly my mother." My reaction to that observation was, "*What?*" "You're kidding yourself," he said, "if you think she isn't." You see, Casey knew my mother and father. Well, okay, I was willing to concede that Mariclare Costello is a redhead like my mother, and I suppose their cheekbones are the same, and their freckles and soft manner. That's all true. So, maybe Casey is right after all. But I wasn't conscious of any resemblance between them during filming, nor was it ever intentional.

> *For more than forty-five years,* Let's Scare Jessica to Death *has threatened to emerge from the cult respectability it has wallowed in and stake a claim to permanence as a deeply affecting and poetic masterpiece of horror. A personal favorite for such acclaimed authors as Stephen King, Charles L. Grant and Kim Newman, it continues to acquire more admirers and there has been persistent talk of a remake.*

Everywhere I go, I still get a lot of people who want to talk to me about *Jessica*. It's one of those pictures that a director makes in a career that simply refuses to leave you—not that I'm complaining. I've met fans who will say things like, "Oh, I really love your movie! It's one of my favorite movies ever!" Sometimes I'll encounter people who will stare rather earnestly at me, then whisper, "Oh God, your picture is so *scary*! I saw it on television," or "I saw it on DVD and I couldn't breathe! I was so terrified!" Some people prefer to look rather accusingly at me as if it's my fault, which, of course, it is. Then I'll meet others who will repeat that exact same sentence, only they'll instead have this reverent tone and tremor in their voice. They'll have a loving smile on their faces like they are saying, "Thank you, thank you, thank you!" I must say that all of those responses are very welcome and very interesting to me.

After all these years, it's obvious that *Jessica* is a cult film as it coldly touches the hearts and minds of a certain kind of horror movie fan; somebody who prefers their horror films to be a little more patient and profound; horror that has some emotional resonance and psychological truth to it. But I'm always surprised and delighted by the various reactions to *Jessica* and the different kinds of people it seems to attract. For instance, I'll receive a phone call informing me that somebody wants to have a screening of the picture someplace at midnight, and I'll go and discover all of these people in attendance that are wearing hoodies like the Unabomber. Sometimes they make more of an effort and come dressed as witches or zombies or vampires, whatever it is, and it becomes more of a celebration. A screening was recently organized in Chicago and there was one guy there that had his teeth filed to points so that he looked like a vampire. Naturally, he just *loved* the movie!

Just recently, somebody on Facebook sent me a link to the trailer for a film called *Queen of Earth*, which came out in 2015. There was a note accompanying it which read: "It appears that somebody likes and admires a certain film of yours." Of course, the film in question was *Let's Scare Jessica to Death* and the apparent admirer, I subsequently learned, was a young director named Alex Ross Perry. I looked at the trailer with great interest and the movie really does look and feel a lot like *Jessica*. *Queen of Earth* is a psychological thriller that stars Elizabeth Moss and Katherine Waterston as two women who meet for the weekend at a lake house where they once spent their childhoods. It's not a rip-off of my movie by any means, but it's made by somebody who evidently loves *Jessica* as it seemingly has the same attention to performance and atmosphere. Also, like *Jessica*, it's a subtle film about women that is directed by a man. It demonstrates to me that my picture still has the power to influence and inspire other directors more than four decades after it was made. I find that very gratifying.

I'm not surprised there was talk of a remake of *Jessica*. Nothing really surprises me in this business anymore. There are so many remakes now it shows you the dearth of good ideas in Hollywood as studios just want to plunder their own past. I'd heard—and maybe this was ten years ago—that Robert Evans was making another picture using the same title. I don't believe he was planning on doing a faithful remake with the same story and characters, but *Let's Scare Jessica to Death* is clearly a good title. As I say it's a cult film, so I imagine the attention it would get would be somewhat modest. But it's such a vivid title it would probably reawaken interest in my movie. I must confess though, I was delighted when Evans' project didn't happen. I mean, *Jessica* has aged so beautifully I liken the film to a fine wine: it's actually gotten better in the barrel as the years have gone by.

Somebody recently asked me if I look back on the making of *Jessica* with fondness. It was a mixed experience, really. I certainly look back on the locations with fondness, as it was such a beautiful and arresting place, and I'm also sentimental about some of the great people I worked with on the picture. However, those debilitating thoughts of uncertainty I mentioned, the terrible doubts and despairs that plague every director on their first film, are still profoundly troubling to me. Yes, there was a lot of happiness and warmth and self-discovery, too, a real confluence of emotions, but I'm not overly nostalgic for those days. Some people look back at the time when they knew nothing, or knew very little, or knew much less than they do now, with blind affection. I try to resist that. I find the time I didn't know anything to be frustrating and scary, not wistful. I look back and say, "I wish I knew *more!*" Every film you make is a learning experience. Even now, after all these years, I'm still learning. But your first movie is always an intense baptismal voyage of discovery. You make mistakes, and you learn from them, and you try not to repeat them.

Bang the Drum Slowly (1973)

After negotiating the numerous challenges and insecurities that arose during the making of Let's Scare Jessica to Death, *Hancock had successfully made the transition from theater to film. Still riding the wave of interest generated by his Academy Award nomination for* Sticky My Fingers, Fleet My Feet, *consolidated by the generous critical reception awarded his unnerving maiden feature, the thirty-two year-old director was eager to find a suitable sophomore project that would further his rather expensive "education" in movies. One remote possibility was a contemporary adaptation of Joseph Conrad's 1911 novel* Under Western Eyes, *which would transpose the story from the political turmoil of early twentieth-century Russia to that of 1960s America. The protagonist of Conrad's book is Razumov, a student in the University of St. Petersburg who has aspirations of pursuing a career as a Privy Councilor in the Czarist bureaucracy. Instead, he becomes entangled in a revolutionary conspiracy after giving refuge to a fellow student who has assassinated the brutal Minister of State.*

I had been working on the adaptation of *Under Western Eyes* in Sneden's Landing. Donny Graham had first suggested the Conrad book might make a good film, so I enlisted my eventual Pulitzer Prize-winning ex-roommate John Casey to write the screenplay. We attempted a modernization of the story involving the FBI and Sixties Radicals rather than the Czarist Secret Police and Anarchists of Conrad's narrative. Looking back now, I don't think it was the right way to go. Conrad's novel is very much immersed in the Russian history of the time—the failed Russian Revolution of 1905 had occurred just six years before its publication. The fact is *Under Western Eyes* still has relevance and power today, particularly in this age of political terrorism we all find ourselves living in. Dorothy Tristan and I later tried again with the book in the 1980s. This time the inciting incident became something that had happened in Los Angeles in 1982: shortly before we started working on it, an Armenian Terrorist shot and killed the Turkish Charge d'Affair. The shooting occurred at an intersection we drove past all the time, Wilshire near Westwood Boulevard. We didn't get very far with this second adaptation, as there's an ending problem in the book that lurked and eventually demoralized us. So, the project drifted away a second time and I think its ship has finally sailed as far as I'm concerned.

> *An alternative possibility for Hancock came his way courtesy of Maurice Rosenfield. A prominent Chicago lawyer, Rosenfield represented such high-profile people as Conrad Hilton, founder of the Hilton hotel chain, and also did some civil liberties work on the side, defending Lenny Bruce before the Illinois Appellate Court in 1964 and earning the controversial comedian an acquittal on charges of obscenity. Rosenfield had recently read Mark Harris' acclaimed 1955 novel* Bang the Drum Slowly, *the second in a series of four books that chronicled the life and career of baseball player Henry "Arthur" Wiggen, the star pitcher for the fictitious New York Mammoths. Preceded by* The Southpaw *(1953), and followed by two further sequels,* A Ticket for a Seamstitch *(1957) and* It Looked Like For Ever *(1979), this bittersweet story (whose title is derived from the lyrics of the mournful ballad "Streets of Laredo") details Wiggen's unlikely friendship with Bruce Pearson, a hayseed third-string catcher from Georgia whom he discovers is terminally ill with Hodgkin's disease.*

The beginning of *Bang the Drum Slowly* for me was somewhat inauspicious. One day, I received a phone-call at my house in Sneden's Landing from a guy who introduced himself as Maurice Rosenfield. He was a successful lawyer who had no experience of making movies, but, like a lot of people it seems, harbored ambitions of breaking into the business. As we started talking, Maury informed me that he wanted to make a film of Mark Harris' novel, and inquired if I would be interested in becoming involved in the project as director. I don't believe I had read *Bang the Drum Slowly* at this point, but I had known Harris a little bit from my time in San Francisco at the Actor's Workshop. Since the Workshop was the significant regional theater there, and Harris seemed to be around a lot back then (they might even have done one of his plays) I recall him being a much admired person. As a matter of fact, people in San Francisco were often recommending his books to me and I would sometimes meet Mark at various fundraisers and parties, that kind of thing, and he seemed like a nice guy.

By the early 1970s, Harris had written three baseball novels that were all concerned with the same set of characters featured in *Bang the Drum Slowly*. A fourth installment would come a few years after our movie was made, but *Bang the Drum Slowly* is probably considered the strongest of the four and is certainly the most famous. Harris really demonstrated an innate understanding of professional athletes and the finer aspects of male camaraderie in his work. Having not read the novel back in San Francisco when people were telling me to, I got hold of a copy shortly after Maury Rosenfield called and finally read it. I thought it was a wonderful book; a simple, straightforward story beautifully told. It was so rich with humor and humanity. I was greatly moved by the central relationship between these two very different men: one a tobacco-chewing country dimwit who pisses in the sink, the other a star pitcher from the city; the latter somebody who has written a book no less (the nickname "Arthur" is derived from the word "Author") and works as an insurance agent on the side, selling policies to other ballplayers. It's a first person book, written by a ballplayer, and a lot of its power comes from the combination of an unreliable narrator, this jaunty wise-guy star, with the depth of the tragedy of his room-mate dying of cancer. It had a way of kicking you in the gut. I knew when I was only a third of the way through the novel that I wanted to make it as a movie.

Now, if you have been nominated for various awards, and certain people are starting to get to know your work and recognize your name, you inevitably begin receiving a lot of calls from different people who say they want you to direct a picture for them. Unfortunately, a very high percentage of these individuals really just want to have lunch, or they are not entirely serious about doing something. They will often claim they've got the money or at least half of it, and things are looking good. In truth, most of them really haven't secured any financing whatsoever. But it came to me slowly that Maury might be different. First, he immediately wanted to fly me to Chicago to meet with him. I then said to myself, "Ah! If this guy is willing to pay for a plane ticket maybe this could be *real*!" So, I decided to just take a chance and meet him. I remember that when I arrived in Chicago, Maury was waiting for me in a fancy car outside O'Hare International Airport. He had parked his vehicle in a place where you were not permitted to park and had duly tipped some guy who was working there in order to get away with it. As soon as I saw that, the same thought occurred to me again: "This one might actually have the money to make a movie!"

Soon after meeting Maury, I discovered that he had not seen *Let's Scare Jessica to Death*. However, he had caught the Thanksgiving television screening of *Sticky My Fingers, Fleet My Feet* and it had fortuitously come to him at just the right time. My overriding impression of Maury was that he had been a big lawyer toiling in a very high-pressure job, and at some point, he'd suffered a serious heart attack and had to stop working for a year or so. During this period of rest and recuperation, Maury had spent a lot of time going to Chicago Cubs games in order to basically chill out and not die abruptly from a stress-related illness. Somehow the obvious combination of attending a lot of baseball games and the fact that somebody had given him a copy of *Bang the Drum Slowly*, which is of course about dying—as well as the sudden realization of his own mortality—had awakened an idea in him. After seeing *Sticky My Fingers*, Maury had said to himself, "Here is a young guy who could possibly do a good job with this material. He understands sports; he understands male psychology and male relationships. He can do this." So, everything had come together perfectly in Maury's mind. The planets were aligned and he now wanted to turn Mark Harris' novel into a movie.

At our meeting, Maury and I talked baseball as well as business. Since I had played the game as a kid, I was able to use what I knew about it to my advantage—this was despite being called "pus-arm" as a kid and being condemned for my catching, throwing and general lack of athleticism. The honest truth was I had long fallen out of love with baseball. I found it boring to watch on television, although I believe I may have kept that view strictly to myself and not mentioned it to Maury. Naturally, when I was a kid, I had loved baseball, but I didn't see the fact that I didn't enjoy it much as an adult to be in any way detrimental or damaging to my ability to make a good picture. I did not recognize that as being relevant. Please understand, I don't like war and poverty either but I feel I could still deliver a damn good movie about either of those subjects that was interesting and entertaining. Whether or not Maury would have accepted that admission when we first started talking, I do not know.

It should be noted that, despite all this, Maury had his own power needs as the financier. I mean, if you hire somebody like Sydney Pollack or Roman Polanski to direct a movie they are going to want to bully you around and maintain a high level of creative control on the picture. Maury obviously took one look at me at this early stage of my career, and reasoned, "Okay, this is a young filmmaker I can work with who won't obliterate me in any power situation." Maury and I got along well at first, and we both decided to press forward with the project and just do it. As I had hoped and suspected, it turned out that Maury did indeed have the money. He actually had quite a lot of money, as well as a rich wife named Lois Rosenfield who would eventually be credited as co-producer on the film. I remember Lois was a rather small woman who had the unsettling habit of whispering things in Maury's ear. She was quiet, didn't say a lot during readings, and mostly just sat there. I also recall that Lois knitted all the time at long meetings and reminded me of Madame Defarge from Dickens' *A Tale of Two Cities*. I gather Lois was the money behind Maury, although he'd done well on his own aside from what she had brought to the marriage.

Anyway, we agreed to do the movie for under a million dollars and, at first, everything was great. The project had come together so easily I initially thought that Maury would be a pleasure to work with and, if we did have any disagreements, he'd be a reasonable and amicable guy. That really wasn't the case at all. In the long run, Maury proved to be extremely difficult and demanding as he didn't know anything about making motion pictures. Also, he was never entirely consistent or predictable, and was sometimes a hard guy to read. He was often subject to wild enthusiasms and very loving behavior, but could suddenly alternate these happy moods with some crazy and angry behavior. My psychiatrist speculated that perhaps because of hardening of the arteries his brain wasn't getting enough blood. I quickly learned that Maury was famous around Chicago for his unpredictable nature. Indeed, so odd and erratic was he during the shooting of *Bang the Drum Slowly* he made everybody else on the production unite and get along with each other. It was clear to see that there was already one maniac on the picture and there would be no room for a second.

Maury and I flew to Los Angeles and drove to Newhall, California, where Mark was teaching at the Disney Institute for the Arts. We worked out an agreement with him for the film rights to the book, and for him to write the screenplay. Interestingly, instead of adapting his own book directly, Mark just wrote a whole other thing. This wasn't quite as unexpected as you might think as I've found this often happens with very good writers—it also occurred when I worked with Tennessee Williams. In actuality, a lot of writers don't really rewrite as such because what they love to do is *write*. Writing makes them feel good, in a state of flow, but they don't enjoy the way rewriting makes them feel. An inevitable result of this is that they often create a new story that is parallel to the story they already have. It ends up being no better and no worse, merely different. But if you are in love with the story you originally discovered, this can be a frustrating and difficult process. Because what you really wanted was for the writer to lose the bad parts of his or her story and augment the good parts. But writers don't always do that. They are sometimes compelled to write something else entirely, which, again, can be a semblance of the thing that you first fell in love with.

In the wake of reading what Harris had done to his own novel, Maury and I got together to discuss the first draft. I said, "Okay, I'll rewrite this script," which I then proceeded to do. Basically, all I really did was go back to the book and include the things that Harris had jettisoned from his story. I was just typing in various scenes that I liked and found interesting. But then Maury looked at what I had written and said, "That's much better, but there are all these other things from the novel that we need to put back in, too." So, we carefully went through the book again and tried to work in all of Maury's favorite lines and moments. Inevitably, this resulted in us ending up with an overlong screenplay. I've often been in that kind of situation and, through a process of screenings, I boil the film down. I manage to reduce it to an acceptable length, but that's not an easy procedure. I tend to shoot stuff that I think I might need, knowing I may have to lose it later. Undoubtedly, smarter directors edit in at the script stage and don't shoot a lot of extra stuff, but that's not what I've done throughout my career. This is why I often find the screening process to be useful. I know a lot of directors don't share that opinion and find screenings horrifically intrusive and damaging. But I feel they often give you an early indication of how some scenes will play with an audience; what things work and what things don't.

During these early days of pre-production, even before the script was finalized, Maury had been busy reading several books of film criticism. Now that I think about it, I believe Maury had purchased *every* single book of film criticism he could find! He devoured these volumes and later brought ideas to the process that he had discovered in them. For example, he would say things like: "Listen, John, when we get started, I don't want you to shoot any close-ups. Close-ups are the crutch of a bad director and I don't want to see any of them in the picture. Do you understand?" I would then reply: "Well, Maury, we have a screenplay here that runs for 157 pages and it's going to have to be made shorter when we eventually release the movie. This means I should shoot all these scenes in a manner that gives me some options later. When we are editing the footage, I'm going to have to lose dialogue and some other things, and so a few close-ups may prove valuable." Maury was concerned about this as he adored Harris' book and loathed the idea of losing anything he felt was wonderful. Aside from not wanting me to shoot any close-ups, Maury had some other issues that troubled him. So, every day there would be this ongoing battle between us. Oddly enough, the problem of close-ups seemed to take precedence in his mind. I'd say, "I have to do it, Maury. I simply have to use close-ups. You'll just have to trust me on this." He would then shake his head vigorously, and say, "But I don't see why we have to!"

> *By the time pre-production had begun in earnest on the film adaptation,* Bang the Drum Slowly *had already established itself as a classic of baseball literature and would later be selected as one of the top one hundred sports novels of all time by* Sports Illustrated. *The book's popularity had first scored a marked increase in the wake of being adapted for television by Arnold Schulman within a year of its publication and filmed live as a studio-bound fifty-two-minute segment of the anthology drama series* The United States Steel Hour. *Broadcast on September 26, 1956, and starring Paul Newman as Arthur Wiggen and Albert Salmi as Bruce Pearson, the episode was directed by Daniel Petrie and remains an accomplished condensation of Harris' 200-plus page novel.*

A strange thing is that I was not really conscious as I was working on the picture that I had seen some of the original television dramatization when it was first telecast. I hadn't seen much of it. All I really remember is Paul Newman talking to the camera, and a bunch of ballplayers in white Yankee-like uniforms with mammoths on their chests. As I think back on it now, I may have this lingering impression that it was pretty good, but I was in high school and concerned with other things and didn't really pay attention. I have no memory of Albert Salmi being in it. As an actor, Salmi was usually cast as the bad guy. He just had that surly and severe look about him. I had previously read him for *A Man's a Man*, but I didn't cast him. In person, he came across as being quite abrupt and unpleasant. I believe his life eventually came to a violent end in a murder-suicide (Salmi fatally shot his wife and then himself in 1990) which is unfortunate.

The dominant theme of Harris' novel as I saw it—and this is present both in the 1956 TV play and my movie—was caring for the forgotten man. That was something Paramount emphasized in the tagline on the poster: "Nothing is more important than friendship. Not fame, not money, not death." Indeed, the shot I'm proudest of in my film, which is a slow-motion shot, is where the team is all celebrating after winning a big game. Arthur and the coach, Joe Jaros, turn back and they go to Bruce, who is addled and still whirling around in a confused way. They give Bruce his hat and bring him a jacket, and it's a small moment that reaffirms this central theme. For me, that captures the essence of what the story is all about: acknowledging the little guy who doesn't have much and isn't even wildly likable. I mean, one of the interesting things about *Bang the Drum Slowly* is the fact that Arthur didn't really like Bruce that much to begin with. When we first started working on the script, I often wondered why Wiggen, a pistol-hot left-hand pitcher, would go to such extremes to protect Bruce, who is a bumbling third-string catcher. Why would he demand that the top brass write a clause into his contract that if one or the other is ever to be traded or sold off to another team, he and Bruce must go together? What makes him do that? What makes a man who thinks mostly about himself, now think of another?

Interestingly, after Arthur makes this stipulation another character points out to him that he and Bruce had no great friendship in the time before his ailing team-mate received his terminal diagnosis. I don't think Arthur understands it himself. It happens slowly. Maybe they discover something as they are driving south together at the beginning of the movie, after visiting the Mayo Clinic in Minnesota and before hanging out with Bruce's parents in Georgia. Maybe that journey they made together, and the time they spent alone, helped them to form some connection. But it goes on from there, through the season, twisting and turning until Arthur at last, almost in spite of himself, recognizes their common humanity. That's how I reasoned it. I mean, human relationships are very mysterious in that way. I don't think that if Arthur had revealed the nature of Bruce's illness to his team-mates upon first discovering it, it would have made any difference to the story. However, it would have certainly ruined the plot! I think the humor derives from the fact that you have a supposed secret and nobody can keep a secret, right? It just gradually spreads and spreads—much like the clap—until everybody knows about it. You then have the manager, Dutch Schnell, trying his best to learn the truth, pestering and probing Arthur and Bruce to reveal it, and those moments provide some of the funniest scenes in the movie.

The thinking and mindset of an athlete, the little nuggets of athlete wisdoms you occasionally hear, is something that fascinated me. I had touched on it before in *Sticky My Fingers, Fleet My Feet*, where you have Norm applying the attitude of a professional athlete to a simple game of touch football he is playing with his friends in Central Park. The way you hear athletes talk, particularly male athletes, the way they motivate themselves and each other, the rituals and behaviors they go through, the close relationships they form, all exist on a very deep level. They all have a purpose, don't you think? I mean, the ups and downs of professional sport, the winning and the losing, the triumphs and the heartbreaks, these experiences are things that allow friendships to cement themselves for a lifetime. As someone who has never been particularly adept at sports, I can only observe these things from afar, but the act of making movies is also a team game with an agreed plan and an objective. On that level I can relate to sports. And when you do a picture you can form profound relationships with your colleagues, although you only work with them for a short period of time. That's why I like to work with a lot of the same people over and over. On that level, too, I understand Arthur and Bruce's bond with each other.

I think another question that is worth considering is to what extent *Bang the Drum Slowly* is actually a film about baseball. I remember that was something that was openly discussed among us all. Let me put it this way: back in the early 1970s, it seemed that movies about baseball in Hollywood were forbidden or, at the very least, actively discouraged. You could take a project like ours to all the major studios and the executives would inevitably crow, "Movies about baseball do not make any money." In fact, various people had done just that. At one point Robert Altman was trying to get it on with Robert Redford as the pitcher and Robert Duvall as the catcher. I remember one guy, an executive named Marty Ransohoff, remarked during one meeting with total incredulity: "Baseball *and* cancer?" So, it was apparent to us that such an unpalatable combination of elements was a serious no-no in terms of studio money. Maury accepted the fact he was going to have to finance it himself, and then try and sell it to a studio. For that reason, we thought it was important at an early stage of the process to state that the film was not about baseball. We would argue, "No, it's really about friendship and fate and young men dying before their time." Obviously, it goes without saying that *Bang the Drum Slowly* is a movie about baseball, too. Of course it is. We just played that aspect down a little when we were meeting with various people in order to give the picture the best chance of success.

If I have to see the game of baseball itself standing for any particular metaphor in the film, it would probably be representative of the game of life. In life, there are winners and there are losers. Also, from a public and media perspective, there are stars and there are nobodies. That's just the way it is in sports (and, admittedly, in the movie business) and always has been. I mean, there are piano players and there are piano movers. I also think the film touches on the idea that no matter how hard you try, you sometimes can't change the result. Baseball seemed as useful an analogy for that sobering fact as anything else, and it wasn't like some kind of "Disease of the Week" movie you saw on TV. I view the manner in which Arthur personally undertakes a mission to make Bruce's last months on Earth a happy and fulfilling time to be a great lesson to us all in humanity; that we must always have respect for those who are in need of care and attention. That's what Arthur really gives Bruce when he fights for him: dignity. He makes Bruce feel important and worthy; that he is actually contributing to a series-winning season, whereas before he was maybe just another face in the locker room, or somebody who was merely making up the numbers in the dugout. That's a wonderful gift to give somebody.

> *Casting sessions for* Bang the Drum Slowly *commenced early in 1972 at the Warwick Hotel, on Avenue of the Americas, New York. Located just a couple of blocks from the William Morris Agency—Hancock's representatives at the time—the firm duly submitted the majority of the actors who attended the auditions. Rick Nicita, who would go on to become one of the premier agents at CAA and represent the likes of Tom Cruise and Anthony Hopkins, served their interests. However, the process of interviewing some of the*

> *best talent the city had to offer tested the patience of all concerned, as the sessions dragged on from weeks to months.*

Casting the movie was a long, thorough and exhausting process. We read everybody. Just name an actor of a certain age in New York who was around at that time and we probably saw them. We had a suite at the Warwick on a high floor and used it as casting and production offices. My wife, Ann, and I were marooned there happily for a weekend during a huge snowstorm when we couldn't get up the Hudson to Sneden's Landing. Okay, maybe we didn't read every actor in New York, but it felt like it as casting went on for months and we were seeing someone every fifteen minutes. John Lithgow was one—a strong candidate for Bruce. Ron Liebman came within a hair's breadth of playing Arthur, but Maury didn't think he was attractive enough. We read Bob Balaban for Bruce, and he was persuasively skilled. I definitely wanted to work with him, but not for that part. James Woods was considered for Arthur—again, I wanted to work with him but not for that part.

Others we saw included Treat Williams for both parts; Tommy Lee Jones and Kevin Conway for Bruce (Conway had been so brilliant Off-Broadway in Mark Medoff's *When You Comin' Back, Red Ryder?*) I also read Bill Atherton for Arthur, as well as Andy Robinson, who had recently played the crazy villain in *Dirty Harry* and would later play John F. Kennedy for me in an episode of *The Twilight Zone* I directed in 1986. Carmine Caridi was another person I saw for Arthur. I found him a charming actor, a big goofy Italian showboat. The first of several tragedies in Carmine's life came after Francis Ford Coppola had originally cast him as Sonny Corleone in *The Godfather*. Coppola later yielded reluctantly to (I suspect) his producer Robert Evans, who didn't want them *all* to be Italian fer crissake! So, that part instead went to James Caan. Too bad this was after Carmine had quit his Broadway show and had enjoyed a big celebration at Joe Allen's. That was a real heartbreaker for him. But, back then, Carmine could have easily played Arthur Wiggen for me.

> *Two exciting young unknowns who passed through the auditions were Robert De Niro and Michael Moriarty, who would both go on to enjoy astonishing success, garnering every major acting award between them. De Niro had already worked twice with Brian De Palma on two of the filmmaker's nascent offerings,* Greetings *(1968) and*

Hi, Mom! (1970), and had played Lloyd Barker in Roger Corman's Bloody Mama *(1970). Moriarty had co-starred in the underrated war drama* My Old Man's Place *(1971), written by Stanford Whitmore. He had also played a small supporting role in the Bill Cosby/Robert Culp crime vehicle* Hickey & Boggs *(1972), and was building a reputation as a powerful theater actor. Hancock was to discover that each would approach the work and their respective characters in different ways.*

Aside from his rigorous training schedule and intensive discussions with Hancock on the finer points of his role, De Niro exhibited his now fabled attention to detail in the realization of Bruce Pearson. Ever the transformative actor, his extensive preparations included the purchasing of clothes from a "country store" that he imagined Bruce would frequent in an effort to achieve a suitably authentic look. De Niro visited the small town in Georgia where the character grew up, and mingled with the locals to capture the cadence of the people Pearson would have associated with. In an interview the actor said of this experience: "The people in the town were really nice, and they didn't mind me copying the way they talked. In fact, they would correct me if I started to sound too much like a New Yorker. After I while I began to move like Bruce and I began to feel like him."

Robert De Niro came to my attention somewhat unexpectedly. Bobby's agent sent him in to read, and I immediately thought, "Ooh, this guy is good!" Despite that, I still think I read him something like seven times before I eventually cast him. I was extremely cautious back then when it came to casting an important role and still am as it's such an important thing. We thought for a while that maybe Michael Moriarty should play the catcher and De Niro the pitcher, because in the book Bruce Pearson is blonde and Arthur Wiggen is supposed to be dark. Sure, either actor could have done either role and delivered a worthwhile performance, but we pondered for a long time about which way to go. That's why we read them so many times. Finally, I settled on Bobby for Bruce because I felt that he was perfect for that part. It wasn't because De Niro was physically smaller than Moriarty, as it would have perhaps been more interesting to have had the bigger guy playing the dying man. It would have been something approaching the relationship between Lenny and George in *Of Mice and Men*, that kind of thing. But anyone who has seen *Raging Bull* or *Cape Fear* knows that Bobby can be quite a robust and physical performer. So, that would not have been a problem for him.

De Niro avidly researched baseball before we started shooting. Bobby had never played baseball, so he worked assiduously on trying to have the technique and movement and mindset of a professional ballplayer. I guess it helped him that Bruce was not as gifted as some of the other members of his team, but he was still a professional athlete. Bobby knew this and so he wanted to achieve some credible semblance of that. I remember we'd shoot all day and then Bobby would go for two hours of batting practice. Then he would go for a three-mile run before coming back and studying his lines for the next day. He was incredibly focused and dedicated, qualities that have been the hallmarks of his career. Bobby even said to me eight years later when we were working on *Weeds* together, "You know, there may be more talented actors around, but no one will ever work harder than me." Everybody knows the stories about Bob getting a cab driver's license for a month before doing *Taxi Driver*; or his gaining a lot of weight to play Jake LaMotta in *Raging Ball* and boxing to a very high standard, all that stuff. But from my own experiences with De Niro on *Bang the Drum Slowly* and *Weeds*, I can certainly attest to the high levels of commitment he brings. His single-mindedness and devotion to the roles he takes on goes way, way beyond the call. It's quite something to witness that up close over a prolonged period of time.

Bobby also researched the symptoms and effects of Hodgkin's disease prior to filming. A lot of actors do extensive research, but can get confused and cluttered by doing too much of it. I mean, ultimately, in terms of the knowledge you've acquired, what do you use and what do you ignore? What can research bring to the role that will be in evidence on the screen, or perhaps help you to get somewhere useful? What I found so interesting about De Niro was the way his mind worked. On *Bang the Drum Slowly*, it was almost like he chose a single physical thing that he knew he could play. Like in the scene where Bruce suddenly wakes up in the middle of the night feeling poorly: before each take we did, I remember Bobby would routinely stick his finger down his throat to the point where he was about to vomit. That was just one example of him selecting a specific means of realizing the different aspects and symptoms of Hodgkin's disease that he could physically perform. It would make him retch and gag and his face turn color, but it got him there. Bobby's little "trick"—if I can call it that — nauseated the crew. Some people were even offended and anxious about it. It was very interesting to see those reactions. The crew thought I was ridiculous to let him do it, but I liked Bob's work and his commitment, and I trusted him totally.

On another occasion, during the shooting of the final game, before each take De Niro would whirl around furiously on the spot until he was uncontrollably falling down dizzy. Then, at that moment, he would try to straighten himself up and we would start filming. So, he didn't have to act dizzy, he *was* dizzy. Once again, the crew thought I was crazy to allow Bobby to do this. They were like, "What are you doing? Are you really going to let this continue?" They simply didn't buy into his approach and were like, "Hey, this guy is an actor, right? Why doesn't he just *act*?" I remember we had seventy-five extras witnessing Bobby do that, watching him whirl around like a crazy person, which aggravated the situation. I'm sure some of them felt rather embarrassed and self-conscious about it, but I didn't. Okay, people didn't know that he was *Robert De Niro* yet. That came shortly afterwards when anything Bobby would have attempted—like standing on his head with a banana sticking out of his ass—would have not only been permitted but praised. But Bobby was just fearless in exploring everything. Another example: I admired his assiduousness in chewing tobacco in character. Have you ever tried chewing tobacco? It's really nasty! It falls apart in your mouth and burns your throat. I tried it once and was sick as a dog, but De Niro just kept chomping away. Despite this, he didn't want to continue the habit on a long term basis. After the film was over, I suspect enough was enough.

Michael Moriarty was recommended to me by John Lahr, who, for a time, was the Literary Manager of the Tyrone Guthrie Theatre where Moriarty was in the rep. That's how Lahr knew him and understood his excellence, and thought he would be good for the movie. I had seen Moriarty playing Octavius Caesar in a production of *Anthony & Cleopatra* in Central Park and thought he was a fabulous actor. In getting him and De Niro involved with *Bang the Drum Slowly*, I now had two actors who each possessed different qualities and attitudes. For instance, Bobby was always very consistent and would just plow through scenes each day in his dependably unstoppable manner. I can recall thinking to myself, "Man, this guy is like a mole. He is going to burrow through and he's not going to be distracted or stopped by anybody." As for Moriarty, I learned he was often subject to sudden mood shifts. He would have his bad days and his good days, and you never knew which was coming. I found this uneven quality he exhibited somewhat peculiar and he was not quite as satisfying perhaps to work with as De Niro. I mean, above everything, you have got to get the day's work done. Even if the actor is not in particularly good shape emotionally, you still have to shoot something because time is money. You can't just say, "Oh well, maybe this isn't working today. I'm not quite feeling up to it. Let's come back tomorrow and we can try it then." No, that was never going to happen. We didn't have those luxuries on *Bang the Drum Slowly*. So, I found Moriarty's behavior a little frustrating—but only a little. You have to say that in spite of everything, he was wonderful in the part. I mean, Michael wasn't moody and uneven compared to other actors, only to De Niro who was so steady. Everyone was kept in line, really, by Maury being so crazy. Again, you can't afford two like that in a single enterprise, and people sensed that.

Admittedly, even before I had cast him, I'd heard that Michael had certain personal issues and hang-ups. About two years before we made *Bang the Drum Slowly*, I had noted a second-hand story that he'd been involved in a strange incident that had occurred at the Alley Theatre in Houston, Texas. Apparently, Moriarty had been on stage during the performance of a Robert Edwin play and had felt that the other male actor on the stage was coming on to him sexually. Moriarty informed the audience that he was finished for the evening; walked off and refused to go back on. Then he played a gay Richard III at Lincoln Center. Michael was great. So spectacular in fact that Neil Simon picked up the idea and used it humorously in his screenplay for *The Goodbye Girl*. Moriarty later won a Tony Award for playing a homosexual in a production of *Find Your Way Home*, so there was perhaps something sexually paranoid and strange going on with him. I don't think he's gay, but there has to be some turbulence there. Maybe the excessive drinking comes out of that, too. Whatever it was with him, I never dug too deeply into it. I had a film to make and just hoped that he could control whatever demons he was fighting long enough to help me do my job. And he could, and did. I'd work with him again. In fact, Michael and I are currently talking about the possibility of doing *King Lear* together.

As for the relationship between Moriarty and De Niro, they got along perfectly fine during shooting. They were not friends exactly, and didn't hang out together after shooting, as Bobby would always go to batting practice and Michael would play wonderfully florid jazz piano in the bar. But as far as I know they never exchanged a harsh word. Interestingly, each one of them had their own particular fans on the crew. There were a lot of people who thought that Moriarty was the superior actor, but then there was another group that thought De Niro was better. These conflicting views continued on into post-production, but I don't think they ever personally responded to them. It was a rivalry created in the minds of others and did not originate from them. However, one thing that did occur before we started shooting was a big fight over billing. Although De Niro had a slightly smaller part as Bruce he would not accept second billing to Moriarty. I was surprised because I was so impressed by him as an artist that I thought it was a little unseemly. I would have anticipated that such a thing was beneath him, to be so concerned with billing. Was Bobby really going to turn the picture down if he couldn't have top billing? It seemed he was. Eventually someone worked out this strange agreement where one actor's name appeared on the lower left of the screen and the poster and the other actor's name appeared on the upper right. This arrangement seemed to satisfy both parties well enough, but I thought it was a little weird.

A lot of times when you are having trouble closing all the deals on a movie, as the director, you sometimes have to get on the phone yourself and try to get the actors to give in. You have to convince them to concede on something that they may be reluctant or unwilling to do. I did that in this case when they were at a total impasse, and there's no question about it, I did find Bobby to be surprisingly intractable when it came to the issue of billing. I didn't know it at the time, but this was my first taste of the person he would become. Of course, a year or two after *Bang the Drum Slowly*, Bobby became a major international movie star. Looking back—and I don't know if this is merely my imagination working in hindsight—but there was a sense of destiny and inevitably about Bob. You just knew that you were in the presence of a truly exceptional actor who, if luck smiled on him, might rise to the top of his profession. *Bang the Drum Slowly* was made the same year as *Mean Streets* and I believe the two pictures led to his playing the young Don Corleone in *The Godfather Part II*. Two such strong performances, in such different parts, for me and for Marty Scorsese, demonstrated an amazing range. *Bang the Drum Slowly* and *Mean Streets* played right next to each other at Cinema 1 and 2 on Third Avenue and 60th Street. They became a potent calling card for a young actor and I think a lot of people took notice of De Niro that year.

Vincent Gardenia came in to read for the role of Dutch Schnell when we were first beginning to cast, even before we were at the Warwick.

Maury and I instantly agreed that he was our guy. This time there was no debate, just unusual unanimity. Vince was so experienced and brought years of accomplished work in the theater to *Bang the Drum Slowly*. I had first seen him Off-Broadway in *Endgame* and some other things and he was always somebody I was eager to work with. He just knew exactly how to time things, his timing as an actor was extraordinary, and he was perfect for the part. What was most impressive about him was the fact I never told him *anything*. I never had to. Vincent didn't need directing. In that regard, he was a very easy actor to work with and it was a wonderful experience (I love not having to interfere). I was extremely happy with his performance and delighted when he was later nominated for an Academy Award as Best Supporting Actor. It was very much deserved, too. I mean, the wonderful scenes where Dutch delivers his idiosyncratic team talks are what probably secured Vincent that nomination. I love those scenes and I also love the scene where Dutch makes Bruce drop his pants as he thinks his medical problem is the clap, not Hodgkin's disease, due to Bruce fraternizing with his call-girl. I particularly adore the moment when Dutch cries, "She'll give it to the whole club! She'll run right around my infield!" I had originally wanted Charles Durning to play the supporting role of Dutch's right-hand man, Joe Jaros. Reading the book and the script, I kept seeing Charlie's face and hearing his voice in my mind. Charlie and I had always worked so well together, and he was a terrific actor, but he had another job and was unable to do the part. So, we started looking around for somebody else to play Jaros, and eventually settled (at Maury's insistence) on the comedian Phil Foster.

> *With principal photography scheduled to take place in May and June of 1972 at locations in Florida, Maine and New York, Hancock began assembling his crew. Hoping to entice a number of familiar faces to rejoin him on his next filmmaking adventure, the director roped in several alumni of* Let's Scare Jessica to Death *beginning with co-producer Bill Badalato, a move designed to combat the relative inexperience and unpredictability of the Rosenfields. Hancock also awarded supporting roles to his old friends Barton Heyman and Alan Manson, who essayed retired catcher Red Traphagen and the Mammoths' team medic Doc Loftus, respectively. He then selected Richard Shore, who had lensed Dan Curtis' atmospheric horror film*

> Night of Dark Shadows *(1971) the previous year, as his cinematographer.* Bang the Drum Slowly *would remain Shore's only other credit aside from a stint as "special lighting consultant" on the animated comedy* I Go Pogo *(1980).*

I chose Richard Shore because I liked him and, ultimately, I was happy with his work. Occasionally you make a decision on someone based on the question of whether or not you feel you will get on with them during shooting. A director's relationship with a cinematographer is vitally important on a personal level as well as a creative level as the first thing often informs the second. I thought Richard was somebody with whom I could get along. I do recall that he also had a rather good commercial reel and was clearly talented. Richard came to me on a recommendation by Dave Golden, who I had known since the days of the dead Greenwich Village movie written by Mark Fine. Also on Dave's list were Bob Bailin, the first DP on *Jessica*, the one I fired after the first week, Dick Kratina, who had operated on *Love Story*, and Dick Mingalone who went on to do wonderful hand-held as well as conventional operating for Woody Allen on a bunch of pictures. I'm not sure how Golden knew Shore, but his recommendation was good enough for me. Be that as it may, there were certain people after the picture opened who felt I could have made a better choice, and didn't mind letting me know it. For example, Stephen Bach at United Artists (who later came to grief with Michael Cimino on *Heaven's Gate*) openly told me, "I bet you wish you had somebody better, right?" I took that comment rather badly and replied, "No, I'm happy with my choice."

I must admit that I never rehired Shore again for another picture, although I did briefly consider him for *Jaws 2* when I was preparing that picture a few years later. That suggestion was swiftly shot down by the production designer on that movie, Joe Alves, who didn't feel Shore's work was of a high enough standard. I do agree that Shore's photography on *Bang the Drum Slowly* was a little conventional and the picture may have benefited from having a more emotive visual style. Back then, the cinematographers union was split between the coasts, and I could only have someone from the New York local—unless we were willing to pay a standby, which we weren't in any position to do. So wonderful West Coast cinematographers like Vilmos Zsigmond, Laszlo Kovacs, Conrad Hall, and Bill Fraker were not available to me. I tried to get Gordy Willis, he was out of New York, but he was busy. I then tried to get Arthur Ornitz, but he couldn't or wouldn't work for the money we had available. Boris Kaufman was another possibility. He had shot *On the Waterfront* and *Baby Doll* for Elia Kazan, and was probably the top guy at that point in the New York local. But I'd heard Kaufman was slow and old, and would be difficult with a relatively inexperienced director. I liked Shore better than Golden's other recommendations, so I hired him and stuck with him. And I'm glad I did. I'm not certain whatever happened to Shore. Maybe he went back to doing commercials.

I thought extensively about how I was going to cover the baseball sequences. I had watched a lot of baseball on television to see what kinds of lenses were being used. I also studied the angles the networks selected during the play, how they would basically cover the game and how much of the crowd was generally visible. I didn't want to duplicate the TV camera coverage because that would have been too static and mechanical, but I wanted to see how it was done and if there were any ideas we could borrow. I wanted to get down there with the team and find the emotion and the drama wherever possible, but a lot of that was about discovering the good moments. More than that, the whole problem with making a low-budget picture is that you have a limited time with a small number of extras. Thus, I deliberately chose to shoot in baseball parks where you don't often see a lot of people in the stands. I also selected longer lenses which minimized the number of people you saw behind the action. Again, I had the seventy-five extras for one day and just positioned them very carefully as we were composing our shots to make it look like there was a big crowd.

Another thing I had to consider was exactly how to shoot the baseball sequences in a way that was interesting and stirring. You see, baseball—in my humble opinion—is not as visually and editorially dynamic as some other major professional sports are. There are a lot of turgid pauses and waiting around and it isn't a real spectacle. It's fair to say that football, basketball, boxing and tennis all lend themselves far more easily to movement and action and speed than baseball does. Oddly enough, just as I had done on *Sticky My Fingers, Fleet My Feet*, I discovered that the use of slow-motion gave the baseball scenes an added weight and grace even though we were effectively slowing the action down even further. There are several fairly impressive slow-motion shots of Michael Moriarty throwing a baseball directly towards the camera that I like very much. What's odd is Michael had pitched in prep school, but he worked very hard to get better. We were shooting him pitching through a pane of plexiglass that was positioned in front of the camera. There came this astonishing moment when Michael threw the baseball so hard and so fast it actually broke the plexiglass right in front of the lens! I recall that took about seven takes to do, but you can't make a guy throw a ball too many times like that. Their arm and shoulder starts getting sore and you don't get what you need. It was a repeat of the same lesson I'd learned on *Sticky My Fingers* when I had tried to rehearse the shot and then shoot it a couple of times: the actors were too exhausted to do the plays again. So, I quickly learned that you had to be very careful and parcel out these moments. The actors were non-athletes and didn't have an incredible amount of stamina and energy. They'd get aching limbs and stomach cramps and shortness of breath, and there was always a finite number of takes we could do.

You may also notice there are a couple of stock footage shots that we incorporated into certain montages. We needed a little more action happening in one or two sequences and so we acquired some baseball footage from a couple of Mets and Yankees games, as well as the shots of the ground crew covering the field with tarp during a rain delay. This stuff came from various sources, mostly stock houses that sent us material to screen, and we then selected what worked best with the footage we had shot. I think the stock footage is integrated successfully, although you can sometimes visibly detect a small degradation in the quality of the film itself. It can be hard to incorporate stock footage into a movie as you can often see that it's slightly grainier and the colors are different. But it still works. It's sometimes wonderful to have stuff in your movie that you could not have created with the limited means and resources available to you. For a long time audiences have been used to seeing movies that have a juxtaposition of various foreign images of assorted grain, color and texture. They seem to accept it, ignore it, or perhaps not even notice it at all.

I should also mention that we rehearsed for four weeks, which was a lot of rehearsal time. Before we started shooting, every morning we would send the actors to Central Park in order to work out. We hired a guy named Del Bethel, who at one time had been a Major League Baseball player, and he taught them the rudiments of the game: how to field, how to bat and how to pitch. So, the actors would train with Del for three hours every morning and we would then rehearse them for three or four hours every afternoon. On all the films I've done since *Bang the Drum Slowly*, I've rehearsed as much as I could get people to pay for as I think it's invaluable. In this case we wanted the actors to really inhabit their characters in a very physical way. They had to think the part as much as look the part.

Incidentally, the baseball uniforms that the actors wore were, I believe, bought from the Yankees and altered with the Mammoths insignia on the chest by our costume designer, Domingo Rodriguez. After the rehearsal period was over and principal photography had commenced, we shot *Bang the Drum Slowly* for about forty days in total. We shot a day in Maine during pre-production for the exterior scene where Bruce and Arthur are coming out of what was the Mayo Clinic. We then shot in Clearwater, Florida, and lived in a hotel there that is now a Scientology building. All the various hotel rooms that Bruce and Arthur find themselves in were sets that we built in a banquet room inside our lodgings. We then shot the spring baseball camp scenes down in Clearwater, at the Carpenter Complex, the Philadelphia Phillies' training facility. After we finished there, we moved the company up to New York and shot at Shea Stadium and Yankee Stadium.

As far as I remember, the actors didn't come up with any new lines during the rehearsals and instead stuck closely to the script. At this stage, we were simply trying to get the actors to understand what the scenes were and how their characters would fit into them, and I was planning how to block things. We had tape on the floor in the rehearsal room like you do for a play, and substitute furniture and props, so I could plan how I was going to shoot things. We were also still trying to cut certain things out, but that proved to be difficult for certain reasons—namely Maury and his unwavering reverence for the material. So, we went ahead and shot the script as it was and then shaped the story in the editing room. However, during shooting there was some improvisation. In truth, some of the things I'm proudest of in the film were improvised. For instance, the very funny little tegwar game that takes place towards the end of the film—tegwar being "The Exciting Game Without Any Rules," which, through misleading gibberish, is designed to separate a sucker from his cash—was an addition. I love the fact that the guys don't let Bruce win despite his terminal diagnosis. I thought that moment acted as a wonderful counterpoint to the fact that the whole team adores him now. It's like, okay, Bruce is truly one of the guys but if there's money involved—forget about it! As a game without rules, tegwar was also a useful analogy for the game of life and the idea that Bruce had indeed been "handed a shit deal," to quote his distraught father.

Other moments that were largely improvised involved all the stuff that occurred in and out of the dugout during that final game. I had two cameras and just rolled them simultaneously. I basically said, "Okay, it's next inning now, out on the field! Okay, it's back to the dugout. Okay, it's back to the field. Okay, it's back to the dugout," and so on. That continued until I got exactly what I needed. I mean, it was all effectively one long shot that I then broke into pieces. I think it's the simple staging of those scenes that felt so natural because, by this point, it was towards the end of the shoot and all the actors were totally into their roles. They were comfortable with their characters, and with each other, and they knew exactly how to do it. The shot I talked about earlier where the team is celebrating after the big win and they go back for Bruce—that whole shot was entirely improvised. It's probably the thing I'm proudest of in my film work and it's not something I was directly responsible for. It was pure luck; creating an environment and just letting things happen organically. A lot of it was the camera operator simply following the action as it was unfolding, trying to capture it, trying to find the good moments.

> *A diverting moment in* Bang the Drum Slowly *features Wiggen, Pearson and a select number of their team-mates performing the song "Please Excuse My Tears" (known alternately as "Look Before You Weep") on a TV show as "The Singing Mammoths." Written by Orville Stoeber, the composer revealed in a 2015 interview with Fox Sports that Hancock had wanted him to essay the role of guitar-playing catcher Piney Woods but admitted he was "too fucked up" to take the part (it eventually went to character actor Tom Ligon). However, he did accept the director's invitation to appear onscreen as the long-haired guitarist who accompanies the men.* Bang the Drum Slowly *would mark the third official collaboration between Hancock and Stoeber following* Sticky My Fingers *and* Let's Scare Jessica to Death, *and he would later work on the scores for* Weeds, A Piece of Eden *and* The Looking Glass. *The "Singing Mammoths" sequence was filmed at Shea Stadium on the set of "Kiner's Korner," the popular post-game interview show that followed every home game by the New York Mets. Hosted by broadcaster and Hall of Famer Ralph Kiner, the program was first broadcast in 1963 on WOR TV (Channel 9) and is affectionately remembered by viewers to this day.*

I adore the musical interlude in the picture. I can watch it all day. I forgot that we shot the sequence at Shea Stadium. My memory told me we did it in a little television studio on the high floor of a building in the West Fifties. Incidentally, I feel I must add that Ralph Kiner was actually one of the people responsible for my boyhood heartbreak with baseball. He was a slugger for the Pittsburgh Pirates and I was an avid supporter of the Chicago Cubs. Year after year, the Cubs would be last in the National League, and the Pirates next to last. One year it seemed that the Cubs might pass them and get out of the basement, but in the last few games of the season Kiner got hot and the Pirates passed the Cubs. I've never taken a huge interest since. I do think De Niro is particularly amusing in the "Singing Mammoths" scene. It plays so perfectly with all the guys singing and dancing in unison, and then Bruce goes off on his very own awkward-looking but enthusiastic little jig. It's just wonderful.

The shooting of that sequence went very smoothly and was a lot of fun to do. The actors were all really into it and they did a good job. I thought it was only right that Orville—being the guy who wrote that song and also did several of the interesting tracks that appear in *Bang the Drum Slowly*—should appear as the guitar player in the sequence. He played the song to the actors, and they learned all the lyrics and just went for it. In reality Orville's hair is probably a little too long for him to be a professional ballplayer, but it was the early 1970s and nearly everybody had long hair. I do seem to remember there was some reluctance on his part to cut his beautiful hair. So, we left him intact. Orville is a guy I've worked with forever and I've mostly enjoyed our many collaborations. I say *mostly* because every once in a while he is a little crazy! But dealing with Orville at his most insane is still a picnic in comparison to handling Maury Rosenfield.

For instance, a lot of people like the "Singing Mammoths" scene and remember it fondly, but the truth is I had to fight to keep it in the movie. It's another pertinent example of the difficulties that would suddenly arise with Maury. As the producer, he was determined to cut that scene out. He absolutely *hated* it and wanted it gone. The way I dealt with this was to say that I wanted to eliminate the whole plot-line involving Katie, the madam played by Ann Wedgeworth, who is trying to cajole Arthur into making her the beneficiary of Bruce's will. That suggestion immediately drove Maury crazy, as I knew it would. He loved all that stuff and wanted it retained. So, after some careful discussions, I got to keep the "Singing Mammoths" if I also kept the scenes with the madam. You see, it was all a game. By this time, I had worked out a few strategies in order to get what I wanted, but none of it came easy. This was not like my dealings with the Mosses on *Let's Scare Jessica to Death*. When the Mosses had suggested I include a séance scene in the movie and the young girl in white, those contributions were made during open and friendly discussions; there was an easy exchange of ideas and opinions. There was also a motive behind the suggestions, although, admittedly, it was sometimes lost on me. But on *Bang the Drum Slowly*, my discussions with Maury were not always as constructive. Maury would often couch his comments in authoritative phrases like, "This is what *I* want!" That's more of a demand or a dictum than an exchange. I had already learned from my time directing theater how to deal with strong personalities and difficult energies without burning the whole house down around me. I'd figured out when to be firm and fight my corner, and when to back down and toe the line a little more.

Believe it or not, another bone of contention between Maury and me—aside from my use of close-ups—was Robert De Niro's hair. Bobby had a kind of 1950s wave which was so wonderful. He really hit it on the nose with that hairstyle, but Maury would repeatedly complain, "Oh, *look* at him! He's just not attractive!" Now, I should mention that we had already shot for two weeks with this hairstyle, but that didn't matter to Maury. He insisted, "I don't care! We have to change De Niro's hair or I'm shutting down production and we can't go forward!" It was always like that with Maury: if I didn't meet his demands immediately (however ludicrous or unreasonable they might be) he would threaten to shut the whole picture down. It was made clear to me that if I didn't do exactly what he required done, it would all be over. I tried to explain to Maury the idea of continuity and the importance of shots matching with each other, but he said, "What do you mean? People get different haircuts all the time. Why won't it match?" I said, "Well, it's like this: I am sitting here and there's a shot of me, okay? Then we cut to a shot of you that was filmed at one time. Then we cut back to another shot of me that was filmed on another day and I suddenly have a different hairstyle from a few seconds ago. Do you understand how problematic that will be?" Maury said, "Oh, okay. Well, I still want De Niro's hairstyle changed or otherwise I'm shutting down. So, you have to do it *now*!"

I then had a difficult conversation with Bobby where I relayed Maury's order to him. I said, "Look, Bob, I'm very sorry but we're going to have to change your hair or this picture is finished." De Niro wasn't happy about that at all and he just looked at me like, "*What*? Are you serious?

I can't believe this." Anyway, despite our protests, we did indeed change Bobby's hairstyle. But it was like that all the time with Maury. Every single day there would be some kind of crazy idea that we had to implement and that continued on throughout the whole editing phase, too. The thing I always accepted about Maury's odd behavior was that some of it was coming from the intense passion he had for Harris' novel and a desire to do it justice on film. But he was often wrong. Despite our disagreements, the fact of the matter was Maury had the money and, most important of all, he didn't fire me.

To this day, Bill Badalato always retells the same three anecdotes about his experience working with Maury and Lois Rosenfield on *Bang the Drum Slowly*: the first concerns Bill having to drive Mark Harris to the airport after "the gruesome twosome"—as Badalato refers to them—had him removed from the production. Bill commends Harris for being feisty and fearless in response to Maury's irrational behavior and considers Maury a coward for what he did that day. From my own memory of these events, I believe Maury wanted to get rid of Mark because he was siding with me. After the whole problem of me shooting close-ups arose, Mark would say, "Leave him alone, he knows what he's doing." Things like that. Maury also forbade us to use any location that was more than half an hour from the hotel. Not dumb, but Mark agreed with me that in certain cases it was too limiting. So, it was a whole range of things and, as I think about it, I believe Mark spoke to the issue directly, and told Maury, "You're a businessman. You have no business interfering to this degree in artistic matters." Maury's reply to that was simply: "*Out!*" He threw Harris off the set and banished him from the location. The truth is Maury didn't want me to have an ally—it was bad enough that Badalato and I were close— and probably felt that the artists were ganging up on him. The second story Bill likes to recount about the production concerns the time Maury asked an actor why wardrobe had to provide him with shoes when he could come to work in his own. The third story, which Bill repeated to me only recently, was his confession that he used to love watching Lois drool over the young lads we were reading for the various roles. Bill suspected that Lois hadn't seen the physical attentions of her husband in decades and remembers the pair of them as "awful people" who didn't really "suffer enough in this lifetime."

> Bang the Drum Slowly *culminates with Bruce's eventual collapse which leads to Dutch and the members of the*

> team learning the devastating truth of his illness. They rally around Bruce, who clearly draws strength from their support and he begins making a temporary recovery. The misfortune that has stricken their colleague seems to act as the cohesive force in bringing the Mammoths together, and they deliver a run of stunning victories with Bruce playing an integral role in one triumph over a Pittsburgh team. All the same, Bruce suddenly becomes too ill to continue playing and takes leave of his team-mates, before heading for his parents' home in Georgia. This leads to an emotional farewell with Arthur at the airport and a somber denouement in which we see that Bruce has died and Wiggen was one of his pallbearers.

I've heard it said that the ending of the film seems to be building towards Bruce dying onscreen, but we always wanted his death to occur off-screen. It was the same approach as the book if I remember correctly, with Bruce dying in the midst of such a triumphant victory, a championship season. *Bang the Drum Slowly* was a novel I loved and I tried to be resolutely truthful to it. When I later read *The New York Times* review, it actually commented that the movie was a faithful adaptation of a wonderful book, and that's exactly what I tried to do. I strived to be honorable to the elegance of Harris' story and the integrity of his characters. I thought it was better to not have Bruce suffering through the final death agonies onscreen and instead just let it happen, and he is suddenly gone. Our approach did have a certain coldness to it, but I thought that was okay. I mean, *Bang the Drum Slowly* is a very sentimental picture, so you have to make sure that you keep a small element of remoteness in one or two instances, of emotional distance. You take a conscious step back because you don't want to get too sloppy and maudlin. I think Harris understood this, too. For example, the team doesn't send a representative to Bruce's funeral. That's a difficult thing for some people to accept, particularly since Pearson has now wormed his way into everybody's affections. But it also seems very authentic to me, too.

It would have been very easy for me to have concluded the picture with Bruce dying in a bed, surrounded by his weeping parents and distraught team-mates, and Arthur gently holding his hand as he passes. That would have been an obvious and conventional scene to do, and as such would have been a disappointment. Although a sense of the inevitable can be deeply satisfying in drama, I think Harris was right to end the book and the screenplay as he did. I personally prefer the slightly more understated and restrained emotionalism of Arthur and Bruce's final farewell at the airport, because what isn't being said between those two men is perhaps more meaningful and powerful than saying everything explicitly. That's why I did not want to do some overtly sentimental death scene. I could have easily shot a scene where the two guys declare their love for each other and then Bruce peacefully winks out and everybody starts wailing. The prospect of shooting something like that did not interest me at all because we've seen it a million times before and since in countless tearjerkers.

The airport goodbye scene seems more realistic to me as Bruce and Arthur both know they will not be seeing each other ever again. All the emotion is in Moriarty's face and in De Niro's face; it's in their eyes, their voices. That's why I really love the dissolve from Bruce boarding the plane to the shot of Arthur walking away from Bruce's grave in the cemetery after his funeral. It's so matter of fact, it doesn't give the audience the death scene that many of them were expecting and perhaps wanting. It's not mawkish as again nobody from the Mammoths even attends the funeral. Of course, they do send flowers. Another thing I love about the ending is Moriarty's famous final line: "From here on in, I rag nobody." It's so totally off the wall but it also feels like another little nugget of athlete wisdom, with all the limited life awareness that such a statement reveals. That was also the last line of Harris' book, too, which has to be one of the greatest closing sentences in modern American literature. The fact that it's delivered as a voiceover gives it a certain poignancy. I had used a voiceover on *Sticky My Fingers, Fleet My Feet*, and to more adventurous effect on *Let's Scare Jessica to Death*, and I would also use it briefly again on my next picture, *Baby Blue Marine*. Arthur's voiceover—which also bookends the movie—was a good way to push some of the themes and emotions, but there was always a danger of overstating what was already inherent in the story. Again, Harris' novel was written from the first-person perspective of Arthur and he used that same voice in his script. But there's something genuinely moving about the whole conclusion of the book and the movie which doesn't feel forced or exploitative. It rings very true for me because, ultimately, life goes on.

I ordered flowers for the funeral scene without having Maury's financial go-ahead. It was probably not smart on my part, but I was busy with a million things. Surely, we had to have flowers for a funeral and I didn't think he could possibly object. But as soon as he learned what I had done, he confronted me about it. I quickly said, "Look, Maury, don't worry. I'll pay for the flowers." And you know what? He *did* make me pay for the flowers! He actually took the money out of my salary! Can you believe that? Being an attorney, I knew going in that Maury was always going to be attentive to the small details, but this was ridiculous. The standard in the industry is when they bitch about something, the director says "Fuck it, I'll pay for it," but they don't in the end make him pay. Not Maury! Many years later, in 1996, nearly a quarter of a century after we made *Bang the Drum Slowly*, I called up Maury and said, "Hey, why don't we have lunch?" Maury warmly welcomed that suggestion and he took me to his club in Chicago. As we were sitting there together, reminiscing, I said, "Well, Maury, we had our disagreements, but we certainly made one hell of a picture." He then regarded me carefully for a moment, his eyes narrowing slightly as he spoke in a voice choked with rage: "What about the flowers in the cemetery scene?" I could not fucking believe it! Maury was still sore about the flowers after twenty-five years! Oh, but that was great. I'll never forget those words and, despite everything bad and unsavory that went on back when we were making the film, it still makes me laugh when I think about it today. But that was Maury Rosenfield for you. If anything, that one moment captured who and what he was right there.

It's interesting and perhaps illuminating to add that Maury only possesses one more feature film credit to his name aside from *Bang the Drum Slowly*: the science fiction film *Wavelength*, which was released a decade later in 1983. The reason why he didn't produce more movies? Well, I can only speculate about it. Speaking from my own fraught experience with him, I can say the guy was pretty damn crazy. There's simply no denying that fact. Maury did go on to produce a Broadway musical or two in later years, such as *Barnum*, and enjoyed some success, but he was a difficult and distracting force to contend with. I'm sure that did not go unnoticed by others he worked with. Indeed, one final problem we had was to do with our relative credits as they appear on the screen. Maury wanted his name last. He felt that due to his contribution as the financer and everything he deserved it—even though it is entirely in contradiction to the way things are done in the industry, where the director's name always comes last just before the picture starts. Maury was adamant, as he was about many things, so I went to the Directors Guild of America and they said they would put a lock on the editing room door unless he immediately desisted. He did.

Post-production on Bang the Drum Slowly *commenced in the summer of 1972. The composer hired for the film was Stephen Lawrence, whose only previous credits were the little-seen comedies* Jennifer on My Mind *(1971) and* I Am Waiting No More *(1972). Lawrence would go on to score* Dragonfly *(1976),* Alice Sweet Alice *(1976), and* Mirrors *(1978) before maintaining a steady if unspectacular career in television. Hancock also secured the services of talented sound engineer Richard Vorisek, who later won an Academy Award for his work on* Reds *(1981), and editor Richard Marks, who would subsequently cut such acclaimed films as* Serpico *(1973),* The Godfather Part II *(1974),* Apocalypse Now *(1979),* Terms of Endearment *(1984) and* As Good as It Gets *(1997), securing no less than four Oscar nominations along the way.*

Richie Marks was just starting out as an editor back then, so I think *Bang the Drum Slowly* was one of his first pictures. He had been one of Dede Allen's top assistants (Dede having cut such highly regarded films as *Bonnie & Clyde, Dog Day Afternoon* and *Reds*) and came to us on her recommendation. We got along entirely and worked very closely. I was there the whole time. We would look at everything before we cut a sequence, choose the best takes, and then set out to cut it together. There was trust on both sides and I don't recall us ever having a single disagreement. You know, sometimes editing rooms can become very unpleasant places, small areas charged with hatred. Not here. Maybe Maury being so crazy helped with that, too, like it did on the set. He would call every afternoon with some strange request—like wanting to cut the "Singing Mammoths" scene—and I felt I had Richie's sympathy for having to field the call. He had my back and I had his.

One of the things I liked about Richie was the fact he didn't take lunch. Maybe I'm a monster, but I like people that work. He and I just had quick sandwiches and kept on going. I also liked the fact that he didn't spend a lot of time on the phone like I understand Dede often did. It was all business for us in that editing room, and we knew we were doing something good. Richie directly called my attention to two great moments in the footage: what Bobby is doing as the camera closes in on him in the locker room while Piney Woods is singing "Streets of Laredo," and, again, what Bobby is doing as he gazes skyward, dazed, and looking for that pop-up which ends the last game. Richie had a more powerful reaction to those moments than I did, and I'm glad he did, because they are two of the best things in the picture. Now, was it clear to me that Richie would go on to have such a big career? I surely thought it was possible because he was so good, but luck plays a huge role and you just never know. I did immediately know from our collaboration that I wanted to work with him again in a heartbeat.

Dick Vorisek mixed the picture, as he had *Let's Scare Jessica to Death*, and did a great job. We found places in the last game to pull the crowd sound down to good effect. Sudden quiet can be so effective. The relationship between a director and the lead mixer is as important as his relationship with his director of photography. He is a key creative element, and Vorisek was certainly one, and on so many great pictures. We cut *Bang the Drum Slowly* at a film building that had offices and editing suites on the upper floors (Aram Avakian was cutting *The Godfather* down the hall from us) and camera equipment on the first. It might have been The DuArt Building on 245 West 55th Street, but I'm not certain. I know it was two or three blocks south of 20th Century Fox because that's where we tended to have our screenings—and we had a lot of them! There was an inexpensive restaurant on the first floor where we would have meetings with prospective composers and things like that. I remember that one day the cabaret singer and pianist Bobby Short came in for an interview. Short was Maury's idea to score the picture and I looked on as he proceeded to order two vanilla malts for lunch, and nothing else. He was probably trying to cure a hangover. Needless to say, we did not hire Bobby Short.

I must be honest and admit that Steve Lawrence was not my choice for composer either. He was again Maury Rosenfield's choice. I had wanted Orville Stoeber to do the music because of our previous associations on my earlier films. Maury didn't want Orville simply because he was my guy and so he instead proposed Aaron Copland. Maury's view was, "Great American game, great American story, great American composer." I love Copland's music, and knew him a little through Harold Clurman, but I didn't really want him. We already had our principal melody from the folk song "Streets of Laredo," and it's not always a good idea to hire a major composer as you can't control them. They serve themselves, not the picture, and you're stuck with what they do. Take, for example, Leonard Bernstein's score for *On the Waterfront*: it's way over the top in my opinion. It's hard to argue with a picture that won the Academy Award of course, and I love everything else about it, but I wonder if Elia Kazan liked what he got from Bernstein. He may have.

Fortunately, Copland wasn't available. So, Maury found Steve Lawrence instead and I don't remember how. At first, I thought Lawrence too conventional, a bit of a hack perhaps. That was unfair on my part but I took it badly that I couldn't have the guy I wanted, and maybe I held that against him. But you can't win every battle on a movie and I had other fish to fry with Maury. So, I set to work with Lawrence in good faith, spotting the picture, giving feedback to his proposed cues when he presented them in dummy form, and so forth. I think we worked pretty well together in spite of my misgivings. I like working with composers, it's easily my favorite part of the filmmaking process. Then came the recording sessions, when I was initially a little disappointed by the conventionality of his orchestrations. I remember a composer friend I'd worked with a lot in the theater, Joe Raposo, of *Nashville, Sesame Street* and *A Man's a Man* fame, stopping by the full orchestra session on some errand of his own, and taking me aside. Joe made faces listening to Steve's opening cue, trying to get the job away from him. I mean, there is very little collegial honor among composers in my experience. However, this ploy didn't work as the die was cast.

But, you know, in the end it didn't work out too badly. What I did was bring Orville in by himself at later sessions of my own—late at night, the studio time paid for by me—to lay down layers of overdubs on his guitar. Orville made it richer; gave the cues feeling. Like especially that slow motion sequence at the end of the big game when they're all congratulating each other: that's Orville wailing away over what Lawrence did. It caught perfectly the bittersweet feeling I love so much. And then too, in a number of places, I came to feel that Steve didn't do so badly by himself. The heavy tympani on the pop-up where Bobby is staggering around trying to see it and catch it, but is too confused and sick—that's all Lawrence, and it's wonderful. I've even come to like the cue over the opening titles, the very one where Raposo made faces. As a matter of fact, I recently screened *Bang the Drum Slowly* for the incoming class at the new Harold Ramis Film School at Second City, where I teach. It was the first time I had seen the film in its entirety for a number of years. I'm happy to report that I liked Lawrence's score much better than I remembered. For instance, I had forgotten about the wonderful banjo stuff that he did. Steve used the same banjo player behind the famous "Dueling Banjos" sequence in *Deliverance*, Arthur "Guitar Boogie" Smith. So, I've recently revised my opinion of Steve's score and I think I've been a little unfair to him.

Released on August 26, 1973, Bang the Drum Slowly *was greeted with instant and near-unanimous acclaim by critics. Roger Ebert lauded it as "the ultimate baseball movie," citing Hancock's facility with actors and comparing his efficiency for "establishing a lot of supporting characters without making a point of it" to the work of Robert Altman. Writing for* The New York Times *Roger Greenspun suggested the picture was "one of those rare instances in which close adaptation of a good book has resulted in possibly an even better movie," adding that "its chief quality is not its pathos, but its beautiful, perhaps heroic, tact." In his review for* TIME *Magazine, Richard Schickel echoed these sentiments, calling Hancock's film, "A funny, gentle and honestly sentimental movie that is easily one of the best of the year in any category, and very possibly the best movie about sport ever made in this country."* Bang the Drum Slowly *would later be recognized during the awards season, with Vincent Gardenia earning an Academy Award nomination for Best Supporting Actor and Robert De Niro winning the New York Film Critics Circle Award for Best Actor.*

The AFI had organized a gala screening of the picture at the Kennedy Center, and it was one of the highlights of my life, actually. Paramount picked Ann and me up in Sneden's Landing with a limo and drove us to the airport, then flew us to Washington. Another limo, a fancy hotel. The Kennedy Center was packed, brimming with senators, cabinet people and Kennedys. They showed *Sticky My Fingers* first, and then *Bang the Drum Slowly*. We got huge laughs for the first which carried over wonderfully to the feature. It was as if it could do no wrong. A lot of times I see my work and I just see the flaws, but this time all I saw was how good it was. And as *Bang the Drum Slowly* moved to its bittersweet conclusion, I got the most intense feeling in my throat. I've had it several other times, not often, but I remember feeling it at a really good performance of *A Midsummer Nights's Dream* in San Francisco. I don't know how to describe it, but it's the feeling I'm working for, and have been my whole life, and when I get it, everything is worthwhile.

I was used from the theater to getting a good amount of personal press, and I had been surprised on *Let's Scare Jessica to Death* when that didn't happen: they reviewed the picture, but there were few interviews with me. I didn't want that to happen again on *Bang the Drum Slowly*, so I discussed the problem with my director friend, Mike Ritchie. He said, "You can't rely on the studio publicists, you have to employ your own." Mike was right. I went to John Springer, who was really the top guy in the business at that point and represented the likes of Elizabeth Taylor, Warren Beatty, and so forth, as well as the AFI. A real gentleman, he agreed to take me on without payment until I could afford to pay. I think he'd done the same for Warren. Anyway, Springer made a great deal of difference in my subsequent career. He had the contacts and called in the favors on my behalf, so there were lots of interviews. Besides, he introduced me to Fred Zinnemann, another of his clients and the director of *From Here to Eternity* and *A Man For All Seasons*, whose work I adored. Springer represented me for years, and yes, I paid him well eventually.

The reviews for *Bang the Drum Slowly* were just about the best I've ever seen. Honestly, if I could have written those notices myself they probably would not have been half as positive and praising. Frankly, the picture was called so many great things I blushed! Oddly enough, I recently re-read some of the reviews—this is something I'm actively trying to give up—and seeing those responses again is still mind-blowing for me. If I'm not mistaken, Richard Schickel cited A.E. Houseman's poem to "To an Athlete Dying Young" in his review, which I felt was quite appropriate. The fact Schickel called it the best movie about sport made in America is something I'll always cherish. I remember Maury was also incredibly thrilled with the reviews. He was very pleased with the film, ultimately, despite his various problems with close-ups and hair and flowers, and everything else he had a bug up his ass about. Maury knew in his heart we had made a good movie and the reviews merely confirmed it for him. Or maybe he really didn't know it after all and needed that fact proved to him.

The film opened big in New York, where people read reviews, but as it spread across the country the box office was unfortunately not quite as stellar as the reviews. Still, it made good money. Paramount really sold *Bang the Drum Slowly* with a good promotional campaign. I remember the studio had a PR guy that I spent a lot of time with, discussing the movie and what we could do to really sell it. This individual was a bright and attentive guy, who had good ideas. They took lots of full page ads with those great quotes all across the country. I wasn't aware while I was doing the picture that the baseball theme might not travel well overseas in those countries where the game isn't played or isn't popular, or that it would ever be a problem. But, undoubtedly, it should have occurred to me. So, in the end I don't know that *Bang the Drum Slowly* played much in foreign territories, especially not theatrically. I believe very, very little. Despite this, Paramount was extremely happy with the picture and Frank Yablans continued to be a big supporter of mine. He really seemed to like my work and was behind a very lucrative development deal I secured soon after with the studio to make a picture called *Ruby Red*.

From my own perspective, I was very proud of the film and always have been. I love it when I hear certain people say it's their "favorite picture ever made," like Al Pacino in *The New York Times*, Kim Williamson in *Box Office Magazine* and Frank DeFord on *National Public Radio*. There are aspects of *Bang the Drum Slowly* that I'm not particularly happy with. I do look at it now and there are some things I'd like to change. Of course, that response is not unusual. I would pick up the pace in certain areas, but pace has changed over these past forty-something years so maybe I'm being unfair. I'd also possibly concede that the film doesn't portray the female characters as well or as roundly as some of the males. Yes, the owner of the Mammoths is a woman as opposed to the men who are often depicted as such figures, but there is Katie the madam and all the ugly business about Bruce's will. That was all in Harris' novel and it was all preserved. I don't feel I can be hung for saying this, but you do get a lot of women groupies, gold-diggers, hangers-on, and whatever else, floating around professional sportsmen. That's generally an accepted fact, is it not? And I suppose we might have made a little more use of Arthur's wife, Holly, played by Heather MacRae, although, again, *Bang the Drum Slowly* is really a story about men and male relationships.

So, yeah, there are times when I see the picture and all I see are the things I missed, the things I didn't get or didn't finesse. Then there are other times when I've seen the movie with an enthusiastic crowd and those same things just seem wonderful to me (and I get that aforementioned feeling in my throat). Or I'll suddenly notice new things I hadn't appreciated before. For instance, there's an interesting scene that takes place early in the film when Bruce is at his parents' house and he burns all the clippings and photographs celebrating his early career achievements. It's a puzzling scene. I suppose Bruce is thinking, "So, it's all come to *this*." Interestingly, when Dorothy's father died, her mother burnt all the photos of him; tore the ones in half where they were together and burnt his half. She was demented, but clearly felt betrayed by his dying. Bruce may be feeling his whole life, including high school stardom, is betrayed by what he's just learned. So, one's response to a movie can be a curious and evolving thing, the way one's opinion fluctuates. My relationships with some of my movies has shifted and changed over the years, but I do love *Bang the Drum Slowly*. I find my mind often drifts back to the time we made it. I was actually thinking as I woke up this morning about an afternoon we had in that rehearsal space in New York, when I first got the idea how good it was going to be. I think we were rehearsing the scenes with De Niro, Moriarty and Vincent Gardenia, where Dutch is questioning his players. Bobby was just so fucking good!

In the picture, one character briefly remarks that "baseball is a dying game," and *Bang the Drum Slowly* may indeed capture a nostalgic time in our history when the sport still meant something important to us. Personally, I believe that baseball still occupies a place of relevance and meaning in American life and culture, but I do think it has now been surpassed by football in terms of popularity and significance. People no longer regard baseball to be the national game in the way that almost sacred view of the sport existed in the 1930s and 1940s, all the way through to the early 1960s. I tend to believe that those golden days are gone, but they could return one day. You never know. I do think that Harris' novel has a quality of a lost past about it, which was perhaps more resonant in 1955 than it was in 1973, but, again, it's not outdated. The story is a timeless one even though it's rooted in traditional relationships and attitudes because these things survive in some form or another. That is why the movie still has legs. You could release *Bang the Drum Slowly* tomorrow and it would still speak to us and tell us something important.

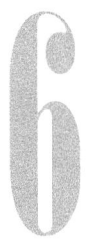

Baby Blue Marine (1976)

FOLLOWING THE ASTONISHING critical plaudits heaped on Bang the Drum Slowly, *Hancock was now, in his own words, "as hot as a pistol." Suddenly thrown into the enviable position of being one of the industry's most visible rising talents, the thirty-three-year-old filmmaker immediately began exploiting his newfound acclaim and connections in any—and every—conceivable way. While heartedly indulging in the assorted delights of the Hollywood social scene, Hancock was still preoccupied with the more serious business of maintaining the upward trajectory of his career. This proved to be more difficult than he had anticipated, as in the three years that would elapse before his next picture* Baby Blue Marine *saw the light of a projector, his name would be associated with a plethora of unrealized projects. These would include a number of absorbing film adaptations of literary works by such diverse authors as Stendhal (*The Charterhouse of Parma*), Dick Francis (*Forfeit*), William Price Fox (*Ruby Red*) and Robert L. Duncan (*The Day the Sun Fell*). Frustration and regret would also trouble Hancock on a personal level with his eight-year marriage to Ann Arensberg experiencing increasing strain and eventually coming to a painful end in early 1974.*

My first taste of how life was going to change for me came in Nantucket. Ann and I had rented a house there for a couple of weeks next to my life-long friend and lawyer Alan Schwartz. I was enjoying surf-casting for striped bass and talking with Peter Schaffer, the brilliant British playwright and screenwriter that had written *The Royal Hunt of the Sun*, *Equus* and *Amadeus*, who was staying with Alan. While we were there, two producers from Los Angeles flew to the island in an attempt to talk me into directing a screenplay they were developing. It was a shock to suddenly be courted like that. We had lunch, and I liked them, but not the material they were offering. So, I turned it down and they flew off. During the time we were in Nantucket, I flew back to New York once by myself for a couple of days to meet with Howard Hausman, my agent at William Morris, and do a press interview that John Springer had set up. I also took the opportunity while I was alone in Sneden's Landing to have dinner with my beautiful neighbor Dorothy Tristan (hmmm, *bad* John, but what the hell). I didn't get anywhere with her, unfortunately. Dorothy said I was married and that she was a friend of my wife. Okay, fine. But things were looking rather more promising with my agent.

I gathered my career was heating up as a print of *Bang the Drum Slowly* had made the circuit of private screenings in Bel Air. Ray Stark, the producer of *Funny Girl*, *The Way We Were* and a lot of other big pictures, had hosted a particularly successful one with his client Barbra Streisand and several other notables in attendance. These private screenings can be brutal—there's almost an obligation to make snotty remarks—but at this one, Ray later told me, there was just stunned silence, laughter and tears. Afterwards, Howard Hausman was very excited, working late, fielding calls from the coast, and dutifully hustling for me. Peter Lampack, then a young agent at Morris, joked that it was wonderful for Howard, "just like the old days." While I was in New York, I also saw my analyst who was back from the Hamptons—it was late August when analysts return. He said that he'd overheard a conversation about me on the beach conducted by some "very important people in the business," he claimed. Maddeningly, my analyst would not reveal to me exactly who it was. I *hate* not to be told things, but, despite my urgings, he wouldn't relent. However, I was assured that what these people were saying was apparently all good.

I then returned to Nantucket where, encouraged by all the good things that seemed to be happening for me, Peter Shaffer and I cooked up a scheme to try and interest studios in a film adaptation of one of our favorite novels, Stendhal's *The Charterhouse of Parma*. The book details the life and times of a young, headstrong Italian nobleman named Fabrice del Dongo. A devoted supporter of Napoleon, he fights in the Battle of Waterloo before returning to Parma where he has several adventures and eventually retires to the Carthusian monastery—the "Charterhouse" of the title—and dies. It's another project that never happened, and was probably too ambitious, but I bet it would have been good because Peter was an incredible writer. You only have to look at *Equus* and *Amadeus* to know that. In truth, looking back on it, we didn't make much progress on how we would actually make such a massive story work as a movie. It was more about us just sharing our love of the novel, and discussing our favorite moments in it. For instance, one important question was raised: were we going to recreate the Battle of Waterloo? I don't remember the answer. I hoped we weren't—not at any great length anyhow.

We did want to center on the triangle in the narrative, the love between Fabrice and his wonderful aunt Gina, and Gina's involvement with Count Mosca, the Machiavellian prime minister of Parma who assists and eventually marries her (Peter and I both saw George C. Scott in the role of the Count). The sequences where Fabrice attempts to escape from his imprisonment in the Farnese Tower, the tallest tower in the city, where he has been detained after killing a man in a fight, would have certainly worked, but we pondered how exactly to fuse it with the character stuff. We weren't sure yet. These were dreams I had while lying on the beach, staring at the Atlantic. I must have still been on Nantucket when *Bang the Drum Slowly* opened in New York because I remember Donny Graham calling me at two o'clock in the morning, all excited and reading me that incredible rave in *The New York Times*. Donny told me he didn't think I'd mind being woken up to hear such a thing. I insisted I wasn't and asked him how he got hold of the review. He said, "We have ways here at *The Washington Post*!" I was thrilled, but then went back to sleep. I returned to New York several days later and saw for myself the long lines stretching around the block for my movie.

Shortly after *Sticky My Fingers, Fleet My Feet* had been nominated for an Academy Award, I got to be friends around New York with Herbert Allen, Jr., the President of Allen & Company, the biggest brokerage house in the entertainment business. Herb was a trustee of the American Film Institute and he'd liked *Sticky My Fingers* a lot. Despite this, over the years I had brought various projects to him, thinking he might finance them as he'd showed an interest in me. Sadly, he never did. Herb later attended a screening of *Bang the Drum Slowly* and absolutely loved it. When the picture opened well and got remarkable reviews, Herb complained, "Why don't you send me something?" I replied, "Well, Herb, because you never buy anything." He said, "Look, things are different now. We're about to buy Columbia. So, please go ahead and send me something that you really want to do." Shortly afterwards, Allen & Company did indeed acquire a controlling interest in Columbia Pictures and Herb—being the impressive, high-powered guy that he was—remained true to his word. He put me in touch with David Begelman, whom he'd just hired to run it. Begelman had been a powerful agent before ascending to the head of Columbia. He was a benignly charming man who would, in the years to follow, become a notorious figure in Hollywood. In 1977, Begelman was implicated in an infamous check-forging scandal after it was discovered he had embezzled money from Columbia. He was deservedly fired, but, incredibly, then became head of MGM—even though he was a proven thief! Back when I dealt with him, Begelman was always unfailingly pleasant and helpful to me.

There were a couple of interesting projects I alerted Begelman to. The first of them was *Forfeit*, a crime thriller based on the 1969 novel by Dick Francis. As you know, Francis was an author who had intrigued me for quite some time. I liked his writing enormously, and thought his narratives and characters would translate effectively into movies. My repeated attempts to make his first book, *Nerve*, into a film had ended in failure. There was another of his novels—the title of which eludes me right now—that I was also interested in doing, but that didn't go anywhere either. But, of all his works, the one that really captured my imagination was *Forfeit* as it was such a well-constructed and tautly-written story. It concerns a journalist in London who uncovers a horse racing scam following the mysterious death of his friend. His subsequent investigations attract the interest of some dangerous people and there are a number of tense scenes and encounters. For instance, the journalist is caring for his wife who is very ill and has an iron lung; there's a terrific sequence where the bad guys are coming to get our hero and he has to quickly move his wife out of the apartment before they arrive. It's fabulously suspenseful and involves time running out; the guy's desperate efforts to take his wife off the iron lung, escort her down the stairs and safely out of the house before it's too late. It would have been a highly memorable passage, I feel.

I'd learned that William Friedkin had at one time been developing *Forfeit* at Columbia, but the project had not moved forward and was presently in turnaround. Happily, I was able to reactivate it and set it up again at the studio as a development deal. The next course of action was to find a screenwriter to adapt the novel. I chose Ernest Tidyman, who had previously written *Shaft* and *The French Connection*. Tidyman had recently won an Oscar and a Writers Guild Award for the latter film, and was now a big name. He and I both shared the same lawyer, so the deal was put together for us both to develop *Forfeit* as a movie. It was not a pay-or-play deal but there was a $50,000 fee to supervise a rewrite and that was lucrative for a director back in 1973. Tidyman then went away and knocked out a draft of the script. I must be honest in saying that I was not happy with what he eventually delivered. His screenplay was extremely flat and clunky, and contained none of the dramatic intrigue and sharpness of Francis' book. I suddenly felt rather deflated and disappointed. Interestingly, by this time I was a trustee of the AFI and I ran into Billy Friedkin at one of our meetings. During a quiet moment, I said, "Tell me about Tidyman." Billy replied, "Well, the first thing I should tell you is he didn't write a single word of *The French Connection*. I had to rewrite that script entirely." This news came as something of a shock to me and I realized what I'd already suspected: we had hired the wrong writer for *Forfeit* and were going to suffer for it. And I believe we did as the project eventually fizzled away. It was a great shame. I had so many ideas about how we could do the picture, and I'd always intended to shoot it on location in England, but none of that mattered anymore. *Forfeit* was dead.

> *Of all the tentative projects Hancock would toil on throughout this period, the dearest to his heart was a proposed adaptation of William Price Fox's bestselling novel* Ruby Red. *First published in 1971, the story follows the fortunes of Ruby Jean Jamison, one half of "The Rose of Sharon Girls," a singing duo she has formed with her good-hearted gasbag friend Agnes. Both of these young women are determined to escape their turgid life in Columbia, South Carolina, and fulfill their dreams of becoming country singing stars in Nashville, Tennessee. After Agnes falls pregnant and leaves the act, Ruby finds a new partner in Irene, and together under the new name of "The Honky Tonk Angels", the two seek fame and fortune in spite of a number of obstacles.*

The failure of *Forfeit* to happen was difficult, but the failure of *Ruby Red* was especially tough to take. Let me preface my comments by saying that a lot of my film work has a discernible ingredient of the bittersweet. One could even go as far as to label me "Mr. Bittersweet," because that's the contrasting tone I've often strived for: a delicious mixture of the pleasant and the painful. Some of the moments I like best in *Bang the Drum Slowly* have that aspect to them and I certainly enjoy experiencing it in the work of other artists. For example, I've enjoyed a bittersweet quality in the plays of Chekhov and I particularly like hearing it in the stirring sounds of country and western music. I had started listening to country music around 1966 or '67, and loved the way the songs mingled feelings of love and hope with those of regret and longing. There was so much honesty and emotion in those tunes that resided beneath this wonderfully tacky surface. I was feeling them deeply and suddenly realized it was possible for something to be both trashy and heartfelt at the same time. I wanted to somehow inject that same bittersweet component into my movies, and what better way to do that than to make a film where the subject or backdrop was the country music scene. In that regard, *Ruby Red* was a perfect fit for me.

My first exposure to William Price Fox's novel occurred while I was out in Los Angeles for the Academy Awards ceremony in 1971. I met with two agents there, Bill Tennant and Marcia Nasitar, who both worked for the prestigious Ziegler-Ross Agency. Tennant was riding fairly high in the industry at this point and represented the likes of Ryan O'Neal and Roman Polanski (it was Tennant who was given the unpleasant job of identifying the bodies of Polanski's wife, Sharon Tate, and her friends after they had been murdered by followers of Charles Manson in 1969). Mike Ritchie had suggested that I talk to Marcia and it was she who then gave me a copy of *Ruby Red*, which I devoured. I immediately loved it and wanted to do it. I responded strongly to the Southern charm and easy humor of Fox's writing; and the assortment of male characters these two aspiring female singers encounter on their journey to Nashville—men who each have their own motives and ambitions and problems.

The rights to *Ruby Red* were held by the aforementioned Ray Stark of Rastar Productions. He had become a powerful force at Columbia by this time and, despite having various deals at Columbia, Ray was actually involved with Paramount in putting the movie together. It then turned out that all those concerned had bigger fish than me to fry as Arthur Penn was suddenly hired to direct the film and I was pushed out—much to my abject misery. It looked like the chance to direct *Ruby Red* was lost, but then Penn failed to put together a version of the screenplay that Ray and the studio wanted to make. After *Bang the Drum Slowly* opened and got noticed by a lot of important people like Ray, I was able to get *Ruby Red* back. The project then remained at Paramount throughout the transition from Penn to myself, and Frank Yablans was still the main guy there at this time. The contract I signed thereafter with the studio was a pay-or-play deal, but maybe I wasn't made sufficiently aware of the difference between a pay-or-play deal and an actual guaranteed go-picture. What I mean is, maybe it would have been a lot smarter and beneficial for me—while I was this hot—to have kept looking around for a picture I *knew* was going ahead; rather than sitting and waiting around for a movie I would get paid for whether it happened or not.

When we were looking for a writer to adapt *Ruby Red*, somebody pointed me in the direction of W.D. "Rick" Richter. He had previously written the crime caper movie *Slither*, which had starred James Caan, and later wrote and directed an offbeat science fiction film called *The Adventures of Buckaroo Banzai*. That movie was much admired but didn't make any money, although I now understand it's considered a true cult item. Interestingly, what we were trying to do with *Ruby Red* was make a picture that was also a little offbeat; something that resided somewhere between what years later became *Nashville* and *Coal Miner's Daughter* in its tone and milieu. Aside from the tangible bittersweet aspect I keep mentioning, I wanted the picture to also be satirical and affectionate and compassionate—all the things I had loved in the book. Obviously, a delicate balance would have to be struck if we were going to achieve all of that. Ultimately, I think Richter's screenplay didn't have enough of these qualities. It didn't have any *pizzazz* for want of a better word. It was missing something—drama, probably. Ironically, and in contrast to Tidyman's tampering with *Forfeit*, Richter was probably (with my compliance, because I loved the book) too rigidly faithful to Fox's novel and didn't take enough chances.

As we were working on the script, we held some preliminary discussions about various casting possibilities. I had my own thoughts about who should play the leading roles, some of which may or may not have conflicted with the views of others. I know that Ray Stark wanted very badly for us to come up with both Liza Minnelli and Goldie Hawn to play the two Southern girls. I wasn't strongly opposed to that idea, but I felt it might be more profitable to cast some unknown—or perhaps lesser known—actors in some of the principal parts. Then, who should come in and read for me, but none other than Sissy Spacek. She was nobody in particular at this point in time and I believe had only recently shot *Badlands* with Terrence Malick. So, Sissy was by no means anybody's first choice but mine, but she could have easily done it. I've always thought she was a terrific actress, a very sensitive and smart performer, and the instinct I had for her that day has been favorably born out through the years. Also, it's worth remembering that Sissy went on to do *Coal Miner's Daughter*, in which she played the country singer Loretta Lynn. She won an Academy Award for that performance, and I believe did all the singing in the role, which makes my wanting her for the role in *Ruby Red* all the more prescient.

Robert De Niro was going to be in *Ruby Red*, too, if I had my way. I'd talked to Bobby about playing an albino record producer the girls encounter and he wanted to do the film. We were discussing how to do the albino make-up, which is not easy. It's difficult to convincingly duplicate the correct pigmentation of the skin, the whiteness of the hair, the distinctive look of the eyes with the red pupils, without it looking like some alien creature from *Star Trek*. I don't believe we did any make-up tests on *Ruby Red*, but Bobby certainly gave it a lot of thought. I think he *wanted* to do the tests. Throughout his career Bobby was extremely concerned about make-up and used a lot of it—appliances, everything—and was meticulous about testing it. I remember when they were shooting *Raging Bull*, Irwin Winkler complained to me about the costs of Bobby bringing his make-up guy and a little camera crew in on a day-off. I asked, "Why does he do that?" Irwin replied, "Because it's his *thing*," which was strange to me because I didn't remember any special make-up on *Bang the Drum Slowly*. But the more I look at Bobby's work I see the extraordinary attention to detail and how beautifully it has paid off, because you're never aware of it.

There's something else worth mentioning here: negotiations on movies often drag on long after both sides are committed and at work. I've even shot an entire picture before I signed the final contract. Letter agreements are exchanged at the beginning, yes, laying out the basics, but there are still a number of points to be worked out. Agents on the whole, naturally, because that's how they're paid, by commission, are more concerned with financial terms than they are with the distribution of power. Conversely, power is far more important to me than money. So, I've usually ended up working out that situation myself and it's often been done during pre-production. This was the case with *Ruby Red*. Now, power in director's contracts is expressed in a series of approvals. You may have the right, say, to approve principal cast, the director of photography, the editor, maybe the composer, certainly your assistant director and so forth; and in the DGA minimum agreement you have the right to a certain number of weeks in the editing room. But beyond that, there's a whole list of other things that are conceivably at play. Do you have the right to approve the schedule, the budget, the locations, the costumes, the line producer, the mix? It can be a long list. And, of primary importance, are all your approvals subject to the final caveat "not to be unreasonably withheld"?

I was still fencing about all these things on *Ruby Red* while I was working with Rick Richter on the screenplay, and it was during this period that Peter Bart suddenly resurfaced in my life. Remember, almost a decade earlier he had written a critical article about me in San Francisco for *The New York Times*. Bart had then left the newspaper and was now working as Bob Evans' assistant, which meant he was second in command at Paramount on the West Coast. We met, just as a mutual courtesy. I guess the plan was to put behind us any lingering animosity, as we really didn't like each other but were going to have to work together. In the course of the meeting the question of approvals inevitably came up. "I don't want to threaten you or anything," he said, "but what you're asking for is out of line." I said, "You are *threatening* me!" "No," Bart protested, remaining calm, but there was something level and deadly in his tone. "You see, Ray Stark and Frank Yablans are relying on you to do this picture and I don't know if this early in your career you want to cross important guys like that." My reply to that was, "What is this, the Mob? You've been working too much on *The Godfather*." "No," Bart said evenly, "I'm just telling you."

Why *Ruby Red* ultimately died a death is an interesting question. I think one reason was Stark, as he proved to be somewhat disruptive. Indeed, as far as I can gather, the project fell apart due to the internal politics within Rastar crumbling. It was either that or the fact we couldn't get the right script. As in the case of *Forfeit*, maybe we hired the wrong guy to write it. Finding the right guy is such an important decision to make, particularly if the status of a movie is fraught or tenuous. Ray was a difficult and dangerous man—charming, but a killer. Other than the time in his New York apartment when he hired me, and once more when he had me to breakfast at his Bel Air mansion and offered to fix me up with Barbra Streisand (the last thing I needed at that point was to get involved with someone else), I didn't see him. His guy on the project was Jack Brodsky. Jack had been a press agent—he and his partner had done a wonderful gossipy book about Elizabeth Taylor's ill-fated *Cleopatra*, and Jack had produced Woody Allen's *Everything You Ever Wanted To Know About Sex But Were Afraid to Ask*. A very funny guy, he had wanted to be a stand-up comedian. Jack and I had a great time working together on the project. We shared an office on a high floor of the Gulf & Western Building overlooking Columbus Circle—that's where Paramount was based in New York at that point. We flew back and forth first class to L.A. all the time, where Jack and I had adjoining bungalows at the Beverly Hills Hotel, all on Paramount's dime. When a mother showed up at my bungalow door with a whip-cream cake and a beautiful daughter, both pretty much on offer, it was Jack who told me not to eat it. We were together when Ann-Margaret and other actresses read for the title role. We told each other everything and had wonderful gossip sessions with Marie Brenner, who was Paramount's East Coast story editor at that point and later became a famous author for *Vanity Fair*.

Jack had been with Ray for several years, all through the Arthur Penn time on *Ruby Red*, which was quite a while. They might have already been on their second or third writer at a certain point. That alone should have told me it might be a hard property to lick. But love doesn't always see reason, and I loved that book. As I said, I didn't properly appreciate the difference between a pay-or-play deal and a go-picture. I thought Paramount's willingness to spend a great deal of money, on us, on writers, on hotels and so forth, meant they were going to make the picture. I didn't anticipate the Borgia-esque inner workings of Rastar. Here's what happened: Jack and I flew out for a big meeting about Rick Richter's first draft. On the flight, Jack somehow lost a front tooth—I don't know, did he bite a nut or what? I don't remember, but there he was, humiliated, without a front tooth, and unable to get to a dentist before the all important meeting. So my cheery partner was somewhat disabled for this encounter, which to make things worse, was with one of his rivals within Rastar, Saul David.

Saul, who at the time was producing *Logan's Run*, was a very sour guy. He immediately made it clear that he didn't like Rick's draft, and actually, now it occurred to him, didn't like us either. That was the message and it was shocking. Somehow, in a moment, I had moved from persona grata to out-kitty. Where was the respect? "It's just a draft," I said. "Let's give Rick notes and he can fix it. Has Ray read it? I'm anxious to hear *his* thoughts." Saul wouldn't say. He was uninterested in any further discussion and cut the meeting short. Poor toothless Jack and I reeled out of the Columbia lot not knowing what to say or do. We decided, over drinks back at the Polo Lounge, that we had to get to Ray. Unfortunately, he was out of the country, but Jack managed to track him down in Paris and left a message. I don't know that he ever returned Jack's call. Nor did Frank Yablans return mine. The project just went away. A big check arrived eventually, but that was not what I wanted.

The same time all of these projects were percolating, my first marriage was slowly coming apart. Allow me to go back to the beginning before I tell you the end: I had first met Ann Arensberg in 1964, while trying to raise finances for *The End of the Road*. Somebody, I don't recall who, had suggested she might be helpful in my efforts. I then met Ann, liked her immediately, and soon after fell in love with her. Back then, she was married to a wealthy lawyer named Pierre Leval, who later became a big Federal Judge in New York. They eventually separated, and soon after Ann and I got together. We got married in 1966, and she was with me when I went to work in San Francisco and Pittsburgh. I wasn't faithful to Ann throughout our relationship and I had a series of affairs with various women including Kit Clarke. I will state for the record here that I've never repeated that behavior in my relationship with my second wife. Not once. I learned that the penalty for being unfaithful was so upsetting and painful no good could possibly come of it.

Back when I first started tasting success with *Bang the Drum Slowly*, there were a lot of temptations. I was suddenly going out with starlets, partying, living the high life. There were a lot of fun times. My marriage to Ann finally threatened to implode when I met Lindsay Wagner, who later starred in *The Bionic Woman*. Lindsay and I started our affair in 1973, I believe, after I met her through Herb Allen. I was having lunch down on Wall Street with Herb in his local hangout, when he happened to remark, "You know, I have an actress I want to bring along. I would like her to meet you." I believe Herb and Lindsay were an item at this point, and he was trying to find her a job by introducing her to a director. By now I was living in a bungalow at the Beverly Hills Hotel—this was all during the time I was valiantly trying to get *Ruby Red* on, and I saw Lindsay for a possible part in the film. She was stunningly beautiful and sweet, and I was quickly taken with her. We got together shortly afterwards and I had to call up Herb, and say, "Uh, do you mind?" He rather generously said, "No, not at all. Go for it!" He then asked me to introduce him to Lauren Hutton, which I did.

My relationship with Lindsay lasted for months, well into 1974. I was out in Los Angeles and Ann was back in Sneden's Landing, so she had no knowledge of what was happening. But that abruptly changed one day when Ann looked at the phone bill and saw there were an inordinate amount of calls to a California number. Naturally, she called the number and enquired as to who was on the other end of the line. A female voice then replied, "It's Lindsay. Who is this?" And that was *it*! Thus began a very distressing time as I was desperately torn between these two women. Lindsay and I started living together in a Malibu beach house, but I felt so guilty about Ann I couldn't find any peace. One day, I announced, "I can't stand this!" I then moved Lindsay's piano back to her Malibu apartment and Ann came out to California to stay with me. Then I couldn't stand to be apart from Lindsay anymore and moved her and her piano back in, and Ann went back to Sneden's. I was literally going mad between the two of them and everything was turning to shit. Whomever I was with at any given time, I would be sneaking out to make phone calls to the other, expressing my longing for them.

To illustrate just how confusing and messy this period of my life was, I think Lindsay's piano was moved in and out of my house something like three times. I was not Good John at this point. I was Bad John. I was acting selfish and irresponsible, and was more than a little cruel. I'm definitely not proud of my behavior and I have some regrets about it. What was happening was very bad for Lindsay in particular. All of this getting together and breaking up—repeatedly—was destroying her. Lindsay told me that she was spending a lot of time lying on the couch fantasizing that she was up in the corner of the room, gazing down at herself from above. She was experiencing odd feelings of dislocation and despair. The whole situation was really kicking the shit out of her in a terrible way—and Ann, too. It was like a form of three-way madness and each of us was suffering. There was one dreadful afternoon when Ann and I were at a party at William Wyler's house in the Malibu Colony and I left the party and walked down the beach to where Lindsay was sunbathing. How surprised and happy she was to see me, but I don't think Wyler's daughter has ever forgiven me for disappearing like that.

Then, amid all of this tumult, Ann suddenly disappeared and I couldn't find out where she was. I was worried about what might have happened to her, but it eventually transpired that she had gone off with somebody whom *she* was having an affair with! The individual in question was a publisher named Dick Grossman and she'd been with him for two weeks. Finally, Ann came back, ostensibly to stay forever. But then I remarked (not to complicate matters further but in the interest of full disclosure) that I'd had a date with Dorothy Tristan while she was away. With that, Ann simply said, "Okay, goodbye," and was gone again within half an hour—this time for good. She wasn't angry, she merely said, "I love you and I know that you love me, but we are just going to continue hurting each other if we go on like this. We have to end it now." And we did. The truth was our relationship had disintegrated into something that was toxic and destructive; where one person would do something wrong and the other would administer their swift revenge. It was not good.

Throughout all of this, I was still getting offers to direct various movies. Lawrence Turman and his partner David Foster brought me two projects when I was living with Lindsay. The first was a script by John Logan called *Running the Wild Red*. It was a period picture about the maiden expedition to explore the Colorado River. It had lots of action on the rapids and bad manly dialogue. The second project was *Raggedy Man*, which was set in Texas during 1944 and concerned a mother and her two children who are being haunted by a disfigured stranger lurking about their home. The picture was eventually made in 1981 starring Sissy Spacek, but, by then, I don't believe Turman and Foster were involved with it anymore. They both wanted me to do the film with Lindsay—and I probably should have instead of ultimately choosing *Baby Blue Marine*—but I knew that doing *Raggedy Man* with Lindsay would have ended my marriage with Ann. I still wasn't prepared to do that at this point.

During this same period, when I was at my hottest really, Daniel Selznick brought me a really charming high school musical movie. I don't remember the title (unless it was *High School Musical*). The script was written by a very talented and nice young guy. He was gay, and in the process of moving from Los Angeles to New Orleans. I didn't see why and wished he wouldn't, and told him so, but he must have had his reasons. The screenplay was probably autobiographical in the sense it was about a girl who starred in her high school musical and the troubles she had with boys. At Danny's suggestion I met with Carrie Fisher and I wanted to cast her in it. She was just a wonderfully interesting seventeen year-old girl at that stage of her life. But Danny never got the money together and it was another one that got away.

> *As he struggled with feelings of guilt and failure prompted by the protracted dissolution of his marriage, Hancock industriously sought solace in his work. Another enticing project he had "cooking" at Columbia around this time was a proposed adaptation of Robert L. Duncan's spirited 1970 war novel* The Day the Sun Fell.

For several years I had subscribed to *Publishers Weekly*, which contained synopses of all the forthcoming books that were to be published. I was thumbing through an issue one day and, after being struck by the dramatic-sounding title, I read the synopsis for *The Day the Sun Fell*. The book was set in Japan during the closing events of World War II and involved three American soldiers who are secretly parachuted behind enemy lines disguised as German Catholic priests. Their mission is to warn the Bishop of Nagasaki that the atomic bomb is about to be dropped on the city, so that peace negotiations between America and Japan can commence or the Catholic community can be safely evacuated before untold death and devastation arrives. It turns out that their mission is in fact an elaborate lie as the military minds behind it had initially anticipated that the three soldiers would be captured and the truth tortured out of them—thus allowing the message to reach the Japanese military all the more convincingly. Despite two of the soldiers succeeding in their warning mission, the novel ends on a rather bleak and devastating note as history records it.

The Day the Sun Fell had the undoubted potential to be a gripping action picture, along the lines, say, of *The Guns of Navarone*. I was excited by it and others were, too. I believe Carter DeHaven, the producer of *The Last Run* and *Ulzana's Raid*, and I had optioned the book from Robert Duncan together, or I had by myself. I do remember that Duncan and his wife visited me at the beach-house, and I then tried to get Columbia to develop it. The studio had a wonderful production guy named John Veitch, whom I liked enormously. He had been John Ford's assistant director, and I always thought we were related because he was big and because I'm a Veitch, too. John was worried that the project might be too costly, but Columbia still seemed very excited about doing it. They thought Duncan's novel contained a fabulous central idea and it really did.

I remember there were two production executives I was dealing with: Robert Littman and Rosilyn Heller. Littman was regarded by some people in Hollywood as a rather colorful character. He was a heavy drinker and, before becoming an executive, had been a highly successful agent with a number of big stars in his stable. Rosilyn was somebody I liked very much and dated briefly. She was involved in developing a number of successful pictures for Columbia such as *Taxi Driver* and *Close Encounters of the Third Kind*. When we were discussing *The Day the Sun Fell*, I was given a list of potential writers that Littman and Heller liked, and felt might be suitable. Two of the names on that list were W.D. Richter, who, of course, ended up doing the screenplay for *Ruby Red*, and Stanford Whitmore, who would eventually write my next go-picture *Baby Blue Marine*. I forget which of Richter's scripts I had perused by this point, but I do recall reading something of his at the same time I was looking for a writer for *The Day the Sun Fell*. I was a little uncertain about exactly whom we should hire, but I wanted somebody who responded strongly to the material.

I eventually went with Stanford several years later because I had a relationship with him from *Baby Blue Marine* and thought he would either be free or not that expensive (Carter may have paid him just $10,000 to write a first draft). I was also aware that Stanford had been part of the American Army that had occupied Japan right after the war, so I figured he would have some familiarity and expertise with a Japanese setting. When I read the draft he eventually turned in, I found his work on *The Day the Sun Fell* to be a little academic, old-fashioned, and with too much exposition out front. "It's a Mission Picture," he said, "and we have to understand the mission." Okay, but I didn't think that we did have to, necessarily. I thought maybe we could gradually figure out what the men were sent to do *while* they were doing it, as the story was in motion. But I didn't insist, because I wasn't writing it, and didn't want to. I probably should have, but it's hard to insist with an author when you aren't paying him his established rate. I had tried a draft myself earlier, while it was still in play at Columbia, but I didn't really like what I was doing. I didn't show it to anyone; I just felt I was at a dead end on it as a writer. The truth is I was having trouble writing, living there at the beach with Lindsay, missing my wife, distracted by beer and pussy and the view of the Pacific. So, I needed Stanford and I didn't want to mess with what he was doing beyond a certain point.

> *Given the excruciating demise of another studio project he had originated, and experiencing a growing unease regarding when and where his next "go-picture" was coming from, it is perhaps understandable that Hancock would begin to entertain more impersonal assignments from producers. One such offer he received came courtesy of Leonard Goldberg and Aaron Spelling, whose company Goldberg-Spelling Productions was then operating out of the 20th Century Fox lot. They also had a deal at Columbia and were looking for a director to helm a screenplay they had purchased in February 1975 titled* Baby Blue Marine.

Written by Stanford Whitmore and set in 1943, the story concerns Marion "Hedge" Hedgepeth, a marine recruit who is ignominiously dismissed from the Corps after five disastrous weeks of boot-camp training. Forced to wear an ugly pale blue uniform that signifies his humiliating failure and brands him a "baby blue marine," Marion is making his way back home to St. Louis (where his father, a successful marine during World War I, awaits him), when he detours to a bar for a drink while waiting for a train. There he meets a highly-decorated but battle-haunted Marine Raider with a shock of white hair who is about to be sent back to the Pacific War. The Raider gets Marion drunk before knocking him unconscious, stealing his clothes and papers, and then disappearing.

Marion has no choice but to dress himself in the Raider's uniform and continues his journey homeward the following day by hitchhiking to the small picturesque town of Bidwell. He stops at the local diner, where he encounters Rose Hudkins, a young and pretty waitress who serves behind the counter. Wearing the Raider's uniform, Marion is mistaken for a war hero and is warmly welcomed by the townsfolk. Mr. Elmore, who has lost his son in the war, treats the out-of-towner to a meal. Attracted to the handsome soldier, Rose suggests that Marion stay with her family for a few days. He accepts, still worried about going home and facing his parents. Marion and Rose quickly fall in love, prompting the bogus marine to reveal his true identity. However, Rose refuses to condemn him. Meanwhile three American-Japanese men escape from a nearby interment camp and flee into the woods of Bidwell. This situation causes much tension in the town between the conservatives and the trigger-happy locals out for blood. A posse is organized to track the escapees down, and Marion joins them. While out searching the forest, he stumbles across the three American-Japanese and convinces them to give themselves up. As he assists the men in crossing a rushing river, one member of the posse who is hiding at a distance fires his gun at them. Marion is shot and wounded, tumbles into the water and is carried off downriver. He is eventually rescued by the townsfolk and the three escaped detainees. Some time after the war has ended, a bus pulls over outside the diner and Marion steps off in a marine's uniform. He is welcomed by Rose who lovingly embraces him.

This was a period of uncertainty for me. I mean, there I was without *Forfeit* going ahead, and without *Ruby Red* or *The Day the Sun Fell* going ahead, and suddenly I started to feel that all the heat and sizzle I'd generated was beginning to cool. I had this growing feeling of desperation, like I needed to get back on a movie set and start directing again—just in case I'd forgotten how to do it! I had been given the script for *Baby Blue Marine* as a writing sample through my connection with Herb Allen and David Begelman, so I was already somewhat familiar with it. I'm always more passionate about my own material than I am about somebody else's, but I would never refuse anything without first considering the script and the people I'm potentially working with and for. I already knew who Stanford Whitmore was, I knew he was a talented writer, but on top of that he was also a truly wonderful guy. When I reread his script I liked it a lot, but, again, the overriding sense I had was one of urgency. I was anxious to get a movie started as quickly as possible and that was probably canceling other considerations out. But I did like the central idea of the story: a failed marine posing as a war hero, who is placed in a situation where he has to live up to the demands of the deceit he's perpetrated. I felt there was mileage to get out of that idea, although, ultimately, we could have pushed that premise even further. We could have had more excruciating moments and dilemmas for Marion to endure in his dealings with the people he encounters.

Now, if you were to ask me what I think the likelihood of such a scenario taking place—a battle-hardened combat marine swapping clothes, and in effect identities, with a baby blue marine—it's a positively artificial set-up. Let's say, it stretches credulity somewhat. For instance, the Raider's uniform just happens to fit Marion perfectly. I'm sure the Raider would have selected his target carefully beforehand, but I think it would have been interesting to have made the uniform a little more ill-fitting and uncomfortable. This would have possibly been too much of a clue for the townsfolk that Marion isn't who or what he says he is, but it might have made things more plausible. More successful I felt (and this was one of the things about the material that I personally connected with) was the idea of failure and rejection. Having been overweight at various times in my life, I know what it is to fail; to feel vulnerable and lesser in the presence of more robust physical specimens who are succeeding admirably all around you. I can be honest in admitting that I don't think I would have been a successful marine. I also identified with the central love story between Marion and Rose, the sweetness and delicacy of it. In my increasing anxiety over my heat evaporating completely, I thought I'd better direct a picture soon. So, I agreed to do *Baby Blue Marine*, even though I wasn't as in love with the project as I had been with *Forfeit* and *Ruby Red*. You see, this wasn't *my* story.

The most important element of any movie is the story. There are other aspects of a film that can distract or partially compensate for the lack of a strong narrative—a flashy style, spectacular special effects, big name stars—but you can't save a movie with these things alone. You must have a good story to tell. Sometimes as a filmmaker you can be looking for a story and you don't know what that story is. Maybe you can convince yourself that you'll know the story when you see it, so you keep looking. Occasionally, despite the millions of stories floating around out there, you may never find *the one*. It somehow eludes you because you're going on a vague feeling, or a desire, that you can't quite articulate and that isn't enough. You want to express this certain feeling, but it's almost abstract in its elusiveness because you need to *see* it. Sometimes you have an image, or a series of images, in your head, but how do you connect them? How do you build on them? It's a curious thing, searching for something you really want to do. It's really all a lottery in terms of whether or not you receive the kind of material that speaks to these ineffable things you want to say. When I had stories like *Forfeit* and *Ruby Red* that I wanted to do, nobody else wanted to do them, or there was some other problem or obstacle. So, I was still looking for a great story to tell, a story that really sang to me and, of equal importance, the studios. Sometimes you see the story you want to do but it's being done—or has already been done—by somebody else. Sure enough, when you do find that elusive story, it can be like unearthing buried treasure.

This leads me to something else that was an unspoken influence on my doing *Baby Blue Marine* and that something was John Ford's *How Green Was My Valley*. I dearly love that picture, but, as I told you, I had never seen it while growing up. It was one of those peculiar movies I'd always heard a lot about. It was constantly cropping up in conversations, or I would read about it somewhere. For instance, I was interested in the House of Un-American Activities Committee's investigations into Hollywood from the 1930s to the 1960s. Back when I was in San Francisco, I had gone to the library and read transcripts of various actors' testimonies and it was fascinating stuff. I found Larry Parks' testimony especially moving. Parks had begged not to testify and was crying as he did so—not that it did his cause any good as he was blacklisted anyway. I found Ginger Rogers' testimony funny, and Gary Cooper's interesting—particularly his admission that he had turned down certain projects he believed were "tinged with communist ideas." After devouring all these records, I actually made an evening of theater out of the testimonies in our experimental theater in Pittsburgh. Following this, in the early 1970s, Ann had gotten Eric Bentley to do a book at my suggestion called *Thirty Years of Treason: Excerpts from Hearings Before the House Committee on Un-American Activities, 1938-1968*, which compiled three decades worth of testimonies detailing the treatment that several prominent artists and intellectuals were subjected to. It's a remarkable document of its age; a time when the nation's fear of radicals, subversion and infiltration was so high certain abuses of power took place. There were a lot of mentions in Eric's book of *How Green Was My Valley* being a movie that embodied communist influences in Hollywood. Be that as it may, not even this had prompted me to hunt Ford's film down.

Then, one day early in 1975, I was caught in Manhattan between appointments. I was waiting to see my agent at the end of the afternoon and was walking along the street when I happened to notice that *How Green Was My Valley* was playing at a theater on 57th and 7th. With a couple of hours to kill, I went in to see it and was just totally knocked out! I was so moved by it, the story, the humor, the emotion, the evocative rural Welsh setting and the wonderful array of memorable characters that inhabited this small mining village. I can remember feeling elated and transformed after watching the film. Uplifted! I then hurried over to meet with my agent, and immediately said, "You know, it occurs to me that there hasn't been a picture made for a long time about love in a family. Wouldn't it be wonderful to do an intimate movie that focused on that?" His assistant then cooed, "Yeah, like *The Waltons*, right?" I shook my head at that. Despite *The Waltons* being a successful TV show that had already been running for several years by this point, I was not familiar with it. But there was now a desire on my part to make a film that was gentle, wistful, that involved ordinary hard-working people in a small rural community existing in a vanished time. *Baby Blue Marine* contained some if not all of those elements and I suppose that was part of the reason why I liked Stanford's script: the sense of community, of family, of love and forgiveness. I think that explains part of why I agreed to do the picture.

When I met my producers, Aaron Spelling and Leonard Goldberg, it was obvious right away that they really wanted me to direct the picture. From the beginning our relationship was generally good, and there were few bumps along the road. I liked Leonard a lot and I also liked his wife. They were both on location with us throughout the shoot and I became close to Leonard and enjoyed his company. Aaron I didn't like as much. Whereas Leonard was charming and personable, there was always something a little distant and business-like about Spelling. During filming, he was mostly back in Hollywood running their company's various television series and attending to other business. Aaron and I got along well when we were doing the picture, but, later, I gave an interview to the *DGA Quarterly* magazine and said a few things that got him quite angry. These comments were in relation to the casting of the movie. I happened to mention that I had felt trapped into having to cast certain actors in certain prominent roles, specifically the lead role, who I felt were not up to the task. Aaron was not happy with that being made public, but everything I said was the truth and he knew it.

The source of my unhappiness was this: I had done two features in *Let's Scare Jessica to Death* and *Bang the Drum Slowly* without stars, and had felt in a way that I'd discovered Robert De Niro and Michael Moriarty—at least as far as the movie audience was concerned. What's more both those films had been fairly successful, particularly artistically. I felt this demonstrated that I knew what I was doing when it came to finding the right actor for the right role. Perhaps understandably, I then found it hard on *Baby Blue Marine* to suddenly have it dictated to me that I *had* to cast the people they wanted me to cast. The narrow pickings made available were these: I was to choose between Jan-Michael Vincent and Richard Thomas for the role of Marion Hedgepeth and nobody else. I bridled at that dictum because I didn't want either one of them. Look, I can see why studios require a star if the star is somebody like Tom Cruise, Jane Fonda or Steve McQueen. Somebody whom people have actually heard of! I suppose at that point people knew Richard Thomas from *The Waltons*, in which he had the starring role, but that was a TV show, not a movie. I was also informed that teenage girls had supposedly liked Jan-Michael Vincent in *White Line Fever*, a trucking picture he had recently made, and that he was supposedly on the verge of stardom. But I've always questioned the necessity of casting stars that aren't *real* stars as opposed to finding a complete unknown. In the process of reading people for the supporting parts in *Baby Blue Marine*, I had found Adam Arkin, the son of Alan Arkin, and thought he was perfect for the part. I made this view known, not that it mattered. Jan was destined to play Marion as he was always the preferred choice.

I then argued that Jan—with his chiseled features and lean, muscular body—would no doubt be a tremendously successful marine. He looked hard and sculpted, and had these eyes that were coldly determined. He clearly would not fail. Conversely, Adam Arkin—with his round face, soft body and doe-like eyes—had a gentler nature and a more vulnerable quality about him. He would not be successful as a marine and, by that rationale, was perfect for Marion. Even the name Marion has a softness and a femininity to it (ask John Wayne) so I pressed the producers to cast Arkin. But they simply would not let me. We eventually hired Adam in a brief role as one of the other Marine rejects at boot camp. It was such a shame. Now, the way you win these kinds of battles is you quit. Would I have won if I had simply announced, "I don't want to direct this picture if you won't let me cast the actor whom I know is right for the role!" Would such a maneuver have ensured I'd have had my way? I really don't know in retrospect. I have a sneaking suspicion such a ploy might have worked and that thought does torment me a little. The reason I didn't do that is a rather uncomplicated one: it seemed to me that I should direct a picture soon and not do anything to seriously rock the boat. Again, since my *sizzle* was slowly dissipating, I felt I better not let another project fall through as time was marching on. Also, I didn't want to acquire a reputation for quitting. So, I decided to play the game by their rules. I basically said to myself: "Okay, Spelling and Goldberg have enjoyed a lot of success. Maybe, just maybe, they know what they're doing. Maybe *you* aren't really the smartest guy in the world, John. Maybe somebody else knows something, too!"

With these considerations in mind I simply relented and went ahead with Jan, but I was never entirely happy with his performance from the first day to the last as it required a further suspension of belief. Needless to say, I never made these regretful feelings known to Jan at any time. He had no idea that I had objected vociferously to his casting (at least, I don't think so) and I had no desire to hurt his feelings. Honestly, I liked Jan and we got along well during the shoot. All the same, right from our first meeting, I knew he was a rather limited actor in terms of his range and instincts. I had seen some of his previous movies and was not overly impressed to say the least. It's not that he was a bad actor—he wasn't. He just wasn't the *right* actor. Jan worked hard and was pleasant enough, but he simply wasn't my choice. During our initial discussions about the script and the character of Marion, he had one or two ideas but no intriguing insights or developments. I like to work with actors who have lots of ideas. Even if those ideas are way-off the mark or conflict with some of my own, you will always find a few things that are useful, even wonderful, if you allow them a certain amount of freedom. I should add that Jan and I remain friends to this day. We're now Facebook friends and he's a good guy.

I was a lot happier with the remainder of the cast we hired. Glynnis O'Connor, who plays Marion's love interest Rose, was a wonderful find. She was the daughter of Lenka Peterson, whom I knew from The Actors Studio. Lindsay had initially expressed an interest in playing that part and I don't recall the reasons why I didn't cast her. I probably didn't think it was a good idea that we worked together as we were in the process of breaking up at this juncture. I had seen Glynnis in *Jeremy*, a picture set in New York in which she had played a ballet dancer who falls in love with a cellist played by Robby Benson. I liked her in that movie and thought she would bring the right level of honeyed chastity to the role, which she undoubtedly did. I then hired the late Bruno Kirby as Pop Mosley, another of the failed marines Marion encounters at basic training. He was great and another actor who could have easily played the lead, too. Bruno came in to read for me and I immediately recognized him from *The Godfather Part II*, which had only just come out. He had played the Young Clemenza and had such an interesting face, voice and physicality. In truth, I think *Baby Blue Marine* suffers as a film once Pop Mosley says goodbye to Marion and disappears out of the story. We kind of miss his presence a little as his character, and Bruno's performance, is immensely likable. There is always a danger of such a thing happening when somebody in a supporting role is so damn good.

The more mature members of the cast included members of my unofficial stock company of players: Barton Heyman, making his third appearance in my third film (this time in a hairpiece), and Marshall Efron who plays the cook in the diner. I also cast Michael Conrad as the Drill Instructor, and Art Lund as the kindly Mr. Elmore, who befriends Marion. After working with Mike on *A Man's a Man*, I thought he would be perfect for the role of this hard-ass disciplinarian whose job is to indoctrinate the would-be killers and dispose of all the washouts; separate the wheat from the chaff, so to speak. As for Art, he was a late replacement for Robert Lansing. I had worked with Lansing back when I was an apprentice in summer stock on the south-side of Chicago and had enjoyed the experience immensely. I grew to love him and thought he was a wonderful guy and a terrific actor. I cast him as Mr. Elmore fairly early on and he was perfect for the role. Sadly, in the intervening years since our last collaboration, Robert had become a hopeless drunk. He couldn't show up at rehearsals sober and would be swaying on his feet and slurring his words. It was a very difficult situation personally for me. So, with great reluctance and sorrow, I said goodbye to him. I then hired Art, whom I liked enormously. He had been a big musical star on Broadway back in the 1940s and '50s, and he was a delight to be around.

> *Awarded even less screen time than Kirby, Conrad and Lund is Richard Gere (here making only his second appearance in a theatrically released movie). The then twenty-six year-old actor plays the battle-scarred Marine Raider, whose hair has turned white from witnessing and participating in the horrors of the war in the Pacific. Several years after the release of* Baby Blue Marine, *Gere would go on to establish himself as a major Hollywood star following such box office hits as* American Gigolo *(1980),* An Officer and a Gentleman *(1983) and* Pretty Woman *(1990).*

I liked Richard Gere a lot and we got along well. Did I know back then he was going to become a big star? Probably not. However, he carried a presence about him and he made the most of his fleeting appearance in the film. One thing I do remember about Gere is he did not want to have his hair dyed white to play the Raider. I can recall saying to myself, "Uh, did you actually *read* the script?!" That aspect of the character was pretty much non-negotiable, but I don't know whether or not he has ever forgiven me for bleaching his hair. The truth is he felt like a fool, but, other than that, Richard was fine and he deftly captured the sense that this was a damaged old man in a young man's body. You look back at that scene now and you notice that he's got a certain something, a charisma that you can discern onscreen, but I'd noticed that when he first auditioned for me. I was extremely impressed with Gere's reading. He had flown out from

New York to do it, and I immediately told the casting director, Linda Otto, that I wanted him for the role. In fact, I was so excited I ran after Gere and stopped him on the way out to tell him he had the part. I mean, why keep people in suspense just so their agents don't ask for more money? I don't like those kinds of games.

We had a number of interesting actors that passed through the auditions but did not get hired. One of them was Dorothy Tristan, my exquisite neighbor who would soon become my second wife. I knew she was an actress of considerable talent after seeing her in *The End of the Road* and *Klute*, and was delighted to see her. She came in to read for the role of Mrs. Hudkins, Rose's attractive mother, but Dorothy didn't think that she was right for the part. Frankly, neither did I, but I very much wanted to work with her. I don't think Dorothy felt particularly comfortable playing somebody's mother at that stage of her life and career. Perhaps she felt it would be a dangerous thing to do, and I'm sure it would have been. Hollywood already has a trigger-happy tendency to consign actresses of a certain age to the supporting roles of mothers, aunts and frigid spinsters. Dorothy had no intentions of assisting that transition. The role of Mrs. Hudkins eventually went to Katherine Helmond, whom I liked a lot. Katherine is billed fairly prominently in the film, although she plays a fairly brief and thankless part. I do remember that Bert Remsen, who played her husband and whom I liked very much, comically crossing his eyes at me once as he gazed at the size of Katherine's magnificent breasts.

At this point I'd like to take a brief moment to talk about Liv Ullmann if I may, as we had met just before I was in pre-production on *Baby Blue Marine*. Someone asked me if I wanted to meet her and I did. We had lunch together in the pretty outdoor area of the Polo Lounge—pink tablecloths, tropical plants; a long sunny California afternoon. We liked each other. She had the rosy coloring of my mother, something I've always found attractive, and, of course, she was *Liv Ullmann*. I never considered her for a role in *Baby Blue Marine* as she was too old for the role of Rose and too young for the role of the mother. Liv was in Los Angeles in connection with her starring role alongside Max von Sydow in Jan Troell's picture *The Emigrants*—it was either an early part of her Academy Campaign or maybe just press associated with the opening, I forget. I do recall her telling me that the film was a real challenge for her because it called for such simple and clear emotions. She was, she knew, more tangled than her screen personae. Liv was staying at Bob Evans's house not far from the hotel.

She hadn't seen *Bang the Drum Slowly*, and I wanted her to, but it was no longer in theaters. So, how could we set that up? "Well," she said, "I have to go to New York to play Nora in a production of *A Doll's House* at Lincoln Center. Maybe I could see it there?" I arranged for William Morris to screen it for her in their little screening room. Oh God, what a disaster! It was undoubtedly one of the more embarrassing things of my life. The picture was shot in 1.85:1, like most things were at that time, wide and narrow, but the William Morris projectionist showed it in an aspect ratio of 1.33:1, deep, like silent pictures, and wrong! Whether the projectionist didn't have the correct matte or was just lame, or both, I was never able to determine, but the result was that I got a phone call from Liv right after the screening saying, "John, it's wonderful, but I saw microphones." I explained (when I found out what had happened) and, being a professional, she understood. But I vowed silently to myself that I would never again shoot something without a hard matte in the camera. That's a vow I've broken, reluctantly, but there's been no repeat of that horrible screening, thank God.

Before I was scouting locations in Oregon and Northern California for *Baby Blue Marine*, there were romantic phone calls back and forth between us. I sent Liv white roses for her Lincoln Center *Doll's House* opening—Jack Brodsky said that was always the safest choice—and I flew to New York to see her in the show. Despite Sam Waterston playing opposite her as Torvald Helmer, it was not a great production and Liv was wasted in it. You understand I feel this was one of the greatest actresses in the history of cinema. I didn't ask her much about Bergman. It didn't seem right. But she did volunteer two things: how careful he is, she said, "not to take your magic," and how she was dreading (in a rather excited way) to be working with him again on *The Serpent's Egg*. I gather they fought a lot. Liv was scheduled to fly to Munich to shoot the film with him when her play closed. This was during the time when Bergman had abandoned Sweden because of some kind of income tax hassle. So, Liv and I had a wonderful lunch and a nice afternoon, but she was going one way and I was going back to California to shoot my picture. I haven't seen her again. I did get a post card a couple years later asking, "How is your life?" But by then I was happily married to Dorothy Tristan.

Anyway, after we had cast *Baby Blue Marine*, and just before we went off to start shooting on location, I had an interesting meeting with Peter Guber who was then an executive at Columbia. Guber had always struck me as a rich boy who had somehow attached himself to the studio in the late 1960s and was kind of goofy nuts. I remember he took me out for cocktails one day at the Bel Air Hotel, looked right into my eyes and in essence said, "Now, John, we are all relying on *you* to make this picture good. So, don't feel that you just have to stick to the script as written. Do whatever you feel is necessary to make it good." I thought that Guber's advice was counter to what it is I do as a filmmaker. I always try to be faithful and conscientious to material once everybody has agreed on the shooting script. But when I think about it in retrospect, maybe Guber was correct. Maybe I should have shown less restraint and less respect. It's not that I was unhappy with Stanford's screenplay and wanted to change anything; I just felt that the script needed to be done in a certain style and with stronger actors. That's all. Naturally, after Guber spoke those words, the first thing I should have done to ensure that we did indeed make a great movie would have been to immediately replace Jan-Michael Vincent with somebody better. Guber plainly wasn't saying or implying that as I believe he was a big supporter of Jan's, but I do wish he had. Unhappily for me, that option was never on the table.

> *Baby Blue Marine was filmed at various locations in Siskiyou County, Northern California. Among the places selected for shooting was the small town of McCloud, doubling for Bidwell in the film, which provided the cozy diner where Rose works as a waitress. The nearby McCloud River is also featured prominently during the climactic sequence in which Marion is accidentally shot and tumbles into the rushing water after finding the three Japanese-Americans who have escaped from the interment camp. The production paid several families who were vacationing at a campsite close to the location to leave for the afternoon while they filmed the action. The football game that Marion attends with Rose and Mr. Hudkins was filmed at a high school in Weed, California, with local students and townsfolk hired as extras. Also making an impression in several scenes is the exquisite Mount Shasta, located near the Oregon border, one of the few instances in which the mountain has been glimpsed in a motion picture. Additionally, the boot camp scenes were shot at the Marine Corps Base Camp Pendleton, located on the coast of Southern California.*

Some of the locations we utilized in Siskiyou and elsewhere were breathtakingly beautiful. I can remember undertaking a scouting trip during the winter when the snow was eight or ten feet deep and everything looked gorgeous. We would be shooting in the summer, but I wanted to capture the beauty of that area. Looking back, this would become a further source of frustration on *Baby Blue Marine* and another battle I failed to win. I saw this film as a decidedly saccharine story and I wanted to do it in a sort of oversweet jewel box visual style. I wanted the images to be like those in *The Umbrellas of Cherbourg* or *Excalibur*, and have a heightened quality that would match with the flagrant sentimentality and romanticism of the story. So, the idea was that we were recreating and rhapsodizing our past; it was an idealized view of our history and ourselves that really wasn't in keeping with the way things actually were. In effect, what I wanted to achieve in *Baby Blue Marine* was a kind of artificial reality. I'm aware of the contradiction of such a statement, but I felt this artificiality would make the story more rich and interesting. With that thought in mind, there were two people I wanted to work with. The first was Ferdinando Scarfiotti, who had been the production designer on Bernardo Bertolucci's *The Conformist*. I felt he would give me my desired look but, unfortunately, Scarfiotti wanted way too much money and was beyond the constraints of our budget. To compound matters, Spelling and Goldberg rejected him as they thought he was not only far too expensive but difficult and demanding. How they had direct knowledge of these things, I do not know, but that was the resounding message I got from them. My old theater collaborator Bob Lavigne was working as a designer on the film, and he wanted to paint lavender shadows on all of the trees in the forest to give *Baby Blue Marine* a kind of Disney-esque *Fantasia* look. But the idea of painting every single tree and then washing it off later was apparently going to exhaust too much time, money and energy.

The second person I wanted to hire was Laszlo Kovacs. Like everyone, I was knocked out by Laszlo's cinematography for *Easy Rider*—the lens flares, the seemingly effortless quality. Then he followed that movie up with his work on *Paper Moon* and *Shampoo*, and I was really sold on him. It was no problem getting Laszlo hired, as everyone wanted him at that point. He and I talked about my wanting an artificial look for *Baby Blue Marine* and Laszlo's solution was to propose shooting the picture on Fuji. John Alonzo had just impressed everyone with the look of *Chinatown*, which was shot on Fuji. We did some tests, and I accepted the tests, which I probably shouldn't have because they weren't going far enough, really, in the direction that I wanted. But I admired Laszlo so much and trusted his work. In retrospect, I realize we should have been doing more with filters and with really long lenses. There was a Swedish picture directed by Bo Widerberg in 1971 that I loved the look of called *Joe Hill*, which was all magnificent long lens footage. I know I discussed the film with Laszlo, but we probably should have sat down and looked at it together because there was, in the final analysis, some failure to communicate. This was largely a fault on my part, as I'm sure Laszlo could have done what I wanted had I made my thoughts clearer to him. There is a wonderful long lens shot in *Baby Blue Marine* of Marion and Rose lying in a field of wildflowers, and you can see the towering snow-capped Mount Shasta in the background. That was what I wanted. For that moment, we dug a hole in the ground and placed the camera down in it, so we could get real low with Jan and Glynnis amid the flowers.

The truth is I discovered that certain people on the production were in the habit—and I'm not only talking about the designers here but actually Laszlo, too—of rejecting or at least discouraging an artificial look. It was obvious to me that they were not particularly adventuresome in this area and wanted everything to look distinctly real. Thus, I was not able to have enough control (or possibly the balls) to get the highly stylized look that I wanted. But Laszlo and I liked each other and got along entirely, which isn't always the case with directors and cinematographers. I liked his crew, too. Len Lookabaugh, Laszlo's key grip, and I became particularly close, and I also liked his operator, Bobby Byrne. I liked Bobby so much that I hired him a few years later when I made *California Dreaming*. I remember that Laszlo had a girlfriend on his crew—I think she was a gaffer or a camera assistant—and it was not an entirely happy relationship, on the set or off. I believe she killed herself a year or two after we finished the film.

Another of the things I found constraining and frustrating on *Baby Blue Marine* was our attempts to maintain the period look of 1940s America at all times on what was a rather limited budget. There was only so much we could do in terms of having the right costumes, the right hairstyles, the right cars, the right wallpaper, and everything else you need to reconstruct a vanished world. Typically, we had to be cognizant of every background and every extra and every object within the frame; was there something in the shot like a digital watch or a modern vehicle, because if the audience spies these things they are going to be removed from the reality of the story. Of course, you don't ever want that to occur. The other restricting factor in all of this was the fact that we simply couldn't grab any footage as we were going along. I couldn't just say to the crew, "Okay, let's set the camera up here real quick and steal a shot of this street." It wasn't so bad when we shooting stuff in the woods or by a river, or in a field of wildflowers, but we still had to be careful. For that reason, it wasn't as freeing and as enjoyable as making a contemporary film where you can hopefully incorporate any new idea or observation you make as you're shooting.

> *In its portrayal of a fraudulent if likable hero and idealized vision of small town America, one might assume that another discernible influence on* Baby Blue Marine *is Preston Sturges'* Hail the Conquering Hero *(1944). This accomplished satirical comedy-drama stars Eddie Bracken as Woodrow Truesmith, the meek son of a First World War hero, whose own ambitions of following in his father's footsteps are dashed by a chronic bout of hay fever. After being discharged from the Marines Woodrow encounters a group of battled-hardened veterans in a bar, who persuade him to return home at the end of World War II masquerading as a valiant hero.*

I haven't seen *Hail the Conquering Hero* I'm ashamed to say, although it's possible that Stanford was familiar with the movie when writing his screenplay. It sounds as if there are some similarities with *Baby Blue Marine*, but I think our intentions were slightly different. I don't know that we were satirizing American hero worship in the manner in which I can only presume Sturges is doing in his picture. I also presume that *Hail the Conquering Hero* is an impersonation story, right? One impersonation story with a wartime background I do love is Roberto Rossellini's *Generale Della Rovere*, which was made in 1959. Vittorio De Sica plays a Roman con man named Bardone who is accidentally arrested by the occupying Nazis, and is sent to a prison in Milan. Word somehow spreads among the prisoners that he is a famous underground aristocratic leader named Generale Della Rovere. Bardone then begins to play the role a bit, and further inspires the inmates to acts of resistance and restores their pride. He eventually finds his calling and integrity when he allows himself to be martyred for the cause, shot as the man he is impersonating.

    I do like war movies, or any films that have a wartime milieu or are about the rigors of military life and how conflicts impact on ordinary lives. Inevitably, war movies often contain a potent sense of drama and emotional power; life and death narratives, stories of personal sacrifice and physical and moral courage. Those things always make for great cinema. I've toyed with the idea of directing a war film in the past, something that involved epic battle scenes and carnage. I've been offered a few things, and developed war projects that still might happen one day. I've always been interested in the question of violence; our fascination with it, our disgust and fear of it. War movies have been consistently popular with audiences during times of war and times of peace. So, human beings clearly have a thirst for seeing conflict and the movies reflect that. My own favorite war films include *Paths of Glory*, *All Quiet on the Western Front*, and, as you already know, I adored *The Sands of Iwo Jima* as a kid. Having grown up during World War II, a period in which we were inundated with flag-waving war pictures, I saw and liked a lot of them. This was part of what made me want to do *Baby Blue Marine*, a powerful feeling of nostalgia. I also like Stanley Kubrick's *Full Metal Jacket*—less than his earlier *Paths of Glory*, but I do like it. That movie also details a marine boot camp that is founded on humiliation, brutalization and the eradication of the individual at the service of the collective. You even see the drill instructor point to Marion's dick and his weapon at one point, saying, "This is your rifle, this is your gun," which is a memorable line echoed in Kubrick's film.

If we are going to talk about this fascination people have with images and narratives of conflict and carnage, I think it's only right that we recognize that it extends to something deeper. I've noticed we often have an allure with those individuals who have fought in wars and directly experienced man's inhumanity to man; people who have perhaps been physically and emotionally scarred by them. Interestingly, when I was doing *A Midsummer Night's Dream* in Pittsburgh, the Polish critic Jan Kott, who was already living and working in America by that time, came to the city and collaborated with me on the play. A few years earlier, Jan had authored a famous book called *Shakespeare Our Contemporary*, which proved to be extremely influential on Peter Brook and a lot of other people in the way it interpreted Shakespeare's plays and saw direct parallels between them and the Twentieth Century Theater of people like Brecht and Beckett. Jan had served in the Polish Resistance and I remember he and I were talking one day when he calmly said to me, "A man who hasn't killed is still a virgin." Obviously, what he meant by that statement was you are not fully grown up until you have taken a human life. No doubt in Jan's mind, and taking into account his personal experiences, the killing of another human being is like a rite of passage. For the rest of us, we sometimes view veterans as people who have somehow gained a secret knowledge or been transformed through the act of killing. I think that's certainly the Michael Corleone narrative in *The Godfather*, isn't it? You cross a line in your life and you can never return to the person you once were. That's also true of the Raider who Marion meets in the bar. He is a changed man and merely assuming Marion's identity will not erase the horrors of his past.

As a character Marion has innocence, or at least naiveté, in the sense he hasn't been corrupted and brutalized by the horrors of war like the Raider has. In some ways Marion is a non-personality in that he almost seems to exist as this benignly charming but somewhat blank screen upon which others project their own thoughts, feelings, hopes and desires. Marion plays to these emotions in continuing the charade he finds himself caught up in, as in the scene where he basically lies to the desperately worried mother about meeting her son over in the Pacific. He tells the mother that her boy is safe and well, and one could argue that it's a good and kind thing that Marion does, but it's also evil and cruel in some ways. I liked that ambiguity and thought it was useful, but we should have played that element up a little more in the film. Again, I feel Marion's reactions to these encounters, these projections, needed to be handled by a far more skilful actor who engendered far more interesting reactions. Jan comes across as very flat in some scenes, and that was not intentional to further the idea of Marion somehow being this blank screen. No, that was merely Jan's limitations as an actor firmly in evidence.

I did little research before shooting the movie, but I was aware that there were actually such things as Baby Blue Marines—the Marine Corps rejects made to wear those pale blue uniforms. Stanford Whitmore had witnessed such a thing happening during his own basic training, shortly before he embarked as a qualified marine for Japan in 1943. He saw a group of washouts in blue fatigues boarding a bus after they were discharged and never forgot it. I didn't research the Baby Blue Marines but I did briefly read about the interment camps for Japanese-Americans and also looked at some photographs. These camps had come into existence following the bombing of Pearl Harbor in 1941, when there was fear of another imminent attack from "the Japs." One can understand the reasons for why the U.S. Government created them, but the question then arises why they didn't also round up the Germans in New York? The Government did make their presence felt with the Italians to some degree. The Italian-

Americans were indeed watched and their movements recorded, but they were not imprisoned in internment camps like the Japanese-Americans were. The truth is there were too many Germans in America to have made such an operation feasible. It just wasn't possible to enforce. The Japanese-American population was much smaller and easier to monitor and subdue. Interestingly, Dorothy grew up in Yorkville which is the German-American section of Manhattan. She remembers there were blackouts where all the lights were put out in expectation of the whole city being bombed. She recalls the German civil defense workers would go around repeatedly shouting, "Out mit da lights! Out mit da lights!" Then, for fear of enemy planes detecting any sources of light and habitation, Dorothy's world would be plunged into darkness.

It's certainly true that people do the most savage and crazy things during wartime—soldiers, civilians, officials, statesmen. They are transformed, really, sometimes abandoning all moral and ethical considerations. For instance, look at the events which led to the Armenian Genocide that occurred during World War I: you had the Ottoman Turkish Empire's systematic destruction of over a million Armenian men, women and children. Turkey was aligned with Germany and Austro-Hungary in fighting Russia and they had within their borders an Armenian minority whose sympathies were with the enemy. The Turks felt this was a potential source of behind-the-lines cohesion, sabotage and invasion that might lead to them being attacked and overthrown. So, their solution to this dilemma was to march the Armenians to Syria where a concentration camp awaited. Of course, we know that the Turks raped and murdered the Armenians along the way, and left others to die from sickness and starvation. Back in the early 1940s, we used trains and trucks to transport the Japanese-Americans to their destinations, and we also fed them, but here's another example of a potential enemy force located within your borders. In California, the Japanese-Americans could have potentially navigated submarines to several possible targets; could have guided airplanes in to bomb the airfields and railroads; could have been relaying information via radios and planning other terrorist activities. So, I can see why our Government did what they did. In retrospect, it is a crime against humanity, but you can see how this distrust of the *other* caused it to happen.

We didn't have any historical or technical advisor present on set as we were shooting *Baby Blue Marine*. I felt I was close enough to having been alive during the time we were recreating (I was five years old in 1944) that I didn't need someone. Again, Stanford had really been there and I made sure he was on the set the entire time. I could direct any questions to him personally. Another question worth considering on a larger scale is how monumental Pearl Harbor was to America's image of itself as this powerful nation and how it affected our perceptions of the Japanese. I don't remember the attack occurring, but no doubt it was like when 9/11 happened and we suddenly felt vulnerable and damaged and afraid. In the years after Pearl Harbor, we were inundated with anti-Japanese propaganda and racist imagery and that stuff certainly got through to me. This race of people we were meant to despise: "evil slant-eyes" with gold teeth, peeping through round spectacles and shooting at John Wayne from their hiding holes. Those were powerful images and in movie after movie the Japanese were depicted as these "little yellow monkeys," and all that obscene stuff. It definitely had its effect and inspired very specific and charged emotions in viewers: fear, disgust, hatred. There was a tremendous anti-Japanese feeling in the country and I felt that hatred too at this point in my life, a time when I didn't know any better.

> *The opening and closing credits of* Baby Blue Marine *feature images which parrot the pleasing style and sensibility of painter and illustrator Norman Rockwell (1894-1978), whose idealized portraits of Americana adorned the covers of* The Saturday Post Magazine *for more than forty years. Fittingly, the paintings depicted in Hancock's film include such things as a young couple signing their marriage certificate before a registrar; a happy family gathering around a table for Thanksgiving dinner; parents watching over their sleeping children; and various soldiers returning home from the war to the commonplace comforts of home. Each reflects, as the narrator informs us, "another time, when there was innocence."*

I did look at a lot of Norman Rockwell's paintings in pre-production, just to draw some inspiration. I had grown up with *The Saturday Evening Post* and had seen all those Rockwell covers for the magazine, so it was very nostalgic for me. We tried hard to make it look like Rockwell's universe, the way he celebrates all the things we cherish about our way of life. It may not represent the reality of what or who we were back then, but it deftly captures what we *believe* we were. The opening narration that is heard over these images was not written in the script; that was also a post-production afterthought. I can't remember who actually delivered that narration. It may have been Art Lund. The Rockwell-like painting that features over the end credits was not done by the great man himself. That was executed by somebody else aping his signature style. The use of Rockwellian art was a conscious attempt to conjure up that lost world, so that it could be contrasted with the contemporary world of America. So, I made an effort in post-production to add another layer of that rosy feeling of nostalgia for a long-gone time.

In the story, Marion getting shot and plummeting into the river is the event which brings the locals townsfolk and the Japanese-Americans who have escaped from the camp together. It's a little sappy and unlikely—the hunter and the hunted coming together like that—but it makes sense within the rose-colored realm of the movie. I do remember that when we were planning that sequence, I spent some time exploring the gorge of the river, trying to find the most effective spots to shoot. There were a lot of jagged rocks, and bushes, and trees, that could potentially obscure the view, and it was quite an operation finding the best place. I can recall walking up and down that canyon to get back to craft services, or back to the trailers, and then back down again to the area where we were shooting. Then, after we'd finished, I'd have to struggle all the way back up the canyon, perspiring and breathing heavily, scratching and swatting away insects. Exhausting! It was getting towards the end of the shoot and I was feeling awfully tired and impatient—climbing up and down, up and down. Sometimes I thought I was going to pass out as the air seemed so thin. Then it occurred to me later that we were shooting at eight thousand feet, something like that, so it was altitude as well as the steep slopes that were affecting me.

The stunt itself—Marion tumbling into the water and being carried away—wasn't dangerous to shoot. Well, not very. There was a safety net positioned further down the river to prevent either Jan or the stuntman from rushing towards a twenty-foot waterfall that lay ahead of them. Jan was also padded up much more than I wanted him to be in that sequence. I always feel that when you watch the movie, you can see the bulky pads and such a sight takes you out of the reality and drama of the moment. It's the same problem when you set a stuntman on fire for a burn sequence; they are often swathed in these thick bandages and wrappings that make them look like The Mummy. Not good. We obviously wanted to avoid the waterfall (I wanted to replace Jan but not that way!) I was actually in the water with Jan most of the time, conferring with him, checking on him, but he was quite safe. I like to believe that I'm fairly courageous in terms of my readiness to do most if not all the things the actors are required to do in any given scene. Such willingness on a director's part often gives the actor a little more encouragement and confidence, too, but Jan was in excellent physical condition. He could easily do it.

It might be true that the area where Marion falls into the river is the same area where he is later seen being pulled out and rescued from certain death. I hope it doesn't appear to be that way in the finished film, but it probably is the same place. The truth is it can often be exceedingly difficult to move the camera, the equipment, the crew and actors up and down a wild canyon like that. The terrain is just too rough and you waste a lot of time negotiating it. I believe that in this instance we might have tried to elude that problem simply by shooting the action in the same place but from a different angle. Always when you are on location, you say, "Okay, this tree is a tree and this bush is a bush and this river is a river. Why the hell should we endeavor to struggle thirty yards downriver to shoot what is basically the exact same thing we have at our disposal right here?" So, we basically fudged it. Not everybody will notice something like that, but there are a few eagle-eyed observers out there who will always pounce on you. They'll take the trouble to list every goof and nonsensical thing you do. I've now gone ahead and confirmed their suspicions for them.

> *Despite Columbia marketing the movie as a period love story (and emblazoning Jan-Michael Vincent's name prominently in all advertising),* Baby Blue Marine *was rejected by most critics and audiences. Few seemed to appreciate a work predicated on "old-fashioned" notions of community, family and personal responsibility, one that evoked a less cynical age. Writing for the* Chicago Sun-Times, *Roger Ebert felt the picture "ends on such a puzzling, inconsequential note that it's easy to forget how many good things came before. The movie's first hour is so absorbingly well done, in fact, that I was beginning to hope this might be the summer's sleeper. But then things go so pointlessly wrong with the story that acting and direction can't save it. … None of the issues raised by [Marion's] deception are ever dealt with, the film's concern with placing American citizens in prison camps is never followed through on, the*

emotional relationship between the boy and the girl is left up in the air and we're left wondering if 30 minutes were dropped somewhere."

Reviewing the movie for Monthly Film Bulletin, Verina Glaessner observantly noted that *"for all its studied evocation of the early Forties ... Baby Blue Marine is blatantly a tale for our time. Although its nominal concerns are with American involvement in World War II, Hancock and scriptwriter Stanford Whitmore deliberately play it as a kind of exorcism of the Vietnam trauma. This aspect becomes most fascinating in the hero's rather ghostly encounter with the white-haired Marine Raider: a veteran wounded, by his own sepulchral account, "where it doesn't show," with a skull and crossbones insignia on his shoulder. He leaves Hedge to don the cloak of heroism (minus the pain), to which, the film suggests, he has every right, making him a clean hero returning to a clean country."*

Speaking personally, one thing I do have trouble with is the ending of *Baby Blue Marine*. The manner in which Mr. Elmore is so forgiving and happy at the climax as Marion steps off the bus a qualified marine troubles me. Considering the fact that his own son died in the conflict and he had given Marion his precious time-piece, Mr. Elmore should be disgusted and angry with him. In that regard, I think the ending is too sentimental and unrealistic. It should have been slightly more abrasive. I should have asked Art to react a little differently than he does in that last scene. I find that working against things is sometimes valuable and it would have been nice to have had somebody in the midst of all that happiness be somewhat bitter and disgruntled. That way, Marion still has some way to go in earning their trust and respect again. It would have constituted a more truthful ending, I feel, and a far more affecting one. As it is, Marion's qualifying as a marine and possibly serving in the bell-lap of the war, appears to be enough. I think my original scheme, with a visual style containing more artificiality and fantasy, would have perhaps made the ending seem more acceptable. I think this is reflected in the reviews the film got, which were indeed very mixed.

Some critics liked the picture and thought it was harmless; others were more frustrated and disappointed with it, particularly as *Baby Blue Marine* was following on from *Bang the Drum Slowly*. I do remember

Roger Ebert praising the first hour of the picture, but feeling that the remaining thirty minutes were not as successful and ended on a confusing note. Honestly, I don't know what he meant by that and whenever opportunities later presented themselves I never questioned Roger about it. Maybe the sequence where Marion is swept downriver didn't really catch fire for him. Or maybe he would have liked Marion to have had a fistfight or a gunfight. Who knows? There was nothing "puzzling" about the film to me. It's not a complicated story by any means. I did find it interesting when Ebert speculated that *Baby Blue Marine* was missing half an hour from its narrative. Again, where he was coming from there I do not know as nothing substantial was ever removed.

We may have trimmed a few individual dialogue scenes a little, but nothing of significance was lost during the editing process. I basically stayed true to Stanford's screenplay and shot exactly what he wrote. I didn't have final cut on the picture, but it was one of those situations where nobody messed with the film. So, even though it wasn't contractually agreed, I did in effect have final cut. Verina Glaessner's comment in her review about *Baby Blue Marine* being something of "an exorcism of the Vietnam trauma" is an accurate one, and I'm glad you brought that up. Behind all this, of course, was the war in Vietnam and it was so much a part of what we were doing. It didn't need saying between Stanford and me, but we were both conscious that we were reflecting, in a strange mirror, how appalled we were at that ghastly folly. We were harking back to a more "innocent time" when there was a war that was worth fighting, but still took its toll on the goodness of people.

Baby Blue Marine was released in May 1976, after the end of the Vietnam War, and the specter of that conflict still fell heavily on our nation. Could that have colored people's reaction to the film? I don't know. Maybe it was too soft and sweet in comparison with what people were seeing in newspapers and on the television news: war, death, destruction, misery. We were talking earlier about the fascination people have with war, but that only goes so far. I perhaps anticipated that the audience wanted to be removed from the harsh reality of the times, the unpleasantness of it, and be taken to somewhere gentler—at least for ninety minutes. In that regard, maybe I didn't understand the audience. As I told you, the 1970s was a far more cynical and distrustful age. So, I made an effort in post-production to add another layer of that rosy feeling of nostalgia for a long-gone time.

For a film that touches on personal failure I find *Baby Blue Marine* somewhat ironic, as I don't think I succeeded with it. I failed to a certain degree and, also, others failed me. They didn't allow me to make the kind of picture I wanted to make. Don't get me wrong, I had great fun doing the movie. I enjoyed it, despite constantly worrying about Jan's performance and the look of the film. Although *Baby Blue Marine* was my third feature, I still wasn't feeling confident as a director by this point. I still didn't feel that I had a firm grip on the technical demands of the medium. Not really. It was the same problems as before. I was still slowly learning what the camera could do—the problems that the camera faces in terms of depth of field, etc.—and the long delay between movies had only succeeded in delaying my education. I look at the film now and I'm only reminded of my regrets—not only Jan, other things, too. For instance, the painfully slow fade-in I employed after the opening titles, where we see a lone figure sitting on the ground in the marine camp and then the marines come jogging over the hill, I think, is a little too slow. I don't know why I did that. It was the rhythm that I wanted at the time, but I see it now and say, "C'mon, hurry it up!"

However, there are other things I like, certain moments. Aside from Glynnis O'Connor's performance, I love Fred Carlin's music in the picture. Although it's a little mushy, I adore Fred's tender arrangement of "I'll Be Seeing You" that plays over the end credits. That was my idea. I'd listened to a lot of period recordings while I was preparing the picture and thought that was a wonderful song. It was very evocative and beautiful, and I love Fred's singing on it, too. Look, I've always been very tough on the movie over the years, and continue to be, but maybe it's not as bad as I remember it. Maybe I'm being unfair. I don't know. What I think inspired my negative opinion is the fact I initially had a singular vision in my mind of what the film should be, something far more sensuous and deeply felt, and I never got close to realizing it. That is still tough to swallow, but there are a few people out there who love *Baby Blue Marine* for what it is. I just feel it could have been so much more.

Portrait of the artist as a young man: a publicity photo of John Hancock taken in 1964 by Hans Namuth. Photo courtesy of John Hancock.

Duncan (Barton Heyman), Jessica (Zohra Lampert), Woody (Kevin O'Connor) and Emily (Mariclare Costello), summon the spirits of the dead in *Let's Scare Jessica to Death*. Photo courtesy of John Hancock.

Madwoman in the attic: Jessica detects a disturbing resemblance between Emily and Abigail Bishop while perusing an old portrait. Photo courtesy of John Hancock.

Emily/Abigail emerges from the lake in a nineteenth century wedding dress, nearly scaring Jessica to death. Photo courtesy of John Hancock.

Jessica defends herself against an onslaught of hallucinatory terrors in the chilling climax of *Let's Scare Jessica to Death*. Photo courtesy of John Hancock.

Henry "Arthur" Wiggen (Michael Moriarty), star pitcher for the New York Mammoths, befriends Bruce Pearson (Robert De Niro), a terminally ill third-string catcher in *Bang the Drum Slowly*. Photo courtesy of John Hancock.

Eccentric manager Dutch Schnell (Vincent Gardenia) and Coach Joe Jaros (Phil Foster) deliver another rousing team talk in *Bang the Drum Slowly*. Photo courtesy of John Hancock.

Robert De Niro, Heather MacRae (Holly Wiggen) and Michael Moriarty relax on the set of *Bang the Drum Slowly*. Photo courtesy of John Hancock.

Scheming madam Katie (Ann Wedgeworth) uses her charms to beguile an ailing Bruce into changing his will in her favor. Photo courtesy of John Hancock.

Image Section I • 223

Marion "Hedge" Hedgepeth (Jan-Michael Vincent) and Pop Mosley (Bruno Kirby) are washed-out of the Marine Corps in *Baby Blue Marine*. Photo courtesy of John Hancock.

Marion shares a drink with the haunted Marine Raider (Richard Gere), an encounter that will forever change his life. Photo courtesy of John Hancock.

Marion, now wearing the Marine Raider's uniform in place of his pale blue "suit of shame," salutes the camera. Photo courtesy of John Hancock.

Hancock shows Stanford Whitmore the sights, after the screenwriter visits the set of *Baby Blue Marine* during shooting. Photo courtesy of John Hancock.

A time of innocence: Rose Hudkins (Glynnis O'Connor) and Marion embrace in a field of wildflowers against the backdrop of Mount Shasta. Photo courtesy of John Hancock.

A morose-looking Hancock in Europe shortly after his dismissal from *Jaws 2* in June 1977, following a year of pre-production and a month of shooting. Photo courtesy of John Hancock.

Hancock and Tristan visit producer Martin Poll on the set of *The Fantastic Seven* in 1978 to discuss his helming a detective movie starring Dustin Hoffman. Photo courtesy of John Hancock.

Hancock with convict-turned-playwright Rick Cluchey (the real-life inspiration for Lee Umstetter in *Weeds*) during a visit to Dunkirk in 1979. Photo courtesy of John Hancock.

Hancock directs Dennis Christopher on location for *California Dreaming* at Avila Beach, as cinematographer Bobby Byrne looks on. Photo courtesy of John Hancock.

Producer Lou Arkoff—afflicted with a contagious case of pink-eye—chats with Hancock during the shooting of *California Dreaming*. Photo courtesy of John Hancock.

Tristan and Hancock share a quiet moment together during happier times on the set of the AIP production *California Dreaming*. Photo courtesy of John Hancock.

7

Jaws 2 (1977)

DESPITE BABY BLUE MARINE *failing to replicate the same levels of critical and commercial success as* Bang the Drum Slowly, *Hancock still found himself a director very much in demand. Nevertheless, even he could not have envisaged his receiving a firm offer during the summer of 1976 from producers Richard D. Zanuck and David Brown to helm the sequel to* Jaws, *the highest-grossing movie in the history of motion pictures. The prototypical blockbuster, Steven Spielberg's terrifying thriller about a Great White Shark terrorizing the shores of a small resort town called Amity Island had been based on the bestselling novel by Peter Benchley. Released on June 20, 1975, in 409 theaters across America, Universal had approved an ad campaign that had cost the studio an estimated $1.8 million ($700,000 of that money allotted to television advertising alone). Made on a production budget of $7 million* Jaws *had gone on to earn $470,653,000 worldwide, inspiring a staggering assortment of merchandise, as well as winning three Academy Awards and irrevocably changing the face of Hollywood filmmaking.*

Within weeks of the bean-counters at Universal tallying the film's unprecedented figures, executives were already formulating plans for a follow-up to their monster hit. After Spielberg refused all overtures to return for sequel duties, Zanuck and Brown commenced their search for a new creative locus, one that would hopefully devise a story capable of rivalling the stomach-knotting tension and visceral thrills of the first instalment. With original co-screenwriter Carl Gottlieb disinclined to script *Jaws 2* following his displeasure at the financial offer made to him, the producers instead turned to Howard Sackler (1929-1982), the Pulitzer Prize-winning playwright of The Great White Hope. Sackler had done a polish on Benchley's initial draft of the *Jaws* script prior to Gottlieb's involvement, and initially pitched the idea of a prequel as opposed to a conventional sequel—a suggestion that had briefly reignited Spielberg's interest. Sackler proposed a story that detailed the soul-scarring experiences of a young Quint, the ill-fated mariner of the Orca essayed by Robert Shaw, and his four-day fight for survival against exposure, dehydration and shark attacks following the sinking of the USS Indianapolis by a Japanese Naval submarine on July 30, 1945. This idea was nixed in favor of mounting a more direct continuation of events that took place at the same location and incorporated as many surviving characters from the original film as possible.

Even though he is one of only two survivors from the fateful expedition of the Orca in Spielberg's film, Chief Martin Brody is depicted as a broken paranoid obsessive in Sackler's draft for the second instalment. Ravaged by the debilitating effects of post-traumatic stress disorder, he is the unfortunate target for ridicule—rather than hero worship—by the community of Amity Island, and is described as having "the look of a survivor, rather than a resident"; a man constantly tormented by recurring thoughts of his experiences who "will NEVER shake off the memory of what he survived." Brody is afflicted with nightmares and sees sharks in every body of water he looks in from the ocean to a swimming pool. Amity itself is a veritable ghost town, its stock failing in the wake of the shark attacks that had earlier devastated it. Enter Len Peterson, a confident real estate tycoon who claims he can restore the island beach resort to its former glory. Mayor Larry Vaughn and the town elders are convinced by Peterson, but are less impressed with Brody's efforts to plunder resources from the city treasury in order to finance the construction of a fence in the water at Amity's premier swimming beach.

> Meanwhile, another character named Boyle has purchased Quint's shack with a plan to transform the site into a tourist attraction called "The Shark O'Rama Shark Den." After the partially-eaten carcass of a dead killer whale washes up on the beach, Brody becomes convinced it has been attacked by a shark and soon afterwards takes a police boat out in the hopes of destroying it. This unsanctioned escapade results in the Chief being fired from his job and obliterates the last vestiges of his already faltering reputation. However, his fears prove to be legitimate as the shark begins terrorizing the island, prompting Brody, Boyle and Peterson to venture out to sea on the tycoon's twin engine boat. The hunters quickly become the hunted as the monstrous shark continually rams their vessel, at one point knocking Boyle overboard into the ocean. Brody attempts to rescue Boyle, reaching down to pull him out of the water, only to discover that he has been bitten in half below the waist. As the shark continues to assail them, Brody orders Peterson to raise the boat's twin engines out of the water and then positions himself between them at the back of the boat. Kicking his feet wildly to attract the shark's attention, the carnivorous fish speeds towards him. At the very last moment before it reaches Brody, the former police chief hauls himself up onto the deck of the boat as Peterson suddenly drops both engines into the churning water. The shark then smashes headfirst into the whirling propeller blades which fatally shred it into a crimson explosion of blood and cartilage.

The first time I heard they were making *Jaws 2* was when Dorothy and I were having dinner with Howard Sackler at a restaurant in Pico called Chungking. I believe this was also the first time I actually met Howard. I got to know him through Dorothy as he had once dated her friend. He and I also knew a lot of the same people from New York who were around *The Great White Hope*, the actors and director, so we shared that connection. During our dinner, I happened to ask Howard what he was working on and he replied, "The sequel to *Jaws*." I was intrigued to learn this as *Jaws* had been a bona fide phenomenon. I can only assume now, since Howard and I felt we liked each other, that it was he who originally mentioned my name to Richard Zanuck and David Brown as a possible candidate to direct *Jaws 2*. At least I've always believed that it was Howard who recommended me and was a considerable part of the reason why I was considered for the job. I already knew Dick Zanuck from meeting him at a party after the 1971 Academy Awards ceremony; and I knew Brown from our lunch board meetings back when we were both Trustees of the AFI. So, I was aware of the plans they and Universal had for the movie, but the first I heard of the possibility of my involvement as director came when Dick called my agent and asked if we could have lunch.

When Dick intimated that he wanted me to direct *Jaws 2*, I was taken aback. I did not regard myself as the natural choice to make that picture, but Dick felt otherwise. He and Brown really wanted me to do it and I was somewhat surprised to discover that I really wanted to do it, too. I mean, even getting an opportunity to make something like *Jaws 2* was very gratifying at the outset. I must be honest about that. I had liked Steven Spielberg's movie a lot and thought it was remarkable—very scary and thrilling. I was delighted to be considered for the sequel, as it was such a high-profile job. It surely meant that I was doing something right. I didn't initially get into the business to make movies like *Jaws 2*, but when a huge project like that comes along you do feel excited and energized about it—about the potential of it—despite any reservations you may have. Ultimately, the whole experience turned sour for me and led me to later question myself; what my desires and motivations had been to even want to make a picture like that in the first instance. But, in the beginning, it was different. I felt different.

People have asked me why I chose to do *Jaws 2* at this stage of my career. My answer is I thought it would be advantageous to do a big commercial picture that had a lot of stunts and special effects in it. By this time, I had already earned a reputation as "an actor's director." So, on one level, I wanted to demonstrate that I could do stunts and special effects as well as work with actors. *Jaws 2* was clearly a chance to do that, to broaden my knowledge and proficiency as a filmmaker. I also felt that, as a scary action picture, it could potentially open up other avenues and opportunities that might have been denied me if I had been typed only as a director of realistic human stories like *Bang the Drum Slowly* and *Baby Blue Marine*. It's often said that a director is supposed to do one picture for themselves and one picture for the business, and alternate them. That idea was very much in my mind at the time. Certain people—such as my agents and Tom Pollock, who was a successful entertainment lawyer back then and would later become a studio executive—were telling me this was sound advice. Clint Eastwood is a good example of a director who moves effortlessly from commercial projects to more personal projects, and is still able to maintain a successful and satisfying career. So, I signed on for *Jaws 2* thinking that it would eventually lead me to more diverse projects down the line that I could possibly deliver while working within the machinery of the major studios.

An important thing to remember is that back in the mid-1970s sequels were not as commonplace as they are now. Movies like *Jaws* and *Star Wars* revolutionized Hollywood filmmaking and ushered in the birth of the summer blockbuster. Today, it seems obvious that a studio would immediately begin instigating plans to do a sequel to a picture with the unprecedented success of *Jaws*. But back in those days, the only sequels being produced were things like *The Godfather Part II* and franchises like James Bond, very little beyond that comparatively speaking. The idea of the big blockbuster summer sequel screaming from every billboard, newspaper and TV set year after year was still a fairly novel concept for audiences to digest. So, I understood that *Jaws 2* presented its own unique challenges: how do you match the kind of phenomenal success of the first film? How do you do something that is as fresh and as thrilling, but also doesn't insult the memory of the original? These were all questions we entertained from the start.

I was aware that Howard Sackler had done some uncredited work on Spielberg's *Jaws* and had written, or at least directly contributed to, the famous speech that Robert Shaw's character, Quint, tells Chief Brody and Hooper about the sinking of the USS Indianapolis. Seeing most of his shipmates being devoured by sharks as they floated around in the ocean waiting to be rescued provided a good motivation for Quint to despise the creatures. But that scene is one of the highlights of the first movie, beautifully played by Shaw. I presume that on the strength of that memorable contribution, Howard was then rewarded with the opportunity to write the sequel. That seemed fine, but the draft he finally turned in for *Jaws 2* was uninspiring and, frankly, terrible. Believe it or not it was written in longhand, and I could only surmise that Howard did not feel particularly excited to be doing another killer shark movie. It definitely showed in his writing. He probably thought the material was not worthy of him—not a second time around, anyway. His script was a rather dull and routine story, not something I was particularly enthused to be directing.

Feeling this, I then made an approach to Nancy Dowd, who had written the ice hockey movie *Slap Shot* for George Roy Hill, to do a polish on Howard's draft. I'd read Nancy's screenplay for *Slap Shot* and thought it was wonderful. I was especially impressed with her dialogue which really leapt off the page. Howard's dialogue was exceedingly bad and stilted, and my idea was that Nancy could make it sharper and also flesh out some of the characters. At the point at which I approached her, however, it wasn't known to me that *Slap Shot* had mostly been the result of a tape recorder. I subsequently discovered that Nancy had toured with her brother's minor league hockey team and had simply recorded and transcribed a lot of what they had said and done. Nancy had secured several rather notable jobs on the strength of *Slap Shot* and later won the Academy Award for Best Original Screenplay for Hal Ashby's *Coming Home*, although on that occasion her script was entirely rewritten. At any rate, it turned out that she wasn't interested in doing *Jaws 2* and, all things considered, maybe that was just as well.

Permit me at this point to take a short but relevant diversion: in the summer of 1975, Dorothy and I started living together and then got married the following Christmas. It was during this period—shortly before *Jaws 2* happened—that I discovered Dorothy could write and this became a very big deal. The first screenplay she completed was a horror film entitled *Motherkill*. It was the story of a couple living in Malibu who experience strange and disturbing phenomena after an evil sister comes to visit them. The inspiration for this tale was the fact we had bought a wonderful house in Malibu that overlooked the ocean and a canyon (it's where we got hitched) that also had a swimming pool. We loved that house and felt very comfortable there. That was until we learned, after we'd purchased the property, that the previous owner's wife had drowned herself in that same pool. This came as a considerable shock to us, so in an attempt to deal with the scariness and unpleasantness of it, Dorothy wrote a script that featured the ghost of a woman in a swimming pool. It was our attempt to exorcise the demons, so to speak, and reclaim our home. You see, we were having trouble sleeping at night knowing that a human being had perished in our pool. Dorothy and I would look out the window in the hours of darkness and see mist slowly rising up from the water and we were *terrified*! It seems rather silly now, but it was unnerving at the time—even for a rationalist like me who rejects the supernatural. I read Dorothy's script and liked it. It needed some work but it was a fairly accomplished and atmospheric effort. We mentioned *Motherkill* to Joseph Janni, an Italian producer who had worked a lot with John Schlesinger on movies like *Darling* and *Sunday Bloody Sunday*. Joe was a wonderful guy and a good friend to us. We showed him Dorothy's script and he was impressed with it. This all occurred right after *The Omen* had opened in 1976 and, after witnessing the commercial success of that film, Joe suddenly developed an interest in religious horror stories. He basically said, "Look, you have got to work God and the Devil into this story." So, in an effort to give the script the best possible chance, we attempted to do just what Joe had suggested. Unfortunately, this messed the whole thing up and *Motherkill* got very silly. We never seriously pursued the project after that and when *Jaws 2* came up, all of our focus and energies were thrown into that.

Anyway, shortly after Nancy Dowd had rejected my offer to rewrite Sackler's draft, I was talking to Dorothy about the various problems I had with his screenplay. She then asked, "Well, can I take a look at it?" So, Dorothy read the script and said, "You know, I have some ideas about how we can possibly fix this. We could work on it together and make the story far scarier and more exciting." She proceeded to tell me some of her ideas and they were all great. By this point, Dorothy had really developed her skills as a writer. She's always had a real affinity and facility with horror stories, and she knew how to effectively punch-up the tepid scares and thin tension Howard had devised in his draft. I liked what she had done so much I went back to Zanuck and Brown and relayed Dorothy's suggestions to them. They both immediately reacted positively, and said, "That all sounds good. Okay, go ahead and do it." It really was that simple. Before we knew it, Dorothy and I were rewriting the script, incorporating several different ideas and scenes that were all new. We altered or dropped some of Sackler's characters and included more teenagers in the story. We wanted to give the movie a few more dramatic set pieces that would get the audience on edge.

As another direct link to *Jaws*, we also added a character named Sideburns. This individual was a mysterious young man who arrives on Amity Island and, at a certain point in the story, is revealed to be Quint's natural son. As I recall, Sideburns was first introduced onscreen as he traveled on a ferry to the island and was quietly whistling "Fair Spanish Ladies" to himself, which is the song that Robert Shaw famously sings in the first film. I always liked that idea and we kept adding new stuff as we went along. Alas, despite what I'd interpreted as his contempt for the material, I don't think Howard was happy when he learned that his work was being revised. As I indicated, he was responsible for bringing us onto the project in the first place and I believe he felt personally betrayed by our actions. In retrospect, I guess he was right, but it was not a Machiavellian maneuver on our part, or an attempt to somehow blindside or belittle Sackler; it was merely our own naivety and over-eagerness in evidence, I guess. The bottom line is we needed to get that script fixed as it simply wasn't good enough. Dorothy and I did not adequately anticipate beforehand that Howard would have a problem with us reworking what he had done. It seemed to us that he couldn't wait to move on to other things and leave *Jaws 2* behind. We were wrong about that and it would lead to some bad feeling down the line.

As we were in the process of writing and planning the film, Zanuck and Brown sent us off to Acapulco to work on the script. The work was intensive, but Dorothy and I were also able to relax and enjoy ourselves a little. We practiced scuba-diving in the ocean as I had a lot of scenes to shoot both on and under the water, and we felt this could only help. As a kid, I had done some scuba-diving so it wasn't hard for me to master it again. It was fun, although I did come face-to-face with a swordfish one day which was rather unnerving. While down in Mexico, Dorothy and I started developing and detailing more of the sequences and set pieces we had in mind. We invented this elaborate and disturbing passage involving two water skiers who are attacked by the shark. It grew into this extremely gory action sequence in which one of them is brutally eaten alive. We also had to come up with a strong climax as there was no ending in Sackler's script—nothing that worked to my satisfaction, anyway. The shark being chewed up by the engine propellers of a boat seemed a little weak and underwhelming to me. Dorothy and I were busting our brains trying to figure out exactly how to kill the shark in a manner that would impress people. We couldn't blow the damn thing up as Spielberg had already done that in his movie, but we had to devise a sequence that was tense, terrifying and spectacular. So, we made a list of the different ways that you can possibly kill creatures but nothing really satisfied us. One day, as we were swimming in the ocean, our eyes and ears always attuned and looking for inspiration, Dorothy suddenly exclaimed, "I know! I've got it! The shark is speeding towards Brody to get him and it bites an electrical cable and is electrocuted! That will kill him, right?" It sounded perfectly feasible to me, as I understand that sharks will bite anything. So, we now had our ending.

When we showed Dorothy's revised draft to Zanuck and Brown, they loved it—as did Sidney Sheinberg, who was the President of Universal Studios and the executive in charge of *Jaws* and *Jaws 2*. Everybody agreed it was superior to Sackler's draft in every way and they also loved our proposed climax. We were all feeling confident and excited about the prospect of moving ahead with the film. I didn't quite know at the time (but would certainly learn later) that there was an ongoing battle between Zanuck and Sheinberg which had commenced on *Jaws*. They had both quarreled a lot with each other on the first movie as Sheinberg had wanted his wife, Lorraine Gary, to play Chief Brody's wife, Ellen, and Dick had promised his wife, Linda Harrison, that she could play the part. Sheinberg had won that particular argument, but it resulted in some negative feelings between the two of them. Then too, when *Jaws* was being made, the picture had tripled its budget and shooting schedule and Sheinberg blamed Zanuck for that. So, regardless of the incredible success of *Jaws*, there was some very bad blood there and this palpable tension that seemed to constantly be on the boil. I believe that Zanuck and Sheinberg also had issues concerning the overages on *Jaws* and that the profit sharing on the first movie had still not been amicably settled. All of this was contributing to the strain and unease that existed in their relationship.

I should add at this juncture that I liked Dick Zanuck, but I did not especially like Sid Sheinberg. I had been Dick's choice to direct *Jaws 2* and soon after meeting him, perhaps even before, I'd arrived at the opinion that he was a gifted and natural working producer who had made some wonderful pictures. I also thought that Dick's father, Darryl F. Zanuck, was a fabulous writer and studio head who had supported some of my favorite movies. Conversely, I considered Sheinberg to be a lawyer and an executive; a non-creative and nothing more. So, I was very much inclined towards the Zanuck camp and, when we working on the script, Dick would often insist that Dorothy and I always did what we felt was right for the movie. As he saw it that was all that really mattered, making a good picture. Naturally, that's what we wanted too. But it wasn't going to be that easy because we would often hear different things from different people. For instance, Zanuck would say, "Ah, don't worry about Sheinberg," and Sheinberg would say, "Ah, don't worry about Zanuck," and this precarious dance between these two enormous egos would continue. I was stuck firmly in the middle of them and, frankly, it was never destined to end well—least of all for me.

I can recall one fateful evening when the Sheinbergs invited Dorothy and me over for dinner to talk about the script. They were both extremely pleasant and, at this point, it's worth noting that Sheinberg was even recommending Dorothy for other screenwriting jobs and was her big advocate. So, we were both looking forward to spending some personal time with the boss and his wife. As we sat around and chatted, Sid and Lorraine proceeded to carefully explain to us exactly why they felt it was important that Ellen Brody should go out on the boat with Chief Brody to rescue the stranded kids from the shark. How it would be good for the picture and, no doubt, good for Lorraine (although I believe the latter consideration was merely implicit). Dorothy and I respectfully listened to this and nodded at all the right times. We then went back and told Zanuck that the Sheinbergs wanted to have Mrs. Brody go out on the ocean with the Chief. Dick immediately responded by saying, "Over my dead body!" Those were his exact words. I didn't realize it at that precise moment, but this reaction was going to have serious ramifications for me.

Now, it's well known that Lorraine pushed very hard to get that part in *Jaws*. She pressed her husband, she pressed Spielberg, and she did indeed secure the role. I liked Lorraine, but I was under no illusions about her abilities. She was an okay actress, but her career had profited from her husband's position and influence. So, I've always believed that her involvement in *Jaws* was a case of nepotism. Maybe I'm mistaken, but I doubt it. Granted, very much like Sheinberg, Zanuck also had his own desires and wishes for the movie, but he was always more open about it. In fact, I can recall talking to Dick one day about nepotism in our industry. I argued that in the movie business it's often a case of *who* and not *what* you know which allows a person to get forward. Dick nodded in complete agreement with this, and said, "I believe in nepotism. I don't deny it." Then, referring to everything his privileged lineage had given him, he added, "I wouldn't be where I am today without it!" I found that comment amusingly honest. As I said, Dick's wife had lost out to Sheinberg's wife for the role of Ellen Brody in *Jaws*. Amid the persistent aggravation between Zanuck and Sheinberg, I remember Dick came to us one day and said, "Can you and Dorothy please write something for Linda to play in the movie? It would mean a lot to me." I believe there was some tension in Dick's marriage at the time and he wanted to make this loving gesture to her. Linda was a beautiful woman, but I think it's fair to say she wasn't an accomplished actress. Again, neither was Lorraine for that matter, but she was marginally better than Linda. So, we thought about it and wrote the part of the oceanographic scientist who confers with Brody when a dead whale is washed up on the beach. Dick was grateful for our efforts, but then Sheinberg intervened again and Linda didn't get to do the part.

Somebody else eventually played the scientist in the finished movie. Sadly, Dick and Linda got divorced shortly after *Jaws 2* came out. But these are just some examples of what went on; two powerful men constantly vying to get one over on the other. It was a very charged atmosphere.

Anyhow, following Dick sharing his disapproving feelings to us concerning the Sheinbergs' suggestions for the story we turned in our next draft—without Lorraine's character going out on the boat to rescue the kids. After that, Sheinberg never met my eyes in the Universal commissary again. Not once. I sometimes think my goose was cooked right from the instant he finished reading that version of the screenplay and realized Ellen Brody was still somewhere on terra firma. Certainly, things were never going to be the same again between us. That much was made obvious. He and Lorraine had initially been so friendly and inviting, so maybe they felt betrayed. The Sheinbergs were possibly thinking they had welcomed Dorothy and me into their home and shared their ideas for the movie, only for us to callously ignore them. That wasn't true at all, but it didn't matter. There was no coming back from it. What's ironic is the fact that Dorothy had fleshed out the character of Ellen in her re-write of Sackler's script and given her considerably more to do. She had felt it was important there be more to Ellen than simply being Brody's wife and the mother of his children, and Lorraine appreciated Dorothy's efforts. In fact, on the surface, Lorraine appeared to like Dorothy very much. We were actually discussing this subject just the other day, and Dorothy remarked, "I liked Lorraine a lot and we got along well." Ultimately, there was just too much ill feeling and subterfuge going on between Sheinberg and Zanuck for everything to function as it should. Now, when you add Verna Fields into this mix things really start to get toxic.

Verna was undoubtedly another important and persuasive figure in this increasingly delicate situation and was then the Vice-President for Feature Production at Universal. I found her to be an extremely interesting and talented woman—very strong and resolute. She had survived a serious bout of cancer (the disease would eventually return with a vengeance and claim her life in 1982) and cancer survivors frequently tend to be incredibly strong and resolute people. Verna was a wonderful editor who had cut *Jaws* for Spielberg. I think she made sizable contributions to the success and power of the film and, let's not forget, Verna had also edited a number of other great movies like *The Last Picture Show* and *American Graffiti*. She'd won an Academy Award for her work on *Jaws* and, shortly afterwards, had ascended to the lofty position of becoming an executive at Universal. It's worth noting that Verna had felt strongly that she should have been the one hired to direct *Jaws 2* based on her considerable efforts on *Jaws*. I personally feel that Verna should have directed *Jaws 2*. I really do. It ought to have been her film. However, Zanuck had not wanted her for the job because he felt that would have transferred far too much power to the studio. I'm sure he had other reasons to oppose Verna securing the job as director, too. For Dick, that prospect was potentially inviting far too many problems because there was already this simmering tension between him and Sheinberg that was always threatening to boil over. In the end, Verna's influence would prove to be just as detrimental for me down the line as Sheinberg's. But, in the beginning, she was friendly and supportive. Indeed, Verna seemed to be very much behind me and liked our ideas for the sequel.

You see, my *Jaws 2* was always intended to be a far darker and grittier film than *Jaws*. It was going to be more somber in tone and we originally started thinking about the story from a totally realistic standpoint: what if a Great White Shark had occupied the waters off Amity Island? Precisely what would the effects of this enormous fish having killed and eaten several people be? How would it affect the local economy and other sections of the community? Would the residue of these events linger and haunt the inhabitants and cause lasting psychological and financial damage? No doubt, if such a terrible thing were to occur, it would be devastating and we wanted to reflect that in our story. So, we had Amity's economy in ruins and Brody suffering the debilitating effects of post-traumatic stress disorder after the climax of the first film. Sackler had the idea that Brody was paranoid, but in our iteration of the character we took it even further and made him a truly bedeviled man. Brody's every waking thought is dominated by sharks and, when he does sleep, he is having nightmares about them. He becomes obsessed with sharks and, to compound everything, another Great White *does* come back to Amity Island and Brody's worst fears are confirmed. We thought that would be a disturbing development for him to contend with: the idea that the absolute worst thing he can possibly imagine is happening again.

A symptom of this situation would be Brody starts seeing sharks everywhere. He'd look in reflective surfaces—mostly in water but maybe in windows and other places, too—and there they would be. Early on, we'd discussed the possibility of doing this using either double exposures or mattes, or by utilizing a simple cut in which the audience would see exactly what Brody imagines in his mind. Another option might have been to reuse quick flashes of imagery and footage from the first *Jaws* to illustrate Brody's recurring nightmares about the shark. A lot of sequels do that, simply quote the original picture. I can't imagine there would have been a rights issue over our reusing this material as the sequel was being made by the same studio. But I do think such an approach would have been too literal and repetitive, and was never something I intended to try. Our initial idea was that these visions Brody is seeing would be like ghostly images, which reinforced the idea of him literally being haunted. Again, that was such an interesting idea, Brody being psychologically damaged. I believe that aspect is mostly gone from *Jaws 2* as it now exists. I mean, he's still frightened and concerned about a shark returning to Amity's shores but he hasn't gone half mad. That is what Brody was going to be in my version—a little crazy.

We scouted *Jaws 2* in Martha's Vineyard, the same location where Spielberg had shot the first movie, only our version of the town was going to be a place of despair and depression: the beaches are empty, stores have been boarded up, holiday homes abandoned, picket fences broken, that kind of thing. In spite of everything that went on in *Jaws*, like the kid being eaten by the shark and the girl getting killed during a night-swim, the sun was always shining in Spielberg's movie. What I mean is Amity Island still looked like a great place to visit if you stayed out of the water. Our incarnation was going to be markedly different: a dark, dour environment that reflected the collective fear and misery the people were feeling. It was not going to be a nice place to visit at all. I reasoned that if I was going to be placed in a position where it seemed like I was competing with Spielberg's film (which was something I never consciously considered) I wanted to do something different. Then, if my picture failed, at least it would be an honorable failure. I couldn't be accused of simply xeroxing another director's movie and approach.

Before we started shooting *Jaws 2*, I had the opportunity to have lunch with Spielberg at some place in the San Fernando Valley, and we discussed the project. This was just before *Close Encounters of the Third Kind* came out and he was about to enter his own personal stratosphere of success. I remember Spielberg was extremely charming, friendly and positive. I was about to do the sequel to his film but he was offering all kinds of advice and suggestions. Sitting beside him I could almost feel this tremendous energy emanating from his body. He would describe things so vividly they would come alive in my imagination and I could really see them. Spielberg had some good ideas concerning the action scenes with the shark and I was impressed with how his mind worked in terms of threading things through a story. For instance, he would say, "Okay, the first time we see the shark it's *this* and then later, after it comes closer, it's suddenly *that*." I would listen and think, yes, of course, that will all work wonderfully well. Thus, I incorporated some of Spielberg's ideas into the screenplay—one of which was the terrific idea of the shark swimming soundlessly and ominously into the Amity harbor at night. As soon as I heard it, I said to myself, "I'm using that!" I actually got the shot of the shark coming into the harbor during our first week of shooting as it only involved one of the fake fins and not the big, cumbersome mechanical shark itself. Spielberg also advised me not to be afraid to re-shoot things that didn't work the first time around as the shark scenes in his movie were often done for the second and third times. He continually kept re-shooting things on *Jaws* that were not successful in an effort to get everything right. It was also evident from our conversations that the camera operator on *Jaws*, Michael Chapman, had been an invaluable and dependable collaborator for Spielberg. He repeatedly praised Chapman for his work on the boat scenes as they were extremely difficult to do. Another thing Spielberg had emphatically said during our meeting was, "Trust Joe Alves!" Alves had been the production designer on his film and at Spielberg's urging I hired him to fulfill that same role on the sequel. I laugh about it now because that was the one piece of Spielberg's advice I should have ignored. It's too bad I didn't.

The shark in our story was originally conceived to be a pregnant female as we decided to go with this idea of "the revenge of the mate." It was going to be bigger than the shark in *Jaws* and even more deadly. I guess we were aiming for a kind of mystical, anthropomorphic quality to the shark that bore no relationship to reality and the natural instincts and behavior of these predators. I mean, Spielberg's film had also done that to a large extent. His shark had exhibited human or "evil" traits in its relentless pursuit of Brody, Quint and Hooper on the ocean. Sure, not all of that stuff had to make sense; it just had to be scary. We felt that our script didn't have to be firmly tied to the facts of nature and biology for this same reason. Really, we weren't going to show the shark a whole lot in our picture. Spielberg told me that one of the first and most effective lessons he had learned during the making of *Jaws* was to "shoot the ripples on the water." He wanted to keep the shark as mysterious as he possibly could because he understood that once you do eventually see the monster, it will be incredibly unnerving. It almost goes without saying that you don't want to over-expose this thing for the piece of rubber, metal and plastic it is. When you really *have* to show it, and reveal it fully to the audience, the hope is that through a careful approach these moments contain far more potency and power.

In considering how to find the correct approach to take with the film in practical and visual terms, one of the most important decisions we had to make was our director of photography. I originally wanted to retain several of Spielberg's camera crew on *Jaws* for the sequel—beginning with the cinematographer Bill Butler. Zanuck and Brown felt strongly that he was no longer a good candidate and I bowed to their wisdom. They claimed that Butler had had some trouble shooting on the ocean, and was maybe a little too old and slow. Personally, I think he would have done just fine. We then all agreed that the next best choice was Michael Chapman, as he'd been Butler's operator on *Jaws* and had also worked with Gordon Willis on a bunch of pictures. Chapman had received the credit in Zanuck's mind for hand-holding the best footage on the boat scenes. He had already done some wonderful work for Marty Scorsese on *Taxi Driver* and would go on to shoot *Raging Bull* for him, too, so I desperately wanted him. Lamentably, Chapman felt he had already done his shark picture and expressed no desire to return for another. Aside from that, he may have also been working on another movie at the time. It was a disappointing loss. I only discovered the true extent of that loss when we started shooting.

I then wanted Vilmos Zsigmond, simply because I had loved his work on *McCabe & Mrs. Miller* and *Deliverance*. I submitted his name to Zanuck, but Dick immediately said, "Nah, no way that's happening. Life's too short!" I gather that Vilmos took so long on *The Black Windmill* Dick did not want to work with him again. I was willing to take Vilmos on despite these considerations, but was blocked. Around this time, we also considered Owen Roisman, who had shot *The French Connection* and *The Exorcist*. I forget why it didn't work out with him. Perhaps Roisman wasn't available. We next turned our attention to William Fraker, who had shot everything from *Paint Your Wagon* to *Rosemary's Baby*. He might have been the best choice, considering everything, because I understand he was also easy to get along with. But Zanuck and Brown were worried that, like Bill Butler, Fraker was too old and wouldn't have the physical stamina required for the boat stuff. Once again, I bowed to their *greater* knowledge. Conrad Hall, who had shot *In Cold Blood* and *Butch Cassidy and the Sundance Kid*, was another guy we briefly considered. I was worried that Hall would be too difficult, but we probably would have been much better off with him. Even so, the last thing I needed in that den of knives was a difficult cinematographer. We also considered three guys I'd worked with before: Bob Baldwin, Richard Shore and Laszlo Kovacs. We flew both Baldwin and Shore out from New York City for interviews, but Joe Alves quickly shot Shore down. As I told you, Joe wasn't a big fan of the visual side of *Bang the Drum Slowly*, which probably should have been my first warning of trouble from his direction.

Following this involved process of finding a director of photography, we eventually settled on Michael Butler (no relation to Bill Butler). Michael had shot a couple of pictures for Don Siegel that I liked and had also shot *The Missouri Breaks* for Arthur Penn. I had hated *The Missouri Breaks*, but I thought the look of that movie was wonderful. I also liked Michael personally, although I've found his subsequent claims that I attempted to make *Jaws 2* more of an "art film" than a scary action picture wildly inaccurate and ridiculous. Early on, I had carefully explained to Michael the look I was after and he appeared to respond to my ideas. We intended to shoot *Jaws 2* without warming filters and were going for a cold, blue look that was in keeping with the concept I had of Amity Island as this destroyed world tinged with tragedy. I wanted it to be a ghost town with a bleak, mournful look—something which has actually become quite modish now. We wanted to do the film with de-saturated colors as a departure from Spielberg's movie which had very bright, conventional American photography. *Jaws* looks like a glossy Hollywood picture, but I was trying to make something that was harsh and downbeat, possibly more European in some ways. I felt that if we were really going to do a story about a character suffering nightmares and post-traumatic stress disorder, this quality should be reflected strongly in all the visual aspects. So, instead of the sun shining like it did in Spielberg's film I wanted fog; where the skies were blue, I wanted them grey. That would have provided a conspicuously different look which would have contrasted sharply with the first *Jaws*. And I repeat: I was trying to do *my* shark movie, not his.

In the final reckoning, I realize this approach was not what the studio liked or wanted. That said, a lot of people received these ideas warmly when they were first suggested. Oddly enough, I read a recent interview with Michael Butler in which he recalled our discussions regarding the specific look I wanted for *Jaws 2*: he claims that after I told him of my desire to make an "artistic" film (an "artistic" film, not an "art film," as there is a difference) he gulped deeply. As strange as it sounds, I can remember that gulp! Isn't that weird? His response, as small as it was, not only registered with me, it has remained in my memory all these years. Ordinarily, I would not have been as sensitive to such a reaction. But Michael certainly got behind the look I wanted at the time. He really did. Only after I was fired from the picture did he ever express any concerns or doubts he had about what it was we were doing. That's always easier to do, but certain people have made strange comments regarding how far I wished to go. There have even been rumors that I wanted the yellow lines in the streets of Martha's Vineyard to be painted black to adhere to the dark visual style I wanted. Again, this is not true. Such a thing would have presented significant liability problems if there were any accidents. I tend not to shoot high shots anyway, so who would have ever seen them? Joe Alves has also recently complained that the boats were "a dark color" in my abandoned version. As I've readily admitted, I did want a de-saturated visual style, but the boats were not oppressively dark, they just weren't overtly colorful. That's the difference. I did not want a kind of Disney/Technicolor look for *Jaws 2*. That would not have served the story I was attempting to tell—this idea of Amity Island as a haunted world in ruins. At a certain point, it seems not everybody bought into my bleak vision. They may have thought it was morbid or was veering too far from the first film.

> *Although the star of any* Jaws *movie was indubitably the shark, Hancock and his producers were mindful that it would be valuable to retain several "familiar faces" for the second installment. The first veterans of Spielberg's film to return were Lorraine Gary and Murray Hamilton, the latter having played Amity's duplicitous Mayor Vaughn. Integral to the sequel's story working was the need to once again secure the services of Roy Scheider who had made such a memorable impression as the beleaguered Chief Brody. Following the immense success of* Jaws, *Scheider had signed a lucrative three-picture deal with Universal that had commenced with William Friedkin's* Sorcerer *(1977), a consummate remake of the 1953 French thriller* The Wages of Fear.*
>
> *The second scheduled film of the deal was to be Michael Cimino's epic war drama* The Deer Hunter, *in which Scheider would essay the role of Michael Vronsky,*

a Pennsylvania steelworker who serves in the Vietnam War. Just weeks before principal photography was to begin, the actor suddenly withdrew from the production citing "creative differences" and was replaced by Robert De Niro. Still contractually obligated to deliver two more pictures for Universal, Scheider refused a succession of projects that were presented to him by the studio—including a proposed sequel to Jaws. *Executives were finally able to entice the actor into reprising his role by allowing him out of his contract if he agreed to star in* Jaws 2 *(the one picture would effectively count as two). Scheider reluctantly complied and signed on for the film in early 1977.*

As several of the principal players were being locked down for the sequel, casting sessions were held in Los Angeles and New York under the stewardship of Shari Rhodes, another veteran of Jaws *who had also worked with Spielberg on* The Sugarland Express *and* Close Encounters of the Third Kind. *The casting director traveled to Martha's Vineyard in February 1977 in a concerted effort to find kids "between the ages of thirteen and nineteen" that were necessary to play the plethora of teenagers detailed in the screenplay. Rhodes also had the unenviable task of locating and convincing many of the locals who had played supporting roles and cameos in Spielberg's shocker to return for the sequel.*

We wrote the script fairly safe in the knowledge that Roy Scheider would be returning to play Brody. Quint, probably the most memorable character in *Jaws*, had been eaten by the shark and Richard Dreyfuss had moved on to other things so there would be no Hooper in the story either. This was okay with me, but without Roy's involvement *Jaws 2* was going to have to be an entirely different film from the one we had conceived—unless we hired somebody else to play the role. I didn't want that and neither did Zanuck and Brown. I understand that Roy was indeed contractually bound to return for the sequel and that he was unhappy about being tied to Universal. From my position, I was excited to be working with Roy. I had liked his performances in *Klute* and *The French Connection*, and later thought he was wonderful in *All That Jazz*, which he did shortly after *Jaws 2*. I'd hoped and anticipated that Roy would respond positively to our script because it gave Brody a definite psychological and emotional dimension. But I don't think any of this mattered particularly to him as he did not want to do the picture. Maybe he was still hurting over *The Deer Hunter* not working out. I don't know. I'm not sure of all the details and I never discussed it with him to any great extent, but I think there was a substantial change to Michael Cimino's script that he strongly disapproved of. I'm sure it was another source of unhappiness for him. So, you could say that Roy wasn't in the most positive frame of mind when he came to work on our film.

After something of a shaky start, Roy and I got along with each other. Did I like Scheider as a person? Well, I think few did. There was something rather solitary and standoffish about Roy. He preferred to work on his tan nearly every moment we weren't shooting. Unless you were willing to physically lie down beside him and catch some rays, you weren't going to have a conversation of any great length and meaning with him. I had far too much to do anyway, so that was never an option for me. Early on, as we were preparing the sequel, I remember Dorothy and I gave an interview to a reporter for *The New York Times*. In it we rather innocuously said, "*Jaws* is a wonderful picture but we want to do something very different with our movie." This was only the truth and nothing we hadn't already openly stated in our many conversations with those involved or associated with the production. At any rate, after Roy read the article, he vehemently objected to this comment—and several other harmless remarks we made. The piece had appeared in print shortly after we'd arrived in Pensacola, Florida, to start rehearsals. Often somebody working on a movie will give an interview to the press that causes a modicum of tension and unrest. That was the case here as, for reasons known only to him, Roy disliked the interview intensely. In fact, Roy hated it so much he went to the trouble of clipping the article from *The New York Times*, annotating it with scribbled words like "bullshit" and "fuck you," before taking the trouble to roll it up in a tampon tube and insert it into my mailbox at the hotel. Doesn't that blow your mind?! I can recall feeling stunned to discover this object waiting for me one morning. I examined it then said to myself: "Christ, this is one hell of a beginning with this guy!" It was odd behavior, a little sick and weird, but Roy never followed-up on it. If you want to know the truth, I think he was drunk at the time he did it. Later, when I talked to him about the article, I said, "Look, what makes you think I was quoted accurately anyway? This appears to be an unfortunate misunderstanding." Roy seemed to accept that explanation and we decided to put the whole sordid episode behind us. We had our little dance with each other, or whatever it was, but the tension didn't last very long.

Other than that one incident, I never really witnessed Roy's tempestuous side. I was never intimidated by him, I was considerably bigger than Roy physically, but he did have a temper that became more combustible when he drank. I understand that he and Jeannot Szwarc, my eventual replacement as director on *Jaws 2*, had a rather difficult working relationship after I was fired from the picture. I was even told that they both got into a physical altercation, or something close to it, at one point. I can assure you that my dismissal from the film was not the cause of the aggravation between them. I never saw Roy again after I was fired and I'm sure that when he received the news that I was history he took it reasonably well. I don't think he was against the decision, let's put it that way. Still, there is no doubt in my mind that Roy was a little nuts. At one point in his life, back when he was a kid, I believe he had been ill and weighed around 300lbs. Then, over a period of time, Roy lost a lot of weight and became rail-thin. As I said, he also enjoyed devoting a sizable chunk of his free time to working assiduously on his tan. I'd heard it was impossible to stop him from doing this and that he couldn't be pried from the reflector he always carried around with him and placed under his chin. He later got so dark during shooting you couldn't photograph him anymore and I believe there were even some continuity concerns after I departed. Roy was definitely suffering from a body image crisis of some kind that was tormenting him.

Aside from Roy and Lorraine, we brought back a few other actors from the first movie such as Murray Hamilton. He had been perfectly fine in the role of the mayor in *Jaws*, but I can't say I was ever a big fan of his work. Murray was kind of an old-fashioned actor to me, very mannered and contrived, but he was okay at what he did. Interestingly, of all the principals on the film, I don't have any particular memory of him during the shooting of *Jaws 2*. Nothing has really stayed with me and I don't know why. Aside from Murray, we initially planned on also bringing back Jeffrey Kramer who had played Deputy Hendricks. Quite why we wanted to do this, I don't know, as Kramer's performance had been one of the few things in *Jaws* I didn't like. There were originally going to be two deputies in our story, and Hendricks was destined to be somewhat secondary to his colleague, Deputy Batliner, played by my actor Marshall Efron. I understand there was some suggestion early on in pre-production that Kramer didn't want to do the sequel as he had read the script and felt his part was too small. It's true that I was trying to minimize the role of Hendricks in the sequel. I don't deny it. I think Kramer took this rather badly. He complained that he didn't have much to do, but there was a reason for that: I thought he was a fakey actor and I tried not to have as much of him in my movie as Spielberg had in his. After I was fired from the picture, Jeannot Szwarc and Carl Gottlieb noticeably restored Hendricks to the story as Kramer's face was around a lot more than I would have liked had I still held the reins. No doubt this has left a bad taste in Kramer's mouth. He claimed in a recent book published about the making of *Jaws 2* that "sometimes there were three units shooting at the same time" on my set and we still "wouldn't get any footage." This simply isn't true. We never had two units, never mind *three*! We only had one as we weren't even into the real hard stuff at this point.

Shari Rhodes had been brought onto *Jaws 2* as casting director by Zanuck and Brown, as she was one of their people. I had no objections to hiring her, as Shari was another *Jaws* crew-member that Spielberg had told me to trust implicitly. So, I did. Shari brought in a lot of young people for us to read for the teenagers in the story—some good, some not so good. One diamond she unearthed was little Ricky Schroeder who we cast as Brody's young son, Sean. As soon as we read Ricky I knew we were in the presence of somebody special. He just had a magical quality about him that was so arresting and commercial. More than that, he was also a wonderful little boy to be around. I don't know much about Ricky's later work as an actor, I'm sure he's still very good, but back then he was a genius. To me, this was clearly a discovery at the level of finding Bobby De Niro for *Bang the Drum Slowly*. I mean, Ricky could do anything. He could cry or be afraid at the drop of a hat; he could be hilariously funny; he was charming, attentive and cooperative. We dyed his blonde hair brown so that he more closely resembled Roy and the kid playing his elder brother, and Ricky was fine with that. Everything was an adventure for him, which is the way it should be for any child actor. We loved each other for the short time we were together, and Ricky is one of the few warm memories from *Jaws 2* that I still carry with me. All of this makes his later firing from the picture one of the most bewildering and regrettable decisions from this whole painful affair, but more on that later.

Aside from casting in Los Angeles and New York City, which is usual on most of the films I've done, I also did some casting in Boston— the only time I've ever done this. Why? Well, because it's near Martha's Vineyard where we were going to be shooting and I thought I might be able to pick up someone for a small role who had a great Boston accent. Additionally, I also wanted to visit Harvard and see if Robert Chapman, my old professor and mentor there, had somebody good to recommend to me for one of the teenagers in the cast. It turned out that Chapman did and he introduced me to an economics major named Alan Stock who was starring in a lot of shows there. I cast Alan in the role of a kid named Eddie, and he was good. I found it was worth auditioning in Boston, not just for Harvard but for all the colleges in the area, as there are a *lot* with strong theater programs. Since I was looking for young people it suited my needs.

After we cast a lot of the kids we went to Pensacola, Florida, to rehearse for a month in the April and May of 1977. The plan was that during rehearsals the kids would spend several hours each day learning how to sail and getting a tan on Navarre Beach before they were brought up to Martha's Vineyard to start principal photography on the film in early June. Those four weeks were spent doing various improvisations and exercises. We worked on scenes and ideas, paired different actors together, and had them discuss their characters and how they related to each other. We wanted the kids to build solid friendships with each other that would give the audience the impression that these relationships had existed long before the story had begun. The way we structured the work was this: the kids would spend half a day learning how to sail in the morning and then we'd rehearse the scenes in the afternoon. We would put tape on the floor to simulate boats on the ocean and sometimes had them reacting to the shark attacking. A lot of the actors responded positively during rehearsals and had some good ideas. Others were far less successful and creative, and were more hesitant. I then realized that I had made one or two poor choices in casting.

Something else we did during rehearsals that apparently caused a little upset was the decision to rehearse the make-out scenes in the script. I only bring this up as certain claims have been made by some of the kids in the cast that I would like to respond to here: a couple of the actors have gone on record as saying they were unsettled to be rehearsing make-out scenes in front of Dorothy and me. I have no idea what they are talking about. Presumably, they had all read the script?! I thought they would have understood that they were teenagers playing teenagers, who were enacting what teenagers do—make-out with each other. Also, if you are going to be kissing somebody in a scene shouldn't you rehearse it? To me, it seems a perfectly useful thing to do. Their delayed objections seem to be one of those after-the-fact situations where people often place a misleading or unfairly negative spin on something. If you were to ask me if actors are occasionally troubled by love scenes my answer would be, yes, in my experience they are to some degree. Love scenes are never easy to do. But if you were to ask me if there was an unseemly or voyeuristic quality to Dorothy and me being present during those moments my answer would be, no, absolutely not! I don't get my kicks that way and neither does Dorothy. Frankly, it's strange and demeaning that they would even imply such a thing.

If I tried to reason it, I'd suggest that one source of their agitation was probably their own inexperience and insecurities as actors and as young people. I do know that from a director's point of view, make-out scenes are one of the things you really have to stage so that the actors don't feel uncomfortable or self-conscious. For instance, you may have to say to an actress, "Can he put his hand on your breast?" Sometimes they are perfectly happy to allow this, other times they are not. It depends on the individual. So, you really have to discuss and block make-out scenes and love scenes, so that everyone is relaxed. A lot of stuff you shoot doesn't have to be rigorously blocked because the actors can do it for you. However, fights, stunts, special effects and love scenes need to be directed. That's the only reason why I did it. A decade after *Jaws 2*, I extensively rehearsed the love scenes in *Weeds* with Nick Nolte and Rita Taggart and both of them were completely nude. Knowing that actors are always so distressed by love scenes I wanted to sidestep that awkwardness as swiftly as possible. On *Jaws 2*, I wanted to get all that stuff over with during the rehearsal period. I've known people who are so nervous about doing love scenes they have a drink beforehand. This can occasionally make them difficult to direct.

This leads me to something else I want to say: I look back now and can identify a couple of opportunities during pre-production where I might have piped-up a little more and expressed my concerns about a few things that were bothering me. I can recall Dick Zanuck arranging a meeting in his office one day before we went down to Florida to begin rehearsals. Everybody was there and Dick basically said, "Okay, does anybody here have any reason why we shouldn't proceed forward at this point?" That was the time when I should have raised my hand and said, "Yeah, I have some concerns I'd like to share. I'm not certain the cast is quite there yet. I have some doubts about one or two of the kids. Maybe we should keep looking for a few more good people. Also, wouldn't it be beneficial to all of us if we knew for certain that the big mechanical shark is working and will be ready for us?" Of course, I didn't say any of these things. I just kept my mouth shut. I didn't want to rock the boat, or slow the momentum down, or possibly bring things to a halt. *Jaws 2* was a huge studio movie costing a lot of money and so you can expect to have the best of everything. You place your full trust and confidence in your co-workers to do their jobs to the best of their ability. But sometimes it doesn't work out that way. I've found that money doesn't always guarantee people's best.

As for Lorraine, I must say that I saw no trace of disappointment or unhappiness during rehearsals—or indeed during shooting—to the fact her character would not be going out on the boat with Brody. I believe she was disappointed by that decision, but she never once mentioned it. There was no adverse reaction that I could detect and Lorraine was always professional. Looking back, could it be she was merely biding her time and knew something that I didn't know? I have no idea, but I don't think so. Lorraine would not have known what was coming at this early point—not during rehearsals. I believe she accepted her subsidiary role in the story and we moved on. All the same, it's worth noting an interesting comment that Ned Tanen, who was President of Universal's film division at the time, made to my agent David Wardlow during the early days on *Jaws 2*. He supposedly remarked, "I think John will be fine on the picture—if he can only survive the women!" Clearly by that Tanen meant Verna Fields, Lorraine, and perhaps even Dorothy. Who knows?

> *From the beginning of their involvement on the project, Hancock and Tristan were determined that their sequel would match the ferocious power and bowel-loosening shocks of* Jaws. *The filmmaker had been impressed with the ruthless skill in which Spielberg had terrorized audiences: "Like everyone else, I almost choked on my popcorn when [Ben Gardner's] severed head leered at Richard Dreyfuss through the hole in that boat," Hancock confesses. One of the first contributions Tristan made to the revised draft was the inclusion of a thrilling and disturbing sequence in which two water-skiers are attacked by the renegade shark off the shores of Amity Island. This gripping passage was greeted with much excitement by Zanuck and Brown, and would later inspire the marketing team at Universal to devise the iconic image of an enormous shark rising from*

> the ocean behind a smiling bikini-clad water-skier for the film's ad campaign. Nonetheless, in order to fully realize the disturbingly ambitious shark attacks detailed in the script, Hancock knew that he would have to place his full trust and confidence in the expertise of the special effects team assigned to the production. This, he would soon discover, would prove to be difficult.

What makes Spielberg's picture so powerful is that it gives you this sense of an ever-present threat lurking in the water. The shark is always waiting somewhere off-camera, ready to suddenly penetrate the frame and attack its victims without warning. It works incredibly well. But Dorothy and I realized that when you read something on the page—a book, a screenplay, even a newspaper article—you sometimes take the events and experiences it describes for granted. You understand everything but you are not entirely conscious of the realities and implications of these situations. What I'm saying is you can see it, but you don't always *feel* it. We did not want to invite that kind of response on *Jaws 2*. Our approach was founded on the idea that the audience should grasp the full horror of what a shark attack would be: the sense of helplessness and hopelessness; the terror and the agony you would feel as this monster devoured you alive. What would those final moments of life be like? Imagine rows of huge, razor-sharp teeth scissoring through your flesh. You're screaming and beating your fists against this cold, hard flesh. Ugh! It's so ghoulish and horrible when you really stop and think about it. Also, it would be happening to you in a different element—water—and there is something terribly primal and frightening about the ocean.

So, among other objectives, I was interested in exploring violence in *Jaws 2*. It was going to be a very violent and visceral picture. This approach would be severely toned down in the version of the film released in theaters, but I initially proceeded by considering what horrors to show and what horrors not to show; what things I would reveal explicitly onscreen and what things I could sell on the faces of those who were witnessing the events unfolding. I wanted to achieve a quality of escalation in the picture; of mounting terror as this monster was on the rampage killing people. I didn't want the audience to be complacent or desensitized to what they were seeing. The way to do that was to keep agitating and surprising them for the movie to consistently work—Spielberg had also known this— because only then would the audience feel the true horror of a person being eaten alive by a shark. Like anything, the way we were going to achieve this was by breaking everything down into tiny little cuts. We had to know exactly what we were going to see in each individual shot and what elements were needed in order to ensure that everything worked.

All these pieces of film would require considerable planning and effort to get. In regard to the attacks themselves, we needed to have a big shark mouth constructed—probably more than one—as well as highly realistic dummies of the human victims that die onscreen. We initially thought we wanted to see (just for a disconcerting flash) rows of jagged, triangular teeth biting into flesh and other violent details. Interestingly, I learned that you don't shoot these moments while you are shooting first unit. You often have to get all the little inserts in post-production, filming in a tank or the lagoon at Universal where you restage all of the action in a setting in which you have greater control. That way you are not battling wind and water. That was always the plan: to do all of these tiny inserts later and incorporate them into a fully-realized sequence. Something that impressed me about Spielberg's work on *Jaws* was the fact he had somehow managed to get a lot of those little cuts on the ocean with the first unit. I discovered that he was able to do this for two reasons: first, because Spielberg works incredibly fast and, second, because the crew was often waiting around so long for the shark to work they'd found enough time to do all the inserts.

Dorothy and I had come up with this terrific sequence in which two water skiers were attacked by the shark (in the finished film it's one water skier, but in ours it was a male and a female). It would have been far more ferocious than it eventually turned out to be in Jeannot Szwarc's version and far more tense. Our shark was going to see the skiers zooming across the surface of the ocean above it in a POV shot, before pursuing them, knocking one haplessly into the water—and then *chomp*! It would have hopefully been a taut and exceedingly grim sequence. The shark would have eaten the male skier slowly and deliberately. That death would have been drawn out in a way I think audiences would have found brutal. It would have been tough to watch. The skier would have eventually been hauled out of the water to reveal he has been bitten in half below the waist. None of this would have happened at once, but in stages, before he was hauled out. I had fished for barracudas in the Florida Keys when I was a kid, and I noticed that they would sometimes attack the hooked fish as you reeled it in. So, you would finally end up with half a fish or less. I'm sure I was thinking of that when we wrote the water skiing sequence.

Having the opportunity taken away from me to do that sequence was hard to swallow—heh heh! Seriously, I had a clear idea in my mind concerning how we were going to shoot it. Again, this would have been a sequence that also played on the faces of the people observing this attack take place. I mean, for a person to watch someone they love gradually be eaten alive by a monster seemed to be the ultimate horror. So, I knew that the reaction shots would have to be strong in order to really sell the horror. A lot of times a character's reaction to some horrible monster or violent event can be what makes a scene work. If you have nobody present to react to something, it's much harder to convey the sense of fear, disgust and alarm the audience is expected to feel. Again, this particular attack would have been rather protracted; it wasn't going to simply happen with one *chomp*! Being so fond of Zanuck, I tried to talk him into playing the role of the male water skier. I thought he would have been good, but Dick quickly turned me down. He said, "You're kidding, right? That's all I need!" He just didn't want to do it. He probably thought it would be beneath his dignity. But Dick was a robust and physical guy, and could have easily done it. His best friend was Teddy Grossman, the stunt coordinator on *Jaws* and *Jaws 2*, who had played the guy who gets his leg bitten off by the Shark in the first movie. I liked Teddy enormously.

One of the more ambitious and spectacular sequences in our screenplay was going to be the passage in which the shark attacks the regatta. The kids are out on their boats and the shark menaces them, so they lash their vessels together in order to form this raft of boats. At one point, a rescue helicopter arrives and lands on the water only for the shark to suddenly attack it; drag the helicopter down into the ocean and devour the pilot. It was a marvelous sequence—absurd but marvelous—and I was looking forward to doing it. I had prepared a series of detailed storyboards for the scene, which were laborious to do. Zanuck had wanted me to carefully storyboard every element of what became known as the "shark versus helicopter" sequence, as well as all the other big action scenes in the film. It was going to be incredibly elaborate. So, I agreed this was something we should do, as it was important to communicate information to the special effects guys, the stunt people, the actors and the camera crew concerning exactly what was required in any given shot. The best way to do that is by having a drawing that they can all scrutinize. Conversely, I was concerned about there being a fixed and mechanical aspect to the storyboard process that would threaten to choke out a lot of the spontaneity I enjoy in my filmmaking. This feeling only increased as for a long time it seemed that every lunch hour on the set was consumed by my working closely with an accomplished storyboard artist. It was exhausting, and I really needed that break, but the results were damn good. At Dick's insistence we drew out each reaction shot from the pilot and the kids, the shark coming out of the water, the helicopter going down into the waves and the destroyed rotor blades tearing through the boat-sails. When we finally finished the storyboards I was satisfied that we had come up with something which would startle and disturb the audience. Sadly, I never got to do it. When I saw the completed sequence in Szwarc's version, it wasn't as dramatic, nor as frightening, as what I'd conceived in my imagination. Of course, a lot of sequences never are once you contend with the realities of shooting—particularly in an ocean environment.

The other big consideration in all of this was undoubtedly the shark itself. Bruce, the big mechanical shark on *Jaws*, had been created by a special effects man named Robert Mattey, who had been head of the special effects department at Disney Studios for a number of years and had worked on pictures there like *20,000 Leagues Under the Sea*. Notoriously, Mattey's hydraulic shark almost never worked during filming and had led to a series of delays and cost over-runs that blighted the original production and placed considerable pressure on Spielberg and everybody else. Zanuck was determined to find somebody else to create the shark for the sequel as he did not want a repeat of these problems. In fact, one of the biggest fights Dick had with Sid Sheinberg on *Jaws 2* was about the re-employment of Bob Mattey. Sheinberg was most insistent that Mattey should return, and even said, "Bob's shark worked well enough for the first picture to make lots of money, so that's who we're going to use on the second picture." Sheinberg then effectively pulled rank and overruled Zanuck on what turned out to be a rather crucial issue. So, Mattey was brought back to realize Bruce II and that was that. What made Sheinberg's decision even harder to accept was the simple fact all Mattey had to do was take the shark from the first movie and actually make it work. That's *all* he had to do!

Instead of doing that, Mattey inexplicably decided to redesign and augment the shark with a much more elaborate set of controls in an effort to "improve" on the original model. Thus, the shark would now have a new platform and be able to dive up and down, weave from side to side, and do all sorts of new and interesting things. It would even have eyes that rolled around in its head as apparently the eyes on the first Bruce were static. All of this was a terrible mistake! As a result of these "state-of-the-art" developments, Mattey consumed a considerable amount of time, money and personnel and the sequel was facing even more serious delays than those endured on Spielberg's film. To this day it's still my firm belief that one of the reasons I was fired from *Jaws 2* was because Sheinberg needed a good reason to shut down the production as Mattey's shark simply was not ready. This is one of the key factors to consider here: Sheinberg had insisted on *his* guy doing the shark and *his* guy had not come through. When you consider this situation from the boss's perspective you realize he doesn't want to be left looking stupid. So, wouldn't it be wonderful for Sheinberg if he could somehow score another couple of months in order to get the shark working? Even then, when he succeeded in this endeavor, they never really did as there were additional technical and act-of-God problems like a hurricane which wrecked the set that forthcoming Labor Day weekend. If Sheinberg could find a reason, or reasons, to fire the director, he could effectively buy himself a little more time at my expense. Think about it.

Not having the shark ready meant we didn't shoot any of the shark attacks detailed in the script during the month of shooting I did on *Jaws 2*. The only shark I had available to me was called the "tow-shark," which, appropriately enough, was a model you could tow along behind a boat (Spielberg had told me that of all the various models of the shark, he felt these were the ones that worked the best). Inevitably, any kind of mechanical contraption like the hydraulic shark that is exposed to saltwater over a period of time is going to have problems. I thought what was so wonderful about the tow-shark was you didn't really have that problem as it was basically like a puppet submerged in liquid. The tow-shark was in essence like a fishing lure in that you used the water to give it movement rather than hydraulic rams. The water made the tail swim from side to side, and the whole thing was hollow so that it would inflate with water. The water would then ripple through it so that its body had some movement. It was very effective. The other shark—the big mechanical shark with all the hydraulics and pneumatics that had to be operated by twelve guys simultaneously—was still being worked on and showed no signs of being ready to shoot. This was the model that was going to be used for all the money shots of the shark coming out of the water, chomping, chewing, and whatever else.

As we were going along and faced several delays, I had the growing belief we'd be better off doing certain things more simply and efficiently. Looking at the complicated mechanics Mattey was deploying, I kept thinking about how effective the creature in *Let's Scare Jessica to Death* had been using a cement block, a cable and pulleys. It had been primitive but immensely effective. I was interested in exploring if there was any way we could repeat the basic approach that Charlie Moss and I had devised for *Jessica* on a slightly grander scale. I felt we could once again use the movement of the water and the buoyancy and motion of the puppet to our advantage. This idea was seen as antiquated by Mattey and Sheinberg. No, they wanted to go the route of complex mechanical effects. Once you start using animatronics to open and close mouths, roll eye-balls, and everything else, and have twelve guys who are each working their own hydraulic rams, you are going down a road to potential ruin as these things can easily fail. They are just so tricky. I mean, just imagine twelve guys doing anything in concert with each other? Do you know how much effort and practice it takes? It's like a symphony orchestra! How do you co-ordinate all these movements and adjustments so that everything runs smoothly and doesn't break down? And how does the crew get enough time to practice and perfect these things that seldom work? When are they going to find the hours to practice and test stuff when you need it *now*? It's incredibly difficult. I could do nothing about the situation I was in. Again, the bottom line is Mattey was not my guy and he was not Zanuck's guy. He was Sheinberg's guy and was working for the studio. So, we had no control over it.

With each passing day on *Jaws 2*, I was learning new stuff about working within the studio system—what to do, what not to do. Perhaps some of these lessons weren't coming fast enough. For example, I remember on one occasion we were on our way to shoot a scene and I happened to look across at the ocean. I noticed these guys on a sailboat who were having a great time hanging from rubber bands on yard arms, dipping and ducking themselves in the water. The colors of the sails and the beautiful blue of the ocean were so visually striking to me. I realized this was one of those serendipitous moments in filmmaking that you try to remain open and responsive to. So, I immediately stopped, got the camera set up and we shot it, thinking it would make another terrific shark attack sequence. I could just see the images in my mind: this kid, who is none the wiser, gets ducked in the water and the shark is coming. They yank the kid up again, and then they dip him back down, and the shark gets closer…and closer… and closer! I thought it would be fabulously tense. Later, after Verna learned about what I had done, she said, "No, John, that's not something you can do on a big studio picture. You can't just take the first unit and shoot things of opportunity like that. You first have to get approval." Now, it goes without saying that by the time lines of communication had been established, and I had sought and secured approval from the studio, those kids would have been long gone. Seizing any chance to shoot new things that weren't delineated in the script was clearly frowned upon, but it was something I had taken for granted on my earlier films.

Indeed, the series of obstacles, misunderstandings and mishaps I encountered on *Jaws 2* would have made an interesting movie in itself. Whether that movie would be a comedy or a tragedy, I don't know. It would probably be a tragicomedy. I mean, certain scenes proved to be more difficult to get than I'd initially anticipated. For instance, there was some stuff that involved the sailboats tied up next to the dock that were pretty tough to do. The main problem facing Michael Butler and I was the fact that the boats were constantly moving and shifting all the time. These movements were causing all kinds of issues, which were troubling for me as I hadn't expected there to be any major problems with these particular scenes. Actually, I was not aware of the full extent of the difficulties until I saw the dailies. Butler had suggested that in order to remedy this problem we should shoot from a huge Chapman Crane that would be sitting on a barge positioned next to the boats. His idea was that the crane, with its arm that could swing, would allow us to make any small adjustments for the perpetual movement of the tide and the boats, as the barge would constantly be changing its relationship with these things. So, he opined, we could, in theory, accommodate for these forces and get all the stuff we needed. It later turned out that this was not a good idea at all. Essentially, the thinking behind it was the same kind of over-elaborate process that later went into having a mechanical shark run by twelve guys. More than that, what the barge and crane did was it effectively cut me off from my actors. As a director, any time it becomes difficult to communicate instructions and comments to people, and you have to shout at them rather than going over and simply whispering a few words, can be hugely problematic. If you are up on a crane, and there is wind and water and physical distance to contend with, to some degree you lose the ability to make yourself properly understood. I found that frustrating and laborious, and I was tempted to junk this whole approach. Then it proved just as hard to do without the crane because that was the way we had prepared and geared-up to shoot those scenes. But it was not how we should have attacked that stuff. We should have just lashed the boats to the dock and shot it from there; or physically climbed onboard the boats themselves with the actors and shot them using a handheld camera. Instead, it was another case of us needlessly overcomplicating matters.

One of the other troubling things that happened involved a scene I was shooting on the harbor. We had a moment where the kids' boats were supposed to set sail from Amity Island and there needed to be no other boats visible on the ocean. It turned out that our production manager, Tom Joyner, was not able to clear the harbor as he had been instructed. In the face of this, I decided to go ahead and shoot it anyway as there were already some pressing concerns over time. In retrospect, I now realize that I should have probably hung Joyner out to dry for his failure. I should have insisted, "Hey, I can't shoot this because there are boats out there." Naturally, you always try to protect your co-workers—or at least I do—so I made the decision to simply go ahead and shoot it anyway. When Verna later scrutinized the dailies she was then able to say, "Oh look, there's a boat in this shot! There's another boat in that shot, too! You can't use any of this. You have to re-shoot it." That caused a little more upset and tension I could have done without. I remember Joe Alves later telling me, "John, you should have just refused to shoot it and allowed Joyner to be fired." I didn't do that. But I should have. My mistake!

Yet another incredibly frustrating and bewildering thing occurred on an entirely different shooting day. This calamity involved the camera operator, John Fleckenstein. I remember we were filming a scene with the actors on a sizable boat, I forget now what it was. This was way back in the days before Video Assist, when you could not view an image of what the camera was seeing as it was filmed. This system made a big difference in my life, and the lives of other filmmakers, in terms of eliminating nasty surprises. We could have done with the technology on this movie as it turned out that Fleckenstein was cutting off the actors at their foreheads in each shot. I'm not kidding. He literally had their eyes right at the top of the frame—if that! Sometimes he even lost them in the shot! It was beyond my understanding how he could have ever done this. It might have been a technical glitch with the alignment of his viewfinder, I don't know, but it was certainly not a viable aesthetic choice. It was deeply horrifying to discover this in dailies and a clear re-shoot was required. Evidently, I somehow took the blame for those terrible dailies as they passed through the studio system with Verna residing back in the Black Tower wishing me ill. I wanted to fire Fleckenstein, but it was really his only mistake up to that point. So, as in the case of Tom Joyner, I decided to keep him. Another mistake!

I was thinking just the other day (I generally try not to think about *Jaws 2* but it came back to me) that Michael Butler was probably not the wisest choice for director of photography. Maybe he was for another director, but not for me. He simply wasn't experienced enough. Michael did have an experienced key grip in John Black, but the rest of his crew, Fleckenstein especially, were not seasoned enough for a big picture on the water. You need to have people who have faced all sorts of technical problems and found effective ways of dealing with them. Michael was a real nice guy, and we became friends, but given my own inexperience and background in theater, I probably needed someone who could have made a bigger contribution to the visual side of the film. Admittedly, I've always been a little wary of that. I don't like a cinematographer who wants to direct or even wants to run the set as that can be a real problem of divided authority. My theory has long been that you're better off with a DP who is slightly less accomplished; someone that you can get along with. I never, for example, hired Gordy Willis, although, again, I was willing to take Vilmos Zsigmond on *Jaws 2* just to get what he had to offer. But all of the mishaps that were occurring on the movie were contributing to a growing discord at Universal. I didn't quite feel it at this point, but certain people were starting to get restless.

At potentially fraught times like these, you really need solid and dependable allies around you and I thought I had one in Joe Alves. I liked Joe, and along with Butler, he and I became good friends during my time on *Jaws 2*. I can say that outside of Bill Badalato, Joe was the person I was closest to on the picture. To what extent he was ever truly my ally, I can't be sure, but Joe seemed a great guy to have around. After Spielberg had recommended that I trust him, I wholeheartedly did. I involved Joe in everything we did. I even had him come to the casting sessions we held in New York and Boston, and was interested in hearing his opinions—even though it was well outside of his duties. Did I sometimes get the impression that Joe felt he could do a better job as director on the film than me? Yes, I think he probably did feel that way. I'm positive he did. Joe later directed *Jaws 3* (which is worse than *Jaws 2*) so I was aware that he had certain ambitions he wanted to fulfill. One other thing I can recall feeling when we were shooting the movie was that Joe was over-building a lot of the sets. He was a very short guy and I felt he had a compulsion to build these huge sets—huge lighthouses, for example—that perhaps, on a subconscious level, compensated for the fact he was vertically challenged. In this regard, Joe was somewhat

Napoleonic in his attitude. I don't mean to say he was power-mad or anything, I'm merely speaking of his predilection for building *big* things. Just like the mechanical shark, I felt that a lot of money and labor was being unnecessarily exhausted on things that could have possibly been done more simply and economically.

This is why I say that allies are important on a movie. I learned on *Jaws 2* that you should always surround yourself with your own choices. As a director, you shouldn't hire the producer's people or the studio's people; you have to bring in your *own* people. There were several crew-members on *Jaws 2* who were veterans of the first *Jaws* and they did not respond well to my new approach. In situations like these you often leave yourself vulnerable to negative opinions and turmoil. No doubt some people were thinking, "Well, Spielberg didn't do it like *that*." I remember Badalato later telling me he felt there were a bunch of people on *Jaws 2* who really wanted to direct the movie. Bill even went as far to suggest I was literally "surrounded" by them. I think those observations are true as there was unquestionably a conspiratorial air. A few people on that production had a sinister purpose. There were certain individuals who viewed me as something of an outsider; an intruder, an interloper, whatever you want to call it. At the very least, I was seen as The New Guy—if not The Wrong Guy. I liken the kind of reception I was afforded to the "stranger ape" phenomenon among primates: the established apes are compelled to drive the stranger ape away from their midst and let things continue as they are or once were. That's what it felt like.

> *On Sunday, June 26, 1977, it was announced to members of the cast and crew that Hancock had officially "left" the picture due to "artistic differences." It would be nearly three weeks before his replacement would be officially unveiled by Universal in the form of Jeannot Szwarc, whose previous credits had included several memorable episodes of Rod Serling's anthology television series* **Night Gallery** *(1970-73) and the William Castle-produced mutant cockroach shocker* **Bug** *(1975).* **Jaws 2** *would be placed on a short hiatus with production resuming in earnest on July 31st, 1977. Originally scheduled to shoot from June until August, the amended shoot under Szwarc would now take place from August until December. This break allowed Carl Gottlieb time to revise Hancock's*

> *shooting script, which he hurriedly wrote on location at Fort Walton Beach, Florida, and turned in to Zanuck and Brown on July 28th, 1977.*

There were several contributing factors to my demise, some of which I was aware of at the time and have already detailed, others I only learned about much later. Allow me to go back for a moment to the rehearsal period in Pensacola as something occurred there which also had some bearing on my dismissal: during rehearsals, I had fired a young actress named Sarah Holcomb whom I was not happy with. Sarah was extremely pretty, but not very real. So, I replaced her with somebody who was not quite as good and that truly was my fault. When we were initially looking for a girl to take over Sarah's role, Joe Alves was determined that I cast Elizabeth Berridge, who would later co-star in Milos Forman's *Amadeus* as Mozart's wife. I wasn't familiar with Elizabeth at all back then, but Joe insisted she was a capable actress. I would have gladly replaced Sarah with her, but Elizabeth was no longer available. So, Dorothy flew all over the country auditioning actresses for me and eventually found Karen Corboy. I now feel we would have done a lot better going with Joe's recommendation as Karen was even more limited in her abilities than Sarah Holcomb had been.

Anyway, it soon transpired that there was a lot of ill-feeling surrounding my firing of Sarah. I couldn't quite figure out at the time why this decision had generated so much consternation. I felt it was necessary and not something that would ordinarily provoke any kind of adverse reaction. I mean, Sarah simply wasn't good enough. That's all there was to it. However, it later turned out that Sarah was actually the girlfriend of Ned Tanen. I didn't discover this fact until several years after the events on *Jaws 2* had occurred. I had no idea she was in a relationship with a high-ranking Universal executive and was surprised when somebody informed me about it. Had I been privy to this information at the time would it have made any difference to my decision? I really can't answer that. I don't know what effect it could have had on the final outcome. This was simply one of several inadvertent missteps I made that were pushing me ever closer to extinction.

As I suggested earlier, the other determining factor in this deteriorating situation was Verna Fields. As we were making the picture Verna was back in Hollywood shooting down the dailies, but doing it in a deviously subtle manner; nothing that appeared too obvious and prejudiced. She would view my footage and say, "Oh, this is very dark. Look at that, it's very contrasty and blue. Do you think we'll be able to fix this later in post-production?" Michael Butler had assured her that would not be a problem at all, but Verna continued to make these veiled and seemingly innocuous comments. She'd say things like, "I really don't see how to cut this. I mean, John is an experienced filmmaker and I'm sure he has his own way of cutting but I just don't see it." Well, if this famous and respected editor is having difficulty finding a way to cut the footage—uh-oh! Alarm bells soon start ringing and then certain people ask all sorts of nervous questions: "What's he doing with this movie? What do we have here? Is this going to work out?" That's really how it all begins—not with big, loud explosions of anger but with little rumblings of discontent. These rumblings then grow in volume until just enough of the right people start to take notice. Verna knew this and she saw to a lot of it.

I guess the final nail in my coffin, the decisive incident that resulted in my being fired, concerned a shot I'd directed where I was apparently guilty of crossing the line. I had done this either inadvertently or because the boat we were using had drifted on the water, resulting in my crossing the line with a close-up of one of the kids getting on the vessel. The editor on the picture, Neil Travis, who had been recommended to me by Verna, was reviewing the footage, and said, "John, you've crossed the line here." I replied, "Well, I'll shoot an insert of a rope being lashed around a stay and that will make the bridge between the shots. It's okay. We can do that in post-production." Typically, the studio doesn't want you to take the first unit out with everybody on salary and shoot little close-ups like that as it's just too prohibitively expensive to keep everybody waiting around while you photograph a rope being lashed around a stay.

Anyway, as I was filming on what would turn out to be my last day on the picture, a Lear Jet suddenly landed in Martha's Vineyard with Sid Sheinberg onboard. Unbeknownst to me, Sheinberg had got off the company plane and marched straight to the editing room to review some of my footage—which Neil had duly showed him—before getting back on the plane and leaving that very same day. I wasn't made aware of this until the end of the day when Neil approached me, and said, "Sheinberg was here today. I'm afraid I had to show him the footage, John. I didn't know what else to do. I'm so sorry, I had to do it." Neil was undoubtedly on Verna's side and was just trying to cover his own ass with me. Obviously, when Sheinberg had walked into the editing room a few hours earlier he did not like what he saw. Verna was then able to say, "Look, John has crossed the line!" Regrettably, there was indeed this glaring close-up of an actress looking the wrong way. I had in fact crossed the line and made it difficult to discern where the actors were in relation to each other. That provided Sheinberg with the last of the ammunition he needed to fire me.

Interestingly, several years later, I tried to shut Sheinberg's mouth up about this incident. I remember my lawyer told me, "Listen, Sid Sheinberg has been making calls and is actually dis-recommending you to people. Why don't you go see him?" So, I called Sheinberg up and said, "Sid, I'd like to talk to you for a few minutes if I may," and he generously agreed to see me. I then confronted him about his comments and he responded by saying, "Well, I honestly didn't think that you knew how to cover a scene." I said, "I know exactly how to cover a scene and I don't appreciate you telling people any different. What I don't know is why I was even doing a picture like *Jaws 2* anyway. That kind of movie is not my strong suit. I do a different kind of picture." We eventually ended our meeting on friendly terms—still positively loathing each other at the same time. But I was satisfied that I had at least talked to Sheinberg about the situation and let him know how upset I was about it. Looking back now, what I find interesting is that Spike Lee has since made a whole film in which he continually crossed the line. As a matter of fact, it's done all the time now. American directors in particular often seem to willfully cross the line as it's no longer considered a sin. But back in 1977, it was a cardinal sin. So, I got nailed on *Jaws 2* over that mistake—and others—but I still feel I should mention it.

I can vividly recall that, on the morning of the day I was fired, people stopped meeting my eyes on the set. They literally stopped talking to me—the cast, the grips, the assistant director, as well as several others including Michael Butler. It was undoubtedly the strangest experience I've ever had working on a movie. I mean, as the director, everybody is always friendly and are constantly talking to you and looking to you for guidance, support and approval. Suddenly, I was a ghost on my own set and was simply drifting through a collection of people. I talked about this incident later with Bobby De Niro. In an odd twist of coincidence he'd had a similar experience which had occurred that very same year while working with Mike Nichols on *The Goodbye Girl*. After the first week, Bob—who'd been cast as the lead—told me that all of a sudden everybody on the set stopped talking to him. A few hours later, he was replaced by Richard Dreyfuss who then went on to win an Academy Award for his performance. When I was fired from *Jaws 2*, De Niro and I had the grim joy of comparing our horror stories. We discovered that in both our cases the first sign that we'd been canned was when everybody abruptly stopped communicating with us. It's quite an alarming situation to find yourself in when everyone has been incessantly asking for your opinion and then *nobody* is. I remember that after an hour or so of enduring this peculiar atmosphere, I called Dorothy on the phone, and said, "Something is terribly wrong here. You need to come over." She then came over, caught the weird vibes and agreed, "Yes, you're right, something is very wrong."

At the end of that final day, somebody informed me that Zanuck and Brown wanted to see me. So, I went over to Dick's motel room in Martha's Vineyard, and he and Brown were waiting there looking rather nervous and solemn-faced. Almost immediately, they said, "John, we have some very bad news. Unfortunately, we are replacing you with somebody else. It's not something we want to do. It's what Sheinberg wants. Please believe us, we're both very sorry that it's come to this." At first, I couldn't quite believe what I was hearing. It was such a stunning moment; I couldn't quite take it in. Then a terrible realization settled on me and I knew it was for real. Of course it was. When I think about these events now, do I believe what Zanuck and Brown told me that day is actually true, that it was all Sheinberg's doing? Yes, I do. Being Dick's choice, he would not have wanted the loss of face in having to fire and replace me unless he had been forced to. After taking a few minutes to gather myself together, I notified Zanuck and Brown that I had to go tell my wife before anyone else did. By now it was dusk, and when I found Dorothy and relayed the news to her, she was understandably very upset. She couldn't accept it at first either, but then she suddenly became furious.

Shortly after this, as we were still trying to process everything, a few people—such as my assistant and a now slightly more verbose Michael Butler—started slowly coming over and commiserating with me. Curiously, when Michael was interviewed recently about *Jaws 2*, he said something very strange about what had occurred that day. He claims that Zanuck and Brown, without ever talking to me personally, simply had me driven to the airport instead of to the location in Martha's Vineyard where I apparently thought I was heading. Butler maintains that a guy was supposedly waiting for me at the airport with my suitcases already packed. All of this is a complete fabrication. It never happened and quite where Michael got this story from I don't know. The events did not unfold that way at all. I distinctly remember that after I was fired, Michael came over and was incredibly sympathetic. He said, "I knew something was going to happen today. I was afraid I was going to be fired, too, but I think they are going to keep me. I don't know anything for certain. I may be gone with you." In spite of his fears, Michael somehow managed to survive. Production on *Jaws 2* was halted for a while, but when the picture started back up again a month or so later, he was retained and thereafter worked with Jeannot Szwarc.

Later that same night and early the following morning, my friends on the movie visited with me one last time. It was a sad and bitter scene. Not a good time at all. Dorothy and I then went for one final meeting with Zanuck and Brown as they wanted to see us before we left. All they kept saying was how sorry they were; how desperately sad and sympathetic they felt. At one point, I remarked, "I suppose it wouldn't do any good to beg?" I was only joking, but the thought had probably crossed my mind. Zanuck in particular felt extremely badly about my getting fired as he and I were friends. We remained friends after *Jaws 2*, but things were never quite the same. It was tough for Dick, but I understood that both he and Brown were pushed into doing it. They fought as hard as they possibly could for me but, ultimately, the axe came down and it was all over. I was gone—just like that—after all the hard work Dorothy and I had put in. I had worked on *Jaws 2* for more than a year of pre-production as well as a busy month of shooting. We had invested a lot of time, energy and emotion into making this picture, and it ended up counting for nothing. That was hard to take, but there was nothing more to be done. It was all over.

Dorothy and I next made plans to leave Martha's Vineyard as expediently as possible. We both agreed that we shouldn't go back to L.A. in disgrace. That would have probably killed me. Dorothy then said, "I know, let's go someplace we love instead." That suggestion sounded wonderful to me. So, we got on a plane and flew down to New York from Martha's Vineyard and from there straight to Rome, Italy. By the way, this was a commercial flight. Universal didn't pay for it, we did. The studio did pay me what was left of my salary which, admittedly, was huge, but we didn't use the company plane or anything. We then holed up at the luxurious Hotel Eden, which was a place Joe Janni had once recommended to us and was located near the Spanish Steps. Joe had told me exactly what room to ask for and it was truly exquisite. Dorothy and I then drove from Rome to Vienna, before moving on to Budapest, and we had a beautiful time together. During the trip I tried to make sense of everything that had happened, how and why it had all turned bad. In Sheinberg's mind I was seriously jeopardizing a valuable asset for Universal and something had to be done about that. But the truth is I never got the feeling during the shooting of *Jaws 2* that the movie was in any way slipping away from me. I never felt I had lost control of the situation and didn't know exactly what it was I was doing. Not once.

This is where it gets confusing as subsequently certain people have agreed there was no indication of any problems, whereas others have claimed the picture was going horribly wrong. It never fails to surprise me how many individuals who were not present at these events are still able to say, "Yeah, that's exactly how it went down. The film got away from him." It's astonishing. Weighing up everything I did have a few trusted allies on the movie—like little Ricky Schroeder! No, seriously, I had Dorothy and Bill Badalato on my side, as well as Nancy Sawyer, a young actress whom we cast that was fired after I was dismissed from the picture. Beyond those three people I was pretty much out there all by myself. Michael Butler was an ally for a time, until the look of the film was openly challenged and then he got very shaky. I thought Joe Alves was another ally, but he really wasn't. Joe was not in Martha's Vineyard when I got my marching orders. He was off in Florida, readying sets for the later part of the shoot that was located there. I would imagine that my dismissal was checked with him, or at least he was informed that it was coming. When I did finally get the chop, Joe probably thought he would be next in line to direct the movie.

In actuality, there was some talk that Universal was briefly considering having Joe and Verna co-direct the picture. However, the Directors Guild of America would not permit this to happen. You see, this was only a year after "The Eastwood Rule" came into being following Clint having replaced Philip Kaufman as the director on *The Outlaw Josey Wales*. That had caused a lot of bad feeling in Hollywood. I was later informed about a shoving match that had occurred in The Polo Lounge at the Beverly Hills Hotel between Robert Aldrich, who was the head of the DGA at the time, and Sid Sheinberg. Apparently Aldrich was unhappy about Sheinberg's rumored plans for my proposed replacements on *Jaws 2*, and told him in front of several witnesses: "No, you will not replace a DGA director with one of your executives, or anyone else on the picture! It simply will not happen!" I was especially pleased when I heard about this altercation, delighted even. It made me like Robert Aldrich's pictures better. Fair enough, if I was the executive in charge of *Jaws 2*, I would have probably thought the best substitute would have been either Joe Alves or Verna Fields, or both. Joe would have possessed the practical knowledge of moviemaking and Verna would have brought her editorial and narrative skills to bear, as well as possibly being able to work with the actors. They were both so steeped in the world of *Jaws* they could have done it together. I'm not sorry the opportunity was denied them.

In the month of shooting I did, I garnered quite a bit of footage. I don't know the exact amount, but it was probably as much as twenty-five or thirty percent of the movie. That demonstrates that we were well on course schedule-wise. Needless to say very little of what I shot was used in the finished film. I understand that Szwarc and the studio reviewed all of my footage, but decided it was too dark to use. It definitely wasn't compatible with their new plans. They did use the great shot of the shark fin gliding into Amity harbor and there is also a scene where a sailboat with a parachute is ducking people into the water that is mine, but precious little else. I have no idea where my *Jaws 2* footage is or if it will ever re-surface. I tend to believe that it won't. I'm sure it was destroyed like everything else. I'm fairly certain that Universal decided not to keep it in their archive and why should they? Be that as it may, some of these things—alternate cuts, deleted scenes, abandoned footage, even entire lost movies—do occasionally turn up. So, you never know. If my footage is ever discovered somewhere, it would be interesting to view some of it now. I thought what I was getting was good. Hopefully, I'm not wrong.

I wasn't the only victim on *Jaws 2*. After I was gone and the production shut down for a little while, they axed some of the actors I'd hired and recast their parts. Again, Nancy Sawyer was one such unfortunate, as was Marshall Efron and the young Harvard man Alan Stock. Dana Elcar, a wonderful actor I cast as a mobster who makes his home on Amity, was also replaced by Joseph Mascolo and the part changed to some kind of official. Even more confounding than losing any of these people was the decision made to let Ricky Schroeder go. I was recently informed that one of reasons why Ricky was replaced by Marc Gilpen in the role of Sean Brody was because he couldn't get scared or be emotional on cue. God, that's such crap! Yes, he could! It's crazy to suggest otherwise and it's just not right. Ricky did *The Champ* with Jon Voight a year or so later, and everybody knows that kid could deliver emotion in bucketfuls. I was profoundly upset when I learned that Ricky was not being retained (he'd already featured prominently in some advance advertising). The fact they saw fit to fire him still astounds me. More than that, I consider Ricky's dismissal to be one of the great heartbreakers on *Jaws 2*. It seems so perverse. I mean, the camera loved him, the cast and crew loved him, but the new broom had to mercilessly sweep everything clean. Little Ricky took this very badly and there was no justification for it—particularly when you see some of the actors they brought in. One of the actors retained on the film was Gary Springer, who played Andy, a teenager. I have a little interpersonal disaster at the moment involving Gary as in an interview I conducted for the *Jaws 2* book, I implied that Steve Guttenberg would have been much more charming in the role than him. That comment makes it awfully hard for me right now because Gary is the PR guy for my latest film, *The Looking Glass*. When I talked to the authors of the book I had no relationship with him, but now I do. So, I've got a large portion of humble pie to eat and a lot of apologizing to do. What could have possessed me to say such a thing anyway? I'm not even a big Guttenberg fan!

> *The movie tie-in of* Jaws 2 *by Hank Searls was published by Bantam Books on April 19th, 1978, two months before the sequel opened. Derived from the revised draft of Howard Sackler's screenplay by Dorothy Tristan that Hancock had begun shooting in Martha's Vineyard, the novelization contained several characters and subplots that were absent from the release version of the picture. This was due to Carl Gottlieb being brought onto the project to revise the initial shooting script after Searls had already delivered his manuscript to the publishers. Thus, the book offers readers a fascinating glimpse into what Hancock's sequel might have been. Even taking into account the discrepancies with the finished film, the unseated director was stunned to later discover that his wife would not be receiving a credit as co-screenwriter for her not inconsiderable contributions. Tristan appealed to the Writers Guild of America, but to no avail. The credit bearing only the names of Gottlieb and Sackler was upheld.*

That decision was simply fucking *evil* and there are no other words I can summon to describe such a despicable action. I mean, they used eighty percent of our script! All Carl Gottlieb did was he altered some names, eliminated a few characters or changed their occupations; removed some of the violence and lightened the oppressively dark tone. It wasn't a great deal of work, all things considered, but he apparently changed just enough to earn the prominent credit. What a deeply sickening thing that was. It still dismays and confuses us to this day, if you want the truth. Yes, there were some differences between our screenplay and Gottlieb's later revision but there were many more similarities. The film lost threads like the mobster and the character of Quint's son Sideburns (the actor we'd hired for that role, Billy Van Zandt, was retained but ended up playing an entirely different person). But it still contained things like the shark attacking the water skiers and the helicopter, and the whole climactic confrontation where the fish is electrocuted. In our script Ellen Brody did not go out on the boat and in the released film she does, but so what? Despite all this, Gottlieb and Sackler were—and remain to this day—the only credited writers for *Jaws 2*. Dorothy did indeed appeal to the Writers Guild but it didn't do any good: the Gottlieb/Sackler credit was approved and we simply had to accept it. It was outrageous because, again, a lot of the sequences you see in the picture are Dorothy's and mine. This has never been officially acknowledged and I don't envisage that wrong being righted anytime soon. Anyway, who even cares about it now beyond Dorothy and me? Nobody!

Here's another important fact about the Writers Guild that may interest you: I thought that when a screenplay was submitted to the Guild for arbitration they faithfully read what you sent them. How else can they possibly determine who is responsible for what? The startling truth is they don't always read the various drafts—or at least they didn't back then. They merely read the covering letter that you sent in to accompany the manuscript. We did not send a covering letter in with our draft because it was so plainly and undeniably evident to us (and anyone else) that Dorothy should receive co-screenwriting credit. Instead we sent a cursory note that basically said: "Please look at the two screenplays and I think your judgment will resolve who wrote this story." But they did not *read* the scripts! Can you believe that? Now, purportedly, Howard Sackler had prepared a careful case and I imagine that Carl Gottlieb did also. Significantly, both of these guys were alarmingly close to the Writers Guild which must have had some bearing on the outcome. Also, let's not forget that Dorothy was the deposed director's wife. The Writers Guild is determined not to replace Writers Guild writers with directors' wives. I honestly believe that was another substantial factor in all of this. Their ruling was grossly unfair and insensible. Not only did Dorothy receive no credit for her work on *Jaws 2*, she also received no money from the subsequent novelization and comic book adaptations of her screenplay that were published. She was effectively erased from everything and that really salted the wound. It goes without saying that Dorothy's friendship with Sackler did not survive any of this. A lot of friendships didn't survive *Jaws 2*.

> *Bolstered by a massive advertising campaign, which included the memorable tagline "Just when you thought it was safe to go back in the water..." devised by copyrighter Andrew J. Kuehn,* Jaws 2 *was finally released on June 16, 1978, nearly a year after Hancock's dismissal. Opening in 640 theaters across the United States and Canada, it garnered mixed notices with most reviewers complaining that Jeannot Szwarc lacked the technical flair of Spielberg and his sequel's best moments were merely regurgitated passages from* Jaws. *Proving itself to be critic-proof the film succeeded in grossing $9,866,023 on its opening weekend, making it the then highest opening of all time. In any event, at a cost of $20 million,* Jaws 2 *was the most expensive movie Universal had ever produced. Despite earning less than half of the first instalment's total gross,* Jaws 2 *had ensured the franchise was viable and would spawn two lesser sequels in* Jaws 3 *(1983) and* Jaws: The Revenge *(1987). For Hancock, as he dealt with the aftermath of his very public expulsion from the production, his fortunes would vacillate alarmingly in the following decade.*

When the movie finally came out Dorothy and I dragged ourselves to a theater somewhere to see it. Call it morbid curiosity. I remember that evening being a fairly unpleasant experience for obvious reasons. The emotions I felt sitting there with an audience were predictably ones of anger, disappointment and regret. It was such a strange situation: watching a film you started but was then taken away from you and redone by somebody else. I was completely removed from *Jaws 2* by this point, but it was still like picking at a painful scab. As I recall, Dorothy was not particularly good at watching the film either. She kept sighing and groaning and shifting in her seat throughout. We'd look at each other occasionally and shake our heads, like "What was *that*?" Gradually, as the movie played out, I began feeling a growing sense of relief when I realized it wasn't as good as what we had planned. Of course, before judging Jeannot Szwarc's version, I do acknowledge my own bias and bitterness here—happily so—but I don't mind telling you that I didn't like his picture. I'm sure that won't come as a big surprise for people to hear, but it's the truth. I understand that *Jaws 2* does have its fans, but I don't include myself among them. I didn't think Szwarc's film contained any trace of the formidable excitement or suspense of our script—or indeed the first *Jaws*. It lacked a little bite. I haven't seen the movie for a long time, so I don't really remember it in any great detail. I do recall being disappointed by the shark attack scenes. Knowing the ideas we'd had, I always thought those sequences with the shark attacking the water skiers, the regatta, and the helicopter would be terrifying. They simply weren't. Also, some of the kids are a little weak and interchangeable. Ultimately, they may have been in my version, too, but the final result is you don't care if they end up becoming fish food or not.

I'm sure the studio was hoping that the sequel would do the same business that the first picture did, but *Jaws* was lightning in a bottle. You can't replicate a phenomenon like that simply by building on the name and goodwill of the original. First and foremost, they should have strived harder to make a better movie. From my position, I was like, "Well, that's what you guys get! You should have trusted us to make a good movie, but you couldn't do that." Knowing the picture didn't turn out so wonderful only offered us a few small crumbs of comfort because the pain was still so big. Sure, it was only a movie and nobody died, but sometimes it felt that way. I believe that what we were up to was considerably more interesting and ambitious than what the movie eventually turned out to be. Maybe the studio didn't want that. They did not like the look of the picture, that's for damn sure. As for the tone and narrative, what I saw as arrestingly bleak, they merely viewed as depressing. Frankly, I regard *Jaws 2* as a missed opportunity—not just for me and Dorothy but for Universal, too. Yes, the film made some money but who really remembers it as one of the great sequels on a par with *The Godfather Part II* or *The Empire Strikes Back* or *Aliens*? Like those pictures, this was a chance to do a sequel with its own unique identity and vision and not some sad old rag. As it is, the movie suffered the same fate as most sequels: it's there to make up the numbers. Today, sequels are even more safe and insipid. They don't challenge you or offer anything new. They are mostly just focused on replicating the highpoints of the first installment with little variation and innovation. What's the point of doing that when you can make a movie that is its own entity, its own self-contained universe? My picture would have been that.

I've never met Jeannot Szwarc. Would I like to? Sure. I understand he's been fairly restrained and respectful to me in regards to my dismissal.

I was an easy target, and there have been plenty of others who've taken cheap shots with relish. Certain people (some of whom I liked and respected when we were making the picture) have insinuated that *Jaws 2* was "too big for me" and I was "ill-equipped" to handle it. Bullshit! I scratch my head when I hear things like, "Hancock was only an actor's director" and "Hancock didn't know how to do stunts and special effects." All that stuff is crap. It's bothersome and I reject it. A lot of these comments are second hand information—or, more accurately, disinformation. It has been passed around and is now being regurgitated by those who weren't privy to what happened. This whole business of "Hancock being over his head doing an action picture" still rankles me. As I've already conceded, back then I had a lot more experience working with actors than I did working with stunts and special effects. I've been honest about that. But when I finally saw *Jaws 2* there was nothing in the finished film stunt-wise or special effects-wise—and I'm talking about stuff which actually works—that I could not have done (and done better) with my hands tied behind me. Even the problems with stuff that didn't work could have been overcome. I always knew we were dealing with the ocean and a mechanical shark that was prone to breaking down. I realized that when the infernal thing worked, I'd better shoot everything I could with it. All I needed was a little more support, cooperation and expertise, and everything would have been fine. I didn't get any of those things. I only got a knife buried in my back.

Despite *Jaws 2* not being the kind of picture I saw myself doing when I first started out as a filmmaker, once I'd committed to the project, I put my heart and soul into it. I reasoned that although I maybe wasn't a perfect fit for the film, it didn't mean that I had to execute a half-assed job. I worked like a dog on it and through that process the movie became a part of me—so much so, when it all unraveled it really hurt. It seems to me that the most important lessons one must learn in life are almost always the most painful. I discovered an awful lot about the business on *Jaws 2*. It was an important turning point as well as a devastating blow. I'm sure my career would have been different had I not been fired. I certainly think I would have directed more commercial action movies down the line. In conclusion, what happened was I got ground-up between these two mighty guys in Zanuck and Sheinberg, and had committed just enough of a sin that they found a reason to can me. Looking back, I now realize that if I had known how to behave in a bureaucracy like that I may have survived *Jaws 2*. But I had insufficient experience and knowledge of how to operate effectively in what was basically a power struggle. I was left lingering precariously between these two dominant individuals, not knowing what to say or do next.

You see, what you have to do is get the two most important figures together in a room and say, "Okay, you guys have to give me clear and precise instructions on what you want me to do here. Does Lorraine go out on the boat or not? How can we proceed in a manner in which everybody is relatively happy?" But I didn't do that. Zanuck would have been mad at me if I had put him in that situation, but I should've taken the chance. I was used to doing my own thing as far as the theater and my previous movies had been concerned. *Jaws 2* was entirely different. It was fraught with dangers and I think cooler heads were needed to work things out. So, it was all politics and when you aren't well-versed in the complexion of the studio game you can suffer for it. There was also the not inconsiderable matter of a conspiracy involving Verna Fields, Joe Alves and several others. I firmly believe that if Verna did not exist in this scenario I would not have been fired. I could have possibly survived Sheinberg as there would have been nobody whispering darkly in his ear. In the final analysis, she is the single biggest influence on the outcome of these events. Verna had initially wanted my job and she used her clout to get me bounced out the door. It took a little while, but she got there.

The damage *Jaws 2* inflicted, and the sense of injustice and humiliation I felt, was considerable, but people in Hollywood still hired me again. It did become more difficult to make the kinds of movies that I wanted to make, as my dismissal raised serious questions and doubts in the minds of some. There were mutterings like, "Hey, if this guy is so good how come *this* happened to him?" It was that kind of thing. I didn't get a chance to explain my side and most people weren't interested in hearing it anyway. I don't mean to be droll when I say the situation was somewhat analogous to farting in a crowded elevator: no matter how desperately you plead your innocence and wave your hands about to clear the air, people still screw their faces up accusingly at the stink before looking away in disgust. That's what it was like and you can't help but take that kind of response personally. The bad smell over *Jaws 2* took a long time to disperse and some folks simply turned their backs on us. To those uncharitable assholes I can now only say, "Fuck you very much!" Over the years, whenever anybody asked me about what happened, I would say, "The shark ate me!" It was a joke but it was also a defense mechanism; a way to disguise some of the pain. I first made that comment during an interview with *The*

National Enquirer and I believe Sheinberg was rather upset about it. He felt it was a direct shot at him as he had been a lawyer. Not that I ever gave a shit what he felt.

I love to work and in order to keep going as a director you have to accept a few unfortunate truths about the business. When you are far removed from an experience like *Jaws 2* and many years have passed by, and you acquire a better understanding of not only movies and how the industry works but of yourself—your own limitations and those of other people—you tend to be somewhat philosophical about things. Being a director is a little bit like being a baseball manager: one day you can be sitting in the dugout doing your job, the next day you are gone and replaced by somebody else. When something like that happens, you try to put that pain in its place and move on. You don't forget and you don't always forgive, but the knowledge you've gained helps you; that's if you don't allow the actions of a poisonous few to overwhelm you. Bitterness can make you go a little crazy and that's not good. It's bad. So, you have to let some things go, you just *have* to, because those emotions are destructive. I enjoy directing. It's not a chore for me; I find it comes very easy. It's all the surrounding bullshit you have to deal with which troubles me. I often think that when you have a bad career experience a general acceptance eventually settles over you. You realize you must keep going because, again, this is simply the way the industry works. That lessens some of the anguish you feel and, sure, time is a great healer. You still have all the dueling scars but each time you get knocked off the horse you just have to dust yourself down, climb back on the saddle and keep on riding.

# 8 *California Dreaming* (1979)

HANCOCK RETURNED *to the United States with Tristan in late 1977 following what he calls "a suitable period of mourning and licking our wounds." Determined to restore the fortunes of his faltering career in the wake of the damaging dismissal from* Jaws 2, *the director let it be known through his long-time agent, David Wardlow, that he was ready to entertain all credible offers. One of the projects Hancock rejected during this difficult period was a thriller called* The China Syndrome, *a decision that would later cause him much remorse. Released in March 1979, the film would eventually be helmed by James Bridges, garnering four Academy Award nominations and competing for the Palme d'Or at the Cannes Film Festival.* The China Syndrome *would also achieve an impressive total domestic gross of $51,718,367 against its $5.9 million budget.*

The trip to Europe had done Dorothy and me a lot of good. It helped us to gain some strength and perspective on everything that had happened, but I was still feeling a little shaky and paranoid. On the flight home I kept wondering what people in Hollywood were thinking and saying about me, and the potential harm the whole *Jaws 2* debacle had done to my career. Then I'd chase those thoughts out of my head, because I wanted to get back to the States and start working right away. I wanted to show everybody that I was still employable. I suppose the official line was that I'd departed over "artistic differences," but I don't think that fooled anyone. Despite my devastating firing from *Jaws 2* leaving a bad taste in some people's mouths, to my great joy and relief I immediately got offered several projects upon our return. This demonstrated to me that I *was* indeed still employable and wasn't going to be consigned to the garbage pile quite yet. One of the first things I was offered was a disaster movie with a neat-sounding title and premise: *The China Syndrome.*

How that project came my way was this: Dorothy had been friends with Jane Fonda since they had done *Klute* together back in 1971, both playing New York prostitutes. Dorothy and Jane later performed in a kind of evening of famous women characters together that was held in Hollywood. Judy Chaikin, the sister of the late Joe Chaikin—the actor/director beside whom I'd been arrested and beaten by cops back in 1962—put together this event and called it *Women Speak.* It was a series of monologues performed by actresses at some nightclub on Sunset Boulevard. Jane did one famous woman, Dorothy did another, Susan Anspach did a third, and so on. Susan drove them all crazy by the way, as she had me on *A Midsummer Night's Dream* and in fact, most of the people she's ever worked with. I forget now who exactly played what, but the list of characters included Contemporary Woman, Sojourner Truth, Susan B. Anthony, Victoria Woodhull, Margaret Sanger, Emma Goldman, Abigail Adams and Eleanore Roosevelt. I went to several of the rehearsals with Dorothy and got to know Jane as we would have drinks afterwards. Jane also attended our wedding on December 29, 1975, and so she was around.

Shortly after *Jaws 2* came to an abrupt end, I learned from Jane that Michael Douglas had a project called *The China Syndrome* that they both wanted me to do. It concerned the core meltdown of a nuclear facility in California and dealt with the hazards of nuclear energy, which I found an interesting and important subject. The screenplay I was given to read featured two or three male characters and one of them was a TV news reporter who uncovers some awful secret of a contaminating leak at a nuclear power plant that needs to be revealed to the public. This character was supposed to be rewritten as a woman so that Jane could play it. Douglas, who was also the producer on the film, came over to my house in Malibu to sell me on the project. He and I had a very long meeting and it was clear that he really wanted me to do the movie. I liked Michael personally and I also liked his work as an actor. Remember, I had wanted to cast him years earlier as the lead in Mark Fine's unmade screenplay. However, I did not like the draft of the script I viewed. It wasn't good to say the least. I also didn't want to work with Jack Lemmon especially as

I'm not his biggest fan. Whenever I had seen Lemmon onscreen, I simply never believed him. I either found him to be overly sentimental and wet in the roles he played or decidedly fakey. To me, he was like an old-fashioned Hollywood actor before the Method arrived and blew everything apart. Of course, there are times when Lemmon can be wonderful, but let's just say he was not on my happy list. It was made clear to me that *The China Syndrome* was a project with Jane, Mike *and* Jack Lemmon attached. That was the deal. So, after carefully considering all these things, I turned it down. That was a big mistake on my part, one that still inspires remorse. Indeed, I consider my refusing *The China Syndrome* to be the biggest commercial regret of my career.

As it turned out, the film was a huge hit. Not only did they succeed in fixing the script well enough to make it work, fate had also smiled on them—if only at the unfortunate expense of others. What happened was *The China Syndrome* opened the very same week as the infamous Three Mile Island accident, in which an actual nuclear facility in Dauphin County, Pennsylvania, experienced a meltdown. From the studio's perspective the picture being released just days after this disaster occurred was a rather fortunate coincidence, one that undoubtedly helped to make the movie a sizable success. So, it was a case of extraordinary luck. I can remember feeling bad that I didn't take the picture on. Very bad! Of all the movies I've been offered over the years, there are really only two projects that I should have done that I didn't. The first is *The China Syndrome* and the other is *Glory*. Sometimes as a director you get involved with a project in its earliest incarnation and it doesn't seem particularly promising or sound. The script may be weak, or the actors attached to it are unappealing, or you aren't entirely comfortable with the people you are working with. Then you may leave the project and it later grows into something far more interesting and successful. Later drafts are stronger and richer, better actors are lured to the project, and the picture eventually becomes a big hit. That's always tough to swallow, but that's what the business is built on: taking chances.

Another of the projects I flirted with in the wake of *Jaws 2* came courtesy of Martin Poll who, a few years earlier, had earned an Academy Award nomination for producing *The Lion in Winter*. He wanted me to consider a script he had and do some work on it. I forget the title of it now, and I believe the movie was never made, but it was a detective story set in New York that also had some half-ass love story in it as well as the detection. Marty thought it was decent and would make a worthwhile picture, but I did not share his opinion or enthusiasm. Frankly, the draft he gave me was a complete mess and very hard to read: limp, clumsy and obvious. Marty wanted me to make a development deal and was also hoping to snag Dustin Hoffman for the lead role of the detective. Again, I did not share his optimism about succeeding with that task. The project was a job, yes, which I really needed at the time, but it was not something that I wanted to do. It's hard to distinguish sometimes, when you're sent a lot of bad material, which are the fixable ones and which aren't. Some scripts are beyond help. The detective script wasn't as interesting to me as *The China Syndrome* and neither was it as good. Neither was it as fixable.

More important than anything was the fact that the detective movie was not a go-picture, it was a development deal. It was certainly nice to feel wanted again, but I eventually turned the project down. I still feel I was right not to do it and, unlike *The China Syndrome*, I have no regrets about doing so. In truth, one of the reasons I didn't sign up for the detective movie—and this is also another important reason why I didn't sign up for *The China Syndrome* either—is that on a lot of development deals they want you to be exclusive. That's the pertinent consideration here. You have to sign a clause in the contract which stipulates that you can't and won't be working on something else at the same time with a different company. The development deal means they are not committing to making the picture, but they insist that *you* commit to make it. In a scenario such as this, there is always the burning temptation to take a go-picture when the opportunity arises. In essence this is what my next film, *California Dreaming*, was.

It almost goes without saying that if I had the chance to go back in time and do it all over again, I would have just cheated. I would have signed two simultaneous exclusive development deals and committed fraud. I would have simply said to the studio, "Sure, yeah, I'll be exclusive." Then, in reality, I would have been working on several other projects at the same time in an effort to get something off the ground. Back then, I felt such actions were how you got sued and perhaps earned a bad reputation in the business. So, in the end, I decided against doing it. I simply refused the deals. I mean, I wanted to work with Michael Douglas and Jane Fonda on *The China Syndrome*, but the insistence that I work on nothing else—although it was not a go-picture—is really what made me drift towards something else. Exclusive development deals tie you up and create pauses and gaps between projects, as you can spend several years developing films that never get made. After *Jaws 2*, I felt I needed to get a movie going as quickly as possible to show everybody I could still do it. I couldn't afford to be inactive.

> *Around the same time he was considering* The China Syndrome, *Hancock optioned the screen rights to a pair of acclaimed novels by two major American authors. The first was* Something Happened *by Joseph Heller, which was published in September 1974 amid considerable expectation and excitement. The narrative concerns Bob Slocum, a successful mid-level executive at a corporate advertising firm, who has a beautiful wife, three loving children and a resplendent house in the suburbs of Connecticut. Now entering a middle-age malaise of misery and introspection, Slocum engages in a lengthy inner monologue that details his fantasies and memories; reflecting on his childhood, his family, his job, and his sexual antics. Although dismissed by some critics as circuitous and oppressively bleak, Hancock was enraptured by the unflinching honesty and meticulous prose of Heller's novel while also admiring its satirizing of American business and culture.*

A long gap of thirteen years had elapsed between the publication of Joe Heller's first novel, *Catch-22*, which he had written in the early 1960s and had become a huge success, a cultural force even, and *Something Happened*. Sure, the follow-up got mixed reactions from critics, but I loved it. It was a stream of consciousness story that contained sections of great dialogue that detailed Heller's experiences at Time Inc., and his problems with his children—his daughter and his little boy. I met Heller through Alan Schwartz, who also represented him, and the three of us had lunch together. I thought at the time the dialogue scenes in *Something Happened* had the brutal honesty of Bergman's *Scenes from a Marriage*. That's what I told Heller at our lunch and it captured his heart. He then agreed to let me option his book for six months for a nominal sum, or it might have been for free, I don't remember. At any rate I had the rights to an important novel by this famous author. I was soon confronted by another of those turning points that I look back on now and wonder about the road not taken. The question was how to set the film up and get it financed? I had, very quickly it was clear, two ways of going:

I had mentioned to George Stevens, Jr., my friend and benefactor from the AFI, that I was interested in the book and I guess he relayed this information to his wife. Now Liz Stevens was and is an extremely powerful Washington hostess, a great beauty, a charmer, a member of the Guest clan (an important family), and as far as I can tell, admirable in every way. So I was delighted when Liz decided she wanted to produce *Something Happened*. She flew to Los Angeles and we had lunch at the Polo Lounge. Liz brought along a friend named Luis San Giorgio that she wanted to co-produce with her. It was a good meeting. I liked Liz better than I liked her potential partner. I had a crush on her, actually—not that I would have ever done anything about it—whereas I wondered about Luis San Giorgio's lack of credits. But it's to be expected that there are always going to be things you aren't entirely happy with and I was open to going into business with them. I was to write and direct the film and, so, shall we make a deal? Well, it turned out they weren't thinking of putting up any money. I imagine Liz felt I was obligated enough to George for funding *Sticky My Fingers* and supporting *Bang the Drum Slowly*, and making me a trustee of the AFI, as well as our personal friendship, that I should have been willing to write the screenplay on trust. Did I rankle at what one might feel was a sense of entitlement on her part? Not really. I liked her and she was indeed *entitled*.

The other way of going came through Alan Schwartz. He had some wealthy new clients who were setting up a production company and looking to get into the film business. They were acquiring projects right and left and wanted to do *Something Happened*. They had money to pay me to write a screenplay—not much, but something like ten or twelve thousand dollars if memory serves. Could I have married them with Liz and her partner? Alan said no, they wanted to be *the* guys if they were putting up the money. I had to choose and I chose to get paid for my work. It was a mistake I regret to this day. Liz took it badly and, as it turned out, Alan's clients were not really serious. By the time I'd turned in my first draft of the screenplay, and like the rich dilettantes they were, these individuals had moved on to something else, real estate or pork bellies, who knows. So much for their venture into the film business!

Was I happy with the draft of *Something Happened* that I wrote? Well, Heller liked it. I found it, though, a hard adaptation. As I said, the dialogue in the novel worked beautifully, but you had to leave out so many great scenes. Also, the ending is probably unacceptably grim by the requirements of commercial cinema: the leading character's much beloved little boy is injured and he holds him so tight in the ambulance on the way to the hospital that he smothers him. Talk about killing the things we love. It was too true to life. What will and will not make a film is something I've had to learn the hard way.

> *The second novel Hancock optioned was* Regiment of Women *by Thomas Berger, author of the epic western* Little Big Man *(1964). First published in 1973, this satirical and chastening science fiction novel is located in a 22nd century New York City beset by pollution alerts and detention centers, where the gender roles of men and women have been completely reversed. The hero of the book is Georgie Cornell, a secretary at a high-powered publishing firm. He goes to work each day in tailored blouses, pleated skirts and high heels, fending off the attentions of his bald-headed female boss who periodically leers at Georgie's silicone breasts. Hancock adapted Berger's novel into a screenplay in collaboration with Dorothy Tristan and his impassioned efforts to realize the film would persist for many years, attracting the interest of some of Hollywood's biggest stars.*

Let me admit something here: I have an interest in science fiction, but no great passion for it. Not really. Generally, I don't like it. The genre often recycles a lot of the same ideas and seems to open itself up to a kind of faux intellectualism and grasping satire that doesn't always work for me. Sometimes it has too much of a message and other times not enough, and feels rather artificial. Granted, you can't restrict that criticism to science fiction alone. A lot of writers and critics dress stories up with meanings and readings that don't really apply. It's easy to interpret works after the fact and take credit for it. All the same, I do appreciate the ability of science fiction to comment on certain social, political and racial aspects of our world. That's a good thing. I mean, you can probably say a lot in a sci-fi novel or a sci-fi film that you otherwise couldn't in a conventional drama without it being dull or preachy. Just by setting a story in the future, or populating it with space-ships and robots and little green men from Mars, whatever it is, people can suddenly accept it and enjoy it. But those kinds of narratives—ones that are solely interested in technology, gadgets and exotic aliens—don't really engage my imagination and I often bridle at them. The science fiction I've enjoyed has always been stuff that is a little more charged and cerebral and character-driven. That's why I immediately fell in love with *Regiment of Women* because it was all of those things and more. It was such a sharp and startling dystopian vision. I loved it and thought it would make a powerful and original movie.

When you are working with a futuristic story in which women have come to power and men now occupy the position that females do in our society, you have to create an all-encompassing world. Basically, in Berger's vision, women hold all positions of authority in life and government. They are our politicians, our business leaders, our law enforcement, our soldiers, etc. Their natural breasts are reduced or suppressed; they wear business-suits and fake nylon beards and moustaches; they have crew-cuts and cuss and play grab-ass. Whereas men wear make-up, dresses and stockings, and routinely shave their legs; they have silicone breast implants installed in their chests through the aid of cosmetic surgery, and cannot serve in the military or the police force. The summit of masculine intelligence is now restricted to thinking about the color of their cashmere sweater and finding the right lamp and carpets for their apartment; they uniformly lack confidence and get screwed in the ass by their female psychiatrists through the use of huge dildos. So, naturally, the male rectum has become the focal point of sexual activity, not the female vagina, and women use these sex aids to penetrate men for their gratification and pleasure. Reproduction is achieved through men being milked of their sperm by special machines.

Dorothy and I obviously toned some of this stuff down in adapting Berger's book into a screenplay. I was going to retain the dresses and stockings in the film, and the fussiness about make-up and getting the right lamp and so forth, the confinement of being cast in a limiting social role, but lose all the stuff about breast implants and the sodomizing by one's psychiatrist (although enough of my female friends have been fucked by their psychiatrists that the latter was sorely tempting to include in the script). It's one thing, of course, to read about these things in a book. It's quite another to see them in a movie. But I thought Berger's novel was brilliant: blackly comic, touching on some painful nerves, and full of neat details and satiric reversals. It was hilarious but also moving, in that it was essentially a love story between two people caught in a chaotic society who struggle towards a level of acceptance and equality. In that way, it presents a future that's still very much like our present. I liked that.

With any novel that is as new and provocative as *Regiment of Women*, the idea of my wanting to do it as a movie prompted a variety of contrasting responses from people. Truth be told, those reactions were mostly negative and ranged from reluctance and general indifference to downright fear and confusion. My representation at William Morris took *Regiment of Women* all around the big studios without a single bite. Not one! I do recall that my London William Morris agent absolutely *hated* the project and thought I was nuts to even try to get it made. I knew early on that *Regiment of Women* was one of those movies that not only required a great actor for the male lead, but someone who was also brave and committed and recognizable to audiences. No doubt some actors were afraid of doing the film or didn't quite understand it. I suspect they were concerned about the damage it could possibly do to their image and their careers. I don't know. Even with all that, I initially succeeded in getting Warren Beatty interested in wanting to play Georgie Cornell.

Warren was extremely enthusiastic and amiable, and really seemed to respond to the material. I was totally convinced by him as he's a real charmer. There is something eminently likable about Beatty when you meet him just as there is when you watch him onscreen. He's also a very busy person. He's always on the move, always full of restless energy. He would say things like, "Oh yes, we *will* do this! We will definitely do it!" Then you don't hear anything from him ever again. But in my dealings with Warren, I found him to be somewhat of an elusive character. I mean, he was always present, always engaged, but I tried to work him out during those early discussions as you do any actor. You try to discover just how smart they are, how interested in the project they are, and if you think you can work with them. I suspect there was the potential within Beatty to be a dominant presence in terms of what he may or may not have wanted in the movie. I would have certainly put up with that because I liked Warren personally, and I admired his work both as an actor and a director. I think he's a wonderful filmmaker, actually. I love *Reds*, which is a hugely impressive film. It was an immense achievement to make a picture like that through the studio system. Beatty's terrific sense of ambition and his attention to detail are admirable. I wasn't intimidated by those qualities; I welcomed the prospect of possibly working with someone like that. In all respects, I prefer to work with a person who is that driven and focused, because you know they will drive you to be the best that you can be. They won't tolerate anything less. I was certain that Beatty was going to do *Regiment of Women*—that was until I mentioned it to the guys at William Morris, who all chorused, "Warren says *yes* to everybody!" Even after that, I still didn't believe them. Alas, it proved to be true. Beatty's interest dissolved and we were never able to work something out with him.

After Beatty was gone, I remember me and David Wardlow tried the project on Lynda Obst, who was David Geffen's development person at that point. We were thinking it might appeal to Geffen, but I don't know that it ever reached him. As time went on, our search for an actor continued and I talked to Dustin Hoffman about possibly starring in the film. I thought the idea of doing a satirical science fiction film would intrigue him, but Beatty had been much more excited about *Regiment of Women* than Hoffman ever was. Despite that, it was interesting to meet Dustin again at this juncture of his career. Our first encounter, which was highly memorable, had taken place back in 1962 when I was doing *A Man's a Man* in New York. I can vividly recall meeting Hoffman when he was a struggling young actor. As I was coming out of rehearsal one day, he physically grabbed me and started pleading with me: "You've got to put me in this play! Please-please-please! You've got to! I could really do it! I could be so good! Please give me a chance! *Please!*" I still have this indelible image in my mind of looking down at Dustin, gazing into his eyes which were these huge pools of desperation, his voice trembling with emotion. I can remember saying to myself, "Geez, this guy is way too desperate to be any good." I don't believe I even auditioned Dustin and I don't think he ever forgave me for that, but he was nice when we met to discuss *Regiment of Women*. By this time—it was 1978—Dustin had tasted considerable success and was now a major movie star. He was receiving multiple overtures and could afford to carefully pick and choose what projects he wanted to do.

I think Dustin recognized the potential of *Regiment of Women*, and the unique opportunities it offered him as an actor, but he was never completely sold on the concept for some reason. This is what I thought, anyway. Interestingly, a couple of years after we had discussed *Regiment of Women* together, Sydney Pollack's *Tootsie* appeared in theaters starring Dustin in the titular role. That movie was similar to my story to some degree, and not merely in the most obvious sense that it's about a guy who wears a dress and impersonates a woman. I wouldn't go as far as calling *Tootsie* a rip-off of *Regiment of Women*, but some people did feel strongly about it—so strongly in fact they felt there was a possible lawsuit that we never pursued. Personally, I didn't think there was any basis for a lawsuit, but others, such as the producer Jack Brodsky, did. I will concede that it's highly likely that, yes, Hoffman probably got the idea and inspiration for playing a man playing a woman from my screenplay. Then again some things are merely floating about in the air, so who knows? The whole affair was certainly irksome, but not something that would justify paying a lawyer to go after. I did not want to possibly acquire a reputation in the business as someone who would do something like that.

Several years after my involvement with Beatty and Hoffman, Jon Voight then expressed an interest in doing *Regiment of Women*. Jon and Dorothy had played Stanley Kowalski and Blanche DuBois together in a production of *A Streetcar Named Desire* in Baltimore. Dorothy and I met with him several times at our Malibu home about the script. Voight wanted to cast his then girlfriend Stacey Pickren, which we weren't opposed to as she was extremely pretty and a good actress. As time passed, we got a strange vibe that Jon was interested in Dorothy romantically and, to compound matters, he also wanted to co-write a draft of the screenplay with us. We thought better about proceeding with him as Dorothy and I have always been careful to protect our marriage. After Voight was gone, there began the slow demise of *Regiment of Women* as a viable movie. This process took a number of years and was profoundly disappointing as the whole idea was so fresh and edgy. It died for good when I got sick of annually paying $10,000 for each year and a half of the option.

Incidentally, just six months ago, my stepdaughter said to me, "Why don't you try to get that one going again? You know, I think its time has come." Alexandra remembered fondly the night she had tracked down Mick Jagger at Mr. Chow's and gave him a copy of the script, and Jagger had flirted with her. So, after our conversation, I inquired as to the current availability of the rights and discovered that, sure enough, they were up for grabs. I showed Berger's book to several people as copies of my screenplay had perished in a devastating house-fire we suffered in 1993 (more on that in a later chapter). They all thought the story was just too difficult and strange. The agent involved eventually called me and said they had received another offer to option the property, but they would go with me because of my long history with it. Needless to say, this was if I ponied up some money. I decided not to. I told them to instead go with the other interested party and *Regiment of Women* was finally, lamentably, out of my life.

> *Early in 1978, David Wardlow was contacted by representatives of American International Pictures regarding a potential project for Hancock. Founded in April 1954 by*

> Samuel Z. Arkoff (1918-2001) and his associate James H. Nicholson (1916-1972), the company had specialized in low-budget films released during the summer and aimed ostensibly at the teenage drive-in market. Seeking to deliver a "quality product," Arkoff was excited by a script he had recently purchased from former surfer turned actor and screenwriter Ned Wynn called California Dreaming. The son of Keenan Wynn and grandson of Ed Wynn, two actors of considerable note, Ned had failed to reach the career heights of his forefathers, having played banal supporting roles in four of AIP's seven "beach party movies"—Bikini Beach (1964), Pyjama Party (1964), Beach Blanket Bingo (1965) and How to Stuff a Wild Bikini (1966).
>
> Drawn from his own experiences of riding the waves on the shores of Santa Monica, the script follows the journey of Tony Thompson (or T.T as he is known), a gauche young man fresh out of high school who has moved from Chicago to California in search of sunshine and excitement. Believing that the people who live in the Golden State are glamorous and fulfilled, he quickly becomes enchanted with the local surfing scene—embodied by the gloriously toned and tanned forms of Rick Chapman and his friends Mike and Tenner. T.T. makes several awkward attempts at ingratiating himself with their clique, but is rejected by the surfers who view him as nothing more than a nerdish Midwesterner. T.T. is then taken under the wing of Duke, an ageing and amiable bar owner who is considered "the biggest bullshit artist on the beach" due to the tall tales he often relates. Shortly thereafter, T.T. meets Duke's attractive teenage daughter, Corky, who urges him to abandon his ambitions of being a surfer and do something more useful with his life. As T.T. becomes immersed in this small slice of paradise, he begins to realize that the lifestyle is not as wonderful as he imagined it would be, and is in fact staid and unfulfilling.

The reason I chose to do *California Dreaming*, and agreed to work for American International Pictures, was the same reason I had chosen to do *Baby Blue Marine*: here was another go-picture! It was that simple, really. Knowing the types of movies AIP had done historically—biker films, beach party movies and other exploitation fare—I was concerned about exactly what kind of picture they were offering me. When I heard the project was another "beach movie" my heart sank. However, my initial fears were allayed by their declaration that they now intended to do a "different kind of picture" to the ones the company had previously been associated with. They basically said, "Look, we don't want to make the typical AIP movie here and that's why we feel this script is so good. It's not your average beach movie; it's a period coming-of-age story that is more refined and emotional. As a matter of fact, it's like *The Last Picture Show* at the beach." I was immediately taken with that description and thought it was a potentially interesting idea.

So, they sent me the script and I liked it. The writing was good, and there were certain shifts in mood that were affecting. The story had that distinct bittersweet tone I often like. To me, *California Dreaming* seemed less of a surfing movie and more of a nostalgia piece. It reminded me somewhat of *American Graffiti* in the way it looked back to a different time, a lost age, and concerned several young people on the cusp of adulthood and awareness. There was an interesting array of characters, nothing too profound, but I often see value in all types of people—like T.T., this fumbling fish out of water who is pursuing his own dream. On the other end of the spectrum was Duke, a nice guy whose refuses to surrender his youth and dreams. Additionally, there were a few offbeat supporting characters I liked, although, admittedly, some of these read better on the page than they eventually would realized on film. I must concede that I didn't connect with the surfers in the script. They mostly just surfed, drank beer and screwed around behind their girlfriends' backs. Interestingly, I saw *California Dreaming* as a story of people who are trapped by their behavior and environment; trapped in paradise. They have spent their entire lives on the beach and some of them have stayed there far too long. It's all they know, and it's all some of them will ever know. In that regard, the narrative had a kind of dual view of the surfing lifestyle: on one hand it celebrated the beach as a place of freedom and frivolity. On the other it condemned it as a place where people behaved irresponsibly and were almost stuck in time. I liked that contrasting tone as I felt there were arguments for both viewpoints. There was also a palpable sadness to the story in that all good things must come to an end. In Duke's case, it would end in tragedy.

Not only did I like the screenplay, I liked the guy who wrote it. Ned Wynn came from a famous showbiz family, and was a terribly nice guy as well as being an interesting and well-traveled man. *California Dreaming* was Ned looking back at his own surfing days as he had really lived that life there on Santa Monica in the early 1960s, on State Beach. It was a cherished time for him; golden summers, beautiful girls, beautiful waves, the folly and excitement and exuberance of youth. After spending several years on the beach doing nothing, he had become friends with members of The Beach Boys, and other musicians and celebrities. He'd also converted into a disciple of the Maharishi Mahesh Yogi for three years and devoted himself to Transcendental Meditation. Ned talked to me about his experiences with the guru, some of which were hysterically funny. He told me there had been some tensions brewing between the various peaceful disciples who were all jostling for the Maharishi's attentions. They would fight with each other for the privilege of spreading the Maharishi's tiger-skin robes, and their cars had actually collided with each other as they attempted to be the vehicle that would be first in line behind his. Crazy stuff!

Now, other than the fact I had once been young myself, there was nothing in Ned's script that related directly to my own experiences. Maybe if there had been I could have made a better film. Thus, there weren't any characters in *California Dreaming* that I could personally relate to in any profound way. Ultimately, maybe that is what's wrong with the picture: my lack of identification. The truth is I had no real interest in the surfing community prior to making *California Dreaming* and I've had very little after making it. I had never really surfed as a youth, as I've never been particularly agile enough to stand up on a moving surfboard. My stepdaughter had gone out with a whole bunch of surfers in Malibu, so I had acquired some second-hand knowledge of *surfdom*. I must say that the impression I got from most of these guys was not an entirely favorable one. From a distance, the majority of them seemed to be rather self-interested and not very bright. For all that, one must admire their skill and tenacity as surfing is not easy, not easy at all. Realizing this before we started shooting, I hired some surfing experts as technical advisors—most notably an ex-champion named Johnny Fain who also appears in the picture as Tenner, the first of the three principal surfers to embrace responsibility and adulthood. We organized Surfing School during rehearsals just like we'd had Baseball School on *Bang the Drum Slowly*, in an attempt to teach John Calvin and Jimmy Van Patten (who play Rick and Mike respectively) how to surf to an acceptable standard. We could fake it to a certain degree, but they still had to look comfortable and confident on the water.

In terms of my own approach to doing the picture, I wasn't consciously influenced at all by any other movies that featured surfers, or surfing as a central theme or backdrop to the story. John Milius' *Big Wednesday* came out around the same time as *California Dreaming*, but I didn't see that movie until later. That picture had some of the same wistful quality I'd wanted for my picture, but it was different. One surfing film I did like a lot was *The Endless Summer*, Bruce Brown's documentary about two young California surfers that traversed the world in search of the perfect wave. That had come out in the late 1960s and I'd always liked the feel of it and the imagery, as well as the real people it featured. We made reference to Brown in *California Dreaming*, when Rick informs Mike that "Bruce Brown is down here! Wouldn't you like to be in a movie?" Ned and I felt it was only fair that Brown got a small mention.

We shot *California Dreaming* for around forty days, something like that, and it was a lot of fun. As I say, the script was originally a period piece and the ending of the first draft featured the characters watching John F. Kennedy surfing in front of those big houses that are situated along the water in Santa Monica. So, it was kind of a dreamy look back at a time when even the President of the United States surfed. That aspect of it certainly had feeling for me. Sadly, AIP would not shoot the film at State Beach. They wanted to shoot it at Avila Beach, which was located on San Luis Obispo Bay, more than 150 miles northwest of Los Angeles. It was a cheaper place to shoot and would be a non-union situation. All the period cars and period clothes, all the money required in the budget for those things, I willingly traded for more shooting days. The question I now ask myself is was that the right decision? Should I have retained the period trappings and trimmings, and given the film a lot more nostalgia, flavor and texture? I didn't want the film to resemble an episode of *Happy Days* or something, because that was a very modish approach in the late 1970s. In that regard *California Dreaming* was a little like *Baby Blue Marine*: it presents a past but maybe not our actual past, if you take my meaning. At the time I reasoned it this way: it's one thing if, in your mind, you see JFK surfing the waves. It's quite another thing if you see somebody who looks vaguely like JFK in a long shot, surfing. So, with that thought in mind, I gave that element up to secure more shooting days.

I should add that we didn't choose Avila Beach merely due to a concession in budget or shooting days, as I thought it was a very attractive location. It was a good place to shoot and it had most of the things we needed. I had looked at a lot of different towns along the coast and that one seemed to be the most practical in terms of where we could house people and equipment, and, importantly, I needed a place where there was a good break surf-wise. In reality, you are limited to where there are really good waves you can photograph and that place was most assuredly one of them. Somebody recently told me that no one has ever drowned on Avila Beach as there is very little undertow there. I don't know if that is actually true or not, but, apparently, it has the perfect conditions for surfing. I'm also not entirely sure if there has ever been a fatal shark attack in the area either, but it was good to hear all of these things. It confirms for me now that we had selected a really great place.

Something that seems to cause confusion in some people's minds is exactly when *California Dreaming* is set. Some insist that it's set as early as 1969 or 1971; others say it occurs later in 1975, or possibly in 1979, the year in which the picture was released. To me, it doesn't always feel like a story that belongs to the end of the 1970s, but I intentionally tried to make a movie that had a timeless feel to it. I wanted the audience to speculate about when these events were taking place. I guess it is 1979 if you look at some of the clothes and the cars, but I wanted the film to be set in a vague and somewhat indistinct period that you couldn't really identify. To what extent we successfully pulled that off is open for discussion. I do think this approach was helpful in my efforts to make it seem like the characters inhabited a kind of poetic fantasy world. I mean, our nostalgia and memories of certain people, places and events are often colored by many factors: the passage of time being just one of them. We don't always remember things correctly, or as they actually were. That is as true of the clothes and the cars as it is of the events themselves. Everything has a golden shine to it; the summers seem impossibly beautiful and so do the girls. Sometimes we don't even remember an event the same way each time we return to it in our minds. Those ideas would have been interesting to incorporate had we done *California Dreaming* as a straight period piece, with characters looking back at their lost youth. But I do think those feelings are still somewhat inherent in the picture as it is now.

The tagline AIP later devised for the film reads: "A state somewhere between fantasy and reality." That makes sense when you consider that California is viewed by many people in the western world as this fabled sun-soaked paradise of near illimitable opportunity and pleasure. It's a place everybody wants to get to because it's seen as this veritable wonderland. There have been countless people like T.T. who have arrived there in search of the abundance of delicious fruits it apparently has to offer. It's interesting, but when I first moved out to California in the early 1970s, I remember Don Graham gave me a book by Reyner Banham called *Los Angeles: The Architecture of Four Ecologies*. Donny had previously lived out in Los Angeles for a year to learn about newspapers before he went on to become the publisher of *The Washington Post* (he'd worked at the *L.A. Times*). I read Banham's book and learned a lot about what things assisted in shaping both the appearance and the personality of the city and the state of California; the geography, the industry, the cultures, and the way that entertainment and amusement came to prominence. The four ecologies Banham identified are the ocean, the mountains, the desert and the fantasy/Disney aspects. That all seemed to be perfectly accurate to me.

Shortly before I arrived in L.A. from New York, everybody I knew was telling me, "John, you are going to *hate* California." So, I arrived there somewhat determined to like it. And I did like it for several months. I became friends with a lot of interesting people including Dick Zanuck, the actor Richard Jordan and several others. Jordan in particular became a close friend, although we never worked together. I don't know why. He drank a lot and maybe I was wary of that. I quickly learned there were people in California who loved everything about it, and then there were others who claimed to hate it, but could never bring themselves to leave. My own attitude towards the place changed after only a short while. I noticed everything that was green and beautiful and flowery eventually turned brown and dry and arid. This had bearing because I don't really like the desert, and I'm not a fan of eucalyptus trees, but I do like the beach. Dorothy and I lived on top of a hill in Malibu looking forward at the ocean and also backward at a canyon. I landscaped two and a half acres that then burned in the fire I mentioned along with hundreds of other properties. I liked our house and I liked our garden. But I did not like living in an atmosphere that was so resolutely dominated by a single business in terms of social interactions and, indeed, the topic of most conversations. I was used to knowing a lot of people in publishing and other creative fields: painters, composers, one thing and another. I found it difficult to remove myself from the circle of people who were in the film business. Ironically enough, *California Dreaming* doesn't really comment on that world because it's fixed almost entirely on the world of the beach.

In accordance with the story, the cast we assembled for the movie was a mixture of youth and experience. Unhappily for me, AIP were determined to stick their nose into the proceedings. You see, *California Dreaming* was originally set up with Robert Carradine starring as T.T., and I actually started rehearsals with Bobby before deciding that he really couldn't act. Also, there was maybe something a little entitled about him I didn't like, a *Carradine* and all that, although Bobby told me that he suspected a certain "Murray" had impregnated his mother. The most important thing was it rankled that yet another actor without a real name was being forced on me—just like Jan-Michael Vincent had been on *Baby Blue Marine*. I'd learned the hard way how key casting was and I wanted to try to do better. So, I fired Bobby Carradine and we hastily cast about for somebody else to play the role.

We saw a lot of people and, in a kind of blind panic, we settled on Dennis Christopher, who had already appeared in a couple of Robert Altman films. I liked Dennis a lot. He was a good guy, who always tried hard, and we got along well. You can't really say it now without possibly being attacked, but I wish he had played T.T. less effeminately. Dennis was gay and was Elton John's boyfriend at the time—or had been right before we started shooting the picture. Of course, I had no problem with his being homosexual as it wasn't important, but I do think he was a little too feminine in his interpretation of the role. I liked the vulnerability and the awkwardness Dennis brought to his performance, but there were times when he could have been a little more masculine—God, I hope that's the right word—in his geekiness. That's all I want to say about that, or I'll probably end up hanging myself!

I then cast Seymour Cassell as the reluctantly aging Duke, and for the role of his daughter Corky, the girl T.T. falls in love with, I hired Glynnis O'Connor as I had enjoyed working with her so much on *Baby Blue Marine*. In the two years between that film and *California Dreaming*, Glynnis had become even prettier and sexier. She was perfect for the part, and I've always liked and valued her both as a person and as an actress. I do recall she had to do the fumbling love scene with Dennis in which they both appeared naked. Glynnis was up for it, no problem, which I find is often the case with actresses with nice boobs. I cast Dorothy as Fay, Duke's ex-wife and Corky's stepmother who runs a bikini store on the beachfront. She also had to appear naked in one scene in which her character is being spied on by these kids outside as she disrobes. Dorothy was not comfortable doing the nudity and I had to talk her into it. She eventually agreed, but had to get liquored-up in order to do the shot.

Like Glynnis, another holdover from *Baby Blue Marine* was John Calvin. I thought he would be great for Rick, a character who was this bullish cheat that is in a troubled relationship with Stephanie, played by

Tanya Roberts. John had made a brief appearance as the drunken soldier who knocks himself unconscious with a bottle as he prepares to fight Jan-Michael Vincent. Like one or two actors we hired for *California Dreaming*, Calvin always had the natural tendency to play things *big*! In one or two scenes he's a little over-the-top and I now ask myself why I let him do it. I guess I was out of perspective and thought what he was doing was funny. Today, I don't think that quite as much. I think he's very hit and miss. But I liked John and thought he was a good actor. Unfortunately, he allowed himself to be misled on the film in other ways, too—mostly by his dick! The problem for him was the beautiful Tanya Roberts, who seemed to cast a spell over him and most of the other guys in the cast.

The unvarnished truth is Tanya fucked nearly everybody on the film and drove them crazy. I'm not kidding. She fucked Calvin and made him crazy; she fucked Jimmy Van Patten and made him crazy. She didn't make me crazy because I didn't fuck her! Even though Tanya had let it be known she was open to us getting it on, I did not take her up on it. No, I resisted and kept my shit together, and not only because my wife was around. Tanya simply never had that effect on me, but, boy, did she have some of those guys completely losing their minds. I mean, she fucked Calvin and then, supposedly, she wouldn't anymore and that suddenly became a problem. John went a little nuts after she'd got inside his head like that. It was difficult for him as they still had several scenes to do together and Tanya was always there.

Aside from Dorothy and Glynnis, we had these two beautiful girls on the movie—Stacey Nelkin, the one with the huge tits who had at one time been Woody Allen's girlfriend—and Tanya, flirtatiously walking around in their bikinis (to be fair they were required to wear them). Naturally, they demanded and received most of the male attention on set and all the guys were entranced with them. Seymour Cassel often referred to Stacey and Tanya rather coarsely as "Trixie and Twattie." He would get liquored-up and valiantly try to get inside their hotel rooms at night. That was amusing, I must say, but Seymour drank much more than I found acceptable and that wasn't quite as amusing. As a matter of fact, the situation got so bad I actually had a scene with his agent about it. But I was happy with Seymour's performance in *California Dreaming* and he was generally a wonderful guy.

As I say, I think some of the actors failed to find the correct register for their performances and were trying too hard for comedy. Alice Playten was one. She is very over-the-top in her role as Corrine the waitress.

I should have reined her in a little more. Alice had appeared in a very famous TV ad for Alka-Seltzer in the late 1960s directed by Howard Zieff, a wonderful director of commercials who then started to direct movies and wasn't quite as good. Alice had played this newlywed housewife who is cooking up outlandish meals for her husband like "marshmallow meatballs" and "poached oysters," as he secretly gulps down Alka-Seltzer in the bathroom. It was a phenomenon and demonstrated Alice's comic gifts. We flew her out for a reading and I quickly hired her. I do find her very exaggerated in *California Dreaming*, but I liked her personally.

I cast Ned Wynn as Earl, Corrine's boyfriend who agrees to sleep in his Pontiac for six weeks in order to win a bet from a rival for her affections. It was great having the writer playing an acting role in the movie, being involved and present during the shooting. I like to have the writer there on the set during filming, and Ned and I became good friends as we were making the picture. I enjoyed him and he was my companion, my friend, my ally, and everything else in between. I wasn't reluctant or self-conscious in any way about improvising or possibly changing anything in his script. At all times, Ned was flexible and accommodating. He was only interested in making the film be as good as it possibly could and having it work. He was always supportive and I valued his support. Dorothy and I were very close to Ned and his wife and we all had a wonderful time together.

> *Having been impressed with his work as Laszlo Kovacs' camera operator on* Baby Blue Marine, *Hancock promoted Robert "Bobby" Byrne to cinematographer on* California Dreaming. *Having recently shot films such as* Smokey and the Bandit *(1977) and* Hooper *(1978) for Hal Needham, as well as* Blue Collar *(1978) for Paul Schrader, Byrne was already building a reputation as a talented director of photography in his own right, and had previously worked with Conrad Hall and William A. Fraker as both an assistant cameraman and operator.*

I guess you could say that Bobby Byrne was steadily climbing the ranks of Hollywood cameramen back then. He'd done some interesting work and I was happy with my choice. However, echoing the negativity surrounding my choice of DP on *Bang the Drum Slowly*, it seemed that others around me were less than impressed with him. As it turned out, they would have good cause. In my conversations with Bobby, we talked about trying to get a sense of a mythic, magical summer. So, we sometimes tried to shoot at magic hour using filters and diffusion to give the film a certain nostalgic look. We tried to invest the images with the feel of a lost world. I thought Bobby was doing a good job of achieving that look, but, as I say, not everybody on the production shared that view. Mike Modor, the production manager and line producer on *California Dreaming*, who was working on behalf of AIP, certainly didn't. Mike came to me after the first week or so of shooting, and said, "Byrne is taking too long to light and he's basically cheating you. You aren't getting enough time to focus on performance as he's eating up so much of the day." I didn't really listen to what Mike was telling me as I didn't particularly like him. But, looking back on it now, there were a lot more faster cameramen than Bobby out there and I would have probably done much better in making a change. What Bobby did looks good, but his methodical approach took longer than was needed. I like to work fast. I don't like to have the actors waiting around for long periods. I feel it hurts performance a little and can be self-defeating and draining on everybody.

What's more is there was a night working with Bobby on *California Dreaming* that I'll never forget. We were shooting exteriors on the beach and it was so cold my teeth were chattering in my skull. Everybody was feeling the chill and it was deeply unpleasant conditions. Apparently, at various points throughout the wee hours, the electricians and the camera department were sneaking into the camera truck and secretly drinking. They probably did this in an effort to keep warm, keep their spirits up or maybe simply because they were bored. I've found this is sometimes the problem with night-shoots: the crew can occasionally be less focused and less attentive, particularly if it's cold—and that particular night was *very* cold. It didn't feel like California at all. Anyway, at one point, I remember Bobby came to me looking rather pale-faced and agitated, and I knew something was wrong. He said, "John, I have something awful to tell you: we've been shooting without film in the camera." For a moment, I couldn't quite believe what Bobby was telling me. I thought it was some kind of joke made in extremely poor taste. Then this sickening feeling settled on me and I knew by the expression on Bobby's face he was for real.

It was a stunning moment, actually, something I've not experienced before or since. I mean, what they did that night was a real violation. There are no other words to describe it. The camera crew was drunk and had simply forgotten to load film into the camera. So, as we were "shooting" we were literally getting nothing. *Nothing*! I reacted very badly to Bobby's revelation. I said, "God, are you fucking kidding me?" Then, fairly quickly, I reasoned, well, it's the middle of the night and my balls feel like icicles, how much can you scream and shout at somebody? What good is it going to do? But I swear, at that moment, the temperature seemed to get even colder. I suddenly had this feeling of bitter resignation and exhaustion. So, I wearily said, "Okay, guys, let's go back and re-do it." And that's exactly what we did. When I told the actors what had happened, predictably, they were pissed off about it, but we had no choice. We simply had to go back because we needed those scenes. Without them we were fucked. In spite of the negligence and lack of professionalism he demonstrated, I would have probably hired Bobby again on another picture. I didn't, but I'm sure I would have.

As you know, I had used slow-motion prominently in my previous films to give moments a subjective resonance and clarity. I talked to Bobby about this and he agreed with my decision to deploy it once again in *California Dreaming* for pretty much the same reasons. I wanted to use slow-motion to give certain scenes the dreamy quality of a memory; of things remembered. Here was a moment in these characters' lives that would remain with them always, and slow-motion underlines the importance of such moments. For instance, there is a lot of it during Duke's death scene as he collapses on the beach from a fatal heart attack during the volleyball game. I thought slow-motion was effective in conveying the wrenching emotions involved. I liked that scene and knew exactly how I was going to shoot it. I wasn't concerned that Duke's death could be seen as being overly melodramatic, coming where it does in the story, immediately after Duke's row with T.T. and Corky, and shortly before he and Fay are about to leave for Hawaii. Yes, it does occur rather conveniently in the narrative, but how many times have things turned sour for people just when life is looking glorious? Many times, I should think. There's also the added poignancy of things being left unsaid, as T.T. and Duke never cleared the air beforehand. I thought that was a dramatic passage, and I was kind of trusting in the structure of Ned's script to provide the most affecting peaks of feeling at just the right time.

I also used slow-motion in moments of ecstasy, as I had done on *Bang the Drum Slowly*. For instance, another scene where it's used prominently is when T.T. is at a concession stand surrounded by girls, and his hand brushes against several glorious breasts (one girl's tit literally spills into the paper cup he is holding in a visual rendering of the quote "My Cup

Runneth Over!") It's a deliberately tactile scene—a hotdog sausage gliding towards a girl's open mouth, and all that stuff. I always laugh at the unaffected joy and exuberance of it. It's a delicious teenage fantasy of the flesh and it's not meant to be subtle. It's meant to be fun. Again, we had a lot of fun doing this picture. Maybe there was too much laughter on the set and in the dailies, I don't know. Maybe I should have exerted more control and seriousness over the shenanigans, but I didn't think it would hurt. People were enjoying the experience, as was I, and following the misery and machinations on *Jaws 2* that felt good and proper. I also thought that good feeling would be conducive to making a good picture and would translate to the screen. I think you can clearly detect that we were having fun making *California Dreaming*. It just shines through, not only in the tits scene, but the sequence where Jimmy Van Patten is beating his head against the restroom door. I like that scene a lot and I liked Jimmy a lot, too. I also like how the tone of the film begins rather light-heartedly then gets progressively more serious until it shifts into tragedy at the end—Duke dying and the rain pouring down. That was always the idea; that the rain would reflect the end of summer; the end of the dream.

> *After the completion of principal photography in the summer of 1978, Hancock entered into post-production on* California Dreaming *at cutting rooms located within AIP's facility on Wilshire near Robertson. This phase would prove to be yet another demoralizing experience for the director as control of the film was wrested from him and his initial cut rejected. Released on April 1, 1979, and assailed by most critics as a thudding attempt to "update" the defunct beach party movie, this bowdlerized version of* California Dreaming *was not the witty and compassionate work Hancock had intended to deliver. Nearly forty years later, the sense of injustice and indignation he feels at being "hoodwinked" by AIP's false promises is as keen as ever.*

My personal dealings with Sam Arkoff were few as he had his son, Louis Arkoff, on the project. Lou was the executive in charge of production and he was very much a presence on the set, whereas Sam mostly kept at a distance. I did have about three or four meetings with Sam, and at one point I remember him saying, "I want you to do really good on this picture. I mean *really* good, you know?" I just nodded at that, and said, "Well, I'll certainly do my best." Despite being Sam's guy, I found Lou to be a rather silly person. He fancied himself a surfer as well as a producer, but I felt at times he had a tendency to be somewhat inflated and frivolous. I mean, Lou was alright, but there were times when I found it difficult to take him seriously. He would be standing there, acting like a producer in his leather jacket, hoping to get laid. Now, there was a lot of cocaine and one thing or another going on back then and I guess Lou had somehow contracted pink-eye from doing coke. The first time he showed up on set, he insisted on looking through the camera's viewfinder and gave everybody else an eye infection! So, Lou didn't exactly get off to a good start with the crew and some of them even thought he was an asshole. I wouldn't go as far to say that Lou was in any way disruptive or intrusive when we were shooting, but he would have these silly ideas that he'd convinced himself were great. It was really later on, in the editing room, when Lou became intrusive. That was when the trouble really started between us.

Basically, in a nutshell, what happened is AIP took the picture away from me and re-cut it. *California Dreaming* is really the only time that I've lost control of a picture and it was a truly miserable and frustrating experience. I delivered my first completed cut, which had more of a measured, leisurely pace that was in tune with *The Last Picture Show* and the easy rhythms of the surfer life. It was in no way cranked up, but it didn't feel slow or labored either—just deliberate. It was representative of the script and our initial ambitions, so was exactly the kind of movie we had strived to make. It had the bittersweet quality, was tough and tender, blending comedy with a love story and tragedy, and had sensitively drawn characters. But when AIP saw my cut, they didn't recognize any of that and immediately demanded that the pace quicken. They wanted the film to be faster, tighter, and they also wanted an entirely different kind of music. My original score was by Fred Karlin, and I had temped *California Dreaming* with not only orchestral music but songs by The Beach Boys and The Mamas and Papas here and there that worked beautifully. I had selected all of these cues with great care and attention in order to create that glowing sense of nostalgia I keep mentioning. It was too bad for me that AIP and the Arkoffs were not impressed with my cut at all and decided differently. They eventually put in a horrible bouncy disco score that pretty much destroyed the feeling I was going for.

Of course, I wanted to know the reason for everybody's apparent disapproval of the job I'd done on the picture. It was then explained to me by Lou Arkoff, actually. He said, "Looking at this movie it's obvious that you hate surfers and that's a big problem." I now ask myself if he was right in that assessment. Did I indeed hate surfers? It was not something I had ever consciously considered. The truth is probably yes, I did dislike them. So what?! I think the surfers do come across in the picture as rather shallow and stupid individuals, particularly Rick who is not a likable or sympathetic character. But that's okay, because not every character has to be a saint for the audience to respond to them. And why should that response be one specific thing? They're human beings and human beings can be many things at different times. What Lou perhaps failed to appreciate was Rick was *written* that way. That was who he was and that's how Calvin played him. The other surfers, Mike and Tenner, were maybe a little more palatable but that didn't matter. I apparently "hated" all surfers and something had to be done to remedy that.

To be sure, that predicament made post-production on *California Dreaming* an unpleasant experience. I've vowed never to put myself in that position again, and I haven't. I was at the mix, but was permitted to say very little. I was also at the scoring sessions but was not allowed any real input. I could express my opinion but no one was required to listen to me. I actually read most of Gibbon's *The History of the Decline and Fall of the Roman Empire* during the mix, listening with one ear and dibbing in occasionally. It was heartbreaking, but I went anyway. Lou Arkoff was not present, just the mixers, but they were under strict instructions not to confer with me. It was a strange and strained atmosphere, not very nice at all. I think Sid Levin, my former friend and the supervising editor on the film, was also there watching over proceedings.

Interestingly, there's a peculiar thing about the editors listed for *California Dreaming* on the Internet Movie Database: I don't recognize any of their names! The second credited editor is somebody called Roy Peterson, whom I think is possibly Sid Levin as IMDb gives *Sounder* as one of his credits, and Sid cut that particular picture. Why is Sid my ex-friend? Well, what happened was this: the first editors on *California Dreaming* were a fairly experienced husband and wife team whose names I can never recall. They started the picture and lasted considerably more than half way through, until I brought in Sid to replace them (these were not happy cutting rooms). Regrettably, Sid then allowed Lou Arkoff to lure him into betraying me in the way he was cutting the movie by dangling the faint hope of his potentially directing something for AIP. By the way, I saw Sid again, many years later, while I was mixing *Suspended Animation* and he was mixing another picture on the stage next door. We were friendly, without ever once discussing our past.

In the face of these tensions, the mixers on *California Dreaming* (none of whom were really stars) did have a modicum of sympathy for me, but they were operating under direct orders and there was no room for sentiment. So, I was just sitting there, reading my book, trying to protect as much of my initial vision as I could; defending certain things to them, explaining and justifying others. It didn't do any good, really, and was very painful. I mean, I don't want to suggest that their injurious tampering with my movie robbed the world of seeing a potential classic. My version of *California Dreaming* was unquestionably no masterpiece, but when you work hard on a movie, and have a clear indication in your mind of what it is and what it isn't, it's extremely difficult to watch it get meddled with and mutilated by other hands. I made whatever suggestions I could get away with and some were accepted and some were not. The vast majority of them were ignored, but I did sneak a scant few through. Then I left in a state of anxiety and depression, and went home.

Before all this occurred, we did organize several screenings of my cut at various times. There were screenings in Hollywood held at different screening rooms and I forget who attended these. Lou was there a lot, but I don't believe his father was. Chris Whittaker, who was also one of the producers, was definitely there. As I've told you, I like to polish films by having repeated screenings. I try to screen every week, or every two weeks, and re-cut in between and make various changes and adjustments. So, we had a couple of screenings of my cut and then Lou Arkoff said, "Okay, we're now taking the picture over. You don't need to come around here anymore." And that was it. That was the point at which I lost all control and input. It was excruciating, but perhaps not unexpected. No question about it, AIP lacked a certain tact. They were not a classy operation, so their behavior probably didn't come as a complete surprise to me. But it did hurt me. There were a few interesting scenes and moments that were excised that I wish had remained in the finished film. It was mostly just looks and reactions, and some more character details and beauty shots. When AIP and the Arkoffs began re-cutting the picture, they seemed to systemically extract the heart out of it. My version had more depth to it, more of a rueful feeling. Their cut was more blunt and heavy-handed, lacking in some things, over-emphasizing others.

I believe we initially tried the film out in the San Fernando Valley at a preview and I remember the reaction being decidedly mixed that day. We scrutinized the cards afterwards and it was obvious that some people had not found the story particularly engaging or the characters enjoyable. It was not the kind of stuff you want to read and was tough to take. Despite that, I still firmly believe in the value of cards and market research because the huge problem with directing is maintaining perspective. I just feel the way you get your perspective back is to put the movie out in front of an audience. You don't have to listen to the cards, you don't have to take heed of the suggestions they scrawl at the bottom, but I think if you try to use their objective eyes and see what they are seeing, it can only be beneficial. I have found it useful to acknowledge what the audience is saying. I've found it helpful in where to cut, and what to cut, how to re-slant or reposition an individual scene, and have a clearer understanding of what works and what doesn't work. Certain things don't quite work as well as you may have hoped or anticipated, and you need to do something about it.

It goes without saying that the more conflicting opinions you receive the more confusing it can be. That's where you have to be smart in what you choose to accept and reject. For instance, it can often be confusing for a preview audience when they answer questions like "Which is your favorite character and which character did you like the least?" Such queries reveal the dilemma for viewers in distinguishing between the actor's performance and the character's overall effectiveness. That's difficult to discern, because sometimes an actor can be incredibly forceful and dominating because he or she is playing a bad or objectionable person—like Calvin plays in *California Dreaming*. So, they may score very low on the approval rating but it's still an effective element of the film because you know it's worked: the villain or antagonist has done what they are supposed to do, upset and agitate the audience. That can sometimes be all it takes to make the viewer dislike not only an individual character, but the movie itself. I've seen it happen. Conversely, it's also easy to be misled by cards. You can suddenly become afraid or disheartened by a negative response from a test audience. This is what makes preserving perspective such a challenge. But, I'll say it again: on the whole, I've found the screening process to be more helpful and insightful than confusing and invasive.

Most directors seem to have this conditioned reflex in immediately rejecting test screenings and market research as an unwarranted violation. I don't think that kind of reaction is realistic, particularly nowadays when some movies are playing for enormous stakes. I've heard certain filmmakers say about their films, "Hey, I cut it so I like it. I don't need to know what other people think." For me, that's the sin of pride as understanding the varied responses to your work can only be a good thing. After having shot and edited a picture for nine months, how can you possibly be objective and have any perspective left on what it is and what it isn't? You need to temporarily extricate yourself from it in order to see it. The problem when you're working on a picture like *California Dreaming*, which has some funny things in it, is that all the jokes suddenly become unfunny. Then you have the strong temptation to take the jokes out because they seem terribly flat or embarrassing. Finally, when you watch the film with an audience and see them cracking up, it can be a revelatory experience. I've seen that happen, too. I think screenings are invaluable as a means of guarding against that kind of thing. You try to remember your initial reaction to something before it was dulled or tempered by repeated viewings. If when you first read the script you thought a particular scene or moment was funny, the audience will probably find it funny, too. Even though the joke no longer seems at all amusing to you, invariably it still gets a big reaction. You reason it by simply saying, "Okay, there aren't many jokes that are funny the nineteenth time you've heard them. So, I'm just going to relax about it." For example, the awkward love scene between Glynnis and Dennis was like that, as was the slow-motion sequence in the theater with T.T. surrounded by a deluge of tits. I do find I am a little embarrassed about those scenes today, but they appear to work just fine for most people.

Ultimately, the mistakes have to be made by the director and not by outside forces tampering with his or her vision. Every film has its own delicate eco-system and when you fuck around with that and take certain things away, or introduce new elements that have no place being there, that natural balance is destroyed. When I talk about the pace of my cut in comparison with the movie as it exists, it still has a fairly laidback and relaxed rhythm to it. *California Dreaming* has an unhurried quality, so, in the final analysis, they were not able to crank up the pace too much. If you shoot a film in a certain way, and attempt to achieve a particular rhythm, and then others try to crank that rhythm up, it can't always be achieved. AIP tried it by injecting quicker cuts and shorter scenes, and by putting their disco music on it, but then the picture was a little bit at war with itself. Internally, it was pulling in different directions and not in a good way where there is irony or ambiguity, or an interesting tension. It just felt hollow and uneven to me, and to the critics and general audience, too.

The reviews were mixed and so were the box office returns, so AIP's interference didn't work. We'll never know if my version would have worked better. Oddly enough, I was recently asked if there was any chance of a restored director's cut of *California Dreaming* appearing anytime in the future. My reply to that was the only chance of it happening is no chance, as they throw all the trims and alternate scenes away. Far greater pictures than *California Dreaming* exist in a state of compromise, so I don't hold out any hope. Maybe it's best left buried. Ironically enough, it's worth mentioning that regardless of all the tampering that came later, I felt I had finally mastered the art of directing. I was far more confident technically during the shoot and could explain to various people exactly what I wanted.

The experience of making *California Dreaming* was another great lesson. I learned that working with smaller independent companies could be just as fraught and perilous as working with the major studios. There were similarities between my situations on *Jaws 2* and *California Dreaming*. Even though the stakes were different in terms of money and personnel, the personal stakes were about the same. I was still dealing with people who had various agendas, who were deceitful and conniving, and I still had a lot to lose. The rules of the game were familiar. In the end, I felt betrayed by AIP. The way they had originally sold the project to me, their stated desire to change their image and do different kinds of pictures, was bullshit pure and simple. I thought I was making "*The Last Picture Show* at the beach," but it turned out, in post, that the Arkoffs and AIP were true to form and true to their history. What they really wanted was another *Beach Blanket Bingo*. So much for the bittersweet, play down the Fred Karlin and bring in The Doobie Brothers! When push came to shove AIP basically fell back on what they knew. They knew how to make brash, bubble-headed pictures and attempting anything a little more subtle and emotionally resonant made them uncomfortable. This was the kind of movie they used to make and they simply made it again. Alas, I don't think the audience for beach party movies of that variety existed anymore. They had all grown-up and moved on.

Despite *California Dreaming* not being what I wanted it to be, there are still things I like about the movie. It's not an abomination by any means, but it's not a film I can easily bring myself to watch. Over the years, I've seen pieces of it—last year I watched a little bit of it—but I mostly resist all opportunities. It's just too painful. From what I have seen of it recently, there were some nice scenes between Seymour and Dorothy. I also think Glynnis is good, but then I always like watching Glynnis. I still feel the subplot between Ned and Alice isn't so hot, and, again, a lot of it tries too hard for laughs. I should have taken a slightly more restrained approach as some of that stuff is awkwardly handled. The humor would have worked better if it was more natural, not so forced, and I recognized some of these problems when I was editing the picture. I can remember feeling concerned about the way in which the story moved from one group of people to another, cutting between assorted characters that were floating around. That approach was not quite as effective as I imagined it would be when I initially read Ned's script. The various plot threads seemed more interesting.

The screenplay had been compared to *The Last Picture Show* and in Peter Bogdanovich's film you follow this collection of disparate characters inhabiting a small Texan town, and it all feels effortless. Maybe the script Bogdanovich was working from was better, and the performances of his actors were more accomplished, but you welcomed the reappearance of each individual character in the story. You were consistently engaged and empathetic, even during quieter moments when not a lot was happening. In contrast, I felt during screenings of *California Dreaming* that the audience was not as welcoming to our characters and neither did they seem especially glad to see them and catch up on their developing story. That response disturbed me and I realized I had failed to recognize what was fundamentally wrong with the film. Looking back now, it was probably the way the script was structured. The first thing I should have done was to fix that, but I didn't.

I think the combination of my firing from *Jaws 2* coupled with the commercial and critical failure of *California Dreaming*, did some further wounding to my career and reputation. Also, accepting a gig at AIP in the first place was not my smartest move. I mean, American International Pictures is not the most prestigious place to work and I would have done a lot better showing a little more patience. I could have worked for Paramount or Columbia, or some other major studio, if I had just sat around a little while longer and waited. There were a number of interesting projects circling around me, but my mistake was not waiting. I should never have jumped in and done a movie simply because it was a go-picture. I had some time available to me and I could have used it more profitably. Sure, it's easy to say these things with the benefit of hindsight. But you know, in all honesty, regret is probably too strong a word for what I feel. It's not like these things torment me. Not at all. None of them.

I have a kind of self-acceptance, which I suppose comes from my mother. Things were what they were, and I did what I did. I never thought I was doing anything but my best. And who knows if the road not taken would have been any better? Somewhere, I forget where, Brecht says the most important thing to learn is *einverständnis*, which translates roughly as "consent." I think he's right. I suppose I felt vulnerable after all the problems on *Jaws 2* and wanted to go some way in repairing the damage it had done. I wanted to bounce right back and show everybody I could deliver a good picture. Unfortunately, that didn't happen and *California Dreaming* only seemed to confirm the worst suspicions of people like Sid Sheinberg, for instance. Of course, if you had told me back in 1979 that it would be another seven or eight years before I directed another feature film of my own I would never have believed you. I would have said you were crazy.

9 *Wolfen* (1981)

PUBLISHED IN AUGUST 1978, *Whitley's Strieber's* The Wolfen *was a fast-paced horror novel that offered a crisp take on the well-worn werewolf theme. It tells of two New York City detectives investigating the deaths of a pair of beat cops killed while on routine duties, who discover that a clandestine species of sentient super-wolves have been living alongside (and feeding upon) humanity for thousands of years. Several months before its publication, producer Rupert Hitzig had been alerted to Strieber's manuscript by his wife, who was working as the author's literary agent. Intrigued by the concept of a pack of ancient creatures roaming the festering tenements and urban wastelands, feasting on the impoverished and disenfranchised who will not be missed, Hitzig had succeeded in convincing Mike Medavoy, co-founder of Orion Pictures, into financing it as a film. The producer's first choice to write and direct* Wolfen *was Oliver Stone, who had made the little-seen horror film* Seizure *(1974) and was about to commence work on a second in* The Hand *(1981). At the time the filmmaker was living in Rome, so Hitzig flew to Italy and spent a week with Stone discussing his hopes and ideas for the project. Unresponsive to the notion of adapting Strieber's novel as a "nature allegory," Stone viewed the film only as a straight detective story. Reaching an amicable impasse, the two men decided to part ways.*

Upon his return to America, Hitzig was asked by Medavoy to consider Michael Wadleigh, the Academy

Award-winning director of the concert documentary Woodstock *(1970), as a possible candidate to helm* Wolfen. *The executive had invited Wadleigh to choose from one of the studio's literary properties and, like Hitzig, had responded to the premise of Strieber's novel rather than its narrative. Medavoy had been developing a relationship with the documentarian since the days he had been Senior Vice President of Production of United Artists, after being impressed with a four-hundred-plus-page screenplay Wadleigh had spent several years writing about the American Revolution. Characterized by Wadleigh as a "definitive movie, an American* War & Peace," *this hugely ambitious project was to comprise eight-hours and two movies at an estimated cost of $11 million. In 1975, Medavoy had provided half the required budget, but a disruptive change in the tax-shelter laws prevented Wadleigh from raising the remaining $5.5 million. Thus, the film sputtered to a standstill, but, in the words of Hitzig, "Medavoy was still fascinated by him." Having secured final director approval, Hitzig agreed to interview Wadleigh and a meeting was arranged at the Beverly Hills Hotel. Three hours later, having realized they shared a common vision for the film in wanting to broaden the novel's scope by adding a social, political and ecological context to its story, Hitzig agreed to hire Wadleigh. The two men then got into a car that same day, drove straight to Medavoy's office and finalized the deal.*

Awarded a budget of $11.3 million (a figure that would eventually swell to a total cost of $17.3 million) shooting on Wolfen *was scheduled to commence in New York in April 1979. However, principal photography did not in fact begin until October of that year, at such familiar landmarks as Central Park, Staten Island, Battery Park, the New York Exchange, the Manhattan Bridge, the Fulton Fish Market, and the devastated South Bronx. Wadleigh also filmed a number of interiors at the sound stages of Queen's Astoria Studios. As production on* Wolfen *continued for the next five months, it became increasingly obvious to all involved that the film would not be ready for its original release* date of Christmas 1980. Subsequent to the excesses and dismal box office performance of Heaven's Gate becoming public knowledge, filming on Wolfen was brought to an unceremonious halt. Wadleigh claimed there were still several scenes left to be shot, whereas the studio insisted the director had completed the work. Throughout the summer as the picture moved into its post-production phase, the producers and executives discussed with Wadleigh the finer points of how the film would be cut both creatively and for length. Shortly after his director's cut was due to be delivered on July 25, 1980, Wadleigh "walked" or was dismissed (depending on whom you talk to) from the production for "political reasons." The filmmaker then challenged the studio over his creative rights as director and demanded that he be permitted to screen his version of Wolfen at a preview before a paying audience. These events led to a lengthy arbitration by the Directors Guild of America that lasted for twenty-one days—the longest case in the then forty-four year history of the organization.

"The arbitration was an unpleasant experience," Hitzig recalled in an interview with the author conducted in January 2009. "The fact is Wadleigh was millions of dollars over budget and six weeks late. I remember Arthur Krim, the chairman of the board at Orion, said, "He's got five days to finish the picture." Wadleigh later claimed he never got to finish the film we had originally approved. He subsequently tried to block the footage, and we went to arbitration. ... Wadleigh said that he had every right to keep me out of the editing room. He insisted he was going to get his director's cut without my interference. So, I went back to New York and returned four months later for his screening. Now, the DGA have an agreement that you get one day of editing for every two days of shooting. So, considering all these factors, we picked a suitable date that Wadleigh was to deliver his director's cut that satisfied the Guild's requirements. Krim, Medavoy, Bill Bernstein and Bob Benjamin all flew out from New York and we went to a screening room. I then stood up and announced to all those present, "Ladies and gentlemen, welcome to the director's cut of Wolfen."

Wadleigh suddenly stood up, and said, "I object! This is not the director's cut as I never finished the picture." I then said, "Okay, let's just show it." Of course, at this point, none of us knew exactly what we had. Well, it turned out that his cut was four hours and four minutes long and had thirty-five SCENE MISSING banners in it! Needless to say, that pissed everybody off and pretty much sealed Wadleigh's doom. I think we had three weeks left for him to do one revision cut and then he was gone."

In a series of lengthy interviews conducted with the author in January and February 2009, Wadleigh insisted that he never intended to screen this cut to the public, and weighed in with his view of the controversy: "[M]any people felt that [Orion] were abnormally leaning on [editor] Richard [Chew] and me to get this film out at any cost. You know, to hell with art! We are just going to get it out there. Of course, a lot of things did go over budget—you better believe it—but I had no control over the budget. I was not the producer. I simply accepted all of these people and was mainly interested in the actors. I did want as the director to choose the actors, but hey, I'm just saying it's a matter of public record that the whole crew was a professional crew and that Orion selected them. I wanted pros, not amateurs, and many people took the position that it was Paul Sylbert, who was a celebrated production designer, who went nuts and really put the budget over the top with the sets and so forth—and they were always consulting with him. I was a nobody by comparison. So, if the next step you might be going to is budget then as I say I think it was pretty well established in the Directors Guild arbitration that any over-budgetings were hardly my fault in the budgetary information that [Hitzig-King Productions and Orion Pictures] brought forward. It didn't seem to have any effect on whether I should not be able to preview my cut of Wolfen."

The arbitrator for the DGA, Edward Mosk, ruled that King-Hitzig Productions and Orion Pictures were within their rights to terminate Wadleigh's services after principal photography on Wolfen was completed. Despite refusing to *reinstate him as director, Mosk determined that Wadleigh would be consulted on any significant changes made to the film during post-production and would also be invited to all previews. Additionally, King-Hitzig was ordered to pay $20,000 in damages to the deposed filmmaker as well as $20,000 to the DGA for their "violation of the hotline procedures of the collective bargaining agreement." During the arbitration, Wadleigh contested that he was not notified of the grounds for his dismissal. In turn, the producers submitted that Wadleigh was indeed responsible for the budgetary increases of* Wolfen *as he had incurred additional costs by writing new dialogue that was not featured in the approved screenplay and had ordered unauthorized props to be included in the picture. While acknowledging that Wadleigh was responsible for the increase in the film's costs, Mosk upheld the director's argument that he had never been awarded a specific budget and that none of the parties involved in the case were ever able to agree on "a mutually acceptable schedule." Thus, Orion could not remove Wadleigh for exceeding the agreed budget and delivering the picture late.*

Amid the air of tension and acrimony that surrounded the production, Wolfen *began to draw some negative advance press attention. In an effort to counter the bad publicity and finish the picture as rapidly as possible, the studio cast about for someone who would hopefully be up to the difficult task at hand. With the movie now rescheduled for release in theaters during the competitive summer season of 1981, Mike Medavoy turned to a filmmaker with whom he had been acquainted for a number of years— John Hancock. Contacted in late 1980, Hancock officially replaced Michael Wadleigh as the director of* Wolfen *at the end of January 1981.*

As I recall, my involvement with *Wolfen* began when my agent received a phone call from Bob Sherman, who was working with Mike Medavoy in a secondary position at Orion Pictures. I was informed that Bob and Mike wanted to talk to me about possibly working on *Wolfen*, which I learned was an expensive movie the studio had been toiling on for many months that was apparently now in "terrible trouble." Medavoy was someone whom I had known and liked for a long time. Mike was a smart and affable guy, not the typical executive you sometimes meet that knows nothing about creativity and everything about profit margins. I was fond of him and respected his good taste and honest intelligence. So, I agreed to meet with him and discuss the project. He and Bob then explained everything that had happened previously, how Michael Wadleigh had become "undisciplined," as well as confused and blinkered about his responsibilities to Orion. This had apparently resulted in a series of crippling cost overruns and delays and recriminations. It sounded like a *real* horror story. The studio clearly had a situation on their hands and they wanted me to come in and help fix the film. They had missed their original release date, and they wanted *Wolfen* finished and out in theaters quickly. I didn't have to deliberate Mike's offer for long. I just said, "Sure, I'll help you guys. Where do I sign?"

When I first got there, everyone at Orion was in a state of panic and confusion—this is my memory of it. It was a tense environment and one or two people were practically tearing their hair out. I do remember it being made clear to me almost from the moment I arrived that I was there to "save the studio." I'm not kidding. This was the rather desperate impression I kept getting. I was like the big hero there for a while which felt good after being fucked by AIP on *California Dreaming*. I did not want Orion to go out of business. I liked the people there and what the company stood for. Nevertheless, I suddenly felt the weight of responsibility on my shoulders. It was a lot of pressure but it was good pressure, as I wasn't the one being held accountable for the state the movie was in. That was the other guy's fault. I know that certain individuals were looking at me to solve all the problems, but there were a number of considerations we had to make. First, the interest alone on *Wolfen* was running to a huge amount every day, and this was back in the early 1980s when the interest rate was exorbitantly high. As I say, Orion needed to have the picture fixed as swiftly as possible, so I did everything I could to make that happen. I worked extremely hard on *Wolfen*. In fact, it was one of the most intensive working experiences of my life; a highly concentrated and demanding effort. But I was determined to do my best for Medavoy and everybody else at the studio.

Let me just say for the record that I never met with, or spoke to, Michael Wadleigh during or after my participation on *Wolfen* to discuss what I intended to do. Now that he was no longer director of the film, his thoughts, requests or suggestions were no longer important. I had actually met Wadleigh about ten years earlier, in 1970, when he was cutting *Woodstock* in New York. I'd visited his editing room, which I believe was located at 62nd and Broadway. He had previously employed people like Marty Scorsese, Albert Maysles and D.A. Pennebaker, all these guys I knew, when he was making his celebrated documentary. Literally every available handheld cameraman in the city had been up to Woodstock at some point shooting Wadleigh's film, so there was that tenuous connection between us. I can remember speaking with Wadleigh that day and being struck by how charming and bright he was. But I don't mind telling you that I had no second thoughts about taking *Wolfen* over from him after he was gone. None at all. I felt no sympathy or remorse for Wadleigh, contrary to what you might expect after all that had happened to me on *Jaws 2*. I did have a degree of empathy, but that's all. You see, *Wolfen* was an entirely different situation to my case as much of the harm Wadleigh had inflicted on himself. He'd been irresponsible and ignorant of his obligations, so the fact is what happened to him was nobody's fault but his own. Nor do I recall thinking how ironic it was that I should now be replacing a director on a picture after being deposed myself just a few years earlier. That's the movie business for you. These things happen.

Aside from Wadleigh and Medavoy, another important figure in this story is Rupert Hitzig, who was co-producing *Wolfen* with his then partner Alan King. I liked both Hitzig and King, although, in his dealings with me, Rupert would blow hot and cold. One moment he would be positive and engaging, the next he could be somewhat brusque and irritable. Also, he had a rat-like competitiveness to him that would often manifest. I can only imagine this would arise because he and I had both attended Harvard, and Harvard boys are not always nice to other Harvard boys. Initially, Rupert had been glad that I was able to come in and help fix *Wolfen*, but there were moments when he would be difficult and testy. One thing that was consistent about him, though, was his frustration and bitterness at Wadleigh. At the beginning, Rupert had admired Wadleigh's visionary qualities as a filmmaker, but he now showed no allegiance to him. With all the problems they had encountered making *Wolfen*, and the lengthy and acrimonious Directors Guild arbitration that followed Wadleigh's firing, Rupert was a little sore. I believe his relationship with Wadleigh had completely broken down and there was bad feeling between them.

From my position as something of a bewildered newcomer entering the fray, I wasn't conscious of the arbitration that had (or was about) to take place after Wadleigh had been removed from *Wolfen*. I knew precious little of the arguments that were being deliberated as I already had enough things on my plate. Although the issue of directors' creative rights is one I feel is of crucial importance, I must confess that Wadleigh's creative rights were of little concern to me at the time—I felt he'd let the occupation down by falling so desperately out of perspective. The exceedingly rare times the subject of the arbitration was even broached, Rupert mentioned some of the points that were raised, as well as the problems he'd faced and his defense against certain accusations made by Wadleigh. I was definitely sympathetic to Rupert and kind of stood with him on several issues. I agreed with his view of things because it was a practical, realistic and commercial view of the situation that was firmly in the best interests of the project and the majority of those associated with it. I liked that about Rupert; that he was willing to fight for the film and do his best for it. He and I may not have always agreed with each other on *Wolfen*, but he was right about one or two things and I respected his opinion.

I've always strongly suspected that Rupert would've loved to have taken over *Wolfen* himself as director rather than have me do it. Just as it had been on *Jaws 2* with Verna Fields, this was made impossible due to the Directors Guild law that stipulates a producer cannot fire a director from a movie and then replace them at the helm. Frankly, I don't know if Rupert would have been acceptable to the cast or not, but that was never a consideration that had to be entertained. I was acceptable to them because I had directed *Bang the Drum Slowly*, which was apparently viewed favorably by the actors and I'm sure figured heavily in Medavoy's decision to hire me. It was anticipated that Albert Finney, Diane Venora and others would be willing to work with me as I was seen as an "actor's director" and, as such, would be cognizant of their needs. It's only natural to presume that Rupert would have liked to have assumed the role of director as he had been the one who had first brought the project to Medavoy. He was heavily invested in *Wolfen*—emotionally and fiscally—and there must have been a degree of regret that he couldn't officially take over the reins.

It's not difficult for a director to step into another director's shoes and finish off or make changes to their vision. Coming in fresh like that you are in a powerful and privileged position, particularly if the production is in difficulty like *Wolfen* was. When people are in trouble on a movie, or suddenly doubt what it is they are doing, you find they tend to listen to you and do what you say. Since I was being received so warmly, even by Rupert, you feel surprisingly comfortable. You also feel you have the necessary perspective, which others may have lost. With this objectivity, you feel you are better able to judge and evaluate what shouldn't be there and what should. I feel a lot of directors who've been in such a position have felt that way. Interestingly, Jerome Robbins made a career out of saving Broadway musicals that had been started by another director. He got so confident of his ability to do this that when it came time for him to direct, for example, *Mother Courage*, he had somebody else block it first! Robbins actually had an assistant block the play. Thus, in essence, it was still like he was coming in as the great savior to change the blocking and rescue the play. I thought that was a fascinating trait Robbins had: that he knew how to fix things, but not necessarily how to originate or create them from scratch. Of course, as a choreographer, he did know how to, but not as a director. Jerry was always more comfortable correcting other people's mistakes.

> Wadleigh had originally sought to transform Strieber's unadorned horror novel into a motion picture that would register not only as a political thriller, but also as a nature allegory that touched on colonial history and race relations, and even contained elements of science fiction. His adaptation would effectively detail the "enlightenment" of Captain Dewey Wilson [Albert Finney], an alcoholic detective who is summoned out of enforced retirement to investigate the baffling murders of tycoon Christopher Van Der Veer [Max M. Brown], his wife and their bodyguard, near a monument to the magnate's Dutch ancestor in Battery Park. The crimes are being attributed to Native American activists who are targeting rich people as part of their terrorist agenda. During the course of his inquiries, Wilson learns of the mysterious deaths and disappearances of several derelicts in the ravaged South Bronx area. Aided at various junctures by criminal psychologist Rebecca Neff (Diane Venora), wisecracking assistant coroner Whittington (Gregory Hines) and eccentric zoologist Ferguson (Tom Noonan), he finally discovers the truth of who—or what— is responsible when he meets Eddie Holt (Edward James Olmos), a high steelworker by day and shape-shifting Indian activist by night. Holt informs Wilson of the existence of

> the Wolfen, a distinct species of highly evolved Canis lupus that has remained invisible to the American imperialists and capitalists who have systematically slaughtered Indians and wolves or driven them to remote areas of the country.
>
> In an interview with the author, Wadleigh outlined his initial vision for Wolfen: "During the discussions I had with Mike Medavoy I talked about the wolves in terms of Moby Dick, which is not to be pretentious, but was just to try to get an idea in there that Ahab was a kind of detective or hunter for his society so to speak, who was obsessed with tracking down and killing the whale. As most people read Moby Dick, the whale stood for nature and Ahab's obsession was misplaced and he went to his death not realizing it. Well, I pitched the idea that the character of Dewey Wilson was sort of disconnected from nature, but then gets obsessed with tracking down the wolves. Eddie Holt shakes him up and says, "Well, you've pretty much destroyed nature in America haven't you? Look at the city—look at the South Bronx area that looks like Dresden and the end of civilization. Aren't you on the wrong side? Why annihilate the last of nature?" And in the end Dewey quits the police force. He literally, in my screenplay, throws his gun and badge away, and says, "Fuck it!" He can no longer uphold the values of a society that he feels is unjust and now begins to question his own role as a defender of those values and a protector of people like Van der Veer. So, that's what I pitched as kind of a way through the piece. Of course, there are no Indians at all in Whitley's novel and no political agenda, so even you can see that the things I added were very strongly along the lines of a political thriller."

Hearing Wadleigh's words, it gives one the impression that he knew his story. Be that as it may, I never got that feeling when I first started working on *Wolfen*. I mean, everybody had been cutting on the movie for so long they were entirely out of perspective. Nobody had any direction about what to do with it. I think the whole process of trying to discover what this film was, what it should be, had completely drained them of insight and inspiration. I was coming in with a clean and objective view. I wasn't tainted by anything and, again, there was a certain freedom and clarity in that. The very first thing I did when I arrived was look at what Wadleigh had done. I remember entering an editing room, which was located in a trailer on the Warner Bros. lot, with the editors Richard Chew, Arthur Coburn and Chris Lebenzon (the latter two being assistants). Inside they screened me Wadleigh's cut on Kems—everything was cut on Kems there—which, if I'm not mistaken, was between three and four hours long and was apparently still *unfinished*! We watched it together in silence. Indeed, the only sound that broke this quiet was my repeated sighs and groans. These were the only outward signs of my displeasure. I sighed a lot that day, I think, because I couldn't quite believe what I was seeing, but I made no direct comments to the editors. I just wanted to take everything in as best I could. When the screening eventually finished I looked at Chew, Coburn and Lebenzon, and said something to the effect of, "Okay, that was very bad. We have an awful lot of work ahead of us."

Although it supposedly wasn't complete, Wadleigh's cut was a mess: labored, earnest, confusing, and *way* too long! He may speak it well, but the narrative didn't make any sense and neither was it engaging. The most damaging aspect of the film was the simple fact it wasn't scary. There were fleeting moments that were unnerving, but Wadleigh had basically taken Whitley Strieber's terrifying novel—and *The Wolfen* was an extremely frightening book about mankind discovering the supernatural in the modern world—and transformed it into a meandering ecological allegory about the beauty of wolves. He threw away some of the more powerful and disturbing ideas in the novel and had no interest in making a straight horror movie about an intelligent monster that eats people. The idea of these creatures with heightened senses that were higher up the food chain than humans was a terrific idea. That's still in the movie, but Wadleigh hampered or diluted his story at nearly every turn. I kept thinking what a shame it was he didn't do the novel as written. To me, it's a creative sin to distort the original author's intentions to that degree. I felt we needed to keep some of the beauty and exquisiteness of wolves that he was evidently interested in, but we also had to make these creatures more terrifying and present. Having read the novel and liked it, I wanted to get back to some of the feeling I had gotten from Strieber's story which Wadleigh had rejected. He had simply used the book as a starting point and had decided to "improve" on it. Wadleigh was going to invest it with more commentary and, dare I say it, *importance*. So, it's safe to presume he had a fair amount of contempt for the material to begin with.

The primary thing I did on *Wolfen* was to extensively re-cut the picture as an editor. I began working with the editors, sifting through all the footage, trying to forge a coherent story. Richard Chew had been Wadleigh's editor and he was displeased that Wadleigh had been dismissed and his version was now being meddled with. I soon learned that what Chew had viewed at that first screening was very different to what I saw. Chew is a good editor, but he was overly committed and supportive of Wadleigh and wasn't afraid to make that view known to me, particularly after I voiced my opinion of the work. Chew liked *Wolfen* the way it was and he wanted to preserve some of the elements in Wadleigh's cut that I regarded as problematic. Aside from him, I don't know if anybody else connected with *Wolfen* behind the scenes felt that same sense of loyalty to Wadleigh and his original vision for the film—at least they never expressed their feelings openly to me. Nobody was ever disruptive or obstructive in any way (Diane Venora was a little frosty later, but that was all). When Chew's attitude became evident I knew we wouldn't be working with each other for long. As soon as he realized I wanted to do a whole other thing with *Wolfen* he quit and followed Wadleigh out the door. Lebenzon and Coburn were then promoted in his place and became the editors. They both supported my changes and implemented them. They were excited not only for the opportunity, but about what it was I wanted to do. Chris later turned out to be a wonderful editor who cut a number of big pictures for Tim Burton and Michael Bay, and also came in and did some cutting for me on *Weeds*, too. Then, around the mid-point of my work on *Wolfen*, Stuart Pappé joined the team and all the pieces were in place.

There were several reasons why *Wolfen* was taken away from Wadleigh: although he later claimed that no budget and shooting schedule had been agreed upon with Orion, his sliding out of perspective in the editing room was damaging, as was his unwillingness to lose extremely lengthy and boring scenes. Basically, he had a three or four-hour picture that had no shape or structure, each scene plodding along at the same weight and pace. His version just lurched from one painful sequence to another and where I saw this near-incomprehensible and grossly inflated story, no doubt Wadleigh viewed it as a richly detailed and interesting film that also had something important to say; a message movie. So, we were coming from two entirely different places. Richard Chew had discernibly slid out of perspective with Wadleigh, as their *Wolfen* was not a releasable picture. Far from it. Wadleigh has claimed he didn't get the chance to finish the film as scripted and the cut that I and others viewed that day was not going to be his release version. Personally, I believe he wanted to preview it before an audience to see if it worked, but I got the strong impression from certain people that he was more than happy with the film and felt it was close to being ready. This shows you where his mindset was at.

During early discussions with Rupert and others, there was this general agreement among us all that *Wolfen* needed some serious scariness injected into it. It was too tepid and toothless. Even though Rupert was difficult to deal with at times, there were never any serious problems between us. He'd already had to deal with the issues concerning Wadleigh, the cost overruns, delays, and everything else, so Rupert and I couldn't afford to bicker and fight with each other. We just had to do a good job with the maximum of speed and effort and the minimum of aggravation. Again, and I can't stress this enough, it was like this movie was going to single-handedly bring the studio down. Orion had spent so much money on the cast, the sets, the special and visual effects, and it had all amounted to what was this chaotic and confused movie. So, surrounded by this odd air of desperation and hopeful expectation, I started studying Wadleigh's cut a little more closely.

Admittedly, some of his ideas were good in theory if not in execution. There was some grisly humor in places: scenes of morgue attendants eating sandwiches over mutilated corpses (everybody does that now in movies and TV shows, but not back then). Another thing Wadleigh had attempted to do was have certain government agencies attempting to simulate or approximate what wolves could do naturally with their heightened senses through the use of futuristic technology. I think Wadleigh was trying to comment on or draw parallels between man and beast, nature and technology, industry and biology. Literally, his whole movie was a series of parallels between Whites and Indians, cops and security forces, and other things. That was all good, but, unfortunately, he never found any kind of compelling balance between all these contrasting elements. It was an ambitious and thoughtful approach, but it was muddled and sprawling. This also extended to Wadleigh's unfinished concept of "wolf-vision"—or "alien-vision" as it was known—which was interesting, but far too involved and over-used. It was designed to show the Wolfen's point-of-view as it stalked its prey in the ghettos and demonstrated their field of vision and incredible senses. There was all this stuff about the creatures being able to see the blood coursing through your body, smell your emotions, hear a cloud pass overhead, and so on. I thought some of this was good, but that other things were a little silly.

Wadleigh had been collaborating with the visual effects artist Robert Blalack in trying to realize "alien-vision." Blalack had worked on *Star Wars*, which was a big deal, and had a company called Praxis. When I took over *Wolfen*, Rupert and I had a series of meetings with him to discuss how the work was going. I visited Blalack's facility and, although I didn't always understand exactly what it was he was doing, I certainly liked it. He was a smart and technical guy, who was plainly trying very hard. Blalack experimented with various colors and visual schemes: in one pass the sky through the Wolfen's eyes would be a certain exotic color—gray, black or pink. In another pass, people and objects would be treated in different ways. In truth, we basically followed Wadleigh's lead on "alien-vision" and never deviated far from his initial ideas. We simply developed them a little further with Blalack. At one point, we had discussions about the Wolfen being able to see their victim's "auras" or "life-force" shining around their bodies. I believe some of that was done to the footage I shot for the inserts. The truth is so much was going on, I felt we should try to simplify some stuff and make a decision. The visual effects were eating up time and money, and we still had to get the picture ready for its release date. In all honesty, we pretty much went down to the wire on that. I felt that Wadleigh had far too much "alien-vision" footage, actually. There were all these uninterrupted steadicam shots done by Garrett Brown of the creatures' point-of-view prowling about. He had obviously fallen in love with this material (and much of it was stunning) but it was interminable. I mean, Wadleigh literally had hours of this stuff.

After watching Wadleigh's version again, I decided I needed to look at the actual dailies: I couldn't tell what they had, with it all cut up into something that wasn't working. So, I had the editors reconstitute everything. First they made a record of Wadleigh and Chew's cut, in case we needed to reference it for some reason, and then they took it apart, laboriously, shot by shot, and put everything back in daily form. Then we screened those reels of dailies—in other words we literally went back to first base and scrutinized all the film they had from beginning to end. Now, please remember, this was way back in 1981. So, it wasn't like it is today with digital editing systems where you can simply store various cuts, outtakes and assemblies and go back to the original files and easily access them. We were working with film. This process is so easy now, but back then it was elaborate and painstaking. It took a lot of time and, in these kinds of situations, there usually wasn't enough money available to just reprint something and recode it. If a shot was damaged in the process of reconstituting it, you could then order it up again, but it was tricky. Thankfully, Coburn, Lebenzon and Pappé were very good editors, and had good assistants, and I don't remember much being damaged.

After we did this, we started work on two sequences: the first was one that featured Dewey Wilson and Whittington searching a dilapidated building in the South Bronx at night in which Whittington is killed by the Wolfen. The second involved Diane Venora's character seemingly being stalked by what turns out to be a cat that suddenly leaps into frame. I went back to the dailies in both instances and reconstituted them to see exactly what we had that could make these sequences stronger. Although the picture was nearly four hours long, for certain scenes we needed to go a little slower in terms of the pace. So, I got Lebenzon to work on the South Bronx scene and Coburn to work on the cat scene with that approach in mind. I suggested we take big snips out of other scenes in the film in order to make time for these sequences to be more effective. In giving Chris and Arthur a scene each to work on, this necessitated my literally running back and forth between two editing rooms to check on their progress. Again, this was all material that Wadleigh had shot and we were simply tearing it apart then reconstructing and reordering it bit-by-bit. It was a case, as it had been on *Let's Scare Jessica to Death*, of retarding the pace and discovering a way to build up moments of terror and suspense. One of the most important things to consider when you are doing a horror movie is to find the correct rhythm of a scary scene. Even if you've managed to capture a uniquely unsettling atmosphere on set with a lot of coverage, and the lighting and the special effects and the performances are all top-notch, you can still negate the impact of a suspense scene by editing it clumsily. From what I saw in his original cut, Wadleigh didn't possess any understanding of how to generate and sustain a palpable sense of tension and fear.

The South Bronx scene in particular demonstrated this inability: Wilson and Whittington are holed-up in these ruined buildings and a wolf suddenly attacks Whittington from nowhere. Now, I felt this sequence had a little more potential to be frightening, but the attack itself occurred (and was all over with) quicker than it took me to speak that sentence. It literally came and went—*boom*—just like that! A big jolt that makes you jump is one thing, but this moment was so ineffectual and arbitrary it bordered on being illegible. We were left asking, "Okay, what the hell just happened there? What was *that*?" This is why I say when you're creating a scary sequence, you have to slow the action down and carefully draw it out. You have to concentrate on the characters physically wandering around and exploring this creepy environment before you hit them with a shock. The audience also needs information. You have to introduce the monster into the sequence in a way that feels right. Otherwise there's no element of dread, no sense of expectation, and you can't build up to the moment when the creature leaps out of the darkness and attacks. That scene, and others like it, needed a lot of work. So, we put in a new shot of the Wolfen making an appearance and growling menacingly before it kills Whittington, just to have it make sense.

Throughout this process, Mike Medavoy would come by the editing room every other day to see how the picture was coming along. He took an interest in the creative aspects of the work and would stay for around twenty minutes or so, ask a number of intelligent questions about what it was we were doing, and then leave feeling happy. Mike also visited the set at Warner Bros. when we shot some of the inserts—as did Bob Sherman—but he was never intrusive or impatient. Mike is a terribly nice guy and everybody in the business likes him. In spite of everything that happened on *Wolfen*, he maintained his good humor. He was always an even-tempered and encouraging presence, which is not easy when you are under the kind of pressure he was. Knowing that these were the days when there was seventeen or twenty percent interest that was running into hundreds of thousands of dollars every week, he would occasionally say with a little more urgency, "Please hurry! *Please*, John!" But that was the extent of his pushing. This is partially the reason why I was getting the impression that Orion could possibly go under from *Wolfen* if we didn't get this picture finished soon.

Also, talking with Mike, I got the unspoken sense that he was disappointed that Wadleigh had lost his way so spectacularly. He had not enjoyed terminating his services in the manner in which he did. Mike had championed him and had expected big things, which Wadleigh wasn't able to deliver. He had bought into Wadleigh's vision and his ideas, and he'd believed in him. Having met Wadleigh several years earlier, I knew what an attractive and intelligent guy he was, and how convincing he could be. I think Medavoy felt he had been seduced by him, for want of a better word. Sure, in hindsight, one might ask why the director of *Woodstock*, which was a concert documentary shot by countless handheld cameramen and cut by seven editors, would be the best choice to direct a movie about supernatural creatures lurking in the dark, decaying regions of New York City. I suspect this is probably the central problem here: although undeniably gifted in the way he crafted visuals, for my money Wadleigh was more of a documentarian than a commercial narrative filmmaker. Rupert and Mike should have approached somebody like John Carpenter or even Wes Craven; intelligent filmmakers who understood how to make a scary movie and were well-versed in the demands and delights of the genre. Both of those guys would have done a far better job than Wadleigh.

Anyway, in our attempts to reduce the movie to less than two hours, I had to be utterly ruthless about what we lost. Inevitably, we left an enormous pile of material sitting on the cutting room floor, but I was never conflicted about what I was losing as a lot of it was purely extraneous. One pertinent example was a scene (and I'll never forget this) that lasted for approximately fifteen minutes in which Dewey Wilson attended some kind of demonstration or trade show of security and surveillance equipment. It more or less began with Wilson simply wandering around this display room, carefully regarding all of this stuff. One by one he picks up the different pieces of hi-tech hardware—all the night vision apparatus and various items of futuristic sound equipment— and he begins examining them methodically. He then strolls to the next table and starts scrutinizing all the gear that's laid out there—again, *one by one*—before moving on to another table. This inspection just went on and on and it was completely fucking nuts! I sat through this seemingly endless sequence once and then quickly threw it out in its entirety. In some ways that scene, and many others like it, illustrated for me what I just said: that Wadleigh was not a movie director. He seemed to have no narrative or dramatic sense whatsoever; no understanding of what an entertaining, accessible film should be.

As we were working through the whole picture, we were attempting different things, experimenting, trying to find a story that was absorbing and coherent. At various times we tried a cut that worked in more of Wadleigh's terrorist and spy threads, in which security forces were combating the activists. I believe we also tried a cut where all of this material was completely omitted, and the narrative was far more direct and linear. We may have also tried a cut where the roles of the Native Americans in the story were lessened to a great degree, but that wasn't the way to go either. We may have emphasized Diane Venora's character a little more in one cut, and then pared the character back a little in another to see how it played. I don't remember everything we tried now. I do recall there were questions about whether or not the Wolfen should survive as a species at the end or be killed off by the cops. We eventually preserved more of the climax as it is now with Wilson and the Wolfen reaching some kind of connection or understanding with each other that humans will not interfere or betray their existence. How Wilson could enforce such a promise, I don't know. Maybe he was just speaking for himself. It does come across as if he's going against his oath in allowing the Wolfen to feed on the very citizens he is being paid to protect. It's the way of nature, I suppose. Maybe that was made clearer in the climax Wadleigh talked about, where Wilson retires from the force and refuses to represent the imperialist forces in charge. I just felt that idea didn't work entirely for me either. So, I tried my best to fashion some kind of viable climax that wouldn't offend anybody too much.

Actually, in terms of deciding what to leave in and what to leave out, I do remember we prepared one initial cut of *Wolfen* that was for an early screening to be attended by Medavoy, and some of the other top brass at Orion: Arthur Krim, Eric Pleskow and Bill Bernstein. When that version finished and the lights came on, Krim approached me and said I had gone too far in leaving out the elaborate activist subplot that Wadleigh had conceived. Orion had spent so much money on the sets for *Wolfen* they didn't want this thread to be excised entirely from the picture. I wanted it gone completely, but Krim asked, "Can we put some of that stuff back in? I think you've taken too much out and we really need to see it." So, I did as he requested, but I didn't see how it added anything substantial or meaningful to the story other than acting as a smoke-screen for the Wolfen—particularly in regard to who was responsible for the deaths of Van der Veer, his wife and their chauffer, which was a sequence I liked. From my perspective, I felt if some of this material impeded the picture from being scary then it didn't belong in it. I later read an article in *The New York Times* shortly after *Wolfen* was released in which Wadleigh claimed that his "red-herring political terrorism" angle had been restored to the release version by Orion in the wake of the attempted assassinations of Ronald Reagan and Pope John Paul II in early 1981. This is not true! As I just indicated, the reason was because Orion had spent so much money on those sets and couldn't stand the loss of face.

You see, if a studio spends a fortune on a number of expensive sets, and they've gone to the trouble of shooting them, it's very hard for the executives to just shrug their shoulders and give all that up. Wadleigh had gotten his production designer Paul Sylbert to build all these futuristic bunkers and laboratories and security areas in which, if my fading memory serves, government agencies were working against the terrorists. Sylbert had been given a considerable budget to work with on *Wolfen* (both he and his brother Richard, another production designer, were excellent at spending dough). The result of this was Wadleigh had shot a prodigious amount of footage depicting various forms of technology including lie detectors and voice modulators and banks of monitors with screens in various colors, lots of stuff. Simply reviewing this material in the editing room, I could see that *Wolfen* had cost a lot. I suppose, in fairness, the footage was really well-photographed and looked rich and good, and they thought a taste of it would add to the production values of the picture. Despite my reluctance, I didn't think it fatally hurt the picture to include one or two of these elements, so I did what Krim wanted. By the way, one of the clips we retained was a brief cameo by Wadleigh as a "Terrorist Informer" who is glimpsed on a thermo-graphic screen. I'd forgotten all about that.

There was very little new material that I shot for *Wolfen*—just a few moments here and there that better explained the plot, advanced the action and knitted certain disparate elements together. The main thing was to make the Wolfen a more visible presence, which I'll come to shortly. As I intimated earlier, when I started shooting with the actors, the only one who visibly showed any displeasure at my having replaced Wadleigh was Diane Venora, who was playing the psychologist. If I gave her a direction, she would occasionally sigh and say something like, "Oh, you want me to do it like *that*?" Diane had this mild impatience with me that would manifest through her voice and body language, nothing that was too obvious. Not that I cared. Some of the other principals in the cast were far more accommodating, like Gregory Hines for example. I can't recall if I shot any additional material with Greg or not. I believe I did, very briefly, possibly for the South Bronx wolf attack scene. I know that I looped his dialogue for some sequences and he was a nice guy. I thought Greg was a wonderful actor who was slightly underused in the film. I was also a big admirer of Edward James Olmos, who played Eddie Holt. When I was reviewing Wadleigh's footage I was particularly taken with his performance. It was bristling with menace and I complimented Olmos on it when I looped him. I had first seen him when he starred as "El Pachuco" in Luis Valdez's play *Zoot Suit*, which was a wonderful production about the Zoot Suit Riots that took place in Los Angeles in 1943 between Whites and Mexicans. I must give kudos to Wadleigh on a wonderful bit of casting there, as Olmos is probably the best thing in *Wolfen*.

I never did any additional shooting with Albert Finney as he was long gone by the time I arrived. However, when I was re-cutting *Wolfen*, I became bothered by Finney's accent in the movie. He was supposedly playing this grizzled New York detective, but I felt he was doing this phony American accent. For me, it was distracting and occasionally annoying. Each time I heard his voice it took me out of the film and I was concerned it would have the same effect on the audience. I felt so strongly about it I actually traveled to Berkley for four or five weekends to meet with Finney and loop him. At the time he was up there shooting *Annie* for John Huston, but I was still surprised to see that he was completely bald when he entered the room. Finney even remarked at one point, "You're probably wondering who this bald old twat is, but I assure you it's really me!" That was funny and a good ice-breaker. I then proceeded to re-record all of Finney's dialogue—his entire performance—in his own voice. This took some doing but then, in the mix, I didn't like the way it sounded either. So, I ended up throwing it out entirely and I played the original sync tracks after all. I still didn't like his New York accent much. In fact, I was agitated by it. Finney is a great actor, but I thought his vocal performance fell short on this particular occasion. If we could have just used his actual speaking voice instead of this fake and faltering American accent he seemed intent on playing, it would have been much better. British actors have gotten much better over the years at doing American accents, but Finney's was at the level of the Lawrence Olivier American accent—which, I can tell you, does not sound good to American ears. Indeed, Finney's accent seemed to drown somewhere in the middle of the Atlantic Ocean.

There was something else I found curious about Finney's performance when I was studying Wadleigh's footage, something that had been missed by everyone: he was playing Dewey Wilson as a *wolf*. I was surprised that no one else on the project seemed to notice or comment on this. They were not sensitive to what it is actors do—and I'm mostly talking about Hitzig and King here—to realize exactly what Finney was doing. I presumed that Finney and Wadleigh had discussed and developed this idea together, or that Finney had just done it on his own and tried to connect the hunter and the hunted in some subtle way. Knowing as I now do that Wadleigh saw the character of Wilson as a kind of contemporary Captain Ahab that was obsessed with hunting down the Wolfen, it makes more sense to me. Maybe that was why Finney was playing the character as a wolf, to find that semblance between killers. But it was clear to me (especially when I viewed both the used and unused footage in its totality) that this was what he was doing. The way he moved, the way he related to other people and objects; the way he tilted his head, the way he used his eyes, it was all there. I don't know how much of that idea comes across in the movie as it presently exists, but that was the distinct impression I had; that his character and his performance had this slightly lupine quality. I thought these physical actions were effective, far more effective than the way Finney spoke.

For all my unchecked candidness in speaking with you, I should add here that at no point did I discuss Wadleigh's controversial departure from *Wolfen* with Finney during the time we were working together. Back then, I saw no benefits in denigrating Wadleigh's work to Finney, or kicking the guy when he was down on the floor. That isn't my style and it definitely wasn't Finney's either. Nevertheless, it was obvious to me that Finney had no feeling whatsoever for Wadleigh and his situation. I don't think he respected Wadleigh very highly, or thought much about him and his compromised vision for the film. During his days looping dialogue with me, it was clear that Finney had moved on. He never gave me the impression that he felt Wadleigh had been treated harshly or unfairly by the studio. As I saw it, Finney simply appeared not to care. I'm sure that as the lead in *Wolfen*, and somebody who had been on the set for so many days, he would have undoubtedly sensed the meandering and grasping quality of Wadleigh's vision. I mean, how could he not?

> *Before their relationship reached the point of schism after principal photography on* Wolfen *was halted by Orion, Wadleigh and Hitzig had taken the decision to shoot with real wolves. For Hitzig, securing permission to use the beasts had been the culmination of two years research and effort that he deemed necessary in order to give the film a greater sense of authenticity. The producer had hired respected animal trainer George Toth, who had supplied a number of creatures for such films as* Across the Great Divide *(1976),* Day of the Animals *(1977) and* Windwalker *(1978). Providing the production with a number of wolves he had raised and trained, Toth worked closely with Wadleigh, explaining to the filmmaker the patience and planning required as wolves "can neither be asked nor*

ordered to perform." In preparation for several scenes that were scheduled to be filmed on the streets of New York, an enclosure was constructed in the areas where the crew were shooting to prevent any of the wolves from escaping. Concerned about the safety of the public, the NYPD sent a dozen police sharp-shooters to the set with orders to shoot-to-kill if any wolves should escape from the fenced-in area.

Despite the necessary precautions having resulted in several delays, Wadleigh explained in an interview with the author why he felt it was imperative that Wolfen rejected utilizing an "artificial creature" in favor of the real thing: "[W]e used real wolves and what really separates a wolf from a dog is their elegance and concentration. Those damn things would look at you and you would break your stare away from them. They had tremendous power and could really stare you down and it scared the shit out of you. I think that worked as a really powerful set-up to then go—pow! There's a shadow, a splash of blood and you are gone! You unsettle the audience by using surreal sound effects on the move and watching a wolf's jaws come up into frame and that kind of thing, but I really still say that one of [Hancock and Hitzig's] huge mistakes was going more animal on them. They should have stayed with the sort of heightened surreal factor that I intended, but instead they inserted shots that I didn't do and didn't approve of, of the wolves growling. I was trying to convince the audience that these creatures not only had a powerful physique capable of delivering instant death, but had an elevated intelligence—not telegraph their presence to their victims ahead of time! ... I still feel very strongly about that one."

When I was gearing-up to shoot the inserts of the wolves that were to be incorporated into the picture, I talked to a few people about Wadleigh's earlier experiences with them in New York. I guess I wanted to get some indication of what to expect. I was then told that for all his initial excitement and determination to be working with them, as soon as Wadleigh had started shooting, the production suddenly discovered just how difficult it was going to be—filming with these creatures in that environment. For one, the wolves tended to be difficult to control and, of course, they didn't take direction as firmly as humans do. Regardless of the fact they had cordoned-off certain areas of the set, there was always the danger of one of these animals escaping and possibly harming itself or a member of the public. More than that, working with wolves ate up a lot of time. Although Rupert had been fighting to use real wolves during principal photography, I seem to recall somebody suggesting that it would have been better to have done all the wolf shots in post-production. That's the impression I received, anyway. Following some of these problems I've described, I think the studio abandoned the idea of shooting more wolves during filming.

Considering all these factors at once, I can remember suggesting to Rupert at one point that we use large dogs instead of wolves. My thought was we could doctor the dogs by placing larger fangs in their mouths, giving them thicker coats of fur, and augmenting their appearance later with optical effects in post-production to make them look even more aggressive and frightening. Additionally, I felt dogs were a cheaper and safer option than wolves. They were also far easier to train and control while we were hastily trying to get all the inserts done. Typically, Rupert reacted negatively to my suggestion. Maybe he feared that *Wolfen* would lose credibility if we followed this path, or maybe it was because he had battled so hard to use wolves. Whatever it was, the truth is we could have done those scenes with doctored dogs. Here's a pertinent example: look how scary the dogs were in *The Omen* during the sequence where Gregory Peck and David Warner are terrorized by a pack of wild Rottweilers in an Etruscan cemetery at night. The way those animals looked in that movie, and the manner in which this passage was shot and edited, combined to create something that was incredibly unnerving. I thought we could do something similarly effective in *Wolfen*, but my idea was quickly shot down.

Wolves are natural predators, but humans have attached a lot of myths and legends to them that have impacted on how we've viewed these animals over time. There are the fairy tales about wolves, like *Little Red Riding Hood*, and movies about werewolves, and all the folklore that has been built up over centuries. So, we've grown to fear and loathe wolves. Wadleigh understood all of that to a degree in his version. He saw wolves as these noble and misunderstood creatures, but that is different to what Whitley Strieber portrayed. You see, Strieber's novel is not about wolves, it's about "Wolfen." It's about these half-human, half-wolf hybrid monsters that are extremely frightening. Since this thing is another creature entirely,

I didn't feel we had to proceed on the assumption that the Wolfen *had* to be wolves. That's why I felt we could have gotten away with utilizing dogs. I mean, what is a dog anyway if not a domesticated wolf? The simple fact is wolves aren't scary. However, the wolf that walked out of my closet on its hind legs when I was a small child suffering with a high fever *was* scary! That's what I thought the Wolfen should be. Unfortunately, what I was presented with on this film was not tremendously unnerving. This is why I said, "Look guys, are you making a frightening picture here or are you making a tract about the environment and social decay, or whatever it is?" I thought they had gone too "worthy" with all that kind of preachy stuff, and they needed to focus on making these creatures far more alarming.

Another idea I may have suggested was that we realize the Wolfen using little people in highly-detailed make-up and realistic wolf costumes. We could have also hired dancers or mimes, or people who were great physical performers, and tried to shoot them in a convincing way. I've known actors who can successfully replicate the movements and behavior of animals (Eddie Olmos for example), so it wasn't as much of a stretch as you might think. This idea was also not acceptable to Rupert. What I've subsequently found interesting—and this may have been something I knew at the time and had actually prompted my suggestion in the first instance—is that Wadleigh and/or Hitzig had at one point also considered having "midgets" play the Wolfen. You tell me that they both deny this fact now, but I seem to recall the idea originating with one or both of them *before* I joined the production. Maybe it was one of Wadleigh's early ideas, but when I first heard about it, I said, "You know, that might be crazy enough to work." Maybe Rupert and Wadleigh now have selective memories, or maybe I have. I don't know. I do know that Wadleigh went in and initially sold Medavoy on doing a different kind of picture about wolves. He was trying to make an A picture out of a B picture. Maybe he felt that by having an "artificial creature" as he put it, like the ones found in *The Howling* and *An American Werewolf in London*, it would remain a B picture. Real wolves kept his project legitimate.

Clearly, if it hadn't have cost too much and everybody was in agreement, I would have liked to have redesigned or re-thought the Wolfen and come up with something more thrilling and eerie. I think Medavoy would have gone for that had we the time, money and the actors available to come back for further shooting. But we did not have any of those things. It would have resulted in a big bill that Orion could ill afford after their already considerable expenditure. Had the studio been willing to re-shoot enough, I would have probably done the wolf scenes as I suggested before: with small actors playing the creatures in heavy make-up. It wasn't like the Wolfen were doing anything overly elaborate, other than just leaping up and tearing people's throats out, or standing there looking ominous. We could have made it work. Many of the most effective scenes in *Wolfen* were really made in the editing, so we could have made these animals very intimidating. It would have also allowed us to really sell the idea that they were a distinct and exotic species, not animals you could observe in a zoo or watch on the National Geographic Channel.

I received no specific instructions from the producers or the executives (aside from Krim's request about retaining a portion of the terrorist subplot) as I was working on *Wolfen*. They gave me a fair amount of creative freedom, although Rupert and I sometimes disagreed on the details. To my memory, I don't recall Medavoy or anybody else insisting that I make the Wolfen a more visible presence in the film. It was me who was really pushing for that, as I thought it was the correct way to go. When we began shooting the inserts, it was with the thought that the Wolfen should be more tangible. I don't believe they were anything like that in Wadleigh's version. As he said, he originally wanted the Wolfen to be these rather elusive and still creatures for the most part that resided in the darkness and are barely seen. We saw a lot of the "alien-vision" but they were more, as he implied, like shadows, or were reduced to quick cuts and movements and indiscernible glimpses of *something*. They would come silently out of the gloom, attack, and then vanish—a little like Steven Spielberg's approach with the shark in *Jaws*. That idea was fine in theory, it was smart, but what Wadleigh had directed was too nebulous and obscure to work. I think at times he was going for something that was ambiguous: could these killers be a man or an animal, or both? This was in keeping with his idea of the Indians being responsible for some of the Wolfen's victims, but it was another of those ideas that were better in theory than in execution.

In Wadleigh's defense, I should say there were a few things he'd shot that did have the necessary bite and aggression I felt was needed. The opening sequence where the Wolfen kill Van der Veer and his companions in Battery Park was good, but the reason it was good was because we played around with it in the re-cut. I should add that Wadleigh also wasn't averse to spilling blood as evidenced not only in that sequence but the one near the end in which Dick O'Neill's police chief has his head severed and it falls to the ground and his jaw keeps silently working. It was wonderfully ghoulish stuff! We probably did emphasize more violence in my cut, but in most cases it was stuff that Wadleigh had filmed. For instance, some people believe that I shot O'Neill's decapitation, but it was filmed by the first unit and directed by Wadleigh in principal photography. We did give the sequence a little more punch in the cutting, and also shot the build-up with the wolf suddenly running out of the mist to attack. The wolf sitting in the back seat of the police car, which O'Neill glimpses looming behind him, may have also been done by Wadleigh, although I could be wrong about that. It's possible it was another insert I directed as there were hardly any wolves in Wadleigh's version—at least not scary wolves. Wadleigh's wolves mostly just sat there, staring.

I know all this sounds rather strange considering the fact Rupert demanded real wolves and Wadleigh had gone to the trouble of shooting them in New York with George Toth (whom I later worked with on the inserts). Toth was an interesting guy. I believe he was Hungarian and was known by some in the business as "The Wolf King" as he was so skilled and experienced at training them. These animals saw him as the pack leader, I guess, more wolf than human. Despite the material they had initially shot with Toth's animals, I seem to recall Wadleigh didn't use much of it. I don't think he wanted the audience to see the wolves as much as maybe *feel* them. I'm merely speculating here on the evidence of his cut as I never talked to him about it. If that is indeed what Wadleigh was attempting to do I don't think he succeeded. They were these slippery creatures, but the various sequences in which they were apparently present were too understated and confusing to make any sense. We really needed to see them. So, Wadleigh is quite correct in his statement, that in my efforts to restructure the film and make things clearer to the audience, I decided to shoot more inserts of the wolves growling and looking menacing. Why? Well, just so we could have *something* in the shot, particularly in the aforementioned scene with Whittington's death.

Even though I now understand Wadleigh objects to these additions, I don't think they were a "mistake." I felt they were necessary. I believe he may have wanted the audience to feel sympathy for the Wolfen. He didn't want them to be viewed as drooling monsters. What price were the deaths of a few derelicts just to have these beautiful creatures remain unseen in our midst? I understood the plight of the Native Americans, but the fact that some of the Wolfen's victims were Blacks and Latinos, and other persecuted minorities, must have escaped Wadleigh's thinking. To be honest with you, maybe it did mine, too, at the time, but looking back, it compromises the purity of his message. Also, there was always a danger that by showing the wolves as they were, a considerable percentage of the audience would perceive them as being rather cute and cuddly. In a strange way, we couldn't get around that problem entirely and it only intensifies my belief that we should have strived for something different. When I worked with Toth on the inserts I talked to him about making the wolves look scarier. I discovered that he had different wolves for different purposes. For instance, he had one growling wolf, one tame wolf, one mean-looking wolf, and so on. I told him what we needed for each individual shot and scene and he would bring the appropriate wolf to set. When you are in fairly close proximity to a wolf you do begin to have a sense of the stillness that Wadleigh talked about. You see them and after a while the tremendous fear these animals can generate begins to dissipate somewhat. Maybe Wadleigh felt that hiding the wolves away remedied that problem.

The original cinematographer on *Wolfen* during production had been Gerry Fisher, who was an excellent English cameraman. I didn't work with Fisher as he had moved on and was unavailable—or possibly unwilling, I don't know—to return for the inserts. I had been impressed with what Fisher had done when I'd watched all the footage. Some of his shots were beautifully composed and lit, just dripping with atmosphere. I knew we needed to make sure that our stuff matched with his stuff, so we needed an equally good cameraman. The guy I worked with on the inserts was Jan de Bont, who had shot some pictures for Paul Verhoeven and later became a successful director himself with *Speed* and *Twister*. I guess Jan was just emerging on the scene in Hollywood at the time, but had already acquired a reputation as a gifted director of photography. I remember Bob Sherman telling me, "We've got this wonderful Dutch guy we're interested in getting into business with. He's very talented. Why don't you use him?" I said, "Sure," and Jan was easily very good. When he and I arrived on the set, one of the first things we shot was the white wolf prowling around on Wall Street. That was filmed on the Columbia lot, actually, as they had a New York street there. The Columbia lot was attached to the Warner Bros. lot, so it was all right there for us.

I remember we tried our best with the wolves, but I don't recall how much we planned in terms of what we were going to shoot. I basically knew what I needed to get going in. We had the wolf-wranglers on set, and I was asking Toth to position the wolves in certain areas and then it was a question of waiting for them to growl and move, or whatever else was required. I forget how we controlled or subdued the animals. I don't think we fenced-off the area as Wadleigh had done in New York. I think the wolves were humanely restrained with fish-line or something like that, but we got the shots fairly quickly and without incident. As I recall, we also shot a scene with the wolves in an office. I know Diane Venora was involved in it and it may have been the scene that appears towards the end of the film where she and Finney stumble into an office having survived their encounter with the Wolfen on the street. Then Wilson looks around and suddenly the Wolfen come crashing through the windows and everything. Finney was not around at that point, but Diane was. So, I probably just shot the inserts of the wolves looking threatening, like they are about to attack, knowing exactly where I was going to put them in the finished sequence. If you watch *Wolfen* now and see there are wolves in any given sequence—particularly growling wolves—and you get a real good look at them, then it's almost certain that I directed that shot.

> *In an interview conducted with the author, Rupert Hitzig made the following comments regarding Hancock's contributions to* Wolfen: *"John Hancock was hired because there was a specific Directors Guild demand that no producer may take over as director of a film if the director has been fired. So, Hancock was named director only for the Guild requirement after Wadleigh was gone. We then did two days of shooting, which John directed on the set at Warner Bros. These scenes included the shots of the white wolf on the steps in Wall Street, and some other inserts, and an additional shot with the Alpha wolf. I had originally wanted Milton Katselas to come in because he was a friend, but Hancock saw a payday and agreed to do it. However, from the outset, it was obvious to me that John did not like the movie. He taunted me about my demand to use real wolves for the inserts. In effect, he merely lent his name to* Wolfen *and was not involved very much at all. So, after getting through a number of trying months with Wadleigh, who as I say was now out of the picture, the DGA insisted that we hire him to finish the shoot—I mean, they didn't know it was in name only—[as Hancock was] a director that was from the organization who was not me. So, we*

> did this, but Hancock's contribution didn't mean much in the end."

First, let me say how shocked and confused I am to hear those comments from Rupert. I can't quite believe he would say such a thing. No, I take that back, I can believe it. I understand how over time memories can recede and become hazy, and the details begin to blur, but Christ, what a *rat*! His words merely serve as a reminder to me of what a terrible business we're in. I can only say this in response: yes, of course, Rupert is right about the DGA requirement, and our lively debates about using real wolves, but his dismissal of my contributions to the release version of *Wolfen* is false and unfair. He knows very well that I worked damn hard on it. I mean, I really killed myself on that picture. Aside from shooting all the inserts and supervising the mix, I re-cut the entire movie from beginning to end! Whatever *Wolfen* is today my influence on it is considerable and wasn't restricted to my simply lending my name to satisfy the DGA's precondition. That's ridiculous. I've already stated that my main contribution was as an editor. So, it isn't what I shot that made the difference, it's the fact that I restructured the narrative and made it tighter and scarier. To me that's a sizable involvement, is it not? Incidentally, I don't recall Rupert being around much during the editing phase. He was there occasionally, but not that much. What troubles me is Rupert was so glad at the time that I was able to come in and help fix the film. He was so complimentary towards me, so appreciative of my efforts.

There is occasionally a temptation for some people in our industry to reduce the importance of other people's input into a movie and take credit for all the good work that's been done. I don't mind admitting that Rupert made sizable contributions to *Wolfen* as both producer and second unit director. I'm sure the thirty days of second unit shooting he did during principal photography dwarfed the couple of days I did in post, but I was the one who ultimately sharpened and focused the film. I see no point in jockeying for recognition with Rupert now, but if he thought my contribution was insignificant why did he later offer me a picture to direct? I'd be interested to know. I wasn't even able to consider his project as it came to me while I was in Israel shooting *Steal the Sky* and was about to do *Prancer*. So, I didn't even read the script, but it confirmed for me that he had valued my work on *Wolfen*. This is what I meant earlier when I mentioned Rupert's competitive edge. I liked him, and thought he liked me, but I believe the fact we'd both attended Harvard brought out an aggressive aspect in our relationship. As evidenced by those comments, he sounds rather like a snotty Harvard boy hitting out at another Harvard boy.

Maybe I shouldn't be so surprised. As I keep repeating, I sometimes found Rupert difficult to deal with. He was often adept at both finding and causing little problems. Occasionally it would be a valid concern, like our discussions on what to do with the wolves, but other times it would be something that seemed rather negligible or petty to me. Here's a good example: I remember we were shooting a scene in an office involving Diane Venora and another character that may have been a government official. I don't recall if this was the same climactic scene as I mentioned before or a different one. I do know there were a couple of wolves present at one point, so it probably was. Anyway, as we were going along, Rupert suddenly pointed to the male actor and exclaimed, "Look at him! You can clearly see he's wearing make-up! *Look*!" He suddenly got agitated and upset about it. From where I was standing, you couldn't see that the actor was wearing any make-up at all aside from base make-up. So, it wasn't even special make-up. But it was enough for Rupert to grind proceedings to a halt and make a situation out of it. Frequently it would be things like that, unimportant details that he was determined to call to my attention. Maybe in those moments he wanted to show me who was boss. Or maybe he was just feeling the pressure as so much had happened by this point. I don't know. I merely recall thinking that we had bigger things to worry about, and I might have even told him as much.

Aside from re-cutting the picture, shooting the inserts, and working on the final mix, my other significant contribution to *Wolfen* was to fire the composer Craig Safan. He had apparently been hired at Wadleigh's insistence, and at no little expense. Wadleigh had either requested or received a sort of atonal and dissonant score for the movie that was highly unusual for a big Hollywood movie. I believe Safan had employed certain Native American instruments and exotic woodwind instruments, like a Peruvian nose-flute and so on. This probably seemed like an interesting way to go, but the results were entirely unsuccessful. I thought the score didn't work at all for the picture and we seriously needed to dump it. I did not want to take such an important decision on my own, so I conferred with Rupert on it. I said, "Okay, listen to what Safan has given us here." I then played him the score and Rupert kept groaning and shaking his head throughout. "God, what is *this*?" he asked. "Is this Schoenberg?" I said, "Whatever it is, it has to go. It's just not scary. We have to fire Safan and start over again." Thankfully, in the face of the terrible time-crunch we were in, Rupert stood strongly with me on that. In fact, firing Safan was one of the few things we were in complete agreement about and Rupert really carried the flag with it. I think he later played the score for Medavoy and Sherman, and convinced them that it was totally unsuitable. I believe Rupert even had our sound mixer Mike Minkler, and our foley guy Scott Hecker, track a couple of reels with Safan's score and then screened them for Medavoy just to ram the point home. When Mike finally saw it our way, I called Safan in and delivered the bad news to him that his score had been rejected. He was understandably upset and hurt. Safan was proud of his work and I understand that Wadleigh, too, had been delighted with it.

It goes without saying that it was extremely costly—and risky—to throw out one score and hire another guy to write and re-record another. By now, we were getting dangerously close to our end-date and we had to find somebody fast. That somebody was James Horner, who was fairly unknown at the time. I had loved his scary score for Oliver Stone's *The Hand*, and thought he'd be good for this. And he was good, too. Horner was enthusiastic and confident (he was only in his mid-twenties). He would later go on to score movies like *Braveheart* and *Titanic*, winning a couple of Academy Awards and enjoying a fabulous career. Horner came into *Wolfen* with some fresh and interesting ideas. I remember he quickly wrote an orchestral score that I felt was a considerable improvement on Safan's effort. I believe he delivered the entire score in just two weeks—perhaps it was even as little as ten or eleven days! It was quite an achievement. Horner was more orthodox and melodic in his approach than his predecessor had been, but he helped to give *Wolfen* a little more dramatic weight and atmosphere; whereas the earlier experimental score was just too avant-garde and agitating and discordant to have ever worked.

> *After losing the bitter struggle to preview his version of* Wolfen *to the public, and having learned the full extent of Hancock's "tampering," Wadleigh petitioned that his name be removed from the credits. This request was vetoed by Orion and their refusal upheld by Edward Mosk. Still bearing the credit "A Michael Wadleigh Film,"* Wolfen *was released on July 24, 1981, in 927 theaters to mostly strong reviews. Although unimpressed with the "platitudinous mumbo-jumbo" that littered the screenplay, Vincent Canby praised* Wolfen *as "a supernatural monster movie*

of extraordinary stylishness in looks and sounds as well as performances." Roger Ebert commended the film for being *"an uncommonly intelligent treatment of a theme that is usually just exploited,"* before castigating its studio for having released Wolfen as if it were *"a sleazy exploitation picture"* of no merit. *"That's a shame,"* wrote Ebert, seemingly unaware of Hancock's diligent efforts. *"Love, thought, care and craftsmanship have gone into this film, which is now, so to speak, being thrown to the wolves."*

Sandwiched between the releases of Joe Dante's The Howling *and* John Landis' An American Werewolf in London, Wolfen *was corralled into a modest revival of werewolf cinema. Despite famously announcing his picture in a pre-release interview as "the thinking man's horror film," Wadleigh strongly objected to the advertising campaign devised by Orion's marketing division. The poster featured a wolf's eye in a cloudy night sky with a full moon at its center, accompanied by a tagline that seemed firmly in keeping with the filmmaker's perception of the Wolfen as this highly resourceful, ferocious and covert species: "They can hear a cloud pass overhead, the rhythm of your blood. They can track you by yesterday's shadow. They can tear the scream from your throat."*

In a conversation with the author, Wadleigh expressed his thoughts on the way his film had been sold to the public and altered irrevocably: "I'll tell you the thing that still most upsets me is the marketing of Wolfen *in general. I really thought that it could have had the horror film audience, because the word would get out, but I also believed it would have captured those people that appreciated the Robert Ludlum sort of thing; a film that was a more of a sophisticated international thriller/detective story. But, of course, that wasn't the advertising campaign at all. All of the wolf material and general treatment that they added brought it more towards what I thought was a simplified horror film—and they thought so, too. They thought that if they went that route it would make more money. As a matter of fact, you may know that Orion was having trouble at the time and were in my view, and I said it at the time, a little bit desperate for a hit. I think the critics for one thing think they made a mistake. They probably could have made more money going the other way. So, that's what I'd prefer to comment on. I only wish that it had gone that way."*

In re-cutting *Wolfen* to make it scary, I assisted in giving the picture a more concrete identity and marketability, which it didn't have before. Okay, Wadleigh complains about what we did, but what exactly was his version? Was it a political thriller? Was it a metaphysical police procedural? Was it a nature allegory? Was it an arthouse film? It certainly wasn't a horror movie, not in the conventional and commercial definition. Wadleigh's *Wolfen* defied categorization in some ways and, although I admire movies that can do that, in this case, with the reputation and financial status of Orion in peril, the picture needed to be classified as *something*. The studio was somewhat confused about the personality of *Wolfen* as a movie, but they knew it needed to become a different beast altogether. Yes, we made it a straight horror film, but that was okay. If Wadleigh had been trying to deliver some kind of political, social or ecological point it wasn't a very intriguing or engrossing one—not to me, anyway. So, Orion then created an ad campaign that made it abundantly clear to everyone that *Wolfen* was indeed a scary movie. They understood that they had gone one way with the film and it hadn't really worked, so they searched for another direction for it. Obviously, I wasn't involved or consulted on the marketing, but it was obvious that they were trying to impose an identity on *Wolfen*. And that was smart, too.

I remember going down to San Diego to a preview screening of *Wolfen*. Orion was a little nervous about how the picture would play that night, but, conversely, there was also a degree of optimism and quiet confidence on their part. Medavoy had liked the changes we'd made, and felt the movie was now stronger in its surer identity as a horror film. He was ready to put *Wolfen* in front of an audience to see how they liked it. So, the studio pulled some people in off the streets to view it and gauge their reaction. When I arrived at the screening I saw there were several important people in attendance such as Medavoy, Krim, Sherman, as well as Hitzig and King. I think they were all hoping that when the cards came back they would be around ninety percent positive with the test audience scoring the movie as excellent. Sadly, I don't believe that was the case. When we later read the cards we saw they were somewhat mixed. Some people had problems with the story and the characters, some with the violence and dark tone. Others had adored those same things and felt the movie was scary and compelling. It was clear the picture was going to work, but that the reviews were going to be qualified. When it was released in theaters, I think enough people liked *Wolfen* that Orion did not feel in any way disgraced in the business. They were happy with the final version of the picture I had prepared for them, but I don't think *Wolfen* did great business. It was not the hit everybody had hoped for. To what extent the controversy over Wadleigh's termination and the subsequent DGA arbitration hurt the picture in terms of its perception, I don't know. It could have done some damage, possibly in terms of the number of theaters that booked it, but probably not too much.

As for Wadleigh's statement about *Wolfen* being "the thinking man's horror film," I can only imagine that in the weeks before the picture was released, he came around a little more to our way of thinking. Maybe he realized he could only benefit from *Wolfen* being a hit and it made no sense fighting what it had now become. But if Wadleigh did in fact make that comment it wasn't very smart of him, as it suggests he has a low opinion of the horror genre. There is an argument that horror movies are fundamentally not a thoughtful genre and Wadleigh possibly agrees with that view. I suspect that in his mind, and I don't know this for a fact, he was probably trying to elevate the horror film out of what he saw as the gutter of nastiness and obviousness it was festering in. He may have thought that by dressing it all up with weighty themes and worthy issues, he was making something of greater value and importance than, let's say, *The Texas Chainsaw Massacre* or *Halloween*—just to throw some titles out there—or even *Let's Scare Jessica to Death* for that matter. I'm just speculating here as, again, I never talked to him about *Wolfen* and his perception of it. I think if he was attempting to do that, Wadleigh should have been conscious of other things, too. He seemed ignorant of the things that make a horror movie interesting, effective and fun.

I feel his was not only a self-defeating and pompous attitude to take, it was also disrespectful. First of all, if you choose to use the words "thinking man's horror film" you are by implication insinuating that the majority of directors who have made horror movies, myself included, produced ones that were mostly dumb and shallow. That's okay, as everybody is entitled to an opinion and there is without question an overabundance of dumb and shallow horror films out there. But, second, and this is more harmful, what you are also saying is that the horror audience is stupid, and they should perhaps be grateful that Wadleigh has come along and given them something that is clever and great. Now, some may argue that that's a noble ambition, but, in effect, you are insulting and alienating the very audience for which your picture is intended. So, no good can come out of making a statement like that. I believe it only invites problems.

In certain Hollywood circles I think my work on *Wolfen* helped in a small way to repair some of the damage *Jaws 2* had inflicted. That was part of the reason why I did the picture, I guess, to get my career rolling again. I don't know that it helped in any meaningful way, but I like to believe it did. I know that my efforts did mean something to Mike Medavoy. A couple of years after *Wolfen*, and having enjoyed such a good relationship with him, Mike wanted me to direct another picture for him. At the time, there were all these *Police Academy* movies being made and Medavoy basically wanted to do *Fire Academy*, a comedy that exchanged policemen for firemen. It was presented to me as kind of a cross between *Police Academy* and Milos Forman's *The Fireman's Ball*—that was what Mike had in mind—but I wasn't able to see a way in which we could successfully bring those two worlds, and two differing comic sensibilities, together. Forman's film is more naturalistic and European in its approach to character and comic incident, and *Police Academy* is far more broad and riotous and distinctly American. So, it was hard for me to understand what tone we should take with it. The project eventually disappeared and, looking back now, maybe that was for the best. But I was happy that Mike had thought of me for it.

To this day, not many people realize I worked extensively on *Wolfen*. I didn't put my name on the finished film, although I do believe that option was available to me. I could have been credited as co-director with Wadleigh, or been awarded a card that read "Additional Direction by John Hancock," something like that. Maybe I could have placed a credit in the end titles that read "Creative Consultant" or "Post-Production Supervisor," just to get my efforts and contributions recognized. But I didn't. To be honest with you, I did not want my name on *Wolfen* as I did not feel it was my work. If I had been able to get rid of all the terrorist/espionage stuff, adequately rework the creatures with a new approach, and shoot a couple of additional scenes with Finney and other members of the cast, I would have certainly put my name on it. As the picture presently exists, I don't feel it's mine. In essence, you could say that the release version of *Wolfen* is my riff or my variation on a film by Michael Wadleigh. I selected and shaped and augmented his material from top to bottom, but it's still Wadleigh's movie. I don't repudiate that.

I'm glad that when you talked to Wadleigh he didn't tell you that I ruined his picture. I've always imagined that he hated what I did with it, and I'm sure he did for a while. Hearing that he expresses his admiration for *Wolfen* these days, in spite of it being heavily re-cut, makes me happy. Evidently, in the years that have elapsed since the release of the film, he's had time to reflect and reconsider his opinion. A motivating factor in his reevaluation may have been due to people having approached him over the years and told him how much they like the movie. Maybe now he thinks the picture is alright after all. It's not the film that he set out to make, but maybe he thinks it's alright. An inevitable result of his revised attitude is he has reclaimed authorship of the picture again. I feel that is only right as so much of *Wolfen* is his. You know, aside from the fact that Wadleigh was over-budget and behind schedule—and suffered for it—his getting out of perspective happens to a lot of filmmakers. It doesn't mean that you are no good as a director.

Wadleigh and Chew simply lost their way and this can happen in an editing room: close quarters, intense work for too long a period of time, seeing things over and over. From what I saw they were clearly no longer able to judge what was good and what was dull. They had long ago lost any sense of what an audience might be feeling from what they were showing them. The electric current that needs to flow between a film and its viewers was gone. The solution to such a debilitating loss of perspective is screenings. There's nothing like a live audience to jerk you up short. In a way, it's too bad they didn't let Wadleigh screen his four-hour cut as that might have restored some sanity to the process. But Orion was probably worried that if they did that, word would spread of what a disaster they had on their hands. I for one would have been interested to see what else Wadleigh could have done in movies—if he could have found the discipline to work within the constraints of Hollywood. When you are making a movie you not only have to fight to preserve your vision and your ideas, you must also accept responsibility for its failings and excesses. Wadleigh pointed fingers and complained about his right to preview his cut, but he should have pointed them at himself as he was ultimately responsible for his own fate.

Wadleigh had a unique vision for *Wolfen*, but it was one he couldn't properly control and articulate on film. It came across like the grumblings of a weary hippie who was using the most expensive medium in creation to hit out at the various injustices of the world. I don't think he fully understood what it was he had and what he needed to do in order to make it work. Again, he's not the first guy to have had that problem and he won't be the last. Naturally, because audiences can't see his cut to compare it with mine, it's easy for people to imagine Wadleigh's version to be some kind of lost masterpiece. Well, I'm here to tell you that it wasn't. His cut had too many flaws to be considered anything but an ambitious failure. If a director's cut ever materializes someday—and I doubt very much that it will—it would put to rest any such notions. Anyhow, in making my changes, it's not like I painted a moustache on the *Mona Lisa*. You can say that I dumbed-down and commercialized *Wolfen* or you can say that I made it work as a movie. It depends on your point of view, I guess. Everything I've told you is merely my memory of these events. It's my truth colored by the passage of thirty-five years and everything else that's happened in between. No doubt Wadleigh, Chew, and Hitzig have a contrasting story to mine. In filmmaking I've often found there is no right or wrong, merely differing views and approaches to things. You may hold certain values and convictions dear as a director, but not everybody is going to agree with them. They just don't see it the way that you do, no matter how hard you try to convince them.

10

Television (1985 – 1999)

Cover Up • *I Had Three Wives* • *Hill Street Blues* • *Lady Blue* • *Dellaventura* • *Cracker*

The first half of the 1980s would prove to be a dispiriting time for Hancock. Forced to reassess his priorities as a director, he now decided to once again commit himself to developing commercial material that reflected his own interests and preoccupations rather than accepting assignments "for monetary gain or straight ahead career advancement." In order to achieve this aim, he and Dorothy Tristan took out a second mortgage on their Malibu home as a means of buying the time necessary to research and write a screenplay that would eventually become one of Hancock's most accomplished works, the inspirational prison drama Weeds. The journey to bring his vision to the screen would mark one of the most intriguing periods of the filmmaker's see-sawing career, consuming several years and depleting the couple's finances considerably. This latter consideration necessitated a rethink in the director's approach as for the first time he contemplated directing for television. Throughout the next fifteen years Hancock would periodically dip his toe into the medium with contrasting results; each time plowing the money he earned into making his feature film projects a reality.

Hancock's entrée into television would be an episode of Cover Up, an action/adventure series for CBS created by Glen A. Larson, the mind behind such popular television series as Quincy, Battlestar Galactica, Magnum P.I., and

Knight Rider. *One of Larson's few duds,* Cover Up *centered on a glamorous fashion photographer named Danielle Reynolds (Jennifer O'Neill) who discovers that her recently murdered husband was in fact an undercover CIA agent. Investigating the circumstances of his death, she recruits a handsome Special Forces Operative named Mac Harper (Jon-Erik Hexum) to assist her in finding those responsible. After succeeding in this endeavor, Danielle is invited to accept her late husband's job by his former boss, Henry Towler (Richard Anderson). She agrees to continue masquerading as a photographer with Mac as her model, so that they can be dispatched to various exotic locations around the world and help American citizens in peril. Hancock's episode, "Adams' Ribs", which was broadcast on March 23, 1985, saw Danielle being sent to Paris, France, in order to root out three thieves who are hiding there until the statute of limitations expires and they can collect a cache of $13 million. Admittedly a minor outing for Hancock by the standards of his subsequent television work,* Cover Up *nonetheless provided a valuable learning experience for the director that would serve him well.*

You know, you get to a certain point in your career and you have to revaluate things. If you've been blighted by circumstances and everything else, you have to stop and think about where you've been and where you're going. After getting fired on *Jaws 2*, and then enduring my subsequent disappointments with *California Dreaming*, I began consciously pulling back in my own mind. So, it was a time of great introspection for me, when I suddenly started asking myself some tough questions: what was my real impulse for doing *Jaws 2*? Is that the kind of story I really want to share with an audience? What are the pictures I *should* be making? Certainly, *Jaws 2* was not the kind of picture I entered the business to make. I knew what my strengths as a filmmaker were and I now made a concerted effort to play to them. I wanted to originate material that really meant something to me and one project that did was *Weeds*. It was exactly the kind of picture I wanted to make—emotional, powerful and provocative. Bringing *Weeds* to fruition was a long and arduous road and there were various ups and downs. After taking out the second mortgage in order to research the project, we then got Robert De Niro involved and

Bob desperately wanted to do it. That whole deal was very high-profile and important, but then it all fell apart for reasons I will talk about later. An inevitable result of all this was I now had trouble paying the mortgage and that kind of stuff, and I desperately needed a job.

It was at this point that I then began to seriously think about directing episodic television. The thought had never really entered my mind before, but I realized it was something I should actively pursue as I like to shoot fast and shooting fast suits the medium. Back in the early-to-mid 1980s, it was hard to make the transition from feature films to episodic television. It felt more like a demotion than a transition, as a lot of television back then was bland. Today it's much easier to make that change and a lot of directors are comfortable alternating between the mediums. There are a lot of TV shows now that have the look and budget of movies, as well as the big-time talent and expertise. The networks were often reluctant to hire movie directors as they didn't think they would be able to finish the episodes on time. Executives considered cinema to be a more expensive and time-consuming activity, which of course it often is, and some movie directors are ill-equipped to deal with the demands of working on a TV show. But the fact that I enjoyed working quickly meant I enjoyed doing episodic television. Another plus is you also receive quite a bit of money for a short and intensive period of time. On top of that, television sometimes provides you with a chance to work with actors that you have admired.

My introduction to TV came through a friend of mine named Don Carlos Dunaway, who also happened to be my lawyer's brother-in-law. It was Don who got me the job of directing an episode of *Cover Up*, as he was the executive producer on the show. The series was being filmed at 20th Century Fox in Century City and starred Jennifer O'Neill, whom I knew and liked. She had been Herb Allen's girlfriend at one time, so I'd gotten to know Jennifer through him. It was good that we had that connection as it helped me to settle in a lot quicker. Jennifer was always very friendly, cooperative and supportive. When Don first filled me in on the whole premise of *Cover Up*—models secretly working as undercover CIA agents—frankly, I thought it was ludicrous. However, I wasn't being paid to critique the series only to help make it. Besides, there were already plenty of other absurd shows on television about talking cars and child robots and futuristic helicopters, so I didn't think too hard about it. There was a nagging feeling in my mind that I was now slumming it a little, but I tried to suppress that. I was happy for the work. I knew *Cover Up* was a silly show, and that I didn't like it, but I wasn't feeling in any way superior.

It did boast fairly handsome production values and had a talented creative team behind it in the form of Don and the creator of the series, Glen Larson. Although Larson had originated the show, my dealings with him were zero. I never actually met him, but Larson was one of those guys back in the 1970s and '80s who seemed to have his name on every major show on American television.

> *On October 12, 1984, Jon-Erik Hexum awoke from taking a nap during a delay in the show's exhaustive shooting schedule. Upon learning that there would be a further delay, the "bored" actor picked up a prop .44 Magnum revolver loaded with several blanks, and reportedly joked with some crew-members standing nearby, "Let's see if I've got one for me." Holding the nozzle an inch from his temple, Hexum pulled the trigger and the gun fired, discharging the heavy paper wadding from the blank cartridge which smashed into the right side of his head. The impact from the blast fractured his skull, driving a bone fragment "the size of a quarter" into his brain and causing tremendous hemorrhaging and irreversible damage. The twenty-six year-old was quickly rushed to the Beverly Hills Medical Center where he would remain in a coma for a week before being officially pronounced brain-dead. Taken off the life-support systems that were sustaining him, Hexum died on October 18 and his organs were harvested.*
>
> *Despite cast, crew and network executives being shaken by these tragic turn of events, plans were quickly instigated to continue the series with a new male lead. English-born Australian actor, model and ballet dancer Anthony Hamilton, who had recently starred in the TV movie* Samson & Delilah *(ironically Hexum was the producer's second choice for the role of the mighty ancient Israelite) was then cast as CIA agent Jack Striker. At the time, Hamilton was also being considered by Albert R. Broccoli as a possible candidate to replace Roger Moore as James Bond, but eventually lost out to Welsh actor Timothy Dalton. Hexum had appeared in only seven episodes of* Cover Up *as Mac Harper including the two-part pilot. Harper's death was written into the show—apparently*

killed off-screen while on a secret mission—and Striker was drafted in as his substitute for the remainder of the season. Hamilton made his first appearance in the episode "Writer's Block", which was broadcast on November 24, 1984, but his presence was not enough to rescue the show. Cover Up was cancelled by CBS after one season due to unimpressive ratings.

I didn't have the pleasure of meeting Jon-Erik Hexum, as his fatal self-inflicted gunshot had occurred before I got there. I began directing my episode of *Cover Up* shortly after that unfortunate incident took place and I'm grateful for that. It was not something I would ever care to witness, never mind having it occur on one of my sets. Hexum's death was tragic and there was an awful sense of futility about it. All the same, and as cold and distressing as this may sound, I don't think it cast a pall over the production going forward. In television you are working so incredibly fast, and you are clocking such ridiculously long hours, it's like you have no time for a pall. You don't get an opportunity to grieve, or to discuss how you are feeling, or share what you are thinking—even concerning something as truly extraordinary as having your lead actor shoot himself in the head with a prop gun between set-ups. Show business has a rather ruthless and entirely necessary tendency of simply marching on. It doesn't stop for anyone. I certainly did not feel the weight of Hexum's passing in the writing rooms, or at the read-through, or on the sets, or at the locations. Nobody ever really talked about it. I felt that the team on *Cover Up* was just plowing onward and there was no hint of a shadow hovering over them. How they might have been feeling inside when they reflected in their private moments, I do not know. I'm sure Hexum was missed and his loss deeply felt, but I saw no evidence of it.

I do recall that Anthony Hamilton, who was essentially Hexum's replacement as the principal male star on the show, was very full of himself. He was tall, blonde and dashingly handsome, but the only lasting impression I have of him is his behavior. Hamilton would occasionally be a little late to the set, which is often fatal to one's career and reputation, particularly if you are a young actor. His attitude was all wrong; especially when you consider the chance he had been given. I can distinctly remember a conversation I had with one of the line producers on *Cover Up*. This exchange has always stuck in my head because what he told me that day has repeatedly proved to be true in my experience. He said, "You know, actors get hired on these series and all of a sudden people start recognizing them on the street, and in shopping centers and restaurants. When this happens to them, they often fail to realize how quickly things can change in this business. There are some who think it will always be this way, that they'll always be stars, so they start misbehaving on the set. They become pompous and self-absorbed, and begin arriving late to the set when you are ready for them. But they don't realize there's always a chance that a year or two years from now the show will be cancelled and nobody will recognize them at all." Hamilton was exactly like that—a little puffy and proud. He suddenly began behaving like he was an important person, but the fact of the matter is I couldn't even remember his name until you just reminded me of it. Isn't that interesting? It just goes to demonstrate that fame can occasionally consist of a fleeting glory and then it's *gone*! It seems not every actor is capable of comprehending this.

I don't mind admitting that I wasn't particularly happy with my episode of *Cover Up*. I thought "Adams' Ribs" was merely adequate. It wasn't an unusually strong script to begin with, and was rather inane, but I did my best with it. I wasn't surprised when I heard that the series had been cancelled after just one season. There was a feeling among those involved with the show that it might not survive. The ratings weren't particularly great and I imagine neither were the reviews. Regardless of CBS's considerable efforts to keep it going after Hexum's death, *Cover Up* never seemed to be on a secure footing. I'm sure the series had suffered a mortal blow and it wasn't going to recover from that. I strongly suspect—and this is only my conjecture—that it would have been cancelled even if Hexum had not died. It simply wasn't a good show, and came across to me as a kind of low-grade reworking of Aaron Spelling's earlier action series *Charlie's Angels*: beautiful people, glossy production values and stupid storylines. I have heard that *Cover Up* enjoys a cult following and is available to watch on YouTube. I'm certainly not tempted to revisit it, but it was an interesting experience for me and one I profited from.

> *Hancock's next assignment in episodic television saw him direct the pilot for the ephemeral CBS comedy/drama series* I Had Three Wives, *which aired on August 15, 1985. The show focused on an "eternally romantic" private investigator named Jackson Beaudine (Victor Garber, starring in his first leading role) who has been married and divorced three times. Blessed with a gift for placing himself in situations*

of trouble, Beaudine often has to call on the assistance of his career women ex-wives to help him solve cases: Mary Parker (Maggie Cooper), a lawyer and mother to his only child, Andrew (David Faustino); Samantha Collins (Teri Copley), an aspiring actress whose only major credit is an impoverished horror film called Hatchet Honeymoon; *and Elizabeth Bailey (Shanna Reed), an intrepid crime reporter for the Los Angeles* Chronicle. *Although enlivened by Garber's likable headlining turn, and featuring a catchy theme tune by Academy Award-winning composer Bill Conti,* I Had Three Wives *was cancelled by the network after just five weeks amid poor ratings and disastrous reviews (Howard Rosenberg of the* Los Angeles Times *dismissed it as "thin-plotted idiocy, a sort of citified* Sleuths of Hazzard, *[featuring] car chases and fistfights with no one even getting bruised or nicked"). The show remains something of an obscurity in the careers of all those associated with it—Hancock included.*

I had developed a fan at CBS Entertainment in Carla Singer, the executive there who was initially in charge of resurrecting *The Twilight Zone*, which I later worked on. When she left CBS in 1985 and went out on her own, the first series she produced was *I Had Three Wives* and Carla hired me for it. The episode I directed, "You and I Know", involved a businessman hiring Garber's private investigator to keep tabs on his estranged girlfriend, who might be involved in some illicit crime, possibly a murder. The other episodes in the series were mostly involved with that same kind of thing. Carla was unhappy with the pilot they had originally shot (which was directed by Bill Bixby and never actually aired). She was hoping that "You and I Know" could replace Bixby's episode, which it eventually did. Garber was good in the lead role, but the scripts weren't as good. Also, the three actresses playing his former wives in the show were so-so. A young David Faustino, who two years later found fame in the sitcom *Married in Children*, played Garber's young son and he was a delight. Unfortunately, he didn't have much to do. I don't remember a lot about shooting my episode, except there was a scene with Garber and Faustino on the merry-go-round at Santa Monica Pier, and Chevy Chase stopped by at one point and was hugging everybody. *I Had Three Wives* was decidedly short-lived, running as it did for just five episodes, and it probably deserved to be cancelled so swiftly. I do know that Carla was under a lot of pressure to succeed, out on her own like that instead of being the person at the network who could bitch at the producer, but the material just wasn't there. I don't know how many people may have actually seen the show.

One good thing that came out of *I Had Three Wives* was meeting the singer-songwriter Melissa Etheridge (it shows you why it's often better to work than just sit). She was nobody at this time, and was singing at bars around the Valley, but she had an important fan in Alan Shayne, who was then head of casting at Warner Bros. He was a friendly acquaintance of mine, and a fan of *Bang the Drum Slowly*, and of Dorothy's. I'd seen him socially here and there over the years, often squiring the screenwriter Eleanor Perry around when she was no longer with her filmmaker husband Frank Perry. Alan suggested that Melissa might be good for the role of the singer in a party scene for the episode I was doing. I met her and liked her immediately. The question then arose about what she would sing so we wouldn't have to pay heavy royalties. "I'll write something," she said—and boy, did she ever! I was thrilled with what she wrote and how quickly she did it, as well as the way she sang it. So much so, that when it came time to add the musical numbers to *Weeds* the following year, I immediately thought of Melissa.

> *For his third foray into network television, Hancock worked on one of the most innovative and acclaimed shows in the history of American broadcasting, the gritty NBC police drama* Hill Street Blues. *Created by Steven Bochco and Michael Kozoll, and broadcast on Thursday nights, the series was set in an anonymous American city and explored the lives of the cops and detectives working in an inner city police station. Running for seven seasons and 146 episodes from January 1981 to August 1987,* Hill Street Blues *was blessed with an exceptionally strong ensemble cast that included Daniel J. Travanti, Charles Haid, Bruce Weitz, Veronica Hamel, Michael Warren, Betty Thomas, James B. Sikking and Dennis Franz. The show claimed twenty-six Emmy Awards from ninety-eight nominations (including four for Outstanding Drama Series) winning eight statuettes in its first season alone. With its reliance on documentary-like realism punctuated by jarring bursts of violence and moments of*

> *dazzling wit, as well as its use of multiple overlapping story-arcs that spanned several episodes,* Hill Street Blues *proved to be one of the most influential shows ever made.*

Hill Street Blues was different to everything else on television at that time. Even how I came to be involved with the show was unique compared to how I got involved with the other television series I did, previously and subsequently. I went to a dinner party one night and met David Milch, who was a writer, executive story editor and producer on the show. It was a party for eight people that was held at the home of a wealthy Beverly Hills or Hancock Park woman named Pike. I didn't know her well, but I know she was from a rich old Denver family—as in Pike's Peak. I forget her first name, or indeed how we met, and I don't know that I ever saw her again after that night. Aside from Dorothy and me, and Milch and his wife, Milch's *Hill Street Blues* partner Jeffrey Lewis and his wife were also there, as well as the Pike woman and her boyfriend (the latter were a middle-aged couple). Speaking with Milch that evening, I was impressed with his confidence and sense of authority. I remember he talked about a writing teacher he and Jeffrey had at Yale grad school and how much he had learned from him: for instance, how you take a scene that needs to be private and play it in public. Shortly after meeting Milch at this party, I suggested to my agent that he put me up for an episode or two of *Hill Street Blues* and that's how I got the job.

I was a fan of the show before I signed on to direct some episodes. I liked the sad and bitter tone it had, and the way it often dealt with characters who were struggling in their lives. That was something that very much appealed to me. I thought the writing was incredibly strong and that Steve Bochco was a genius and Milch just wonderful. They had provided a gritty examination of what it really was to be a cop that seemed a world away from things like *Starsky & Hutch*. Additionally, what made *Hill Street Blues* stand out was its whole visual and editorial approach. It was realistic and incredibly fresh. It was shot in a very distinct style and before you set foot on the set the producers had you look at a whole bunch of previous episodes and discuss your reactions to them. They wanted to know what *your* thoughts and observations were. So, you had to spend a certain amount of time with the supervising producer, Scott Brazil, and receive an education—or re-education as it were—in filmmaking. You basically had to attend "*Hill Street Blues* School" and learn how to shoot it and I found that interesting. I learned an enormous amount in terms of how to do things in one shot, how to move the camera and how to use longer lenses. I basically learned how to weave—how to take an 85mm lens and weave together a shot where one thing led directly to another and then to another. I found the experience a very useful exercise in a certain style that I've returned to and used since.

It was somewhat daunting coming into a successful television series which, at that point in time, had already been running for five or six years. It's difficult sometimes to direct a show that has already been established because a lot of the episodes are fixed in terms of how they look, feel and unfold. You are not supposed to try anything that is too experimental or remotely detached from what has come before. So, television is entirely different from doing a movie. Aside from the fact it's more impersonal and anonymous, you are working for *them*—for the network and the executive producer—and you are supposed to come in and not rock the boat. You are expected to fall in line and do it in the designated style that they've adopted season after season. You definitely don't want to fight with the actors about their performances, because they think they know the characters better than you. Despite being familiar with the show as a viewer or a fan, you are still somebody who has only just arrived on set. The actors have been living with their characters for years and wear them like a second skin. Also, the cast work with a different director every week or so, which effectively makes you more like a cog in a machine than a new and vital component that is going to bring something new. That's why television (certainly back then) was not as creative or personally rewarding as film. It's more strictly defined as a job of some kind and the only pleasure you can draw from it is by doing that task well, and contributing to an ongoing and overall vision of which you are merely a part. But *Hill Street Blues* had such a unique look and feel to it, I never really felt that way. It was exciting and invigorating just being involved with it, learning how they did it. In fact, I found the experience enormously rewarding and stimulating in comparison with *Cover Up*. I also thought the police station and squad-room was a beautiful antiqued set that had been designed by Jeffrey L. Goldstein, a talented art director. I almost hired Goldstein on *Weeds* as I liked his work a lot, but I went with Joseph Garrity instead. However, I was happy to later work with Goldstein again on *Cracker*.

> *Hancock's involvement with* Hill Street Blues *came at a time of considerable turmoil and transition for the series. Steve Bochco had been asked to leave the show at the end*

of season five by Arthur Price, the then President of MTM Enterprises Inc. which produced the series (co-creator Michael Kozoll had already left during the show's second year) and was replaced as the "guiding force" by Milch and Lewis. Beginning with season six, the producers and writers were instructed to "simplify" the show's plots and reduce the number of characters (with fewer featured extras and regular cast members appearing less frequently) in an effort to combat cost overruns. Another contributing factor rumored to be pertinent to Bochco's dismissal was the fact that the series had hit the 100-episode milestone and could now be sold into syndication. The first of Hancock's contributions to Hill Street Blues *was "Oh, You Kid", the sixth episode of season six, which was broadcast on November 7, 1985.*

There were a lot of changes during season five, but from my perspective as a relative newcomer to the series I never got the sense that *Hill Street Blues* was a show in any difficulty. Obviously Bochco was not involved with it anymore by the time I came aboard, but Milch and Lewis weren't in any way struggling. It was quite the reverse, as everything seemed very steady. They appeared to be confident and completely in charge. They were not hands-on in terms of their dealings with me, but Scott Brazil was very hands-on. He liked to make his presence felt from time to time, but not in an obstructive or difficult manner. He was a smart guy who was very competent. I've heard it claimed that later seasons of *Hill Street Blues* were accused of being formulaic and tired, but I don't agree with that view at all. I don't believe the show lost much of its potency towards the end, although familiarity to viewers and critics alike would have dulled its impact slightly over time. Also, the considerable influence of the series on other shows—and not just police dramas—would have contributed to that. It's inevitable, really, as there would have been more of the same thing around. Seven seasons is a long time for any show to exist and maintain a strong output. I thought *Hill Street Blues* was still exciting and relevant even though Bochco was not involved with it. When I arrived there in preparation for season six, I quickly learned from certain people that Bochco had been tough in his dealings with the network. There had been some tension on the show from time to time, which of course happens. Interestingly, although Bochco was gone, his presence was still felt. For instance, he was often quoted by the executives and writers during discussions.

One of Bochco's innovations was the way you had these multiple characters and storylines moving along nicely. Each episode of the show had three or four narrative threads that would run concurrently and sometimes intertwine with each other. "Oh, You Kid" had a few interesting subplots: one had Buntz, Dennis Franz's character, catching a mugger and beating him up. The mugger then gets away when his victim won't press charges, eventually leading to Buntz shooting the mugger dead as he attempts to rob a convenience store. The second thread concerned a Black artist named Castro who has made a fifteen foot street monument that resembles a gigantic penis he has called "Man's Pride." The third thread involved Detective Washington, played by Taurean Blacque, getting shot with his own gun by the child of his girlfriend. I can recall doing a low tracking shot on "Oh, You Kid" that I was quite proud of. It started behind the child during the scene where he takes the gun out of the cop's holster and shoots him in the apartment. I liked that shot, because I felt it built up suspense with the adults arguing in the background and this little kid looming in the foreground like an ominous shadow. It really worked well. So, there was plenty of meat in my episode which I was happy about.

My favorite of the threads was the Black artist and his telescoping phallic statue. Now, there was the need to secure network approval on whether this work of art can and should have testicles or not, and be even more clearly defined as a gigantic cock. I remember at one point Milch said, "Steve used to say, 'When you've got 'em, bounce 'em!' It's like a drug-dealer thing: when you've got them on your thumb, bounce 'em!'" Apparently, Bochco would trap the network in a certain way and then make them crawl. Probably, in the long run, they took their revenge and pushed him out. I don't know if Bochco had shot something that the network felt they couldn't cut, or he had stepped on too many toes, but, whatever it was, there existed a feeling that he had fostered a confrontational relationship with the executives. This is what I gleaned anyway in general conversations. It's interesting, but I only recently learned that certain characters, like the ones played by Barbara Bosson and Ed Marinaro, were being phased out either at the beginning or the end of season six. I didn't know any of this at the time, as I was not on the inside of the show.

Because each episode had so many scenes, so many continuing plotlines, subplots, principal characters, supporting characters, guest stars, locations, etc., directing *Hill Street Blues* was hard. Just to be shooting in downtown Los Angeles was difficult enough as you were shooting L.A. for Pittsburgh or Chicago, or some other northeast American city. Sure, the actual city in the show was unnamed, but "Hill Street" is actually a section of Pittsburgh. I knew that Bochco had gone to Carnegie Tech, which is in Pittsburgh, so I always believed the series was set there. They would occasionally shoot second unit in Chicago, as in the case of the famous opening credits montage that commenced the show. Being able to find suitable locations in downtown L.A. that resembled those places was not necessarily easy. Also, there were often a lot of street people wandering around—some of whom would occasionally be disruptive or abusive. But the crew on *Hill Street Blues* was always incredibly proficient and thorough in everything they did. I remember we had an early scene in "Oh, You Kid" where Buntz is pursuing the mugger and they eventually fight in an alleyway. I was impressed by how the crew had quickly taken all of the junk out of the alley and beautifully dressed it with various crates, boxes and a mattress. They had removed all the soiled and stinking junk out and sprayed the area down with disinfectant. Then, immediately after we shot the scene, they put all the filthy junk back! Can you believe *that*? I thought that was operating way beyond the call.

During my second or third day of shooting on "Oh, You Kid", I was setting up a shot with Robert Prosky, who was an actor I liked both professionally and personally. I believe that Prosky's character, Sgt. Jablonski, had been a replacement for my old pal Mike Conrad who had played Sgt. Esterhaus, the guy at the beginning of each episode who does the roll call in the squad room before the assembled cops and finishes with, "Let's be careful out there." Mike had died about a year or so earlier from cancer. Whatever problems we'd had on *A Man's a Man*, I was sorry not to be getting an opportunity to work with him on *Hill Street Blues*. Had he still been around, Mike and I would have been on good terms as by that time he'd already appeared in *Baby Blue Marine* and we were friendly again. He would also come by my house in Malibu on his horse and we would talk. Anyhow, we were doing a sequence that involved Jablonski and several other characters in the squad-room, and I was discussing how I was going to cover the scene. As I was doing this Scott Brazil gently tapped me on the shoulder, and said, "John, can I talk to you for a second?" I said, "Sure," and walked off to the side of the stage with him. Scott then whispered, "It looks to me like you are shooting a master." I replied, "Uh, yeah, that's correct. I am." He then shook his head and quietly muttered, "We don't shoot masters on this show. You need to execute this shot by moving from Prosky to another actor, and then to another actor, and then back to Prosky. You must not shoot a master. That's not what we do." I nodded my head and whispered back, "Okay, Scott, I won't."

One of the principal cast members of *Hill Street Blues*—and certainly one of the most recognizable and beloved—was Charles Haid, who played Officer Andy Renko. I'd had some previous history with Charlie as I had fired him during the making of *Bang the Drum Slowly*. He had originally played the small part of the private detective who Dutch Schnell hires to follow Bruce Pearson around and report on his various activities. Charlie just had that one scene in the picture, but he was so hokey I replaced him in the role with Arnold Kapnick, the still photographer on the film. Charlie took this decision badly, not terribly badly, but badly enough to let me know how disappointed he was. I was glad that Charlie seemed, at least on the surface, to hold no grudges against me when we crossed paths again on *Hill Street Blues*. If he did, he managed to disguise it well. I had first met him back in the 1960s when I was in Pittsburgh. Charlie was at Carnegie Tech and I recall that he and his incredibly beautiful blonde girlfriend had come in to read for me for one of the productions I was doing at the Pittsburgh Playhouse. Despite us not sharing a profitable working history, Charlie welcomed me to the show and was just fine to work with.

Bruce Weitz was an actor I'd always enjoyed watching on the series. He was undoubtedly one of the best things on *Hill Street Blues*. His performance as Detective Mick Belker was so consistently good and inventive, I was eager to work with him. To my great happiness, I discovered that Bruce was a joy to be around. Like Charlie, I think he was also from Carnegie Tech. As a matter of fact, there was a whole Carnegie Tech element on *Hill Street Blues*. In "Oh, My Kid", the fourth narrative thread involved Belker going undercover as a vagrant to discover why a number of street people have been mysteriously falling off buildings to their deaths. He meets two rich kids (one played by Alex McArthur whom I later worked with on *Suspended Animation*), who are encouraging vagrants to commit suicide. Belker was a scruffy, unshaven guy, so he was the natural choice for this assignment. Bruce was great in the scenes where he's jousting with these two villains, and it's still confusing to me how Weitz never became a huge star. He has such big chops and charisma, and really comes through the screen when you watch him. I mean, I always thought that Weitz could have played some of the roles you saw Bruce Willis playing. He would have brought tremendous depth and feeling to them.

The other members of the cast varied in terms of their skills. You had great people on *Hill Street Blues* like Prosky and Weitz, but then you had actors that were not so accomplished—Michael Warren for instance, who I'm not a huge fan of. I was crazy for Dennis Franz right from the beginning. We were both from Chicago and maybe that cemented our easy working relationship. I also liked Ed Marinaro, who played Officer Joe Coffey. He had been a running back for the Minnesota Vikings before becoming an actor, but I thought he had ability. I remember his character getting blasted by a water hose in "Oh, You Kid," which I don't think Ed enjoyed particularly. Joe Spano, who played Lieutenant Goldblume, was also very good—maybe not as charming or as attractive as Bruce Weitz, but very skilled. James B. Sikking was another guy I loved working with. He played Lieutenant Hunter, an Oliver North type; a rightwing gun-nut who heads the SWAT Team. Hunter was the flipside to somebody like Goldblume, a wonderful character who perhaps merited his own spin-off show. Interestingly, Sikking really seemed a lot like his character to me. He was a little scary at times, but maybe he was just in character the whole time. But I enjoyed him so much I've looked for another project to do with him, as I thought he was wonderful.

> *The second and final episode Hancock directed of* Hill Street Blues *was "The Virgin and the Turkey", which was broadcast on December 12, 1985.*

"The Virgin and the Turkey" was the last episode telecast before Christmas 1985. So, it had a little festive feeling to it and the various narrative threads were tied into the holidays. I recall one thread had Ed Marinaro's character dealing with a dispute between the landlord of a tenement slum and a resident who has discovered the image of the Virgin Mary on a water-stained wall. Val Bisoglio played the landlord and it was great to be working with him again so many years after *Sticky My Fingers, Fleet My Feet*. I believe we shot most of the scenes in the shadowy tenement building handheld, as I felt that rough approach worked particularly well in such a confined and dark area. The other stories in the episode had the guys at the police station competing in a tug-of-war competition, which was quite funny. Some of the humor was a little forced, but, as it was something of a Christmas episode, it was probably intended to be lighter than some of the other episodes featured that season.

The main thread I enjoyed doing involved Buntz and "Officer Giblet", a dope-sniffing turkey he has recently acquired and is using to bust drug dealers. Buntz employs this animal so that he will have probable cause to search dealers and arrest them. That was a funny idea and Dennis was great in those scenes. Now, the turkey is a huge part of the episode (for one thing it's mentioned in the title) and it features all the way through the segment as Buntz is busting these pushers. I remember we had a series of meetings before I was going off to shoot the episode to discuss the script. At one point Milch came to me, and said, "For a final payoff at the end, I think Buntz should twist the turkey's neck and kill it." I was both shocked and disturbed to hear this. I said, "David, for God's sake no! You can't do that. The audience will have fallen in love with this turkey by the end of the story. It will horrify them if we simply slaughter it on camera." Milch then gave me a hard look that clearly conveyed his disapproving thoughts without words: "You pussy!"

When I finished the episode the climax left the eventual fate of the turkey unknown, but he was alive and well just before the closing credits. Whatever happened next is merely left to the imagination. Maybe Buntz and Officer Giblet live happily ever after, or have a series of exciting crime-fighting adventures in an alternate universe. "The Virgin and the Turkey" may have been a Christmas episode, but the reality of Christmas is that millions of turkeys absolutely do get their necks twisted every year and are plucked, cooked and consumed on millions of dinner tables. Milch wanted to give the story a rather dark climax where this animal was killed, right at the very last moment. He might have been right about doing that, too. It would have indeed made an interesting and truthful climax. At the time, though, I really didn't want to do it. I have strong objections concerning cruelty to animals. I don't like to enact cruelty to animals onscreen and I don't like to see it in other movies and TV shows. I just don't like it. So, the implication is either the turkey found a good home somewhere or Buntz ate it. I'd like to believe the former.

In my opinion another of the best things about "The Virgin and the Turkey" is Betty Thomas, who played the role of Sgt. Lucy Bates in the show. I was very fond of Betty. I liked her and I think she liked me, too. She was a good actress and I enjoyed working with her. I found her performance very nuanced and sympathetic. When we were shooting the episode, Betty had a couple of nice intimate scenes in her bedroom with this guy she is having an affair with. I can remember liking what she was doing a lot. There was a scene where Lucy phones this man at his home several hours after they've made love, and she can't bring herself to speak to him. The camera just sits there and we played it all on Betty's face. She now works as a director herself and has directed several successful movies like *Private Parts* and *Dr. Dolittle*. What's interesting, looking back now, is that I could tell from working with Betty on *Hill Street Blues* that she had an interest in directing. She would ask me questions about why I chose to frame something a certain way, or move the camera a certain way, when we were doing the various scenes. Betty was always intrigued by the decisions I'd made when covering a scene and I hope our short time together proved edifying for her in some small way.

Another actress I found interesting to work with (for different reasons) was Veronica Hamel, who played the public defender Joyce Davenport. She was soft and sexy—not wildly sexy, but sexy enough—in her performance. I liked her and believed there was more of an actress lurking somewhere inside than what she was giving on the show. We worked together fairly nicely on "Oh, You Kid", although, admittedly, she didn't have much to do in that episode except represent Buntz's mugger. But I felt that when we were working on "The Virgin and the Turkey", I finally got through to her. I liked Veronica, but, again, always felt she could perhaps give a little more. There was something remote and removed about her, but maybe it was the way she was used to playing her character. I do think that certain people on *Hill Street Blues* felt that Veronica was like a model: she looked great, but you could only get so much out of her. I thought I drew some good things from Veronica in that second episode. There were several scenes where she and Daniel J. Travanti, who played her husband Captain Frank Furillo, drove off to the home of his elderly parents in an attempt to repair their relationship with them. They hadn't seen each other in a number of years, so there were a number of delicate scenes in the script where the family members confronted each other. Veronica had a nice moment with Furillo's mother where she confessed that they couldn't have children of their own. Those were the scenes where I felt Veronica finally responded to me and tried a little harder.

As for Travanti, like Charlie Haid he was one of the most familiar faces on *Hill Street Blues*. However, unlike Haid, Travanti was not well liked on the show or nearly as popular. He was quite a difficult person and I quickly understood why people were generally not fond of him. I remember we were shooting a scene for "The Virgin and the Turkey" one day that exemplified who and what Travanti was. After we did a take, I said to him, "That was good, but let's do one more where you do *this* instead of that." Travanti regarded me for a moment, then sighed and calmly said, "No, I don't think so. I think what I did is perfectly fine. When you see the dailies I think you'll agree that what I did is right." For a moment, I was taken aback by his response, but then I gathered myself and said, "I see. Okay, let's move on." The truth is I had never heard such a comment from an actor before in anything I'd done in any medium. Later, during that very same day, Travanti proceeded to tell me in his now familiar condescending tone, "I've got to say it: I'm looking forward to the end of this show. I think it's coming to the time when I can finally take my place where I belong." I was totally confused by this statement. So, I asked him, "What do you mean? Take your place where exactly?" Travanti replied, "Oh, you know, with my contemporaries: De Niro, Fonda and Nicholson. That's where I really belong. Not here." What could I say to that? I just nodded absently, but there was no doubt in my mind that Travanti had a huge ego and then some.

If I had to pick a favorite from "Oh, You Kid" and "The Virgin and the Turkey" I would go with "Oh, My Kid." I thought the script was just wonderful—humorous and light, but balanced with enough dramatic weight and emotion. Both of my episodes were written or co-written by Robert Ward, a talented screenwriter and novelist who remains a friend to this day. He wrote the Western novel *Cattle Annie and Little Britches*, which was made into a movie, and has also written a number of successful crime novels. Ward and I have tried to get various projects off the ground over the years (he also recently contributed some additional dialogue to the script for *The Looking Glass*). I tried to get him involved in a project I want to do about steelworkers called *American Steel*, and he also has some noir idea based on his childhood that he's interested in doing. Bob once pitched me an idea for a dramatic comedy film about evil boy scouts, which was quite interesting. I didn't see any foreign potential in the project, although I was going to try raising some money at Cannes. The story concerned a young boy who is sent to a terrible summer camp where everybody is extremely violent, vicious and delinquent. It had some good things in it, but I believe that project is dead now. Ward and I are always bashing ideas back and forth. Just last week, he said, "I've got another great idea! I'll lay it out in cards and I'll be in touch the day after tomorrow if it still seems good." I haven't heard back from him, so who knows?

Something that surprised and disappointed me about the experience of doing *Hill Street Blues* was the fact I didn't have an offer to return to direct any episodes in the seventh and final season. I didn't understand that decision at all. Interestingly, in season seven, the producers accepted scripts from acclaimed writers outside of television such as Bob Woodward and David Mamet. I don't know if that was an effort to reclaim some of that "lost" potency or not, but it would have been fascinating to have possibly worked with them. Milch, Lewis, and the network told me they were happy with both of the episodes I directed, so their apparent reluctance was most unexpected. Maybe it was the result of my uncomfortable encounter with Travanti, or maybe it was due to my not wanting to kill the turkey. I don't know for certain, but I suspect it was the latter. Perhaps Milch thought I wasn't quite malleable enough for him as a director in terms of his ability to control and influence me. None of this really mattered anyway because not too long afterwards I got *Weeds* going, but it was still displeasing that I never got a call from them. But Milch was an unusual guy in some ways. He was kind of an addict and had a huge gambling problem. I was fascinated when I later learned he did *Luck* for HBO, a series that was set in the world of thoroughbred horse-racing and gambling that starred Dustin Hoffman and Nick Nolte. Several horses broke their legs during filming and had to be euthanized, which I believe caused considerable controversy. Then, suddenly, Milch didn't want to do the show anymore and *Luck* was cancelled despite all the heavyweight talent that was attached to it—including Michael Mann who had directed the pilot. So, David has had a fascinating career and he's an interesting figure. He has a big ego but also the talent to match it, and I enjoyed doing *Hill Street Blues* with him. It was great fun and I carried all I learned on the show with me moving forward.

> *For his fourth excursion into television, Hancock would direct five episodes of CBS's* The New Twilight Zone *(covered in depth in the next chapter) before tackling an action-packed first season segment of the short-lived ABC crime drama* Lady Blue. *The series starred Jamie Rose as Katy Mahoney, a flame-haired homicide detective whose father and brother were police officers killed in the line of duty. Following the death of her partner and lover during a botched drug bust, Katy begins using excessive force in her dealings with the criminal elements of Chicago. After*

> her trigger-happy tactics culminate in a gun fight with drug dealers that gets a civilian killed, Katy is transferred to the Matron Squad under the command of Lieutenant Terry McNichols (Danny Aiello). Brandishing a Colt Python .357 Magnum (an appendage that prompted several critics to variously label the character "Dirty Harriet" and "Skirty Harry"), Katy and McNichols clash over her uncompromising methods in fighting crime. Broadcast on January 11, 1986, Hancock's episode, "Scorpio's Sting", was the eleventh of the season, and saw Katy hunting down a motorcycle gang of armed robbers led by a psychotic former Green Beret who murders for pleasure. Despite good ratings, Lady Blue *was cancelled by the network shortly before its fourteenth and final episode was scheduled to be telecast in early February, 1986. It has been claimed that the reason for its termination was due in part to complaints about the show's apparent predilection for excessive violence.*

Once you have demonstrated to executives and producers that you can finish a show on time and on budget, and can deliver work that is coherent and halfway decent, then you suddenly become very employable to the networks. You see, that's really what the fundamental concern for everybody is: hiring a director who can bring it off in the number of allotted days. Whatever my feelings were about the overall quality and integrity of *Cover Up* as a show, it was a potent calling card for me. As a result of doing it, I was then able to work steadily in television. The opportunity to direct an episode of *Lady Blue* came courtesy of my agent, actually. Mostly you don't get jobs directly through your agent, but some of these television gigs happened that way. I don't remember which agent it was now, probably David Wardlow, but possibly not. Yeah, I think David was off being a UA executive at this point. The creator and executive producer of *Lady Blue* was a guy named David Gerber, who had done a number of successful police procedural shows like *Police Story* and *Police Woman*—the latter series having predated *Lady Blue* and starred Angie Dickinson as a sexy female cop in Los Angeles. So, Gerber was well-versed in the genre, but he was kind of like your typical bullish executive. He was relatively hands-on as a producer—certainly in comparison with others I've known—and was always conscious of his own success and track record and wanted you to be, too. I do recall that people were a little scared of him. Gerber was the kind of guy who would enter a room and the atmosphere would change and people would get nervous. Fortunately, he was not on the Chicago location more than once so I didn't have to deal with him much.

I felt comfortable with most of the other people working on the show, particularly the two stars of *Lady Blue*: Jamie Rose and Danny Aiello. Danny and I had worked together previously on *Bang the Drum Slowly* and would later work together again on *Dellaventura*. I remember he was very happy to see me again and we had dinner a bunch of times and enjoyed many long conversations. Danny is an interesting guy to be around. He almost has this mobster-type role that he enjoys playing in real life. It's really something worth seeing. He likes to preside at a dinner table laden with great Italian food in the company of a bodyguard and some borderline figures who may—or may not—be from certain mob-related families. It's all very nebulous and fascinating. You know, a lot of people pose as mobsters in the film and television business, and carry this mildly threatening aura or aspect with them. It's a very curious thing. I've encountered several such people in my career and they never fail to amuse and intrigue me. Of course, I'm not saying that Danny is in any way threatening or criminal. He's a wonderful guy, very warm and giving, but he does like to be thought of as "connected."

As for Jamie Rose, I liked her a lot, too. She had red hair like my mother and was rather striking. She was also a pretty good actress and was definitely enjoying her newfound status as the lead of her very own primetime show. It was too bad for her that *Lady Blue*, like *Cover Up* before it, would only survive for one season and this prestige would come to an end. In fact, it's a recurring example of the validity of what that line producer once said to me about Anthony Hamilton: circumstances can quickly change in this business. For a while you are a big star and then you are suddenly a jobbing actor, looking around for work. I do know that since the days of *Lady Blue*, several times I've been auditioning people for various projects and Jamie has come in looking much subdued, hoping for a small role or bit-part in something I was doing. I never cast her in anything as I didn't think she was necessarily right for the particular role she was vying for, but I've always appreciated her talent and remembered her fondly. Shortly after *Lady Blue* was cancelled, I believe she came in to audition for the role of Nick Nolte's girlfriend in *Weeds*, but I finally went with somebody else. I think I also saw Jamie for a promo I shot in the mid-1990s for *Bohemian Nights*, a comedy I was trying to raise financing for. She might have come in for some of the other television shows I did in subsequent years, too.

Naturally, shooting *Lady Blue* in Chicago was a lot of fun for me because I'm from Chicago. I love the city and know it well. I know the people and I feel extremely comfortable there. There were a number of excellent people located in Chicago who were working on *Lady Blue*, some pretty good secondary personnel who would stand in for David Gerber and keep everything ticking over. They had an associate producer named Christopher Chulak, who was very capable. Chris was Serbian and later became a pretty good director of episodic television himself, helming segments of *E.R.* and *Southland*, among other things. I was particularly impressed with the gaffer on the show, Robert Hudecek, who owned a light rental place in Chicago. What immediately struck me about Bob's crew was they ran. They literally zipped around and worked at a trot. I had never really seen that before, at least not with that kind of sustained energy. I was surprised because mostly on a set there is a lot of moping around, and setting lights, and what have you, but not with Bob's crew. They always moved with urgency and purpose, and he had them organized in such a way that they galloped around with the instruments and equipment. This was so attractive to me that I employed Bob on my next film, *Weeds*.

There was also a terrific stunt co-coordinator on *Lady Blue* who doubled Jamie in a number of scenes. Her name was Glory Fioramonti and I employed her many years later on *Suspended Animation* because she was so good at what she did. The show was fairly packed with stunts and action, and there was a lot of stuff to do in a fairly short stretch of time. There was one rather daring motorcycle stunt we filmed at Marina City, which is located on the North Bank of the Chicago River. The complex, which has spiral parking lots and various apartments, has two circular towers that are shaped like enormous corncobs. It's very distinctive-looking and has appeared in several movies and television shows. We had a sequence where one of the motorcycle gang drove off a balcony that was two thirds of the way up one of the towers and plummeted into the water below. It was pretty spectacular. I also got to control the bridge over the Chicago River which was located near where my father had worked in the Merchandise Mart. It was wonderful to be there as a grown up ordering when the bridge goes up and down, and that kind of thing. It was like living out a childhood fantasy in some ways.

I must say that I was never aware that *Lady Blue* was considered by some to be an overtly violent show, even when you measure it now against the delicate sensibilities of television in the 1980s. There was violence in the series, sure, but I never thought it was in any way excessive or extreme—certainly not enough to get it removed from the air. I don't recall there being any discussions or concerns expressed about violent content from anyone connected with the show, or indeed anybody unconnected with the show. No doubt there were other reasons for its cancellation as only thirteen episodes were aired before it was axed. I haven't actually seen "Scorpio's Sting" in a long time and I don't remember it too well, but memory seems to be telling me that it was fairly tame. I do recall there were several shootings in my episode, but there probably was in *every* episode! I believe my segment—at least I think it was my segment, but I could be remembering a different episode of the series—featured a scene where Jamie's character is having her hair done in a beauty salon. She's sitting under the hair dryer, getting a pedicure done, when she glances out the window and notices some armed robbers are exiting the bank across the street. She then hastily pulls on her boots (ruining her pedicure), comes whirling out of the salon with rollers in her hair and a smock draped over her, and proceeds to blow the bad guys away!

If you were to ask me if I felt *Lady Blue* was a series that deserved another chance, I would probably say no. *Lady Blue* was not a classy operation like *The Twilight Zone* and *Hill Street Blues* were. It was more like *Cover Up* in that regard, and you always had the sense it was borderline in terms of it being picked up for a second season. My main problem with it (and I'm sure this was at the forefront of the network's mind when they decided to terminate it) was the show was insufficiently entertaining. Be that as it may, unlike *Cover Up*, I thought the basic premise of a tough female cop patrolling the streets of Chicago was sound and would make for a good action series. I mean, it seems like a concept that should work and could bring in other elements such as her relationships with her co-workers, her superiors and her family, how they react to her and what she does for a living. So, there was a lot of potential material there to be mined. The best things that *Lady Blue* had going for it were Jamie and Danny. They were worth watching, but I think some of the scripts could have been a lot stronger. Also, *Lady Blue* was up against some stiff competition in its Thursday night slot, coming directly up against juggernauts like *Cheers*, *Night Court* and *Simon and Simon*. It probably didn't have much of a chance against those shows.

> *It would be more than eleven years before Hancock directed another hour of episodic television. During the decade-long gap between the release of his films* Prancer *and* A Piece

of Eden, Hancock tackled a segment of the CBS detective show Dellaventura (1997-1998). Created by Julian Neil, Bernard L. Nussbaumer and Richard Di Lello as a starring vehicle for Danny Aiello, the show concerned a former NYPD policeman who now works as a swaggering private investigator with a heart of gold, taking on cases that the criminal justice system has either failed or abandoned. He is aided in his efforts by a trusted team of similar-minded people that includes Teddy Naples (Rick Aiello), a beefy ex-cop, Jonas Deeds (Byron Keith Minns) an electronic surveillance expert, and Geri Zarias (Anne Ramsay), the tough token beauty. Another one-season wonder, Dellaventura once earned the unwanted distinction of being voted the worst private eye show in the history of American broadcasting after an informal poll was carried out in 1998. A wildly uneven retread of more successful programs such as Griff (1973) and The Equalizer (1985-89), Hancock's contribution, "Dreamers", the tenth episode of thirteen, proved to be one of the better entries. Broadcast on December 11, 1997, the storyline featured Dellaventura and his recruits being hired by a breeder (Tony Darrow) to find out why his prize thoroughbred horse stopped during an important race and never seems to win.

When you examine the whole premise of *Dellaventura*—a retired cop toiling as a private investigator—it's hardly a groundbreaking concept for a TV show, is it? We have seen this set-up several times before: a series built around a charismatic older man who is operating alone against the system. On any detective show, whether it's *Columbo* or *Barnaby Jones* or *The Rockford Files*, whatever it is, the strength of the series always rests in the writing, the personality of the lead character and the magnetism of the star. Is the character an interesting or unusual guy? How is he going to save the day this week? Yes, we know that he's going to solve the case at the end of the episode and make everything alright, but do we want to take that journey with him and see how he does it? Dellaventura is kind of a champion of the people, a savior of the little guy, who is fighting against all the abuses of authority and bureaucracy. He has a tough exterior but he's sweet and compassionate on the inside. I think it's better when these kinds of TV detectives are not quite such benevolent figures without flaws. It isn't so interesting to me, dramatically. But, in this case, I was willing to forsake that opinion just because I wanted to work with Danny Aiello again. I thought he'd be just great playing the part.

My involvement in *Dellaventura* came about simply from my having known Danny for so many years. I think my agent initially proposed me and then Danny immediately welcomed that suggestion. Now that I think about it, I may have written Danny a letter asking to be involved. I forget which it was now. Anyway, I was happy to see him again. My relationship with Danny at this juncture of our careers was still very affectionate and friendly. If I was to compare the Danny Aiello I knew back in 1973 when we were making *Bang the Drum Slowly* to the Danny Aiello who was now the star of his very own show, I can honestly say there was no difference whatsoever. He was the exact same guy. In spite of everything that had happened in the interim, he never once *lorded* it over me for want of a better word. I've had experiences of working with certain actors early in their careers, and then met them later when they were big stars, and discovered they have changed considerably—and not for the better. Danny was never like that. Danny was always unfailingly Danny. He's consistently been a wonderful guy and success has never changed that.

When I first received the script for "Dreamers," what I found interesting about it was the horseracing milieu of the story. Back in the early 1960s, when I was working in the Off-Broadway Theater, I used to regularly play the horses and got quite immersed in gambling for a while. I had developed a system that involved my watching the pattern of a certain famous trainer named Buddy Jacobson, who would later become a rather infamous figure. Jacobson owned a lot of thoroughbred horses, but he was a betting trainer. He would move horses from one track to another and run them in easy races. In horseracing there is something called a claiming price and in order to get the horses into a given race they have to be fairly equal in terms of ability. This means you have to offer to sell them at a $10,000 or $12,000 price if somebody wants to claim them. So, this procedure gets horses of roughly the same value into the same race. Jacobson would have a horse that was racing at $12,000, but then he'd move it to another track and have it compete in an $8,000 claiming race. This meant that the horse had an extremely healthy chance of winning, so he would bet heavily on it. This is what I *believed* Jacobson was doing and, through my repeated observations of him, I noticed that whenever it happened, the horse usually won. That's how my own system evolved. Naturally, it took a lot of careful scrutiny of the racing form to nose out these opportunities with Jacobson, but I followed him steadily for a year or two. I generally made money on these races, but I did the math one day and discovered to my consternation that I was making about 29¢ an hour with the amount of time I was spending just studying the racing.

Anyway, in 1980, Jacobson was sentenced to twenty-five years imprisonment for the murder of a rival for the affections of his stunning *Cosmopolitan* model girlfriend, Melanie Cain. She was many years younger than Buddy, and had left him for this other man. Jacobson had responded by shooting and stabbing and bludgeoning this individual several times. The subsequent trial made huge news in the tabloids. In a bizarre twist of fate that reconnected me with Jacobson in a tenuous way, Melanie Cain—who was now an actress and had changed her name to Melanie Norris—played Dellaventura's old flame in "Dreamers." How she came to be involved with the show was interesting: I had taught acting and film directing at the State University of New York for two or three years around the time I was doing *Bang the Drum Slowly*. I had a couple of wonderful students there who were brothers of Pete Hamill, who was an important columnist for the *New York Post* and *The New York Daily News*. One of them, Brian Hamill, was a still man for features around New York. I believe it was he who first suggested I cast this rather colorful and beautiful woman that Buddy Jacobson had adored and even killed for in a mistaken effort to keep. As soon as I met Melanie, I recognized her from the news reports I'd seen many years earlier. It was undeniably odd that she should be doing a horseracing story with her particular history and association with one of the most famous and notorious horse trainers in American history. You would think she would have been sensitive about this, but she never seemed to be. By the time we did "Dreamers" Jacobson had died several years earlier in prison of cancer, and I think Melanie had gotten married and had a child. Her involvement in *Dellaventura* didn't earn the show any additional press attention or anything, neither did it worry anybody on the production, but it makes for a fascinating piece of trivia.

Danny had a lot of good people working in front and behind the camera. For instance, "Dreamers" was cast by Todd Thaler, who was a wonderful casting agent, and it was shot by Tony Jannelli, who had been a camera operator on movies like *The Silence of the Lambs* and *Philadelphia*, and later shot episodes of *Law & Order*. My episode was cut by Mark Laub, who had been one of Aram Avakian's assistants (an old family friend of the Avakians, actually) but I hadn't known him previously. Mark had also directed some episodic television, so he knew what he was doing.

The cast of regulars was also good, as were the guest stars. Anne Ramsey had co-starred opposite Helen Hunt and Paul Reiser in *Mad About You*, which was an extremely successful comedy series during the 1990s. I was crazy for her and thought she was a terrific addition to *Dellaventura*. Both of Danny's sons were also heavily involved with the show, so there was a bit of unabashed nepotism there. Ricky Aiello was playing one of Dellaventura's subordinates and Danny's other son, Danny Aiello III, also directed two episodes and was the stunt co-ordinator. Sadly, Danny, Jr. has since died.

We had Tony Darrow of *Goodfellas* fame guest-starring as Victor, a trainer who is having trouble with his prize horse which seems incapable of winning and allowing him to be a success. At the end of the episode it is revealed that Victor has in fact been messing around with his own horse in order to prevent it from winning races. He was trying to make money for his young daughter, played by Rebecca Harrell of *Prancer* fame, and was doing all this illicit business for her. That twist to the story worked fine, but just getting to it was the problem. What I mean is *Dellaventura* was a well-organized show but it was unfortunately a somewhat self-indulgent one. As executive producer, Danny had full control of the series and this extended to not only who was hired but what elements would feature in each episode. For instance, in "Dreamers", he actually sings! Another of the things Danny insisted upon was that an extremely sweet and sentimental subplot be included in each episode. The overly saccharine subplot of "Dreamers" happened to be his relationship with his old flame, played by Melanie. So, in some ways, there was a certain amount of feeling that *Dellaventura* was a vanity project for Danny, but he was always passionate about the show and wanted to do his best for it.

Obviously, since "Dreamers" was an episode about horseracing we needed horses. Somebody on the crew had brought in this former jockey to co-ordinate all the horses and, soon after meeting this individual, I quickly grew to loathe him with a passion. At one point I even wanted to kill the ex-jockey and even threatened him over the on-set radio. This "informed" guy was hired to provide us with twelve racehorses and twelve jockeys for use on the show. He was doing this for $6,000, or possibly as much as $8,000, something exorbitant like that, for each race that we shot. We agreed with his price but then, at the very last minute when we were all set up and the whole company was ready to shoot, he suddenly said, "I'm afraid I've changed my mind. I now want $12,000 a race." To say I took this unexpected rise in his already generous fee extremely badly is an understatement. I was enraged, but I felt he had us trapped. We were simply going to have to pay the money, or we couldn't shoot. But I wanted to let this piece of shit know in no uncertain terms just how much I hated him. I think he felt it, too. I really do. I was supported in my anger by several other members of the production who were disgusted with his behavior, but there was nothing that anyone could do. He had us by the balls and so we gave him the money and shot the scenes.

In many ways *Dellaventura* was a feel-good show. Again, the characters weren't seriously conflicted or flawed. I certainly don't think there were enough flaws to Dellaventura as a person. You kind of always knew that he and his team were going to solve the case. They were always confident and strong. That took something away from the show, too, I guess, because you knew things were going to work out wonderfully well by the end of the hour. I was fairly happy with "Dreamers"—well, happy enough—but it was compromised somewhat. I had improvised some interesting takes during filming and had used one or two scenes merely as points of departure for something else. Regrettably, the producers ended up not using this material and instead just played the script as written. I felt we had done some good things that never appeared in the transmitted episode. You see, I didn't have final cut on *Dellaventura*—you don't have anything like that kind of authority on episodic television. But I intentionally deviated from the script at certain junctures because I thought Danny's scenes with Melanie Norris were a little sickening as written. I sensed we could find something better, so I encouraged the actors to add a few new things. We then came up with some pretty good ideas that were better than what was scripted. I seem to remember Danny in particular being happy with those new scenes. I think he was quite proud of what we had done, but somehow he was too busy to insure that they survived. So, all that stuff ended up getting lost. I don't know if Danny had approval of the final edit or not. In truth, I don't imagine he ever saw my cut but it was exceedingly better than what was eventually aired.

When I worked with Robert Pastorelli on *Cracker* later that same year, he said something hilarious to me that I've never forgotten: "Italians are only embarrassed about two things: the Mafia and *Dellaventura!*" That quip still makes me chuckle. Was the show as bad as Pastorelli and others will have you believe? No. *Dellaventura* had some serious things wrong with it, but they were all things that could have been fixed. But aside from that same self-defeating contrast of tone, and the fact the series trod a well-worn path in terms of its central idea, each segment had an interminable voiceover that wasn't always pertinent to the story. If you get a main narrative thread going, a hard plot of some sort, and then you interrupt and saturate that plot with long sugary sections and intrusive narration you are going to fail. The audience will sense how patchy and uneven the story is. These distracting interludes were not only present in my episode, by the way. I watched a bunch of episodes of *Dellaventura* and a sappy subplot was always in there. Always! I felt those saccharine sections needed to be cut, or at least tempered, but that was easier said than done. I couldn't just leave them out in the edit as they literally comprised half the show. I think if these problems had been addressed earlier, *Dellaventura* could have possibly survived cancellation. But that never happened, much to Danny's great disappointment and regret.

> *To date, Hancock's last involvement with episodic television has been* Cracker, *the American remake of the acclaimed British crime drama. Created by Jimmy McGovern, the original had starred Robbie Coltrane as Edward 'Fitz' Fitzgerald, a troubled forensic psychologist who assists the Manchester Police Force in solving some of their most difficult cases. A potent mixture of the police procedural, cutting social commentary and unflinching violence,* Cracker *was a critical and ratings success in its native land. Broadcast on ITV from 1993 to 1995 (with two one-off specials produced in 1996 and 2006), it remains one of the finest U.K. television series of the last thirty years. No surprise then that it attracted the interest of American networks hungry for original programming. Produced by Granada Entertainment for ABC, many of the hour-long episodes of the U.S. incarnation were derived from the teleplays of the original series—including the two installments that Hancock directed. The first of these, "Madwoman", which aired on October 2, 1997, saw Fitz helping an amnesia victim who has been arrested by police having been found covered in blood near the scene of a murder. Hancock's second episode, "Best Boys", broadcast on March 5, 1999, detailed Fitz's investigation into the brutal murder of a landlady, which embroils him in a combustible standoff between a youth and his former stepmother.*

I came to be involved with the remake of *Cracker* through Scott Brazil, who was co-executive producer of the series and had remembered me from my time on *Hill Street Blues*. He called my agent to hire me for the show, but I didn't know Scott was there until I arrived at the office for pre-production. I was glad to see and work with him again as he was highly competent. As soon as I heard more details about *Cracker*, I immediately liked the premise and the central character of this troubled maverick psychologist. I then watched every episode of the original British show in preparation and loved them all. I thought it was an exceptional series and its writer, Jimmy McGovern, an exceptional talent. He clearly had a uniquely weird and wonderful mind, particularly when you compared his work with what most American television writers were doing in the 1990s. McGovern's writing was so rich, dark and bristling, and Fitz such a comprehensive and three-dimensional character, I was excited to see what we could possibly do with it. There were good guys and bad guys, but the good guys had very real and relatable problems. Also, I liked that McGovern never shied away from showing his audience how horrible and destructive murder and hate can be, and the toll these things can take on those who fight evil.

It almost goes without saying that the other thing which struck me about *Cracker* was the consistently brilliant performance of Robbie Coltrane in the lead role. He and McGovern was truly a match made in heaven. Fitz was so complex and compelling—so spiky and unconventional—you couldn't take your eyes off him. One of the alluring things about the character as played by Coltrane is he's this troubled anti-hero: an alcoholic chain-smoker, who is overweight and addicted to gambling. On top of that he curses like a sailor and is difficult and sarcastic and self-loathing. You didn't see a lot of people like that in American shows—*Dellaventura* being an obvious example. Despite being labored with all these personal faults, Fitz is incredibly smart and is the best at what he does. Coltrane was able to play those flaws with such charm and dexterity, he made Fitz irresistible. You can watch that show today and I think you'll agree it remains one of the best performances and characters that have ever been devised for television. So, we knew the bar had been raised very high by the Brits and if we were going to even approach those same levels of quality we were going to have to work very, very hard.

The creative team on the American incarnation was headed by James Steven Sadwith. He was the showrunner on *Cracker* and one of the principal writers tasked with adapting many of Jimmy McGovern's teleplays and transposing them to the States. Sadwith was a talented guy, but, like a lot of showrunners it seems, he was not without ego. He had assembled all the regulars on *Cracker* and, ultimately, I think he made some good choices and he made some bad choices. Casting Robert Pastorelli as Fitz was a fairly sound choice all things considered, but some of the supporting actors he selected were not. For instance, Angela Featherstone, who played the female detective Fitz has an affair with, was not as strong as Geraldine Somerville, the equivalent character in the British show. Somerville had nearly been as great as Coltrane and her performance was fabulous and very, very real. I've never seen Somerville in anything else, which, oddly enough, only seems to reinforce the feeling for me that she was indeed a real person. I didn't think Angela Featherstone was capable of matching her in the same role. This led to a little unrest further down the line, but more on that later.

Sadwith also cast R. Lee Ermey as Lieutenant Fry, another of Fitz's associates at the police department. Ermey was a nice man, but I was not entirely convinced by him. He had been a drill sergeant at one time, which led to him being famously cast as the drill sergeant in *Full Metal Jacket*. But he always had the faint whiff of somebody who was really catching up as an actor a little bit and still had a lot to learn. Two of Sadwith's better choices were Carolyn McCormick and Josh Hartnett, who played Fitz's wife and son respectively. Carolyn was a charming lady and almost as good as the English actress who had originated her part in the British *Cracker*. As for Josh, I was just crazy about him. I felt that kid really had *it*! He was perfect for the role and had an authentic charisma to him. He was also very good-looking and could actually act. From the first day I worked with him on set, I said to myself: "This kid is going to be a star." I still think that way. And he was for a while, and may be again. I recall that Josh and Pastorelli got along very well. They respected and liked each other and they never had a problem. The same couldn't be said of Pastorelli's relationships with some of the other members of the cast, which were often fraught with difficulties.

Interestingly, continuing on the subject of Sadwith, I felt that he and others gave me a lot of creative freedom on the show as a director, but, strangely, not when it came to casting the guest stars and supporting roles. Sadwith wanted to instruct me on whom to cast in each specific part when we were preparing my first episode, "Madwoman". We eventually crossed swords on that a little bit as I disagreed with several of his choices. Scott Brazil and I had initially wanted Felton Perry (with whom I'd worked with on *Hill Street Blues* and *Weeds*) for the role of John Doe, the villain in the story, but Sadwith would not let me cast him. He made me cast Adewale Akinnuoye-Agbaje as Doe, who was a little younger than Perry and was not a great actor in my opinion. Adewale has since gone on to do some interesting films and television series, but I don't think he was as good in the role as Perry would have been. Sadwith continued to be fairly insistent about whom he wanted in certain roles, so I finally said to him, "Okay, why don't you direct this episode then?" He quickly caved in after that and allowed me to cast whomever I wanted, but it's safe to say that Sadwith did not appreciate my dissent.

I really should talk a little more about Bob Pastorelli. First, let me say I liked him a lot as a person. He had a warm and engaging manner about him and was very funny (his quip about *Dellaventura* exemplifies that). However, he definitely had his demons. Pastorelli had a troubled history with heroin which undoubtedly cast a shadow over his life and would eventually kill him. No doubt his addiction contributed to his erratic and occasionally violent behavior. The year after *Cracker* was cancelled in 1999, Bob apparently, or quite possibly, shot his girlfriend, Charemon Jonovich, in the head with a handgun at his home in Hollywood. He claimed that Charemon had shot herself during an argument, or something of that nature, so there was some question over whether her death was a suicide or homicide. Back when we were doing *Cracker*, I liked Charemon and was very sad when I learned of her death. Like me, she was from a fruit farm family and I think we shared certain values because of that. Charemon would often be on set with Bob, trying to keep him straight and happy and concentrated. After she died in these mysterious and violent circumstances, Bob was viewed as a "person of interest" by the police. I recently read that he was going to be arrested by the cops before he died of a heroin overdose in March 2004 and charged with Charemon's murder. This was not something I knew about at the time he passed. I must add that Bob was clean during the making of the two episodes I did with him, at least I don't believe he ever took anything. I was never conscious of any changes in his mood or behavior beyond what I already knew of him. The fact is Bob had a plateful of lines to learn on *Cracker* and he was never going to learn them if he was wasted on drugs.

Speaking of learning lines, this brings me to a night on "Madwoman" that I'll never forget. As we were shooting the episode I could see Pastorelli approaching me looking rather nervous and agitated. He said quietly, "John, I don't know any of my lines. I don't know what else to tell you.

I'm sorry." This was a big problem as we had a *huge* scene to do next that consisted of four pages of dialogue, ninety percent of which were his, and it was already something like 9:30 at night. So, I said, "Well, Bob, I guess we'll just have to wait until you do. Why don't you go off, learn the lines, and when you come back we'll take it from there." Pastorelli nodded gratefully before hurriedly disappearing into his trailer. It then took two hours for Bob to get those lines inside his head—two hours with the entire company sitting around waiting for him. Of course, the network and everybody else gets extremely angry at you for doing something like that. They won't tolerate any delays or stoppages, but there was no other alternative available to me. I simply made the decision to lay down our tools and give the actor the time he needed. Occasionally, you have to make decisions as a director on the day that upset one or two people in high places when they eventually hear about them. The fact is we had to get the day's work done, and Bob had assured me that he could learn the scene in a reasonable amount of time. And he did, too. He came back out of his trailer and was focused and ready. We then shot the scene and everybody went home.

If it hadn't happened already, I think that evening firmly cemented my place in Pastorelli's affections. He knew I had looked out for his best interests, and the best interests of the show, and he appreciated that. Bob and I liked each other a lot, and I felt I was able to talk to him about addictions and about how one should conduct themselves at various times without upsetting people or getting in trouble. I mean, Bob would often do that terrible thing I mentioned earlier: arrive late to the set. He would come surrounded by an entourage like he was a Mafia don flanked by his dutiful henchmen. I remember that after he did this one day, I took him aside and said, "Bob, don't do that. Don't arrive late to the set and act like it doesn't mean anything. Everybody is here for you. Everybody is working hard to make this show the best it can be. Don't treat them like that. Don't do it." Bob apologized, but I really felt that he heard what I said that day as his behavior steadily improved—at least during the two episodes I did with him. But you always had to be a little wary of Pastorelli. The week before the incident where the whole company had sat and waited for Bob to learn his lines, he had punched or shoved Angela Featherstone. Needless to say, the two of them did not get along and there was this thickening tension in the air. Apparently, they had both been in his trailer when an argument had erupted that culminated with Bob physically manhandling Angela. The producers then *rewarded* Pastorelli by sending him a basket full of cookies and fruit and flowers! I felt that was not the correct way to deal with this situation. You don't buy gifts for a man who hits a woman, even if that woman is a thoroughly disagreeable and agitating person such as Angela. I'm not in any way condoning what Bob did, but I could certainly see how he—and quite possibly some others on that show—could view her as eminently hittable.

It's worth noting at this point that Angela and I hadn't gotten along with each other at all during the making of "Madwoman." This was simply because I didn't like her. I disliked her so intensely in fact I thought the producers had made a mistake in hiring her. I felt she should be replaced in the role of the female detective and went as far as presenting a strong case to them about why I felt it was necessary. "One of the big problems here is Angela," I argued. "This actress has no feeling or finesse in her performance. It's just dead. Look at how wonderful this same character was in the British show; how beautifully and sensitively she was played by Featherstone's English counterpart. You seriously need to change this member of the cast and have Pastorelli be partnered with somebody better." Alas, the producers were not prepared to do that. So, after accepting their decision, I just got through "Madwoman" with Angela as best I could. By the time "Best Boys" came along, my second episode, I tried a little harder to get through to her. I began discussing the part with Angela more deeply. I wanted to help her, but we then had a conversation that confirmed certain suspicions I had. We were talking one day and Angela revealed to me that she was playing her character as a man. I was startled by this and gasped, "You're *what*?!" She said, "Yeah, it's how I see it. I tried to figure out exactly what kind of cop I would be. I came to the conclusion that if I was going to be a cop I would try to be a man. I don't know how I could possibly be a cop as myself." I said, "Well, that's the problem you are having right there: you are losing yourself in it." She then gave me a rather confounded look, and said, "You really think so?" After that, we tried very hard in "Best Boys" to have her not play the character so much as a man. We tried to soften and feminize her slightly, and Angela put a lot of make-up on in one of the scenes and was rather good. I then began to thaw slightly and like her more as a person, but I thought Angela was totally out of perspective on how to play that part.

> *Even though the series had been cradled in much optimism and excitement,* Cracker *was to suffer the ignoble fate of being abruptly cancelled by the network in January 1998*

after only eleven episodes of its sixteen-episode run had been transmitted. The remaining five shows were quietly screened a year later on the A&E Network.

The cold, hard truth is I don't think the network was happy with the series and so maybe the writing was on the wall. I mean, *Cracker* hadn't met with anybody's high expectations and was clearly missing something. It was missing what the British show had in abundance and there was the distinct disappointment of that. I also think the American version was watered down slightly and made a little more palatable for viewers in the States. Certain parts of the British show were very dark and I saw the American version and felt it wasn't quite as confrontational and ballsy as its predecessor. It took less chances and was more middle class somehow, whereas the original *Cracker* had a lot more grit and bite and was all the better for it. The American Fitz probably wasn't as angry and as troubled as the British Fitz either. He was more attractive and less conflicted, and was in better health, both physically and mentally, than Coltrane's incarnation was. I also don't think that Los Angeles was the correct city in which to transpose the American series. It was too beautiful. The British series had been set in the dour Northern English city of Manchester and that location had assisted in giving the show a lot more character and texture. Maybe Sadwith and the network should have selected a corresponding American city that had some of those same characteristics and qualities.

I also feel that the British storylines did not always transfer well to an American setting and American characters. On occasion certain aspects were lost in translation and had worked much better in the original show. Sadwith and Jim Leonard—Leonard being the executive producer and a writer on *Cracker*—were both talented guys, but they made their mistakes. I thought Leonard was rather skilful at adapting some of the original teleplays, but that Sadwith occasionally took this material in some rather conventional and formulaic directions. Instead of taking McGovern's ideas and characters and trying to do something equally interesting and affecting with them, they diluted and simplified them. Maybe Sadwith should have taken the format and created new scripts that had their own identity. Then, if it failed, it would have done so on its own terms. It's been said by some critics that the relationship between Fitz and the cops is different in the American version than it was in the British version, in that the police seem to be "fawning" over him. I don't know if this is true or not, but I do think Pastorelli was never quite as charming and accomplished as Coltrane was in the role. That too is another big reason for the difference between the two shows. Neither did I agree with the decision to have the American iteration of Fitz be a movie buff that made references to movies in his dialogue. To me that seemed misplaced and false, as if being an aficionado of cinema was somehow a meaningful character trait. It really isn't.

Robbie Coltrane actually guest starred in the final episode of the American *Cracker*, "Faustian Fitz", as a former child actor turned studio mogul. I understand that Coltrane has proved himself adept at American accents in his work, so it may have been a good move on ABC's part to have approached him about reprising his role as Fitz in the U.S. version. The question is would he have done it? I don't know, but maybe they should have given Coltrane an offer he couldn't refuse. Ultimately, when you assess the American *Cracker* and compare it with its British counterpart, it pales by comparison. Again, it didn't have the cast and the scripts weren't as good, but Pastorelli tried hard. Oh God, did he try *hard*! I just can't think of any American actor who could have played that part as well as Coltrane. I mean, possibly Robert De Niro or James Gandolfini. Joe Pesci would have been another interesting choice. He would have had the charm, maybe not the physical presence. The truth is anyone would have had big shoes to fill in replacing Coltrane, but Pastorelli did his best. He really did. I was only thinking about Bob just yesterday, actually. I was thinking what a gifted and versatile actor he was. After the cancellation of *Cracker*, I don't think I had any contact with him before his untimely death, and I only learned about his passing in the news. Nobody told me about it. I wish he and Charemon were still around. Bob had far more to give as an actor, but he was a troubled soul. The only comfort I can draw from knowing he's no longer around is that he is at peace now.

The year that followed *Cracker* I happily returned to directing features with *A Piece of Eden*. That's really where my heart belongs—in making movies. Do I harbor any thoughts about possibly returning to direct some more episodic television? Sure, I'd love to do it. There are a number of current shows I'd love to contribute to. I'd love to do some of *The Americans*, which is a series about two KGB sleeper agents posing as a married American couple in the suburbs of Washington DC. I've enjoyed that show immensely. I haven't had any offers from anyone, but I think that's merely a case of my advanced years. I certainly feel prejudiced against in terms of my age—absolutely I do—but then so does everybody. I think certain producers, networks and studios feel that filmmaking is a young man's game, so they question your energy and commitment levels as well as your ability to tell a story. Some of them believe that older directors are out of touch with the demands and details of modern filmmaking. They fear that older filmmakers don't understand the "style" (I use that word cautiously) of the work being produced today. All the blistering edits, motiveless camera moves and furious pacing they think is beyond your capability. It would be funny, if it wasn't so depressing. I mean, that approach is decidedly easy. Anyone can do it. It's very easy to shoot a movie or a TV show with five cameras running simultaneously and cut it all together. My dog could do it. Experience and wisdom do not seem to be as valued today in our industry as they once were.

11 *The Twilight Zone* (1985 – 1986)

CREATED, HOSTED AND PRINCIPALLY written by Rod Serling, The Twilight Zone *remains the most enduring and culturally significant anthology series in the history of television. Airing for five seasons from October 1959 to June 1964, and totaling 156 episodes, its stories ranged from science fiction/fantasy to horror, from comedy to the Western, from period drama to futuristic tales. Despite most television series of its era being consigned to memory by the mid-1980s,* The Twilight Zone *remained in the public consciousness due to its episodes being repeatedly aired in syndication for more than twenty years. Additionally, its title was borrowed for a successful horror/fantasy magazine,* Rod Serling's The Twilight Zone Magazine, *which ran from 1981 to 1989, and there was even a major Hollywood feature,* Twilight Zone: The Movie *(1983) co-produced and partially directed by Steven Spielberg. Although the film was not a huge commercial and critical success, executives at CBS realized they owned a valuable property.*

In what later turned out to be a bad business decision in the wake of the stunning success of The Twilight Zone *in syndication, Serling had sold his forty percent share of the series back to the network in March 1965. This eventually paved the way for CBS to revive the series in 1985 as an in-house production under the stewardship of executive producer Philip DeGuere, as the network stood to earn more profits than if they acquired a new series produced independently of the organization. Accompanying DeGuere on this journey were producer Harvey Frand, supervising producer James Crocker, executive story consultant Alan Brennert, story editor Rockne S. O'Bannon and creative consultant Harlan Ellison (who would controversially leave the show at the end of the first season due to a dispute with the network's standards and practices).*

Dramatizing stories by such acclaimed authors as Ray Bradbury, Stephen King, Richard Matheson, Robert Silverberg, Arthur C. Clarke and Theodore Sturgeon, the roster of directors hired by DeGuere to helm them was no less illustrious and included William Friedkin, John Milius, Joe Dante, Wes Craven, Jeannot Szwarc and John Hancock. Presented in a different format from the one thirty-minute stories of the original series, The New Twilight Zone *as it has come to be known, featured as many as three stories per hour. DeGuere and his team also decided against having an onscreen host introduce each segment as Serling had earlier done, instead opting for the soothing narration of Charles Aidman (an actor who had made two appearances in the original series). Hancock would go on to direct five segments of the show, a number that was only bettered by Wes Craven (six episodes), Peter Medak (seven episodes) and Paul Lynch (nine episodes).*

Like a lot of people back in the 1960s, I was a big fan of *The Twilight Zone*. The idea of becoming involved in *The New Twilight Zone* was certainly an attractive proposition for that reason alone. I still fondly remembered many of the iconic episodes of Rod Serling's original series, particularly the famous one where William Shatner is on the airplane and sees this horrible creature lurking out on the wing, tearing it apart and driving him crazy. Everybody talks about that segment and with good reason—it's terrific! I remember the distinctive theme music, of course, and Serling's voice and image. I think an entire generation of viewers was affected by *The Twilight Zone*, as well as a generation of writers, producers and directors. If something is still being talked about with reverence more than fifty years after it was first transmitted, it obviously has considerable value and importance that goes beyond mere nostalgia. I think we can all agree on that. So, there was already a built-in brand recognition and it made sense to bring the show back.

I don't recall when I first heard that CBS was resurrecting *The Twilight Zone*, but I believe my agent was the one who informed me about it. After doing *Hill Street Blues*, it was the very next thing I was asked to do. Right from the beginning I could see that the show was a tight operation. It had a strong creative team behind it: Phil DeGuere was the executive producer and also wrote several of the best episodes. He was an incredibly bright and warm guy. I liked him as a person and thought he had good taste and intelligence. Phil was a charmer, but he was not somebody with a hidden agenda or sinister purpose. He was always accommodating and supportive of his directors. I was so impressed with Phil I tried to get him to produce *Weeds* at one point during 1985. He really liked the project and tried to get it on, but wasn't able to. I only recently learned that Phil died back in 2005. It's shocking to me. I'm somewhat embarrassed to admit I had no knowledge that he had passed more than a decade ago. I'm sure if you talked to most of the directors who worked on *The Twilight Zone* they would all speak as highly of Phil as I have. There aren't a lot of smart, generous and talented men working in television today and there is one less now.

The rest of the team on the show was also excellent. Harvey Frand and James Crocker were the producers, and, like Phil, were both intelligent and amiable. I enjoyed working with the resident cinematographers on the show Bradford May and Chuck Arnold. They also had the most wonderful ADs on their staff, one of whom was a guy named Paul Deason who was a great help to me (I later hired Paul for *Weeds*). It was such a class outfit, and was being run by people who had a lot of knowledge and passion for science fiction, horror and fantasy. It was clear that they were trying to do a show that was much more accomplished than the likes of *Cover Up*. I didn't have much to do with Harlan Ellison, as he wasn't around whenever I was there. I do recall the author and journalist Hunter S. Thompson being there for some reason, though. I don't exactly know why. At the time, I guess CBS was possibly trying to adapt some of Thompson's stories for the show or maybe he was working on an original story for them; or maybe he was involved in some other project entirely. I really don't know. I would occasionally see Thompson lurking in and around the writer's block at CBS and he often impressed me as an asshole. He had a kind of silly, puffy attitude and a facile cynicism that seemed rather fake and inflated to me. In my few encounters with the man, I remember him as being wholly unconvincing.

The producers had managed to secure some great directing talent for the show, people like William Friedkin. As you know, Billy and I already knew each other from our days as Trustees of the American Film Institute, so we spent a certain amount of time chatting about Phil DeGuere and gossiping about the management, that kind of thing. Billy is an incredibly interesting and articulate guy; one of those people it's always rewarding to listen to. He's had a terribly interesting career and has such extraordinary courage and single-mindedness as a filmmaker. I remember that when I was working on *Twilight Zone*, it was made known to me that one or two members of the production team had "hated" Friedkin during the making of "Nightcrawlers." I believe they felt he was making too many demands. They assumed that because Friedkin had come from making big movies like *The French Connection*, *The Exorcist* and *Sorcerer*, he was not used to doing episodic television where the ambitions of your vision are considerably more modest and confined. They felt he was trying to make "Nightcrawlers" as if he were making *Sorcerer*. I don't know what it was exactly, but it was not a happy encounter with some of the staff—this is what I was told and maybe Billy would refute it. Nobody can deny the fact that he delivered one of the best—if not *the* best—episode of *The Twilight Zone*. "Nightcrawlers" had the scope and feel of a movie, and as such, I think it elevated the show. Regardless of any demands he did or didn't impose, Friedkin made something special.

I had no such lofty ambitions for my episodes. I fell in line, which is probably the reason I was invited back so many times, that and the fact I was efficient. In order to work successfully in episodic television, you must set your motor at a whole different register when compared to making movies. As I implied before, you are working for *them*—the network and executive producer. So, if you want to alter a line of dialogue or change a piece of action, the assistant director has to get them on the phone. You ask if you can do it and the executive producer usually says yes, or they come down to the set and discuss what the problem is. Essentially, on a movie set, the director is like a dictator with all the powers such a position affords you. On a television set, the director is merely an employee—a cog in the machine—and you must be cognizant of that fact if you want to continue working. Despite not enjoying an enormous amount of creative freedom as directors on *The Twilight Zone* in terms of altering or revising the scripts, we did have a lot of freedom stylistically. The producers didn't care how you interpreted the script visually as long as you completed the episode on time and stuck to the structure and details of the story. This was in direct contrast to *Hill Street Blues* which had a fixed style they wanted you to shoot in—something I loved doing. But *The Twilight Zone* wasn't as restrictive or as repetitive as some other TV shows I directed afterwards. The teleplays were always interesting.

> *The first of Hancock's episodes to reach television screens was "Kentucky Rye," which was broadcast on October 11, 1985, as the third and most memorable entry of a three-segment hour that also comprised Sigmund Neufeld's "Healer" and Wes Craven's "Children's Zoo." Written by Richard Krzemien and Chip Duncan, this macabre tale stars Jeffrey DeMunn as Bob Spindler, an alcoholic businessman. Ignoring the protestations of his wife and co-workers, he insists on driving himself home after consuming large quantities of alcohol while celebrating the closing of a major deal. Driving along a lonely road at night, he veers into the wrong lane and almost collides with a car hurtling towards him in the other direction. Spindler crashes into some trees and is knocked unconscious. Coming to some time later, he staggers, bleeding, out of his vehicle and into an isolated roadside tavern nearby. Within moments of entering, Spindler's head-wound miraculously disappears and he is immediately struck by the warm atmosphere and friendly regulars. He engages in an arm wrestling contest with one of the customers and buys everyone inside a round of drinks, before noticing a somber-faced stranger (Arliss Howard) and an earnest-looking woman glaring at him. The elderly bartender (Philip Bruns) offers to sell Spindler the business for the paltry sum of $1600, but the offer only stands for the night. Spindler tries to negotiate an even lower price, insisting that he only has a check for $1500 on him. The somber-faced stranger intervenes and gives him the $100 he needs. As Spindler takes the keys from the bartender the once gregarious mood in the tavern immediately darkens and it soon becomes apparent that the businessman has acquired much more than he bargained for.*

"Kentucky Rye" was an interesting introduction to *The Twilight Zone*. The casting of each episode involved a casting director hired by the producers, but you could request actors if you wanted somebody specific for a particular role. They would bring in anybody that you wanted to see who was available and affordable. If you decided the actor was right, they would duly cast them. *The Twilight Zone* afforded me the opportunity of working with several actors that I had always wanted to work with, so that was fun. On "Kentucky Rye" we were looking for somebody to play the lead role of this alcoholic businessman and somehow Jeffrey DeMunn came to my attention. I think he was possibly recommended to me by Phil DeGuere, I don't recall, but I agreed he would be a reasonable choice. Jeffrey has gone on to do some wonderful work and he did a good job for me on the episode.

Interestingly, although he only played a brief supporting role in the segment, the actor that really excited me on "Kentucky Rye" was Arliss Howard who played the ghost of the other driver involved in the road accident. I must admit that when we started shooting, I didn't realize at first how good Arliss was. I mean, once the cast was assembled on these *Twilight Zone* episodes there was never any rehearsal time. I think there would be a table read, something like a two-hour session where we would all sit around a table and read the script twice. That was it. But as soon as we began shooting and I saw what Arliss was doing, I said to myself, "Oh boy, this guy is good!" I hadn't heard of him before, but it never ceases to amaze me how you can work with an actor and, all of a sudden, one day you wake up and say, "Geez, I've really got something good here." Arliss was not conventional, not typical, in his approach to things. Of course, he was playing a ghost, but he had an interesting and unearthly presence about him in those scenes that really served the story well. I'm not surprised how well Arliss did in the following years. In fact, he went on to work with Stanley Kubrick on *Full Metal Jacket* right after we had finished shooting.

When I read the script for "Kentucky Rye", and even when we were shooting it, I never had the sense that it was in any way different from other *Twilight Zone* episodes in its use of flashbacks. The way the story moved backward and forward in time at the beginning of its narrative structure was all detailed in the script. That was not something arrived at by restructuring the scenes in the editing; that was all on the page as written by Richard Krzemien and Chip Duncan. I simply followed what they had carefully laid out and I was happy that it worked so well. There was always a great respect for the writers on *Twilight Zone* by Phil and his creative team, as there is on many television series. In a lot of ways, in TV, the writer is king, but with so many good directors on the series

Twilight Zone seemed to be as much a director's show as it was a writer's show. I can remember Richard and Chip visiting the set when we were filming, so their involvement continued after they delivered the script. Now that I think about it, I don't recall Chip being around as much as I do Richard. I remember Krzemien very well and I think he went on to write for *Star Trek: The Next Generation* and *War of the Worlds*, and did quite well for himself.

The Kentucky Rye itself, the interior of the bar, was a set at CBS studios. The exterior of the bar was someplace located in the San Fernando Valley that I believe was, or at one time may have been, an actual roadside tavern. We shot all the scenes of the barroom in its working condition first—replete with customers, working lights and flowing beer taps—and then covered the set in cobwebs and dust and grime to make it look like it hadn't been used or inhabited for years. It's plainly much easier to deteriorate or antique a set afterwards than it is to clean all that stuff up and work backwards, so to speak. Thus, I believe the scenes where Bob Spindler suddenly learns his terrible fate were among the last things we shot on the segment. That seemed strangely fitting somehow.

> *"Kentucky Rye" features several amusingly sinister touches including the elderly bartender calling Spindler by his name even though the injured interloper hasn't identified himself, as well as the portentous moment when Bob finds the Charlie Pride song "In Heaven, There is no Beer" on a jukebox. The episode ends on a decidedly bleak note with Spindler waking up in the now deserted and gloomy-looking joint the morning after the night before. He looks around and notices that the furniture is knitted with cobwebs, and all the bottles and glasses are empty and caked with dust. The somber-faced stranger then appears from nowhere, startling him. He reveals that Spindler ran him off the road the previous evening, killing him and making the earnest-looking woman his widow. Peering through a boarded window, Spindler spies both his own bloodied corpse—and that of the stranger—being loaded into the back of ambulances. Spindler then realizes to his horror that he is dead and has unwittingly purchased his very own private Hell from which there is no escape. He*

> *collapses to his knees in despair and regret as the screen quietly fades to darkness.*

Was concluding the episode with a lingering shot like that—Bob falling to his knees and then simply fading to black without any music—an unusual approach for *The Twilight Zone*? I don't recall enough of the episodes to pass comment on that. I don't remember if we had a problem about where exactly to put the closing narration on "Kentucky Rye" or if we experimented with a few different ways to end it. Maybe we just felt the climax played much better if we put the voiceover a minute or so before the old man appears sitting behind Spindler, laughing his ass off and telling him the bar is "all yours!" By the way, is that old man really the Devil? I think he probably is. The Devil was a frequent guest on Serling's original show, wasn't he? So, that idea makes perfect sense. But maybe the quiet fade-out we did worked out better and was more affecting than something loud or dramatic. Sometimes silence and emptiness can be more terrifying. Also, there are times when there is no room for a voiceover, or the narration feels intrusive, or it's merely repeating what is already inherent in the imagery. I don't recall if the closing narration was included in the script or was added sometime later by Phil or a member of his writing staff.

True, it's a dark and depressing ending—an alcoholic seemingly trapped forever in a bar without booze. It's very morbid, but it's good. I like it. I also like all the malignant hints Bob gets that the bar isn't quite what he thinks it is; clues he fails to pick up on but the audience receives loud and clear. For instance, I love the moment when Bob reads the Charlie Pride song "In Heaven, There is No Beer" on the jukebox. It's great, but that was all in Richard and Chip's script, as was the addition of the popular Rod Stewart song "Some Guys Have All the Luck" sung by a different singer. No doubt it would have cost CBS a fortune to have used Rod Stewart's cut. I enjoyed all those details because those are the things that assist in giving the final payoff a little more resonance. I think there is a—I don't want to use the word predictability—but there is an inevitability about the ending in that you can kind of see it coming. But that's okay, because what you really want when you do a creepy story like "Kentucky Rye" is something that has a sound internal logic to it. The story may be fashioned out of total fantasy, but it still has to have a sense of coherence and believability about it if it's really going to work.

In the best episodes of Rod Serling's *Twilight Zone*, there was always this sense of justice, of cosmic justice, where the guilty are punished for any crimes and misdemeanors they may have perpetrated. I think "Kentucky Rye" definitely falls into that category but, in my personal view, I don't feel that Spindler is entirely deserving of this horrible fate that's suddenly been thrust upon him. He has made a mistake, a very bad mistake, and he may be a rather disagreeable fellow, but the question of whether or not he deserves to reside for eternity alone in a dusty hovel is open for discussion. Maybe this excessive supernatural revenge is really a kind of purgatory. Granted, I've rejected religion for most of my life, but I'm still intrigued by the idea of one having to atone for one's earthly sins in an afterlife. Also, if it only works as one thing, I think "Kentucky Rye" succeeds spectacularly as a very powerful anti-drunk driving commercial. That issue was quickly becoming a very important one back in the early 1980s—and indeed still is. But back then you had the formation of MADD [Mothers Against Drunk Driving] and other organizations, which were gaining a lot of publicity, and I think "Kentucky Rye" captures that same sense of anger and indignation. The idea that a twenty-minute television episode I directed more than thirty years ago might have had some small influence in making somebody change their mind about driving home drunk would be a wonderful thought to entertain. If it has just saved one life, boy, wouldn't it have been worth it?

> *The second of Hancock's* Twilight Zone *episodes to be aired was "If She Dies". Paired with Peter Medak's "Ye Gods," the latter an insipid tale of yuppies and star-crossed deities, it was screened on October 25, 1985, and was the only contribution to the series from writer David Bennett Carren. The story concerns a widower named Paul Marano (Tony Lo Bianco) whose young daughter Cathy (Andrea Barber) goes into a deep coma following a car accident. After being informed that his only child's chances of surviving are remote, Paul leaves his bedside vigil at the hospital and heads for home to get some rest. Going to his car, he suddenly sees the form of a little girl standing on the roof of the nearby St. Amelia's orphanage. He tells a nun named Sister Agnes (Nan Martin) what he has seen, but is informed that there are no children in the orphanage as it is about to be torn down. Sister Agnes then tries to interest*

Paul in some items from the orphanage that she is selling in a rummage sale. He declines but then glimpses the same little girl on a swing, pointing to an antique children's bed. He is compelled to purchase the bed and takes it home, placing it in Cathy's room. Later that night, Paul is visited by the little girl (Jenny Lewis), a sickly-looking child whose luminous form and icy touch reveal she is a ghost. The girl asks Paul if he will tuck her into bed, enquiring if he has seen somebody called Toby. Moments after escorting the little girl to the antique bed and placing her under the blankets, the child vanishes. The following day, Paul visits the new orphanage and learns from Sister Agnes that the bed once belonged to a child named Sarah who died of tuberculosis many years before he was born. Paul also discovers that Toby was the little girl's teddy bear, a memento that the nun has kept since Sarah's death. Paul asks Sister Agnes to give him Toby as he is convinced that Sarah's restless soul has a greater purpose to fulfill before departing the earth.

As directors on *The Twilight Zone*, we did not have the freedom to select what material we wanted to do. We were simply assigned the various stories to direct and you were in no position to say that you didn't want to do the one you had been given. So, you couldn't suddenly demand to be given "Nightcrawlers" or "Shatterday" instead of "Kentucky Rye" or "If She Dies." Not that I would have done that and nor was I ever unhappy with the scripts I was given. I was just happy for the work and excited to be making my contribution. I have to think that Phil was smart enough to place certain stories with certain directors whom he felt would not only be adept at handling them, but would respond to the material positively and deliver something that was worthwhile. For instance, I remember that both Phil and Harvey were big fans of *Bang the Drum Slowly*. More than once Phil complimented me on the balance of humor and pathos in that movie, and how the story had touched him. I imagine for that reason he felt I would be a good fit for something like "If She Dies" which involves bereavement and the idea of death before one's time. I must admit, it does seemingly appeal to my sensibilities, but I didn't have any special feeling for the script. "If She Dies" was a rather small, sad, sensitive little ghost story, very bittersweet and nothing that was too taxing on the brain.

I find that a lot of these kinds of stories, tales of ghosts and restless spirits, are more emotional than cerebral anyway. A lot of them are strongly connected to human emotions, feelings of sadness, grief, love, hatred, and many have an almost anecdotal quality. What's interesting is a lot of ghostly encounters seem to have happened to a person that somebody else knows but whom you don't know personally. So, you are removed from the events by several degrees—unless you've experienced the supernatural directly. Then it becomes a different thing entirely. You already know how a lot of these ghost stories are going to end, but they still succeed in giving you the shivers. It's a little like hearing the punchline to a good joke and, like a joke, the best ghost stories have the directness and simplicity of folk tales and fairy stories. That is what makes them effective in most instances. I don't believe in ghosts and I've certainly never seen one. Even the story I told you about the woman who died in our swimming pool, Dorothy and I never actually saw anything. We just scared ourselves, really. Obviously, the question of whether or not I believed in ghosts was not an important consideration to make before agreeing to do the episode. Dorothy does believe strongly in the existence of ghosts, but I feel there is always some kind of rational or psychological or biological explanation for why people think they have seen or felt a ghost. I think these sightings or sensations are related to who, what and where we are; our environment, our emotional states, lots of different things.

I thought "If She Dies" was a lot like the kinds of anecdotes about ghosts that you hear. It has that same sense of simplicity. Also, you have a widowed father in there and a little girl without a mother and those elements echo *Prancer*, which I made a few years later. Looking back now, those sentimental aspects may appear familiar but they did not draw me to the material as, again, this was an assignment. I think the haunting in "If She Dies" derives from a mutual sadness and grief that Tony's character shares with the spirit of this little girl who has died of TB in an orphanage. They both feel this sense of loss and the fact that someone very close to Tony, his only daughter, is near to death brings them together. It probably opens him up or tunes him in to other dimensions, though, in reality, I think such emotions can be misleading and can cloud a person's rationality. I mean, some people have that desperate *need* to believe don't you think? They need to know that the personality or the soul of their loved one has somehow survived death and continues to exist in some form. A lot of people don't want to accept the possibility that we are finite;

that we die. I don't want to either, but the quicker you accept the reality that all things must perish perhaps the happier you will be; or perhaps not. I don't know.

What's interesting is I never had a sense of the budgets we were working under on *The Twilight Zone*. I've always been fairly conscious of the budgets on the movies I've made, and also on some of the other television shows I directed, but I couldn't tell you what any of my *Twilight Zone* episodes cost. I do know that it wasn't a huge amount of money. I will say that it never seemed to be a case of balancing out the cost of casting a name actor with reducing some of the special effects in the script, or restricting the number of locations, or dropping a stunt. That said, unlike "Kentucky Rye" before it, we did not show the car crash in "If She Dies." We instead cut to a shot of a nearby boy on a bicycle looking on and merely heard the vehicle colliding with something. That was not an artistic decision; that was simply a budget consideration I made as we could not afford to stage the car crashing in this instance. Also, stunts can be difficult and potentially dangerous to do, so I sometimes prefer to take the approach of what you don't see is often more effective than what you do see.

Realizing that we were operating under the constraints of time and money, I seldom exceeded more than three or four takes before moving on. If I could get the shot in one take, I would move on right away. I don't always insist on protection—in my movies as well as in my television work. If I think I've got it, I go on. I've always been fairly secure that way. Yes, working with kids requires a little more patience and you do sometimes have to do a few more takes than usual. The two actresses I hired to play Tony's injured daughter and the ghost of the little girl, Andrea Barber and Jenny Lewis respectively, were both pretty good as I recall. I remember Jenny had a suitably sad and vulnerable quality to her that was perfect for the ghost, but beyond that I don't recall that much about her. I looked on IMDb recently and saw that both Jenny and Andrea have gone on to have good careers in the business which is wonderful. They were both perfectly fine to work with. Having worked with several child actors before and after *The Twilight Zone*, I've often found it's better to treat kids as adults. Some directors don't do that, and have no affinity for children. Some even view them as a necessary hindrance, an obstacle you have to overcome. That's not a particularly healthy or productive attitude to take when working with child actors. I think you can achieve better results if you find a way to communicate with them on the same level.

I remember one of the things Bradford May and I had to do was create an ethereal effect for when the ghostly little girl approaches Tony late at night when he awakes in his bed. We put pale make-up on Jenny's face to give her the necessary sickly look that the character required and I think we used a filter that diffused it a little bit and assisted in giving the child this slightly luminous glow in the darkness. I didn't want anything too weird and over-the-top for that, just something that confirmed for the audience that this girl was clearly a spirit—not that they didn't know that fact already. I think it was something Brad and I had first attempted briefly with Arliss Howard on "Kentucky Rye." His character was also a ghost and at one point we put a light on his face and really flared it up. I don't remember if some of these things we did were augmented with a post-production effect of some kind or was something we were able to achieve in-camera. It may have been a mixture of both. Brad was an interesting and inventive cinematographer, who was always brimming with good ideas. He had a system of using prime lenses and camera moves that I found interesting. I learned quite a lot from him. Brad also directed a few episodes of *The Twilight Zone* himself and still works as a director.

> *A saccharine and somewhat predictable ghost story,* "If She Dies" *still succeeds due to its rich atmosphere and delicate performances—particularly those of Lo Bianco as the grieving father and Martin as the holy sister who rejects belief in the supernatural. The episode culminates with Paul removing his ailing daughter from the hospital and placing her in the antique bed at their home. Falling asleep he awakens in the morning to see no change in Cathy's condition. Despairing at the thought of losing her, he suddenly hears his daughter's meek voice calling for him and sees that she has awoken from her coma fully intact. Overjoyed, Paul is startled when Cathy suddenly asks for Toby. He gives her the teddy bear, which she embraces warmly. This ending has led to confusion in the minds of some viewers as to whether or not the conclusion is a happy one. The sentimental music appears seemingly at odds with the slightly ominous freeze-frame of Cathy clutching Toby, begging the question has Sarah's restless spirit been laid to rest or has she now taken possession of Cathy's body?*

To be honest with you, that's not a question I've ever asked myself. I always believed that it was a happy ending, and that father and daughter have been reunited with the help of this little ghost girl. I never felt it was a downbeat or dark ending. The sweet music and the freeze frame are not meant to mislead or confuse or unsettle the audience—quite the reverse. If there is a problem in the way that scene is read, it's simply in the way I directed it. I do think the ending could have perhaps been a little clearer in terms of what has happened. I mean, has the old bed itself restored the dying daughter to full health? Or has the ghost girl somehow sacrificed herself, or passed on her energy, her soul, her force, whatever it is, in order to push Tony's daughter back from the brink of death? Or, as some people clearly think, has the ghost girl entered the body of Tony's daughter so she can continue her existence? If anybody knows the answers to these questions I'd be very interested to hear them.

I don't believe there is any closing narration at the climax of "If She Dies", which might have helped to make things a little clearer for the audience. Maybe we thought that if we put some narration in there it would be a little intrusive or over-explanatory. We were probably wrong about that. I thought the ending was obvious and upbeat, but maybe I should go back and look at the episode again. On the other hand, I do enjoy an element of mystery and ambiguity in a story. I don't see that as a problem and it may even make "If She Dies" a far more interesting segment. Everybody seemed to find the ending a satisfying and warm one, but who knows? Some may feel that it doesn't work entirely. I will say that, all in all, I like "If She Dies." I like it well enough. I like Tony Lo Bianco's performance and I like the cozy economy and purity of the story. Again, it's that anecdotal quality we discussed earlier and the way it plays on a parent's worst nightmare—the idea that something terrible could happen to their child. That's where the real power of the episode lies, I feel.

> *The third and perhaps most accomplished of Hancock's* Twilight Zone *episodes was "Profile in Silver", which was broadcast on March 7, 1986, alongside Peter Medak's "Button, Button." Originally conceived by author J. Neil Schulman as a possible feature film, the story attracted the interest of producer Robert Jaffe, whose previous credits had included* Demon Seed *(1977) and* Motel Hell *(1980). In 1985, two years after first pitching his idea to Jaffe, Schulman*

was invited by Alan Brennert to submit an outline for an episode of The Twilight Zone. After receiving "Profile in Silver," Brennert grew concerned at the potentially sensitive nature of a segment that revolved around the assassination of John F. Kennedy. As a result, Schulman wrote two versions of the story: the first contained real names and historical events, while the second was termed the "Greek Tycoon" version after J. Lee Thompson's 1978 drama of the same name which was loosely based on the relationship between shipping magnate Aristotle Onassis and Jacqueline Kennedy. Brennert's initial apprehension appeared to be well-founded as Carla Singer, the executive first charged with developing the reboot of The Twilight Zone for CBS, found the story unpalatable. After Singer departed from the series before it aired, Tony Barr, her replacement, was far more receptive to the proposal and approved Schulman to write his teleplay with certain provisos in place. The most sizable of the restrictions imposed on the author was the removal of a second assassin from the story, with Barr insisting: "The CBS television network is not going to rewrite history."

Schulman's teleplay concerns Dr. Joseph Fitzgerald (Lane Smith), a Harvard professor who is in fact a field historian from the year 2172. He has secretly traveled back in time to 1963 in order to observe the fraught historical events of the era. Retiring to the privacy of his office, Fitzgerald produces a silver coin from his pocket from the year 1964 that has the image of President John F. Kennedy engraved on it. Moments later he is visited by Dr. Kate Wang (Barbara Baxley), a friend and colleague from his own time who suddenly appears in the room. They discuss his mission, which is to witness the assassination of Kennedy the next day, and Fitzgerald reveals his contrasting emotions about watching his own ancestor being murdered in cold blood. Undeterred, Fitzgerald dutifully teleports himself to Dallas, Texas, and begins recording the Presidential limousine as it descends fatefully down Elm Street. As he moves the camera up to the sixth floor window of the Texas School Book Depository and glimpses Lee Harvey Oswald raising

> his rifle to kill Kennedy (Andrew Robinson), Fitzgerald is overcome with the urgency to intervene. He shouts for the President to take cover and, as he does so, Oswald's bullets miss their intended target and the assassination is prevented. Fitzgerald is hailed a hero by Ray Livingstone (Louis Giambalvo), a trusted Secret Service agent, and is invited to meet Kennedy onboard Air Force One. However, Fitzgerald's intervention causes the fabric of time to be bent and distorted out of its normal shape, triggering a series of disastrous events such as the assassination of First Secretary Nikita Khrushchev and the subsequent Soviet invasion of Berlin. Fitzgerald learns from the calculations of his wrist-computer that the situation will culminate with a nuclear exchange between the USA and USSR that will end all of mankind. The only way to avoid this alternate time-line is for the Kennedy presidency to end as history originally recorded.

Time travel and time machines are used as a rather easy device in movies and in literature. It's just the McGuffin that gets a character somewhere or some-when and their predicament and adjustment to their new surroundings becomes the meat of the story. That's okay, but it's not enough to make a really strong story. Time travel is rarely used in a truly interesting way I feel. What impressed me when I first read J. Neil Schulman's script for "Profile in Silver" was the fact that the repercussions of time travel were an essential ingredient of the narrative and not just a simplified excuse. The character of Fitzgerald, by occupation, traveled through time, but there were certain ethical questions that were addressed in the story. I don't think that it's theoretically possible to travel through time, but, if it were possible, those same questions would become important. For instance, should we even do it? What are the dangers and consequences if it all goes wrong? All of that was in Schulman's teleplay. I also liked the idea that the alternate time-line had a seismic environmental and physical effect on the earth as it meant the stakes in the story were very, very big.

Interestingly, I don't remember there being a strong reluctance on the part of CBS to go forward with "Profile in Silver" either for political reasons or for reasons of taste. I'm sure the network was a little nervous, but nobody asked me to be careful or mindful of certain elements. If they did have any fears or reservations—which I think is understandable when you consider the fact that some of the people involved and their family members were still alive, and the events depicted still fairly raw—I didn't notice nor was I informed about them. As a matter of fact, memory seems to be telling me that there was considerable excitement about the episode on the part of the network as well as the creative team. Everyone agreed that Schulman's script was exceptionally good and I was glad that it came to me. I wasn't familiar with his work before we started shooting. I do remember that Schulman was fairly young at the time. I don't know where he came from, but I do seem to recall that "Profile in Silver" was his first piece of writing for television.

The writers on *The Twilight Zone* would occasionally visit the set and be present during the shooting of their episodes, but not too much. Schulman was the exception in that he was around all the time. A result of that was he and I saw a lot of each other and became very friendly. It was good having the author there as I could directly ask him questions and would receive an immediate answer if there was a problem. Not that there were many of them as his script was so strong and had a very interesting and emotive central concept: the idea of changing a huge historical event so that it alters our present reality. That in itself was by no means an original idea, but applying it to the assassination of John F. Kennedy was an inspired notion. I mean, there's a certain wish fulfillment in there; the idea that we can possibly right a terrible wrong and make everything better. Of course, Schulman posits the idea that in righting this wrong, we inadvertently create a future that is even worse. It's a destiny that is far too horrific to ever come to pass, one in which the human race is doomed.

"Profile in Silver" is probably the most popular of all *The Twilight Zone* episodes I directed and I think one reason for that popularity is because it's about JFK. His premature death still resonates with people; the waste of unrealized potential and the loss of a brighter future for everyone. Again, that's such a profoundly powerful idea. The episode was made twenty-three years after Kennedy's assassination and was among the first to treat the assassination in a science fiction context—probably the very first. The memory of this tragic event was still surprisingly painful, even though a lot had happened to us in those intervening years like Watergate, the end of the Vietnam War and the rise of Ronald Reagan's Conservative revolution. My own memories of the day Kennedy was murdered, and the days that followed, are full and elaborate. I remember that on November

22, 1963, I was coming back from a meeting with a producer and all of a sudden every car abruptly stopped on 57th Street. We were all wondering, "What the hell is going on?" I looked out the window and saw that people on the street were visibly upset. They were crying en masse, or had their hands clasped over their mouths. It was the most unnerving experience, actually.

I don't know if my memory has embellished this event over the years, but I do recall having the powerful sensation in those moments that something truly monumental had occurred. We quickly turned on the radio and that was when we learned that the President was dead. It was profoundly shocking and nobody could quite accept it at first. I mean, who would do such a thing? Surely not an American! Then, two days later, I happened to be watching the live television broadcast of Lee Harvey Oswald being shot by Jack Ruby as he was being led out of jail by cops. I remember getting the sense in those moments that our country was unraveling and everything was turning to shit. Everybody was depressed and there was the obsessive and continuous watching of the news reports, and the President's funeral, and the interviews with eyewitnesses, and everything else. It was quite a traumatic and turbulent time for America. You can ask anybody who lived through those days where they were when they first heard JFK had been killed and they can tell you.

Many Americans view Kennedy's death as the exact moment we lost our innocence. They point to that event as the reason why everything turned sour for us. I think it's somewhat dangerous and naive to restrict our view of history like that, as a lot has happened to us in our relatively young history as a country. I mean, earlier in the twentieth century, before Kennedy's assassination, we had Prohibition, World War II, the bombings of Hiroshima and Nagasaki, Joseph McCarthy and the House of Un-American Activities Committee, and several other dark and troubling things. I don't think JFK's death was the one instance when we lost our innocence. Yes, our political system went a little haywire and we later had Lyndon B. Johnson and Richard Nixon, the assassinations of Bobby Kennedy and Martin Luther King, as well as further involvement in Vietnam and the Watergate scandal. We might still have had some of those things happen to us even if Kennedy had completed his time in office. I think you can even go further back in our history to various other wars we've engaged in, as well as the attempted annihilation of the Native Americans, to see that maybe the United States never had any innocence to lose in the first place.

When we were casting "Profile in Silver" I was looking around for two actors to play Fitzgerald and Kennedy who had a passable physical resemblance to each other as they were supposed to be related. How much Lane Smith and Andrew Robinson, the two guys we cast, look like each other is open for debate. I don't think it's important as a plot point because the historical time-line has been altered anyway. Lane's face (when he eventually takes Kennedy's place in the motorcade) is the only face the American public would know anyway as history has been changed. I was very happy with Andy's performance as JFK. I knew him from New York and had seen him in some Off-Broadway Dostoevsky play there that I had liked. I also remembered him from the casting sessions we held for *Bang the Drum Slowly*. After playing the memorably disturbed villain in *Dirty Harry* opposite Clint Eastwood, I'd heard that Andy couldn't get a job for a long time as he'd been so convincing as this sickening psychopath. Isn't it interesting how that happens to actors? I've always been fascinated by the tendency audiences and studios have of only viewing an actor as one thing and nothing else. It's ridiculous, really, but you see it all the time. Anyway, Andy was my choice to play Kennedy as the producers never forced actors on you. I could cast whomever I wanted and nobody objected to Andy.

I find it's occasionally a dangerous proposition for an actor to play a famous person—particularly a Kennedy—onscreen. They are riding that careful line between the impersonation of a recognizable figure that has lived and their interpretation of the character as written. I think JFK is often one of those people where it's a question of whether or not there is too much of an impersonation in the actor's performance or not quite enough. When an actor goes over the top with the New England/Boston accent they can start sounding like Mayor Quimby on *The Simpsons*! That's not a good thing within the remits of serious drama or science fiction— not that I'm making a distinction between the two. Fortunately, I think Andy was good. He looked something like Kennedy, which always helps, and he had the voice down. Again, when you are doing these kinds of well known historical figures it's not like doing Julius Caesar or Jesus Christ. We know exactly what JFK looks and sounds like, how he moved, how he wore his hair, because there's a wealth of archival footage out there that we can view. I'm sure Andy did his research, but it can sometimes be hard to get these things right because the audience carries certain expectations.

An integral scene in "Profile in Silver" was going to be the Dallas motorcade. When we were preparing to restage that event, I carefully studied the stock footage and planned the shots out so that they would inter-cut together. We only used a few brief clips, so we didn't dwell on anything too long. Needless to say, the Zapruder Film, which shows the bullets smashing into Kennedy's head and body, was far too grisly to include. You'll notice that due to network restrictions on violence during the assassination scene that appears later in the story, Lane Smith simply jerks spasmodically and we see no trace of blood or brain matter. The Zapruder footage was not as readily viewable back then as it is today. I mean, you can now go online and examine the bullet hits in forensic detail. But it's such a fascinating historical document, perhaps the most remarkable in existence in terms of the magnitude of the event it captures. When we were shooting the motorcade sequence I decided to venture into what would look like documentary coverage of the event, like the moment when the cameraman falls down with the camera and that kind of stuff. I thought that worked and added to the sense of fear and confusion the bystanders felt that day. Having incorporated stock footage into my previous films, I think it's harder in this instance to detect the difference in quality between our footage and the stock footage. It was all pretty seamless. We also had a few antique cars and the costumes to really sell it. We also used an additional stock footage shot of The White House for one brief establishing shot.

The removal of the second assassin from Schulman's script at the insistence of CBS executives meant very little to me as I don't personally ascribe to any of the conspiracy theories surrounding JFK's death. Some of them are highly ridiculous and some of them are more plausibly argued. I can understand why certain people believe in them, particularly the idea that there was more than one assassin present that fateful day— one in the Texas School Depository Building and another on the grassy knoll. I'm not certain, but I do feel it was just Oswald, the lone gunman, that killed the President and he did not conspire with others. I mean, the crazy lone wolf is a potent weapon as we now know from examining all kinds of shootings and assassination attempts throughout history. I think it's another element that ensures this whole unfortunate business lives on in the American consciousness. It feeds the conspiracy theorists. Dropping that element of the story and restricting it to just one assassin also simplified and streamlined things as we were trying to get this story in at just under thirty minutes and didn't want any unnecessary diversions.

For the later scene where Kennedy arrives at Dallas Love Field Airport and meets Fitzgerald before they board Air Force One, we shot that entirely with a handheld camera. I don't think handheld camera was employed very much by some of the other directors on *The Twilight Zone* (with the possible exception of Billy Friedkin) but I felt it gave the sequence more urgency and immediacy. My previous episodes had been shot by Brad May, but I worked with a different cinematographer on "Profile in Silver." Chuck Arnold was the cameraman and he was also good, very imaginative and amenable. I thought the documentary look for the airport stuff would go with the "stock-a-mentary" look we'd devised for the Dallas Motorcade sequence. Chuck agreed that the handheld approach was the way to go, and he was willing to try it. Actually, in my dealings with Brad May on "Kentucky Rye" and "If She Dies", I discovered he was not a handheld guy. Brad liked to use a dolly and a crane, and get a smoother and more controlled look. We had a lot of scenes to get through on "Profile in Silver" but we didn't use the handheld camera out of necessity—meaning we did it for reasons of speed and efficiency. It was purely an aesthetic choice.

> *The segment builds to an affecting climax. Kennedy and Livingstone discover that Fitzgerald is from the future after finding his silver coin with the President's face engraved on it after he drops it aboard Air Force One (it is against U.S. policy for any living American to have their image on money). They also learn that Fitzgerald's camera is not what it appears to be as Government metallurgists cannot open the device or determine what it is made of. Under questioning Fitzgerald tells Kennedy and Livingstone the truth, demonstrating that the camera is a holographic recorder. Kennedy theorizes that Fitzgerald was sent back to 1963 to observe the fraught events of the Berlin Crisis, but the time traveler reveals that he had no knowledge of it. The President then realizes to his horror that Fitzgerald came to Dallas to witness his assassination. Bravely resigning himself to his fate, Kennedy decides to restore the original timeline and perish as history recorded. However, Fitzgerald slips his time ring on the President's finger transporting him to the future. Aided by Livingstone, Fitzgerald then travels back in time to November 22, 1963, and assumes Kennedy's place and identity in the motorcade. Moments later, he is shot and fatally killed.*

> *"Profile in Silver" finally ends with a coda depicting a man in futuristic garb with a familiar Boston accent addressing a classroom of Harvard students in the year 2172. The subject of his rousing lecture concerns the sacrifices of honorable men in difficult times, and we see it is being delivered by none other than John F. Kennedy. Aside from a brief establishing exterior shot of Harvard University in the 22nd century, Hancock executes this final scene in one uninterrupted tracking shot that begins with a glimpse of Fitzgerald's time ring and ends with the reveal of Kennedy's face. Schulman's script originally climaxed with the students rising to their feet to applaud the speaker, accompanied by a cursory narration that simply stated: "A fitting tribute of the sort only to be found in…The Twilight Zone."*

Like "Kentucky Rye" before it, "Profile in Silver" presented another small problem in finding a way to best end the episode without it being clumsy or repetitive. You do that by experimenting, by trying out one or two different things, and then deciding what works best. When I first read Schulman's script, I seem to remember thinking that the final scene would work best in one continuous shot where we see the students of the future sitting in the classroom and then we finally unveil Kennedy's face at the podium. I mean, the viewer already knows that it's JFK because the voice is unmistakable and we see the time ring, but I still felt it was more satisfying to draw that reveal out without a cut and just let it flow without interruption. I probably did get a shot of the students rising to their feet to applaud the President—just to cover myself—but I was happy with the way it worked. I'm sure Phil understood that this was one of those rare instances in *The Twilight Zone* (along with "If She Dies") where we didn't require the closing narration. It might have worked out okay, and I'm sure Phil tried the narration in post-production as it was just one line, but we didn't need it. The speech was enough. It was more than enough.

One of the questions we could have asked ourselves is why the authorities of the future would have permitted a relative or descendent of Kennedy to go back in time and observe the assassination in the first place. Surely they'd have realized that such a thing would have been a potentially damaging and emotive assignment for any time traveler to undertake? Certainly, that addition gave Schulman a sound dramatic excuse for having Fitzgerald interrupt the established flow of time, even if you think it doesn't bear much scrutiny. More than that, perhaps we shouldn't let these kinds of questions get in the way of a good story—and "Profile in Silver" is a very good story. It's rather immodest of me to say, but I think it's one of the best *Twilight Zone* episodes ever made. There are so many things going for it, one of them being the great score composed by Basil Poledouris. That was a hell of catch there as he had written the music for *Conan the Barbarian*, *RoboCop* and *The Hunt for Red October*. I thought Poledouris was wonderful and he wrote some emotive music.

> "Profile in Silver" *had been awarded a shooting schedule of ten days and a generous budget of more than $900,000, making it one of the more expensive* Twilight Zone *productions. In spite of this expenditure and their initial reluctance to proceed with the story, CBS were ultimately delighted with the finished episode. Indeed, the hour containing Hancock's segment was the only one the network ran three times in prime time before the 1980s incarnation of* The Twilight Zone *went to syndication (where it was repeated many more times in subsequent years).*

"Profile in Silver" has proven to be influential. There was the recent novel and miniseries *11/22/63* written by Stephen King that involved a man traveling back in time to 1963 in an attempt to prevent Kennedy's assassination. Just as in my episode, this honest intervention by the hero of King's story proves to be disastrous for the future of mankind. Several years before *11/22/63* even appeared as a book, I went to a film festival in Muskegon, Michigan about ten years ago and encountered a director there from Detroit. He handed me a copy of a screenplay he'd written and I discovered it was a total rip-off of "Profile in Silver." In fact, it wasn't a screenplay; it was a movie that was playing at the festival! After watching this movie I approached him, and said, "Hey, this film is very much like an episode of *The Twilight Zone* I directed in 1986 called "Profile in Silver."" He said, "Yes, it is. Yeah, that's where I got the idea. I stole it." He just spoke those words like it was no big deal. I do remember that rather than being embarrassed or concerned about it, he was impressed and excited to learn that he was talking to the guy who'd made it. I don't know how Schulman feels about this movie, or if he's even aware of it. I recently heard talk that Schulman and others are planning on doing their own feature film version of "Profile in Silver." It's such a rich and emotional story with so many possible avenues to explore, it doesn't surprise me. I'll be very interested to see the movie if it ever comes out.

> *Costing less than its predecessor, the fourth of Hancock's* Twilight Zone *episodes, "The Library", aired on March 28, 1986. The third of a three-segment hour that opened with Gus Trikonis's "Take My Life…Please!" and continued with Ben Bolt's "The Devil's Alphabet," the story concerns Ellen Pendleton (France Conroy), an aspiring writer in need of money who is hired to work at a vast private library run by Gloria (Uta Hagen). Ellen is warned by Gloria not to read the contents of the books as such a practice is strictly forbidden by her unseen employers. Disregarding this advice, curiosity overtakes Ellen one day after she notices that each volume has the name of a person inscribed on it. Ellen quietly opens up one of the tomes and discovers that they are detailed up-to-the-second descriptions of every person's daily lives on earth. When Ellen later arrives at the apartment she shares with her sister Lori (Lori Petty), she is disturbed by the activities of her noisy neighbors Edwin (Alan Blumenfeld) and Carla (Candy Azzara). The following day she decides to administer her revenge by rewriting a chapter in Edwin's book so that he is now a priest who abstains from physical relations with women. However, when she arrives home that night she finds Lori comforting a despairing Carla who is on the verge of a breakdown due to her terrible loneliness.*
>
> *The next day, Ellen is determined to remedy this situation and rewrites the latest chapter in Carla's book so that she is happily married to Doug (Joe Santos), one of her more benign neighbors. This too ends disastrously as Doug reveals he is bankrupt from all the gifts he has bought Carla. Ellen then rewrites Doug's book so that he is wealthy, but this in turn goes wrong when she later learns that he is now the landlord of the building and has unfairly increased the rent of all his tenants. In an effort to remove herself from this tangled milieu, Ellen rewrites her own book and relocates herself and Lori to a house*

by the sea. Finally believing she has achieved peace and contentment, she comes home from work to discover that her sister has drowned in the ocean while attempting to rescue a little boy. Distraught, she rushes back to the library and confesses to Gloria that she has been tampering with the books. Enraged and fearful of what her "employers" will think, Gloria orders Ellen to collect all the volumes she has interfered with before ushering her out of the library as the ominous peel of a bell shakes the building. To her relief and amazement, Ellen is met outside by Lori who is alive and well. She rings the doorbell of the library to apologize to Gloria for her actions, but is greeted by an unknown man who claims he has been living at this residence for ten years.

"The Library" shared certain surface similarities with "Profile in Silver." Both stories deal with time and a central character faced with the temptation to interfere and change present and future events. So, it was another exploration of the perils of messing with things beyond our control and understanding. To a certain extent, I think "The Library" was warning the audience: "Do not mess with fate! If you do, you'll be sorry!" One of the strengths of the episode was its suggestion that one's destiny is perhaps pre-ordained or inescapable; whereas "Profile in Silver" has a character actually sacrificing themselves in order to maintain the events of history and preserve the future of mankind. I thought the idea of a huge library that contained the continuing, ever-evolving life stories of every human being on the planet was a rather novel idea. The whole notion that one could directly alter one's own reality is a very interesting thought because it's another wish fulfillment thing. How many people have longed for such a thing to be possible? How many feel they've been dealt a rough hand in life and wish they could somehow change the deck? I know I have and I'm sure you have, too. It's only human to think that way. You have the character of this young woman who discovers a new and easy way in which she can change her life, and the lives of those around her. But, in true *Twilight Zone* tradition, she learns that it comes with a price. "The Library" isn't as bleak or as sad as "Profile in Silver." It's a little more upbeat, playful and gentle. But it hasn't got as much dramatic meat for that same reason, even though we are hopefully invested in this woman and feel the difficult predicaments she finds herself placed in from tampering with reality.

When we were casting "The Library" I believe I initially had a different actress in mind to play the role of Ellen Pendleton. I don't recall who it was now, or the reasons why this person couldn't do the episode, but Frances Conroy was not my first choice. I think she was suggested to me by the casting director who said she would be wonderful in the part. I thought in this instance I would go along with that suggestion as we were getting fairly close to our start date, but I ended up liking Frances a lot, too. She had just the right vulnerable qualities that were needed for the character and she also had a believable chemistry with Lori Petty, who played her sister. I don't recall how Lori came to my attention (she may have also been suggested to me), but I was happy with her. Both Lori and Frances have gone on to enjoy good careers but very little was known about them when I cast them in *The Twilight Zone*.

Uta Hagen on the other hand was very well known. By this time she'd maintained a long career on stage and screen, and was greatly respected in the business. Uta had written a well-received book on acting and had won various awards including the Tony. I was eager to cast her as the woman who runs the library as I thought she was the right age and had the right qualities needed—that balance of delicacy and authority. Before we started shooting, I'd heard that Uta had the unfortunate capacity of being "very difficult." Eric Bentley had once told me he'd had terrible trouble with Uta when they did the production of Brecht's *The Good Woman of Szechwan* on Broadway in 1955. Uta had played Shen Te opposite Zero Mostel as Shu Fu the Barber, and she had not been easy to deal with. Eric had not enjoyed the experience of working with her at all and found her demanding. I could have been forgiven for anticipating there'd be some problems with her, but I really wanted to work with Uta and we got along splendidly during filming. She took direction well and seemed happy to be there. Uta was a terrific actress and I liked the way she paused with emphasis each time she mentioned "her employers." I suppose they were meant to be the Advisory Board of Heaven, or God's angels, or whatever unseen force was behind it all. Uta's pauses are probably a little bit too much—she was primarily a theater actress let's not forget—but I liked them. She seemed to enjoy the subject matter and found it stimulating, so I didn't fret about it. It's an episode of *The Twilight Zone*, so you don't always have to be subtle and restrained about every little thing.

I feel "The Library" is a very lean and linear story and that's not a bad thing. *The Twilight Zone* segments varied in terms of their length from under ten minutes to more than thirty, but I think "The Library" was just the right length. It kind of worked within the parameters of its simple concept. I don't think we cut anything from the script to make it smoother and faster. I don't remember Anne Collins, the writer of the teleplay, at all. I don't think I had as much, or possibly any, contact and interaction with her as I had enjoyed with some of the other writers on the show. If I had, I would have brought a loose end in the story to her attention: if Ellen works in the library her time there will be recorded in the book of her life. So, when Ellen eventually dies, Gloria's "employers" would no doubt read this material when determining her "final chapter" and will know about all her indiscretions anyway. That thought never occurred to me when we were making the episode. I don't recall any scenes being cut during the editing phase. In fact, we never had to trim any of the episodes I directed in order to fit them into the hour of programming. Not that I remember. I think each episode was written concisely.

Conversely, I don't think any of the segments had to be padded either, which sometimes happens. Having the three-episode presentation, everything had to be fairly exacting anyway during the writing, shooting and editing. I can say that Phil never made any dictations to me about length requirements for the stories I directed. Incidentally, *The Twilight Zone* was my first experience of working with Video Assist and digital editing. This was before Avid was available, so we were using a different and somewhat primitive digital editing system. Inevitably, this resulted in certain technical problems that we encountered during post-production. For example, it was very laborious and tricky doing dialogue overlaps. Thankfully, they later improved the technology with the next generation, so Avid was much better than the days when we were toiling on *The Twilight Zone*. All *The Twilight Zone* episodes that CBS made were originally shot on film, and then transferred to video and edited on video. I can't speak for the other directors who worked on the show, but I actually liked that process.

Of all *The Twilight Zone* episodes I directed, "The Library" is probably the one I remember the least about—certainly in terms of the day-to-day stuff. I haven't seen it for many years. Indeed, I probably haven't seen it since its original broadcast in the mid-1980s. I bought a collection of *The Twilight Zone* series recently, but I still haven't looked at that particular episode. I don't know why, because I remember liking it when I saw it. I think the actual shoot itself was a little more anonymous and perfunctory than some of the other episodes I made. It quickly passed without incident as a lot of TV work does. I can remember thinking that "The Library" could have been a little punchier, and perhaps darker. It may have benefited from a more downbeat ending like the climax of "Kentucky Rye"—well, maybe not quite *that* dark, but a shade darker. I mean, Frances' character basically gets away with it in the end. She isn't punished for all the trouble she's caused. Maybe she is just left to learn some great cosmic lesson, I don't know, but perhaps her sister should have remained dead at the end. If that price was a little too much, maybe it would have been nice if there was some lingering trace of Ellen's tampering in her current reality. Maybe her sister now has a false leg or hates the water—something that gives the story a little added kick at the end; a lingering warning. If "The Library" had been one of my movies I would have done that without hesitating. As I said, you did occasionally get an opportunity to change things in the scripts on *The Twilight Zone*, but when you are working so fast—unless something is egregious or you are getting terrible trouble from some actor on a particular line—you are inclined to just steam ahead and shoot it as written.

> *Hancock's final contribution to* The Twilight Zone *is* "The Saucer of Loneliness," *which opened the second season of the show on September 27, 1986 alongside Jim McBride's wistful time travel story* "The Once and Future King." *Based on the acclaimed short story by Theodore Sturgeon, which had first appeared in the February 1953 issue of* Galaxy Science Fiction *magazine under the title* "A Saucer of Loneliness," *the story concerns a lonely woman named Margaret (deftly played by Shelley Duvall) who works as a waitress at a Los Angeles diner. One morning, while walking to work, she spies a small, glowing flying saucer in the sky. The craft pursues Margaret, hovering directly above her, relaying a private message moments before she collapses in a dead faint. Upon regaining consciousness, she tells a crowd of onlookers that the mysterious saucer "spoke" to her. In the wake of divulging this information, Margaret becomes something of a celebrity. She is hounded by people who want to know the contents of the message or suspect that she now has the God-given power to heal the sick. Embarrassed by the unwanted attention, her alcoholic mother (Nan Martin, making the second of two appearances for Hancock) throws her out of the house. In*

> *desperation, Margaret scrawls notes which she places in bottles and hurls into the ocean. Finally, one night, she decides to commit suicide by walking into the waves, but is rescued from death by an equally lonely man (Richard Libertini) who reveals that the saucer's message was one of loneliness and hope.*

I don't remember what elements of "The Saucer of Loneliness" initially attracted me to the story. I do recall thinking it offered an original take on the theme of UFOs and alien encounters, something that has been exhausted in science fiction over the decades. What I liked about the script was it offered a quiet meditation on loneliness and isolation in our world, and I think Shelley Duvall's performance as the lonely woman captures that. I must be honest in admitting that my attachment to "The Saucer of Loneliness" came more from the possibilities of working with the actors, particularly Shelley and Richard Libertini, than it did from my adapting the work of a celebrated science fiction author—in this instance Theodore Sturgeon. I think that was true of all my *Twilight Zone* episodes, actually. What appealed to me about doing "If She Dies" was the opportunity to work with Tony Lo Bianco, whose work I had always admired, not the script. We managed to get Shelley to play the lonely woman and that was quite a prestigious catch at the time, I must say. Shelley was a highly-regarded actress and had previously worked with people like Stanley Kubrick and Robert Altman. Interestingly, I do recall that she had a kind of consequential air about her on the set and regarded herself as an important person. It was the way she carried herself and spoke to people that gave me that impression. It wasn't that she was in any way unfriendly or obstinate, not at all. As a matter of fact, she and I got along very well. I would have gladly worked with her again as she was an extremely talented actress. Now that I think about it, I tried to get another project on with her shortly after *The Twilight Zone*. I forget now what it was, but it never happened.

    I remember watching the making of documentary on *The Shining* and seeing Shelley butting heads with Kubrick. My sympathies were with Shelley as I don't treat actors the way Kubrick did. I just don't do that. Even if she was being demanding or was attention-seeking, you find a better way to negotiate the problem. On *The Twilight Zone*, I think Shelley was not overly happy to be doing a science fiction television show. Perhaps she felt a quiet sense of slumming. If you look at "The

Saucer of Loneliness" you'll see it's a very human story rooted in very real emotions. It's unlike some of the other *Twilight Zone* segments I saw that spotlighted the effects and the fantasy elements more prominently. Aside from the saucer itself, it's really an intimate character study and that may have been Shelley's doing, actually. I don't know this for a fact, but I suspect she may have insisted that some of the fantasy aspects of the script be reduced before agreeing to do the episode. I may be wrong about that, but somehow I did get that impression. I really don't know the extent of Shelley's interest in science fiction. Maybe it equates somewhat with my own.

Richard Libertini immediately entered my mind for the lonely man when I read the script. He has this warmth about him, although he looks a little wild and woolly. I just saw Richard's face for the part, just as I saw Nan Martin's face for the lonely woman's mother. Obviously, Nan plays a very different character in "The Saucer of Loneliness" to the one she played in "If She Dies." I've always thought that Nan had this wonderful, haunted face that could look at various times either compassionately inviting or unnervingly sinister. She has such an interesting and strange face, and you can see how malleable it is in the two roles she did for me. I mean, she went from playing a nun to this total harridan. Nan was wonderful to work with; very easygoing and positive. We had kind of known each other a little bit from New York, or at least we thought we did, and that made our relationship easier. I was happy with what she and Richard gave me. As I told you, I really had no sense of the budgets on *The Twilight Zone*. I wasn't aware, for instance, that "Profile in Silver" was more expensive than most of the other episodes I directed. I don't know if all the actors were paid the same or not as I wasn't in on the contract negotiations. They probably weren't. Certainly, they would have paid more for Shelley Duvall, Richard Libertini and Tony Lo Bianco than they paid for Frances Conroy, Lori Petty and Jeffrey DuMunn. Maybe Phil DeGuere reserved the best roles for the best actors.

> *Adapted by David Gerrold, the teleplay of* "The Saucer of Loneliness" *features several marked differences from Theodore Sturgeon's story. Aside from altering the title slightly, the character of Margaret is just seventeen years-old when she first encounters the saucer and is not the middle-aged spinster portrayed by Duvall. Also, the timeframe of the original story spans several years and is narrated from*

> the perspective of the lonely man. Another addition by Gerrold is the appearance of the glowing orb at the climax, an idea that met with Hancock's approval.

I did not read Sturgeon's short story before we started filming, and I still haven't, so I'm not aware of the differences between his tale and the finished episode. I do find it interesting to know that Sturgeon's story is told from the point of view of the lonely man on the beach as he makes such a late appearance in the teleplay, coming in at the end as he does. I also didn't know that the glowing orb was a new addition to the narrative, but I liked that idea. It's a very direct and visual way for Shelley's character to suddenly open up to this man, a stranger who has just saved her life. She is giving him the one thing she has kept for herself and, in doing so, can perhaps find love and companionship. She can now start her life over again with this man who knows how she feels. I liked the idea of the messages in the bottles, as the saucer itself is something of a galactic message in a bottle. I also liked the truthful poetry and humanity and hope of the message the lonely woman places in the bottles.

> There is in certain living souls
> a quality of loneliness unspeakable,
> so great it must be shared
> as company is shared by lesser beings.
> Such loneliness is mine; so know by this
> that in immensity
> there is one lonelier than you.

I think the way the story reserves that hopeful message for the climax works rather nicely, don't you think? I imagine that sense of mystery and anticipation gives the episode a more haunting and resonant quality. It makes the viewer long to know what the secret of the saucer is. Just as the millions of people around the world want the lonely woman to give up the secret of what the saucer told her, I suppose we want her to give it up, too. We want to know because, naturally, we're curious. If "The Saucer of Loneliness" works at all it should make the audience feel that way. What Shelley's character receives is a gift, but it's a gift from *The Twilight Zone*. So, it's another of those gifts that comes with a price—in this case the gift of instant celebrity. So, ironically, although people now know her, she is more alone than ever. Can you imagine if such a thing happened today—a woman given a message from aliens? It would be seismic for sure; filmed by hundreds of camera-phones, and uploaded and shared and broadcast around the world in minutes. Undoubtedly, it would cause wonder and terror in equal measure.

On *The Twilight Zone* episodes the shooting schedule generally ran to something like five or six days, certainly not ten days ("Profile in Silver" must have been an exception). "The Saucer of Loneliness" was more involved and more detailed than say "Kentucky Rye" or "The Library" as we had a lot of exteriors and special effects to do. There was also a number of night-shoots on "Saucer" that proved very difficult and time-consuming. I hate shooting nights and just reading the script I quickly realized it required a fairly big night-shoot. Whenever I think of doing the episode I immediately remember filming the climactic scenes on the beach when Shelley's character is pulled from the surf by Libertini, who suddenly comes running out of the darkness. We shot those scenes by the Santa Monica Pier and those nights were incredibly cold and uncomfortable. I'd learned on *California Dreaming* how surprisingly chilly it could get shooting at night in California, but it must have been particularly distressing for Shelley and Richard as they both had to get their clothes and hair soaking wet. They were both real troupers about it and didn't complain much. We had a lot of dialogue to get through in that sequence and it was tough for them.

Another reason I don't like to shoot at night is because it interrupts my practice of going to bed early and getting up the following morning early. That's just how my body and mind are set, and it's difficult for me to mentally and physically readjust. I also think—and this is a far greater problem—that you generally get about two-thirds as much effort and concentration from the crew during night-shoots as you get from them during day-shoots. In my experience, I've often found that they are not always as focused and as energized as they are during the daylight hours. Also, people start drinking alcohol sometimes during night-shoots and that can be very detrimental and unfortunate. I told you of another rather painful lesson I learned on *California Dreaming* when the camera crew got drunk that one night and forgot to put film in the camera. This is the kind of crazy stuff that can happen. Fortunately, nothing remotely that crazy happened during our nights on "The Saucer of Loneliness." There wasn't enough time to sneak off for a drink as there was too much to do.

I didn't feel that the visual effects of the flying saucer itself were especially successful, but they were okay for the budget we had at our disposal. The show had these basic light effects they would do that were primitive by today's standards. We did one where we created the glowing orb that Shelley reveals to Richard, but I wasn't present in post-production to oversee the creation of those effects. Well, maybe I was there for a little bit, but I would have liked to have supervised the saucer and orb sequences more closely—particularly the saucer scene. I had shot some stuff which was from the point-of-view of the saucer as it chased after Shelley on the beach. I knew we were going to have something in the shot, perhaps a section of the craft, but I didn't know it was going to look like it eventually did: a rather nondescript luminous object hovering about her. There was a rush in trying to get the episode finished for its impending airdate as "The Saucer of Loneliness" was the first episode of that second season. So, it needed to be ready and I believe CBS had an in-house visual effects company do the saucer effects. Whatever the reason was I'm not entirely happy with what we got. You see, is the saucer a machine made out of some extraterrestrial alloy or is it a living thing? Or is it a mixture of both? I don't know. That detail is probably not that important. On *The Twilight Zone*, there was not much you could do in terms of the visual effects and the work was often executed before you'd even had a chance to see it. That's just the way things were done and I had to accept it. But I think the saucer could and should have been a lot better as it was a pivotal element of the story.

Despite the dodgy effects, I do like "The Saucer of Loneliness." It's a nice, leisurely-paced story. There are one or two shots of Shelley walking along the beach that drag on for far too long. I don't know if there was a time problem there and we needed to stretch one or two scenes out a little more (I realize this conflicts with what I told you earlier about not "padding" any segments). If I could go back now I'd trim a few shots, but I always say that the demands of pacing have changed so much. In my defense, I could argue that those interminable shots are easily selling the feeling that the lonely woman's existence is mundane and monotonous. Would you buy that? I hope so. I should add that the dedication to Theodore Sturgeon that appears at the end—Sturgeon died in 1985 shortly before we went into production—was not my idea. It was probably Phil DeGuere who did that, as he and his creative team were students of science fiction and all who practiced it. "The Saucer of Loneliness" was the only episode I directed in the second season. That may have been because *Weeds* was beginning to move forward at this time and I also replaced Hal Ashby on *8 Million Ways to Die*. I don't remember the exact chronology of these events, but I believe those three things all happened fairly close together. So, I wasn't able to do anymore of *The Twilight Zone*, but I enjoyed my time on the show and I look back on it with great fondness. The main reason for that is undoubtedly Phil. He was such a good guy.

> *In its first season,* The Twilight Zone *had been scheduled for eight o'clock on Friday nights, facing tough competition from several more established shows. DeGuere had lobbied CBS for a ten o'clock slot, fearing that the series was too dark and disturbing for the family audience, but his request was denied. Network executives were delighted with the strong ratings for the show's first few episodes, but viewing figures steadily began to drop over the following five months. Despite not garnering the critical praise and commercial success of its iconic predecessor, CBS renewed* The Twilight Zone *for a second season. However, the network removed the show from its Friday night slot and shuffled it around various times and dates, effectively killing any chance it had. Several weeks into its sophomore season, the show was predictably cancelled due to low ratings. In 1988, a third season appeared in syndication under the guidance of executive producers Mark Shelmerdine and Michael MacMillan. A further thirty stories (most of them staid and derivative) were then filmed in Canada on reduced budgets and were screened with the eighty stories from the 1985-87 series.*

Looking back, I was pleased with all my episodes but if I had to pick a particular favorite it would be "Profile in Silver." Along with "The Saucer of Loneliness," it had the strongest concept and richest characters. As far as where *The Twilight Zone* stands among the rest of my television credits, I would say that overall I found it less interesting than my work on *Hill Street Blues*, but more interesting than my work on *Cover Up*, *I Had Three Wives*, *Lady Blue* and *Dellaventura*. The experience was neither as edifying nor as satisfying as *Hill Street Blues*, and the style in which *The Twilight Zone* episodes were shot was not as uniform. Also, *Hill Street Blues* was shot and edited on film, so they retained that look and texture that *The Twilight Zone* may have lost due to being edited on video. When you look at those *Zone* episodes today, do they look grainy or like they went through some unfortunate video process? I'd like to hear people's judgment on that. The question I now ask myself is this: was the cut video from the editing machine broadcast, or was the film negative cut so that it conformed to what was on the editing machine? Also, were the broadcast materials then made from a print from that conformed negative? I think the latter is what happened, but I could be wrong. Anyway, just working on *The Twilight Zone* was a lot of fun, and the fact that each segment dealt with the scary and the fantastic rather than the realities of the world, always made each of them interesting and challenging.

One of the strengths of the original series was, of course, Rod Serling who made huge contributions to the show not only as creator and host, but by the fact he wrote more episodes than anybody else. Someone once told me that Serling was a great fan of *Let's Scare Jessica to Death*. Apparently, he went around recommending it to everyone. I would have enjoyed the opportunity of telling Serling how much I admired his work. What I think is interesting about *The Twilight Zone* is that, in a way, Serling accessed a darkness and a climate that was perhaps unavailable to Phil DeGuere. What I mean is, Serling was a very serious man and I'm not saying that Phil wasn't, but I don't think the second incarnation of *The Twilight Zone* had the same profoundly thoughtful quality that the first show had. The original arrived at a tumultuous time in our history of great social, political and cultural upheaval. There was also the sheer novelty and newness of *The Twilight Zone* back in the early 1960s. Today, we see a lot of anthology shows that are interchangeable and have no real identity or personality. Serling *was* the face and voice of *The Twilight Zone*. As soon as you saw or heard him, you were immediately transported and knew exactly what you were watching. I think the second show lacked that kind of iconic presence.

Additionally, I believe that Serling was a soldier before he became a writer and the shadow of World War II falls over his *Twilight Zone*, as maybe the shadow of Vietnam falls over Phil's *Twilight Zone*. In fairness, I don't think you can say that the second show lacked the social and political commentary of the original series. It was in there, but I don't know if Phil's writers had any direct experience of war. I'd be interested to find out. Another thought I have about Serling has to do with The Theatre of Cruelty, the invention of the crazy/brilliant Antonin Artaud. At one point in his madness, and confined in a French institution, Artaud felt natives in the Amazon Basin were trying to measure the distance between his navel and his anus. However, in a sane moment, he said one of the important functions of theater was to teach you that the sky can fall on your head.

I'm sure he knew nothing about it, but it seems to me that Serling was a subconscious adherent to The Theatre of Cruelty, and Phil DeGuere wasn't. But I still like Phil's incarnation a lot. I just feel that—as good as it is—it's probably doomed to forever reside in the shadow of Serling's original.

Another problem with the second *Twilight Zone* might have been the format. I don't believe audiences welcomed having three different stories in the same hour. I think it worked better in the past when Serling's show featured one story in one half-hour episode as opposed to three stories in one one-hour episode. People don't want to suddenly get used to a new story with new characters and a new setting; they want to continue with the one story and the same characters and I think Phil's show was always battling against that. I don't think the portmanteau structure was effective on *The Twilight Zone*, and the Achilles heel of the anthology format is you will almost always have at least one weak chapter.

It occurs to me now that it would have been interesting to have done some episodes of Phil's show in black and white, although impractical and potentially confusing for most of the TV audience. Naturally, Phil was trying to create his own show and going down that route would have been steering too closely to the look and atmosphere of Serling's series. But there were no new black and white shows on American television in the mid-1980s, just as I don't believe there are any now. It would have been interesting to have done an individual episode in black and white as a nostalgic nod back to the past. Something like "Profile in Silver", which was mostly a period piece, or "Kentucky Rye", which was an atmospheric little horror story, would have made interesting stylistic exercises. This is why there's something great about guys like Rod Serling and Billy Friedkin, guys that have a fearless quality. It's that unbottled aggression certain creative people have that I think the show needed a little more of. It needed to be edgier and darker, but I don't think a lot of television shows back then were permitted to be truly dark and edgy. People had to be a lot more careful in the 1980s, because there were certain restrictions and codes you had to abide by. I'm sure Phil would have liked the freedom to have made a darker show.

If you assess the program within those confines, Phil's *Twilight Zone* was certainly no failure. It produced individual episodes that were really quite brilliant. I do think, all things considered, the show was a success. It's also worth noting that if you go back and look at Serling's show from episode to episode, you'd probably see that overall there were an equal number of weak segments. It's weird how nostalgia can often affect one's judgment. The memory can play tricks on you and things from the past appear better in the memory than they actually are. Maybe Serling's *Twilight Zone* is like that. Maybe it's no better or no worse than our series when you examine it in the cold light of day. I just have this strong suspicion that the old show *is* better. I think Phil and the executives at CBS expected *The Twilight Zone* to be a big success, because of that brand recognition I mentioned. I don't remember the shows we were up against on those Friday nights, but any night in a primetime slot is competitive. I don't recall them pulling *The Twilight Zone* from its Friday night slot, but if CBS did do that then they probably signed the show's death warrant. When you mess around with a timeslot that's already been established, the audience doesn't know where the show's gone. And if they don't know where to find the show, they don't see it. That's when the ratings start to suffer. I suspect that the network probably tired of *The Twilight Zone*. That happens a lot in television, you know.

12 8 Million Ways to Die (1986)

EULOGIZED BY SOME as the "lost genius" of American cinema, Hal Ashby (1936-1988) was one of the radiant lights of the New Hollywood movement that emerged in the mid-to-late 1960s. A liberal-minded filmmaker of uncommon sensitivity and skill, Ashby's first job upon leaving Utah State University was toiling in the RKO mailroom. He gradually worked his way up to becoming an editor, working first as an assistant on the B-Western The Naked Hills *(1956),* before joining the Society of Motion Picture Editors and cutting such films as The Loved One *(1965),* The Cincinnati Kid *(1965)* and Norman Jewison's In the Heat of the Night *(1967), the latter winning him an Academy Award for Best Editing. Jewison then produced Ashby's first feature as director,* The Landlord *(1970), which starred Beau Bridges as the affluent white landlord of an inner city tenement in Brooklyn who plots to evict his Black tenants. Ashby's sophomore effort,* Harold and Maude *(1971), which detailed the unlikely love affair between a death-obsessed young man and a life-obsessed eighty-year-old woman, was a romantic black comedy and existentialist drama that has achieved near-fabled cult status over the last forty-five years.*

It was followed by The Last Detail *(1973), a gritty comedy-drama about two Navy patrolmen who decide to show a naive eighteen-year-old offender a good time on his way to the brig. Ashby's career continued its upward curve with his next two films:* Shampoo *(1975), a droll satire on*

Beverly Hills sexual mores that served as a roguish vanity project for its co-writer/producer/star Warren Beatty, and Bound for Glory *(1976), a hagiography of legendary folksinger Woody Guthrie. His next work, the post-Vietnam melodrama* Coming Home *(1978), was a soapy but affecting three-sided love story that concerned a woman and two Vietnam veterans she loves—one of whom has suffered a paralyzing combat injury. The film won Oscars for its two stars, Jon Voight and Jane Fonda, with Ashby earning a nomination as Best Director.* Being There *(1979), Ashby's final offering of this defining decade, was arguably his most accomplished and ended a remarkable run of fine highly individualistic films. A melancholic satire of American culture and politics, it features a mesmerizing performance by Peter Sellers as the childlike Chance, a middle-aged and illiterate gardener who involuntarily becomes a national celebrity. The four features Ashby managed in the 1980s—with the exception of his documentary* Let's Spend the Night Together *(1983), which followed The Rolling Stones on their 1981 American tour—were all critical and commercial failures, marking a decline in his reputation.*

Ashby's final picture before his death of pancreatic cancer was the crime thriller 8 Million Ways to Die *(1986). Adapted by Oliver Stone from the 1982 novel by Lawrence Block, it starred Jeff Bridges as Matt Scudder, an alcoholic Los Angeles Sheriff's Deputy who fatally shoots a small-time drug dealer in front of the man's wife and children during a narcotics raid. Crumbling in the aftermath of this violent encounter, Scudder's drinking problem exacerbates and his addiction quickly claims his job, his marriage and threatens his life. While attending an AA meeting, Scudder meets a mysterious stranger who invites him to a party at an exclusive gambling club owned by Chance Walker (Randy Brooks), one of his former busts. At the party, Scudder meets Sunny (Alexandra Paul), a dark-haired call girl, and Sarah (Rosanna Arquette), a blonde-haired woman who may or may not be a hooker. Also attending the shindig is Angel Moldonado (Andy Garcia), a drug dealer obsessed with Sarah who it later transpires is in business with Chance.*

Scudder learns that Chance is a pimp and Sunny one of his workers. She begs Scudder to help her get away from Chance, and the former cop is drawn back into the sleazy underworld of vice. Shortly afterwards Sunny is murdered and Scudder crawls back into a bottle, waking up in a drunk ward several days later. Attempting to piece together the events of the last few days (which have implicated both himself and Chance in Sunny's death), a clue throws Scudder into direct conflict with Angel, whom he suspects of the murder.

8 Million Ways to Die *was originally slated for Walter Hill, director of* The Warriors *(1979) and* 48 Hrs *(1982), with Nick Nolte starring as Scudder. After this iteration fell through, producer Steve Roth brokered a deal with PSO (Producers Sales Organization) for Ashby to direct Stone's script with Jeff Bridges, fresh off his Academy Award nomination for* Starman *(1984), headlining as Scudder opposite Jamie Lee Curtis. When Stone was unavailable to revise his draft due to his shooting commitments on* Salvador *(1986), Canadian author R. Lance Hill was brought in to rewrite his script. This was followed by further uncredited revisions made by Robert Towne, acclaimed screenwriter of* Chinatown *(1974), who emphasized the subplot of Scudder's alcohol addiction. Towne even wanted to change the title of the film to* Easy Does It—*a slogan used by members of Alcohol Anonymous—and relocated the action from the New York setting of Block's novels to Los Angeles. Indeed, so extensive was Towne's revision, Ashby considered* Easy Does It *to be an original work and not an adaptation of Block's novel. Coming in at a total cost of $11 million (the initial budget had been projected to be in the region of $13 million), the film wrapped on November 26, 1985, after eighty-six shooting days.*

In his 2009 biography Being Hal Ashby: Life of a Hollywood Rebel, *Nick Dawson notes that:* "On December 16, 1985, just twenty days after Ashby finished shooting 8 Million Ways to Die, *a five-ton truck arrived at the cutting rooms where [Ashby's editor] Bob Lawrence was working. Producers Sales Organization representatives confiscated the footage and refused Ashby and Lawrence access to the film." This drastic action was taken, according to producer Charles Mulvehill, as PSO feared that Ashby would "take the film to Malibu and cut it as some unreleasable art film." Despite these unfortunate turn of events, Ashby (who had spent the last two weeks lounging on the beach as Lawrence began assembling the footage) still believed he would be allowed to return and deliver his cut of the picture. His contract stipulated that he had full creative control over post-production and PSO could not interfere until Ashby had completed three cuts. This provision was either ignored by executives, or apparently meant nothing, as Stuart Pappé was duly hired to edit the footage. This led to Lawrence's departure from the production, although he was invited to remain involved with the picture. Shortly before Christmas 1985, as Pappé was preparing a cut for PSO, it was decided that a series of re-shoots would be required to augment and explain the meandering plot. With the "Eastwood Rule" coming into play as it had done on* Wolfen, *Hancock was once again brought in to fulfill the DGA requirement that prohibited a producer or actor from firing the director and taking over the directing of the motion picture.*

My involvement with 8 Million Ways to Die came directly through Stuart Pappé, whom I'd met back when he was one of the editors brought in on *Wolfen*. He and I had become firm friends on that movie and we'd enjoyed working together regardless of the pressures we'd faced. I believe Stuart had replaced Bob Lawrence on 8 Million Ways to Die, who was originally Hal Ashby's editor on the picture, after Ashby had been fired by PSO after principal photography had finished. Mark Damon and John Hyde, the guys running PSO, were then looking for a director to come in and "repair" what Ashby had done, as they were concerned about the current state of the film. Stuart had said to them, "You know, John Hancock is a friend of mine and he did a terrific job on *Wolfen*. Why don't you ask him to come in and finish the movie for you?" I'd had such a positive experience with Stuart previously I was attracted to the opportunity of working with him again. Not only that, there was also the cachet of replacing a major Hollywood director, although, in the end, hardly anyone knows that I worked—however briefly—on 8 Million Ways to Die. I had worked on *Wolfen* for six months, possibly more, I don't remember exactly. In contrast, I ended up working on *8 Million Ways to Die* for a little under two months. I basically came in, shot a couple of scenes and helped Stuart work on the cut, but he was already pretty far along with it by the time I got there. So, all things considered, it was a fairly minor involvement compared with my efforts on *Wolfen*, but it was still an interesting time.

After my own experiences on *Jaws 2* and *Wolfen*, I was well aware of how destructive tensions could arise between directors and studio executives and producers. There can be different approaches, conflicting ideas and personalities, and something always has to give. I knew that when a director is dismissed from a picture the reasons are all placed under the trusted banner of "artistic differences." But I don't believe Ashby's dismissal from *8 Million Ways to Die* made any big headlines at the time. His name was still on the picture as director, so I slipped in under the radar so to speak. I do recall hearing about the hullabaloo of the trucks arriving at the editing rooms and confiscating the footage from Bob Lawrence and not allowing Ashby to do his cut. I remember there was this definite fear that Ashby was going to run away with the movie and do his own thing with it. PSO thought he would simply take the film and disappear, and they would be fucked. Whether Ashby would have actually done that or not, I don't know, but I doubt it. That incident just goes to demonstrate the high level of mistrust and the breakdown of communication that had occurred between Ashby and PSO. This whole scenario brought to mind Blake Edwards' amusing comedy *S.O.B.*, which was about a Hollywood director who does that same thing—steals the negative of a movie from a major studio. Of course, nobody in this case found that idea particularly funny, but there seemed to be a lot unfounded paranoia floating around.

By 1985, I don't think executives had as much confidence in Ashby's abilities as they'd once had. They knew he was uniquely talented, but they always regarded him with a degree of suspicion. Was he truly a commercial filmmaker who could deliver the movie they wanted? That's the question they were asking themselves. Rumors of drug use had also chased Ashby around on his last few pictures, and this production was viewed as being very much part of the cocaine scene. I do think that was one of the factors in Ashby's dismissal. I never witnessed anything personally as I wasn't there, but certain people told me that Hal was on drugs during filming. Now, maybe they had their own reasons for saying such a thing, and I can't corroborate if it's true or not. Contrary to this, I'd heard that Ashby had apparently cleaned up his act (he'd even cut his hair to appear more respectable and employable). I've also subsequently learned that Ashby was experiencing difficulties in finding work and *8 Million Ways to Die* was almost being viewed as the last chance saloon for him. The question I'd like to ask is why someone of his considerable talent was having difficulty finding work? Aside from the drug rumors, I had heard stories that Ashby had spent several long months cutting just one scene in a recent movie of his. Again, how much of that is true and how much is bullshit? I can't answer that. I mean, sure, I was getting a sense from some people that Hal was a borderline personality who was having addiction problems and several other issues, but he was still doing good work. PSO possibly saw Ashby as some kind of loose cannon hippie, whereas a lot of other people saw him as a genius. Okay, fine, but it's possible to be both isn't it?

A lot of things had happened before I got there, things I had no knowledge of but was informed about later. Nor did I ever ask too many questions when I did get there. I just did the job that was asked of me and moved on. Now, officially, I was told that the reason Ashby was axed from the film was because he was "talking all day and not shooting." Apparently, what had happened was Hal had gotten into trouble by involving the actors entirely in making the script better—ostensibly better. He and the principal players such as Jeff Bridges would spend at least the entire morning, and sometimes the whole day, congregating in someone's trailer, dissecting the various scenes and revising them. The PSO people would drop in on the set, see this and be very concerned. In fact, they dropped by so often that Ashby eventually grew irritated as he felt there was some suggestion he was losing control of the movie or was being made to feel that way. The first day I came onboard *8 Million Ways to Die* certain people were quick in telling me, "You know, there were days when Hal shot *nothing*! It would just be people sitting in trailers, talking about the script, and nothing would get done." If what these individuals were saying was true, that's always a serious problem. I think Ashby was under pressure with the schedule and the impending release date, as well as the intrusive presence of PSO on the set.

That said, another of the things I've subsequently learned is Hal was over schedule but only marginally over budget on *8 Million Ways to Die*. I didn't know that at the time I was working on the film, but it suggests to me that PSO overreacted. They were disturbed by Ashby's filmmaking approach, the way he did things. Some people have claimed that Hal was being constantly visited and distracted by the "money men" during shooting; he was apparently questioned about what he was doing and how he was doing it. If that's indeed accurate, I'm sure it placed a lot of undue stress on his shoulders. I was not subjected to similar pressure during my time working on the picture. To a certain extent, it was similar to my situation on *Wolfen* in that when you come in under the specific circumstances that I did, the top brass can't torment you in the same way they messed with the first guy. The company are in trouble and they have to let you do what you need to do in order to put things right, or they are back to square one again. I was the second director on the picture and they had no desire to hire a third. But whatever the reasons for his dismissal were, I do think that Ashby was treated shabbily. He deserved more respect, but I believe that Mark Damon ultimately made a business decision. That's all it was. He did what he felt was right, regardless of whether or not it was just.

Let me be clear though, Mark was somebody whom I liked. He has unusual and unexpected tastes (*9½ Weeks* is his favorite picture of his own, so he's not your ordinary producer!) I'd had dealings with him before I became involved with *8 Million Ways to Die*. Mark had pre-sold the rights to *Weeds* when Robert De Niro was attached to star. When that deal fell apart, Mark had to lose face with all the foreign people he had sold the project to. I wanted to get Mark involved in several other projects I was doing, as aside from liking him personally he is a very capable and powerful guy. I was also friendly with Mark's assistant, too, who at one point optioned (for quite a bit of money) a screenplay I had written called *Fire Music* which was about Adolf Hitler's life as a young art student. Now, it should come as no surprise that Mark wasn't too fond of Ashby. The truth is he had not wanted him to be the director of the project right from the beginning. I understand Mark wanted somebody like Walter Hill, who was more used to doing those kinds of tough action-thrillers involving cops and car chases, and so on. There's no getting around the fact that Ashby was an unlikely choice to direct a violent crime thriller like *8 Million Ways to Die*. The movie lacks the humanity, the offbeat comedy and subversive quality of his other films like *Harold and Maude* and *Being There*. Do you really want to hire the director of *Coming Home*, which is a movie I happen to like a lot, to make a robust picture about a private investigator trying to bust a drug dealer and rescue a hooker?

I remember the producer on the film, Steve Roth, was very well turned out and had the most wonderful shirts (you must understand that shirts are important in Los Angeles). Roth came to the mix, but was a very low-key presence. I believe he was distressed about Hal's firing and had grown a little disillusioned with the project. After all, I understand that it was he who had effectively sold Ashby to PSO. It's not a feather in his or anybody else's cap if they have hired the wrong guy—although I'm not entirely certain that Ashby was in fact the wrong guy. I feel he was more than capable of delivering a great action movie. It's just that maybe it was the wrong set of circumstances and the wrong group of people; an environment in which he couldn't do his best work. I think the constraints of Hollywood filmmaking in the 1980s were not a good fit for Ashby. New Hollywood was dead and the freedoms directors had enjoyed only a few years previously were now rescinded. From a purely personal perspective, I would rather see a Hal Ashby film than a Walter Hill film. I mean, both are fine directors, I just like Ashby's movies more. They are a little more profound and human; the characters are a little more complex and empathetic, and speak to me on a deeper level. It would have been fascinating to have seen Ashby successfully marry his natural quirkiness and individual sensibilities with a commercial Hollywood crime flick. It just didn't work out that way.

There's no doubt that Ashby was desperately wounded about having the picture taken away from him. It must have been devastating for him both professionally and personally. When I first got the job of replacing him, I do recall feeling a lot of sympathy (I had more compassion for Ashby than I'd ever managed for Mike Wadleigh on *Wolfen*). I never actually met Hal in person, but I did ask Mark Damon for his number. I said, "Look, I'd feel a little more comfortable if I could talk to Ashby. I really feel I should call him." Nobody objected to this idea, at least not openly. Hal had been informed by someone of my desire to talk with him, so he was expecting my phone call. We only spoke for about ten minutes. It was a fairly quick chat, the only interaction we had, but I'm glad I made the effort. I began by saying, "I'm sure you know they've asked me to come in and take over the movie. What can I do to help protect your stuff?" Ashby replied in this quiet voice, "Just use your own judgment and do the best you can. That's all I can ask of you. Do what you think is right." I then queried him about what I should avoid doing and who he thought would make good allies for me. Ashby was helpful in that regard. Finally, I told him that I thought he was a wonderful director and how sad I felt it had come to this. That was the truth, too. At one point during our conversation we briefly got onto PSO and Ashby suddenly hissed bitterly, "Those bastards! Those lousy bastards!"

Other than Stuart, I didn't work with any other editors on the film. It was just him and me. Neither were we heavily supervised during the re-shoots and post-production phase, which didn't really surprise me. I mean, when you come in on a movie the studio merely wants you to give your best. You have a clean perspective, so they don't second-guess or judge you. They've already second-guessed and judged the first guy. Instead of firing you or supervising you, they tend to trust you and leave you alone. When I first started working with Stuart on the film, I looked at some of the material that Ashby had shot but not all of it—by the way, Stuart had had no contact with Ashby and was really answering to Mark Damon. When we were reviewing some footage, there was a lot of stuff about Scudder's alcoholism and how it affected his ability to function. Some of this was good, some of it was over-indulgent. Indeed, I seem to have a vague recollection of a "drunken dream" fantasy in which Scudder is deliriously pouring champagne over a hooker. We didn't use any of it. Frankly, it was difficult to assess exactly what Ashby had planned to do when we were cutting. It was a movie that clearly existed in his mind to a large extent and how do you find a key to unlock someone's brain? To what degree we really tried to do this, I don't recall. I suspect we were merely trying to make a picture that we would want to watch. It really was that simple and banal. We just wanted to make something that we liked.

As I said, before I had come in, Stuart had already assembled quite a bit of a cut and didn't want to delve back into the dailies with me to see if there was anything else of value we could use. So, my efforts were much less extensive than they had been on *Wolfen*, in which I reconstituted the dailies entirely and went from there. Several important sequences such as the climactic confrontation between Scudder and Angel were already cut, or were close to being finished, and Stuart was happy with them. I must admit, I was less happy with them, but I didn't feel entirely comfortable pushing Stuart to revisit and re-cut this material as there were concerns about time and money—as there always are, of course. In this instance, I wasn't being hired to rework the entire picture from beginning to end. I was being asked to help make a presentable, workable film both from the material we had to work with and the hastily written additional scenes I was required to shoot. How much of Ashby's excised material would have made his final cut had he been allowed to edit the film, I don't know. The footage I viewed was kind of a mess. Again, I didn't have a strong sense of what he was up to. It was rather diffuse and confusing in places, a little loose and unfocused. So, we tried to clarify the plot a little bit. Stuart and

I also briefly conferred with the actors about their characters, in an effort to get a firmer grasp of the story and decide where it should go.

I believe I may have read Oliver Stone's original draft before coming onboard, but I don't remember anything about it now. I'm actually a huge fan of Stone's work, but I quickly discovered that his draft had been extensively altered by Ashby, Robert Towne and several others. I did peruse a later version of the script while working with Pappé on the editing, as I thought it best to look at the screenplay to try to see what the film was, or had been. It was obvious that Ashby hadn't followed the draft I read and had taken several diversions. I mean, the best screenwriters in Hollywood were working on *8 Million Ways to Die* at various times. PSO had literally employed The A-Team on the project, but maybe there were too many wonderful cooks stooping over the pot as there were still several sizable problems with the narrative. I wasn't familiar with the character of Matt Scudder in the series of books by Lawrence Block, so I had no emotional attachment to the changes that had been made by Stone, Towne or Ashby. I didn't think the script offered anything new from the standard detective story and plot devices, and seemed to me to be somewhat routine in its execution.

Matt Scudder was considered by Block's readers to be the ultimate New York detective. Apparently, Scudder lived and breathed the city in the same way Raymond Chandler's Philip Marlowe is inextricable from Los Angeles. So, the idea of transposing him to L.A. pissed off some of the fans. Again, not being familiar with the character or the novels in which he features, none of this meant anything to me. What I did find interesting was that Ashby had wanted to steer *8 Million Ways to Die* away from the thriller and procedural elements into more profound psychological territory with the whole notion of Scudder being an alcoholic. I think Ashby could relate to the experiences of addiction, and probably wanted to explore that idea more deeply. Scudder is an obsessive character seeking redemption after blowing away this lowly criminal in front of his family in the opening sequence. Ashby probably found an ally in Bob Towne in venturing down that path. Towne had apparently left room for the actors to improvise, so his screenplay was not a complete version in the conventional sense. There were spaces or gaps left for the actors to contribute ideas and dialogue. Very dangerous! This obviously encouraged the cast to work closely with Ashby on the script and fill in those gaps with various pieces of business.

A lot of the actors had signed on for the film because of Ashby as he was viewed, quite rightly, as an actor's director. He had tremendous facility for developing and refining performance, involving actors in the filmmaking process and treating them as artistic equals. However, in this instance, I do feel that Ashby let it get out of control. You can't involve actors in the script beyond a certain point, and I think he went beyond that point and got into trouble. You see, here is what happens when you involve actors too much in revising the dialogue in a script: in highly plotted narratives, which *8 Million Ways to Die* evidently was, there are certain lines that have to be spoken and certain actions that need to be performed by the characters in order for the audience to successfully follow the plot. Those lines are usually fairly obvious and are not necessary on every occasion, but they are not lines that actors want to say. They are merely pieces of exposition and plot-driving dialogue. Now, if you involve actors in the scriptwriting process, they quickly get rid of those lines because they are not always good lines from an emotional or dramatic point of view. They are good lines from a writer's position as they serve the story and help to construct things. But if you excise or alter that expository dialogue you sometimes render the narrative incomprehensible. That was my strong feeling when I first started working on the film and saw what Ashby had shot. Hal, his actors, and probably Bob Towne, too, had done away with everything that allowed you to understand the plot.

In this kind of situation, you tend to fall in love with performance and can't be objective. You can't see what is missing or what needs to go. You drift out of perspective. That's what Mark Damon and PSO were picking up on, and maybe they didn't know what to do to stop it. I don't exactly know how you *can* stop it. I mean, directors have a lot of power if you don't fire them. It's hard to control them on the set and Mark waited until principal photography was finished before getting rid of Ashby. I felt we desperately needed to shoot some additional scenes where certain characters revealed or illustrated what was going on—just to make things comprehensible again. When my name was presented to the cast as the director who would be supervising the additional shooting, it was received fairly warmly. The actors had been fiercely loyal to Ashby and were upset at his dismissal. Nevertheless, they were sufficiently at ease in learning that they were now dealing with another director who was sympathetic to actors and their needs. Some of the cast were already familiar with my work (particularly *Bang the Drum Slowly*) and were also aware of my theater background, so they welcomed the prospect of working with me. That made the transition a little easier. I'd gathered there was a good atmosphere on set with Ashby and the actors had been comfortable and happy with him. So, I strived to keep that same atmosphere for the re-shoots and maintain good relations with everyone.

The first guy I tried to get onside was Jeff Bridges. He was a friend of Hal's and, naturally, had been against his firing. Jeff certainly didn't hold anything against me for my having replaced Ashby, as he understood it was a decision that had come from the top. If it hadn't have been me warming Ashby's chair it would have been some other director. After I started shooting I discovered that Hal had at some point told Jeff, "Do exactly what John Hancock says, but be sure to look at the monitor." This advice was something Jeff endeavored to follow at every opportunity. After each take he would approach me and I would have to play everything back for him. He would scrutinize what we had done, but it was always done in a friendly and constructive way. I never had any run-ins with him at all. I saw no possible advantage in fighting with Jeff and was always happy and willing to accommodate him. I liked what I was getting from him anyway. He is a truly wonderful actor, but I was surprised at how little control Bridges appeared to have over what he did. I believe Jeff had researched the role and attended AA meetings, but on the whole he just *did* it. His performance always had great energy and spontaneity, and I was surprised that he wasn't able to shape what he was doing more. In that regard, he really seemed like a method actor. He just took a *whang* at everything with great aplomb, and I invariably liked the result.

I don't think I shot anything with Rosanna Arquette, who played the glamorous hooker Scudder falls in love with. At least, I have no memory of working with her. I did shoot scenes with Vyto Ruginis, who played Scudder's partner. I liked him a lot and thought he was very skilled. I also shot several scenes with Andy Garcia, who was playing Angel Maldonado. *8 Million Ways to Die* provided me with my first contact with Andy. I was not aware of him before starting work on the movie, but I quickly became a big fan of his and remain one to this day. He was a delight to work with and I also liked him as a person. Andy was another one who was hurt by Hal's dismissal, but he was very welcoming of me. I do remember we were shooting in a residence in Beverly Hills known as the O'Neill House, which betrayed the influence of Antoni Gaudi in its architecture. Andy and I were talking between set-ups and he was very excited by the look of the house, and commented astutely on the Gaudi influence. He struck me as a rather interesting and cultured guy. Another thing I recall about Andy is his strongly objecting to a ring I showed him that I felt Angel should wear. We had obtained this big, fat pimp ring but Andy took one look at it, and cried, "Oh, that's *so* tasteless! Angel would never wear that kind of jewelry. Are you kidding me? He's a very cultured and discerning kind of scumbag. He would never wear that *thing* on his fingers! Keep it away from me!"

I do recall that Andy was anxious to play the part of Navarro the pimp in *Weeds*, which was a project that had received the green light just as I was finishing up on *8 Million Ways to Die*. Somebody had given him a copy of the script and he had fallen in love with it, and was lobbying me for the role. Unfortunately, when the moment came when I actually wanted him for Navarro, Andy was doing *The Untouchables* with Brain De Palma and he couldn't get out of it. We had a whole series of lengthy phone-calls, trying to work something out in terms of his schedule. But there was no way of possibly extracting him from *The Untouchables* and we had to surrender the possibility of ever casting Andy in *Weeds*. It was too bad. Both he and I were desperately disappointed at the time as we'd had such a good experience together on *8 Million Ways to Die*. Andy would have been an interesting choice for the role and even today I find myself imagining what he could have done with it. If you look at *8 Million Ways to Die*, he is just phenomenal. I think he steals the picture, particularly during the fiery warehouse confrontation between Angel and Scudder when they are ranting at each other. Andy was playing this raging criminal—and when actors deliver that kind of maniacal performance it sometimes threatens to go over the top—but he always kept it together. He didn't resort to any moustache-twirling antics, he was just crazy-evil.

When Stuart and I were editing some of the dialogue scenes Ashby had directed, we could clearly see that some of it was improvised. It felt rather flat and meandering, but some of it was razor-sharp. Ashby was an exceptional editor, so it's bitterly ironic that the film was taken away from him before he had a chance to cut it. He is one of those guys who started out as an editor and worked his way up to being a director. That's a good way to become a director. It's certainly not an easy way, but I think in terms of being good at the job and having a greater understanding of filmmaking, it can be invaluable. As an editor you're in the same business of judging performance, and you already know how to construct a scene. Also, you aren't victimized by the things people say. What I mean is you have more willingness for fearless experimentation because you know what will work. Ashby had shot the film with a lot of overlapping dialogue. Usually you are told: "Do not overlap dialogue in close-ups!" But Stuart knew how to cut overlapping dialogue in close-ups and make it seem dynamic and energetic. This ability gave sequences like the warehouse confrontation a credible momentum that you would not otherwise have had if the actors had been pausing between each line. Jeff had looped a lot of his dialogue with Stuart. Neither Stuart nor I were fond of ADR, and there was nothing wrong with the sync tracks, or with Bridges' performance. The grand finale yelling was filmed with overlaps which might have required ADR, but Stuart cut it masterfully preserving the sync tracks.

> *By early March of 1986, Hancock's duties on the production were completed. Several weeks later, on April 26,* 8 Million Ways to Die *opened to negative reviews and lackluster box office returns. The notice published in* Variety *was indicative of most, although it did publicly acknowledge Ashby's displacement: "What could have been a better film delving into the complexities of one tough-but-vulnerable alcoholic sheriff out to bust a cocaine ring, instead ends up an oddly-paced work that is sometimes a thriller and sometimes a love story, succeeding at neither. … Respected director Hal Ashby was reportedly fired from this picture before it was finished, which could explain its unevenness as he wasn't privy to what happened in the editing room." Writing for* The New York Times—*and seemingly unaware of the behind-the-scenes shenanigans that had led to the filmmaker's sacking*—*Walter Goodman traduced Ashby in stating that* 8 Million Ways to Die *was a detective story that contained no detecting in it and no story. "[Ashby] seems to have been made desperate by the desultory and disjointed nature of the material. He has the characters constantly shoving and yelling insults at one another, fills the many interludes with headache-making music and winds things up with as clumsy a burst of bang-bang as you've ever seen. But by then, you may feel you've died eight million deaths."*

I must admit, I wasn't too surprised when *8 Million Ways to Die* was met with such a dismal reception. I didn't have much confidence in it, although I know that people tried very hard to make it good. So, I think the critics got it right for the most part. They saw the picture as some kind of big-budget mounting of an episode of *Miami Vice* and it was interchangeable with a lot of the anonymous stuff that people saw on TV. Again, Andy

Garcia is definitely worth watching, and there are several sequences that carry a distinct charge—there just aren't enough of them. From what I can recall of the film (and I haven't seen it for a long time and have no strong yearning to reacquaint myself with it) I thought it was okay. Memory tells me it suffers from a lack of tension in one or two places and the plot stumbles occasionally. I think PSO wanted the picture to be better than okay, and Stuart and I tried our best. From a personal standpoint, I don't think working on *8 Million Ways to Die* helped my career in any way. It was merely a few weeks or so of income and the fun of working with Stuart, Jeff and Andy. I had *Weeds* on the horizon and that was where my focus was heading. So, unlike Ashby, I didn't feel the hit.

Looking back, it would have probably been better for all concerned if Ashby had been allowed to finish the picture himself. He had the overall design in his mind, and could have delivered something worthwhile—or perhaps not. Who knows? I don't know what Ashby's final assessment of the film was after we had gotten through with it (or for that matter if he ever saw it), but I imagine he hated it. I guess we tried to inject more commercial and conventional elements into the movie than some of the things he had attempted. We lost some of his subtleties and quirkiness, but a lot of those decisions had been made before I got there and some of them were necessary as the story was muddled. *8 Million Ways to Die* is seen as something of an aberration in Ashby's body of work, but I don't think it's a complete failure. It just doesn't fit comfortably alongside everything else that he did. With everything that happened to Ashby at the end of his life, it's tempting to view him as this tragic figure or persecuted talent, or whatever epithet you choose. I tend to resist some of that. I prefer to concentrate on the wonderful movies he did make. All the bullshit eventually dries up and blows away and, in the final analysis, the only thing that remains is the work itself. And his work is very good indeed.

13 *Weeds* (1987)

AS HE WAS COMPLETING work on 8 Million Ways to Die, *Hancock received confirmation that his long-cherished project* Weeds *would finally receive the go-ahead after a frustrating eight-year struggle to the screen. Written by Hancock and Dorothy Tristan, the screenplay was loosely based on the life of former San Quentin inmate Rick Cluchey. In 1955, Cluchey was convicted of the crimes of armed robbery and inadvertently inflicting bodily harm after the .44 Magnum he was carrying discharged and the bullet "grazed" his victim's arm. Just twenty-one at the time, Cluchey was handed a life sentence without chance of parole. He unexpectedly found a source of hope and salvation in the form of the San Francisco Actor's Workshop who performed a production of Samuel Beckett's* Waiting for Godot, *directed by Herbert Blau, at the facility in November 1957. Profoundly affected by the existential play's adroit blend of comedy and tragedy, Cluchey founded the San Quentin Drama Workshop soon after and began reading and studying modern drama as well as acting in a total of thirty-five prison productions.*

In 1965 Cluchey wrote Le Cage, *a prison drama that ostensibly concerned three characters, each a convict, one of whom is driven homicidally insane by the rigors of his environment. Cluchey, who would often play the mad inmate himself, felt the play was an attempt to capture "the disintegration of the human animal behind walls and the less tangible rigidity of prison." In December 1966, after*

> being incarcerated for twelve years, Cluchey's sentence was commuted by Pat Brown, the then governor of California, amid much press attention. Shortly afterwards, he was escorted from the gates in a Silver Dawn Rolls Royce and would never return to prison. Cluchey subsequently reformed the San Quentin Drama Workshop with other ex-cons and, in 1969, performed The Cage (as it is more popularly known) Off-Broadway following runs in San Francisco and Washington. He would go on to enjoy a successful career as a theater actor and director, mounting well-received productions of Krapp's Last Tape, Endgame and Waiting for Godot—finally meeting his mentor Samuel Beckett in Berlin, in 1975, and later collaborating with him. Cluchey died in Santa Monica on December 28, 2015, at the age of eighty-two.

My predecessors at the San Francisco Actor's Workshop had regularly ventured into San Quentin every other week or so to work with the prison drama group there. Herb Blau had taken his famous and award-winning production of *Waiting for Godot* into the prison and performed it for the inmates—a truly captive audience. Some of the convicts had gotten excited about the play, as they felt it captured what it was like to be caged. It was an all-male production that spoke to their sense of desperation and the interminable confinement of being stuck behind bars. One of these convicts was Rick Cluchey, who at that point in time was wallowing in the third year of a life sentence without possibility of parole. It was Cluchey, and the editor of the San Quentin newspaper, who had fallen head over heels in love with *Waiting for Godot*, and been directly inspired to create a drama group inside the prison. At the time of Cluchey's death it was reported by some sources that he had been considered such an escape risk he was not permitted to attend the performance of Beckett's play. Instead, they claim he actually listened to it from inside his cell as it played over the public address system. Not true! I know this is bullshit because there's no way they would have broadcast something like that over the prison PA. Think about it. Five thousand inmates, a third of them members of Hispanic gangs, a third of them Black. You can't subject them to Beckett on loudspeakers, you'd have a revolution. Maybe Cluchey listened privately to a recording that had been made by the inmate who ran the prison newspaper. Or maybe, as he said elsewhere (and always told me), he was there, but didn't really appreciate it for what it was until he got to talking about it with the inmate editor and some of the prison intellectuals. I'm not certain of the truth, but I am certain that *Waiting for Godot* could not have been broadcast on the prison PA.

Anyway, when I took over the running of the Actor's Workshop in '65, I too started going into San Quentin every two weeks to work with the prisoners. I found Cluchey in particular to be a thoughtful, sympathetic and softly-spoken man, who clearly had some talent as an actor. Interestingly, Cluchey had a kind of Richard Burton vibe about him when he performed. He had been the assistant to the Catholic chaplain in the prison and the chaplain had a record of *Camelot* featuring the original cast of Richard Burton, Julie Andrews, et al. Cluchey had obviously listened to *Camelot* too much and began to talk like Burton. When I first saw his play about prison life, *The Cage*, I realized immediately that it was a rip-off of Jean Genet's *Deathwatch*. I still thought it had some strong qualities, enough in fact that I agreed to have it mounted at our experimental theater. I then requested that Ken Kitch, who was the managing director of the Actor's Workshop, direct the play and *The Cage* received decent reviews and did good business. Naturally, Cluchey couldn't come out to see the production as his custody was such that they would not let him out. The authorities had emphatically insisted that he would "never" be set free and would die in prison. As the men from the San Quentin Drama Workshop would be released from incarceration, I would occasionally employ some of them—the ones I thought had some modicum of talent. Sometimes this would work out and other times the ex-cons would show up drunk or high, and I would have to get rid of them.

Time passed and Cluchey was still incarcerated. After a while, a bunch of us were compelled to do something about this as we felt Cluchey had been reformed and had something valuable to offer the world as a free man. So, a number of us wrote letters to Governor Pat Brown to campaign for his release. This included the Catholic Father at San Quentin, and, through him, we also got the Cardinal of San Francisco to write one. Another valuable supporter was Alan Mandell and his wealthy wife Liz Heller. Alan had been the managing director of the Actor's Workshop under Herb Blau and Jules Irving, and had gone off with them to Lincoln Center (Jules probably wrote a letter, too). Alan's wife's letter, I imagine, was particularly useful, because she and her family were big donors to the Governor's political campaigns. Finally, through the efforts of all these people, we got Cluchey's sentence to be commuted and he was liberated from San Quentin. Cluchey then got some of his old group of ex-cons together and formed the Barbwire Theatre Company, which consisted entirely of former convicts, and took *The Cage* on a national tour of colleges and regional theaters. They ended up taking the play Off-Broadway and got bombed by Clive Barnes, the formidable English theater critic for *The New York Times*.

During the time I was editing *California Dreaming*, it suddenly occurred to me that Cluchey's experiences would make a terrific movie. In essence, it was the ultimate underdog story: the desperate sense of hopelessness and struggle, and then redemption and triumph, made it irresistible to me. So, I got together with Ken Kitch and we eventually tracked Cluchey down in Chicago where I believe he was performing in a Beckett play at the Goodman Theatre. I flew there from Hollywood and quickly optioned the rights to Cluchey's life story. It was at this point that Dorothy and I took out the second mortgage on our home, so that we could have the time and money to research and write the script for *Weeds*. Thus began the protracted process of interviewing all the members of Cluchey's prison drama group to get more information on its inner workings and the people involved, recording our conversations and making detailed transcripts. We did a lot of work and it was both exhausting and exhilarating. We were getting massive amounts of valuable material and information, enough to make a whole series of movies that could have veered off in different directions and tangents.

By this time, Cluchey had famously become friends with Beckett and later the pair started working together. In 1977, Beckett directed Cluchey in a production of *Krapp's Last Tape*, and a subsequent production of *Endgame*, and they remained close until Beckett's death in 1989. When Dorothy and I decided to sit down and talk with Cluchey at length about his experiences, we learned he was over in Essen, in what was then West Germany. He was again working with Beckett as they had managed to secure a big grant from the German Government to tour a number of German cities. So, we flew to Essen and saw the drama group over there and discussed the movie project with Cluchey. He then accompanied Dorothy and me when we later drove to London and spent a bit of time there. Following this, Cluchey came back to America and we saw a lot of him over the course of several years as we were laboring on getting the movie off the ground. We also spent time with a number of the other ex-cons in Cluchey's group. There was a guy named "Bagdad" Everhardt who I tracked down in San Francisco and spoke with at length. I also interviewed a man named Kenneth Whalen—I think I found him in New Jersey or Philadelphia—who had been Cluchey's cellmate in San Quentin. Unlike Cluchey, Whalen was more of a white-collar criminal than the blue-collar types he was mostly surrounded by. We didn't base the character of Claude Mullens in *Weeds* on Whalen. In fact, I discovered that the real cellmate did not like Cluchey much as Whalen had come to feel that Cluchey was a hopeless alcoholic. So, we made up our own Claude and imbued him with more loyalty and sympathy than what had actually existed in that relationship. There was a character called Claude in one of those *Young Lust* underground comic books that appeared in the early 1970s and we initially visualized him like that. Then, when we later began casting, we just depended on who the actor was and how he looked.

Another member of Cluchey's drama group we interviewed was an African-American guy named Bobby Poole. He was a pimp and a drug dealer, who had written the screenplay for the 1972 blaxploitation film *The Mack* after he'd gotten out of prison (there's a legendary story I don't believe that Poole had ardently written a forty-page treatment for the film on prison toilet paper). *The Mack* had starred Richard Pryor and was a big success. The distributors of the picture then cheated Poole out of his money and he was in no financial position to sue them. So, he had to just swallow it down and that was tough for him. Poole then had difficulty in getting his other screenplays on. Finally, he returned to his old nefarious lifestyle and began pimping and selling drugs once again. He basically did the only other things he knew how to do. At one point Poole talked to me about possibly producing or directing some of his subsequent scripts. He had written one about two girls that are smuggling heroin from Mexico using carrier pigeons. I forget the title now, but he wanted me to lend my name to it. That project didn't go anywhere, neither did a subsequent serial killer story he tried to interest me in called *The Fulfillment*. I spent a lot of time with Poole, talking about his life and experiences in prison. He was a colorful and charming character. However, he was none of those things for Dorothy as she is not a fan of pimps. But I found him to be a rather moving and interesting personality, and I came to understand some of the reasons why his life took the lamentable course that it did. Finally we met extensively with Barbara Bladen, the Bay Area food and drama critic who picked Cluchey up in a limousine on the day he was released from Quentin, and with whom he became romantically involved. We were intrigued by the idea of a love story across class lines, and created the character of Lillian Bingington. In Lillian, Dorothy saw an opportunity to write a good part that she herself could play.

> *The first draft of* Weeds *was, in Hancock's estimation, completed "sometime around late 1980, early '81." Drawing selectively on details of Cluchey's life story as well as their voluminous research materials, Tristan and Hancock concocted the story of Lee Umstetter, a self-destructive inmate who is serving a life sentence in San Quentin for armed robbery without possibility of parole. After two failed suicide attempts in which he first leaps from a forth-floor balcony and then almost immediately after tries to hang himself in his cell, Umstetter wearily drifts into the prison library and tells the librarian, "Gimme a thick book—I don't care what it's about." After being handed a copy of* War and Peace, *he returns for more and begins devouring the works of Nietzsche, Sartre, Dostoevsky, Solzhenitsyn, Camus and Genet. Three years later, Umstetter is enthralled by a performance of* Waiting for Godot *that is mounted by a professional acting troupe inside the institution. Inspired, he begins writing his own play about prison life titled* Weeds, *which is dutifully typed-up by his embezzler cellmate Claude Mullens.*
>
> *After convincing the associate warden of his intentions to stage the play for the convicts, Umstetter and his cohort Reuben Navarro, a pimp (styled after Bobby Poole) with acting ambitions of his own, supervise the auditions that are attended by an assortment of jailhouse toughs. They include Burt the Booster (who recites "Eeny-Meeny-Miny-Mo") and Elliot "Bagdad" Everhardt, a Muslim serving time for three counts of murder in the first degree, who impresses with a soulful rendition of "The Impossible Dream." His cast now in place, Umstetter and company stage* Weeds *inside the prison for an audience of convicts and invited civilian guests. The performance is attended by Lillian Bingington, a middle-aged drama critic who exchanges letters with Umstetter after being touched by his writing and acting. Lillian successfully campaigns for Umstetter's release and he eventually receives a pardon and*

moves into her apartment. Once freed, Umstetter sets about reassembling his combustible band of ex-cons and forms a traveling group he christens the Barbwire Theatre. The men embark on a modest tour that begins in San Francisco and continues on to Iowa, Illinois and finally New York, encountering a number of adventures and difficulties along the way.

I don't know how other writing teams work together, but Dorothy and I like to exchange pages back and forth. On *Jaws 2*, I had—without receiving credit—co-written the screenplay with her, and on that project we worked in the same room across a big desk from each other. By the time *Weeds* rolled around, we had started working in separate rooms and were continually passing scenes between us, offering comments, suggestions and encouragement. We had a good and productive system. The work was being done on these big IBM Selectric typewriters that were popular at the time. Our rule was if you were willing to retype it, you could change whatever you wanted in the other person's scene. I've found that way you don't get into fights with your co-writer. The bad things just tend to vanish as you discard all the problematic material with very little fuss and aggravation. I think our approach worked well because we always had a unified sense of what the overall story was and who the characters were. I understand people think when you are married to your co-writer, and enjoy a personal relationship as well as professional one, it can be fraught occasionally. But Dorothy and I have never had a huge row when working together. We've had rows about drinking, and other personal issues, but never about the work itself. We seem to mostly agree on which direction a particular story should go.

With the huge quantity of information and anecdotes we had at our disposal on *Weeds*, we couldn't squeeze everything into our screenplay. Thus, we dropped a number of interesting ideas, characters and scenes during the writing stage. There was originally a whole thread in the script that was excised before the final drafts were completed: it involved an investor in San Francisco who plans to give Umstetter the money that will allow him to keep the group going. This person then drops out at the last minute and, in a blind panic, Umstetter flies to New York to see his father who sets him up with a local loan shark. He gets on a hook with this oily individual, which eventually leads to more tension and problems down the line. It was a good subplot because Umstetter's father got mad at him when he couldn't pay the loan shark, so we had a few good father and son scenes. All that stuff was cut, as was another wonderful scene (based on reality) where the police come in and threaten to arrest Bagdad during a rehearsal. He has apparently gone into a building and is not able to explain why he was in there, and this action has violated his parole. Umstetter then manages to get the police not to arrest Bagdad and he escapes further problems.

Another sequence we had involved something called a pimp ball. Bobby Poole had flown Dorothy and me to a pimp ball in Oakland, California. It was an astonishing thing to witness as it was like a fashion show for pimps, replete with music and close-rhymed rap lyrics about their clothes and coolness, etc. It was called "The Top Star Award" and we had a scene in our screenplay that was a version of this event. It was a very colorful scene that was much-loved by many people, but we ended up cutting it as it was something of an unnecessary detour. Another lost thread concerned Umstetter having a slightly retarded brother who is incarcerated. We had a wonderful scene where, halfway across the country, he visits his brother in the joint and they share some moments together. I liked that material and it was difficult to cut. Nevertheless, all that went, and there were a lot of other things that were dropped. Someone once said something interesting about the collaborative process of two screenwriters working together: there is something about the span of ninety minutes in that it's specifically like a dream cycle. If you have two people writing, you tend to end up with two dream cycles. So, instead of ninety pages, you end up with close to 180 pages if you aren't careful. Inevitably, there were a lot of scenes dropped at both the writing and editing stages.

> *Further refinements were made to the screenplay for* Weeds, *with Hancock and Tristan rooting out several fascinating diversions and details that were deemed superfluous. Both writers now felt confident that they had crafted a narrative of uncommon emotional power. Indeed, this early iteration was strong enough to attract the attention of Robert De Niro, who, in the eight years since the release of* Bang the Drum Slowly, *had risen to the summit of Hollywood, securing two Academy Awards for his epochal performances in* The Godfather Part II *(1974) and* Raging Bull *(1980).*

When Dorothy and I were writing *Weeds*, we always had either Bobby or Al Pacino in mind for the role of Umstetter. So, I sent the script to De Niro and he read it and loved it. He was enraptured by the character, the story and the subject matter, which was gratifying. As soon as Bobby wanted to do the film, everybody was calling up offering to finance it and the interest was intense. Bob wanted to do *Weeds* with Robert Chartoff and Irwin Winkler (he was especially close to Irwin) as they had produced *New York, New York* and *Raging Bull*. Bob was pushing the project in that direction and I was completely agreeable to this. So, we went with them. The picture was then set up at United Artists, where Chartoff/Winkler had a deal—the *Rocky* movies and so forth—many deals actually. Following this, Bobby and I were suddenly boarding private jets and flying to different places to look at prison drama groups. We also got houses next door to each other in Montauk, New York, in order to work closely on the script and deliberate every aspect of *Weeds*. Right off the bat, it soon became apparent to me that Bobby had changed since the days we had made *Bang the Drum Slowly* and discussed *Ruby Red* together. It was now like I was dealing with The Godfather or Jake LaMotta. Clearly, he had become very tough and confident in those intervening years, having worked with Marty Scorsese and Francis Coppola and bagged two Oscars. Bob was always unfailingly polite to me, and even remarked at one point, "You know, I'm really in the position I'm in today due to luck. So, it's not like I'm better than you now or anything." Despite that, I realized he was an entirely different proposition to the guy I'd once known.

For instance, De Niro had it stipulated in his contract that he had approval of every cast member, every music cue, every prop, every costume, etc, etc. He literally had the final say on *everything* and I found that difficult to swallow. I felt going in this might result in some tensions between us further down the line, but I thought our friendship was strong enough to survive any problems. Fairly early on, Bobby made it known to me that he did not want Orville Stoeber to do the music for *Weeds*, which greatly concerned me. I had already committed to Orville and that put me in a difficult position. Bob felt the picture should have a harder, rockier score and, in a way, perhaps he was right about that. But I had obligations to certain people, individuals I had worked with for a considerable period of time and developed close relationships with. I couldn't just shrug them off because Bob didn't like them. More to the point, like a lot of actors, De Niro was coming into the project later than others who had been attached to *Weeds* pretty much since its inception. Basically, as the writer/director, you have been working on a movie for as much as two or three years. The lead actor may have only been working on it for two or three weeks, but they suddenly think it's theirs. Naturally, you think it's yours, but when you make any picture it involves a large group of people. Little-by-little, step-by-step, you surrender more and more of your film to them—at least the film you've conceived in your mind's eye—as they contribute to your vision. That's just the process of making movies, and I accept that. What I find hard to accept is people trying to compromise or squeeze you in that process. Bobby and I had gotten along so well on *Bang the Drum Slowly* I really found it hard to take this change in him. But worse was to come.

As I said, Dorothy had written the part of Umstetter's girlfriend, Lillian, for herself. Before we signed the deal I relayed this information to Bob, and he replied, "Yeah, of course. Dorothy is a wonderful actress and it's only right that she should play her." So, we went ahead and signed, but as soon as we'd put pen to paper De Niro suddenly said, "You know, John, I think we should see other actresses for this role. I just don't feel comfortable making love to your wife on camera." That started alarm bells ringing in me, but I still felt confident that Dorothy would indeed be playing Lillian. Then, one day, Irwin Winkler took me aside, and said, "I must tell you something: Bob had a terrible problem during the shooting of *New York, New York*. He was revolted by the fact that Liza Minnelli was sleeping with Marty and they had to play romantic scenes together. It just made the whole situation nearly impossible for him." I knew Bob had a problem acting with women anyway. If you look at *The Deer Hunter* it's really Meryl Streep who is doing all the work in the scenes they share together. Winkler then continued: "Look, Bob is not good with women and I'm afraid you'll have to give in on this. You'll simply have to cast somebody else in this part." I then said, "Geez, Irwin, I feel a little betrayed here. I mean, Bobby said that Dorothy was wonderful and now all of a sudden she's not?" Winkler said, "It's purely a psychological thing, it's nothing personal. You must understand that."

Well, the truth was I didn't and couldn't understand it. I felt tricked, and I thought if I allowed De Niro to bust my balls on this issue, so close to home, I was possibly going to lose all my power and influence on the project. Bob already had every contractual approval and I had none to speak of. To compound matters the feeling I was getting from certain individuals was along the lines of, "Hey, Hancock, you are lucky to even be doing a picture with a big star. When was the last time you did a movie with this kind of budget and this many shooting days?" That really grated on me, I must say, but I always liked Irwin and thought he was a fabulous producer. Be that as it may, I was occasionally made to feel that I was fortunate to be involved with my own project and be associated with such a successful actor—despite the fact that Bobby and I had a history together. Winkler even said to me once: "You do know that Bob cast *The Deer Hunter*, right? Michael Cimino didn't cast that movie, Bob did. Bob also cast *Raging Bull*. Marty didn't cast it. So, you should listen to him. Let Bob cast who he wants in this movie. He'll do it right." Well, I had my own pride in my casting ability. After all I had cast De Niro when he was an unknown. Anyhow, soon after this advice was imparted to me Bob did something that demonstrated why it was imperative that I also had a say in casting: we could have gotten Gene Hackman to play Claude Mullens, but Bobby did not want him for the role. He said, "I know it puts more pressure on me being the only star in the film, but I'd rather have it that way." So, the opportunity to work with Hackman vanished—just as it had twenty years earlier when we were going to do *The Wild Duck* together.

Another thing De Niro wanted to do was cast actual ex-cons in a lot of the supporting roles. This was fine with me, but not to the significant extent he was advocating. My feeling was, okay, Bob works a lot with Scorsese and maybe Marty is better at working with amateur actors than I am. Maybe he is adept at drawing good performances out of people with little or no experience, but I've always relied on people literally being able to *act*. I try to cast the best available actors in each role and then just leave them alone to do what it is they do. But Bobby was excited by the idea that *Weeds* would somehow be a more authentic and evocative piece of work if he was surrounded by people who were "real." Again, I welcomed that idea, but within reason. Bob and I had such a good relationship I believed I would eventually wear him down about Dorothy and he'd suddenly realize, "Geez, the girlfriend isn't a large part anyway. For Christ's sake, what am I worried about? How many love scenes are there in this movie? I'll just suck it up and do it." No doubt, at the same time, De Niro was also thinking he could win the argument because he was a big star now. So, we battled on about it for weeks and months without either of us relenting.

The pain of it—for both of us, I imagine—was, again, that we had been so close. We had adored each other on *Bang the Drum Slowly*, and I kept looking for the boy who'd trotted up to me on that picture begging to do another take. I couldn't believe that I'd be unable to talk Bobby into something that was so incredibly important to me. Dorothy was willing to step aside, but I insisted, because I couldn't afford to let him win this dispute and still maintain authority. Later, in an attempt to make it clear to me that Dorothy would not be permitted to play Umstetter's girlfriend, Bob made us read everybody (and I mean *everybody*) for the role. I'm not kidding. We read nearly every actress of a certain age you can possibly think of: Susan Sarandon, Karen Black, Raquel Welch, Melinda Dillon, Barbara Harris and Sally Kirkland to name just a few. This process went on and on, day after day, and it was deeply humiliating. It left a bad taste in my mouth that didn't really go away.

Then, quite out of the blue, Bobby decided he was going to do *The King of Comedy* with Scorsese. I took that decision badly as we had both been entirely focused on doing *Weeds*. It had literally consumed us, like total tunnel vision, and now here he was somewhat unexpectedly changing lanes. Bob said, "Look, I understand you're not happy. I'll give you $50,000 because I know you have to wait for a year or two." I said, "Oh, fuck you! Just go do the picture with Marty and then we'll do *Weeds* right after. I don't want your money." I was very angry and very stupid. I should have taken the $50,000, but, instead, I considered it even more humiliation being heaped upon me. That was a difficult moment for me, being forced to take my foot off the gas after I was steaming ahead with the picture. Anyway, while De Niro was off doing *The King of Comedy* in New York, I saw that Chartoff/Winkler had accidentally let the option on *Weeds* lapse by one day. Just one day. I then realized that I suddenly had an out, and said, "Look, I want to renegotiate the contract. I don't want Bobby to have all the approvals and I not have any. I have to secure a somewhat equal number of approvals." Essentially, the power in movie-making is all about the right to say no to something. De Niro could say no to the director of photography, to the costume designer, to the set decorator, and to all other personnel and details, and I wanted an equivalent set of approvals.

As soon as De Niro's agent, Harry Ufland, learned of this, he called me up and hissed, "Hancock, you lowlife scumbag! No wonder you never made it!" I quickly responded with, "Well, fuck you too!" I then hung up on him. Within minutes Chartoff and Winkler got on the phone with me, both at the same time. They were worried, trying to smooth things over and saying that Harry was entirely out of line. I explained to them the problem: I didn't think I could do a good job of directing the picture if De Niro had all the controls and I had so few. I said it was a huge movie with a big cast, a lot of sets and a cross-country journey, and I had to have the autonomy to direct it without running to De Niro for approval of every little prop and music cue. Inevitably, that same night when he was finished shooting, Bobby called me and without preliminary pleasantries asked in a hostile tone, "Okay, what's your side of it?" I saw red, and said, "Bob, I'm afraid I no longer want to do the picture with you. If your agent can talk to me like that, it shows an intolerable level of disrespect. I just won't—I *can't*—make this movie with you." I felt a great relief when we got off the phone, after months of being bullied and having my authority questioned. And there was another more important thing. You see, it was my belief that if his agent felt free enough to say those kinds of things to me, and had De Niro to defend him, I was in a precarious position. I was worried that if it was *starting* with this kind of hostility, I could even get fired at some point. I mean, what might happen when we were in the trenches and things really got rough? After my damaging and harrowing experience on *Jaws 2*, I knew I couldn't afford to get fired again. That would have meant almost certain career death. I for sure wasn't going to sign a contract that could permit them to ever take *my* project away from me, a project I had conceived and developed and pawned my house to write, and of which I was prouder than anything I'd ever done. I could not take that risk and so I killed it. I killed the deal over the issue of sharing power with Bob. And that was it.

Afterwards, De Niro and I ostensibly remained friends. Our last meeting after our association on *Weeds* came to an end was actually a pleasant one. We had breakfast together at The Rose café in Venice, California, in a sincere effort to be friends again. We wanted to wish each other well and for things to somehow be alright, but things were never the same between us again. In fact, I remember that sometime during the 1990s I was in New York shooting a Kmart commercial and I stopped by Bobby's Tribeca Grill Restaurant. I tried to see him, I talked to the Maitre d', but Bob declined to come talk to me. Our intense experiences together on *Weeds*, and the way it all unraveled, had taken its toll. You must understand, Bob had appeared on *The Tonight Show* and raved about the project and I know for a fact that *Weeds* meant the absolute world to him. I recall Irwin Winkler once telling me: "Bob does some pictures merely as an actor, but there are certain pictures he does as a passionate creative partner. *Weeds* is one of those pictures and Bob is deeply and emotionally invested in it. This movie is the equivalent of *Raging Bull* for him. You do realize that, right? It's not just something that Bob wants to add to his resume. He wants to be on the inside and control everything." Evidently, De Niro was very mad that I wouldn't surrender the control and that *Weeds* was one passion project that got away from him. To this day, I don't know what Bobby thinks of the finished film. I can only assume he hates it.

Thinking back on all of this though—and it's been a long time—I remember something I felt strongly when I was going through it: that it wasn't just about power and face, it was about love. Bobby wanted me all to himself. He has this peculiar relationship with his directors, some of them—Marty certainly, and me at this point. It's some complex father-son thing probably, I don't know, but I haven't had it with any other actor. It's very pleasant in that you feel close and adore each other, but there can be problems when a third party comes in. I think it's possible that Bob had trouble with Liza Minnelli not because she was sleeping with Marty, but because she was splitting Marty's sole focus on Bob, taking him away. I'm not talking gay. It's something else, but strong. At any rate, Bob was really asking me to choose between him and Dorothy. He didn't want her around—at all! Not just in the part, not in script conferences, not in the limo, nowhere, *gone*! He always talked to me about wanting to work "one on one." Okay, one on one is good. I like that, too. But was he so swollen with success and everyone saying yes to him, that he actually thought he could split Dorothy and me up? She was my partner, professionally as well as in life. I needed her to write together. She was my meal ticket. My mother saw the situation clearly. She said I couldn't allow anything to hurt my wife like that.

> *Following this early iteration of* Weeds *with De Niro as star falling apart, Hancock's focus and enthusiasm for the project remained undimmed. His search for a suitable actor to play Umstetter resumed and would continue over the ensuing four years with a roster of leading men attached at various junctures. Only when Nick Nolte was cast in the role late in 1985 would* Weeds *finally receive the go-ahead after legendary Italian producer Dino De Laurentiis was enticed to finance the film through his fledgling company, The De Laurentiis Entertainment Group.*

Okay, back when De Niro first decided he wanted to do the picture, there were only two producers he would accept: the first, his preference, had been Chartoff/Winkler. The second was Barry Spikings with whom he had done *The Deer Hunter*. Either was fine with me, as I knew them both. Like myself, Barry was a client of Alan Schwartz and I saw a lot of him and his wife Dot at dinners at the Schwartzes. I was also fond of his ex-partner on *Deer Hunter*, Michael Deeley, and his wife Ruth. I knew them better than I knew Chartoff and Winkler, but all these guys were accomplished producers. After the picture was set up at United Artists, and amid all the casting squabbles that occurred during pre-production, U.A. suffered a near fatal blow: *Heaven's Gate*. They no longer had the money to finance *Weeds* by themselves, so Barry Spikings came aboard with his film fund from the U.K.—a deal that Alan Schwartz put together. More money came through Mark Damon, pre-selling foreign territories. Then, when the whole thing with me and De Niro came to a head and he was gone, Chartoff and Winkler tried to help keep the project alive. They said, "We can still do this picture. We just need to find somebody good." So, we next got the script to Mickey Rourke and he liked it. I don't know if Barry would have gone along with Rourke, he might have, but Chartoff and Winkler were unable to find another studio that wanted to do it with Mickey. No one would buy him as the lead. After Mickey departed, we tried to get the film on with Danny Aiello but nobody wanted him either. We then huffed and puffed to get *Weeds* activated with several other actors who wanted to do it—including Robert Davi—without any success.

A few years passed. Chartoff and Winkler drifted away from the project, and then from each other. I was still searching for my Umstetter and, after trying different people, we finally found Nick Nolte. How Nick came to be involved with *Weeds* is an interesting divergence: Dorothy and I had secured a deal at Tri-Star Pictures, when Gary Hendler was head of the studio in the mid-1980s, to write a movie for Nick—the title of which has long vanished from my memory. I do remember that Dino Conte was the producer and Linda Palmer was the executive in charge of the project. Several other writers had worked on the script and then we did our own draft. The screenplay had a lot of laughs in it, but it was an action picture with a love story as well. Nick was going to play a food critic in San Francisco that—I suppose a bit like Cary Grant in *North by Northwest*—gets involved with spies. There were various scenes where Nick and his love interest are being chased around Napa by the bad guys, as well as on the streets of San Francisco, so the movie could have been a little bit like *Bullitt* if we weren't careful. I remember at one point the two of them were pursued around the city by a garbage truck and then in a vineyard by a grape picker (I eventually worked the latter sequence into *A Piece of Eden*). Nick and I took a trip up to Napa Valley to research the different restaurants and wineries up there as the script also featured a big scene in a winery. Although the movie never came to fruition, throughout this process Nick and I got to be friends. He was living with his then wife, Rebecca, and they shared a house nearby in Malibu. But they were also spending a lot of time in another of their properties that was located in Charleston, West Virginia.

I flew down there with a draft of the Tri-Star project and Nick and I read it aloud in his living room. He had a mirror with several lines of cocaine on it and every ten or fifteen minutes during the reading Nick would dip his head down and snort up the coke. This was a rather strange and unique experience for me: reading with an actor who was ingesting quantities of cocaine. I can honestly say that I did not participate at all. I've tried coke a couple of times and, frankly, I've never seen the point of it. After Nick and I had read through the script and discussed it a little, I was feeling tired. Nick, looking anything but, said he was going to stay up for a little while longer. So, I said goodnight and traipsed off to bed. The following morning I got up and as I was sitting down to breakfast, Nick was coming into the house wearing the same clothes as the night before. He distinctly had the fragile look and chagrined manner of a man whose tail was now firmly between his legs. I asked him what was wrong and he explained what had happened: it turns out that Nick had ventured out after we had finished our reading and had gone to a bar. He was feeling humiliated because at one point he'd run out of cocaine and had proceeded to remedy this problem by snorting a biker's snot in order to get the coke that was contained within it.

Obviously, Nick felt this behavior was pretty low and desperate. I had a history of taking more amphetamine that I should have at a certain point in my life, so we were able to talk about things on that level and deal with the situation. It was good in a way, because we confronted the problem before we had even started working together. When we finally did *Weeds* together I can remember saying directly to Nick, "We're not going to take drugs on this movie, right?" He promised me that he would remain straight during the course of filming, and he was ninety-five percent of the time. I was grateful for that, just as I was grateful for having the opportunity to work with Nick. You have to remember that all of this occurred during the 1980s when it seemed like nearly everybody was doing cocaine. It was as accessible as candy. At any rate, the following night after this incident, I pulled out the script for *Weeds* and we started to read it aloud instead of the Tri-Star movie. Within an hour, Nick was like, "Oh, my God! I *really* want to do this!" That's how I hooked him in.

With Nolte, you are dealing with contrasting energies and qualities: the tough physicality, the growling voice, but then there's this vulnerability, too. In many ways, much like Cluchey and Umstetter, he was "a sad and tangled thing" himself. He had what I needed. It seems strange to label criminals working class guys as you can't restrict criminality to just one class. We do mention the class bias of incarceration in the film, but in the case of *Weeds* we were dealing with a central character from a lower class background that has developed an unlikely interest in avant-garde theater. It was important to always keep that contradiction alive. If you cast somebody who is upper-middle class—and many actors are from that background—it's not going to seem odd that they are interested in Genet and Beckett, and other art forms. The interesting thing about Nick is he has that roughness and that proletariat culture. He's definitely not a middle class boy. Beneath his gruff veneer there is something very likable and sensitive about Nick when you see him onscreen. More than that, in reality, he is a wonderful guy. Sure, he can be a little crazy and impulsive at times, but when you get the opportunity to work with somebody that good, you seize the chance with both hands. Nick and I got along terribly well on *Weeds* and we became close.

After managing to attach Nolte, indeed as soon as he wanted to do it, we got *Weeds* on. Nick's agent, Sue Mengers, said she was going to send it to Dino De Laurentiis, and I was enthusiastic about this. Dino had interviewed me for his 1976 remake of *King Kong*, a job that eventually went to John Guillermin. I can remember asking Dino what it was about, thinking, maybe he was taking an anti-colonialist slant with the material or something. He looked at me strangely and said, "What's about?! It's about a bigga monkey!" Then, in 1984, I ran into him outside an early screening of his movie *The Bounty*, and he was pleasant. It was like Dino knew he had a picture in some trouble there, but he wasn't going to be destroyed by it. I felt we liked each other. Happily, sometime in early 1986, Sue Mengers was able to set *Weeds* up very quickly with Dino. I believe she sent the project to four or five different places and gave them a week to respond, and Dino bit—largely because his story guy, Gary DeVore, loved it. Things had to be translated into Italian in order for Dino to read them. So, I don't know if he'd read the script before they bought it, but he may have. DeVore was really the guy who made it happen. Plus the fact that Dino was bullish and needed product for his new company, DEG. One of the most impressive things about Dino is that he let me have my own producer in Bill Badalato. Bill is and has been an important person in my life, both as a friend and a collaborator, and I really wanted him with me. When you are putting a movie together, whose person gets hired and whose person does not can become a huge subterranean battle around the office. It can get real cold and brutal, and you don't expect to be able to have your own guy as producer. But Dino was different. He met Bill and looked at his credits, like *Top Gun* for instance, and he knew he was dealing with the best. So, after receiving Dino's approval, it was really Badalato and I who put *Weeds* together and scheduled it.

Now, there were in effect two versions of the *Weeds* cast that featured different actors in respective roles: there was the De Niro cast in 1981/82 and then there was the Nolte cast when we shot the film in 1986/87. Cis Corman was De Niro's casting director and she was wonderful. Cis was a close friend of Barbra Streisand's—that was her principal claim to fame—but she had a profound knowledge of the New York acting community and, to a lesser degree, the California acting community. Cis had cast a lot of big pictures such as *The Deer Hunter* and *Raging Bull* (officially anyway), as well as *Heaven's Gate*, *Wolfen* and *Yentl*. So, she was a pretty big deal. There were a bunch of people that we read with Cis, then, when we actually got the movie going several years later with DEG, we had Dino's casting directors, Barbara Hanley and Cathy Henderson. There were one or two holdovers between both versions, but no one was ever set in stone for the Cis Corman/De Niro version—partly because we didn't have a definite schedule yet and partly because of Bobby and me being somewhat at odds on what kind of actors we wanted. For example, I thought Ted Ross (who had played the Cowardly Lion in the original Broadway production of *The Wiz*) was a conceivable candidate for the role of Bagdad, and Mandy Patinkin was a possible Navarro. Again, De Niro's tendency to want more non-actors who had done hard time came to the fore as he thought Ross and Patinkin were "too theatrical."

One of the most important supporting roles in *Weeds* was that of white-collar criminal Claude Mullens. In the original cast, Cis had brought in Tom Noonan for the role. I had known Tom from *Wolfen* and was a big fan of his. I thought he'd play well opposite De Niro as physically they looked so different and that contrast worked well for the story and the relationship between the characters. I don't recall why Tom didn't eventually play Claude in the Nolte version, as I was delighted with him. Maybe he was busy doing another movie at the time, possibly *Manhunter*. In the subsequent cast we eventually hired an actor for the part of Claude whose name (I'm embarrassed to admit) I can never remember. This actor is not listed on IMDb and I'm not the only one who has forgotten his name. I recently asked Badalato if he could recall it and Bill couldn't either. If I close my eyes I can see this guy's face in my mind, but his name is lost in the dark backward and abysm of time. I should remember it as he is the only actor I've ever worked with who has died during the shooting of one of my movies. I believe he succumbed to AIDS during the Christmas of 1986 while we were taking a break from shooting. Now that I think about it, I don't know that he died in 1986, but he did indeed have to leave the production over the Christmas hiatus due to the ravages of his illness. In actuality, he might have died as much as a year or two later. This is what has made it difficult for me to locate his name.

Anyhow, the result of his departure meant we had to recast the role with Lane Smith, and go back and re-shoot a bunch of scenes. So, we simply collected the insurance and continued on shooting. I had just worked with Lane on the "Profile in Silver" episode of *The Twilight Zone*, so there were no problems there. Even though I and others have forgotten the original Claude's name he hasn't been completely erased from the picture. He's discernible in a couple of shots, so you can still see him in *Weeds* if you look carefully. This gentleman was not an important actor in terms of reputation or celebrity, but he was an interesting and unnerving presence. In fact, he played Claude like he was the ultimate creepy cellmate. It gave his relationship with Umstetter an interesting tension. I remember feeling disappointed to have lost the actor in the picture, and, that he later lost his life to the disease. That said, I was happy with Lane's interpretation—or reinterpretation—of the role, but I did feel it was to the detriment of the picture that we lost our first guy. The original Claude just had this uniquely unsettling quality about him and was so strange. I also remember the actor had these tremendous scars on his head that were clearly visible. Apparently, he'd been suffering with AIDS for quite a while and had endured several brain operations. So, it looked like his skull had been cut open a couple of times. Yeah, that was a remarkably good bit of casting and it's a shame he isn't really in the movie now.

Another big role was that of Bagdad Everhardt. I only ever considered two actors for that part: Ernie Hudson and Ving Rhames. Ernie had been brought in to read by Barbara and Cathy and I liked him immediately. Oddly enough, even though it had been a huge hit just two years earlier, I didn't remember Ernie from his role in *Ghostbusters*. To me, he was something of a new face, as was Ving Rhames at the time. I do recall that Ving made a mistake in his audition: he literally came through the door in character. I've experienced this several times over the years with actors where they arrive in character. In this particular instance, I thought, "Christ, this guy hates White people so much I'm not going to be able to direct him." I mean, the character of Bagdad hates White people, but of course, in reality, Ving turns out to be a pussycat. He cries on television about his mother all the time and gives his awards away to other actors, and is a great guy. However, back then, he entered the room as *the* most hostile Black man I've ever encountered. Dorothy thought he would have been a much better Bagdad than Ernie and, okay, he might very well have been. The truth is Dorothy has had problems with Ernie's performance as she feels he is too soft in the role. She felt Bagdad needed to be a more dangerous physical presence initially and then is gradually revealed, or is transformed, into a pussycat. But I was happy with what Ernie gave me. I didn't agree with Dorothy on that at all. I particularly love the scene where Ernie auditions for Nolte by singing "The Impossible Dream." Hudson does it with such conviction. While we were shooting the idea came to me that all the other convicts should join in, too. I'm so happy I thought of that. It's a terrific scene and it's such a perfect song for those guys to be singing.

I could be wrong, but I believe William Forsythe was left over from the Cis Corman sessions and was brought in again later. I then cast him as Burt the Booster after being impressed with his reading. I remember Bill told me that he was saved from a life of crime by a teacher who got him into acting as a kid, which was a charming story. Unfortunately, Bill later proved to be difficult to work with. I hear that a lot of directors have hated him, and I was certainly one of them for a time. I think Forsythe more than returned that feeling to me and we clashed a lot. To be honest, he and I almost came to blows during shooting. One of the things that inspired our confrontations was his unwillingness to say the lines as written. Bill even went as far as to call me a "Nazi bastard" one day, among other things, for wanting him to recite the dialogue in the script. I actually threw him off the set in front of nearly three hundred extras and, I must say, that action endeared me to crew. The truth is Bill was not well-liked at all. Back then, he was rather inexperienced as an actor—I believe he only had two or three film credits under his belt before doing *Weeds*. You would imagine that he would have been a little more compliant and amenable. Not at all!

At one point, Nolte came to me and said, "I'm having terrible trouble with this guy." He then proceeded to explain that Bill was possibly thinking he was a better actor than Nick and perhaps there was a lack of respect there. I just laughed the comment off, but it was clear that Forsythe was getting under his skin. Nick said, "He just doesn't knuckle under, he doesn't give me anything in the scenes. What the hell can I do here?" I thought about it for a moment and then came up with a possible solution to this problem. I said, "Okay, I've got it: in previous drafts of the script you had a retarded brother, right? Why don't we just use the Stanislavski system here and employ the magic *as if*. Every time you have a scene with Forsythe and he pisses you off, just look at him and play it *as if* he was your retarded brother. How does that sound?" Nick was pleased with that suggestion, tried it, and found it worked for him. But the working relationship between him and Forsythe was somewhat strained. In the story Umstetter and Burt are supposed to be close, but in reality Nick and Bill were anything but. In spite of this, when you look at *Weeds*, the two men do appear to be close and that was important. I subsequently heard that Bill greatly admired Nick's commitment to the role, so I think he eventually came around. I do know for a fact that his part in *Weeds* is Bill's favorite of all the parts he has played in his career. He's stated this in interviews and, after we finished the picture, he came around and stated it to me. He said, "You know, I love it! It's wonderful! I'm sorry I was such a prick." We then talked and I saw a more agreeable side to Bill, one that I liked.

The character of Navarro, the pimp "who is tired of misusing women," was another important figure in the story but for different reasons. I was always keen that we should find somebody really good to play him. In the Corman/De Niro cast, Eddie Olmos—with whom I had briefly worked on *Wolfen*—was a strong candidate for the role. When we finally got the picture going in '86, I cast Michael Cristofer, who is a rather good playwright and screenwriter as well as an actor. He had read for a part in *Baby Blue Marine* a decade earlier and I'd remembered him. I cast him in *Weeds*, but, when we started rehearsals, I didn't like what he was doing with the character. It just wasn't how I saw Navarro at all. Michael was too intellectual and didn't have the surface gushiness of Bobby Poole. So, I fired him and I do recall he didn't take that decision well. It was at this point I wanted Andy Garcia, whom I had enjoyed working with on *8 Million Ways to Die*, to play Navarro. He would've been wonderful in the role, but, as I said, Andy wasn't available as he was doing *The Untouchables* with Brian De Palma. There were many phone calls trying to talk him into jumping ship but to no avail. So, Michael was eventually replaced by John Toles-Bey, who Dino's casting people had found working on the street in Venice as a stand-up comedian, right on the waterfront there. When John came in I discovered that he had not acted before, but I immediately saw him as Navarro. He had the smooth charm and chutzpah the character required, as well as the warmth and likeability. I really like John's performance in the film. I think he's got great appeal and believability.

I was initially considering Bobby Poole for the part of Lazarus, another member of the company. In fact, I wrote that character for him as he could act as well as write. Sadly, by the time we got around to doing *Weeds*, Poole was back inside prison for armed robbery and it proved impossible. Lazarus then ended up being played by a wonderful actor that I found named J.J. Johnson, who had once been part of The Family, an acting group of inmates from Rahway, New Jersey. The rest of the ex-cons fell into place quite nicely. Bill Badalato had seen Joe Mantegna in something and thought he was wonderful. So, on his recommendation, Joe came in and we quickly cast him as Carmine Vaccaro, an actor from New York who the guys devise a criminal bio for. I then cast Mark Rolston as Dave the flasher. He was brought in by Dino's casting people and, at the time, I believe Mark had just made his film debut playing a futuristic marine in *Aliens*. He's gone on to play a variety of different characters for me and other directors, appearing in a lot of big pictures like *Lethal Weapon 2* and *The Shawshank Redemption*. After all the tumult over finding an actress to fulfill the role of Umstetter's love interest, we eventually cast Rita Taggart. Again, Dino's people brought her in and I liked Rita. At this point, Dorothy felt she was now too old to play Lillian. In her mind too much time had passed and she didn't want to do it, but there would be some lingering regret there.

Another great find was Anne Ramsey, who played Umstetter's elderly mother. It was Nick who first suggested we cast Anne as he knew her. Despite her roles in movies like *The Goonies*, I did not know Anne, but, boy, did she turn out to be good. I did know Anne's husband, Logan Ramsey, as he had been in The Actors Studio. Logan had also appeared in several of Tennessee's productions on Broadway, playing Southern degenerates mainly. He was a nice guy, but what an unwholesome-looking couple he and Anne made! Like her husband, Anne was always cast as a certain type in movies: harridans and dragons of one variation or another. I believe she came to acting rather late in her life, but she was always great to watch. I loved working with her and *Weeds* turned out to be one of Anne's final films before her death in 1988. I believe at the time Anne had endured a series of painful oral surgeries and operations for throat cancer, which noticeably affected her speech. She went on to appear in *Throw Momma from the Train* the year after *Weeds* and earned an Oscar nomination for her role as yet another battleaxe. But she was not well. By the way, I should add that Anne had a remarkable resemblance to Dorothy's own mother. That's how she looked, talked and acted. Dorothy's mother had suffered a whole bunch of strokes and also had Alzheimer's, and one thing or another. She was a very vulnerable woman.

With all the cast in place, we rehearsed for four weeks in a loft in Hollywood. There was a great moment deciding on that loft. We were having trouble finding a place to rehearse—I think there was money in the budget to pay the actors for rehearsal but perhaps nothing for a place in which to do it. So, at one point, Badalato and I told Dino that if necessary we would buy a loft and lease it to the film. Dino gave us the most wonderful look, with a tolerant little smile that said in so many words, "You boys are amateurs at stealing compared to me! You actually think you can put one over on *me*?" He was such a great character. For my part, I'm sufficiently naïve about how to steal that I still don't know how he thought we could manipulate that situation to our financial advantage, but he sure did. I forget what happened, but I guess Dino ended up paying for the loft. The rehearsals were structured as if we were doing a play—tape on the floor, substitute furniture, etc. We built the walls of the cell so we could rehearse the prison scenes in a confined space. This helped me to visualize how I was going to cover those scenes during filming.

You know, rehearsals can be edgy and difficult. It's the time when you discover that some ideas, and even some actors, are not as strong as you imagined they would be. Other suspicions you have are merely confirmed. As I mentioned earlier, Cluchey had done this odd thing where he talked like Richard Burton during performances. I didn't want Nick to do that in the movie. I just felt it was too bizarre and distracting a choice. Also, there was going to be the extended nude scene between Umstetter and Lillian, so we brought in a bed and rehearsed the scene with both Nick and Rita completely naked. People are often incredibly self-conscious in love scenes and this approach was designed to get all of the discomfort and difficulty out of the way as quickly as possible. Aside from the two actors, the only people in attendance during this time were me, Dorothy, and the assistant director. As I anticipated it would, rehearsing the love scene made it easier to shoot during principal photography, and Nick and Rita were more relaxed with each other and their own bodies. After rehearsing in Hollywood, we then moved the company to Wilmington,

North Carolina, for a further period of rehearsal. This time we worked on a soundstage, which was helpful as a lot of the musical numbers and choreography came together more there.

There wasn't much improvisation during rehearsal or shooting. We had worked on and lived with the script for so long it was inviolable. Thus, we were determined to adhere to it. I depend very much on improvisation as a director, but sometimes I don't. Even Bill Forsythe was eventually made to understand this. All the actors got along fairly well with each other and no serious conflicts or rivalries surfaced between them. We were trying to make a lot of picture for the money we had available to us ($12 million), so everything needed to go fairly smoothly. I convinced Nick to fly coach as the first class air-fares can eat up a sizable portion of your budget. You see, if the star agrees to fly coach then everybody else flies coach, too. Another stipulation I made early on was that I didn't want to have make-up on the film. After announcing this, I then became the enemy of the make-up and hair departments. My reason for doing it was because I felt—and still do in some ways—that the make-up and hair areas become a kind of cabal. The actors arrive, sit down in the chair, and the make-up and hair people just go *yada-yada-yada* in their ears first thing in the morning and don't stop until they're finished. The actors then come to the set already feeling somewhat hostile and negative, jazzed-up by gossip. I wanted to eliminate that tension right at the source. Aside from that, I often don't like the way make-up looks. So, we had just one make-up artist on *Weeds* and that was Nick's make-up guy. Nick believes in using make-up, so we had his guy practically servicing everybody. Also, having worked extensively in the theater, I had seen actors doing their own make-up and thought why can't actors in movies do their own make-up?

> *Musician and songwriter Orville Stoeber, who had worked with Hancock since the days of* Sticky My Fingers, Fleet My Feet, *was among the first to be involved with* Weeds *and would remain with the project from beginning to end. Cast as "Lead Guitar" in the company's modest but proficient orchestra, some of Stoeber's songs and musical numbers were composed as the screenplay was being written. Singer-songwriter Melissa Etheridge would later become involved with the film shortly after it received the greenlight from DEG. Almost a year to the day after the release of* Weeds, *Etheridge's self-titled debut album would be released by*

> Island Records to considerable acclaim and commercial success. She would later win two Grammy Awards for Best Rock Vocal Performance, Female, and in 2007 collect an Academy Award for her song "I Need To Wake Up" which featured in Davis Guggenheim's Oscar-winning documentary An Inconvenient Truth *(2006)*. The rest of the score for Weeds was composed by Angelo Badalamenti, whose previous credits had included Blue Velvet *and* Tough Guys Don't Dance. *The film would mark the beginning of a fruitful collaboration between Badalamenti and Hancock that would continue on several of the director's subsequent films.*

I felt it would only be helpful to develop both the script and the songs simultaneously because the music was going to be integral to the success or failure of the film. We had to know that what we had was good and that it worked. Orville Stoeber was living in Los Angeles at that point, so I saw a lot of him socially. Having collaborated so many times with Orville, I knew how talented he was. So, I talked to him about the project and he started writing songs for *Weeds* very early in the process. When I heard what he was doing, I thought it was terrific. He wrote and performed the song "A Prick or a Noose," and there's also a fragment in the finished film of a longer track he wrote called "Pimp Song." It features in the sequence where the ex-cons open the play in New York—Joe Mantegna, J.J. Johnson and Essex Smith principally perform it. Having worked with Melissa Etheridge on *I Had Three Wives*, she immediately entered my mind for *Weeds*. I had been impressed with the quality of what she'd been able to deliver for my episode in such a short turnaround. I also liked her enormously. Melissa then composed the songs "Weeds," "Burn," and "I Wanna Go Home," which are all songs that I love dearly. Another valuable contributor to the score was Richard Peaslee, who co-composed the song "Lock & Key" with Orville and Adrian Mitchell that the men sing at the end. I'm particularly fond of that song. It's beautiful and stirring. Dick was widely respected and had worked both for Broadway and Off-Broadway, writing the scores for the Royal Shakespeare Company's *Marat/Sade*, directed by Peter Brook, for *Animal Farm* which was directed by Sir Peter Hall for the National Theatre, and for my production of Robert Lowell's *Endicott and the Red Cross* at the American Place Theatre. He was a significant talent.

All other music was composed by Angelo Badalamenti, whose score for *Blue Velvet* I had loved. I thought it was haunting, threatening and beautiful. Angelo came onto the project after Orville, Melissa and Dick, and I was delighted to have him onboard. Our collaboration on *Weeds* was harmonious. I had a temp score that I was enamored with that contained a lot of Mahler and Wagner. Angelo was willing to incorporate and reproduce these selections, which not all composers are willing to do—at least not happily—but he was. There's a lovely piece of music that plays during the scene where Umstetter is released from prison and he's traveling by limousine with Lillian to her apartment. That is Wagner's *Das Rheingold* that you hear. Also, Angelo was willing to build some of his cues on Melissa's chord progressions. So, he was a delight to work with, completely collaborative and without ego. I also asked Angelo if we could use the non-vocal track of "Mysteries of Love," the exquisite song he'd earlier co-composed with David Lynch for *Blue Velvet*. I've used that track subsequently in other movies of mine such as *Prancer* and *The Looking Glass*. It worked wonderfully well in the sequence where Umstetter delivers his speech to the convicts at the end, which rouses them to violence.

You may notice that in the end credits I thank Garth Hudson from The Band. I didn't know Garth personally, but I had been impressed with him when I saw Marty Scorsese's concert film *The Last Waltz*. When we were doing the score for *Weeds*, I decided to track him down. I felt that some of the Mahler and Wagner cues, which were lush and big, would benefit from being brought a little closer into the world of the convicts. So, I had Garth overdub the symphonic tracks several times with his accordion, which made them more suitable for the picture. It was subtle. I didn't clobber the symphonic tracks volume-wise with what he was doing, and he just laid it in there sensitively and nice, responding emotionally to what we already had. It added an appealing tackiness without losing the emotionality of the Mahler. I was delighted with the work Garth improvised, and that's why I thanked him. One other interesting thing that involves Mahler: during the brief montage where we see Umstetter and the ex-cons excitedly climb aboard the RV in San Francisco and leave for their tour we hear The Four Tops song "I Can't Help Myself (Sugar Pie, Honey Bunch)" playing. Towards the end of the montage, a gorgeous orchestral accompaniment is heard playing with the song. For that cue, I asked Angelo to do something that was fairly challenging: to modulate as seamlessly as possible from The Four Tops to Mahler. And he did it! I'm always glad when people appreciate that cue as it's probably my favorite musical moment in the film. It catches what is happening inside Umstetter.

> *Since* Weeds *was evidently a film that featured multiple scenes set inside and outside a prison, Hancock realized that he needed a recognized facility where he could shoot as many interior and exterior scenes as possible. Having visited San Quentin State Prison back in the mid-1960s while working as artistic director of the San Francisco Actor's Workshop (and knowing that it was the same institution where Rick Cluchey had served his sentence), the filmmaker investigated the possibility of shooting at California's oldest and most notorious lockup.*

San Quentin was the natural first choice. Early on, back when De Niro was still involved with *Weeds*, Bobby and I went there to discuss the idea officially. We flew up to San Francisco to meet Rick Cluchey and go through the prison together, looking at various areas and talking to different people about the facility. It was an unfortunate meeting. Cluchey had been partying the night before with Bagdad Everhardt and other veterans of the ex-con drama group. He was hung-over and kept us waiting for forty minutes outside the Quentin gate. Bobby was miffed, with good reason I felt (I'm always a hundred percent punctual). As the morning progressed, and we wandered through the yard and so forth, it was clear that Bob did not like Cluchey. He was put off, I think, by the Richard Burton voice and the smug in-the-know airs. Nor for that matter did Cluchey like Bob. I suppose Rick thought he should have been playing the part of Umstetter, since after all he was an actor. In short, it certainly was not a marriage made in heaven.

Quentin was considered far too dangerous to shoot by the warden, by the associate warden, by Cluchey, and, ultimately, by me. The prison was effectively being run by the inmates at this point in time and there were a high number of stabbings and other violent altercations frequently taking place. In spite of the volatile atmosphere, I must say it was interesting being there with De Niro. At one point, a convict came up to him and politely introduced himself. "I'm so glad to meet you," he said. "I'm just sorry it's under these circumstances." I then heard another inmate mumbling to somebody nearby, "What makes him think *he* can act?" Neither of us responded to this comment, but as Bob and I continued on into the next cellblock somebody threw urine down at us from a high tier as we were walking below. The piss didn't hit us, but it wasn't a good sign. There was this growing unease in the air, that's the only way I can describe it, which I suppose our presence was exacerbating. Bobby was sensing it too, and he was beginning to feel nervous.

Another thing that added to the increasing disquiet was the fact that our tour was steadily taking us into more precarious levels of the prison. If you don't already know, there are all kinds of distinct sectors in lockups that detain prisoners with different custody and different levels of dangerousness. As Bobby and I were going up a set of cramped stairs, we were met by a group of convicts that was suddenly coming down towards us to play basketball outside. Now, these were clearly some threatening-looking individuals that we should not have been anywhere near and there was nowhere for us to go. I took one brief look at these guys as we got up close to them—I didn't want to come across like I was eyeballing them or anything—and knew it was a serious situation. This was confirmed when I glanced over at the guards who were accompanying us and noticed they had tensed-up, the color having drained from their faces. It was obvious that this little encounter was quite unexpected. The guards realized they'd made a terrible mistake and were now visibly scared. Of course, when prison guards get scared in the joint, it's like when the stewardess on an airplane gets scared—you do not want to see that! So, it was another bad sign and I was starting to think that Bob and I should get the hell out of Quentin sooner rather than later. Luckily, that particular brush with the inmates passed without incident but it was a hairy moment. Then, as the tour was coming to an end, Rick took me aside and repeated gleefully what he'd overheard the inmate saying earlier about De Niro: "What makes him think *he* can act?" Afterwards, Bob said he didn't think any further contact with Cluchey would be beneficial. He felt he was already far enough along in his own identification with the character of Umstetter, and didn't need that distraction.

Aside from San Quentin, De Niro and I scouted a number of other maximum security prisons including Rahway and at least one other place in New Jersey. Another facility I looked at with Dorothy was Stateville Correctional Center in Joliet, Illinois. At that point, the prison had been open for over fifty years. I probably scouted Stateville on three or four occasions over the years and we ended up shooting a lot of *Weeds* there. I'm not certain of the year, but the first time I went it was just Dorothy, me and Jim Brubaker, who was Chartoff/Winkler's head of transportation.

The Illinois Film Commission flew us to Western Illinois in the governor's helicopter to scout something around Galena and I remember De Niro joined us in Chicago. We all stayed in huge suites at the Drake Hotel with great views of the lake. Bob then went off to have lunch with Barbara Harris to see if she would do the movie, while Dorothy, Brubaker and I went to Stateville and then the next day to Galena in the helicopter, while Bobby flew off to L.A. or New York City for some obligation or other. I remember that helicopter ride so well, flying over these endless flat Illinois cornfields like the place where my mother grew up. It was stuffy in the cabin, and Dorothy and I were heartsick and anxious about the growing tension with De Niro.

On another visit to Stateville, Dorothy and I went to see Cluchey perform *Krapp's Last Tape* for the inmates. That trip was interesting because, once again, the guards made a mistake in their organization that might have proved costly: they inadvertently brought in two groups of prisoners that were not supposed to be together. This error resulted in the play having to be stopped as they reshuffled the convicts. They eventually got rid of half of them, which was strange to see. What also contributed to the weird atmosphere that day was the fact the guards all had these radios on their belts that were crackling loudly all the time. They were constantly barking into them as they patrolled the aisles and it was very distracting and unnerving. One minute I would be lost in Cluchey's performance and then this blast of sound would suddenly erupt near my ear. Not good.

Despite *Weeds* being a fictionalized account of Cluchey's life, I wanted to show how culture and art had been introduced not only into his life but the lives of other prisoners through various forms of in-prison entertainment and events, and through prison libraries. Knowing that Cluchey had literally been transformed by his exposure to *Waiting for Godot*, we kept that specific work in the screenplay. We were then able to secure permission from Samuel Beckett to include a scene from *Waiting for Godot* in the picture. As *Weeds* was more or less the Rick Cluchey story, I'm sure Beckett would have smiled on it anyway. More than that, he was paid whatever he asked for the privilege of our using it. I then shot the carefully selected scenes with Barton Heyman and Walter Charles playing Vladimir and Estragon. I thought Barton in particular was wonderful, and I was very happy with what he did. *Weeds* marked the fifth and final time we worked together on a movie before he died of a heart attack in 1996. I think the last time I saw Barton was probably at the screening of *Weeds* in New York. So, I didn't see him for a while, but I look back on our times together in the theater with affection and respect. He was a good actor.

Before the performance of *Waiting for Godot*, however, the convicts get a little taste of Charlie Rich. As you know, I was a tremendous fan of country music and I thought that "Behind Closed Doors" would be an appropriate song to use in the film for obvious reasons. I didn't want Beckett's absurdist play to be the first piece of entertainment that was brought into San Quentin. I thought I would have something that was more popular in the form of "The Silver Fox" as Rich was known to his fans. There's a lot of driving in Malibu—half an hour or so to get to Fox or MGM, fifty minutes to get to Universal or Warner Bros. —so you listen to a lot of the car radio. At one point, that meant hearing a certain amount of Rich's music. I had seen quite good documentaries where Johnny Cash or Joan Baez had gone into San Quentin or Sing Sing, and performed for the prisoners, so a vocalist seemed like a good introduction to in-prison entertainment. I believe that Bill Badalato tracked down Charlie for me through his manager. I didn't have much to do with him on set, other than saying hello and telling him he'd done a fantastic job. Charlie just came in, did his thing, and then went, but he was an entirely pleasant fellow and I was happy to meet him.

> Hancock selected the Danish cinematographer Jan Weincke to shoot *Weeds*, after first considering a number of other possibilities including Roy H. Wagner, whom he would later work with on *Cracker*, and Dante Spinotti, who had shot *Crimes of the Heart* (1986) and *Manhunter* (1986). "Spinotti was Dino's candidate," recalls Hancock. "He might have been good, but I hesitated to hire him because he was Dino's guy." Weincke had come with a strong recommendation from Arthur Penn, and had recently lensed the veteran filmmaker's Gothic horror/thriller *Dead of Winter* (1987), a troubled production Penn had taken over several weeks into filming following the dismissal of its original director, Marc Shmuger.

I wasn't crazy about *Dead of Winter*, but I had liked the look of that picture. Arthur Penn had been impressed with Jan's work and how dependable he'd been. So, I hired Jan and he truly was a good cameraman who had some excellent ideas. It was Jan who suggested the opening shot of *Weeds* where all the cell doors on each of the tiers slide open in unison and the inmates march out. I thought that was terrific and it evinced a certain understated theatricality that I liked, the choreography of the action also capturing the dour machine-like monotony of prison life. We devised a color progression that occurs at a certain point in *Weeds*. The first half hour of the film we are entirely locked inside the closed world of the prison. For as long as Umstetter was in the joint we tried to restrict the colors to different shades of grey, black and white—barring the obvious exception of the flesh tones of the actors.

Then, once Umstetter is released from captivity and becomes a free man, we wanted to suddenly introduce an explosion of vivid colors to try and convey the overwhelming sensuous feeling of what it would be like to re-enter the outside world after being confined for so long. You suddenly see the blue of the sky and the water, the red of the Golden Gate Bridge, the pinks and purples of Lillian's apartment. Jan and I approached the shooting of the scenes where the ex-cons are performing the play on stage very simply. We decided to cover the action from different directions, making sure we always had a reverse. Sometimes we shot with several cameras in an effort to capture more of a continuous performance. We would have two cameras and then Jan would have a third camera. He would be fishing with a 300mm lens in order to get cutaways of inmates and people watching the shows. Jan was adept at finding good stuff, zeroing in on interesting faces and moments.

> *Seeking to craft a deeply personal work that traversed a range of themes and emotions, Hancock was also resolved to make an inspirational film that addressed not only his feelings about art and the struggle to find one's own creative voice, but a narrative that touched on a variety of subjects that interested him: plagiarism, criminality, punishment, compassion, redemption, rehabilitation and transformation being just some of them. Hence,* Weeds *observes the tragedies and triumphs, as well as the realities and absurdities, of life as an ex-con through the prism of artistic ambition and a society that is not always welcoming of those who have transgressed.*

It's probably too reductive to label *Weeds* a prison film, but the fact that prison looms large in the story opened up a number of avenues for me to explore and comment on. I mean, when we meet Umstetter he has to look up just to see the bottom and that's a good place to begin dramatically. When Umstetter writes to Lillian after she writes a positive review of his play, we hear Nick's voice-over utter one of the most pertinent lines of dialogue in *Weeds*: "Could it be that even in the least of us, there are crumbs of all abilities and potentials." That's something I believe is true. I think we all have creativity inside us, the ability and desire to contribute. It's just discovering that creativity, bringing it out and developing it. The fact that art can transform us is a wonderful thing. One of the central themes of *Weeds* is this idea of redemption through art. Art has certain restorative and transcendent powers that I feel are positively vital to humanity. It's terribly important that a human being expresses themselves creatively and feels free enough to lead a creative life. I believe strongly in that, too. The ex-cons feel this urge to perform, to entertain, to bring value and meaning to their lives and, at the same time, possibly atone for their past sins. They've been given this chance to do something creative and they are going to seize it—that's if they don't fuck it all up by resorting to their criminal ways. They are artists but they are still criminals, and that duality interested me.

I've always thought that writing a song, or a play, or a screenplay, or making a film, is an act of bravery. When I teach directing at Second City's new Harold Ramis Film School in Chicago, it's something I often stress to my students. I repeatedly say, "The truth is you don't have to be terribly smart to do this job. You don't have to be a genius. One thing you do have to be is courageous, both in forging your vision and in telling other people what to do. You have to possess the courage to stick to your guns and go up to an actor, and say, 'No, I don't think what you're doing is quite right. Can you try this instead?' That's not always easy, but you must be brave." I believe that art can make a difference in people's lives—Cluchey is a glorious example of that. One of the things I've thought about so much in my own life is the fact that, as I told you, I started out as a disciple of Bertolt Brecht. I did my first productions very much in that Brechtian aesthetic (and to some degree with those politics), thinking that if I did works a certain way, and they were entertaining enough, I could influence the world. But I was never entirely certain that you *could*. I'm still not certain that you can, if you want the truth. But, my God, exposure to these things can forever change you. I mean, reading *War and Peace* certainly changed me. It changed how I felt about myself, about humanity, about literature. Seeing *Cat on a Hot Tin Roof* and *Death of a Salesman* helped me to understand certain facets of my relationship with my father. So, I've gotten a lot out of art as a person and as an artist.

Another of the interesting themes in *Weeds* is this discussion of the rights and wrongs of plagiarism. After a learned professor notes similarities between Umstetter's play and *Deathwatch* following an early performance at a college, Umstetter justifies his own plagiarism of Genet by saying, "It was more like osmosis than stealing." He then later admits to Lillian that he did crib some of it. With that element, I wanted to make a comment about how common plagiarism is and how certain artists sometimes comfortably re-label it as "inspiration" or "influence," or they simply refute it. For example, when we were writing the script, I remembered the stink from the case of Alex Haley's novel *Roots* supposedly being partly plagiarized from Harold Courlander's *The African*. To be honest, I had been guilty of plagiarism myself when writing some of the papers for my philosophy courses at Harvard: I had managed to successfully "paraphrase" Bertrand Russell. I just had Russell's book in front of me and I guess I took what I needed. Guilty as charged! Also, I was close to Eric Bentley and Eric had once been accused of plagiarizing somebody's earlier translation of a Brecht play. He was caught because the same errors of translation that were present in the other guy's work were also present in his. So, a lot of great people have plagiarized and I do think that cribbing another person's work is a prevalent practice.

Conversely, it is entirely possible for an act of plagiarism to be unconscious and for the perpetrator to not even be aware that he or she has done it. It's just something that is locked away inside your brain that you mysteriously summon forth. The human mind is an inscrutable thing in the associations it sometimes chooses to make. I believe even Brecht himself was once accused of plagiarism and he had a very indifferent reaction to it. He believed in the freedom to draw upon other artist's works as he felt that art was not private property. Once you created a book or a play or a film and you put it out there, Brecht felt it was there for everybody to pick at and pirate. I also happen to believe that this can be a productive route for a frustrated artist who longs to be creative. It's not simply a case of stealing; it's that first faltering step you take. It clears up a path. It's been said that a burgeoning artist should draw on all their inspirations and influences in order to find his or her own voice. I think that's true. I don't think it's wrong to start out parroting the things that you like.

That's exactly how Cluchey started out, isn't it? He had done his own unmistakable rip-off of *Deathwatch* with *The Cage*. I had been struck by the similarities between the two plays and added that element to *Weeds*. This implied that Cluchey was a plagiarist, but he denied it to me. He said, "No, I didn't plagiarize *Deathwatch*. I plagiarized something else!" Cluchey claimed he'd gotten the idea from some other work, not a play set in a French prison, but some other source (I believe it was some Frenchman's memoirs or fantasy memoirs of incarceration). *The Cage* is set in a French prison and is very much about inmate-on-inmate violence as a means of freeing yourself. During the maiden performance of Umstetter's *Weeds*, the play within a play, the inmates speak with French accents. Then Umstetter drops the accents in an effort to distance himself a little further from Genet. Aside from *The Cage*, Cluchey had also done *Waiting for Godot* in San Quentin, and there were things in those works that related to the themes and characters in *Weeds*. Again, you could understand why an inmate in prison for life without the possibility of parole would like both *Deathwatch* and *Waiting for Godot*. Convicts already live in an extreme world and Genet's works have an extreme aspect to them. The idea in *Deathwatch* that you kill somebody in order to be free struck me as a rather silly idea that was worth sending up a bit. I'm not a fan of Genet's work, actually. At one time I did want to do some of his plays, but I've definitely cooled towards him over the years. By the way, Umstetter's play never existed in a complete form. Dorothy and I only ever wrote sections of it. We had full use of *The Cage*, but we weren't able to use that much of it as we had our own story to tell. Also, it didn't seem to work entirely for our needs.

    What did serve our needs was the unexpected irony of the ex-cons' dealings with those in the outside world. Some of the men found it difficult to readjust to civilian life and encountered problems, not all of which were from their own making. I mean, there was a code in prison, a way of life, and the inmates had their own system of policing and punishment. Even taking into account the brutalities of life on the inside, we learned there was a certain security and trust among the prisoners that, oddly enough, was somewhat absent in the outside world. For instance, I told you about Bobby Poole being cheated out of his money by the distributors of *The Mack* and his subsequent career difficulties. He was dismayed to be treated that way by seemingly "honest" people. The same thing had happened to others, too. Cluchey told me about a trip he took to Italy to perform *Krapp's Last Tape* and the Italians had simply stolen the box office receipts from him. He was like, "What the fuck?!" That was a particularly painful lesson for him. Criminals were everywhere and they didn't need a "Born to Lose" tattoo on their arm to do bad things. The outside world had no rules, no code, by which the men could function. At any rate, who cares if a criminal—even a reformed criminal—gets screwed over? A lot of people feel they deserve it.

This led me to another interesting thing about the ex-cons' experiences on the outside: Cluchey and the acting company would hold these Q&A sessions after some of their performances in which they would invite audiences to remain behind and ask them questions. These events were sometimes disappointing and frustrating exchanges for the men as they revealed the public's general ignorance of inmates and the hardships of prison life. Crowds were more titillated by their crimes rather than being intrigued by the work they were doing. Sure, that was part of the whole attraction and was what made those guys unique in the first instance. So, Dorothy and I decided to incorporate some of these sessions into our film as it was another way to demonstrate the trepidation and fascination these men inspired in people. We even had some fun with it in the scene where the ex-cons are arguing over their official biographies—who has done what and to whom. Nobody wants their bio to be cocked-up so that they are viewed as a child molester. Some misdeeds are irredeemable. So, the crimes must be specific not various. I also liked the idea of all these obstacles, big and small, that stand in the way of the ex-cons' pursuit of success and acceptance: the constant threat that one of them might commit a crime and be arrested, or die on the road; the waiters at Sardi's bringing in an ice sculpture of Alcatraz instead of San Quentin; dealing with negative reviews and sub-par performances. Nothing is ever easy or comfortable for them. That's what good drama does: it presents problems that characters must overcome. But I also did it for another reason in that I wanted to address the idea that life on the outside is difficult for ex-cons.

At one point, I believe it's the associate warden at San Quentin who says, "We don't have rehabilitation anymore, we have punishment." Navarro then replies, "Yes, and we welcome it," which is a line I find both amusing and pertinent. Personally, I think the American penal system is a disaster. It plainly doesn't work and is a non-viable system. Racially, it's utterly unfair and the conditions the inmates are subjected to are often inhumane. Any convict will tell you that there are men who should be locked up, but not nearly so many as there are. I don't know if it's still in the movie or not, but Umstetter originally had a wonderful line in the script: "I believe in punishment…for other people." I don't know how other countries manage without caging the incredibly high numbers that we do here. It's crazy and, again, not everybody should be in there. Norman Mailer once said, "Some of the bravest are incarcerated." Think about that. The system also breeds brutality and crime; you effectively learn how to be a criminal in prison. Then, having been exposed to the festering inhumanity and savagery of the system, you get out feeling so angry you're determined to hit back at society. That inevitably sends you back to prison. So, it becomes this vicious circle.

As Dorothy and I were working on the script, and going on our research visits to various prisons, we got to know and like some of the inmates. Not only that, we even identified with them and felt a certain amount of sympathy for their personal situations. All the same, something occurred that deeply affected us and caused Dorothy and I to once again question our views on criminals and criminal behavior. One night, I was outside our Malibu home putting scraps of food out for the raccoons that frequented our swimming pool. At one point I happened to look up and saw through one of the windows that two armed guys—one with a mask and one without—had entered our home in the meantime and were now terrorizing Dorothy and her Anne Ramsey-esque mother. They didn't catch me as I was outside the whole time. It was a rather surreal and frightening experience. I took a few seconds to gather myself, trying to think of a way to get to my shotgun, before slinking off next door to my neighbors' house. They called the police for me. I then attempted to convince them to give me a gun, as they had one. But, to my immense irritation, they wouldn't give it to me as they "did not want to get involved."

So, I crept back toward our house again through the bushes and saw the guy with the mask violently going through the drawers in my office. I waited out there, breathing hard, adrenaline pumping, and watched as he eventually left the room. I waited some more, trying to catch another sight of him. Then, as the police *still* hadn't arrived, I went back to the neighbors' house and called them myself this time. A voice calmly said, "We understand your impatience, we're on our way." Then I went back outside again and did some more lurking around in the dark, trying to figure out what was going on in the house; worrying that my wife would feel I had abandoned her in the face of danger. My mind was racing. I was also imagining various scenarios and possible heroic actions I could undertake. Aside from the fear and the desire to protect one's own, there was this growing anger inside me: how dare these people enter my home uninvited? To be honest with you, I was quite prepared to shoot another human being that day. I can clearly remember saying to myself as I was trying to get to a gun, "Well, if I do happen to splatter blood and brain matter on the walls I can always clean it off." It was very revealing; a strangely cold and matter of fact consideration to make, unlike anything I've felt before or since. I wasn't prepared to shoot it out with somebody. I thought if I could just kill them from behind without them ever knowing I was there, that would be ideal.

Eventually a number of police cars came rolling slowly up the darkened road with their lights off. The officers got out and—I'll never forget this—their flashlights were literally *shaking* with nerves as they came toward the house. It gave me a brief glimpse of what it is to be a cop and be expected to approach a building with armed intruders inside. A blond, rather attractive lady officer then proceeded to throw me against the side of my house, and in a trembling whisper said, "I don't care who you are, just don't move!" Once inside, I learned that the cops had called the house earlier, telling Dorothy, "We are magazine salesmen and we're on our way." She then thought carefully about the situation and, not wanting a bloody shoot-out, told the robbers that the police were on their way. The two men vanished into the night. Dorothy quickly got out her .22 rifle and blew two shots off in the air—just to keep them from coming back. Then she got under the bed and waited. The cops had to yell at Dorothy to get her to put the gun down. The crooks had gotten away with about four or five hundred dollars in cash. They were never caught.

We really had to put this incident out of our minds as Dorothy and I were toiling on the script. The truth is the armed robbery could have resulted in death for one or all of us, and that was a deeply troubling thought. It did not negatively affect my view on inmates and I remained steadfast in feeling compassion for them, but it was a reminder to me that there were some bad and desperate people out there that could inflict serious harm. Even the "good" convicts I had met had done some very bad things, and we always had to be conscious of that fact. Ken Kitch reminded me of a story he once told me of the time he was helping to remount *The Cage* in New York in 1969 and get the play in shape for its cross-country tour. He and Cluchey were rehearsing one day and Cluchey had done something that Kitch felt hadn't worked. "What are you doing?" he yelled at Cluchey. "No! Don't do it like that! What's wrong with you?" Kitch recalled that as soon as these words left his lips, Cluchey fixed him with an ice-cold look that just froze all the blood in his body. At that moment, he saw the face of the old Rick Cluchey and it chilled him to the marrow. Ken quickly remembered exactly who he was dealing with and how careful he needed to be.

An important event in the story—one that, since we're on the subject of compassion, I hope engenders sorrow in the viewer—is the death of Navarro in an automobile accident. This occurs shortly after the scene at the gas station in which Navarro and Umstetter talk about "the Brotherhood of the Doomed," and how some ex-cons get homesick for the joint (I'd learned of this phenomenon during my research). Navarro also tells Umstetter he loves him. It's something he repeatedly says, and that's Bobby Poole's influence there. Poole would constantly say, "I love you, man! I'll always love you!" So, that phrase came straight out of the mouth of our pimp. For all the times Navarro declares his love for him, Umstetter never tells Navarro he loves him back. He never responds to it. That's in keeping with the kind of man Umstetter is: wounded, guarded, tacit. I put those two scenes close together in the narrative in order to give Navarro's death even more resonance. When we shot the stunt where the car flips over from the highway, it looks like the vehicle hits the camera. We got lucky there, as it's a terrific shot. We used a crash camera that was unmanned, so there was never a possibility of an operator getting injured or killed. After the crash, Umstetter races to the car and peers inside; he and Navarro then share a look. You think he's going to be okay, that he's intact, but then we immediately cut to the funeral parlor and see Navarro lying peacefully in a casket. It's a very jarring transition, unsettling even, but I felt it was effective. Umstetter then touches Navarro's cold hand, returns the love. There are no words spoken. What can be said in such a moment anyway? "I love you" would have been bathetic and anything else redundant.

Sometimes, in reality, the last words you exchange with a person have tremendous poignancy and they live with you. Other times the import of a final conversation can be, "Sure, I'd love mayonnaise on my sandwich." But that's what life is: a series of accreting moments. We don't know what waits for us around the corner and perhaps that's for the best. There is a continual battle I have to combat, my sentimental side and my realist side, if I can call it that, and I wonder now if I should have spaced those scenes out a little more in the narrative. I juxtaposed them directly because it felt right at the time. I don't regret doing that now as much as I regret killing off Navarro. One of the questions I ask myself is whether or not he should have died. Was it a mistake? Like Bruno Kirby's character in *Baby Blue Marine*, I think his presence is missed when he goes. His death is heavily felt by Umstetter and it does serve a purpose beyond emotional manipulation or just having some action occur. Perhaps it's never adequately articulated in the picture, but Navarro's death is the event that enables Umstetter to compose original material. He draws inspiration from tragedy, and plunders the depths of his own emotions, so he no longer feels the need to rip-off Genet. By going back to his motel room alone at night and writing a character called Navarro in tribute, somebody he loved although he never found the words easy to say, Umstetter is empowered to make a breakthrough. He finds his own way. He becomes his own man and a better artist.

> *Following Navarro's death and the excoriation of their subsequent Off-Broadway performance by the New York critic Fisher Cobb, Umstetter and the acting company next perform* Weeds *at the less illustrious environs of a maximum security prison. During the show, Umstetter is compelled to deliver a passionate anti-authoritarian soliloquy that incites the crowd of watching convicts to violence and insurrection. At first amused at the vigorous reaction his words have aroused, Umstetter and the rest of the troupe are soon forced to flee the stage and desperately struggle to find an avenue of escape as the prisoners fight with the guards and attack the associate warden (played by Felton Perry). The melee quickly disgorges out of the jailhouse and into the yard. During the fierce altercation the actors are mistaken for inmates due to their prison apparel. Umstetter is attacked by the guards and, when Burt intervenes to save him, he is viciously beaten to death by the officers.*
>
> *In order to realize this sequence (and several earlier scenes set in San Quentin), Hancock, his cast, and up to seventy crew-members, entered the Stateville Correctional Center for ten days of shooting that commenced on February 12, 1987. At the time, the facility contained no less than 1,830 inmates (thirty-six percent of whom were convicted murderers). The visitors were instructed to "dress down" as not to appear "too Hollywood," and were also told never to carry more than $30 dollars on their person at any time, or wander through the prison unaccompanied by a guard. Undeterred by these warnings, Hancock and Badalato still wanted to employ as many convicts as possible as*

background extras. The inmates—who mostly ranged in age between their mid-twenties and early thirties—were each paid $20 a day to participate and some were members of The Con Artistes, Stateville's resident theater company. On February 16, Hancock deployed two cameras to shoot the dramatic stunt that takes place during the opening sequence of Weeds in which Umstetter first attempts suicide by hurling himself off the fourth tier of the cellblock and tumbling fifty feet to the concrete floor. This scene required 120 inmates, who all observed with keen interest a stuntman plummeting into an assemblage of empty cartons and mattresses that were positioned below.

Hancock had already begun shooting the exterior sections of the prison riot on February 14. This would prove to be one of the most ambitious and complex sequences he had yet attempted, requiring a number of cameras, technicians, actors and extras to realize. First opened in 1925, Stateville was famous for its F-House, or "roundhouse," a large 300-cell block that featured a huge guard's tower in the middle of an open area that was surrounded by several tiers of cells. Initially scheduled for demolition shortly after filming was to be completed, F-House survived until 2016 when, after various complaints from organizations that attacked it as "unsanitary, inhumane, and degrading for prisoners and staff alike," it was finally bulldozed. Given permission to make any changes he wished to the site, Hancock was dissatisfied with F-House's clean look. He then ordered that the cream and brown railings were daubed with grey paint that was then "painstakingly peeled and dirtied" by his set decorators. Hancock also asked that the cell's small window panes be painted black to diminish the quality of sunlight, although he later changed his mind and requested that the paint be scraped away. The prop team provided many of the convicts with sledgehammers and other tools and weapons that were fabricated out of foam rubber. Shortly before Hancock yelled action, the guards positioned nearby each banged their clubs on the floor as a reminder to the prisoners that their "tools" were the real thing.

We shot a few scenes in Durham, North Carolina, moving the company there from Wilmington. We filmed on the old Duke University campus, and also in the theater there for one of the troupe's performances, as well as in and around the dormitory (we also shot a different theater scene at North Carolina University, going back and forth between the two colleges). After this we then moved on to Joliet, Illinois, to shoot the prison scenes. All the prison stuff was tricky to get for a variety of reasons. We shot some of the interiors at a couple of facilities in North Carolina, but the majority of the prison scenes were shot at Stateville. During the shoot we had many convicts working as extras and the number rose to between 250 and 300 during the filming of the riot sequence that occurs near the end. So, it was a big deal and required a lot of careful planning—although I did not use storyboards. The riot was actually filmed at two locations: for the interior scenes where we see the performance for the convicts and the subsequent disturbance it inspires, we took over a cement factory in Wilmington and built the prison auditorium in there. This was necessary as we needed a place where we could start a fire and that would have been impossible to stage inside an actual working prison. I do remember that factory being very cold during filming but it served our purposes. For the moments where the riot spills outside onto the yard, that portion was filmed entirely at Stateville. I think in total we shot the performance and the riot stuff for about four or five days. It was hard work and, aside from being terribly cold, I also had a toothache that greatly troubled me. Sometimes you look back on your career as a director and certain days you feel you worked extremely hard and earned a good result. Those were certainly some of those days.

Now, I should add that I've always been concerned about using extras in movies. They always seem so uniform and rigid in terms of their behavior: when they laugh, cheer, talk, whatever it is. I wanted individuals in the crowd who looked interesting. So, we searched for guys who looked the part—bandanas, tattoos, muscles, beards—and a lot of them did. I was very happy with the extras that were watching the performance. Because of his experience with convicts, Ken Kitch came in and, for three or four weeks, organized a special school for extras. Ken held auditions with the inmates who were screened for their suitability and temperament, as well as their acting ability. He then put them through their paces and helped them to focus on what we needed them to do—and, of equal importance, what *not* to do! We also had a wonderful casting director in Wilmington who assembled all kinds of ex-cons, bikers and other assorted toughs for the production. As a matter of fact, some rather famous former criminals were recruited as extras. We had one guy who had been a member of the Wilmington Ten, a group of Black nationalists that had famously shot it out with the Federal Government back in the early 1970s. This individual had served something like fifteen or seventeen years in a penitentiary and had only recently been released. So, it was an interesting group and they all did a good job.

Since we were hoping to shoot with real correctional officers fighting real inmates, it was quite a negotiation to secure the go-ahead to do all that. The guards were not only concerned about the disruption to the convicts' routine, but the fact we were filming an actual rebellion where people were enacting violence and destruction. The authorities did not want the inmates to get too excited or agitated and end up hurting or killing one another. In such a charged environment there is always animosity between rival gangs, and people of different races and religions, as well as the tension that exists between guards and convicts. No doubt going through the minds of some inmates was the thought, "Man, I've always wanted to hit the sergeant. Here's my chance!" Despite that fear, there were no incidents. All of that tension seemed to disappear during the time we were shooting at Stateville. Everybody was just concentrated on the work and the convicts took direction exceedingly well. In fact, they were more disciplined and attentive than some of the civilian extras. Soon after we packed up and left Stateville, I'm sure the harmony was broken and all the old tensions resurfaced. That was only to be expected, but it was remarkable to see all these dangerous men—murderers, rapists, kidnappers, armed robbers—keeping the peace with each other. For many of them this was a totally unique experience in their lives, working on a Hollywood movie, and they wanted to enjoy it. Everybody saw it was a positive thing for all those involved. Sure, some of the actors, particularly Nick, were worried that the fake riot would suddenly erupt into a real riot due to a mistimed blow or something. There was this palpable fear that somebody would choose to settle a score with someone who happened to be close by in the melee.

I say that everything passed without incident, but, truth be told, on the last day of shooting at Stateville, something did happen. One of the convicts we hired was a guy named Daniel Duane, who had done some painting for us and had also been one of our extras. He was serving a fifteen-year sentence for armed robbery and had made previous escape attempts for which he had been punished. Somehow, Duane had managed to persuade the wardrobe girl (who was susceptible to male attention) to give him street clothes. He then shaved his beard, cut his hair, and, slipped into the civilian clothes he had obtained. Another thing he had procured was a radio. This was important as everybody on the crew had one, so a radio was almost like an official badge that stated you were a crew-member. Duane then jumped into one of our vans and rode out in it. He'd calmly said to the driver, "Can you drop me off at the parking lot outside the gates?" On the way there some question had been raised by the crew, and the driver said to him, "Can you call and see if they need a 50mm lens?" Without missing a beat, Duane got on the radio, called the set, and asked, "Hey, do you guys need a 50?" Somebody replied, "Yeah, we do." He said, "Okay, I'll be back with it." And, of course, he never returned with the 50mm lens. He was gone!

The guards would count the inmates a couple of times during the day—at least two or three times—and at 4:30 in the afternoon they had a count and came up short by one. So, they immediately stopped everything and locked down the entire institution. What the guards do then is they resume the count until it comes up right. They did this and, inevitably, came up short again. As you can imagine, this was not good for them or us. Nobody was allowed to leave the facility and we were kept there—locked down on the clock—until nine or ten o'clock at night. This was costing us time and money, and the waiting itself was agony. Not only was it bitterly cold and boring, we'd been burning tires all day to make smoke for the riot, and the choking smell of burning rubber was just appalling. It was in my hair, my clothes, filling my nostrils. It really got to me. I remember talking to one of the guards about the escape and he said with steely confidence, "Oh, don't worry, we'll get him. Make no mistake about it." I didn't understand exactly how they were going to succeed with that, but they did indeed apprehend Duane just as the guard had promised. Three days after he had escaped from Stateville, Duane was stopped for a broken tail-light in South Dakota. The state trooper that pulled him over had read reports about an escaped fugitive with a butterfly tattoo on his neck, and noticed the driver had a band aid covering that area. So, he was captured and quickly returned to prison.

> The original ending of Weeds, as devised by Hancock and Tristan and retained through several drafts, was different to that of the final shooting script. Instead of Burt being killed by the guards during the prison riot, it was initially going

> to be Umstetter that would suffer this fate. Despite fighting to preserve his preferred climax, Hancock was forced to change it—a decision that still vexes him.

I liked the idea of an assistant in a secondary position who is close to the leader and eventually ends up taking over from this person. The way the screenplay was conceived, Umstetter was supposed to die at the end and his long-time ally Claude was going to rise to the occasion and take over the management of the troupe. The climax was going to be much like what happens now in the film with a few variations: Umstetter sees Claude being beaten by the guards that are quelling the riot, and he goes to defend him. He's hit by one of them, and the homicidal rage that's always been in him to some degree wells up, augmented by his fury at *The New York Times* review and everything else, and he lashes back, attacks the guard and tries to choke him. They beat him to death. There was an important moment a bit later when the riot has been put down: the local inmates are being stripped and forced to run a gauntlet of guards. The members of the acting company are ordered out of the prison. Some of them don't want to leave Umstetter's body inside. Claude says, yes, that's what we're doing. And they do. Then it's Claude who carries on, takes the lead, and keeps the company together. That's why I initially felt we needed someone with the stature of Gene Hackman for the part. Claude has the final soliloquy on a European tour, about the Berlin Wall being overgrown with weeds—instead of the climactic voiceover delivered by Umstetter when he visits an abandoned prison. Thus, this thing that Umstetter has created lives on after his death, and so would he in some way, through the creativity and love of these men he'd assembled and struggled to hold together.

In a way I felt the story required this conclusion. It was better, but Dino wouldn't do it. He initially bought that ending when we discussed the project, but he later changed his mind and said, "I no make the picture if this a man dies. He *musta* live!" Dino and I persistently fought about this without either of us conceding an inch. Finally, I had waited so long to get the project on I relented and said, "Okay, Dino, Umstetter won't die at the end. I guess Cluchey is still alive in real life, so maybe it's false to have Umstetter croak in the movie." For me it was a case of six of one, half dozen of the other. Even so, in retrospect, I still believe that Umstetter needed to die as he was a deeply flawed human being who was always courting death. He was both a criminal and an artist, but despite his redemption he remained a crook to some degree and was always fighting against his darker impulses. In my original ending, he kind of succumbed to those impulses and lost control. I also felt strongly that Umstetter should die simply to fulfill the artistic and dramatic need for it in the film. I thought the climax would contain a lot more power and poignancy if he was killed.

A sentimental and fantastical touch to the climax, one that I still really enjoy, is having the deceased Burt and Navarro appear on stage in fancy clothes with the other ex-cons as they perform "I Wanna Go Home"—this time on Broadway. I don't know why I did that. It was not in any of the scripts. The idea came to me while we were shooting and I instantly knew that it would work. In my mind their return has to do with art not only having this redemptive power, but also the ability to raise the dead and give people an interesting and unique afterlife. I thought it was fitting to provide a curtain call for these men, and it supports the suggestion that the spirits of Burt and Navarro will somehow live on through these other ex-cons in the things that they do. When I think about shooting that sequence now, I distinctly remember it being a happy working day; a very happy working day, actually. There was a wonderful and intoxicating atmosphere on the set and everybody felt that they were doing something really creative, and I did, too.

I always felt it was important to work out the timeline of the events in *Weeds* as it's a span of twelve years from Umstetter's conviction until he is released and reforms the acting company on the outside (just as it was with Cluchey). Then there is a further period of time that follows the ex-cons on their tour right up to their triumphal final performance on Broadway. In the original draft, we had much more of a sense of the passage of time in the way we structured the narrative. For instance, we used the assassinations of John F. Kennedy and Robert F. Kennedy as reference points to establish a particular year, and we saw the national history through the eyes of the inmates as they were locked behind bars. That approach was abandoned in subsequent drafts and I still think that was a wise thing to do as, in some ways, it placed their lives in what felt more like a hermetically-sealed world. The men had no direct experience of the outside world during their years of incarceration and some details just weren't important anyway. Furthermore, when they were on the outside, the ex-cons were dedicated to what it was they were trying to do. So, the historical information was not integral and just seemed like window dressing.

When we were editing the picture, some sections of the story had to move with great speed and precision, particularly during the montages.

It's a credit to Nick that, early on, his transformation from suicidal lifer to liberated artist is a credible one. We squeezed a lot of stuff into what was a two-hour movie, and I was concerned that some things would appear a little rushed or scanty. In truth, we lost a couple of interesting scenes that I liked. One featured Bagdad attempting to kill Fisher Cobb after his scathing review of the production (incidentally, that's pretty much a word-for-word reiteration of Clive Barnes' disheartening review of Cluchey's play that is read aloud during the party at Sardi's). Bagdad gets so mad he tries to shoot the critic in the street outside his apartment, and the other men succeed in stopping him just in time. Ultimately, I cut that scene for two reasons: first, because I felt it slowed down the picture at this juncture and, second, because the idea of Bagdad killing a critic did not seem true in a way. Part of the problem with these men being ex-cons is, if they want to be respected and accepted as artists, they can't afford to go murdering the critic if they receive a terrible review—never mind how angry they are. Of all the scenes I dropped, looking back, this is probably the one I regret losing the most. I think it worked well and it was a good moment for Ernie Hudson. I probably should have kept it, but, at the time, it felt right to lose it.

There was also a scene that I thought was very funny where Carmine's agent attends the last performance of *Weeds* and Carmine refuses to die on stage at the appointed moment. He milks his death scene unmercifully until Umstetter finally has to actually hurt Carmine in order to get him to die. I cut that scene because it seemed too humorous and light for that particular passage in the story, although, like Ernie's aforementioned scene, it was a good moment for Joe Mantegna and he played it wonderfully. Ordinarily, I do love to move between serious and humorous moments, but sometimes the contrast can be shrill; or one emotion cancels out the other. I felt that moment unbalanced the scene somewhat and it was only right that we should cut it. There were also originally more performances of the play in the film at different colleges across the country that we dropped during the edit. Some of this stuff was really good, and I felt these scenes showed the audience how the play gradually changed and was refined as the tour progressed from place to place. In keeping with my usual approach, we held a series of previews of *Weeds*. I did this in order to boil the film down to what I deemed both necessary and unnecessary. After each screening, I kept cutting more and more stuff in order to keep the story engaging and the length acceptable. It was the various performances of the play that suffered most during this process. My agent at the time thought we'd made a terrible mistake in leaving out so much of it. He kept stressing to me how richer and more interesting the picture was in previous versions where these performances were intact. He may have been right about that. Regrettably, all this excised material is now lost, which pains me.

> *Released on October 16, 1987,* Weeds *grossed a disappointing $2,325,444 despite critical reaction being mostly favorable. Kevin Thomas of the* Los Angeles Times *was high in his praise, citing Nolte's "large-scale, emotion-charged performance" and the "terrific group" of actors he plays off.* "Weeds *is the kind of film that makes us realize how hungry we are for genuine, rousing emotion onscreen," wrote Thomas, "and then proceeds to do an exceptional job of providing it." Janet Maslin of* The New York Times *was equally glowing in her appreciation of Nolte: "He combines a tough, hard-bitten manner with great reserves of energy and optimism for [the] role, and the result is a galvanizing performance," prefacing her words with the observation that "Mr. Hancock's methods seem outrageously heart-tugging at first, but they work." Pauline Kael offered a marginally more cautious appraisal, affirming that "[Weeds] encompasses way too much, and it never goes very far into the issues it raises, but the messy collision of energies keeps a viewer feeling alive." While acknowledging Hancock and Tristan's industrious efforts in researching prison theater groups, Kael contended that "the movie gives the impression that they piled together the stories and anecdotes they liked best, and left the job of unifying them to Nolte. (He does it)."*

Weeds was indeed well-received critically, but not well enough. It needed to get absolute raves as it was such a difficult subject. Among the supportive reviews was one by Kathleen Carroll of the *New York Daily News*, but it needed much more than that. I do recall being particularly unhappy with Roger Ebert's review in the *Sun-Times*. I thought *Weeds* contained a unique and emotive premise, and it turned out to be a wonderful picture. When I read Ebert's review (he gave the picture three stars out of four) I thought he had missed something. He called the final prison sequence "less than convincing" and felt that Nick's big speech contained "recycled

'60s leftist panaceas" that were "a little too pat." After reading those words, I felt obliged to write to Roger and say, "You've liked my previous pictures, why don't you take another look at this one?" I then received a reply that said: "I'm afraid I can't do that. I'm sorry. I must stand by my original review." And he did. The truth is *Weeds* really needed the prestige of De Niro attached to it. It needed to have a spot at Cannes and come at the public with considerable critical weight behind it that signified it was an artistically valid picture. Frankly, Nick Nolte is not as prestigious as Robert De Niro. I'm sure Bobby would have been better in the role of Umstetter, too, but even apart from that, *Weeds* required a star of that stature—certainly in the eyes of critics I feel. Maybe I'm being unfair here. I don't know if Bobby would have been better than Nick. It's hard to tell. No question about it, the way Nolte ferociously committed himself to the role was so heartfelt and un-self-conscious. I looked at *Weeds* again just recently and was impressed with the strength of Nick's work. Yeah, I take that back: maybe De Niro would not have played Umstetter as well as Nolte did.

DEG initially opened *Weeds* big with a sizable television campaign, but then they quickly ran out of gas. Suddenly, there was no money available to pay for ads and they weren't able to keep pushing the movie and giving it the kind of presence I felt it required. So, *Weeds* didn't have the necessary follow-through that kept it alive for people. That was, of course, disappointing to accept. DEG was experiencing some difficulties at the time and they badly needed a hit after a series of well-publicized bombs at the box office. Dino was quite a figure, an intelligent and passionate guy. I liked and respected him and, despite our arguments over Umstetter's eventual fate, he was not destructive in the editing room. I got along with him throughout the process, but there was, I don't know, perhaps a history of misuse of money. Dino had been responsible for some costly duds like *King Kong Lives*, but DEG had also produced interesting films like *Manhunter*, *Blue Velvet* and *Near Dark*. Those movies were not breaking box office records but, like *Weeds*, they were solid films of great worth. What we all needed was for our picture to be a hit and it wasn't. There are a number of reasons for why that happened, many of which were beyond my control as they so often are. After DEG declared bankruptcy in 1988, a lot of their pictures were released by other studios and their projects taken over by other companies.

The fact that *Weeds* had an eight-year gestation period from the time we researched and wrote the script to the time it was released in theaters, still amazes me. It was a shame that it took so long to get made as you can't really take that long on projects. To be involved with a movie for that length of time, your thoughts and feelings towards it can change. Sometimes your passion dims or you feel it's too late and the right time has passed. One thing I was conscious of was this feeling that we had sort of missed the national zeitgeist. *Weeds* would have done much better if it had been made and released during the time it was first written in 1981 or '82. The film would have plugged directly into the public sentiments of the time. One thing that's always been apparent to me is the pendulum motion of popular opinion in relation to the penal system. It constantly swings this way and that way. One year it swings towards punishment, the next year it swings towards rehabilitation. It's always shifting with each new movement and moral outrage that occurs. The picture was originally conceived a few years after *One Flew Over the Cuckoo's Nest* was released, at a time when inmate rights were being discussed and people were more favorable towards rehabilitation. *Weeds* eventually opened in the closing years of the Reagan administration, which was a period that was not so kind to inmates. Society was not as sympathetic or as warmly embracing of a story about reformed criminals.

Today, *Weeds* is something of a lost film—literally and figuratively. It gets precious little love and appreciation. I hope that changes sometime soon because, again, I think it's a wonderful movie. I remain incredibly proud of it (the only thing that irks me is the ending as I still feel Umstetter should have died). *Weeds* is the story of a broken soul; a man with no freedom, no hope, no salvation, who longs to die, but who discovers something that restores all that he's lost and more. That idea resonates with a lot of people who feel as Umstetter once did. I'd love for the film to be discovered, but what limits the chances of that happening is the fact the negative of *Weeds* is lost. I do have a laserdisc and I make DVDs from that, but owing to Dino going out of business shortly after the picture was released the negative cannot be found anywhere. It's probably sitting idly someplace, but, so far, no-one has been able to unearth it. Believe me when I say many people have been diligently searching for it. That's one of the reasons why there's never been an official DVD and Blu-ray release, despite a lot of people requesting it. Oddly enough, the title itself is now more readily associated with the TV series of the same name than it is with my movie. You mention *Weeds* to people and they'll tell you it's about a widowed housewife who sells marijuana. I think the popularity of that show has assisted in some way, along with the unavailability of

Weeds, in plunging my picture further and deeper into obscurity. In truth, I don't know if *Weeds* was a good title to begin with. I know that De Niro never liked it. More than once he said, "Let's find something else for it," and I agreed with him on that. I forget all the alternatives we had in mind. I believe one of them was *Umstetter*. We probably came up with all kinds of suggestions, but nothing else stuck. It's funny how a working title can settle in your head and be difficult to shake off. I've never been particularly adept at coming up with good titles.

I know that Nick liked the picture a lot back when we did it. He was as proud of *Weeds* as I was, and always expressed his happiness with it when we'd talk about the film in the years that followed. Rick Cluchey was a fan of it, too, although he had a more see-sawing relationship with the movie than Nick did. When Cluchey saw *Weeds* he initially loved it and said some very complimentary things. But then he started to hear from several ex-cons who were questioning him about certain aspects of the picture. They would say things like, "Jesus Christ, man, you plagiarized? Tell me it isn't so!" Cluchey was not happy about that reaction and his attitude began to change. He suddenly got real sore about it and, at one point, didn't actually talk to me for over a year. Eventually he came back around and apologized. He said, "I love it! I love the movie and I love you!" People have often asked me exactly how much of *Weeds* is based on Cluchey's life and how much isn't. I would say that in terms of real events the film is between forty and forty-five percent true, perhaps slightly less than that. There are some things that are based on historical fact and there are other things we took dramatic license with or compressed slightly in order to make an interesting narrative that would keep the audience engrossed. I don't feel it was a crime to do that. We just had to make a good and entertaining movie, and I believe we succeeded.

> *One thing that may assist in bringing* Weeds *back into public consciousness is a proposed musical of the film that Hancock has been developing for several years in collaboration with others. Also titled* Weeds, *it is a project that has attracted considerable interest and hopes are high that it will brighten a stage in the near future.*

The present status of the *Weeds* musical is this: it's on hold. I'm still not quite happy with the score at the moment and I'm trying to find a composer to complete it. I don't want to throw out Melissa and Orville's numbers, which are wonderfully stirring, as well as the other numbers that a noted composer named John Fournier has written for it. Fournier was initially working on the project back in 2012, but I feel he has taken it about as far as he can. However, it's incredibly difficult to find a composer who doesn't want to completely start over from scratch. Everybody that has credits writing musicals wants to take it over entirely. They don't want to use or incorporate any other composer's work and that is the problem I'm having. So, I still need to find a few necessary things for it. I need an opening number as well as what they call an "eleven o'clock number." Plays used to start at 8:30 PM and around about 11:00 PM there would be a song, an "eleven o'clock number", that the principal actor would come out and sing which people loved and would fulfill the story. This would come right before the concluding sequence and we need a number like that. I would love to find an accomplished composer who can give *Weeds* the kind of ambition and emotional dimension it deserves. Essentially, it's a combination of aggression and criminality with something sublime and artistic, and to catch all of those qualities musically—and also be willing not to throw everybody else's work out—requires somebody special. I've not been able to find this special person thus far. So, I'm still looking.

Hancock's long-gestating project *Weeds* is finally realized in 1987. The uplifting story of Lee Umstetter (Nick Nolte), a man who is both a criminal…

...and an artist, serving life without the possibility of parole in San Quentin.
Both photos courtesy of John Hancock.

Journalist Lillian Bingington (Rita Taggart) helps Umstetter adjust to life on the outside after twelve years behind bars. Photo courtesy of John Hancock.

William Forsythe as Burt the Booster. Hancock clashed with the actor during the filming of *Weeds*. Photo courtesy of John Hancock.

After his impassioned performance incites a prison riot, Umstetter and his troupe become embroiled in a violent fight with guards. Photo courtesy of John Hancock.

A billboard on Sunset Boulevard announcing the release of *Weeds* in theaters on October 16, 1987. Photo courtesy of John Hancock.

Image Section II • 495

Ben Cross as Munir Redfa and Mariel Hemingway as Helen Mason in a publicity photo for *Steal the Sky*. Photo courtesy of Yoram Ben-Ami.

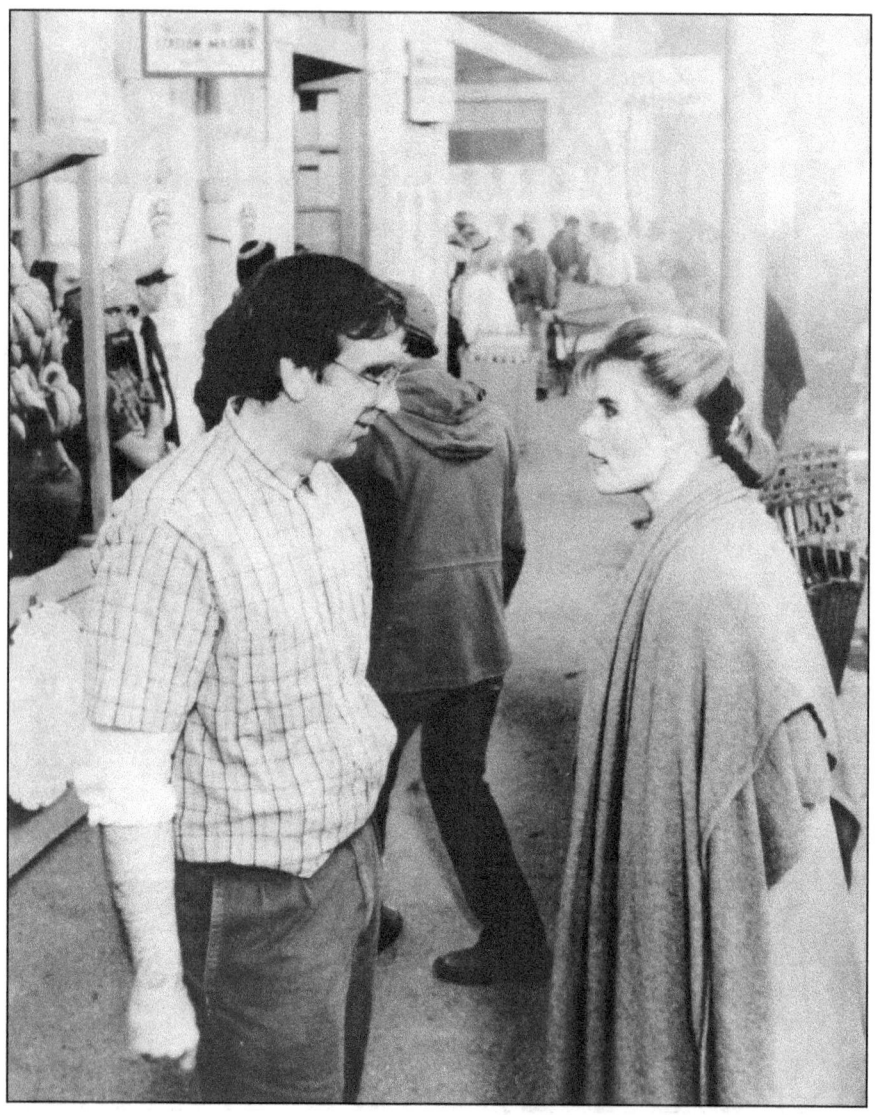

Hancock confers with Mariel Hemingway on the set of *Steal the Sky* in Israel. Photo courtesy of Yoram Ben-Ami.

Making glad the heart of childhood: Jessica Riggs (Rebecca Harrell) restores an injured deer she believes to be one of Santa's own in *Prancer*. Photo courtesy of John Hancock.

Sam Elliot as John Riggs. "The interesting thing about Sam's performance is how fierce he played [Jessica's] father," remarks Hancock. Photo courtesy of John Hancock.

Elliot and Hancock "freezing their asses off" while shooting exterior scenes for *Prancer* in a dependably bitter Midwestern winter. Photo courtesy of John Hancock.

Hancock and cinematographer Misha Suslov (seated and looking through viewfinder) line up a shot with Rebecca Harrell's double. Photo courtesy of Bob Wellinski.

The impressive exterior country road set for *Prancer* constructed inside the former AP Parts warehouse in LaPorte, Indiana. Photo courtesy of Bob Wellinski.

Some of the "perverse" reindeer utilized in the film. Borrowed from a Christmas parade in Alabama, the animals were not used to the cold climate. Photo courtesy of Bob Wellinski.

Misha Suslov filming the scene at the mall where Jessica asks Mr. Stewart (Michael Constantine) to get an urgent message to the real Santa. Photo courtesy of Bob Wellinski.

"Mad as a hatter": a behind-the-scenes snapshot of an impish Cloris Leachman as kooky Mrs. McFarland. Photo courtesy of Bob Wellinski.

Rebecca Harrell proudly displays a prop copy of the *LaPorte Herald-Argus* used in the film. Photo courtesy of Bob Wellinski.

A desperate Giuseppe Tredici (Andreas Katsulas) attempts to save his sheep from a dreaded family curse in *A Piece of Eden*. Photo courtesy of Andrew Tallackson.

Hancock directs on the set of *A Piece of Eden*, his first movie after an enforced hiatus of eleven years. Photo courtesy of John Hancock.

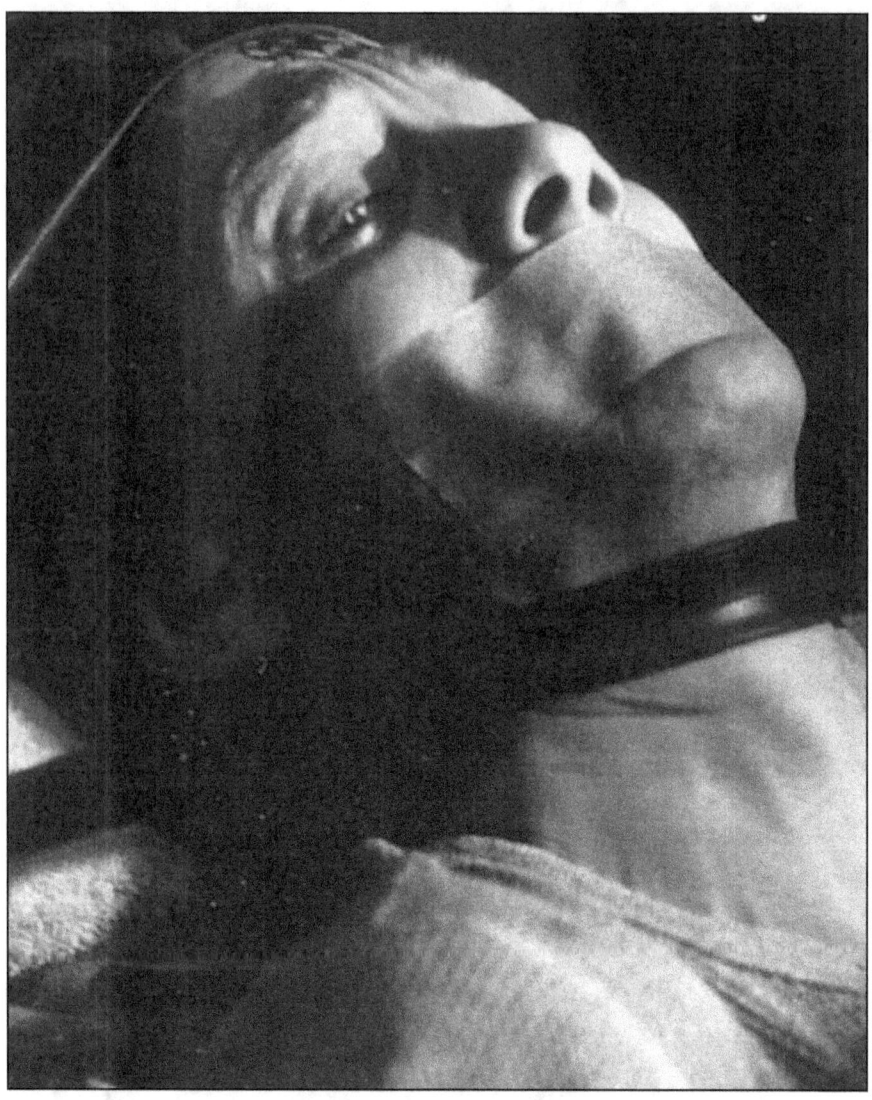

Tom Kempton (Alex McArthur) finds himself being tortured by two crazed sisters in *Suspended Animation*, Hancock's undervalued return to horror. Photo courtesy of John Hancock.

Ann (Sage Allen) and Vanessa Boulette (Laura Esterman) show Tom the "pickled pecker" that belonged to their last victim. The severed penis contained in the jar is real! Photo courtesy of John Hancock.

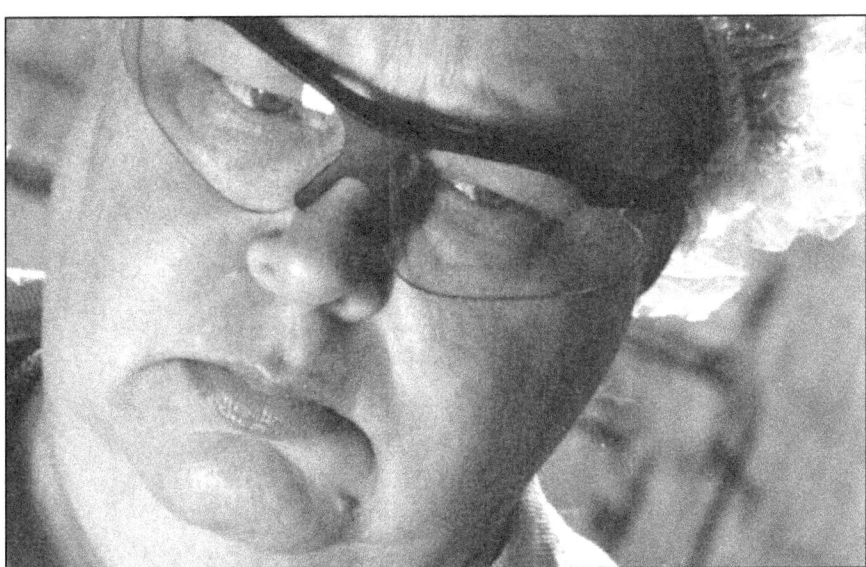

The face of evil: Ann Boulette coldly sets about drilling into Tom's forehead in *Suspended Animation*. Photo courtesy of John Hancock.

The resurrected Vanessa Boulette terrorizes Tom and his wife Hilary (Rebecca Harrell) in their Hollywood home. Photo courtesy of John Hancock.

Karen (Dorothy Tristan), a retired actress battling Alzheimer's, tries to bridge the generational divide with granddaughter Julie (Grace Tarnow) in *The Looking Glass*. Photo courtesy of Andrew Tallackson.

Image Section II • 505

Hancock approaches the graves of his parents as he prepares to shoot in a cemetery near Three Oaks, Michigan. The scene was later cut from the film. Photo courtesy of John Hancock.

Grace Tarnow and Hancock observe a take on the set of *The Looking Glass*. Photo courtesy of John Hancock.

Karen is briefly reunited in a dream with her deceased husband, John (Allen Turner). Photo courtesy of John Hancock.

Hancock and Tristan get cosy during a break in filming *The Looking Glass* inside their own home. Photo courtesy of John Hancock.

A star is born: Julie performs the tender song "The Promises We Keep" with The Caterpillar (Orville Stoeber) during the *Alice in Wonderland* musical. Photo courtesy of Andrew Tallackson.

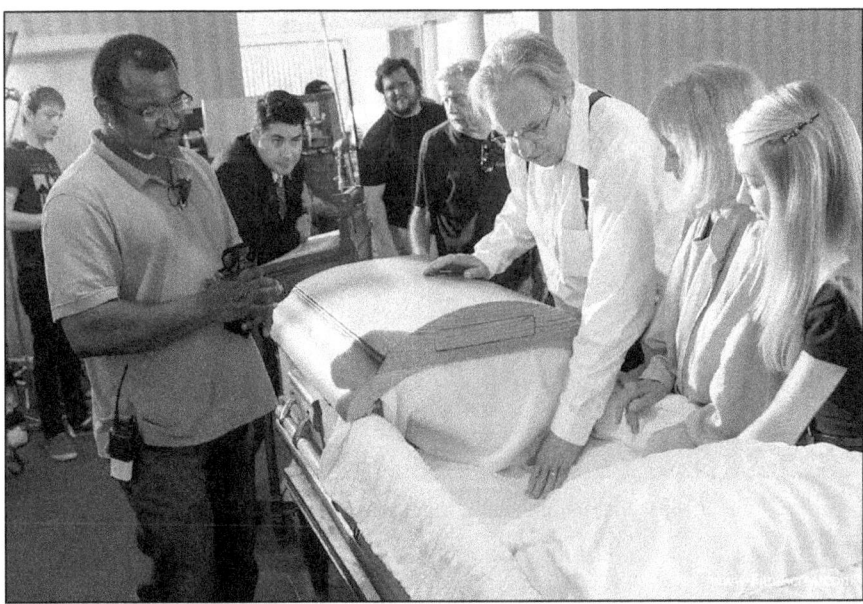

Dorothy Tristan prepares to reluctantly climb into a coffin as Anthony Panzica (Arthur), Hancock, Tarnow and assorted crew-members look on. Photo courtesy of John Hancock.

The provincial filmmaker. Photo courtesy of John Hancock.

14

Steal the Sky
(1988)

HANCOCK'S NEXT FILM *was an unexpected choice. Steal the Sky was a period espionage melodrama made for HBO, the first production released under the cable network's co-financing agreement with Paramount that was launched in 1987. The story was based on the true events of Operation Diamond, a bold mission undertaken in 1966 by the Mossad, the national intelligence service of Israel, to acquire a Mikoyan-Gurevich MiG-21. First developed in the early 1950s, it was the most advanced fighter jet of its time and the crown jewel of the Soviet fleet. Nicknamed the "balalaika" due to its planform resemblance to the Russian stringed instrument, the MiG-21 was a highly adaptable all-weather interceptor that was small, fast and maneuverable. Capable of hitting a top speed of 1,351 mph, and boasting a service ceiling of 50,000 feet and a range of 940 miles, the aircraft was often used by Arab air forces and other Soviet allies in Asia.*

The Russians had begun secretly introducing the MiG-21 in the Middle East in 1961 under conditions of maximum security. Two earlier attempts had been made by the Israeli high command to coerce an Arab pilot into defecting with a MiG-21, but both had ended in failure. The first mission had involved efforts by Mossad operatives to lure an Egyptian pilot into deserting with the jet following an offer of $1 million. An Egyptian-born Armenian named Jean Thomas, and several of his accomplices, were arrested after the pilot refused and reported the men to Egyptian *authorities. Three conspirators were hanged in December 1962 and another three were handed long prison terms. The second attempt to recover a MiG-21 targeted an air base in Iraq. Mossad agents were forced to flee the country after they assaulted two Iraqi pilots who refused to cooperate and threatened to expose their covert plan.*

By 1965, when the idea of a third operation to capture a MiG-21 was broached by Israeli Air Force commander Ezer Weizmann, Mossad had learned that Egypt had thirty-four MiG-21 jets in their arsenal, while Syria had eighteen, and Iraq had ten. Following a tip from an Iraqi-born Jewish contact who was working for a wealthy family in Baghdad, the Mossad learned of an Iraqi Assyrian fighter pilot named Munir Redfa. Captain Redfa was disillusioned by the poor treatment he had received as a Christian in the predominantly Islamic Iraqi military, and had also been disturbed at having been forced by his superiors to drop napalm bombs on dissident Kurdish targets. Additionally, it has also been claimed that Redfa—who was a deputy commander of a MiG-21 squadron—felt a "sneaking admiration" for the tenacity and bravery of the Israelis in the way so few fought valiantly against so many.

After this intelligence had been gathered, a female Mossad agent living in Baghdad was deployed to persuade Redfa to defect with a MiG-21. A beautiful woman (it has never been confirmed whether she was Jewish, or indeed if she was working on the behest of Israel or on her own initiative as sources conflict) she first encountered Redfa at a party. After engaging him in conversation, the pilot liked her immediately, and confessed that although he was a patriotic Iraqi, he found himself "in violent disagreement with the current war being waged by his government against the minority Kurdish tribesmen in northern Iraq." Armed with this information the agent developed an intimate relationship with Redfa, despite knowing that he was married and had two children. At her suggestion, they both took a short holiday together in Europe in July 1966 and, during the course of the break, the operative revealed that she had friends in Israel who might be "of service to him."

> Following this, secret negotiations were held and the Israeli Government offered Redfa $1 million, as well as new identities and Israeli citizenship for himself and his family, and a guarantee of full employment in the country. Redfa succeeded in leaving Iraq for three days without arousing suspicion where he met with an IAF pilot who flew him to Israel. He then secretly visited the area where he would be landing the MiG-21, and held a series of briefings with high-ranking Israeli personnel on details of the operation and their plans to safely evacuate his family. Mossad arranged for Redfa's wife and children to be vacationing in Paris when he was to undertake his dangerous mission. The remainder of his extended family were picked up by embedded Mossad agents (who had hired vans for the trip) and were hastily driven across country to the Iranian border. The family had told friends they were leaving Baghdad to have a picnic and were not missed for some time. Once across the border they were guided to safety by Iraqi Kurdish guerrillas before being collected by a helicopter and flown to an airfield, where a waiting airplane took them to Israel.
>
> On the morning of Tuesday August 16, 1966, Redfa completed his mission and successfully landed at the Hatzor Air Force Base in a MiG-21.

First let me say I was not familiar with the story of Munir Redfa before signing on for *Steal the Sky*. I knew nothing about Operation Diamond, or the circumstances that led to it. When I was first informed about the mission, I did find the idea of an Iraqi pilot defecting to Israel with a state-of-the-art fighter jet an interesting and provocative subject. The film actually came to me from a combination of different things. The producer, Yoram Ben-Ami, had seen *Weeds*, and loved it. He then contacted me about *Steal the Sky* and felt it was a project that might be of interest to me. As soon as I met Yoram I liked him, and wanted to work with him. Our relationship on *Steal the Sky* was very good from start to finish. He is a wonderful guy and we remain friends to this day. Yoram has led a strange and interesting life. For the last ten or fifteen years he's been traveling all around the world, experiencing different countries and cultures. That's what he's been doing with his life. His wife belongs to an original settler Israeli society. So, Yoram literally married into an important and respected family whereas his own parents were poor Romanians and he grew up on a kibbutz. He hasn't been involved much in film recently. I don't know why as he is a tremendous producer.

Like *Jaws 2* a decade earlier, *Steal the Sky* provided me with another chance to do an action picture. Believe it or not, even this far removed from *Bang the Drum Slowly* I was still being typed as the "warm and human guy." Maybe the initial perception of *Weeds* had done little to change that view. *Steal the Sky* offered an opportunity to do something that had a lot of breathless action and high tension. That prospect, along with the chance to do something commercial, probably attracted me above all others. *Top Gun* had been released the year before *Steal the Sky* and I do think the immense success of that movie assisted in getting our picture off the ground. It certainly did not impede its chances, let's put it that way. I had already seen *Top Gun* before committing to *Steal the Sky*, as Bill Badalato was the line producer on it and had done a terrific job. So, I got to hear all the behind-the-scenes stories from Bill regarding the shoot which were interesting. I was impressed with the visual look of the film, and marveled at the stunning action sequences Tony Scott had directed. Those can be extremely difficult to co-ordinate and choreograph, as I later discovered myself. However, I disliked *Top Gun* politically and for all its surface sheen and posturing, thought it was jingoistic and a little empty. But it did contain the same blend of frenetic action, danger and romance that we were going for in our movie.

Aside from Yoram, another important figure in my getting *Steal the Sky* was Steve Scheffer, who happens to be one of my oldest friends in the business. I first met Steve when he was fresh out of Harvard Business School, where he had taken a number of courses in the entertainment business. He went to work for Jim Aubrey, a successful television and film executive who at that point was running MGM. Steve had been one of the various development people at studios who had seen *Sticky My Fingers, Fleet My Feet* when it was doing its rounds back in 1970, and had been instrumental in passing it on to others and encouraging me generally. So, I've known him for a long time and, as a matter of fact, he tried to sell the cable rights to my latest film *The Looking Glass*. Back in 1988, Steve was second in command at HBO under Michael J. Fuchs—they were the two guys running the network at that point. Steve had always wanted to find something for me to do there and, now that *Weeds* had come out, he saw the opportunity to put me on their list of prospective directors. This meant that if a suitable project came up and the timing was right, they could get the guy they wanted and go off and make the picture. So, my involvement with *Steal the Sky* came partly through Yoram's enthusiasm for my work and partly through my connections at HBO insisting they would move ahead with the project if I signed-on.

> *The script for* Steal the Sky *was written by the English novelist and screenwriter Christopher Wood, whose previous credits (under the pseudonym Timothy Lea) had included the low-budget British sex comedies* Confessions of a Window Cleaner *(1974),* Confessions of a Pop Performer *(1975),* Confessions of a Taxi Driver *(1976) and* Confessions from a Holiday Camp *(1977). Under his own name, Wood had followed these harmlessly puerile and highly successful films with more illustrious assignments such as the James Bond movies* The Spy Who Loved Me *(1977) and* Moonraker *(1979). Among his later credits is the amusing action-adventure curio* Remo Williams: The Adventure Begins *(1985) directed by Guy Hamilton, himself a veteran of four entries in the James Bond canon. Wood's draft of* Steal the Sky, *which was completed in mid-1987, would be revised by Dorothy Tristan shortly after Hancock agreed to direct the film.*

Before Yoram sent me Christopher Wood's screenplay, he told me the title. I didn't like it particularly and, truth be told, still don't to this day. It sounded a little like the title of some corny romance novel. Not being very adept at conceiving titles myself, I couldn't think of a better alternative to *Steal the Sky* and so it quickly stuck. When I finally read the script, I was happy to discover that the story was stronger than the title. Nonetheless, I still felt it contained dialogue and character problems that needed to be addressed if it was ever going to work as a movie. The central love story also needed to be a little juicier as the lady spy initially came across as somewhat bland and unappealing when she had to be a vivacious seductress capable of convincing this Iraqi pilot to turn against his own country. It's my understanding that Wood had tailored his story after some war picture from the 1940s—I've never been able to discover exactly which film it was—and I felt one of the script's core strengths was its structure and clarity. It really worked in the way the action and tension steadily built up, particularly during the climactic sequences. All of that stuff was solidly constructed and I was visualizing it in my head as I was reading, which is always a good sign.

Another potent aspect of Wood's story was the timeless notion of the honey trap. To me that's a really compelling set-up, one I've always been attracted to in stories. It resonates with audiences as it presents them with a question: would they succumb to temptation and be held in the thrall of a nice piece of ass, or would they remain resolute? It's such a good element to play with. By remedying a few of the deficiencies in the screenplay, I felt we could have something really good. At no point before or during *Steal the Sky* did I ever get the opportunity to meet with Wood to discuss his script. I must admit that I'm not familiar with the *Confessions* films he'd written previously in England. I've never even heard of them, although I'd be interested to see them as nobody specializes in embarrassing sex comedies quite like the British! I had seen both *The Spy Who Loved Me* and *Moonraker*, and I can see the relationship between *Steal the Sky* and the two James Bond movies he wrote in terms of their blend of international espionage, romance and action. But with Wood not around, Yoram thought Dorothy would be great to come in and fix all these problems. She did a page-one rewrite, revising the scenes between the pilot and the lady spy so that they carried a little more sparkle and charge.

> *One of the most disheartening aspects of making* Steal the Sky *for Hancock was the casting process. HBO refused several acclaimed actors he submitted for the principal parts of pilot Munir Redfa and Helen Mason, the beautiful American spy dispatched to seduce him, as well as rejecting various names Hancock proposed for the supporting roles. Notables such as David Suchet, Alfred Molina, Charlotte Rampling and a pre-Academy Award-winning Joe Pesci (whom Hancock had wanted to play a heavy) were dismissed by the network—much to the filmmaker's astonishment. "HBO's reasoning was founded on reasons of 'commerciality and convenience'—whatever the hell that means," he recalls with exasperation. Casting sessions spanned continents, with Hancock and Ben-Ami interviewing actors for the film in Tel-Aviv, London, Los Angeles and New York, in an exhaustive search for international actors. They were aided in their efforts by Rosemary Welden and her associates Carolyn Long and Irene Stockton (the latter a veteran of*

Weeds) *with additional assistance coming from a casting agency in Israel that helped with the hiring of ethnic players. One actor Hancock suggested that was met with immediate approval from HBO was Julie Christie, the Oscar-winning star of such films as* Darling *(1965),* McCabe & Mrs. Miller *(1971) and* Don't Look Now *(1973). Sadly, Christie would refuse the starring role of Helen Mason for "political reasons."*

I found the casting process extremely frustrating with HBO at that point in time. I think it's changed to some degree since, but, back then, it was difficult and tedious. The situation on *Steal the Sky* was something of a repeat of the unfortunate business I'd encountered on *Baby Blue Marine*. It was basically another case of battling over actors who just weren't suitable or special in my view. Now, I can understand why you might want to cast Tom Cruise as Munir Redfa and Julia Roberts as Helen Mason, but there are certain actors who just won't do anything for your movie in terms of their marketability and the quality of their performance. They don't have a certain cachet. What I'm referring to here is the mini-names that people have heard of, actors who have enjoyed moderately successful careers and are somewhat recognizable, but aren't big draws. Indeed, when their names appear in the credits and ads of certain pictures it's taken as an indication by some that the movie is not very good in a way. HBO were intent on hiring these mini-names for *Steal the Sky* at the expense of actors who I felt were better and stronger. I argued that we didn't need any "name" actors, we needed the *right* actors. HBO thought otherwise, and I could see the validity of their position without liking it. They maintained that we needed people the audience had heard of, since they only showed the picture a limited number of times and there would be no chance for word-of-mouth to build. They've learned since then to either do series like *The Sopranos* and so forth, which do provide an opportunity for word-of-mouth to build, or program their one-shot shows with real names—like Barry Levinson's recent Bernie Madoff movie, *The Wizard of Lies*, which starred Robert De Niro and Michelle Pfeiffer and was excellent. But things were different back in 1988.

We auditioned a lot of people for the different parts and looked at a lot more. In moving from the United States to Israel to England in an effort to find our cast, it was quite an operation. When we were casting in London we worked out of the Dorchester Hotel, which was nice. Yoram always took good care of the casting sessions and scouting trips, all that stuff, and *Steal the Sky* was easily one of the most international movies I've made in terms of the traveling and the personnel involved. Ben Cross came to my attention for Munir Redfa through his agent, who submitted him when we were casting in London. I had liked Ben in *Chariots of Fire* in which he had played an Olympic athlete, but I must be honest in saying he was not my first choice for the role. I had earlier looked at several wonderful English actors including David Suchet, who has since achieved international fame for his starring turn in *Poirot*. He really wanted to do the film. Suchet actually said to me during our meeting, "I'd like to play something straight," which I found amusing. He is a fabulous actor and I would've liked him to have played Redfa, even though it would have possibly been a little bizarre.

My first choice for Redfa was Alfred Molina. That's who I initially wanted for the part and was excited by. I had recently seen Molina in Stephen Frears' film *Prick Up Your Ears*, which was derived from the biography of the British playwright Joe Orton that had been written by John Lahr (Lahr appears as a character in the movie and is played by Wallace Shawn). Anyway, Molina had played Kenneth Halliwell, Orton's lover and eventual murderer, and I was immediately struck by him. His performance really captured a tormented and somewhat pathetic soul. I thought the interesting thing about Molina playing Redfa, which was something I felt Ben Cross ultimately lacked, was a certain vulnerability and ordinariness. Molina would have been slightly overweight and kind of goofy-looking, as opposed to Cross's lean handsomeness. I thought Ben would not be as susceptible to seduction in some way, at least not to the extent that Molina would. I felt Molina looked like someone who would be more prone to the charms of a beautiful American woman and could possibly be persuaded to defect. Unfortunately, Molina wasn't a star yet and despite him being a tremendous actor whose career was on the up, HBO would not allow me to cast him. So, I relented and somewhat reluctantly agreed on Ben Cross for the role.

As for the part of Helen Mason, there were several candidates. I had initially tried to get Julie Christie to play the part. I thought she was capable of bringing not only the alluring beauty but the cool intelligence and bravery the character required. Julie and I had wanted to work together for some time. Back in the mid-1970s, I almost did *Demon Seed* with her, the horror movie in which she is somehow impregnated by an organic super-computer. The truth is I'd always had such a mad crush on her. For that reason, I thought *Demon Seed* would be a dangerous picture for me to do. I had only gotten married to Dorothy the year before and my philandering days were well behind me. Still, despite being so blissfully happy with my wife, I asked myself if it was worth risking my marriage for a movie. In the end, it didn't matter. Daniel Melnick and Sherry Lansing were two of the people setting *Demon Seed* up at MGM—this was before Sherry became one of the first women to head a major studio and was President of 20th Century Fox. I remember Sherry—so pretty—took me aside one day and said, "John, are you kinky enough to make this picture?" I looked right at her and said, "Oh, absolutely! You bet I am!" So, they offered me the picture with a fairly low-ball fee, and my agent was in the process of trying to get more money when for some reason they withdrew the offer. Maybe after careful deliberation, they decided that ultimately I was *not* kinky enough to direct *Demon Seed*, or maybe it was just that the guy they may have originally wanted—Donald Cammell, not my favorite director in the world—decided he wanted to do it. Frankly, I thought Cammell screwed the picture up. I don't think he did a good job with what appeared to be a fairly original, if rather weird, story.

Anyway, as I said, when *Steal the Sky* rolled around more than a decade later, we offered the part of Helen to Julie. I hoped for the best, as I was aware she was not accepting many film roles at this point in her career (I believe she was living in Wales at the time). A little while afterwards, I received a letter from Julie. It was a very personal and heartfelt letter in which she basically said, "John, how could you possibly do this film? It's so pro-Israeli. Don't you realize what their activities are doing to the Palestinian people?" She then proceeded to give me her reasons for why she couldn't do the film. I then wrote Julie back, saying, "I'm aware of the difficulties with the Israeli-Palestinian conflict. I'm just sorry that we find ourselves on opposite sides of this issue, but I do understand and accept your reasons for not wanting to do the picture." The fact is Julie felt that I should not proceed with *Steal the Sky*. She even directly asked me, "Why in the world are you making this film?" That's always an important question for any director to ask themselves before taking on a movie and the reasons can be different every time: financial reasons, career reasons, personal reasons, and, yes, political reasons. Let me be clear though, I was making *Steal the Sky* because it was a job. Needless to say, I haven't had any contact with Julie since I made the movie.

After Julie's refusal, I wanted very badly to cast a beautiful young actress by the name of Shannon Tweed, who was a former Playboy Playmate of the Year. I had seen a couple of pictures she had done, one of which was a horror movie called *Of Unknown Origin* that concerned a man who wages war against a monstrous rat which has invaded his New York brownstone. None of them were good pictures, but Shannon had been quite charming in them. I read her for the part of Helen on three or four occasions and firmly believed that she could do it. She had this sexy, soft, broken quality that I thought would be perfect for the character of this female spy. On top of everything, I had anticipated that the fact Shannon was a former Playmate of the Year she would satisfy HBO's desire for "commerciality." I couldn't have been more wrong. They thought it was an utterly tasteless and undignified choice, particularly following on from Julie Christie. They argued that giving her the role would be the equivalent of slumming it, and indicative of the kind of inappropriate stunt casting that Cannon or AIP specialized in. I felt they were being unfair and narrow-minded, and that Shannon deserved a chance. It didn't matter. The network would not let me cast her and insisted that we continue the search.

After Shannon was shrugged aside, we then flirted with Charlotte Rampling for a while. I think she would have been excellent, as she had the same sexiness and glacial intelligence that Julie had. Charlotte also has a morose and remote quality in some of her performances that would have worked for the loneliness and dissatisfaction the character felt. I forget now what happened with her. For some reason it just didn't work out. Throughout this casting phase, I remember HBO was pressing me to hire Anne Archer as Helen Mason because she was just coming off *Fatal Attraction* in which she had played Michael Douglas' wife. That movie had been a huge box office hit and received several Academy Award nominations, including one for Best Picture and one for Archer as Best Supporting Actress. I thought she was pretty good in *Fatal Attraction*, but I was not really a big fan of her work. There was something about her that I didn't find entirely convincing for the role of an international spy, although she was undeniably pretty. When I suggested to HBO that I didn't feel she was especially right for the part, they were not impressed. It was obvious that we had very different ideas about who should be playing the principal roles in the film.

Then Mariel Hemingway came into view. I had seen her in *Manhattan* and *Star 80*, and liked her performances in both movies. She came in, read well, and was also very likable. As a personality, Mariel is an extremely straightforward girl. You look at the prose of her grandfather, Ernest Hemingway, it's very simple declarative sentences, and that's very much

Mariel. She has an unaffected way about her in that what you see is what you get. That's an attractive commodity, particularly in the double-dealing circles of Hollywood, but, in the final analysis, was she the right choice to play a spy? I would have to say no, she wasn't. It didn't really work and that was probably my mistake. A big part of directing is determining whether or not the actor has the character *in* them. I was so dazzled by Mariel's work in *Manhattan* and *Star 80*—and was impressed enough by her initial reading—I failed to recognize she was not the ideal person to play this heroic seductress. There were some things Mariel simply couldn't do. She was comfortable doing the nude scenes, but she did have it specified in her contract that she had the right to edit them. So, Mariel literally sat in the editing room with me and duly eliminated several shots of her breasts in the shower scene. She had gotten a boob job for *Star 80* in which she had played Dorothy Stratton and I believe she decided she had gone too far with it.

The disagreements with HBO over casting continued when we were looking at some of the supporting roles in the film. One incident that particularly aggrieved me was the casting of Aziz, the head of the Iraqi secret police. You may find this hard to believe, but Joe Pesci actually wanted to play that part. This was several years after Pesci had appeared alongside Bobby De Niro in *Raging Bull* and just before he did *Goodfellas*, which won him a well-deserved Academy Award. I met with Pesci to discuss the film and he was a wonderful and funny guy. He's one of those actors who can switch effortlessly between various states and colors in his performances; one moment he's incredibly charming, the next he is a sickening psychopath—and yet he's still incredibly charming. You only have to watch those remarkable scenes in *Goodfellas* where Pesci holds court with the other gangsters and is telling his amusing stories. The moment when he seemingly turns on Ray Liotta's character, Henry, and you fear the confrontation will explode into violence, is so arresting and disturbing. We could have had that in *Steal the Sky*. I knew Pesci would be terrific in the role, but, yet again, HBO would *not* let me cast him. I just found them a near-constant hindrance to deal with. It was crazy! We eventually hired Yossi Shiloa, an Iraqi-Israeli actor who is sometimes billed as Joseph Shiloach, to play Aziz.

Some of the cast was made up by people I had worked with previously, like Richard Libertini whom I'd done a *Twilight Zone* episode with. There was also Nicolas Surovy, who'd been in *Bang the Drum Slowly*, who I cast as Helen's husband. Mark Rolston, who was in *Weeds*, is adept at international accents, so I cast him as the Soviet Colonel stationed at the Al Rasheed Air Base in Iraq. I also formed some new associations on *Steal the Sky* that survived the film. One was with Andreas Katsulas, whom I later worked with on *A Piece of Eden*. I was just crazy for Andreas. He was trained in Peter Brooks' international theater company in Paris and had performed all over the world for fifteen years. Another actor I enjoyed working with was Sasson Gabai, who we cast as Kamel Djem, an Iraqi pilot and comrade of Redfa's at Al Rasheed. I loved him. He was the leading actor in the Habima Theatre at that point, which is the national theater of Israel and is located in Tel Aviv. Interestingly, Sasson was born in Iraq but had lived in Israel since his early years. A lot of the people around the edges of *Steal the Sky* were Iraqi-Israelis—that's how Yoram and the Israeli casting people thought of casting the Arabs and the Kurds, using Iraqi Jews. I also liked Etti Ankri, the Israeli actress who played Mrs. Redfa. She was very beautiful and very real in her performance.

If you look at *Steal the Sky* now, hopefully you'll agree that the film looks far more expensive than what it cost. The budget was around $7 or $8 million, something like that. I don't know the precise figure. Maybe I'm exaggerating, as it could have been as little as $5 million. It was a fairly modest production by most standards of the day, but the money did not impact on my ambitions for the movie. I pretty much got everything that I wanted and asked for. First, to assemble the six or how many MiGs that we used on the picture was not easy. That took some doing. There wasn't anything I wanted to do in the film that I couldn't get, and the locations were so beautiful and so exotic it really gave the film a great look. We shot around sixty percent of *Steal the Sky* in Israel, and I think we shot for three or four days in Rome, Italy, which was great fun. The rest of the stuff, including the aerial footage, was shot in the desert of Reno, Nevada. It was considered extremely dangerous and foolhardy to even attempt to stage the aerial sequences in Israel. If we had tried, no doubt we would have been blown out of the sky.

Even with the tensions, it was surprisingly easy to secure permission to shoot in certain locations in Israel that we'd identified. There wasn't a lot of red tape involved with inquisitive officials demanding to read the script before granting permission, not in the way you might imagine there would be with all the troubles. We shot a lot on the West Bank and were surrounded by soldiers. Well, they weren't soldiers exactly but members of Shin Bet, the Israeli internal security service. We were well protected throughout the shoot and it was an extraordinary experience living and working at that location. You'll notice there is also an exterior shot of Baghdad that is glimpsed early in the film. That's a matte painting. We employed a bunch of matte paintings on *Steal the Sky*. The shot of the Iraqi train station is one of a number of mattes, for instance. Additionally, there is a wide-shot of the airfield upon which stands around twelve MiGs— that is another well-executed matte painting. My production designer on the film was Keith Wilson, who was British and had worked on a number of television shows. I thought he and the set decorators did a wonderful job of recreating the past on a budget. Keith made considerable efforts to make it seem like a 1960s period piece as we did not want the film to feel like a contemporary 1980s movie; a Middle Eastern *Top Gun*. That attention to detail also extended to our having the correct military uniforms, weaponry and vehicles of the time and place as well.

I don't believe we had any historical, military or technical advisor on *Steal the Sky*. At least I have no memory of conferring with such a person. I do recall that I did a lot of research myself before we started shooting the film, just to make a small effort at trying to understand some of the complexities of the nations involved. I read a lot of books about the history of Iraq and its people. I also have a neighbor here in Indiana—in fact my parents had sold him the property where he built his house—named Marvin Zonis, who is a specialist in Middle Eastern affairs at the University of Chicago. I spent a lot of time discussing various things with Marvin. He shared some intriguing insights with me into Arab nationalism, how the nationalists despise the "decadence" of the Western world and seek to eradicate its influence in the Arab world. All of this was helpful and gave me background information. I tried to quickly grasp some of the social, cultural and religious factors, as well as some of the political events, that have assisted in shaping that territory. I found Iraq to be a deeply fascinating country, and I discovered a lot of interesting stuff about it.

During my research I also learned about a real-life incident that I thought would make an exciting visual scene in *Steal the Sky*. I discovered that several years before he came to power in 1979 as the fifth President of Iraq, Saddam Hussein was involved in a conspiracy that was organized to overthrow the previous regime. In 1959, Saddam was part of a botched operation that was designed to assassinate a high-ranking target who was going to be riding in his car through a certain street at a certain time along with his entourage. Saddam and his soldiers were positioned across the road from each other and they managed to kill a number of their own party simply by stepping out and shooting at the motorcade as it rode by. I believe the idea was that the first line of Saddam's men would kill those sitting in the front of the car and the second line would kill those sitting in the back, something like that. The insurgents succeeded in killing many of their own people as they failed to comprehend that two rows of gunmen shooting at a passing vehicle from opposite sides of a road at the same time was a dangerously bad idea. Surely, it would have been better for them to have all been shooting from just one side. Saddam himself was wounded in this operation and scurried off to Syria or Egypt to recover for a year and a half until the heat died down. I was astonished to read about this episode and wanted to work it into the screenplay somehow. Ultimately, there really wasn't any place for it, but it's still lurking in the back of my mind as something I'd like to use in the future.

Research is important. It gives you different avenues, choices and details you can always draw from, although if you use too much of it the picture just comes across as dense, wieldy and boring. On *Steal the Sky*, I discovered that it's also good to research the place where you are filming. It's often hard to work abroad as you are working in a new and unfamiliar environment. There are always hidden communication problems that need to be overcome as the international crews have different styles and different working methods, as well as other idiosyncrasies that—from your comfortable American perspective—can be confusing and frustrating. As a director, it's never a case of simply catching a flight to another country populated by people that speak a different language, and just making your movie. There are lots of things you must be cognizant of, things that don't enter your mind until the moment they become apparent. For instance, something you often have to contend with shooting abroad is getting ill on location. I remember I got sick on part of the shoot on *Steal the Sky* and it was a difficult situation. I was coughing terribly, had a debilitating sore throat and no energy. It was awful.

Like me, Mariel also got desperately sick from encountering germs that our bodies didn't know anything about. There are certain foods you're not accustomed to that can make you decidedly ill. You can't afford to be sick when making a picture as there's a lot of money involved. You can take a crew to Mexico for a shoot and suddenly everybody has turista (diarrhea, the disease of tourists) for three weeks. I mean, a film crew can parallel invading armies who are exposed to strange new germs, like Sherman's troops marching across Georgia, and Hitler's in Russia. About the latter, I was reading recently that the Germans were ordered to slit open the back of their pants because they were having to shit so often in the middle of winter they were literally dying of exposure as they were taking their pants down so many times to do it. So, I think you always have to give careful thought and consideration to every possibility when you are in a foreign country. Thankfully, on *Steal the Sky*, these problems did not extend our schedule. We shot for something like forty days and I think we only lost one day. Mariel had such a bad sore throat on that occasion we collected insurance for that one day.

As I implied earlier, I was not well-versed in Middle Eastern politics before embarking on the film. What I did know was confined to what I'd read and seen on the news, even if I'd often thought about the problems. When we first arrived in Israel to scout and shoot the film in early 1988, it was during the First Intifada, which I believe had begun in December 1987 and lasted for the next five or six years. That was a terribly interesting time to be there. I remember Dorothy and I expressed a desire to go scout in Jericho, in the Palestinian Territories, near the Jordan River. When we got part of the way there on the West Bank, we suddenly saw an ominous column of thick smoke rising out of the city that was coming from burning tires. We stopped and said, "Okay, maybe we should scout it another day." This happened more than once; we'd head for Jericho, see the smoke in the sky and would then turn back for the relative safety of our hotel. We were warned by certain individuals never to go into Palestinian areas on our day off; that if we did, some harm may come to us. Despite this we consistently did just that and found these trips fascinating and rewarding. Dorothy and I went to Nablus, a city in the Northern West Bank, and to Hebron, as we were intent on seeing and experiencing as much as we could.

My stepdaughter, Alexandra, who now works as a photojournalist for *National Geographic*, *LIFE* and *TIME*, stayed with us while we were in Israel. This was back when Alexandra was just starting out and she really seized the opportunity. At one point, she ventured off and stayed overnight in a Palestinian village. The next morning, she awoke to the sound of the neighboring kids throwing rocks and stones at the Israeli soldiers. She then went outside, her camera in her hands, and was basically dodging bullets with them. Alexandra managed to get some incredible photographs that she later sold to *TIME*. One was a rather famous picture of an Israeli soldier moments after a Palestinian had calmly walked up to him and shot him in the head. She just happened to be there and quickly snapped off the immediate aftermath of this incident. In fact, Alexandra was there so fast the Israeli soldiers thought she had some foreknowledge of their comrade's assassination. They tried to confiscate her film and bent her thumbs back in an effort to make sure she surrendered everything she had. Fortunately, Alexandra had managed to secrete the roll containing the crucial shots in the door of a car. She later smuggled that film out of Israel and it got her started as a photojournalist. She has since enjoyed a successful career photographing conflicts in the Middle East. Alexandra was also present when the Berlin Wall came down in 1989, and when Boris Yeltsin was on the tank after the Moscow Coup of 1991. So, her time with us on *Steal the Sky* proved to be profitable for her.

One thing we quickly learned was that people in Israel are extremely observant and intuitive about exactly who are what and what is who. I mean, the Israelis are astute about what kind of Jew you are and where you are from, and what kind of Arab you are and where you are from. It was the same thing with the Arabs, who were also remarkably perceptive. They immediately determined from taking just one look at us that Dorothy and I were not Israelis. I don't know if they deduced this from our clothes, or our mannerisms, but whatever it was they simply knew it before we had even uttered a word. Had we been Israelis wandering around their territories we would have been in serious trouble, but we were not and they clearly understood this. Be that as it may, I did get a little scared when we were in Hebron because there were so many burning tires as well as this discernible restlessness. I felt the atmosphere was decidedly different there than it was in Nablus. Historically there is a lot more guerrilla violence—violence on both sides—in Hebron and you could see that tension hanging in the air as surely as the smoke.

Despite what Julie Christie had feared about the film being "pro-Israeli," I was interested in being as objective as possible in *Steal the Sky*. Admittedly, some of the Iraqis are scowling villains, but I wanted to make a well-balanced film that presented the conflict evenly in terms of these opposing viewpoints. One example is the moment when Redfa has a meeting with the Israeli high command. At one point he looks at a fleet of toy jets attached to a military map on the wall that are all pointed toward Israel, and says, "This is how you see the world?" He then turns the jets around so they face outward: "This is how we see it!" So, I wanted to show his side of things. I should point out that when I was shooting the film, I was surrounded by the rightwing of the Mossad and several other important and committed Israelis. Yoram was actually friends with Ariel Sharon who at that point was the Minster of Trade and Industry and would later become the Prime Minister of Israel. So, I was ringed by people who believed passionately in their own cause and country. For instance, there were occasions when we'd be driving along a road and Yoram would see Palestinians being searched by the Israeli soldiers. He would then roll down the window of the car as we glided past, lean his head out and shout, "Yeah, good! Fuck 'em! Fuck 'em!" It's my understanding that the transportation co-coordinator on the set was one of the Mossad guys who had gone around and rang the doorbells of the people who had assisted or participated in the killing of the Israeli athletes during the Munich Olympics of 1972 and had shot them. That was the reality of who I was working with.

I felt, and still do, that it was important that Israel exist, because of the Holocaust and other factors. It's unthinkable to me that it should not survive. Of course, like anything, it all comes down to your point of view: who is the oppressor and who is the oppressed? Who's in the wrong here? It's such a fiercely divisive and wide-ranging issue, conflated with a number of other emotional considerations, one must be aware of all the facts before one aligns oneself with any particular cause or position. Yes, the Palestinian people are being persecuted and, as I see it, the tragedy of the Israelis is this passing-on of violence from generation to generation. It's so ghastly and unremitting. On the other hand, it must be said that the Palestinians are blowing up Israeli cafes in Tel Aviv as well as committing other damaging activities. So, it's a historical tragedy where Israelis feel their very existence is imperiled, and Arabs point to the fact that the creation of the state of Israel is what really soured relations between these races. The truth is we can talk about dispossession and historic rights and forced exile and land claims, all that stuff, but the amount of people who have died—and are continuing to die—in this conflict is appalling. I don't think anybody can refute that. Sadly, nobody seems capable of resolving this situation peacefully.

I recall that during the shoot, Dorothy and I were staying at a hotel in Tel Aviv. It wasn't the Hilton, it was another big hotel in the city. Our room was up on a high floor that was overlooking the Mediterranean in all directions. It was an exceedingly nice suite, very comfortable. While I was out shooting the picture, Dorothy would be ensconced in the hotel, toiling on the script. There was a janitor working in the building whom she had befriended, and I guess this guy had developed a crush on her. He would come up to our room and do rather sweet things for her; bring her snacks, make sure that her typewriter was working, little things like that.

This guy took good care of Dorothy and I know that she enjoyed talking with him. One day the janitor said to her: "You don't know it, but down in the basement of this hotel there are swastikas painted on the walls. It's my belief that we won't last here. This country is not going to survive. The Arabs are eventually going to out-breed us and surround us, and, one day, finally push us out into the sea. This Israel is just a temporary phenomenon." When I got back to the hotel later that night, Dorothy told me what the janitor had said and I was struck by the apparent sadness and fatalism of his words. I've never forgotten them. The Israelis are a defiant and proud race of people, but when you live in a state of unceasing conflict and anxiety like that it takes its toll. I hope I don't sound too glib when I say you can see why some of them want to go to Los Angeles. I mean, if I were an Israeli Jew I might be tempted to move from Tel Aviv to the San Fernando Valley.

I never really discussed the conflict with the actors, or asked them where their own sympathies lied. That was a big question to ask anybody, but I occasionally heard and observed things that troubled me. Ben Cross was good to work with, but he sometimes behaved bizarrely while we were shooting in Israel. I never quite got a fix on him, although he was always pleasant to me. I remember one night we were going out to dinner, and Dorothy and I met him in the lobby of the Tel Aviv Hilton. Ben came walking out of the elevator and suddenly yelled at the top of his voice, "I *hate* Jews! They have absolutely no taste at all!" Dorothy and I just stood there for a few uncomfortable moments, dumbfounded. Ben would openly repeat these sentiments on occasion and we would simply choose to ignore them. I do recall that we had an extremely Israeli costume lady working on *Steal the Sky*, and I actually said to her one time after Ben had expressed this view in her presence, "How do you feel about that?" She just shrugged and said, "It means nothing to me. I don't care what he thinks, or what he says. It isn't important." But it was strange and potentially disruptive behavior on Ben's part and I never quite understood where it was coming from. I certainly thought it was the kind of thing one should *not* do in that environment, but I never talked to him about it. Perhaps I should have.

> *Wood and Tristan's screenplay is careful in the way it parses and parcels out bits of historical information about Operation Diamond, but, perhaps understandably, some liberties were taken with the facts. Always conscious of "the*

> dramatic imperative," Hancock and Ben-Ami never strived to make an authentic portrayal of these real events and people at the expense of entertaining an audience.

In filmmaking, when it comes to the question of sacrificing a little truth for the sake of narrative clarity and propulsion, I'm all for it. I really am. As a writer and a director you have to condense actual historical events that took place over days, weeks, months and years into two hours or so. Not only that, you have to make it a piece of entertainment that will engage and inform the audience. In that effort, I believe you should strive to create a higher kind of truth. Basically, what I mean is you should in effect attempt to communicate the essence of those events as you can not precisely duplicate what happened. It just isn't possible. The medium won't allow it. Thus, you have to compress and approximate what these affairs mean in a historical and political context. What your objectivity or opinion is, that's another matter. I mean, what is *truth* exactly? In selecting and editing the events you are recreating, you are attempting to convey impressions to an audience of what might have happened and not the surfaces of what happened. You try to imagine what people were thinking and feeling at various moments either by measuring it against the limits of your own imagination, your own physical and moral courage, or by taking a swinging guess at it. I don't feel by doing this we distorted too much of the truth in *Steal the Sky*.

Not being very keen with all the facts, I still think our batting average is good in terms of veracity. As far as anybody knows, the portrayal of Helen Mason in the movie is as accurate and respectful as it's going to get. Maybe in reality she wasn't an American spy; maybe she was an Israeli spy or possibly a French spy, but that's never been confirmed. My understanding is that the character is true to life in regards to her ultimate objectives: the continued security and preservation of the state of Israel. To the best of anyone's knowledge, Redfa was coerced to defect in the same way we present in the film: he met Helen at a party, began an affair, and was convinced to flee Iraq with a MiG-21. I don't think it was a decision Redfa made quickly. It clearly took him some time to decide if he was going to go through with it; $1 million, Israeli citizenship for himself and his entire family and the guarantee of full time employment, means nothing if you're dead. We had to hurry these events along to keep our story moving, but any mission of that importance would have required a lot of planning. Obviously, back then, in the chill of the Cold War, the idea of a citizen defecting to an enemy country and giving away their secrets and technology was a huge thing. It still is.

Some events we chose not to dramatize or speculate about in the film, or we simply weren't aware of them. This included the fact that Redfa had secretly visited the airfield to view the area where he would eventually be landing with the MiG. We didn't need that scene in the movie and I knew nothing about it at the time of filming. But it would have made sense while he was in Israel—and if he indeed was going through with the operation—to have taken a look. I also recently discovered that Redfa had been secretly photographed by the Israelis on his visit, so that this evidence could be used to force him into defecting if he refused or changed his mind. In the movie, we had the Israelis threatening Redfa with photographs of him and Helen together romantically, as well as a picture of him arriving at an Israeli airport. The truth is Mossad were determined to capture a MiG-21 at whatever cost. They were prepared to sacrifice their agents in this task because they understood the value of the prize. No doubt Redfa knew they meant business. Dorothy and I felt it was important to have this threat hanging over Redfa as it made him a far more sympathetic character and, conversely, made the Israelis look a little tougher.

One decisive thing that made Redfa a viable candidate for the mission was the fact he was a Christian serving in the Iraqi military. As part of an ethnic and religious minority, my sense is he felt discriminated against by those in authority. I believe one of the questions that's often been asked in relation to Redfa's religious beliefs is could it have made him suspicious to the Iraqi command. Did they not anticipate that he could be a potential defector? Well, the truth is more complex than that. The Ba'ath Party had also experienced trouble with the Kurds and yet there were still Kurdish generals in the Iraqi Army. In a way, you can understand why Saddam Hussein was so ruthlessly brutal in his efforts to hold his regime together. If you start off by saying, "Okay, we are not going to have any Kurds or Christians in positions of responsibility because we simply can't trust them," you are eliminating a whole bunch of effective and able people who can contribute to your power base. You may end up with a number of people whom you don't entirely trust, but at least the organization continues to function—if you can scare 'em enough! That's exactly what Saddam did by applying executions, torture and other forms of oppression as a means of keeping his subordinates in line. Naturally, there will always be disgruntled individuals who are vulnerable to betraying the regime. Redfa was undoubtedly one of those people.

Even considering this, it would not have been easy for Israel to get an Iraqi to turn against his own nation. If you research the history, you'll see that the men appointed to a MiG-21 squadron were receiving the highest honor that could be bestowed to a pilot. It was a big deal. They had been carefully selected because they'd met a certain criteria and skill level. They were brave, capable, ambitious, but above all patriotic. These were not guys who would just throw it all away for nothing. This is why Mossad had made no progress in learning about the MiGs. They couldn't gather the necessary intelligence together to acquire one. Thus, they had to try a different approach: seduction. That's why there is always the temptation to adopt a poetic license when making a movie that concerns real people and events. Maybe the real stuff is not as juicy and dramatic enough to meet the requirements of a commercial action film. So, you have to give it a little more *buzz*! Nonetheless, you must be careful about what fictional aspects you add to the story. I don't know of many times in *Steal the Sky* we did that, but I believe one instance is the aerial dogfight that Redfa engages in after he defects and is trying for the Dead Sea. I was not told any differently, but I imagine that in reality there was no dogfight and Redfa simply flew to Israel unopposed. I think Christopher Wood wanted to have him be chased there and it probably was the right thing to do. If I remember correctly Redfa may have even been accompanied or escorted by two Israeli jets for the closing stages of his flight to insure he arrived safely, but I may be wrong about that.

Granted, I very much doubt that Redfa knocked out an Iraqi Colonel at Al Rasheed before jumping in the MiG-21 and taking off. That was all invented by us, as I believe was Helen's escape with Mrs. Redfa and the children over the mountains. The shoot-out on the airfield didn't happen either, but, again, I understood why we had to do that stuff. We had to turn up the heat and make the situation appear more exciting and pressurized. The whole thrust of the picture was building towards it. We didn't want it to seem like Redfa had just climbed in a jet and flown to Israel (even though that's pretty much what happened). After his comrades saw on their radar that he'd veered off course, they ordered him back. Redfa ignored them and switched his radio off during the flight. Not very exciting! One other thing worth pointing out about the movie is that Redfa actually escapes with a MiG-15, not a MiG-21. This was due to the fact that we could not obtain a MiG-21 for the purposes of shooting. It was interesting dealing with the kind of guy who lives in Texas and wants to own MiGs and loan them to productions. That in itself is a fascinating underworld and would make a compelling subject for a movie. Collectors of military paraphernalia—uniforms, weapons, medals, vehicles, whatever it is—are obsessive and possessive about their collection. They are curious personalities to encounter. Some collectors are eager to loan things to a film company just for the notoriety and amusement; other collectors cannot bring themselves to part with as much as a wheel-nut or a button.

One detail in *Steal the Sky* that we didn't have to juice up was the fact that Redfa only had a certain amount of fuel in the MiG-21 to complete his mission. In what one could say was a very clever addition, the Russians had imposed strict limits on the amount of fuel that could be carried by the MiGs on approved flights. Clearly, this was designed to prevent any possible defections from occurring. A smart move! Any pilot who would dare steal a MiG-21 would not be able to make it very far, certainly not as far as Israel. All the same, Redfa had somehow convinced the ground crews on the Iraqi airbase to completely fill up his tanks. This did not alert the crew to Redfa's possible defection, or arouse their suspicions in any way, and they merely did as he instructed. The flight to Israel from Iraq was something like 900 kilometers and that was as far as the MiG-21 could fly with a full tank. That was its complete range. So, it was very, very tight and Redfa pushed that jet to its absolute limit. I believe he landed in Israel with only fumes in his tank. He was basically down to his last few drops of fuel, so it was an incredibly close run thing. That is all confirmed as having actually happened.

The MiGs themselves were a curious mixture of elegance and ruggedness. They were impressive machines to behold, but, upon closer inspection, I noticed several interesting details about them. The MiG-15s we worked with, when you stood up close to one, you could see, for instance, the quality of the rivets. You could detect that these jets had been built by workers and not by Stanford graduates. They were surprisingly rough and somewhat rudimentary in appearance; functional, even primitive. The construction of these aircraft was sturdy and they tended not to break. They were designed to be fast and tough and durable. There was plainly a high level of sophistication and ingenuity in certain areas, but there were also what appeared to be more basic attributes in others. Looking inside the cockpit one time, I noticed they had instructions on the dashboards in Chinese and Czech. I don't know whether the MiGs were constructed in Russia for Czechoslovakia, or whether they were constructed in Czechoslovakia itself, but I do believe they were built under license in other countries. My point is the MiG-21 was considered to be the most advanced fighter jet of its time, but, in coming from Czechoslovakia, you would have expected more accomplished riveting than what I saw on display. For that reason, I always suspected that they were built in Russia.

Interestingly, since we are on the subject of truth and authenticity, another matter I'd like to touch on is actors' accents. Some directors are not consistent, or even insistent, about actors speaking dialogue in the character's correct accents. That is definitely the case with certain American actors, who may not feel adept or entirely comfortable with the foreign accents they're doing (Mark Rolston being an obvious exception). Many times they speak in their own accent when they are playing French, Russian or Mexican people and the audience may even forget that they are playing someone from another country. We've all seen Biblical epics like *The Greatest Story Ever Told*, or adventure films like *Robin Hood* set in Medieval England, where characters speak with thick American drawls. Now, do these unlikely accents remove one from the reality of a film or is it even important? This is why I think actors like David Suchet and Alfred Molina would have excelled as Redfa; they specialize in foreign accents and can still be understood and appear sympathetic. But it also depends on what the artistic motives of the film are and the integrity of the people who are making it.

Something I've recently heard, and I don't agree with it, is the apparent problem of "identification" American audiences have when presented with a leading foreign character in a movie. For instance, it's been claimed that a foreign protagonist can sometimes be an unappealing prospect for an American viewer. I don't believe this is true, but if Hollywood studios prefer an American protagonist in a movie it's always done for reasons of box office. It's what studio executives *believe* an American audience wants to see and will tolerate. It's okay if the bad guys speak with foreign accents because they are distinctly defined as different, as other, but there is a need for affinity and identification with our heroes. Ironically, one thing I did find particularly frustrating on *Steal the Sky* was the thick accents of some of the Israeli actors we used. It was often hard to understand them when they were speaking English dialogue. I thought the Israeli casting people were not sufficiently cognizant of the problem they were presenting me with. I mean, they understood perfectly well what the actors were saying as they were attuned to their accents and mode of speech, but I didn't think an American audience would understand a lot of it. That's the flipside of this argument, I guess: what you sometimes have to sacrifice for the sake of authenticity.

Here's a final anecdote concerning truth: when Dorothy was revising the script, she wrote a lovely scene that we had to cut. During their trip to Rome, Redfa and Helen visit the Mouth of Truth, the huge mask carved in marble which rests against a wall in the Santa Maria in Cosmedin church. It's this big bas relief face and legend has it that if you stick your hand in the mask's mouth and tell a lie, your hand gets trapped. Dorothy wrote a scene in which Redfa and Helen visit the mask on their romantic getaway and one of them puts their hand in its mouth. She conceived it in good faith and, later, included this moment in the draft she turned in to HBO. During a meeting, one of the guys at the network said, "You do realize that this scene you've written is almost line-for-line the same as a scene featuring Gregory Peck and Audrey Hepburn in *Roman Holiday*?" We didn't know what he was talking about. It turns out that this was a rather famous and well-loved scene in which Peck takes Hepburn to see the Mouth of Truth and he pretends that his hand is stuck. We were totally confused about it, but how do you plead your innocence? I hadn't seen *Roman Holiday* at this point, and if I had, I could not recall the scene. It was the same for Dorothy. She didn't know she had watched the film once upon a time, and I believe her. She thought it was an original conception and was quite proud of it. Dorothy must have drawn this memory out from a dim corner of her mind and wrote it down.

> *If the prevailing aspiration of* Steal the Sky *is finally one of excitement and intrigue, it is mostly down to the film's robust third act which features one of the most ambitious and nerve-jangling sequences in Hancock's filmography. The aforementioned aerial dogfight between Redfa and two jets deployed from the Al Rasheed Airbase to take down his aircraft before he can reach the shores of Israel is inter-cut with Helen Mason escorting Mrs. Redfa and her children to safety over the desert mountain.*

I'm very proud of the dogfight and aerial footage as that stuff was particularly difficult to shoot. But it was exciting to do as we had Navy Blue Angel pilots piloting all the aircraft. I remember we were shooting from a Lear jet—our camera plane was piloted by James Gavin who was the aerial co-coordinator on the movie. As we were up in the air trying to get the shots we needed, James was never once sick and, thankfully, neither was I. However, the entire camera crew was. They would be sitting down, swallowing, sweating, their faces drained of color, throwing up into paper bags on their laps as the plane kept zipping around. I actually got the chance to fly in one of the two-man MiGs and it was an experience I'll never forget. I quickly discovered that fighter pilots have a whole different personality and nervous system compared to those of bomber pilots or Pan-Am pilots. They have amazingly fast and highly-developed reflexes. It's very easy to get sick as the jets move up and down and all around with such speed it can be extremely disorienting and unpleasant. I was thrilled to be in one of these machines and savored every moment. Maybe that excitement and concentration was what kept me from depositing the contents of my lunch everywhere like everyone else.

All the scenes down on the ground featuring Helen and Redfa's family fleeing probably involved the most energetic and exhausting day I've ever spent as a director. It involved running up and down a mountain-side on the West Bank in considerable heat, directing actors, setting explosions, getting the helicopters in and co-coordinating the goats. Actually, during the making of *Steal the Sky* I got to be very fond of goats. We shot one sequence in a cave and I found the goats would nuzzle you. They were very affectionate animals. It was also interesting to see the desert; how certain areas of it bloom in the spring. We were there when the desert was blooming and it was a wondrous sight. It had an otherworldly and timeless quality. I would say that day (and maybe a day or two of shooting the big riot sequence in *Weeds*) are the hardest and most satisfying working days I've ever done. I was incredibly happy with that sequence. I thought on the strength of it, I should have directed a James Bond film afterwards! Certainly, *Steal the Sky* is my most epic film in terms of the scope and logistics of the action, locations, and other elements. I like seeing those big action and spy movies. I find them empty and ludicrous, but entertaining. I admire directors like Tony Scott, John Woo and James Cameron who can orchestrate enormous action sequences where so many elements are important. I've heard that a lot of action directors don't like watching action films, but maybe I'm coming to it from a different perspective. I felt comfortable shooting the aerial battles and gunfights. I got satisfaction from creating a visceral sequence that hopefully met its objectives: getting the audience to squirm in their seats, getting their hearts racing, and so on.

Less enjoyable for me was the apparent over-concern people had with safety that I encountered doing all the action scenes. I'm treading on dangerous ground here as it's almost a form of political incorrectness to question such things, but I'm being honest. I think the infamous helicopter crash that killed Vic Morrow and two child actors on the set of *Twilight Zone: The Movie* changed everything in our industry. It was such a devastating and tragic event; it was always going to be a big game-changer. No doubt the heavily publicized aftermath of the accident, which included several people connected with the production being brought to trial, ensured that something had to be seen to be done in Hollywood. Thus, there was a tremendous worry and preoccupation with safety on subsequent movies and it's sometimes been to our detriment as directors. I do understand the need for precautionary measures as no movie is worth dying for, but it does get out of hand occasionally. I've seen things done in the name of safety that, in my estimation, have inadvertently contributed to making things less safe—for example, when a person is securely tied to a speeding motorcycle. It can be very dangerous. So, I definitely felt the after-effects of the *Twilight Zone* accident when we were doing *Steal the Sky* because we had these big planes and helicopters around actors and people were afraid.

Having just admitted that, I must say that the shooting of *Steal the Sky* did not pass without incident. I remember one day we were filming the MiGs in Reno and the crew was all positioned right next to a runway. At one point, I saw that a MiG was thundering down to the ground in our direction. It was landing and was suddenly coming right towards us. Somebody yelled and there was that awful moment where you dimly say to yourself, "Okay, this might be the end of me right here." So, we all turned and started running for our lives. We just fled and left the camera behind to be destroyed. Fortunately, the jet landed a short distance away from us and the camera didn't get hit. It was a hairy moment that revealed the awesome power and speed of these machines. As I said, we had Navy Blue Angel pilots that were very expert, but that particular pilot came awfully close on that occasion. It was an experience of pure terror for the camera department and it really got my blood going.

We did some of the most dangerous-looking jet maneuvers using radio-controlled models. In actual flight situations you have trouble convincing pilots to steer close enough to other aircraft or to the ground as they don't want to be killed. I didn't think I was being unreasonable or reckless, but I found my constant efforts to urge James Gavin to get closer to these things tiresome and frustrating. He was extremely reluctant to do it and was overwhelmingly safety-conscious. I didn't want Gavin to crash either, but we weren't getting the shots we needed. Naturally, if the model jets collide or crash you aren't killing anybody. So, you can be far more daring and adventurous in some of the stunts you're attempting. Inevitably, that's the route we decided to go. Yoram located some guys in Israel who had models of various aircraft and he brought them in. These were not film guys; they were model airplane enthusiasts who simply enjoyed their hobby. The models we acquired were highly realistic and detailed and we got some excellent footage from them. We shot the models from the ground and in reality they weren't that high up in the air above us. Like the real thing, we had to co-ordinate with the model pilots (who were equally skilled in their own way) which direction they were going in so we could follow them with the camera. Those sequences cut together seamlessly and I find it pleasing that a lot of people can't distinguish between the model shots and the shots of actual jets.

My editor on *Steal the Sky* was Dennis O'Connor. We worked so well together that I've pretty much used him on every picture I've made since. Together, we followed the screenplay fairly closely in terms of our structuring the film and didn't change too much. For instance, the intercutting back and forth between the mountain escape and Redfa's dogfight in the skies was mostly specified in the script. Dennis and I played around with it a little in the cutting, but those sequences were still designed on the page in terms of when we moved from one thing to another. We simply selected the best moments in which to cut in order to ensure the maximum charge of tension and excitement. There are also title cards inserted throughout the movie at various points to illustrate the time, place and political situations the movie deals with. I don't recall if they were specified in Wood's script or were added later in post-production in order to better clarify some things for the cable audience. Now that I think about it, yes, I believe those cards were indeed written in the script. Another thing we took from the screenplay, something I always liked, was the last shot: the empty chair and discarded drink on the table where Redfa was sitting only moments earlier. That was all described by Wood and I thought it was redolent of the idea that Redfa has become a ghost. He still has a life ahead of him, but he must disappear. He's now invisible and must remain so. That's what he even confirms at one point: "It's wonderful, but it's empty for me." A shot of a vacant chair is a direct and strangely emotive image to convey that idea.

> *Hired to compose the score for* Steal the Sky *was the Greek-born American New Age composer Yanni, who would later achieve astonishing success with the release of his 1994*

> *multi-platinum selling album* Live at the Acropolis. *The soundtrack for* Steal the Sky *was eventually released in 1999 on the Rhino Entertainment label, peaking at #17 on Billboard's "Top New Age Albums" chart.*

Yanni was recommended to me by HBO and I had no objections to that suggestion. Since we'd had such a rough and combative time during the casting of the film, I wanted this stage of the process to run a little smoother. I could hardly be described as a rabid Yanni fan, but I had seen a television show he had done and thought that some of his music was rather beautiful. It was a combination of electronic music with a full scale orchestra; very nice and inoffensive. I believe at this point in time, Yanni had only ever scored one movie and *Steal the Sky* was to be his second. I also thought that the project was right up his alley in terms of the ethnic and exotic character of the music and that he could bring something interesting to the table. I guess it was his chance to finally write like a Greek. When I met him, he was a nice guy, and I would work with him again as I liked his score very much. Yanni ended up composing a lot of music for the film, which is good as I like having a lot of music in my movies. I thought his score accomplished what it had to: it succeeded in sustaining the tension during the fighting sequences and was suitably affecting during the romantic scenes. It should be noted that Yanni was not a superstar in the music world at this point. All his success and acclaim exploded about five or six years after *Steal the Sky* came out. It's always a good time to catch a superstar early on in their careers as you find they are a lot cheaper to hire!

> Steal the Sky *premiered on HBO on August 26, 1988, to excellent ratings but mixed reviews. Howard Rosenberg, writing for the* Los Angeles Times, *was less than effusive in his praise, feeling that Hancock's film "begins intriguingly" but then "swiftly diminishes in credibility and ultimately succumbs to the big, boffo, preposterous, Rocky-esque finale, in which Munir and Helen inflate to super-hero and super-heroine." While acknowledging its "beauty" and "superbly filmed locations," Rosenberg found Hancock's picture to be "a spy/adventure story that lacks suspense, a love story whose lovers lack intensity, [and] a Middle Eastern story— set in the months preceding the history and politics-shaping*

> six-day Arab-Israeli war of 1967—that lacks historical and political definition." In 1989, Ben Cross' performance as Redfa was nominated for a Cable ACE Award for Best Actor, but he lost out to Danny Glover for his starring turn in Philip Saville's Mandela (1987), a British production that had also premiered on HBO.

HBO didn't have any problems or restrictions with the content of *Steal the Sky*. They seemed to be very happy with it, delighted even. The film proved to be the network's top-rated presentation at that point in time. It did exceedingly well, but HBO never offered me anything else after the movie was aired. I was somewhat surprised about that, I must say. I couldn't understand it. No doubt one determining factor in this decision was that the administration changed at HBO. Of course, it changes all the time, but I'm sure that had something to do with it. Also, I don't think HBO liked Mariel's performance. They felt I had made a mistake in casting her when there were several more accomplished actors available. I went for some of their suggestions, but others I ignored. I'm sure that dissent did not go unnoticed. Looking back, I guess Mariel was something of a concession to me as they had so desperately wanted to cast Anne Archer. In this instance, they yielded and let me have my way. I was then later blamed for it when they felt she wasn't entirely convincing in the role. That's the way it goes sometimes and you just have to accept it. I agree with some of Rosenberg's review—some, not all—that the love affair between Ben and Mariel needed a little more fire and passion. I don't think Mariel was right for the part, but, given that limitation, I still do like the film, and her.

> *After it was returned to Israel from the United States, the MiG-21 that Redfa acquired in 1966 was placed in the IAF Museum in Haterzin, near Be'er Sheva, where it remains to this day. As for the pilot himself, little is known of Redfa's activities in the years following Operation Diamond. Some sources have speculated wildly on details of his life, with one unlikely report even claiming he later ran a petrol station in Israel. What has been confirmed is that Munir Redfa died of a heart attack sometime during 1998 at the age of sixty-four.*

For many years, I didn't know whatever became of Redfa after the events depicted in *Steal the Sky*. I never followed up on him. For a long time I merely assumed he was still living comfortably somewhere in Israel under an assumed name. I only recently learned—just a couple of days ago, actually—that he had in fact died nearly twenty years ago. The Israelis were true to the deal they'd struck with him, but it's tempting to wonder how Redfa *really* felt about his mission in the years that ensued. In his private moments, did he ever regret it? Did he feel it was worth it, that it was just? Or was he a contented man? I'm sure he never set eyes on his homeland again and that's a tough thing for anybody to do: turn your back on the country of your birth and never return; never again look upon the land and feel the soil under your feet, breathe the air, for as long as you live. Although he endured discrimination, it was a huge sacrifice to undertake, even for the rewards of greater freedom and finance. In his heart, did Redfa long to return to Iraq and his own people? I'd be interested to know, if only to satisfy my curiosity. Needless to say, I had no contact with him prior to, during or after the shooting of the film and I don't believe many others connected to the film did either. I don't know if Redfa ever saw *Steal the Sky*, or what his thoughts on it were. That's something else I'd be interested to know.

At the end of the film Redfa says of his actions, "I'm a hero to some; a traitor to most." It's interesting to consider how history remembers his mission, if it's remembered at all. I don't believe there are many who really think about Operation Diamond today. They evidently don't attach any great significance to it. If you asked most people about it, they would probably admit they'd never even heard of Munir Redfa. Frankly, I don't believe that Redfa's actions were important in terms of the Middle Eastern conflict. It was a blow, a wounding, a betrayal, but, ultimately, not much more than that when taken in the great scheme of things. It didn't settle anything, really. Based on the knowledge the Israelis had gleaned from conducting an extensive study of the MiG-21 that Redfa delivered to them, they were able to assess the various strengths and weakness of the jet. "To know the weapons that the enemy has is to already beat them," as the Israeli commander says, and I understand they did detect a number of flaws and blind spots in its design. They learned what maneuvers and tactics they could adopt to beat the MiGs. This later enabled Israeli pilots to blow a number of MiG-21s out of the sky during The Six Day War. But was Redfa vital to the success of The Six Day War? I suspect the Israelis were confident of victory regardless. Maybe Redfa's actions merely shortened the war and prevented it from being the Twelve Day War or Thirty-Three Day War.

After the Israelis had turned the MiG-21 over to the United States in February 1968, so our guys could conduct their own thorough analysis of the aircraft, the American Government duly rewarded Israel by giving them more advanced planes such as the F-4 Phantom fighter bomber, which were used in a series of air-to-ground and air-to-air missions. So, it was well worth it for them. Everybody gained. America had earlier been somewhat reluctant to give these jets to Israel (there had, until this time, been a twenty-year U.S. arms embargo on Israel that was suddenly lifted), but the prize the Israelis offered was significant enough in helping Uncle Sam to change their minds. So, the gift was seen as being deserved. The Phantom then replaced the French Vautour II and Dassault Mirage III attack aircraft, which had both been around since the mid-1950s, and were what the Israeli Air Force had been using up to that point. On that evidence, you can clearly see that Israel did positively benefit from Operation Diamond and Redfa's bravery. He did make a difference from a political standpoint.

It's somewhat ironic that the Iraq War should explode just two years after we made *Steal the Sky*; and that it would eventually lead the U.S., in the early 2000s, to wage the War on Terror and invade Iraq under George W. Bush in search of Weapons of Mass Destruction. My thought on all that is it's been an absolute unmitigated fucking disaster; a mortifying turn of events. Additionally, all this torture that has gone on with our soldiers mistreating and maiming prisoners is a shame that will take some time to go away. It seems to me that our country has taken a terrible wrong turn somewhere. We've veered down a long, dark road and we are still paying for it. It's disgusting and reprehensible. I believe that George W. Bush, Tony Blair and others should be prosecuted for war crimes. At the time we were all told that Iraq had WMDs that they were planning to use against us. Okay, did I buy all that? Yes, I did. Like congress, I initially believed this was a serious threat and agreed that we should do something about it. I felt we had to be assertive. We had to show them that we were tough. Unfortunately, all of that was unconscionably misleading. It was lies! It was bullshit! As it turned out, there were no WMDs and the entire world was duped.

In this country, I find it tough to accept that these torturers are not being punished for their crimes. The events at Guantanamo Bay and Abu Ghraib, and the secret torture program carried out by the CIA in facilities over in Poland where they are using renditions and water-boarding on detainees, it's like a nauseating national disgrace. Interrogation is one thing; torture, rape and murder is quite another. The Bush Administration tried to claim these were isolated incidents, but it was obvious that it was part of designated U.S. Government policy. These abuses were a concerted plan designed to violate other human beings. It's a sickening thing to accept that an "advanced" and "honest" country like America should be responsible for these crimes. Incidentally, I recently toyed with the idea (and this is just a projection of what I would actually like to do) of doing a film that featured a character who thinks these crimes are such a national disgrace he feels it's his job to execute these people himself. I didn't go very far with the idea because I knew it would face the charge of inciting political assassination and, consequently, be almost impossible for it to secure funding. And, indeed, there are fresh national shames now.

I would not describe myself as a proud American. In truth, there are times when I dislike my country and feel deeply ashamed of it. I like the standard of living here, and other freedoms that I enjoy, but I think for a long time our foreign policy has been imperialistic and uncompromisingly brutal. That's no big revelation, of course. Our history is a rather regrettable one for such a relatively young nation. It's a history that the American public simply isn't aware of, or chooses to ignore. Even when you consider the wounds of Pearl Harbor and 9/11—and those were two traumatizing events that happened to us on our own territory— you have to place them in a full historical and political context. You must remember the multitude of despicable atrocities that America has perpetrated throughout the world; the terrible things we have done to the people of other nations in the name of "freedom" and "justice." We must also consider the terrible things we have done to the people of our own nation such as our treatment of the Native Americans and Blacks. It's not very pretty. In that light, I can certainly understand why it might make one want to turn against one's own.

15 *Prancer* (1989)

ALTHOUGH THE CRITICAL *and commercial success of* Weeds *and* Steal the Sky *was less than spectacular, Hancock discovered that he was once again an attractive and viable proposition for the major studios. After turning down the opportunity to direct* Glory, *a film about the 54th Massachusetts Volunteer Infantry, one of America's first African-American military units formed during the Civil War, he then rejected an offer to helm the "revolt of nature" horror comedy* Arachnophobia *which concerned the deadly mass infestation caused by a vicious Venezuelan spider that has been mistakenly transported to a small quotidian American town. With his career now effectively revived, Hancock continued to develop his own more personal projects alongside entertaining a variety of lucrative offers from several other companies.*

The late 1980s was an interesting time for me as there was a lot going on. I felt like I was really back in business. I believe *Glory* first came my way sometime between *Weeds* and *Steal the Sky*. I'd always had a profound interest in the American Civil War and was intrigued by how those events had shaped our country. I've worked on one or two projects about the conflict over the years, as I think it's a fascinating and fraught period in our history. There have been lots of movies made or set during the Civil War. Some of these films have merely used the conflict as a backdrop and haven't explored it too deeply, but there are so many interesting stories yet to be told about that time. I'd heard about the exploits of the 54th Massachusetts Volunteer Infantry and agreed that it could potentially make a wonderful movie. Be that as it may, the script I was offered was not good. It had been written by Maurice Jarre's son, Kevin Jarre, and had apparently been derived from the personal letters of Colonel Robert Gould Shaw, the White officer who had led the first all-Black regiment and was killed at the Second Battle of Fort Wagner in 1863, as well as Peter Burchard's 1965 novel *One Gallant Rush*. Despite plundering such rich source material, the script I read was terrible. Really bad! I thought the problems with Jarre's draft were legion and I did not believe that they were going to be able to fix them.

I also felt strongly that the version I received was not only a little clumsy, it was racist. It was very racist, actually. I can remember thinking to myself that Black people were going to despise this movie and I did not want to be any part of it. Another factor in my decision to turn down *Glory* was the fact it was being produced by Freddie Fields. Fields had been a powerful agent and had founded CMA with David Begelman. He had represented a roster of big stars like Judy Garland, Henry Fonda and Marilyn Monroe before producing movies like *Looking for Mr. Goodbar* and *American Gigolo*. Frankly, I had no desire to work with Fields as I was afraid of him and thought he was some kind of monster. The project was then handed to Edward Zwick, who succeeded admirably in fixing all of the unfixable problems I had identified. He cast Denzel Washington, Morgan Freeman and Matthew Broderick as the leads and *Glory* went on to win three Academy Awards. When I saw it, I did think that some of the battle scenes were a little underwhelming, but Zwick was working with a modest budget and didn't have the money he perhaps needed. Still, he made a good movie and turning down *Glory* is—alongside my turning down *The China Syndrome*—one of the two biggest regrets of my career. It was a pretty substantial mistake on my part. I should have amended Jarre's script myself and tried to dance around Freddie Fields. Maybe Fields wasn't as much of a monster as I had feared. But it just wasn't to be.

Conversely, I was content with my decision to turn down *Arachnophobia*. That movie was a co-production between Amblin Entertainment and Hollywood Pictures, but it was really a Jeffrey Katzenberg project at the point in which it came to me rather than a Steven Spielberg project. Katzenberg was a huge fan of *Weeds* and he generously proposed my name for several things. *Arachnophobia* was one of them, but I simply didn't respond to the concept or the screenplay. It read a little bit like a tired variation on *Jaws*, only it was set on land with deadly spiders instead of on the water with a shark. Maybe it was the lingering bad taste in my mouth over *Jaws 2*, I don't know, but I thought if I do this movie I'm going to be killing a lot of creatures. I did not want to do that, even though, in the story, the spiders were causing the deaths of the innocent inhabitants of this cozy town. In the same way I had earlier objected to David Milch's suggestion that I snap the turkey's neck at the end of my Christmas episode of *Hill Street Blues*, I balked at the prospect of killing all these highly aggressive arachnids. The movie was eventually directed by Frank Marshall, who was Spielberg's producer for many years and still is, and I believe it did some good business. Sure, a lot of people in the world have a terrible phobia of spiders, but I felt *Arachnophobia* was really a diluted monster movie in some ways; a safe and comfortably commercial horror film. Again, it certainly didn't have the bite that *Jaws* had and I have no regrets about not doing it.

> *After rejecting one "animal picture," Hancock soon received an offer to direct another.* Prancer *was the slightly more benign story of an eight year-old girl named Jessica Riggs who, one cold winter's night, discovers an injured reindeer in a snow-covered forest. Believing it to be a member of Santa Claus's fabled flying sleigh team, the child endeavors to nurse the wounded animal back to health so she can return the creature to its rightful owner on Christmas Eve. Written in 1986 by former Hollywood costumer turned screenwriter Greg Taylor—who would go on to script* Jumanji *(1995),* Harriet the Spy *(1996) and* Prancer Returns *(2001), the latter a lesser direct-to-video sequel—the first draft grew out of a bedtime story the author had relayed to his seven year-old daughter (also named Jessica). Raffaella De Laurentiis, who had worked for her father, Dino, on such films as* Conan the Barbarian *(1982),* Dune *(1984),* Tai Pan *(1986), and* Weeds, *related to the determined nature and potent imagination of Taylor's young protagonist and quickly acquired the property. De Laurentiis then began developing* Prancer *as the maiden project of her newly formed company Raffaella Productions, securing a deal with Cineplex Odeon to finance the film on a budget of just under $7 million.*

During the making of *Weeds*, Raffaella De Laurentiis had served as her father's person on the set. She was always a supportive presence, a charming and funny lady, and we got to be friends. I liked her a great deal and still do. Aside from all those things I thought she was incredibly smart. Sometime after *Weeds* opened, I called Raffaella and took her out to lunch. As were talking, she said, "I have something I want to send you. I think you'd be a wonderful choice for it." Shortly afterwards I received the screenplay of *Prancer* and duly read it. My first impressions were less than positive as I felt the story was too sappy, too hokey, and wholly derivative of *E.T.: The Extra Terrestrial*. There were certain things that I liked, the simplicity of it, the way it touched on the themes of magic, love and faith—not religious faith, a more personal and tangible belief. But I did not like the dialogue or the reassuringly safe Disney-esque world that Greg Taylor had created. The heavy sentimentalism didn't ring true to me and was rather bland. Also, I didn't want to make a movie for kids at this point in my career. I do like watching subtle movies about children and their perceptions and misperceptions of the world around them; something like *Whistle Down the Wind* for instance, or Guillermo Del Toro's *Pan's Labyrinth*. Both of those pictures deal with children exposed to the harshness of the adult world; how they interpret events and people through the prism of their limited awareness. They demonstrate how fantasy and reality can merge and distort a child's reality, and even shield them from the difficulties of life they must face—Del Toro's wonderful film is especially affecting at capturing that. I thought this same quality was present in Taylor's script to a degree, but it was far too cloying and indelicate. It needed work.

Another reason I didn't want to do *Prancer* was the simple fact I had no desire to make a Christmas picture. Frankly, I'm no great lover of Christmas movies, although I appreciate the fact they are a genre unto themselves. I love Christmas time itself, and always have, but there are very few seasonal films that I like. One I don't particularly like is *It's a Wonderful Life*, which is high up on everybody's list of the greatest festive movies ever made. I find it has a moralizing tone—be sure to count all your blessings and know your place—and people look at it now almost as a means of measuring how far our values have declined since World War II. I recently saw a reading of *It's a Wonderful Life* at our local theater here and I was offended by its content, actually. As I told you, I don't like Frank Capra's work that much, so maybe I've carried that prejudice with me. One Christmas picture I like well enough (I haven't seen it for a long time) is *Miracle on 34th Street* with Maureen O'Hara and Edmund Gwenn. It's a film of some charm, I think, and is more honest and endearing than Capra's movie. There are also some parallels between *Prancer* and *Miracle on 34th Street* in the way both movies contain cynical characters and the idea that the Christmas magic might in fact be real. I also like the old black and white version of *A Christmas Carol* starring Alistair Sim as Ebenezer Scrooge. That's an unqualified classic and I'd be a real humbug if I didn't like that one!

 Anyway, getting back, I was about to inform Raffaella that I didn't want to do the film when Dorothy happened to pick up the script and start reading it. She immediately said, "Don't be so quick to dismiss this. There's a lot of potential here and it could even become a Christmas classic. I can fix the dialogue and one or two other things. Why don't I give it a try?" By this time, Dorothy and I had already written *Weeds* together and then she had come in and re-written the script for *Steal the Sky*. I told her, "Look, if people think I'm going to be continually bringing you in to revise their stuff once it's submitted, it's going to cut me off from good material." She agreed this could be a problem. I then went back to Raffaella, and said, "Dorothy will do a full re-write on this script for no money and no credit. If you are happy with the results, you can give her a present after it's all over—or not. It's entirely up to you." Raffaella welcomed this suggestion, but I wasn't exactly finished. "Aside from Dorothy fixing the script, I will only direct this picture if we can find the right little girl to star; and if we have enough money in the budget to pay for a big special effects department to make our own snow that will match whatever the natural snow happens to be. If you can meet those conditions, I'll do it." That may have seemed a little forward of me, but the truth is *Prancer* was not a movie I felt I *had* to do. I'd just made two pictures back-to-back and this would now be my third in a row. So, I was able to adopt a strong position which allowed me to issue a few small demands.

 In feeling that I did not have to make the deal, some of the pressure I'd perhaps felt in previous years was slightly removed. But then all my requirements were accepted by Raffaella as she really wanted me to direct the film. Further to the conditions I had stipulated, I was also able to negotiate that I controlled the editing through the mix, which was very important to me. I did not want to have another experience like the one I'd suffered on *California Dreaming*—not that I expected such a thing to occur on *Prancer*, but you never quite know what will happen during the course of making a movie. I believe Raffaella was working out of Universal at the time and she had cleverly made the deal with Cineplex Odeon. At one point, they were the biggest chain of exhibitors in North America and the company was being run by an extremely colorful Canadian gentleman named Garth Drabinsky. I've still stayed in touch with Garth all these years and he's quite a legendary character as a producer and entrepreneur. Later, Barry Spikings' company Nelson Entertainment became involved with the film, but they were not involved in setting up *Prancer* as it was entirely a Cineplex Odeon entity. However, when the picture was eventually finished, Garth showed it to 20th Century Fox and Universal and Nelson. Fox offered $4 million and Barry and Universal offered $6 million, so Garth went with them.

With everything agreed, Dorothy set to work on revising Taylor's script. In our early discussions we talked about making the characters more believable and the milieu of the story more gritty and realistic. A lot of Christmas movies are inordinately sentimental and sugary by their very nature, but I didn't want to make a picture that was too much. I thought about my own childhood, my own sense of wonder and fear as a kid, and, inevitably, my thoughts drifted back to the times I'd spent on our farm. As I had done on *Let's Scare Jessica to Death*—and would later do on *A Piece of Eden*—I introduced a lot of autobiographical content to *Prancer*, and so Jessica and her father now had a fruit farm. I also used a lot of my father's machinery in the film and even included some of the things my mother had said to me. I told you about that memorable flight we took together from Havana to Key West when I was more or less the same age as Jessica, where I thought the plane was going to crash and we were going to die. The way my mother had calmly said, "Well, we've had a good life," stirred certain emotions in me. I thought about my mother and her view of the world, and my relationship with her, and how bad things can happen to good people simply because that is the way of the world. I think my mother was very much in my mind when we were discussing the scene near the end where Jessica's father tells her they might lose the farm one day. In consciously attempting to make *Prancer* not only more real but more personal, I grew a lot closer to the material.

One of the first things that happened after I'd signed on was Raffaella and I embarked on a long scouting trip together. We flew from Los Angeles to Toronto and looked at some studios there that I believe Garth would have liked us to have used for the film, possibly because he had partial or even total ownership of them. We definitely felt obliged to check them out for reasons of common courtesy, but we soon decided to move on elsewhere. Raffaella and I then went to Montreal and took a look around, before we drove down through Vermont to investigate possible locations there. I had envisioned the town in the original script as looking like somewhere in the Pennsylvania Mountains with a river and a ridge; but we never scouted Pennsylvania as it would have been out of our way. We then visited the grave of Raffaella's brother, Federico De Laurentiis, which was located outside New York. Federico had also been a young producer, but had been tragically killed in a small plane accident in 1981 while shooting a documentary about salmon in Alaska. Needless to say, his death was a huge tragedy in the De Laurentiis family and, when they buried Federico, Dino was so grief-stricken he threw himself into the grave. As you can imagine, it was a big Italian emotional scene. Devastating!

Raffaella and I next flew to Detroit and drove from there to my family's fruit farm in Indiana. The truth is it had always been lurking in my mind to show her this area, as it not only had personal significance for me, I felt it would also be the perfect place for the film. Now, when you're trying to sell a location to a producer or a studio you ask yourself, "Okay, should I show my preference first or last? What will make the biggest impression on them?" I eventually decided to show Indiana last and, thankfully, that ploy worked as Raffaella quickly fell in love with the place, too. That impressed me, I must say, and was another thing I always liked and admired about Raffaella: she was a very thorough, hands-on producer but she had great warmth and humility. She was receptive to ideas and suggestions that may have conflicted with her own and, above all, she was supportive. I remember Raffaella once shared with me her view of what she felt a good producer should do: "My job is to create an environment that ensures that the director can do their job. That is the most important consideration and is something I always strive to do." Obviously, those words were music to my ears, but Raffaella meant everything she said. The fact she recognized that I wanted to do the picture here, and chose to okay the shooting of *Prancer* in Indiana, demonstrated this to me. Raffaella instinctively knew she would get a little more out of me if we shot here and she was probably right about that.

Our family had three separate farms that could have been used as the location for the Riggs farm. Each was situated several miles apart and, excruciatingly, the tool you needed was always at the *other* farm. I showed Raffaella all three and she picked the one that we used in the movie, which is about a mile from where we live. Looking back now, boy, did she ever make the right choice! She selected that farm because you could see the house, the barn and the pond in the very same shot. It was a real eye-opener to me about how to select the correct location and I often use it as a pertinent example to young directors that I meet. I would have actually shot the movie at a different farm, one that did not have that tie-in. I must be honest, I thought one of our other properties was the correct place to do *Prancer* and I was pushing for us to go there. Raffaella said, "No, John, this is the one. Believe me." It's difficult to explain, but when you visit a location your field of vision is clearly very wide and all-encompassing. You are looking around, trying to take in as much of the environment as you possibly can. But, in doing so, you can easily forget that you will ultimately be restricting your view of this expansive place through the little box of a camera. You have to line up all the things that are inside that little box if you want them in the shot. It's sometimes hard to retain that fact in your mind—at least it was for me. Fortunately, Raffaella was on hand to make the correct choice.

> *As Hancock had rightly anticipated, the casting of the child actors in* Prancer *would be pivotal as so much of the action and emotional content depended on their competence. Thus, an extensive search was conducted to find the best talent in the eight-to-fourteen age range, with hundreds of children being interviewed over the course of several months. For the key role of Jessica Riggs, Hancock and Raffaella De Laurentiis finally settled on a pixie-faced eight year-old newcomer by the name of Rebecca Harrell. Despite her previous acting experience being restricted to a small part as a singing Litterbug in a school play back in her native Vermont, Harrell was a precocious and highly intuitive talent. She was also dyslexic and unable to adequately read at this point in time. To combat this obstacle during her auditions, Harrell had to be patiently taught the lines of dialogue in the screenplay by her mother. Indeed, after she had secured the part, this practice would continue throughout the shooting of the film.*

We started looking for child actors on both sides of the coasts and there was no shortage of them to consider. There were a surfeit of good child actors to choose from, but I seem to recall us still having some trouble trying to cast the role of Jessica's older brother, Steve. We eventually settled on a good-looking kid named John Duda, who I don't think had appeared in a movie at that point. I thought he was a little hokey in his performance, but he's still alright. We did manage to unearth some kids who went on to have great careers: Johnny Galecki, who has now become a very important television actor in *The Big Bang Theory*, played one of Steve's friends, and we also found Ariana Richards in Los Angeles, who later went on to do *Jurassic Park* with Steven Spielberg. We cast Ariana as Jessica's best friend Carol, but she was also one of the candidates for the role of Jessica. She was a capable little actress, but Ariana wasn't quite what I was looking for. She had a highly commercial look and was more conventionally pretty than most little girls, but was a little mannered in her style. I was looking for somebody who was a little more *real*.

I had emphasized how vitally important it was that we locate the right little girl to play Jessica, as so much rested on our choice. The movie would stand or fall on this child's ability to convey the wide range of emotions the character required. All the same, I did not want to hire a "child actor" per se. What I mean is I was looking for a kid who had that ineffable spark of natural magic about them. One of the reasons I was so insistent about finding the right girl before agreeing to do *Prancer* was because, shortly before I started work on the film, I had seen Spielberg's World War II picture *Empire of the Sun*. Today, Christian Bale is rightly regarded as a wonderful and adaptable actor. Back then, when he was a twelve year-old boy, I thought Spielberg had made an unfortunate choice in casting him as this privileged English kid whose life is dismantled by the Japanese invasion of China. Spielberg may have liked Bale's performance, but I did not. I thought it was dead and artificial. It was an example to me that if you hired the wrong child actor for a lead role, and you started to shoot, you couldn't suddenly go back and replace him as you'd have to restage and re-shoot everything. So, you would effectively be trapped in a place where you didn't want to be. I certainly did not want to be stuck in that situation on *Prancer*.

I had started working with a casting person named Susan Willett and it was she who eventually found Rebecca Harrell, after we'd undertaken our sweeping search and seen nearly every young actress. We had undertaken a sweeping search on both coasts and seen nearly every young actress. Then, like some beautiful gift, Rebecca had come to New York with her mother and had read for Susan. I can remember getting the call from Susan and her simply telling me: "I've found her! You're going to love this kid!" At one point, Raffaella had stopped on our big scouting trip and traveled to Rebecca's house in Vermont to read her again. Both she and Susan were convinced they had found our Jessica. When I met Rebecca soon afterwards, I became convinced, too. I can recall reading some lines with her and it was an incredible thing to witness. Here was this eight year-old girl with no previous acting experience whatsoever, who sounded like she was saying the lines herself. She didn't have that horrible cuteness and annoying artifice that a lot of child actors have. There was something decidedly real and natural and feisty about her. Rebecca struck me as a child with a big imagination and an innate ability to improvise. Susan remarked of her, "She's like an old soul in a young body," and that observation proved to be very true. Looking back now, I have no idea how Rebecca did it. To this day, I still don't know if you want to know the truth. She gives a quite extraordinary performance in the film. She was simply able to throw herself into every moment and just do it. Her mother was without doubt a great support to Rebecca, but this little girl had a magic inside her. Full credit must be laid at Susan's feet for finding her, as *Prancer* could not have been what it is without her diligence.

> *In the role of John Riggs, Jessica's irascible father, Hancock cast forty-five year-old Sam Elliott, whose breakout performance in Daniel Petrie's* Lifeguard *(1976) as the passive beach beefcake Rick Carlson was followed by memorable appearances in* Mask *(1985),* Fatal Beauty *(1987) and* Road House *(1988). Although habitually typecast as a tough cowboy or hirsute biker, Hancock had always suspected Elliott to be an actor of considerable versatility and emotional depth.*

Sam Elliot was an actor I'd admired for a while. I believe he was initially suggested to me by Raffaella and I immediately responded to the idea. I don't recall if I had anybody specific in mind for Jessica's father when I read the screenplay, but at one point we did fly Paul Le Mat, who had been in *American Graffiti* and *Melvin and Howard*, to Indiana from Los Angeles for a reading and an interview. He was good, but I eventually decided to go with Sam. I had seen Sam in *Lifeguard* and *Mask*, and several other pictures, and had enjoyed his performances. He was one of those actors who was capable of transmitting masculinity and strength, but could combine those qualities with something that was a little more vulnerable and sensitive. That isn't always easy to do. A lot of actors know how to play taciturn tough guys, but when it comes to playing emotional scenes they can falter. We needed an actor who could play this no-nonsense farmer: a guy struggling to hold his family and farm together, who finally experiences an unguarded moment of truth with his daughter and realizes what life would be without her. I had the strong feeling that Sam could do all that. So, we flew him in and he read for us. Right off the bat I agreed that he was perfect—the deep gravelly voice, the big moustache, the feeling, it was all there—but Sam proved to be better than I ever hoped or imagined he would be for the film. He was also a wonderful guy to have around and everybody on the crew loved him.

When we started shooting *Prancer* we were negotiating thigh-deep snow and it was exhausting just moving about. One day, I happened to look around and saw Sam helping the grips to move the dolly track. This was hardly an unusual act for him, except for the fact that Sam wasn't even shooting that day! He had just come in on his day-off and was ably working away with the grunts. It was the kind of deed which endeared him not only to me but to everyone else on that movie. That was not the typical behavior you saw from a privileged Hollywood actor, but he was always doing stuff like that, making an effort with people. Sam was also very good with the community. He was invariably courteous and friendly to the locals, and was nice to businessmen in bars at night, that kind of thing. That may sound rather unimportant, but I have directly benefited from the many small kindnesses Sam showed during this time. In fact, he is the primary reason that we've been able to raise money in this community for several other pictures I've done subsequently. It's because Sam was so wonderful with rich people in this area. To this day, his name is still spoken in quiet reverence. I'm not kidding. Occasionally I'll get a phone-call or somebody will stop by the house, and excitedly whisper, "Hey, I hear Sam is looking at houses! I hear he's moving back!" I mean, it's like Zapata, who is in the hills and will one day return. Sam had that effect on people and it was nothing he ever had to force. He was just a natural, unaffected, affable guy. Sam and I have never worked with each other again, but that's just by accident. I would work with him tomorrow.

> Hancock rounded out his supporting players with an eclectic array of respected and recognizable character actors. These included Rutanya Alda as Jessica's kindly Aunt Sarah; Michael Constantine as Mr. Stewart, a department store Santa whom Jessica encounters at the mall; Mark Rolston as Herb Drier, a butcher who buys Prancer from John Riggs

> with the plan of making burgers out of the beast after he's finished displaying it for the holiday season; Abe Vigoda as Orel Benton, an aged and cantankerous veterinarian Jessica enlists to heal the deer's injured leg; and Academy Award-winning actress Cloris Leachman as Mrs. McFarland, an eccentric widow whom Jessica helps to rediscover the transformative spirit of Christmas.

Rutanya Alda was another actress who came to my attention through Susan Willett. She was based out of New York and simply came in to read. Rutanya and I had a lot of mutual friends and she was married to the late Richie Bright, an actor whom I had used a lot in the theater. Rutanya also knew Bobby De Niro and some of the other people who were involved in *The Deer Hunter*. She had played John Savage's pregnant bride in the wedding sequence which dominates the early portions of the film, and I was delighted to cast her as Jessica's Aunt Sarah. Michael Constantine was another actor I'd shared a tenuous history with. I had almost cast him in some play once in New York that didn't happen. He was somebody I had known from reading countless people in the theater and I'd always wanted to work with him. When we were looking for somebody to play the rumpled Santa Jessica meets at the mall—she knows he isn't the real Santa Claus, of course—his face kept hovering in my mind for some reason. Michael has a wonderful face, wonderful eyes. It's really only his eyes that you see beneath that big white beard when we first encounter him.

I also cast Mark Rolston again, this time as the butcher. It was the third straight movie we had done together and by this time we were like old pals. I also rehired Walter Charles, who had briefly appeared in *Weeds*, to play the local minister in *Prancer*. Another familiar face was Abe Vigoda, whom I remembered from my days at the San Francisco Actor's Workshop (how could I forget him!) Like Constantine and Rolston, he was somebody I specifically requested to play the grumpy old vet. I thought Abe would be wonderful in that role as he was another guy with a distinctive face and voice. He resembled a tired, decrepit, old hound dog of some kind that somebody has left tied up in the yard. He had that weary quality about him that simply shines through the screen. To be honest with you, Abe had not been the easiest guy in the world to work with back in San Francisco, but, as long are they aren't too obstructive, I never let things like that get in the way of casting the right person for the right role. That said, by the time we were making *Prancer*, Abe was having some trouble remembering his lines. But we got through it and I do enjoy his performance in the film.

Like most people, I had loved Cloris Leachman in *The Last Picture Show*. She gave a beautifully measured and delicate performance as the coach's neglected middle-aged wife who has an affair with one of her husband's students, and Cloris deserved the Oscar she won for it. We had to find an actress of a certain age to play the old woman who Jessica meets and restores the Christmas spirit to. When Cloris's name came up as a possibility for the role, I jumped on it. Oddly enough, I do recall getting the feeling during shooting that Cloris was acting in a slightly different style to everybody else in the film. She played her character with a heightened realism and that troubled me somewhat. It just seemed to be moving in a peculiar register. I was tempted on one or two occasions to inform her about this, but I didn't and still let it happen. Despite these misgivings, when I look at *Prancer* now in retrospect, I do like her performance. Before we started filming, I learned that Cloris was as mad as a hatter. She spoke so fast and was so animated I hardly understood a word she said to me about anything. There are actors who will come to you on the set and say certain things—ask a question or seek an approving word—and you simply cannot understand what the hell they are saying. Cloris was like that. On such occasions I tended to just nod and smile politely whenever she rabbited on. That seemed to satisfy her for the most part.

> *Principal photography on* Prancer *commenced in late January 1989 for eight weeks at locations in LaPorte and Bendix Woods, Indiana; Three Oaks, Michigan, and Starved Rock State Park, Illinois. LaPorte provided a number of venues for the film including the press room of the* Herald-Argus *newspaper and Galena Township Elementary School, the latter serving as the backdrop for Jessica's classroom and Christmas pageant. The Jeremiah Service House, known more commonly as the Old Republic, which had been built in 1860 and was located on E. Michigan Street, New Carlisle, provided the glorious exterior of Mrs. McFarland's mansion. The Old Republic was in a state of disrepair at the time and so another house in LaPorte was utilized for the interiors. The citizens of Three Oaks left their Christmas decorations up on Elm Street and other places until*

> March for the duration of filming, a decision that led the filmmakers to change the name of the fictional Midwestern town in the film from Fall River to Three Oaks as a token of their gratitude. The local United Methodists Church doubled as the church Jessica and her family attends with members of the congregation and choir recruited as extras. The producers later bequeathed the Christmas decorations to the church after filming was completed.

The community of LaPorte was fabulously helpful and accommodating during the shoot, as were the other communities where we shot. They were always patient and friendly and enthusiastic about what we were doing, so we got tremendous co-operation. I believe the fact that my parents had been successful in the fruit business in this area also helped, as a lot of goodwill had been built up over many years between them and the locals. Their relationship was excellent and my folks had in the past invited people to come over and pick their own apples, that kind of stuff. Those small things seemed go a long way with some people. I look a lot like my father and I still run into people at the local supermarket who say, "Hi, Ralph!" Oh, but I can't tell you how amazing and pleasant it was to be making a movie about a child in the very area where I had grown up. Just to be shooting on the same road where as a little boy I had fallen off my bicycle and cried, or standing near a tree I had once climbed as a youth, was wonderful. All these years later, here I was back home and I was now The Boss. I had at various times between fifty and a hundred people doing my bidding, helping to make the film a reality. It was so much fun.

As we were making *Prancer* the LaPorte Civic Auditorium, or the Chamber of Commerce or some other organization, actually sold tickets to the townsfolk inviting them to come and watch the cast and crew eat onstage. I'm quite serious. The Civic Auditorium holds about 1,500 seats and has hosted various regional and community events over the decades, but this has to be one of the strangest. We sat at tables positioned on the stage and were served dinner, which the locals observed us devouring. I've likened this experience to something like the court of Louis XIV of France—it had that same perverse sense of grandeur and spectacle to it. Of course, the people of LaPorte were also eating little snacks, too. They did not go without. The Hispanic mayor then sang "La Bamba" and I must say there was this very warm and interesting atmosphere that was generated. It felt a little weird and uncomfortable, but it also felt rather glorious. I mean, here I was, having returned to the place where I had grown up, the area where I was from, and I was eating with my people. For a few fleeting moments, I felt like a king. So, it was both strange and wonderful.

We even employed some of the locals as actors in supporting roles and cameos. One such person was Marcia Potter, who played Mrs. Fairburn, the school teacher in the opening scene of the movie who is distracted by Jessica's shrill singing in the classroom. I think you can detect that Marcia was not a professional actress, but her performance is still good. It works, and has warmth. You can always spot local hire in movies and I'm not happy with it in some instances, I must be honest about that, but it was entirely necessary due to the budget we were toiling under. We even lost an actor because we couldn't quite match a financial offer he had received from someone else. Mike Starr was originally going to be playing Bert the cop, but he couldn't do it. I believe Mike got a job for more money, I forget what it was now, and departed. So, I instead hired Michael Luciano as the cop. Luciano had played the guard in *Weeds* who briefly speaks with Nick Nolte at the beginning of the film after Umstetter attempts suicide for a second time. He was wonderful in the part.

Getting back to Rebecca Harrell, over the years many people have asked me, "How did you get that performance out of that little girl?" There was no great secret to it. I just treated Rebecca like an adult and told her what was happening in the given scene if I needed to. Often I didn't need to. Miraculously, she would be able to just do it. In my experience, one of the most fascinating and wonderful things about working with children is how uninhibited and pure they are as performers. They don't carry any baggage and filmmaking simply becomes another form of imaginative play for them. They can be conscious of what it is they have to do in a scene, but they can also have a freedom that is invigorating to behold. Sometimes, when you explain too much to a child actor, he or she becomes self-conscious and distracted. As a director, you have to know when to say a little and when to say a lot. The secret is, again, to make sure that you are on their level. You want them to see you as their friend, their protector, their confidante, someone whom they can depend on to get through a performance. Some child actors are so experienced in all facets of the business they become either arrogant or apathetic. It's a weird and unsettling thing to experience. I could not have made *Prancer* with a blasé kid like that. Not only would the magic have dissipated, it would have somehow seemed phony and plastic. You can't communicate on the necessary level of wonder and curiosity that you need. I had that with Rebecca, and I was unfailingly nice to her in an effort to keep it that way.

On one of the first days of principal photography, I remember we were shooting outdoors in the thigh-deep snow. As she was so small, I had to pick Rebecca up and carry her from one area to another. It was a rather sweet and intimate experience for the both of us, and helped us to bond quickly. We would always be talking and laughing as I gently lugged her along. Those shooting days were incredibly cold, with temperatures getting as low as twenty-two degrees below zero. We had erected a tent where we could house the actors between set-ups in an effort to keep them warm, but it was still tough. I was wearing thick and heavy down clothes as well as boots with felt-linings like the Russians and hog-farmers wear. So, I was more than comfortable when we were out in the open filming. Many of the actors were not so padded and protected from the elements, and were freezing. It was especially difficult for Rebecca as, unfortunately, we had earlier made the mistake of establishing her character without mittens. That oversight proved to be a painful one for her. To be shooting in the snow for so long, at that bitter temperature and without anything covering your hands, was tough for any adult to endure never mind a child. The crew was standing around with gloves on and here was this little girl valiantly struggling along. Understandably, there were occasions when she would just break down crying as her hands became raw and were hurting so much. Each time she would cry I would comfort Rebecca, and tell her how brave and wonderful she was.

Early on during filming, I decided to do a lot of takes with Rebecca—some involving the words as scripted, others that were entirely improvised. I would get a good take with the dialogue as written and then I'd say, "Okay, now say it again in your own words." That was when we got some of the most wonderful stuff from Rebecca. She'd get to the core of something quicker, or would rephrase the lines in a manner that was somehow more truthful and affecting. I would often take her back over the same scene. By the third time, it would start working extremely well. I would also keep the camera running and tell her to keep going without stopping whenever a take broke down. This helped Rebecca to maintain her fluidity. Another thing I did was get her to run a lap before shooting a scene. This was a ploy designed to get her blood going. I mean, there is so much waiting around in filmmaking that the actors sometimes go dead; their blood pressure and adrenaline goes down, and they lose a lot of energy and concentration. That is one of the tricks I use a lot and it's often proved profitable. I've had actors doing push-ups on a set, or jogging laps around the soundstage, or running up and down the steps of a house, whatever it takes. After doing this, they often arrive at the scene with their blood flowing. Conversely, if they're about to play an emotional scene and are feeling physically or mentally tired by their exertions, I find it also aids them in getting to the right state of weariness.

When you have the kind of instinctual or impulsive performance like the one delivered by Rebecca, it can sometimes grate against the more conventional or mannered approach taken by an adult actor, or another experienced child actor. An instinctual approach from a child is more mysterious because the performance is simply happening before your very eyes, to your own astonishment, like it's coming from some place you don't know. Sam Elliott is a method actor, but it was never a question of combining his method approach with Rebecca's more intuitional approach as I've always thought that she was a method actor in a way, too. I mean, method acting is really just instinctual acting. It basically involves the actor trying to get rid of any preconceptions and just letting it all happen in the moment, using and recalling any sensations to foment an authentic emotional state. So, on that basis, Sam and Rebecca were able to act together and improvise together remarkably well. They were simply playing off each other and it was beautiful to see.

Indeed, I still marvel at the tender scene between Sam and Rebecca that takes place in Jessica's bedroom towards the end of the film. Again, this is what I referred to earlier that I feel comes from my mother's wisdom: an acceptance of life and seeing things as they really are. Jessica's father says to her, "I can't tell you that everything is going to be alright." That is a very revealing and honest moment, I think. He knows that they may lose the farm one day and be in a difficult place, but they will always have each other. And that's enough. You might not get a moment like that in a Spielberg picture. Everything *would* be alright. It's enough that these two people have come to a new place in their relationship, a better understanding of each other. The father realizes how wonderful his daughter really is and the daughter knows that her father loves her. It's not worth pouring more sugar over a scene like that because the oversweet taste just makes you want to throw up. What I find interesting is a certain amount of that scene, especially on Rebecca's part, was improvised. The way she allowed herself to find such emotional truth still amazes me. I mean, how did she know to be so withdrawn in those moments? That's a question I've often asked myself. Where did that instinct or insight come from? Also, if you watch it again, you'll notice that she did not give Sam an inch for a long time in that scene. You know, good actors give each other obstacles and it's very important to do that. You have to give your scene partner an obstacle that they must respond to, or negotiate, and Rebecca really gave Sam one. She made it hard for Sam to get her to forgive him.

The interesting thing about Sam's performance is how fierce he played the father. He pushed it right on the edge—to the point where he comes across at first as a rather disagreeable and unnerving presence. When you're making pictures for children you don't want to give them nightmares, but he made this angry father somewhat scary. It wouldn't surprise me to learn that Rebecca was a little afraid of Sam. She wasn't terrified of him or anything, as Sam liked her very much and she liked him, but he played that character so forcefully. The way Sam pressed it in that manner made Jessica's father appear more real and rounded. I think the crankiness and abruptness he exhibited was fairly unusual and refreshing in American movies of that period. You didn't often see a father portrayed like that—not back in the 1980s and particularly not in family films, or movies made for children. Parents were not always presented as these difficult and fallible human beings with their own faults and problems. They may be divorced or out of work, but they consistently seemed to be very middle class for the most part; dependable, affectionate, and capable of expressing love to their kids. That was especially the case in Christmas movies where there is an attempt to portray a cozy and wholesome Disney world. You still see it today. But life isn't always like that, is it? The reality can be decidedly different. Additionally, there is the idea that some parents have to prepare their children for the grim and bitter realities of the world, where things are not always going to be handed to them on a plate. So, there isn't as much tolerance and softness. Occasionally, there are some very good reasons to be tough and miserable and pessimistic.

As adults we can easily forget what it was like to be a child. I find there are grownups that often have a bristling and complicated relationship with children, and it isn't entirely dependant on them being a parent themselves. There are people with no children who have an inexhaustible patience with kids and there are parents who can't stand to be in the same room as their own offspring. Either in real life or in the movies, what one adult views as being cute and charming in a child another sees as annoying and exasperating. This can be further complicated when placed in a working environment. I saw evidence of this during the shooting of *Prancer*. As we were filming, Rebecca had some things she would occasionally insist on doing that, over time, started to aggravate certain members of the crew. For instance, it would be late at night after a long and tiring day of working in the cold, and she would want to do the slate—the board held in front of the camera at the beginning of each take. I was completely fine with this as it kept her happy and, let's not forget, she was just a little kid. But I do remember that towards the end of the shoot, and I don't recall exactly what scene we were doing, something interesting happened: Rebecca fell and hurt herself and she started crying. Earlier in the schedule, people would have rushed to her aid but nobody moved. I looked around and saw that some of the crew were actually chuckling with satisfaction. I said, "Oh, I see that the suffering of a small child amuses you." And it really did. The truth is if you spend enough time with a child that age you do develop a variety of different feelings and responses.

Even though we had a healthy amount of snow during filming, from the first day everybody began to understand why I had been so adamant about the whole business of making our own snow. For one thing, they could see how important it was in terms of continuity and atmosphere. Snow is synonymous with Christmas, with wintertime, so there was no way of getting around that perception. We needed it. It may not be a well-known fact but snow is hard to match on film. Aside from the fact it can turn dark and dirty over time, or melt away, there are other considerations. Snow can be composed of big flakes and it can be composed of little flakes, and you can't cut back and forth between two people in a dialogue scene with the snowflakes constantly changing in size between the two close-ups. It's just too obvious and distracting. Thankfully, we always had the option of using a lot of potato flakes during shooting that we blew up into the air with big fans. They looked like real snowflakes and were consistent in their size and shape. We had a huge art department on *Prancer* and were also able to "snow-in" the whole of the Main Street of Three Oaks and other areas where we shot using large consignments of fake snow. This looked very effective on film, which made me happy.

The fact is we tried not to shoot outdoors in the winter more than we had to as the icy temperatures were so difficult to negotiate. To solve this problem, we constructed a duplicate of the street in Three Oaks inside a former AP Parts warehouse located in LaPorte. We also built a country road in that same warehouse replete with overhanging trees, bushes and snow, which looked quiet impressive. So, we were able to shoot several exteriors indoors and the conditions were much more conducive to a happy working environment. We kept it cold enough in there so that you could see the actors' breath but we weren't shooting at ten below zero and freezing our asses off. I mean, you get so cold when you're shooting outside at night you can no longer think effectively. You just look at a take and say, "Yeah, that's okay," and then simply move on because you are mostly conscious of the need to be somewhere warmer. You get tired, and when you get tired, you get sloppy. Later, you look at what you've shot in dailies and say, "Christ, why did I let them do *that*? What the hell was I thinking?" Well, the truth is you weren't thinking about anything at that point other than the fact your balls felt like icicles!

My cinematographer on *Prancer* was Misha Suslov, who hailed from the Soviet Union. Misha had already shot a couple of American movies like *Black Moon Rising* and *Nobody's Fool*, and had also done some of the post-production re-shoots on *Weeds*. He had then shot *Steal the Sky* for me and I was impressed with not only his keen visual sense and work ethic, but the fact he was a great guy. When the opportunity to do *Prancer* arose, I insisted on using Misha again. That took some doing, as I seem to recall there being some initial resistance to my suggestion for some reason. Maybe the studio had somebody else in mind for the job, I don't remember, but I stressed that I would not do the picture without Misha. They relented and we proceeded forward. There are three very good reasons for why I wanted Misha so badly for the film: first, I knew he could comfortably make the schedule. Second, being from the Soviet Union, I knew he would be able to endure the cold. Third, it was simply because Misha was, and remains, a good cameraman. Misha has this tradition where he will break a plate against the camera on the first day of shooting for good luck. It's something he does on every film. I gather he has done it ever since his first film in the Soviet Union; whether it's an actual Russian tradition or not, I don't know. I suspect it's just Misha.

When Misha and I had our early discussions about the visual style of the picture, we realized there is always the temptation in a movie with the subject matter of *Prancer* to give it a heightened realism. We shot using star-filters and that kind of stuff, in a concerted effort to achieve a Christmas or festive look as they would turn the lights into diamonds and other interesting arcs and shapes. For instance, the shot where Jessica and her father are driving at night to release Prancer into the wild, you can see the lights of the town have this certain look that almost resembles the lights on a Christmas tree. We had a lot of exterior night scenes that were going to involve a large area that we would have to light. We lit the exterior night scenes using these huge lights that were mounted up on

Condor Cranes. We'd drive the cranes around, set up our lights, and it was a fairly expedient way of working. We had a lot of expensive equipment on this picture, but we still encountered some problems with the cameras regarding condensation. I believe we sometimes had to keep the lenses cold at night, maybe leave them outside, or they would fog-up when we started shooting our exteriors after keeping them indoors overnight.

You'll notice there are a couple of day-for-night shots in the picture that we achieved using blue filters, but they don't trouble me at all when I see the film now. Importantly, they don't resemble those awful American television movies you used to see in the 1970s which were so obviously shot during a bright sunny day and the images later darkened in post-production. I forget now which specific scenes in *Prancer* we shot day-for-night. I think the brief shot near the climax where Prancer leaps from the truck and gallops away through the forest towards the cliff-edge was certainly day-for-night. There was simply no way we could haul our equipment up into that freezing pine forest in complete darkness—and with a little girl in tow. So, we had no other alternative but to shoot that particular moment during the daylight hours. It still looks okay, I think. As far as some of the daylight exteriors are concerned, Misha mostly tried to get a kind of clean, wintry look. We were careful in trying to manage the whites of the snowy landscapes without burning the images out.

> *Another essential ingredient for the shooting of* Prancer *was, of course, a reindeer. To fulfill the titular role the production secured the services of Boo, a female reindeer whose only previous experience in the field of entertainment was working the Christmas parade circuit in Alabama. Transported to the colder climes of an Indiana winter, Boo took several weeks to acclimatize. Another concern for the filmmakers was the fact that Boo was pregnant during shooting and there was a chance she would give birth to her calf before the end of the schedule. On the last day of shooting, twelve hours after Hancock announced the film was a wrap, Boo gave birth to a calf that was named Raffaella in affectionate tribute to the producer.*

In total, I believe we managed to locate six reindeer for use in the film. Working with these creatures was difficult and they presented us with a number of problems that we perhaps did not entirely foresee. They were rather stubborn and contradictory animals during shooting. In fact, there was a certain percentage of the crew that wanted to eat them at the wrap party! The source of their frustration was the simple fact that you can't train reindeer. They don't respond to direction, or to rewards, or to punishment, or to anything. They are wild animals and the only way we could even get them to look in a certain direction was to put a screen up in front of a couple of reindeer that were positioned off-camera. Then we would suddenly reveal the reindeer from behind the screen to the principal reindeer we were shooting and, because they are instinctually herd animals and are always desperate to join their kind, they would immediately turn and try to get to the other reindeer. That trick was essentially the only means at our disposal that would get them to turn this way or that way. But it invariably took some time to organize and coordinate this maneuver.

We were fully aware beforehand that Boo, the main reindeer we mostly shot with, was pregnant before we started shooting. You see, we had been reliably informed that pregnant reindeer tend to keep their antlers long in order to protect themselves. That was the theory, anyway. It was important that our hero reindeer consistently had a healthy pair of antlers as that is the way we often imagine Santa's reindeer to look, particularly young children. That was one of the fundamental reasons why we hired six reindeer on the picture; we were always afraid they were going to drop antlers halfway through shooting and we'd be left with major continuity issues. I honestly don't know what we would have done if that had occurred. There was no way we were ever going to be able to tie the antlers back on their heads, or add them later as a visual effect in post-production. It would have been disastrous for us. Honestly, I think there was considerable anxiety and concern about possible antler loss from day one. Something I only recently discovered—or perhaps I'd just forgot it over time—was that some of the reindeer had to arrive in Indiana a certain time before shooting commenced. This was done in order for them to properly acclimatize themselves as, unlikely as it sounds, they were not used to such cold conditions. The head wrangler was a guy I knew from Wilmington, and I believe the person who was in charge of Boo was from Alabama. So, these animals were not accustomed to biting temperatures as they were kept in places that were far warmer.

Boo was a rather perverse creature in many ways. She had the strange and disturbing habit of relieving herself every time I yelled "action." It was like the word would literally inspire her to take a leak whenever it was uttered. Her reaction to the word "cut" was equally problematic. I didn't feel that Boo was my enemy during shooting, but I was pretty close to feeling it. I mean, here's another example of her perversity: somehow Boo got attuned to the very faint noise that the camera made when it started rolling. She would hear this sound and would immediately turn her head away every time I tried to get a shot of her face. As soon as I yelled cut, the beast would then turn its head back around again. *Every fucking time*! It was quite incredible. At first, I thought it was merely some kind of coincidence or possibly a behavioral tick, something like that. I didn't think at this point that it was directed at me personally. I quickly changed my mind about that as each time we'd start over and roll the camera, Boo would immediately turn away again! Then again! And again! Feeling exasperated, I said to Misha, "Okay, I know what we can do: we'll just let the camera run and she will eventually turn her head back around and we'll get the shot of her face." Misha agreed this was a good idea. So, we let the camera run and waited…and waited….and Boo still didn't turn around.

After a few minutes, in complete irritation, I yelled cut. At *that* very moment the animal turned around to face us! This conduct continued on and on; me saying cut, Boo turning back around as if on cue. I then whispered to Misha, "Okay, I have another idea: I'll say the word 'cut' aloud, but do *not* cut! We'll just let her think that I ordered you to cut. Understand?" Misha nodded. Well, we did this, but Boo still did not turn around! It was now getting a little spooky as well as profoundly maddening. We ended up running through an entire thousand-foot magazine of this reindeer looking away from camera. I boldly tried to wait her out, but it was all in vain. Then Film Finances, the bond company that had also been involved with *Steal the Sky*, got to hear about it and grew somewhat concerned about this expenditure. They basically said, "We were very happy with the John Hancock who shot *Weeds* and *Steal the Sky*, but the John Hancock who is shooting *Prancer* is shooting far too much film. I'm afraid you're way over on your allotment here." My inevitable reply to this observation was, "I'm sure you've heard of the old adage about working with children and animals, right? We are doing a lot of stuff with children and animals here. What did you expect?" I was shooting with two cameras and we did indeed exhaust a lot of film, but it was entirely necessary.

A further consideration we had to make in regard to the reindeer was the safety of our cast and crew. This was brought into alarming focus one night when we were shooting the scene where Jessica and her father are driving along the wintry road in the hours of darkness and almost hit Prancer with their pickup truck. Most of that sequence was shot in the relative comfort of our warehouse soundstage. However, for the section where you see the vehicle screeching to a halt with the reindeer in the foreground, we had to shoot on an actual exterior road at night. This necessitated our having to fasten Boo down to the spot where she needed to be positioned. So, the wrangler secured a bolt into the road and attached heavy duty 60lb fishing line to it that was fixed up to a harness concealed around the reindeer's body. As they were preparing this rig, Boo suddenly jerked her head around and hooked the wrangler in the cheek with her antlers, putting a huge hole in his face that began bleeding profusely. Very shocking!

If the thought hadn't occurred to us before it quickly became apparent just how potentially dangerous it would be to bring Rebecca in and place her in close proximity to this wild animal. I mean, what if that had happened to *her*?! It would have been horrific. After careful deliberation of all the risks involved, we decided to go ahead and shoot all the reindeer scenes under close supervision and care. Rebecca had previously spent a certain amount of time going to the stable where we kept the six reindeer for the duration of production. The stable was near to where I live and every day she would go in there and spend an hour with Boo and the other reindeer either before or after rehearsal. This was done in order to get her used to the animals and, more importantly, get the animals used to her. Despite this, I was still greatly concerned about doing the scenes where Rebecca would have to get close to the beasts as I don't believe that reindeer recognize people. Well, perhaps they do recognize humans, I don't know, but from what I observed back then I would have to say that I doubt it.

Another scene that required careful planning was the passage where Jessica attempts to free Prancer from the butcher's cage where the animal is on display for the customers. Jessica falls heavily to the snowy ground from a tree and is knocked unconscious. Prancer realizes this and approaches her, so we needed a shot of the reindeer lying down beside Jessica. That was difficult to accomplish and we ended up having to reverse the film to make the scene work. The wrangler positioned Boo down on the ground beside our stunt double, Bobby Porter, as on this occasion we did not want to put Rebecca in the shot. Bobby, who was also our stunt co-coordinator, is only 4' 10" and made an excellent double for Rebecca as he was around her size. As soon as we got Boo down on her stomach, we rolled the camera and the wrangler released her. Seconds later, Boo got back up on her legs and absently trotted away. We later printed the footage backwards and it looked like Prancer lies down beside Jessica to comfort her and keep her warm.

Actually, there's a moment that occurs after that where Prancer wanders onto the deserted street. That night is the coldest I've ever been at any time in my life, as we were shooting some of that sequence outside in minus fifteen degrees. I remember that we simply let Boo go out on the street and we got incredibly lucky. She slowly loped out onto the icy road, looked around, and then started back towards the direction from which she had come. So, we were able to then cut that shot into the action of Prancer coming back to Jessica's unconscious body with the reverse printed shot of the child lying down on the ground. It worked out rather well. We also had a shot of Boo sniffing or nuzzling the tiny unconscious figure. I think we achieved that simply by placing some reindeer food down around Bobby's head, so that it looked as if Prancer was tenderly seeing if Jessica was okay.

To cover ourselves a little more in certain scenes we also hired a special make-up effects artist named Lance Anderson, who had worked on John Carpenter's remake of *The Thing*, to construct a mechanical reindeer that we could use for some shots. I guess the idea was that a fake reindeer would be much easier to control and subdue than a real reindeer, and would remain still for us. We could also deploy it for some of the moments where Rebecca was physically close to the animal and there'd be no safety concerns. So, Anderson created a life-size animatronic puppet that was operated by five guys who were all making the head turn left and right, the eyes blink up and down, the mouth open and close, and the ears move forward and back. The puppet was fairly detailed, but we only used it sparingly. As a matter of fact, I believe you can only see it in one or two shots of the scene where Jessica is alone in the Riggs family barn with Prancer. I originally shot a lot more footage of the mechanical reindeer, but I was sufficiently unhappy with it that I decided to stop using it. After struggling to get the shots of Boo simply turning her head, I didn't feel entirely comfortable using too much of the puppet as it simply didn't look real enough—even when we carefully controlled the lighting and angles.

> *The climax of* Prancer, *in which Jessica and her father release the fully recuperated creature back into the wild, is*

> *luminous in its gentle beauty and ambiguity. Hancock leaves the question open as to whether the animal has tumbled to its death over the edge of a dark forest cliff, or has instead taken its rightful place alongside Dasher, Dancer, Vixen, Comet, Cupid, Dunder, Blixem and Rudolph, as a member of Santa's team of flying reindeer charged with pulling his slay through the night sky.*

The question remains has Jessica imagined it all or is the magic real? I tend to believe that she was merely imagining Prancer flying up out of the forest to rejoin Santa Claus and the other reindeer. I feel that moment does not occur in reality, only through the innocent and wondrous eyes of this remarkable little girl. I do enjoy the fact that some people don't know if it's real or fantasy, but, originally, in the first cut, I did not want to see anything at all. Nothing! We merely had Jessica and her father standing there at the edge of the cliff, contemplating the reindeer's fate. Not many people have commented on this but a moment before Prancer soars into the sky, a dappled patch of colored light moves over Jessica's face. This reveals that at one point I did consider a different approach; one that did not actually show the reindeer flying. You notice it, perhaps, because the light traveling over her face does not match the timing and trajectory of Prancer's flight in the scene as it presently exists. I initially felt that the light would be a more subtle indication of what exists in Jessica's mind. That's all I wanted to depict on film. I wanted to play it all on Rebecca's face.

Even so, in their capacity as the financing entity, Cineplex Odeon felt differently. They wanted to have some explicit revelation at the climax of Prancer's flight. Raffaella pretty much agreed with that opinion and felt we needed to confirm the magic for the audience. Several other people also contended that it was kind of a jerk-off to have come all this way with Jessica, and witnessed her love and belief that this creature was genuinely one of Santa's own, only to have it be a figment of her imagination. Having the attitude of a staunch realist I personally do not believe that reindeer fly, so I felt the ending worked just fine as it was. But following all of these conflicting reactions I was receiving, and the studio's strong desire to see *something*, we created a visual effect that we incorporated into the sequence—one that is not in the finished film. As I remember it showed Prancer having difficulty in taking off at first, shakily struggling to fly, before finally gathering pace and soaring really fast into the night sky. I thought this shot was rather good, all things considered, but others were not of the same opinion. I do recall that upon seeing this ending, Joel Michaels, who was the executive in charge of Cineplex, said, "No, we can't use that. It's just not going to work." Maybe I was out of perspective at this point, I don't know, it's certainly possible, but I thought he was mistaken.

Following this, we decided to try a third time. After some discussion, we settled on the idea of having a visual effect that depicted a glowing trail of colored light ascending out of the forest and into the sky, finally merging with Santa's sleigh as it glides past the full moon. That seemed to work just fine for everybody and by this point I'd resigned myself to it. So, that's what we did. I still believe the ending worked better without descending into total fantasy as it seemingly does now. Artistically, it would have worked better. Commercially, I don't know. Perhaps not. Maybe the audience would have rejected the movie had we not seen something fantastic happening. Of course, coming back around to my first point, just because we do see Prancer gliding up into the sky does not make it *real*. You'll notice that the camera is mostly restricted to a shot of Jessica's face before and after the reindeer flies, which was done to subtly reinforce the idea that it's all in her head. Ultimately, I guess it works both ways and ambiguity can still be gleaned from it. The events of the film could merely be Jessica's imagination running away with her as, at the beginning, she witnesses the plastic Prancer decoration fall to the ground on Main Street and break apart. That incident might have triggered her illusion to begin with. Then she just ran with it as a lot kids so often do.

This leads me to something else I want to talk about in relation to imagination: in his address during the church service, the minister sermonizes to Jessica and the congregation about the "electronic age" and "children growing up too fast." That seems more relevant now than ever, don't you think? *Prancer* is a film about a child with a fertile imagination and how that imagination feeds her sense of adventure and allows her to combat her fraught reality to a certain extent (a cynical reading of the film, one I don't encourage, is that the story details the total mental collapse of a child who is rendered insane by a cruel parent and an isolated existence). Jessica is a little girl who has got no mother and a mean father, so she has to find this imaginary playmate. These days, in my opinion, children don't live in their imaginations so much. I feel it's something that is getting rarer and rarer these days. I think it's a real problem now that has gotten worse since the late 1980s when we made the movie. Back then, kids used to go outside and play, and lead very active lives. Today, it seems like most children are content to remain indoors with their iPads, computers, and other electronic devices. I ask you, where is the adventure in that?

Notwithstanding the visual effect of Prancer's flight itself, the whole climax was put together from a variety of elements. First, there is no cliff within a hundred miles of where I live. Thus, in order to get the scenes where Jessica and her father release the reindeer into the wild, we had to drive the company to the southwest of Chicago. There is a cliff there known as Starved Rock, which is a tree-covered mountain that overlooks a section of the Illinois River. There are several legends attached to that place and it's said that Starved Rock earned its name after some Indians took refuge there after an attack and were systematically cut off and starved to death. It's a grim story, but a beautiful location. Anyway, we shot the action there and then later did a very nice matte shot of the moon-washed forest and added the effect of Santa's sleigh traversing the night sky and flying past the moon. All of that stuff worked out very well. There are a number of other impressive matte paintings sprinkled throughout *Prancer*. For instance, aside from there being no cliff available locally, there was also no sledding hill. So, the scene where Jessica slides down the snowy hill on her sledge and trashes the old woman's garden incorporates a matte painting that was built out of the actual location. The final shot of the movie which shows Santa's, or possibly Prancer's, point of view as the sleigh glides unseen over the town towards the Riggs farm was a model. It was a good model, very meticulous. It was carefully lit to give the impression that moonlight was throwing off the shadows of the trees and buildings. Lights were also placed within the tiny houses and there were tire-tracks in the snow, lots of nice details. Part of that model is presently on display in the LaPorte County Historical Museum.

> *Much to Hancock's delight, the veteran French composer Maurice Jarre (1924-2009) agreed to score* Prancer. *Nominated for nine Academy Awards, and winning three, he was noted for his fruitful collaborations with David Lean on such epic pictures as* Lawrence of Arabia *(1962),* Doctor Zhivago *(1965),* Ryan's Daughter *(1970) and* A Passage of India *(1984). His other notable credits include* Mohammad, Messenger of God *(1976),* The Tin Drum *(1979),* Witness *(1985) and* Ghost *(1990). Working with his longtime orchestrator Patrick Russ, Jarre's remit was to*

create a score for Prancer *that deftly captured the "magical" elements of Christmas and childhood wonder.*

I was initially excited to be working with Maurice Jarre. How could I not be? Like everyone, I had adored his exquisite scores for *Lawrence of Arabia* and *Dr. Zhivago*, and he was undoubtedly a towering figure among movie composers. Truth be told, I was less enamored with some of his more recent scores, the stuff he'd done in the years directly prior to *Prancer*. I don't know, I guess Maurice was going through his experimental "electronic phase" throughout much of the 1980s and was writing a lot of music for synthesizers. Things like *Witness* and *The Mosquito Coast* were okay, but I felt those scores weren't as majestic or as moving as his earlier epic orchestral compositions. All the same, Jarre did possess the ability to marry synthesizers with orchestral music to great effect and not every composer was as adept at doing that as him (with the possible exception of Jerry Goldsmith). Maurice had something he called a EWI, which I believe stood for Electronic Wind Instrument. It had a unique, warm sound. He had a house in Malibu, so I would travel from my home to his. I'd then listen to what he was doing and offer my comments on it, which were politely received. Maurice had his computer set up, and maybe he had two recording sessions with seven people playing a variety of different wind and string instruments: an Irish harp, piano, one thing and another. He then had another session with a full orchestra and a chorus of voices singing.

I try to have a good relationship with a composer when I'm working with them on a movie, as it's such an important relationship. I've not always liked what a composer has given me, but, having been a musician at one time myself—admittedly not a particularly great one—I've always appreciated what it is they do and what they can bring to a picture. A great score can have a truly transformative effect on the images in a way that is quite wonderful and spellbinding to behold. I try to communicate any suggestions and opinions I may have to a composer in a manner that does not appear dictatorial or disrespectful. If you have a favorable working relationship with somebody that can be easy; if you've worked with them more than once you can even talk in a kind of shorthand. But from the moment I met Maurice, there was a certain formality to our relationship and that never changed. He was nice, I liked him, but I didn't feel personally close to him as I have done with other composers like Angelo Badalamenti and Orville Stoeber. Maurice and I did have a mutual respect, which was equally important, and I do recall that he liked *Prancer* very much and found it suitably "inspiring." Coming from a man who had worked repeatedly with David Lean, I took that to be quite some compliment.

Before Maurice was hired, I had principally temped *Prancer* with the music of *E.T.* and several other scores by John Williams, as well as some classical pieces. Again, since *Prancer* is in some ways a more abrasive variation on Spielberg's film, in that you have a child developing a friendship with an exotic creature, Williams' music worked exceedingly well. It had an enchanting and childlike quality about it, as well as an enormous amount of feeling. That was useful in helping me to discover exactly what I wanted: something magical and emotional and uplifting. My temp score was all of those things. Lamentably, and this is the disease of most directors, I had fallen in love with the temp score very, very hard. The classical pieces complemented the images beautifully to the point I couldn't separate them. When I eventually heard Maurice's score for *Prancer* in its entirety I was not thrilled, I must say. I do like it and, undeniably, it works. His music has great sweetness and a nice Christmas feeling, which were the prerequisites for it. It's just that, in my mind and in my heart, it doesn't work as well as the temp. It's also not of the same high quality as Maurice's wonderful music for *Lawrence of Arabia* and *Dr. Zhivago*. Maybe I'm being unfair here, but that was my honest response.

For the final sequence where Prancer rejoins Santa and the other reindeer and they fly over the snow-covered town, I had originally intended to use Giuseppe Verdi's *Nabucco*, the famous "Chorus of the Hebrew Slaves." I thought that would provide a glorious and inspiring climax. For me, and for nearly everybody else I'd shown the temp score, it was far more powerful than "Prancer is Free," the cue Jarre had composed for the ending. Everyone agreed that the fly-over sequence accompanied by *Nabucco* was stirring and built towards the moment that the camera soared through the window of the farm and into the blinding light—oh, it was wonderful! Regrettably, the one person who disagreed was Raffaella. This was to be the only friction that occurred between us, the only fight we had on the film. I stressed to her that Verdi's music was the correct way to go, but Raffaella was unmoved. She said rather firmly, "John, I've enjoyed a long relationship with Maurice and I want to work with him again after *Prancer* is finished. I know that you are in control of the final mix, and you can mix the film however you see fit, but if you include

Nabucco at the expense of Maurice's cue I will be forced to remix it. I would rather not run up that money and cause any ill feeling between us, so please, John—*please*—don't do it!" And I didn't.

We used Jarre's final cue at the end, which, again, is still very good and melodious, but I do miss hearing *Nabucco* in that scene. I can't help it. To this day, I mourn that decision. The original climax had such a great spine-tingling feeling, it was exhilarating. Perfect! As a matter of fact, I just used that same piece of music in *The Looking Glass*. So, *Nabucco* has never quite left me and, like any music that nourishes your soul, it never will. This is why I say its loss is so hard to take: once you have a piece of music in your mind for a sequence nothing else will quite do, no matter how wonderful the alternative is. Maurice did use *Nabucco* in a comic version for the scene where the reindeer escapes from the barn and wanders outside the house, bothering Sam while he's trying to read his newspaper. In truth, it's not the same. It's more playful and doesn't carry the same emotional frisson. I mean, they played *Nabucco* at Verdi's funeral in 1901 and the people of Milan spontaneously began to sing it as his coffin was carried by. So, it has become a kind of Italian national anthem and it still contains such tremendous emotion and power.

> *Whatever his concerns with the film were, Hancock was pleased to see the generally warm response* Prancer *received from critics that was typified by Roger Ebert's ebullient review: "[Prancer] sounds like a cloying fantasy designed to paralyze anyone over the age of 9, but not the way it's told by director John Hancock and writer Greg Taylor. They give the film an unsentimental, almost realistic edge ... And what really redeems the movie, taking it out of the category of kiddie picture and giving it heart and gumption, is the performance by a young actress named Rebecca Harrell as Jessica." In his notice for the* Los Angeles Times, *Kevin Thomas labeled* Prancer *"the perfect Christmas gift for the whole family," and highlighted among several things Maurice Jarre's "shimmering" score, and the "splendid" interplay between Harrell and Sam Elliott. "John Hancock is ideally cast for this material, for in films like from* Bang the Drum Slowly *to the recent* Weeds *he has revealed an ability to deal with highly charged emotions with directness and without apology," noted Thomas. "Of course,* Prancer *is*

a sentimental Christmas heart-tugger, but it's not ashamed to be so, and it is not unduly manipulative."

Writing in the Chicago Tribune, Dave Kehr proved a dissenting voice: *"Prancer is the story of an emotionally disturbed 8-year-old who transfers her grief for her dead mother onto an obsession with a wounded deer found in the woods. Told like that, it doesn't sound like much of a Christmas movie, and yet John Hancock's film does harbor a dark sensibility beneath its often excessive tinsel. Hancock is hard to classify. As a filmmaker, he seems compulsively drawn to sentimental material that can't help but contradict his unmistakable gifts for social realism and complex character psychology. Prancer is a typically perverse Hancock project. It's drawn from a screenplay that's meant to be slick and heartwarming in the Spielbergian mode, but rendered in a gritty, joyless style that sabotages most of [its] themes. … Hancock's rendering of the Indiana countryside is insistently unpretty; this is no Frank Capra fantasy of small town life but a surprisingly real, contemporary place, in the grip of economic stagnation."*

Prancer *was released in theaters on November 17, 1989, during an intensely competitive festive period. The final two months of the year saw a glut of high-profile big-budget family and fantasy films appear such as* The Little Mermaid, Ghostbusters II, Back to the Future Part II, All Dogs Go to Heaven *and* Always. *Other studio movies scheduled for that same Yuletide season included* Born on the Fourth of July, Driving Miss Daisy, Harlem Nights, Steel Magnolias *and* Tango & Cash. *In spite of this opposition,* Prancer *still collected a respectable $18.5 million at the box office. The film was also screened in twenty different cities across the United States to benefit the Make-A-Wish Foundation, a non-profit organization that fulfils "wish experiences" for children with life-threatening medical conditions.*

I'd forgotten how many big movies came out that Christmas. All things considered, *Prancer* did amazingly well. We released it fairly early, before Thanksgiving, and I was pleased with its performance in the face of such unremitting competition, particularly as it's difficult to retain theaters during that season. Shortly after *Prancer* came out it started to share weeks at a certain point with other major films, but it still managed to hold its own. One of the chief motives for why Raffaella chose to do a Christmas picture, despite it being hard to keep theaters during the holidays, was because she was making a Christmas picture financed by Cineplex Odeon; a company that owns most of the theaters in America. Thus, it was going to be able to hold the theaters even though it was contending with the likes of *The Little Mermaid* and *All Dogs Go to Heaven*—which were released on the same day as *Prancer*—and *Ghostbusters II* and *Driving Miss Daisy*, which followed soon after. Unfortunately, by the time *Prancer* came out, Garth Drabinsky had lost control of Cineplex Odeon. He had somehow quarreled with Lew Wasserman and Sid Sheinberg, and gone up against the real superpowers of Hollywood. That was a substantial mistake on Garth's part and the inevitable result of it was he had been kicked out of his company. So, instead of Cineplex Odeon releasing *Prancer* they got Nelson Entertainment and Universal to release it; and those entities were not able to hold the theaters as unmercifully as they otherwise would have if Garth had still been around. The fact that *Prancer* still managed to gross more than $18 million regardless of these problems is impressive.

Based on the evidence of my previous movies, some critics felt I had fallen back on doing sentimental material. I found those responses somewhat amusing, as we had strived to give *Prancer* a more somber and sober quality. If I had shot Taylor's original draft, the critics would've had more of a right to complain. The film would have been mushy and silly, and there were already enough fantasy movies foisted on the public that served that need. Why make another? Naturally, you always have high hopes for any picture as you are making it. You hope it will do well and find an audience. You hear some directors refer to their movies as their kids: you raise them, send them on their way into the world, and only wish them the best. Sometimes they disappoint you and don't turn out so well, but they're always yours. *Prancer* was a picture crafted with great care and love, and I think you can see that. When we finished it, and looked at it, we were all so proud. Raffaella in particular really liked the film and she hadn't forgotten our conversation about Dorothy receiving a "little present" for her efforts in revising the script. After the picture came out, Raffaella paid for a tile floor for our Malibu home and we were delighted with it. We enjoyed that tile floor for the next four years before a fire destroyed our house. So, I remember all the good feelings people had about *Prancer*. My memories of the premiere are like that: feeling a sense of happiness and satisfaction. Actually, the premiere was when I finally met Garth in person, as he was not around at all during filming. Garth and I have remained friends from that day to this.

After doing *Weeds* and *Prancer*, Raffaella expressed an interest in us making a third movie together. For a while we considered mounting a remake of Mervyn LeRoy's *The Bad Seed* with Rebecca playing the role of the evil, murderous little girl that was made famous by Patty McCormack in the 1956 original. We were going to do our version right after *Prancer* and had some preliminary discussions about it. We set about trying to acquire the rights and were talking about what we would like to do with it. Although we never had a screenplay written, Raffaella decided that we couldn't make the ending work (the little girl is struck dead by a God-like bolt of lightning at the climax of LeRoy's film, something we felt would not work for a contemporary audience). So, she bowed out of the project and it eventually drifted away. There had already been a remake of *The Bad Seed* made for television in the mid-1980s, and I now understand they are currently preparing to do a third film version. I would've liked to have taken my shot at it, as I think Rebecca would have been great playing the psychopathic flip-side of Jessica. I should add that Rebecca and Raffaella have continued to see each other socially over the years. They have remained firm friends, which is nice. I've also used Rebecca three times since *Prancer* and have always enjoyed seeing and working with her.

Of all the movies I've made, *Prancer* is the one that people want to talk to me about the most. It seems to resonate strongly with audiences in a way that some of my other pictures perhaps don't quite as much. I mean, *Let's Scare Jessica to Death* has its share of passionate fans, and there are those who adore *Bang the Drum Slowly* and *Weeds*, but *Prancer* appears to hold an enduring significance. The local librarian often dutifully reports to me how many people have rented *Prancer* each week from the library and when the holidays come around each year it goes out a lot. Part of the reason for why it's still cherished is that it continues to be played every Christmas on television and people readily associate the movie with that time of year. It also stirs in them memories of their own childhoods; a period in their lives where they still believed that fantastical and wondrous things could happen. They once believed that an old man in a red and white suit was able to deliver presents to all the children of the world—despite being grossly overweight and working against a tough schedule—

with the aid of his flying reindeer. There is something quite beautiful about that; the purity of innocence. I believe it's important to have a sense of awe and wonder in our lives and I've repeatedly been struck by the ability of children to live in their own hearts and imaginations. Sometimes they use this as a survival mechanism to escape abuse, poverty, grief, whatever it is that might be troubling them. There is something so sad and moving about that, and I think *Prancer* taps into that feeling.

I can also tell you that *Prancer* remains a huge deal here as the movie is treasured by the people of LaPorte and Three Oaks. In Christmas 2014, Three Oaks celebrated the 25th anniversary of *Prancer* by organizing a special screening in grand style as well as a parade that Dorothy and I marched in. The screening was held in a packed theater and I hadn't seen the picture for a long time at that point, certainly not with a full house. Before the movie started I was curious to see how it played with an audience. I had some doubts that it still worked, but I couldn't believe the response it got. It was wonderful! Even after all these years, people were crying and cheering and laughing. It was an incredibly rewarding experience for me. I mean, you see your work every once in a while and, as I often declare, all you can see are the mistakes. You don't always recognize the good things because you're too busy saying to yourself, "Ah, I should have done that differently. I wish I could go back and re-shoot that." But then you see the picture again with an audience and you realize that it retains the power to move and amuse them. I sat there watching *Prancer* that day, observing and listening to all these reactions, and I realized, "My God, this movie is okay. It works! It really does work!" That's more than enough for me.

16 *A Piece of Eden* (2000)

THE 1990S WOULD PROVE to be a decade of great personal and professional upheaval for Hancock, in which his fortunes would fluctuate wildly and his cinematic voice would be silenced. Ironically, this period would mark a time of considerable activity and productivity for him as he directed more than four-hundred commercials for the big box department store chain Kmart, in addition to helming episodes of the television series Dellaventura *and* Cracker. *Hancock would also co-write or conceive a number of compelling film projects that would fail to acquire financing (for more details on these ventures see the chapter entitled Future Projects). Nonetheless, these disappointments were soundly put into perspective as disaster would strike both he and his wife in 1993.*

Shortly after *Weeds* opened, I got a call from a guy named Eli Feldman. He was Vice President and Executive Producer of a company called Directors' Chair, which was a commercial house in New York City. Eli said, "If you're agreeable to the idea, I could sell you for directing commercials. I can make you a lot of money." I thought that sounded wonderful. So, after Eli brought me in, I initially directed one commercial for Stanley Tools and the money was indeed very good. I then got busy doing *Steal the Sky* and *Prancer* back-to-back, and had to inform Eli that I could no longer take time out to do any more commercials. After *Prancer* was released, and with no go-picture set up, I suddenly did have the time. Eli was then able to sell me as a director to Kmart. There was an agency in New York that had done a campaign where everything in the commercial was executed in one shot. They had actually based this approach on certain techniques developed on *Hill Street Blues*. The ads would feature customers wandering around Kmart. Sometimes they'd be looking for each other, since people often get separated in Kmarts, other times just chatting, but always finding something to buy. These commercials were light and humorous; a very inoffensive campaign designed to establish the idea that Kmart people were funny and human, and that amusing things happened to them in the store. Having directed the two episodes of *Hill Street Blues*, Eli was able to convince them that I was a director capable of doing these commercials like they wanted them to be done—in one shot.

The Kmart gig lasted for several years and it involved my going to New York every five or six weeks for ten days at a time and shooting a whole bunch of them. It proved to be profitable for me, and not just financially. What made it so rewarding was I felt I'd finally learned how to use a camera. Honestly, it was like I had mastered how to direct a shot and had a greater understanding of the camera. Oddly enough, that knowledge did not come entirely from the movies I had directed up to that point. The Kmart commercials posed several technical challenges and they also provided opportunities for variety in the work. Certainly, I exhausted every possible and conceivable way of doing something in just one shot. Aside from the technical demands the commercials also involved working with actors, which is something I always enjoy. We had a revolving company of around twenty people that we used in ninety percent of them (they were all cast by Susan Willett). These weren't celebrities endorsing products; they were just actors around New York. They were supposed to appear like normal people, as it was important that they seemed like real customers who were in a Kmart. I spent the next four years doing these commercials and—in regards to my movie career—one could say it was a rather depressing and fruitless time. The money may have been good, but I was getting restless throughout this period as several strong film projects I'd developed didn't go anywhere.

> *Monday, November 2, 1993, was a day that would dramatically alter the course of Hancock and Tristan's lives as Malibu endured one of the largest and most ferocious wildfires in its history. The blaze, which started about thirty miles from their residence before heading northwest towards them, roared down from the Santa Monica Mountains to the Pacific coast. It would eventually burn for ten days*

> engulfing close to 18,000 acres, reducing 430 homes to ruins, destroying countless wildlife and vegetation, and leaving three people dead and many more severely injured. Although some of the properties would be rebuilt and the ashen landscape would eventually replenish itself, the scars this tragedy inflicted on all those who directly experienced it would take far longer to heal.

About a year or so before the great fire of '93, Dorothy and I had seen a column of white smoke rising in the air from a blaze located further up the hill from our Malibu home. That particular fire did not reach us, but it was still an ominous warning. We had seen fires previously in the area, but nothing that had been truly devastating to property and wildlife. From our house, you look out in one direction and there is the Pacific Ocean. You look the other way and there is a canyon with a pass between two mountains. Now, what happens in this area is the Santa Ana wind blows and it's a sixty to eighty mile an hour wind that comes whistling and swirling down these hills. If somebody goes to the top of the canyon and lights a fire, and it gets out of control and spreads, the flames are fed by this near-inexhaustible supply of wind and oxygen and they get carried. The heat and gusts combine and then sweep down through an area of arid brush. In the past, Dorothy had always rather gloomily predicted that our house would eventually burn one day. I must admit I thought this forecast was just an indication of her pessimistic nature, as she had been beaten as a child and often tended to look at the darker possibilities and outcomes in life.

However, on the morning of November 2nd, we looked out and over the top of the mountain pass at the summit of the canyon we saw this towering plume of white smoke reaching up into a cloudless sky. Dorothy immediately became afraid, but I tried to reassure her that the fire would probably miss us just as the previous one had a year earlier. We didn't know how big and fast-moving the fire was, so there was no cause for alarm quite yet. This is honestly what I believed. The Santa Ana wind was picking up all morning, stirring the vegetation and knocking over garbage cans. Dorothy had noticed this and was becoming even more agitated. I had two and a half acres of landscaped garden as well as a big sprinkler system and a swimming pool. So, to satisfy her, and as a safety precaution, I began wetting down the property. I had planted fire retardant shrubs and perennials all over this hillside, and thought that if I kept them moist the fire wouldn't reach us. On the chance that it did reach us, the fact this area was wet might protect us from serious damage.

Dorothy and I then climbed up on the roof of our house and I hosed that down, too, just as another precautionary measure. Again, I felt fairly confident that if I kept the roof wet, as well as the vegetation that stood between us and the big column of smoke, we would be okay. I mean, we still hadn't seen any flames at this point, but the wind was still howling and blowing. We then noticed that several of our neighbors had emerged from their homes and had packed their vehicles with valuables. Within a short time, we saw a solid trail of cars working their way down from the top of the hill. Then, as we sat huddled on the roof, we watched the fire suddenly crest the summit of the hill. Minutes later, the flames were eagerly but slowly crawling down the side of the mountain pass. There were a couple of helicopters flying around dumping water onto the fire but, frankly, it was a pitiful effort. At this moment, the police came by with a loudspeaker and announced, "You have to evacuate now!" I said to Dorothy, "No, let's not go just yet. I don't think the fire will hit us. There's still some time. I don't want to just surrender the house if it comes. I want to try to keep things wet."

Dorothy reluctantly agreed, but suggested we should start loading everything of value we could into my car. So, we quickly started putting in our check book, insurance policy, house plans, photographs, scripts, contracts, awards; everything we considered to be essential or important. I grabbed my silk shirts from Turnbull and Asser, while Dorothy left her expensive Italian boots behind but did manage to grab her jacket from Kmart! I could understand her confusion and dismay. Think about it: what exactly do you take from your house at a moment's notice and squeeze into a car? What do you choose to leave behind? It was terrible, agonizing. As we were going in and out of the house, filling the car up with stuff, I noticed that our neighbors' dog—a big blue hound of some kind—had suddenly gotten very melancholy. To me, the animal looked like it had resigned itself to dying and that was quite disturbing to see. It just started to wearily mope around and then settled down to sleep in our garage as this chaotic event was building momentum. I picked the dog up and put it in the car (on top of my precious Turnbull & Asser shirts), then got behind the wheel.

We moved one car of possessions down to the Pacific Coast Highway, which was about a mile downhill, and parked it near the water along with many other vehicles that had congregated there. We saw our neighbors and returned their despondent dog to them. They hadn't been home during the fire and were glad to be reunited with him. Dorothy and I then rushed back up towards the house and filled up our other car. We climbed back up on the roof and watched as this inferno finally arrived. It was the strangest feeling, one that will probably remain with me forever. I remember Dorothy commenting at this sight: "Something monumental is happening to us. It's somehow euphoric, isn't it?" I understood exactly what she meant. It was like something tremendous was happening in our lives and we knew it, we really did. Just observing this huge fire hungrily working its way closer and closer to us was weirdly exhilarating. Then, at a certain point, it became clear that it was *not* going to miss us. It was not going to disappear over the hill on the side, or change direction; it was coming right at us! Of course, throughout all this, I still kept trying to keep things wet. I had all the sprinklers and the hoses going full tilt.

Then a truck pulled up in our driveway and a big guy clambered out, and said, "I'm a friend of Tony DeVivo's." Tony was our neighbor. He lived downhill from our house, between us and the fire. "Put everything you can in my truck," this guy bellowed, "and I'll take it down to the highway for you." I was reluctant to do that as I didn't know this man from Adam. He may have been a friend of Tony's, but he was a perfect stranger to me who could have driven off with our most treasured possessions. So, I politely refused his offer. He then shrugged, got back in his truck and sped away. Shortly after he disappeared, Tony showed up and confirmed that the guy had indeed been his friend and that he had sent him to help. Tony then asked me if he could borrow my chainsaw as he wanted to cut down the huge eucalyptus trees that were in his garden. He was afraid they would catch fire and ignite his house. So, I hurriedly gave him the chainsaw and he climbed back in his car and drove off.

Around this time the fire seemed to suddenly pick up speed. It was jumping in that awful, greedy way that fires jump and was devouring everything in its path. The air grew thick with big plumes of smoke and burning embers were flying about. The wind had also picked up some more, and this roaring sound was getting louder and louder. By now it was the afternoon and it was starting to get late. I figured that the water pressure would go at a certain point as the pipes got overheated and burnt. So, I brought out a small sump-pump that I'd purchased from Sears and prepared it; filled it with gas and rigged several hoses so that it could pump the contents of the swimming pool onto the roof and keep it wet. All this time I kept checking on the progress of the fire, which was getting nearer and nearer. Finally, I knew it was time for Dorothy to go. My intention was to send her down the hill and remain with the house, but I didn't tell her this was what I planned to do. I just told her to take the car to the Pacific Coast Highway and that I would follow her soon enough, once I'd finished watering everything down.

You see, what people occasionally attempt during wildfires is they get in their swimming pools and wait until the fire passes over. This was something I thought I could do: hide in the pool then get out and use the sump-pump to smother what was left of the flames. Sometimes the fire passes and only leaves the eaves of your house burning. When that happens, you can clamber out at an opportune moment and extinguish the eaves and save your house. So, it's a wildfire that can sweep over your property without totally igniting and incinerating the house; it just gets little parts of it burning that can be controlled. If you're patient and diligent and brave enough, you can extinguish the flames before they engulf and destroy everything. That's the idea anyway, and it was something I intended to do myself. Not letting Dorothy in on this plan—she would have immediately rejected it—and with the fire now fairly close to the house, I sent her away. I again told her that I would follow on momentarily, but that I was going to wait for as long as possible; I would keep the roof wet and then bail. In the end, she reluctantly got into the car and drove down the hill (for an equally vivid account of what happened next from Dorothy's perspective, I urge you to read her autobiography *Joy Street*).

I watched her go and then continued with my efforts to saturate everything. But within a few short minutes the water pressure failed and the sprinklers died. It simply stopped, just as I'd feared. I then relied entirely on the sump-pump and was pumping water onto the roof. Alone at the house, I noticed that the smoke had gotten so thick it had suddenly grown dark. It was getting close to the end of the day and the shadows were thickening and the air was thinning. That was the moment when I really got scared. I quietly said to myself, "Okay, this fire is going to suck all the oxygen away and I'm going to die—and for what? For possessions, that's what!" My mind was dancing between what course of action I should take next: should I stay or should I go? Weighing everything up, the fact I was alone, it was dark, the fire and wind were roaring, and breathing was becoming increasingly difficult, I made my decision: I was going to haul ass! So, I did just that, and left the pump spraying the pool onto the roof. I realized it was still full of gas and thought there was a chance the gas would ignite, but what the hell? I had this nagging feeling of dread in the pit of my stomach, like, "Have I made the decision to bail too late? Is it out of my hands now anyway? No! Just get going *now*!" I then turned and started running downhill.

On my way down I rushed through evacuated properties, climbing over gates and fences, dashing over patios and gardens, and negotiating my way around swimming pools. The fire was coming fast behind me and some houses were already starting to burn as I moved past them. That came as something of a shock to me because I had been saying to myself, "Gee, I'm chickening out here, running away like this." But then there were all these houses between me and the ocean that were actually aflame, and I became terrified. I was lucky that I'd made the decision to go when I did. A few more minutes of delay could have been the difference between life and death. I hadn't realized that the fire would jump and leap in the manner that it did. I then started roughly sliding down these cliffs on my ass, barely conscious of the pain. As I was doing this, I was abruptly struck by a terrible thought: what if I break a leg or an ankle as I'm hustling along? Any injury that potentially slowed or stopped me would have meant certain death. I knew that. So, I tried my best not to damage myself as I kept moving down, and was holding onto shrubs and things as I went.

Now, there were lateral roads running across the hill between our house and the ocean. As I breathlessly stumbled along one I came upon a fire-truck containing several firemen who were pulling a hose out from their vehicle. This was literally the only fire-truck I saw all day until I got down to the Pacific Coast Highway where, incredibly, there were hundreds of 'em! These firemen saw me and started pointing and shouting, "Go that way! Go that way!" I looked in the direction in which they were gesturing and instantly knew it was the wrong way. I shook my head, but they bellowed again, "*That way!*" These guys were from Montana or someplace, so they were not local firemen who were familiar with the region. They had just come in to assist. Anyway, they made me go this certain way and ended up sending me into a dangerous area where there were five houses burning! Quite literally, I had been pushed into the blaze. As for these guys from Montana, I later learned that the fire had jumped again and had trapped them. They ended up surviving by hiding in somebody's swimming pool with their oxygen tanks as their fire-truck was consumed and destroyed by the flames. So, their limited knowledge of the area had resulted in them not being in the right spot to preserve their equipment.

After being sent to my doom by these firemen, I passed by these burning houses and continued on my way. Once again I started sliding down the slopes on my butt as best I could. It was clear to me that the fire was going to burn down to the ocean and I had to stay ahead of it. Finally, after a huge effort, I got down to the Pacific Coast Highway which was jammed with cars and fire-trucks. Here were all these firemen and their vehicles—again, literally hundreds of them—and a very strange thing occurred: I saw several firemen haltingly, almost like they were in slow-motion, unrolling their hoses, staring up at the burning canyon with stunned faces. It was as if they were saying, "Gee, maybe we better do something about this." Looking back, they were positively awestruck by the magisterial power of the fire. Evidently, they had never seen anything quite like it before. I mean, it was so devastatingly *big*. They were gazing up at the flames, repeatedly saying, "My God! Sweet Jesus! I guess we better fight it, right?" It was a total clusterfuck. With the exception of that one company from Montana, the fire department did not venture up to defend the houses on the hill. Instead, they stayed down and saved their equipment. They did not try to safeguard all the people up in the canyons of Malibu. They simply allowed this inferno to burn down to the Pacific Ocean. Then, suddenly compelled to take action, they saved the houses as much as possible on the Pacific Coast Highway—although the fire jumped and burned beach houses on the water-side of the highway, too.

After reaching the highway, I started looking around for Dorothy. I ran up and down the line of cars, my eyes searching for her, swallowing down the panic that was building inside me. Then I saw her and she ran to me. That was quite a moment, as you can imagine. It was like, "Oh God, there you are! Thank God!" She was afraid that I'd remained with the house and been killed. So, there were a lot of grateful tears. Then, in the midst of this chaos, we had to figure out where we were going to spend the night. Now, before either one of us had bailed—before we had even seen a flaming lick of fire—we had received a phone call at the house from Nick Nolte's wife, Becky, who was in Santa Monica. She had seen the wildfire on television and had learned that it was heading northwest towards us. Becky had kindly invited Dorothy and I to leave Malibu as quickly as we were able and come stay with her and Nick. So, that's where we ended up. We showed up, exhausted and bedraggled and black from smoke. We had a shower, got cleaned up and ate something; then all of us settled down to watch the news coverage of the fire on television. It was depressing, as we didn't know at this point if our house had survived or not.

It was a further two or three days before we could even attempt to get back to Malibu as the police had closed the coast. They wouldn't let us go up the hill, so it was an agonizing period of not knowing what was waiting there for us. We couldn't make the journey by car as the bridges had burnt out, so Dorothy and I walked for a mile up the hill. On the way, we could see the utter devastation left behind: houses had been reduced to ashes; trees and roads were smoldering; the charred carcasses of animals strewn about. Terrible! Despite seeing all this horror, we maintained hope that our house would still be there. I know I was thinking there was a chance it would be, as I saw that several of our neighbors' homes were intact. It was not until I walked ahead of Dorothy, and discovered all that remained of the place we'd called home for nearly twenty years was the chimney—that and a filing cabinet in my office that was somehow still upright. Our hearts immediately sank and for a few moments we were in shock. But then I said to myself, "Okay, I'm going to retrieve all the photographs and documents I stored in that cabinet. At least that will be something." I opened up the drawer, peered inside, and saw that everything in there was scorched and brittle to the point that if you touched it, it fell apart.

This was only the beginning, as more anguish was to come. There had been a bobcat that Dorothy and I had loved seeing. It would come visit us and drink in our pool and was a lovely creature. It lay blackened and dead downhill in my garden, my beautiful garden which was now all gone. It was heartbreaking, and hard to take in all at once. The top soil had burnt and the whole area now looked like the surface of the moon. In every direction you looked from our property you couldn't see anything that wasn't burned, except for the neighbor's house. As I walked about, I noticed that all the fire retardant vegetation I'd planted had burned very vigorously with the exception of two plants: Echium and Jade Plant. There were also ants, which had survived underground, that had come out in their millions and were crawling around everywhere. Most grim of all was the ghastly sight of our pool which was choked with the drowned and burnt remains of dead animals. They had either fallen in there in a blind panic to escape the flames, or had gathered to drink the water, or simply crawled in and used it as a place to die. It was an awful scene.

We then trudged around the rubble of our house, sifting through the ashes of our lives, trying to salvage whatever we could. We found a few pieces of crystal that had survived the blaze, as well as a lot of guns we had purchased following the armed robbery that had taken place several years earlier. The guns were all loaded and had gone off during the fire, the ammunition exploding in the flames. I found other items in the ruins, such as my tools. I glimpsed my table saw and, after realizing it was burnt beyond the point of usability, quickly moved on. The loss of some things was much harder to take than others. For example, I was greatly saddened by the loss of all the books I owned, as well as the paintings and clothes. Aside from the bobcat, most distressing of all was the fact that this was the house where Dorothy and I had gotten married; a place of happiness for us, that was now a place of utter misery and despair. Thankfully, in the coming days and weeks when we were mired in this terrible low, we had friends like the Noltes, and Alan Schwartz and his wife, who provided us with a lot of support. The Schwartzes brought their little boy along and he helped us go through the ashes, looking for quarters and things. I've never forgotten the Noltes and the Schwartzes for all their help.

Throughout this time we saw the kindness of some, but also the heartlessness of others as, in the days that followed, the looters came. They had no human feeling at all and were prepared to take whatever they could. Tony DeVivo's house had survived the fire. Tony had stayed in his hot-tub and saved not only his home but that of the Federal Judge who lived next door. Both had suffered tremendous smoke damage, but at least the houses were still standing. Tony was badly burnt in performing his heroics. At one point, holed up in the hot-tub as the fire was going over, he'd resigned himself to the certainty he was going to die. But Tony was a fighter pilot in World War II and is one tough customer. He managed to endure and saved those two houses single-handedly. Afterwards, Tony had seen the looters start to enter the Judge's house and managed to chase them away. Aside from the looters, there were also these despicable and opportunistic people who brazenly arrived—while we were still going through the smoldering remnants of our home—and tried to buy the property! In contempt of our abject misery and grief, these individuals saw their chance at a possible bargain. They thought that because we had experienced this disaster, we might want to get the hell away from Malibu and they would get a good price.

In the wake of the fire, we stayed with the Noltes for a couple of days and then moved to a hotel. Becky and Nick were reluctant to see us leave, but we felt we had to. It was like Dorothy said, "We have to grieve in private." Besides, we had gotten soot on Becky's lovely expensive white rug and we didn't want her to find out about it. Our insurance company then moved us to a beach house as we had a policy that stipulated we were to be awarded similar accommodation to that of our home. So, we lived in a place on the beach in Malibu that was located a little further down the hill. From that vantage point we could look up to the canyon and see our surviving chimney which, perhaps appropriately, resembled a kind of tombstone. It was so bizarre and upsetting. In a way, we felt like vampires. Dorothy and I kept going back up to what we called "our native soil." It was still our home even though it wasn't there anymore. We'd be pottering about, sifting through the ruins in this mournful and methodical manner. Believe it or not, after the fire, we then had a tremendous earthquake! We woke one night with the whole house shaking. It was like, "Oh, c'mon! Are you kidding me?" And after the earthquake we had a violent aftershock! It was then that we first started thinking seriously about moving out of Los Angeles. I said, "You know what? Let's go to Indiana for a while." And we did and we've been here ever since.

I can't think of an aspect of my life that the fire didn't impact on. It was pretty seismic overall. At the time I thought, "Okay, these are finally just possessions. I'm alive, my wife is alive, and that is what's important." Be that as it may, even realizing this fact and being thankful for it, the fire was still harder to get over than I'd ever anticipated. As time passed, it became a much bigger blow than I thought it would be. It was just as Dorothy had said: "Something monumental is happening to us." I mean, you do feel like you've truly lived when you lose everything like that. There's nothing more life affirming than a scrape with death. It puts things firmly into perspective. The fire did impact on my career as I had to get my life back in order before I could possibly entertain the idea of working again. I had to stop whatever it was I was working on at that point and pay attention to collecting the insurance claim. That process took about a year. Our insurance agent had told us, "You need to employ the top insurance adjusters in the world," and we did just that. These individuals helped us a great deal. Indeed, we would not have collected as much money as we did without their assistance.

Nevertheless, this procedure was painful, protracted and emotionally draining. For one thing, we had to write everything down—all that we had lost in the fire. The insurance adjustors teach you a system where you go around every room in the house, and ask, "Okay, what was in the top drawer? What was underneath this cabinet? What was in that closet?" You have to remember each item and scribble it down. Finally, after cataloguing all these possessions, it comes down to where you got them from and how much you paid for them. So, you produce receipts from credit cards and other evidence of transactions having taken place, or you contact the company and find out what something would have cost when you bought it. Thus, collecting such a big insurance claim (and ours turned out to consist of 135 singled-spaced pages) was like losing everything twice. I mean, they forced us to recall the minutiae of our suffering: the glasses that Bobby De Niro gave me, or the plates that Sam Goldwyn, Jr. gave us, all of these vanished belongings. They make you drag it all up again and it was extremely distressing. It's like they inflict the pain of that, rather than simply giving you the money. Of course, I understood why they did it, but that still didn't make it any easier to deal with.

For a time after the fire, we kept some of the guns with melted barrels and other damaged objects. We considered these things to be some form of "burn art"; relics of this extraordinary event that had happened to us and changed our lives forever. We certainly didn't need any reminders of the fire, but I do think we dwelt on it a lot. There was definitely a period of wallowing in our own misery for a little while, but, eventually, we got rid of all those things. Also, I had a lot of cans of paint that had burnt in the blaze. There was a concern that all the incinerated paint and industrial building materials contained carcinogens—especially if charred—that would be perilous to us. All this stuff had to go. Subsequently, the county, or somebody from Malibu City, came and bulldozed everything. We didn't have to pay for this job; the authorities just ordered them to show up and clean away all the trash and rubble. After this waste had disappeared all that remained was a naked burn site. There was a peculiar finality about that, which left us with mixed emotions.

Dorothy and I then thought long and hard about what our next move should be. We reasoned that if we rebuilt the house on the same site one of these days it would burn again, and it almost has as those canyons so easily ignite. We could not go through a repeat of such a harrowing ordeal. To have absorbed that kind of soul-destroying pain again would have killed us, possibly even physically as we might not escape with our lives a second time around. I couldn't bear the prospect of working closely with an architect, seeing the house built again from the ground up, and then going to the hardware store for the doorknobs and the hinges and the drawer slides and the floor tiles and the rugs and the lampshades and the thousands of other things that constitute a home. The idea that it could all disappear again in flames was too horrifying to consider. We just couldn't face it, living in fear and expectation like that. So, as I said, in 1996, we moved to LaPorte, Indiana, a place I knew and loved so well.

However, the fact remained that we still needed a base in Los Angeles to operate out of. So, we bought two mobile homes—one to use as an office and another to live in—and erected them at the burn site.

I then installed natural gas heating pipes and water pipes, and did all the plumbing myself. Following this, we had to have the place inspected to make sure that the cesspool and the natural gas lines were acceptable. It was a huge job that took up a lot of my time and energy. Directing was pretty far from my mind for a time, and I did kind of get the sense that life was passing me by. After a while, I lived and worked in the mobile homes when I directed the episodes of *Cracker*. I would come out to L.A. from Indiana and stay in one of them, and I was comfortable. We did eventually sell the land several years later and finally cut our ties with Malibu. It was sad as so many happy memories were wrapped up in that place. But moving back to Indiana, I very much got the sense that I was coming home. Over the years, Dorothy and I had taken certain things from Malibu and brought them to LaPorte. All of a sudden these things became extraordinarily precious to us. We spent a lot of the money from the insurance settlement expanding the house in Indiana and working on it, and it did very much become our home. Dorothy and I have been very happy and fulfilled here ever since.

> *In 1999, three years after his return to Indiana, Hancock formed a production facility in LaPorte that he christened FilmAcres. The first movie on the company's slate would be* Tredici, *a romantic comedy that would once again affectionately draw on the rich source of his family history. "We needed a name for the limited liability company that was going to produce this film," Hancock explains. "Susan Willett, my casting person on it, thought FilmAcres would be fun because of the farm setting in* Tredici, *and it stuck. We still used the name FilmAcres with slight variants for the subsequent films I've directed: FilmAcres Independent LLC produced* Suspended Animation *and* The Looking Glass *was produced by FilmAcres Summer Film 13 LLC. Really, they're all just me!" Shortly before filming commenced in the summer of 1999, it was agreed that the title of the movie should be changed to the slightly more inviting (and appropriate) label of* A Piece of Eden.

If you asked most filmmakers they'd probably say the most frustrating thing about being a director is the long gaps between projects. Sometimes they can stretch on for years and it can be profoundly depressing and disheartening (believe me when I say it helps if you have a hobby!) These periods of inactivity can be difficult to endure. You can lose confidence and feel like you're somehow out of the loop. Directing is a thing that, ideally, you need to do on a fairly regular basis if only to maintain your skills and knowledge. Granted, not everybody feels that need. There are some who can take a long break and step onto a set like they were just gone for the weekend. For others, the break can have more impact; it can be like forgetting a language you once spoke and you have to learn it all over again. It's upsetting that we now have to jump a decade between *Prancer* and *A Piece of Eden* as it was more than ten years between the releases of those two movies. Yes, I directed some television and did the 400 Kmart commercials, but it was a considerable amount of time to not be doing a feature. When that happens, you have that aforementioned sense of your life just passing you by. That's not a nice feeling, but, as I've taken great pains to tell you, a lot happened in the interim. I always kept working and developing movie ideas throughout the 1990s, so I hesitate to call this period my "wilderness years."

After forming FilmAcres the first project we got going was *A Piece of Eden*, which had been percolating in our minds for a little while. Now, let me confess something that may surprise you: I like romantic comedies. I'm not cynical or dismissive about them, even when they are at their most gooey and silly. I've enjoyed things like *Pretty Woman*, which is a highly implausible movie but still a very entertaining one. The notion of doing my own romantic comedy, something affectionate and personal with a lightness of tone, was appealing to me. I wanted to try one myself, a commercial movie that would reflect my feelings about home, family, love and responsibility. So, I was very much operating on familiar terrain, literally and figuratively. You'll notice that Dorothy receives sole credit for the screenplay, but I did contribute. Dorothy and I have an understanding where I get to direct the picture and she gets sole screenwriting credit. The truth is she helps me cast my films and I help with the script. Thus, it's very much a team effort.

You may notice that I share credit with Dorothy for *A Piece of Eden* in that the opening titles read: "A John Hancock/Dorothy Tristan Film." I'm well aware that it's highly unusual that a director shares credit with a writer. I've done this before on *Weeds*, where I even put Bill Badalato's name in there: "A Hancock/Tristan/Badalato Film." A lot of directors are very serious and adamant about what, when and where their credit is placed. Some directors even have their name above the title as possessory credits. I'm not in any way insecure or demanding about those kinds of things. I value the contributions of the screenwriter, as writers are not always properly acknowledged and treated it seems. I don't like possessory credits. I'm against them, actually, but I do understand the need for them occasionally. I also understand why some writers object to them as film is a collaborative medium. I mean, just try to direct a movie without a good script. You can be as possessive as you want, but it will still be a piece of shit. I too have the desire to be recognized for my efforts, but not at the expense of other peoples' contributions to the success of my movies.

Dorothy's strengths as a writer are numerous, but she has a real facility with dialogue. She's able to write an extended dialogue scene that is consistently engaging and interesting. The dynamic of our professional relationship is the same as our personal one: it simply works. I tend not to examine why that is in case the magic is somehow broken. There is a certain element of self-hypnosis in creative work where you get your mind to think in certain ways. When you collaborate closely with somebody it's like there's a connection of some kind between you. As I told you, Dorothy and I have found it easy to reconcile a professional relationship with our marriage. We've been able to balance the two successfully, but I realize not everybody can. One advantage of collaborating so closely with your spouse is that you are working from a solid foundation of trust and recognition. Sometimes you can anticipate what the other one is thinking and feeling, what they want; other times, you haven't got a clue! With a lot of other people you work with you feel they may have another agenda or purpose. Since our careers and fortunes have been inextricably linked, and our finances joined, I don't think Dorothy is out to get me in any way. I feel she's always there for me and I'm there for her. If she happens to feel strongly about something and is pushing hard for it, it's not coming from a bad place. It's her honest and heartfelt opinion, and that kind of truth is priceless in my experience.

> *The narrative of* A Piece of Eden *encompasses three generations of the émigré Tredici clan, who are supposedly cursed to forever encounter misfortune and grief in their dealings. One unfortunate event in their fraught history occurs in the 1930s, when the sheep owned by Giuseppe*

Tredici are suddenly startled and charge to their deaths over a cliff in his native Corsica. This calamity prompts Giuseppe to leave his homeland for America, eventually settling his young family in northwest Indiana in the hope of starting a fruit farm and lifting the hex that has plagued his bloodline. In the present day, Bob Tredici, Giuseppe's grandson, is a successful New York publicist who, several years earlier, left behind the 240 acres of the family orchard to pursue a career in show business. One fateful day he is summoned back to Indiana after his own father, Franco, suffers third-degree burns in a drunken accident. In the time since Bob rejected farming duties his cousin, Gregory, has eagerly supplanted him in Franco's affections to the point where the nephew fully expects to take over the running of the farm after the ailing patriarch dies.

Suddenly alarmed at the prospect of his birthright being placed under another's supervision, and with his agency having recently hit a rough patch, Bob decides to stick around the homestead a little while longer. With his father confined to a hospital bed, Bob takes it upon himself to revitalize the flagging farm by updating the running of the operation. Armed with his flashy show business acumen, he introduces a computer system and modern marketing techniques in order to bolster profits and interest in the orchard. As a desperate ploy to convince Franco of his newfound maturity, Bob persuades his effervescent secretary, Happy Buchanan, to come to Indiana and pose as his new bride for the duration of his visit. In a further effort to win back his father's shattered trust, Bob informs his relatives that Happy is three months pregnant. Despite feeling the pressure to maintain this facade, Happy effortlessly charms the Tredicis, including Bob's matronly Aunt Aurelia, and succeeds in helping Bob rescue the fortunes of his family business by transforming the farm into a successful tourist attraction.

As I say, there is a lot of autobiographical content in *A Piece of Eden*, some of it subtle, some of it explicit. For example, aside from the story being set on a fruit farm, my father caught fire just like Franco does in the film. What happened was one day Dad had been drinking and was burning brush that he had cut out of the pear orchard. He had poured gasoline over it and then, rather foolishly, knelt to light the brush with his cigarette lighter only for it to blow up in his face. He was very badly injured in this incident and was in the hospital for six months. He had to endure several extensive skin grafts and it was a bad time. I wanted to include this rather painful episode in the screenplay as it was bringing the story closer to my reality, and reflected the kind of man my father was towards the end of his life. It occurs to me now that when you restage certain events from your life and resurrect people from the dead as I did in this case, it's a way of keeping them alive in your memory and the memories of others. There is also something primary and valuable to me about *A Piece of Eden* in that it has such truth in it. Another autobiographical element of the story is the idea of the city slicker son coming back and trying to help his folks out with the farm. All of that happened to a certain extent, too, as I had returned to our fruit farm from Hollywood after my father's death to help my mother. The thread involving the famous actor coming to help publicize the business was also based on reality: I had once asked Nick Nolte to come to Indiana at one point, and he did well for me.

Coming from English, Scots-Irish and German descent, one thing that is obviously not from my own history is the nationality of the Tredici family. I decided to make them Corsican when we were writing the script as I thought it would be different. Basically, it was done merely to keep them from being Italian! I felt it would be too corny and too obvious to have them be Italian émigrés. Calling them Tredici (which translates in English as the Italian word for "thirteen") was another way of underlining another thing I wanted to touch on in *A Piece of Eden*: the theme of unluckiness. It's something people have obsessed about for centuries, the idea that there is something hanging over a person or persons that determines or adversely affects their reality. The notion of a family curse, or an unlucky clan who have been consistently plagued by accidents and hardship throughout their history, is something I enjoy. It's like a kind of hereditary guilt and misery being perpetually passed on from father to son. In this case, the curse of the Tredici family pertains to ships sinking at sea and an incident where Giuseppe's flock of sheep has thrown themselves over a cliff like lemmings. These things are then interpreted or explained as a curse—an irrational way of rationalizing misfortune—and it puts a black cloud over successive generations.

You do find these things happen: a tragedy or catastrophic event strikes a family and its repercussions echo through the years. Also, the notion of a curse that involves sheep is specifically a rural thing, but then there tends to be more superstitions in the country than there are in the city. Why, I don't know. One could argue there is a cynical worldliness to urbanites, but that implies that country folk are dim and lack ambition, and that's definitely not the case. Furthermore, the script for *A Piece of Eden* came after the devastating fire at our Malibu home, and my decade of unemployment in movies, and various other lamentable things, and I started to get preoccupied with the vagaries of fortune—good and bad. I've always been struck by the huge element of luck that occurs in the business that I'm in; how so many coincidences and unexpected meetings and unforeseen events have determined much of my career. It can make you go a little crazy thinking about how being in the right place at the right time—or indeed the wrong place at the wrong time—can affect so much of your life; how different things could have been if a certain incident did or did not happen. I really wanted to work that element into the picture somehow.

The financing for *A Piece of Eden* came together in an interesting way. Dorothy and I put up part of the money for the movie and I raised the rest of the budget from local guys around where we live. A lot of people from this area put up around $25,000, which was wonderful. There was a well-respected businessman in LaPorte named Robert J. Hiler who owned a foundry here called Accurate Castings. It's a very successful and lucrative company, which makes things like bicycle parts, parking meters, one thing and another, casting them in aluminum and selling them all over the world. Bob actually put up more money for *A Piece of Eden* than even I did. A lot of that dough was raised on the goodwill of *Prancer*, which was an experience that was still cherished by the locals a decade later. That goodwill and general excitement about possibly making another movie in the region circumvented a lot of problems we would have otherwise encountered trying to secure the money. When you're shooting in LaPorte, people will let you use their homes for free and they'll go stay at a hotel at their own expense. That's the kind of wonderful people who live in this place. It was the same thing when it came to finding extras for the scenes where the crowds flock to the Tredici farm. One day we had 1,200 extras turn up for absolutely no payment. We gave them each a bag of apples and they still came back the next day. Incredible!

We filmed *A Piece of Eden* right around my house. We have two farmhouses here, so we shot the exteriors where I live and shot the interiors in the other house we own. Filming it in our properties saved us a lot of money, as no sets had to be constructed for the movie. There were also a number of details that were already here that added to the mise en scène, which bypassed my having to hold lengthy conferences with an art director or set decorator or prop guy. A lot of it was here. I think *A Piece of Eden* could have been set in some other rural area of America, say in New England or Virginia, or maybe somewhere in California, and it wouldn't have made much difference to the story. That said, to me Indiana is a richer and fresher area—fresher in the sense that I feel it's been untapped on film. There have been a lot of movies set in the West, in California, in the Great Barrier, and in New England, but Indiana is unbroached in a way. I saw that as an advantage. Some filmmakers are interested in examining the American psyche through the landscape of our country and how it has shaped and affected us. That doesn't interest me as much as telling a good story which happens to take place in an area of dramatic beauty or vitality. All I really want to do is tell a story. I'm fascinated with the ordinary lives of ordinary people who occasionally experience extraordinary things.

> *The cast for* A Piece of Eden *is an assured mix of newcomers and experienced thespians, as well as several members of Hancock's unofficial stock company of players (which includes longtime friend Marshall Efron making his fifth appearance for the director). Chicago theater actor Robert Breuler was hired to play the sickly Franco Tredici with Andreas Katsulas cast against type as his deceased father Giuseppe. Recognizing the need to inject a few familiar faces into the production, Hancock brought in Tyne Daly to play Aunt Aurelia. Daly, who proved to be somewhat difficult during shooting, was most famous for her role as the married working mother and detective Mary Beth Lacey in the popular CBS police procedural show* Cagney & Lacey *(1982-1988). Academy Award-nominated actor Frederic Forrest—noted for his work with Francis Ford Coppola on such films as* The Conversation *(1974),* Apocalypse Now *(1979) and* One From the Heart *(1982)—was then cast as Paulo Tredici, Franco's scheming brother who has been bought out of the farm and plots to have his own son assume control.*
>
> *Essaying the role of Bob's elderly grandmother was veteran Ukrainian-born actress Irma St. Paule, who had*

previously appeared in Twelve Monkeys *(1995) and* Thinner *(1995), with Australian daytime soap star Tristan Rogers playing Victor Hardwick, a client of Bob's Television Publicity Bureau, who is enlisted to appear at an event he has organized to boost the farm's profits and profile. A Piece of Eden also reunited Hancock with Rebecca Harrell, who had so impressed the director during the shooting of* Prancer. *The third of four collaborations they have enjoyed, Harrell was cast as Happy Buchanan, Bob's eventual love interest. The last piece of the jigsaw was the film's star, Marc Grapey, who came aboard to play Bob shortly before shooting began. Interestingly, Grapey bares more than a passing resemblance to a younger version of Hancock—a consideration the director insists was purely coincidental even if the character of Bob can be viewed as representing him.*

It's true, Grapey does somewhat resemble me, but that was not intentional. We do share a physical resemblance (he doesn't have my blue eyes), but Marc was not cast for that reason as he was a late replacement for another actor. We would have probably done a little better casting a more conventionally handsome lead, but Marc still made a good Bob and he is attractive. I realize it's ironic to even suggest such a thing, especially after earlier citing Ben Cross for being too handsome to play Munir Redfa in *Steal the Sky*. But every situation is different and on *A Piece of Eden* it was the reverse: I needed a more glamorous male lead as the star. As I intimated, I had initially cast somebody who was attractive and had started rehearsals with him. I forget his name now, he was a Chicago actor, but I didn't like what I was getting and fired him. Then, in a panic, as we were getting close to our start date, we looked around and thankfully found Grapey in Chicago. He was a theater actor there who had appeared in a couple of TV shows and movies. Since I was putting up part of the money for *A Piece of Eden*, I tried to hold the budget down by not having to bring in people from Los Angeles. So, I cast it with discriminating austerity.

In the time since we'd made *Prancer* together, I had used Rebecca Harrell in the episode of *Dellaventura* I directed, so we'd remained in touch over the years. She had matured into a capable actress and was now an attractive young woman. After *Prancer* had come out in '89, Rebecca went back to Vermont and had suffered a little. Apparently, the girls at her school were rather mean to her because she had been in a movie, which saddened me to hear. Rebecca came to my mind for Happy and I think her performance in *A Piece of Eden* is awfully good. She's ditzy and funny and sweet, just wonderful. There was a nice onscreen chemistry between Rebecca and Marc, which is ironic as in truth they did not like each other off-camera. Thankfully, they do appear to in the film when it's necessary. One of the things I've discovered is that people who are supposedly playing characters who fall in love almost never do on the set. As a matter of fact, they tend to despise each other. It's very strange. I feel this tension arises because the atmosphere and situation itself is too charged, too expectant and artificial. It's like the human animal rebels at what you are *supposed* to be feeling. I don't know exactly what caused the animosity between Marc and Rebecca, but, truth be told, I think Grapey disliked Rebecca more than she disliked him.

Tyne Daly was an old friend of Dorothy's. I thought she had a suitably matriarchal quality and look about her, so we cast her as Aunt Aurelia. I don't have much to add on Tyne. You see, the problem is I have such terrible things to say about her. She started each shooting day sane, but, in the course of the day, as far as I could tell, she would medicate herself with some kind of upper. Thus, by the late afternoon, she would be talking non-stop and having problems controlling her temper. I eventually fired her around thirty-five days into our forty-day shoot—after being careful, of course, to have covered all her important scenes (John is not a stupid boy!) I then gave some of her lines to Frederic Forrest, who played Aurelia's Viagra-taking brother. Fred was an actor I had always liked and wanted to work with for several years. I had hoped to cast him in some of my previous movies, but for some reason it never worked out. I was delighted when he signed-on for *A Piece of Eden*, as I think he was perfect for Paulo. Curiously, Fred always did a wonderful thing during shooting: before I called action he would make this peculiar whooping sound: "Whoa-hoo!" Every time he would do it, the moment before we rolled—"Whoa-hoo!" I don't know why he felt compelled to repeatedly make this sound, or exactly what it was meant to signify, but it was okay.

I found Robert Breuler for Franco when we were casting the picture in Chicago. He was sent in by a casting agent and I recognized his name. Robert was, and I believe still is, a long-time member of the Steppenwolf Theatre Company. He had only done a handful of movies before *A Piece of Eden*—the most notable of which I suppose is the 1996 adaptation of Arthur Miller's *The Crucible* with Daniel Day-Lewis and Paul Scofield.

Other than that Breuler had appeared in a few modest television movies but he was a good actor, particularly for Steppenwolf. I also liked Bob personally, and cast him again in my next movie. There are one or two scenes where he is especially strong. Andreas Katsulas, who I cast as Giuseppe, Franco's deceased father, has bucketfuls of charm and warmth. I remember Andreas being grateful that I'd cast him in the role and that he wasn't playing another stern-faced villain. The truth is he was sick of being the bad guy at this point in time and really embraced the opportunity of playing this loving farmer. I adore his performance in the film and I loved him, too. He was a wonderful guy and I was terribly sad when I learned of his death in 2006. I feel privileged to have worked with Andreas more than once.

Two additional actors I cast were Tristan Rogers and Irma St. Paule, who played Victor Hardwick ("the sexiest man alive") and the elderly Maria respectively. They were both easy to work with and got along with people. We cast Tristan because he was the star of the popular soap *The Bold and the Beautiful*, and we thought he might bring in that audience. That didn't prove to be the case. We actually chose him over Michael York on the advice of a Hollywood marketing guy. Not the best advice I've ever received. I should have known better and gone for the actor, but Tristan was good, too. Now, would Michael York have been better? Maybe, I don't know. As for Irma, I was crazy about her. I just adored her. What a face! I thought she would be wonderful in the part of the grandmother. Irma smoked like a chimney and had *the* worst sounding cough I've ever heard in my life. There's a wonderful tracking shot of her on the porch seeing the crowds of people that have flocked to the farm. I told her to think about dying for that shot and, boy, she really delivered.

> *After finalizing his cast, Hancock organized a three-week rehearsal period to be held at the Elks Country Club in LaPorte. The actors would gather each morning to work on the scenes in a specially designated meeting area that was loaned to the production. Unfortunately, after firing his original choice for the role of Bob Tredici, the cast were only able to manage five or six days of rehearsal before principal photography began. Due to budgetary constraints, Hancock also hired a number of locals in LaPorte to play supporting roles and cameos, as well as serve as crew-members.*

We burnt up a lot of our rehearsal time with the first lead actor, which was frustrating. It was a necessary blow, as he just wasn't right for the picture. I would've liked to have had more time to rehearse with the actors, but it wasn't possible and so we simply marched on. Even though *A Piece of Eden* was my first film in a while, I still felt like a confident and accomplished director. I never doubted myself, not for a minute. The enforced absence didn't unsettle me in any way and, as I indicated earlier, I even felt I'd improved and sharpened my skills over those ten years. From the first day on the set, even throughout the problematic rehearsal period, I felt very much in control of the movie. I wasn't at all nervous about stepping behind the camera, dealing with actors and technicians. It felt perfectly natural to me, and I was excited to be back making movies again. Employing locals as actors and on the technical side as crew-members only made the experience more interesting. It wasn't a hindrance. For instance, the mayor was our location scout and his wife did props; the assistant director, Ryan Juszkiewicz, was also local hire. So, it was a real community film.

Despite this, I still felt it was important to employ professionals in certain key areas. I brought in Jim Thornton, a sound mixer whom I'd worked with on *Weeds* and *Prancer*, and would later reunite with on *The Looking Glass*. I also hired Dan Zarlengo, who was Misha Suslov's gaffer on *Prancer*, as a lighting technician and second unit director. The art director was Wendy Jo Martin, who had previously worked in the art department on *Prancer* as a scenic artist; our special effects coordinator was Mike Menzel, whom I'd worked with on *Weeds* and *Prancer*. So, it was a nice blend of professionals and non-professionals. I find that when you're working with non-professionals it's always a matter of communicating to them exactly what you want in a manner in which you've clearly made yourself understood. In terms of amateurs, you try to treat them as if they are professionals. A lot of times they respond to this positively. You have to hope that they will do a good job for you, but I don't think you can afford to cut them any slack. Obviously, when you work with amateur actors in a low-or-modest-budget situation, they don't prepare in the same way as professional actors do. They don't have the same range and technique in finding a performance. Thus, you have to demonstrate a little more patience. Similarly, with inexperienced crew-members you have to be cognizant of what tasks you give them.

When I'm working on a script I often see the film in my mind. Then, later, when I'm shooting, I'll make a lot of the creative decisions on the day. There is still some pre-planning involved, but I like to remain open and flexible. Sometimes as a director, you're confronted with a location and what you thought would be on the left of the area turns out to be on the right, and vice-versa. You then ask yourself, "Okay, do I have to find a location where it's laid out left-to-right just as I envisioned it, or can I adapt to this situation and work with what I've got?" It sounds trivial but it's sometimes one of the key decisions you have to make. On the whole, I've found I tend to do better if I find a location that is laid out as I saw it in my head. You can't invariably do that because there are wonderful locations that aren't as you envisioned, and you don't want to lose them. Occasionally, you are in danger of crossing the line if you violate the way you initially saw something in your mind and have to now reverse it. You are likely to break the 180-degree rule in coverage, and make mistakes in the spatial relationship between the actors in the frame. So, you have to be especially careful about that and make sure that you stay on the same side of the axis that connects the two or three actors in the shot.

As a matter of fact, I must identify a scene in *A Piece of Eden* that takes place early on in a kitchen which features Tyne Daly, Marc Grapey and Jeff Puckett, who plays Greg. During the filming of the scene, I evidently broke the 180-degree rule without realizing it at the time. That mistake came about for a different reason in this instance, which I'll explain: something I like to do is shoot the close-up first because if you shoot the master first and then follow it with an over-the-shoulder shot and then the close-up, by the time you arrive at the close-up the actors tend to be somewhat stale. I find their energies are slightly lower and their faces are moderately less emotive. You don't want this, as it's the time when the actors should really be selling the shot as all the emotion and drama is in the close-up. So, I like to work my way out *from* the close-up as a means of ensuring that I've got the money shot and it feels strong and fresh and has feeling. But that approach is another way that you can get involved with problems with the 180-degree rule. I don't think anybody notices my mistake in *A Piece of Eden*, but me. I detect it every time I see the picture.

> *Conspicuously,* A Piece of Eden *features an extended series of flashbacks that deftly trace the history of the Tredici family and their journey from Corsica to America. Hancock has rarely used flashbacks in his cinema, favoring a more linear approach to narrative, and their anomalous inclusion in the finished film appear to be almost accidental.*

The flashbacks were shot rather conventionally in black and white but then, rather unconventionally, I wanted the images to suddenly blossom into color. I thought that was an effective way of conveying not only the passage of time, but the gradual flourishing of the farm. As *A Piece of Eden* was written, the script started with the events of the past: the sheep, the cliff, Giuseppe and his family arriving in America and founding the farm. They were not intended to be flashbacks at all, but an introduction to the family's story before we jumped ahead to the present day. You see, we discovered in early screenings that this approach started the story too late and even confused one or two people. It also confirmed something I had found in editing, that it was a big bump when we finally got to Bob, Happy, Franco and the others. So, we went back and restructured the narrative and played the original opening passages as flashbacks. We then wrote the accompanying narration that Andreas Katsulas speaks, and that seemed to work. I'm still not certain that I was right to do this. One shot I do like in the flashbacks is the moment when Franco is born in the hospital and the nurse holds the baby and he spits right up as if on cue. Talk about luck, right?

By the way, I've been asked by certain people if there really is such a place as Fail Road where the Tredici family purchases a property. Yes, there is. I live on it! That wasn't invented for the purposes of dramatic irony, that's an actual place. Incidentally, we've tried to officially change the name several times without success. It came about originally as there was a Mr. Fail who happened to be a very important Klansman who lived during the early days of LaPorte. The road is named after him in tribute. I've tried to get it called something else, even if it's something equally pessimistic like Despair Way or Misery Road. But I guess people appear committed to it remaining as Fail Road, at least for the foreseeable future. Also, I thought the sign that reads Fail Road looked suitably authentic in the film. I was incredibly happy with that. We had a wonderful propmaker who made that sign for us. It's easily one of the better props I've ever had in my life.

Knowing how diligent the American Humane Association and how hard they come down on people who mistreat animals on movies, we had to be careful in staging the moment where the sheep tumble over the precipice in Corsica. In the area where I live, there are a lot of guys who've worked in the steel mills in Gary and in various local industries. There was an engineer in town named Jack Whitted, who was an expert in the engineering of remote control devices for furnaces. We hired this gentleman and he built ten mechanical sheep for us using rotisserie motors. He bought the sheep skins from a farmer and fabricated them. They were rather impressive and rudimentary creations as simply by pulling a string their articulated legs moved realistically and their heads wobbled in a perfectly lifelike way. When we were shooting the moment where the sheep tumble over the edge, we launched these mechanical animals off the cliff with catapults. It looked quite effective and I was happy with it. We also had real sheep, but the sheep that get their necks broken were all decidedly fake. What I find interesting is that on *Prancer* we spent $150,000 for a Hollywood special effects artist to make one dodgy animatronic deer that was operated by several people, and which we hardly used at all. On *A Piece of Eden*, we spent $500 for a local guy to make ten mechanical sheep that all worked wonderfully.

During the flashbacks, there is a montage that shows the passing of the changing seasons—summer, autumn and winter—on the farm. While we were cutting, winter came and we were able to shoot some snow and then some of the spring that followed. Over the editing period we were able to reassemble a camera crew (not with the same cinematographer as Misha had moved onto something else at this point) and get more footage. Of course, we were able to keep shooting at the location because we live here and it was easy to return to the area. We simply walked out of our front door over the course of several months, set the camera up and got the shots each time. As far as the actors were concerned, I believe we used doubles in one or two instances—like the flashback sequence where they are peeing in the show. We may have also gotten Rebecca and Grapey back for a short time to get a couple of additional shots we needed. I particularly like the memory montages: the shot of Maria as a young woman preparing her hair which dissolves into the image of her as a ninety-year-old woman. I also like the shot of Franco's wife waving goodbye in front of the house. We signified her passing by simply fading her away. I wanted to keep those elements very simple and emotive.

> While A Piece of Eden *seems to brandish what Hancock playfully terms a "surface lightness," strong themes do emerge in its story. The film deals with the tension between one's desire to participate in the bustling urban rat race and being drawn "back to the garden," where the leisurely simplicity of a rural paradise awaits. In keeping with the zealous plundering of his own history, Hancock confesses*

to having felt this conflict acutely at certain times in his life.

Whether you grow up in the city or you grow up in the country, or you do both as in my case, you see the beauty and ugliness of life in equal measure. You see the truth of people, the reality of what we are, how we live, what we do. It's not just a question of size and distance in regards to personal intimacy or the number of opportunities that are available, whatever it is. I think it's a mistake to merely assume that one experience is somehow more revealing or relevant than the other. It's not. I've witnessed the best and worst of both worlds, because people will always be people. What I mean is people are alike all over: loving and hating, good and bad, wherever they hail from. There is a battle in Bob's mind about what life is best. So, it's a clash between the materialism of living and working in the city and the more spiritual way of life that one supposedly finds in the country when close to nature. Yes, that's certainly a tension I've felt in my own life, but I don't feel that country life is about resisting change. Moving back to Indiana was a tough decision to make, but it was the right one. After our house burnt, and the earthquake and the aftershock that followed, we simply asked ourselves where our Eden was. Where would we be happiest? We decided it was Indiana and here we are still. In leaving L.A., I kind of felt I was letting go of Hollywood. Admittedly, this made me very nervous. I thought I could operate from Indiana, and go back and forth, which is what I did, but I did feel like something was changing. I feel a sense of contentment here, like I'm where I'm meant to be.

Not to accentuate this whole country versus city debate, but I wanted Bob to be right at the end. I wanted this city slicker with the cynical veneer to bring some of what he'd learned in his New York life to the farm that would assist in making it a big success. It's not that he's outgrown his family or anything, or that he now considers the community he left behind to consist of uneducated hicks, he's just forgotten how wonderful home can be. In effect, Bob brings together the best of both worlds which is as it should be. The idea that he uses computers and organizes a petting zoo and a cherry pit spitting contest was a nice means of marrying sophistication and technology with tradition and good old-fashioned rustic fun. I thought it would be too simplistic and false to say that city life is bad and country life is good. That would be preposterous. There are a lot of wonderful and intoxicating things that can happen to you in the city. Just because you have a lot more anonymity and isolation in urban centers does not mean there are a multitude of great and vital things there, too. I saw value in entertainment and big business as potentially positive forces for good.

> *Death has long been a preoccupation of Hancock's film and television work beginning with* Let's Scare Jessica to Death. *Moreover, like* Bang the Drum Slowly, Baby Blue Marine, California Dreaming, "If She Dies", "Profile in Silver", Weeds, Prancer, Suspended Animation *and* The Looking Glass, A Piece of Eden *features characters and families dealing with the expected or sudden passing of a loved one. For all that,* A Piece of Eden *points to a more hopeful rendering of death by including a sequence where father and son are reunited in a kind of afterlife. Hancock's own father, Ralph, had passed away in 1981 shortly after the filmmaker had completed his duties with the re-shooting and re-structuring of* Wolfen. *His mother, Ella Mae, would succumb to bone cancer nine years later.*

Death and the process of grieving is, indubitably, an important part of anybody's life. One of the inevitabilities of our existence is dealing with the sure and certain knowledge of not only our own deaths but the deaths of our loved ones. How do I feel about that? Well, it's simply unavoidable. Never mind how much we scream and fight against it—or, if you are so inclined, choose to ignore the reality of death—you can't stop it from happening. Even if you do finally accept death, it doesn't make it any easier to deal with, particularly if you have to watch someone you love die. I felt my father's death very deeply, very strongly. I can recall being left incredibly upset and despondent by it. I had been distressed by his catching fire and seeing the serious injuries he'd sustained. In fact, he never really recovered from that incident. My father lived a number of years after it happened, but I think he inhaled some of the flames and it damaged his lungs and aggravated his emphysema. Until you just mentioned it, I've never been entirely conscious of death and grief being a recurring element in my work. The specter of death, the inevitability of death, yes, but grief is something else, isn't it? I mean, you see death in lots of movies but you rarely see a character's grief—the terrible weight and consequences of it.

I find the scene where the recently departed Franco is reunited with the long-dead Giuseppe a rather moving one. Sure, that can possibly be read by some as a kind of wish fulfillment scene: father and son happily dwelling together on the family grounds, in the pear orchard, now and forever. Is that something I wish were true? I don't believe that it is true but, yes, it's something that I wish *was* true. I don't believe in any kind of afterlife, but, over time, I've come to learn there is this terribly fleeting, temporary, transitory quality about life that disturbs a lot of people. The idea that once our lives are over that's it, there's nothing else, troubles many of us. Look at it this way: we can either treasure the wondrous fact and privilege that certain factors and coincidences and events have conspired in the universe to make us alive, and really savor each moment of our time on earth; or we can worry about a continuation of our consciousness on "The Other Side" or in Heaven, wherever it may be. We'll all get our answers one day and be let in on the big secret, so why worry about it? What happens to those characters in *A Piece of Eden* is something that I would welcome for myself. I'd love to be able to linger around the old home-place with my loved ones after I'm gone, but I just don't see it happening.

As I told you before, I don't believe in God. I'm very much afraid of death, of an end to consciousness and a surrendering to the void, but there's also a kind of peace that can be gleaned from that. Something I have inherited from my mother—and we keep coming back to this—is the acceptance of things as they truly are. I'm so grateful that I have a little of that same unshakable quality, too. What a gift! I mean, I watched my mother die of bone cancer and it was a painful death. But I saw this remarkable recognition and peace that she had and it was inspiring to witness. It was not a defeat. I had seen it on that memorable flight we'd taken from Cuba when I was a child ("Well, we've had a good life," she had said) and I saw it again when she was dying. As the cancer was claiming her, my mother said to me, "You know, I've been to Egypt, I've been to Russia; I've been to so many wonderful and interesting places. When I think of how much I've seen, and the people I've known, I know I've had a good life." She was ready. I can only hope that when my time comes I'll be ready, too.

I wasn't present when my father died. I got a call from my mother telling me he had passed and then I flew back from Hollywood to be with her. I can still recall his funeral and how tearful and distraught I was. I saw his body as this area is very much for the practice of open casket viewings and wakes, the full obsequies. I guess some of those things do feature in my films. I later put Dorothy in an open casket in *The Looking*

Glass, and of course, Breuler is seen in the coffin in *A Piece of Eden*. There is also the shot of John Toles-Bey in *Weeds* lying in an open casket, so I don't deny anything. Somebody once said that creating art that embraces or confronts death is an attempt to control what cannot be controlled. I think that's true in some ways, just as sex is a way of temporarily staving off death, warring against the inexorable. Ultimately, I included that hopeful moment of fantasy between father and son because Dorothy wrote it and it had that familiar bittersweet quality that I like. Dorothy would like to believe in Heaven, or an afterlife of some kind—does not, but would like to. So, that was the way the story was bent. It was kind of like us saying, "Ah, wouldn't this be nice if it was true?"

If I could meet my father one more time like we depict in the film, or if he was brought back from the dead for a few short minutes, I know exactly what I would say. I would tell him that I know he loved me. At the end of his life my father became rather difficult and abrasive. I think his brain had atrophied to some degree from emphysema, and he got to be quite profane. I can remember proudly showing him the screenplay for *Weeds* shortly before he died. He read it and said without a moment's hesitancy or discretion, "You have wasted your time." I did not want to hear that. Ironically, his rejection was largely founded on the bad language present in the script. "There are too many 'fucks'," he said, despite the fact that he was now cussing *all* the time! But I can honestly say that he was a fan of my movies. He liked *Bang the Drum Slowly*, but, more than anything I had done up to that time, he particularly liked *Let's Scare Jessica to Death*. I suspect it brought back some memories for him of the time he'd spent spraying the pesticides on our fruit farm. It seemed to be close to his heart for that reason. I think he would have loved *A Piece of Eden*, too. My decision to feature a series of black and white photographs of my parents and grandparents working our farm seemed fitting. I did that as a kind of homage to them, to the departed members of my family. It was a direct way of announcing the fact that *A Piece of Eden* is an autobiographical film. It was openly saying to the audience, "Look, this is real to some degree. These were real people. They lived, they loved, they worked, they died, and some of these things actually happened."

The final cut of *A Piece of Eden* is nearly two hours long. The film has an unhurried pace, but it's crowded with comic incident and character development. There were only a few things we excised during editing, nothing significant. There was a little more stuff with the dog, something in the middle of the narrative where Happy has to go tend to him when he's boarded in New York. I don't remember exactly, but it wasn't much. There was also more to Happy and Bob's conversation in the truck when he picks her up at the airport, but it was nothing I hated losing. *A Piece of Eden* was not another example of the dream cycle I talked to you about on *Weeds*, where if two writers are working on a script you are likely to end up with a story that is twice as long as it should be. We didn't have that problem on this particular picture, or for that matter on the next one *Suspended Animation*. We did encounter it again to a degree on *The Looking Glass*, because I wrote more of it. Why didn't we on those two previous movies? I suppose we had learned that it was a potential danger, but more I think it was merely an accident of the creative process, in that Dorothy wrote much more of *A Piece of Eden* and *Suspended Animation* than I did (it was maybe eighty/twenty in her favor). I know that might seem odd as *A Piece of Eden* is inspired by my family, but the truth is she did the bulk of the work.

When I finished *A Piece of Eden*, and looked at it, I felt proud. I felt I'd succeeded in making a film about my family and about my own life. In that regard, the picture was fulfilling for me on a personal level, and I still derive a great deal of satisfaction from it. As for the community's feelings about the movie, they were ecstatic! Truly, *A Piece of Eden* provided me with one of the great screenings I've ever had the privilege to attend. They showed the picture at a big high school auditorium and 1,500 people squeezed in there. The response was beyond terrific. This was to be expected for certain reasons, namely because everybody was seeing themselves and the place where they live onscreen. There were all these extras in it and the audience was looking for their cars, their streets, their houses, their stores, their neighbors—people, places and objects that were so familiar to them. That made it a uniquely wonderful experience, and the audience was a very vocal and happy one. I think the spitting montage in particular drew a huge response as the people that featured prominently in that sequence were all locals. I put that in because I knew I could work in a lot of people and acknowledge the community in a direct way. Big Jack Hurley, who wins the cherry pit spitting contest, is a man named James R. Lewis. Jim pumps out all the local cesspools and I thought he made a rather fitting victor.

We released *A Piece of Eden* ourselves, in a limited theatrical release, on September 15, 2000. This became necessary as there were no recognizable stars in the picture that we could use to sell it. I remember screening the film for Sherry Lansing, who at the time was the head of Paramount.

Sherry loved the picture, and really responded to its sweetness. All the same, she said to me, "John, I don't know how to sell this." I must say, that was the general attitude to the movie from all the big distributors. With no stars in the picture and no big commercial hook, it was a tough task. So, we set out to release the movie ourselves and put it out in forty-five cities. In regard to our efforts to sell the film, I have an interesting foreign sales story. Actually, it was a terrible experience that involved our first foreign sales agent on *A Piece of Eden*. This person was a guy named Eric Louzil, who had a company called Lion's Share. In retrospect, the company's trade name should have been a big tip-off to me about how this individual operated, as Louzil sold foreign territories on the film and simply kept all the money!

My dear old friend and former partner Ken Kitch, whom I had worked with in San Francisco, Pittsburgh, New York and Los Angeles, came out of retirement to kindly co-produce *A Piece of Eden* and help me raise the financing. Like me, he was pissed-off and tried to collect our money himself by threatening legal action against Louzil. Kitch lives in San Francisco, but he flew down to L.A. where Louzil was based, walked into the guy's office on Sunset Boulevard and confronted him directly. Sadly, this effort got us nowhere. Louzil basically shrugged his shoulders, and said, "So, sue me! What are you going to get?" It was infuriating, but we just had to swallow it down. Then, some time later, a woman who was a big fan of *A Piece of Eden* showed up at my office one day. After proceeding to tell me how much she loved the movie, I asked, "Out of interest, how did you see it?" She replied, "Well, I'm in the wholesale seafood business and a gentleman named Eric Louzil traded me a DVD copy of your film for 10lbs of shrimp." So, there you go. Sometimes the world has a nasty way of spitting in your eye even when you're smiling.

I should add here that in some DVD copies of *A Piece of Eden* that are available, around the forty-eight minute mark after Happy and Bob leap into the pond, there are several shots of Rebecca Harrell's wet T-shirt that are pixilated. Needless to say, I was not responsible for that and it did not appear in my original cut. It was Walmart who did that, and they did it without permission. I was hugely irritated by their effrontery and contacted them about it. Naturally, I never heard back from them. Their silence was effectively a big "Fuck you!" I presume the reason they did it was because Walmart customers would object to a woman's nipples being visible through a wet T-shirt. They were afraid it would be deemed offensive and controversial. I happen to very much like that passage in the film—Happy and Bob have their honey fight, rubbing the stuff all over each other's bodies, and jump in the water. I think both Grapey and Rebecca are very good in that sequence, which is interesting considering they did not like each other. They appear to enjoy each other in that scene. Maybe the joy of being able to smear each other with honey was a way of working out their hostility. They put aside their feelings and just did it. That was mostly improvised, and the scene does feel very loose and real.

> The delicacy of Hancock and Tristan's character observation is matched by the quirkiness of their humor and faith in the enduring strength of family. Alas, not every critic responded to these wholesome qualities. Marc Savlov of The Austin Chronicle wrote of A Piece of Eden: "Hancock's messages here—the family that farms together stays together, or something along those lines—is straight from the John Mellencamp school of rural oversimplification. The homilies being taught here are so broad in their scope, and so obvious, that they come less as surprises than simple speed bumps on the road to The End. And that's too bad, because the plight of the American farmer—and the American family—remains as fertile a ground for powerful cinematic storytelling today as it was sixty years ago when John Ford let the ghost of Tom Joad loose on the blighted American consciousness."
>
> Dave Kehr was far more sympathetic in his lively notice for the Chicago Tribune: "Warning signs for urban audiences ought to be posted at theaters playing A Piece of Eden: 'Danger! You are entering an irony-free zone.' ... [This picture] has sincerity, warmth and a few cliché-shattering surprises. Though its tone is one of homemade simplicity, it is not at all a naïve work. ... Commercial calculation, for what may be the first time in film history, emerges as a force for good—a refreshingly unhypocritical attitude on the part of Mr. Hancock, who clearly sees no contradiction between his love for nature and his affection for show business."
>
> Roger Ebert, so often a supporter of Hancock's work, was more stinging in his assessment: "A Piece of Eden is a good-hearted film with many virtues, although riveting entertainment is not one of them. It's a family comedy that

> *ambles down well-trodden paths toward a foregone conclusion, neither disturbing nor challenging the audience.... The only review it has collected so far comes from a Utah critic, Fawna Jones, who finds it predictable, and describes it quite accurately: 'This is a movie for those who generally stay away from the theater for fear of being offended and who like their movies to have happy endings.' ... Watching* A Piece of Eden, *I found myself wanting to be shocked, amazed or even surprised. ... But the storyline runs out of steam about four-fifths of the way through, and the closing scenes lack dramatic interest, dissolving in a haze of landscapes and blue skies and happily-ever-after music."*

Waiting for reviews to come in can be like, I don't know, trying to date a cheerleader: it's not a great analogy, but it rhymes in the sense that you kind of hope for the best but are fully prepared for rejection. *A Piece of Eden* did receive some favorable reviews, but some qualified reviews. I read a lot of them and the notices generally used adjectives like "inoffensive" and "safe" and "sentimental" to describe it. Sure, the picture was all of those things, but there's nothing wrong with a nice slice of soothing, unsullied entertainment. In the ads Walmart sold the movie as being "chicken soup for the soul." We intended to make something that was unabashedly heart-warming and contained homespun views (I do have sympathy for the plight of the American farmer, but I was making a romantic comedy not a polemic). For those qualities to be attacked or dismissed by some was disappointing. The only motive I can find for critics who couldn't get behind the film is that maybe it was too much of those things. Maybe it should have been a little tougher, more ironic, or like *Prancer*, possibly a little grittier. The idea that everything works out in the end—Bob and Happy get together, father and son are eternally reunited, the farm is saved—was I guess too syrupy for some.

I do recall that Roger Ebert's vociferous review hurt me a lot. To be honest with you, I was extremely bitter and pissed-off about it—the fact he saw fit to quote from a similarly negative notice was I felt a particularly mean gesture. Roger didn't think *A Piece of Eden* worked quite as well as *Prancer*. I believe one of the only things that amused and excited him about the film was the machine that shakes apples out of the trees, a comment I found more than a little confounding and insulting. He also did not like the character of Franco and I have a theory about why that is: even at this point in his life, Roger had suffered terribly from cancer and had always been unwaveringly valiant about it. I believe it bothered him very much that the father was lying prone and miserable in his hospital bed, complaining about his ailments. That aspect really seemed to agitate Ebert. I contend it was a perfectly normal and justified response for a person suffering with cancer to have, but it was not one that Roger appreciated particularly. I think Ebert was way off base there as not everybody can stoically face down cancer. Some of us wail and plead and moan about the injustice of it. We throw our fists up to the sky and cry, "Why me?" But not Roger.

    I feel I should also mention that Ebert was something of a neighbor of ours. He lived about twenty minutes away from us, up on the lake, and over the years we became friendly. Aside from *Prancer*, Roger had loved *Bang the Drum Slowly* and would often bring that movie up in conversation. I believe he also admired *Let's Scare Jessica to Death* as well, but, as I told you, he did not like *Weeds* as much as those aforementioned films and only gave it a lukewarm review. That's when, in 1987, I wrote Roger the letter asking him to take another look at the picture, which he refused to do. Anyway, shortly after this cordial exchange, Roger and I got to know each other socially and he would invite Dorothy and me over for dinner. By the time *A Piece of Eden* was finished in early 2000, and having gotten to know him a little better, I made a conscious attempt to co-opt Ebert and get him on my side. I basically wrote to him and said, "Dear Roger, would you please look at a rough cut of *A Piece of Eden*? I'd be very interested to hear your thoughts on it." He then wrote back and, rather snootily, said, "No, I'm afraid I can't do that as it will compromise my abilities and neutrality as a critic. I have to judge any and all films in their finished form. There are no exceptions to that."

    Ebert was not a stupid man. He smelled a rat and quickly realized what I was trying to pull. So, right away, he busted my effort to get him onside. Despite failing in this attempt, I had previously enjoyed success at co-opting critics and had done it a couple of times. During my theater years in San Francisco and Pittsburgh, I always got close to the critics and they gave me wonderful reviews—not that they weren't deserved in many cases I might add. I'm not the only one who has done that. I recently read a series of letters Tennessee Williams once wrote to Brooks Atkinson, *The New York Times* theater critic and, oh man, was Tennessee ever working him! He was clearly feeding Atkinson a nice line of bullshit, writing things like, "How valuable I'm finding your reviews in my creative work."

It's terrific stuff. Unfortunately, Ebert proved more impervious, at least in my case. When *A Piece of Eden* finally came out, Roger seemed especially determined to demonstrate his objectivity and only awarded the film one-and-a-half stars out of four. I felt betrayed by that and even struggled with it. Shortly after his review appeared, Ebert was flying to the Virginia Film Festival. On the very same flight was Rebecca Harrell and the two of them happened to be sitting near to each other. At one point, Roger leaned over to Rebecca, and whispered, "Is John mad at me?" I can laugh about it now.

Roger died of cancer in 2013, and I'm sure he was stoic to the end. One of the last times I saw him was during a screening of *Suspended Animation* in 2003 at the Lake Screening Room, which was where he would review movies in Chicago. I ran into him in the men's room—he was leaving as I was going in—and we were pleasant to each other. There's no denying that Ebert was passionate and highly knowledgeable about cinema, but I do think (like a lot of critics) he was a frustrated filmmaker. Just knowing him socially he talked more than he had any right to about *Beyond the Valley of the Dolls*, a terrible picture he co-wrote with Russ Meyer in 1970. Roger would talk to me about that film as if it was an unqualified masterpiece, but, other than finding it a modest satire at best, I didn't think it was ever worth mentioning twice. Roger thought otherwise. But I liked him, and felt he was a nice guy. Sure, he was rather full of himself and always aware of the power he held, although I personally believe that his importance as a critic has been overstated. I'm not pissing on his grave here, that's just my personal opinion. My overriding feeling about his response to *A Piece of Eden* was that Ebert had punished me. He had chastened me for deliberately trying to get him on my side in advance. There's no doubt about it, Roger had a spiteful streak in him that would manifest from time to time. On the other hand, looking back, maybe I deserved to be punished for even attempting such a ploy.

The reviews for *A Piece of Eden* didn't change how I felt about it. I love both Misha's photography and Angelo Badalamenti's score for the movie. Angelo wrote some wonderful themes for it—even before we started to shoot, he'd written a stirring melody. He did a great job as did Orville Stoeber who also worked a lot on the music. We used the Italian song "Fenesta Vascia" in the picture, which is a tune I love dearly. I'd used it previously in *Steal the Sky*: a soprano sings it in a restaurant in Rome. It's a song that has a special meaning for Dorothy and me. It conjures up memories of the first time we went to Rome together. In truth, if I'd had a larger budget at my disposal on *A Piece of Eden*, there would not have been a lot of stuff I'd have done differently. Maybe I would have shot a little more helicopter stuff to make the film seem a little bigger. I've often seen movies begin with some kind of ambitious aerial shot that is designed to give the immediate impression that the movie is big. They try to start off with a helicopter shot to give the picture a sense of grandeur and scope, that kind of thing. This would have probably grated against the subdued and intimate experience I wanted to give viewers. So, I don't lose any sleep over it. Looking back, the experience of making *A Piece of Eden* was an extremely pleasant one. It was a very happy time for me, and just thinking about that time brings a smile to my face.

17 *Suspended Animation* (2003)

AFTER THE DECIDEDLY UNEVEN *critical reception awarded* A Piece of Eden, *Hancock and Tristan immediately began looking for a project that would provide them with a conscious departure from the family-oriented fare of their previous films. Having threatened at various junctures to originate another horror picture in the thirty years that had elapsed since* Let's Scare Jessica to Death, *the director encouraged his wife to develop an idea she had first started writing in 1995 as a screenplay and then subsequently as an unpublished novel. A riff on the "urbanoia" themes of John Boorman's* Deliverance *(1972), with its delineation of vulnerable urbanites coming unstuck in a hostile backwoods environment, the script also absorbed the influence of* The Texas Chainsaw Massacre *(1974) and* Misery *(1990) in its unblinking examination of the themes of madness, cannibalism, and the obsession "civilized" human beings have with those who commit extreme acts of evil.*

Tristan's wintry campfire tale revolves around Tom Kempton, a successful Hollywood animator who goes on an ice fishing trip with two friends in Northern Michigan. While traversing the frozen near-wilderness on snowmobiles, Kempton rolls his vehicle and is separated from his companions. After becoming lost, he takes refuge in a small cabin inhabited by a pair of middle-aged siblings named Vanessa and Ann Boulette. At first the women seem benign and helpful, if somewhat eccentric, but Kempton quickly discovers that in reality they are two homicidal

> *cannibals and he is now their hapless captive. Rescued mere moments before he is to be slaughtered—but not before he is viciously tortured—Kempton returns home to California and is haunted by his exposure to such voracious evil. He soon becomes fixated on the figure of Vanessa Boulette (who perished in an avalanche while murderously pursuing Tom and his friends across the desolate snow) and uses the traumatic experience as inspiration for his next animated feature. Kempton then tracks down a young woman named Clara Hanson who appears to have no knowledge that she is the daughter of Vanessa. Fearing that she may exhibit some of her mother's depraved tendencies, Kempton is equally alarmed when he meets Clara's psychopathic fifteen year-old son, Sandor, who appears to be every incarnation of his deceased grandmother.*

I thought it was about time I did another horror picture as a lot of time had passed since I'd made *Let's Scare Jessica to Death*. Waiting thirty years was a mistake. Of course, in the interim I'd lost *Jaws 2* and there had also been *Wolfen*, but the latter really wasn't my movie. I thought it would be good to revisit the genre and have some fun with it. I also like to do an entirely different picture from the previous one I've made as not to repeat myself. So, once again, it was an effort to move against my image as this maker of safe and sweet pictures. Around this time Dorothy had been struck by the idea of doing a kind of Grand Guignol horror film that we rather blithely referred to as "*Deliverance* on snowmobiles." It concerned this city slicker who stumbles across a pair of demented female cannibals in the wilderness who want to torture, kill, cook and eat him. Something amused and excited me about that concept, but I think for Dorothy it was a slightly more serious affair. She was interested in exploring the idea of how evil can contaminate and destroy us; how good people who are exposed to this kind of darkness, and survive it, can then find it difficult to return to a state of normalcy. They are forever changed, simply because they have stared into the face of the Devil. I also liked the fact that it was a story of oppositions where the forces of civilization and rationality (embodied by Tom Kempton and his friends) are pitted against the forces of deviance and irrationality (the Boulette sisters).

Dorothy had first started writing *Suspended Animation* as a screenplay and then as a book, before coming back to it again as a script. She wanted to try the story out as a novel in order to describe the events and characters in more detail. In a screenplay, you can't really do that. The form doesn't allow it. *Suspended Animation* made an extremely scary book. It's a hell of a good read and anyone that's perused the manuscript has not been able to put it down. In adapting the novel into a screenplay, we learned this unorthodox approach was not a bad way of working. I mean, one of the interesting things about writing prose is how one sentence leads directly to another. You make all kinds of associations in the third sentence that you would not have thought of had you not written the second sentence. The more you write, the more this exploration deepens and can take you to some amazing places you may not have otherwise considered. Screenplays are so incredibly tight, they are a little like lyric poetry; you are writing so precisely you almost never write the second sentence that leads to the third. There are no such constraints imposed on you when creating a novel. You can investigate these hidden places and that's really how *Suspended Animation* evolved. The story expanded beyond these pair of cannibal sisters and incorporated elements such as a lost adopted daughter and her disturbed teenage son. Interestingly, despite turning the novel into a screenplay, there weren't many significant differences between the book and the final script, aside from the extraneous stuff we had to leave out. We didn't lose anything particularly exciting, although the novel originally began with a house-fire, the same one that had claimed our Malibu home. We abandoned that opening for the film and tried to get to the meat of the story much quicker.

Another unexpected thing that occurred as Dorothy was writing *Suspended Animation* is the script gradually became what I can only describe as a form of vengeance she intended to take out on Allegra Kent, with whom she shared an unfortunate history. Allegra Kent was one of the Russian choreographer George Balanchine's principal ballerinas and had danced with the New York City Ballet. Her connection to Dorothy is this: back when she was modeling, Dorothy used to live for several years with Bert Stern, the famous commercial photographer. But then she broke up with Stern and married Aram Avakian in 1957 and had two children with him, Alexandra and Tristan. A couple of years later, Stern married Allegra Kent and, I don't exactly know why, but Dorothy and Allegra never got along with each other. Then, after Dorothy and Aram got divorced in 1972, and Stern burned out on amphetamines and divorced Allegra in 1975, Allegra and Aram began living together. When Aram died of heart failure in 1987, Allegra suddenly threw Dorothy's kids out of the house and took all the rugs and lamps, and would not permit Dorothy to come to Aram's funeral. This situation then deteriorated into a rather ugly and regrettable thing, and Dorothy seriously had it in for Allegra. As a result of all this lingering ill-feeling, Dorothy wanted to include the character of an evil, twisted, self-obsessed former ballerina in her story. That was how Vanessa Boulette came to be born.

It goes without saying that when you come up with an antagonist like Vanessa, you need to devise a good protagonist; someone the audience can like and root for. A lot of heroes in movies and books are not as charismatic and flawed as the villains. That said, I think there's something quite liberating and attractive about being evil; not caring about the laws of decency, decorum and morality. There's a sense of freedom about it, of being unbridled and unconfined, as you're not conforming to the norm. You're transgressing; you're getting crazy. Fuck propriety! Dorothy understood how that can be an appealing thing as well as an abhorrent and disturbing thing. So, we needed a force for goodness to oppose the evil. One of the decisions we made early on was to make Tom Kempton a director of animated features. I thought that was an interesting choice, rather than making him a writer, or an actor, or a live action film director. Not only did it give Kempton an intriguing occupation, his creativity would allow him to vividly express his most profound thoughts about the horrors of what happened to him the day he crossed paths with the Boulette sisters. He could filter some of his darkest fears through his work. We felt Tom would seek a catharsis of some sorts through his art, as that is something that a lot of artists do. In this instance, it's a means for Tom to investigate and perhaps tame the awful memories of that experience. Also, in our writing *Suspended Animation*, Dorothy and I were really writing about artists. So, it was an effective disguise for us.

Upon completing the script in mid-2000, we set about trying to secure financing for the project. As we had previously done on *A Piece of Eden*, we hoped we would be able to attract potential investment for *Suspended Animation* from several local businessmen based on our good reputation and the success of *Prancer*. The budget eventually came to $3.5 million and there's no denying that once again the film only came together financially due to the generous participation of Robert J. Hiler. Bob put up the money for *Suspended Animation* and I was extremely grateful about that. Bob's previous involvement on *A Piece of Eden* amounted to his not only being an investor and co-producer, but also a kind of interested on-the-set observer. It was clear to see as we were shooting *A Piece of Eden* that Bob was totally enamored of the filmmaking process. He had caught the ever-contagious movie-making bug and that's a difficult thing to just shake off and forget. It's fairly addictive. Immediately after we'd finished that picture, I remember Bob excitedly said to me, "Okay, let's do this again! Let's make more! This is wonderful!" That was sweet music to my ears.

Through Bob's financial muscle and enthusiasm, we were able to take over what had once been a cannery factory and a set of offices near town. We then converted part of this disused factory into a 20,000 square-foot soundstage and that allowed us the space inside to build some sets. In there we constructed the interior of Tom's studio office and the interior of Clara Hansen's home. We built each set with removable walls which gave us a lot of maneuverability; we could extract a particular wall at any given time and place a camera there, or rig up some lights. Also of importance was the fact the location of the factory meant we could mostly keep the work centralized, which always saves a considerable amount of time, money and energy. You get more value if you don't have to move the trucks, equipment and personnel from one place to another. Aside from shooting some of the film on our soundstage, we also shot at various local houses situated around the area. The cooperation from the locals was wonderful, just as it had been previously on *Prancer* and *A Piece of Eden*. We secured building materials to construct our sets, vehicles to transport our cast and crew, and food for them to eat—all on deferment. Once again, we also succeeded in coercing the mayor's wife into making props for us.

> *With the financing and locations for* Suspended Animation *now firmly in place, Hancock began interviewing actors for the film with casting directors Rosemary Welden (who was based in Los Angeles) and Susan Willett (who was operating out of New York). The latter had previously cast* Prancer *and* A Piece of Eden, *and had also been a production associate on* Weeds. *Willett worked in close consultation with Hancock to find the best actors on the East Coast who were "available and affordable," a process that was not without its challenges. This may have prompted Hancock to include the knowing line of dialogue Tom Kempton delivers to Ann Boulette as he is tethered to a chair in an early scene: "Casting is always difficult."*

Casting is indeed *always* difficult. It involves a lot of uncertainty and seemingly endless deliberation. Have I made the right choice here? Is this going to work out? You can have a strong instinct about an actor based on their reading, or from viewing their previous work, and feel they have a quality that can give the character an extra dimension. Then, during rehearsals, you might have the sudden realization that you've made a terrible mistake. You always strive to get the best possible people you can for each individual part, but it's incredibly difficult to acquire a name actor for a low-budget film. There are certain things you have to accept and contend with when you work with a star; you have to woo them and stroke them, and that soaks up a lot of precious time for a director. A name actor almost inevitably brings in a circus of trailers, entourages and assorted hangers-on. That kind of dampens the hearty esprit de corps you have on a low-budget movie, where everybody is on the same level and is willing to pull together and sacrifice. Some of the supporting actors gaze at the star and say, "Hey, why isn't *he* trying so hard?" So, you have to convince everybody to fall in line and keep struggling with you, but it's not the same.

The central issue for us on *Suspended Animation* was finding the right people for the right roles at the right price. A fundamental problem facing all independent filmmaking is the acting. Many people are preoccupied with the visual style of a low-budget picture, but the thing that often betrays a movie's modest origins and limitations is the quality of the acting. I've seen many independent films that look wonderful, but the acting is atrocious. Sometimes this is because the director has cast his friends and acquaintances, rather than professional actors. Now, this isn't always a question of money and necessity, it's because the director is afraid of dealing with real actors. Real actors have needs and expectations; amateurs tend not to. The key to directing is securing the right actor. I don't presume that I can create or forge a performance for them. They have to be right, so you can just let them go. Even though some fairly accomplished actors read for *Suspended Animation*, I made some mistakes in my choices. We didn't completely succeed despite the best efforts of Rosemary Welden and Susan Willett. Incidentally, I do recall that during the same time we were casting our film, Sam Mendes was casting *The Road to Perdition*, his big-budget gangster picture starring Tom Hanks and Paul Newman. We lost a couple of our actors to that production, which Mendes eventually filmed in Michigan and Illinois.

Two roles I felt were important to get right were those of Vanessa and Ann Boulette. They were the villains of the piece, and both had to work or we were in trouble. I was looking for two distinctive-looking females that didn't necessarily have to look like they were related. In fact, it was more interesting to me if they did not appear as if they shared the same bloodline. The first of the pair we cast was the role of Ann, the fat sister. We found Sage Allen in Los Angeles after she was brought in by Rosemary. It soon transpired that I had actually met Sage many years earlier, back when I had directed a play at the American Place Theatre. It turned out that she had been an intern there, or an observer of some kind. Sage remembered me and greeted me warmly, although I must admit I did not remember her. The truth was she'd been much thinner during the time we had first met and now looked somewhat different. But as soon as I read Sage, I liked her immediately. She quickly got a firm grasp of the character, that sense of a frustrated and ignored woman who has probably resided in the shadow of her more attractive and talented sibling all of her life. I think Sage is wonderful in *Suspended Animation*. I particularly enjoy the moment where this psychotic woman whispers to Tom about her equally psychotic sister: "She's crazy! I *hate* her!" That always gets a big laugh from audiences.

Having found our Ann, I knew we had to find somebody just as good to play Vanessa. It was going to be crucial to the success of the film, as the specter of this character ominously falls over the entire narrative even when she isn't onscreen. Laura Esterman came to my attention for the role as she was an old friend of Dorothy's. They had worked together when Dorothy had played Nora Helmer in a production of *A Doll's House* at the Center Stage in Baltimore. Laura had played one of the other parts and Dorothy was always complimentary about her. Laura lived in L.A., so we saw a lot of her socially for a time. She was a good actress, more technical than I like, but a competent performer. Laura came in to read for Vanessa in New York and was wonderful. She was funny and insidiously wicked, and this was one of those aforementioned instances during casting when you believe you've found *the* one. So, I felt confident we'd made the right decision in giving Laura the part. We actually began rehearsals without Laura, as she had a job and couldn't come until right before we were scheduled to start shooting. So, we rehearsed with Dorothy playing Vanessa opposite Sage as Ann. Then, just a couple of days before principal photography was to commence, Laura arrived and was clearly—and quite unexpectedly—teetering on the edge of suicide. I'm not kidding. She turned up looking agitated and mournfully depressed. I quickly realized that Laura had developed an incredibly grim view of life and was literally out of her mind. She couldn't sleep and was addicted to sleeping pills, and was taking far too many of them for my liking. So, her situation was desperate.

Now, on the evidence of her reading, I'd anticipated that Laura would have been very strong in the part. However, in the final analysis, her performance is plainly lacking something. If you're playing this female cannibal who is torturing and killing men, and devouring their flesh, it seems to me that you ought to get something out of it. When Dorothy and Sage played those characters in rehearsals, they both relished what they were doing. They brought the terrifying gusto that was needed. Laura never quite achieved that quality on film. Really, Dorothy *should* have played Vanessa. I certainly thought so and everybody from Bob Hiler and my assistant, Beth Behler, to Sage Allen agreed with me. We would repeatedly entreat Dorothy during rehearsals and say, "You would be so great in this part. Why don't you do it?" But she would repeatedly refuse. In the end, it was only Dorothy's vanity that kept her from playing Vanessa. She did not want to be shot in the face and wear special make-up, and have former boyfriends now see her onscreen looking old, scarred and bedraggled. I still feel that Dorothy's refusal was something of a tragic mistake for the picture, as Laura's portrayal ultimately drained most of the humor out of the subject. You see, scary pictures often get a lot of laughs when they are done correctly. They ride the perfect storm between terror and laughter, two extreme reactions that are closely related when you think about it. Laura found nothing remotely amusing about her character—or about anything else really. She was in terrible emotional shape and her reluctance to find traces of humor in the role had a blunting effect on the film.

Don't get me wrong, I did not want to encourage Laura and Sage to bring a sense of farcical theatricality to their portrayal of the sisters. I merely wanted them to have fun with their roles. I was hoping for something that was realistic, but also revealed that these women really savored what they did. Sage brought that perverse sense of enjoyment to her performance, but Laura simply couldn't. She was in such a black mood on the set it cast a dreadful pall on the work. For instance, while the crew would be lighting, instead of just leaving the set and getting herself a donut or a cup of coffee, Laura would just sit slumped in a chair and sob. I can't tell you how difficult that was for everybody. What exactly do you say and do in a situation like that? We were all working against a schedule and a tight budget, and we had to contend with an actor who was visibly in a very dark place. You can't ignore it, but you can't continually bring everything to a grinding halt either. Actually, when we first see Vanessa Boulette in the film, she's a little like that: she's morose and sleepy and distracted, but then the deliciousness of Vanessa then showing Tom her snatch and all that stuff, I felt something was missing from those moments: a kind of knowing depravity. Interestingly, in some of the later scenes when Vanessa invades Tom's home for their final confrontation, Laura brings a quality of underplaying to her performance. She is probably better in those later scenes than in the early portions of the picture, but she could have brought so much more to the role.

We also encountered major problems in finding the right actor to play our intrepid hero, Tom Kempton. We originally cast Richard Grieco in the role. He had a fairly modest track record in movies and in television, and had co-starred opposite Johnny Depp in the TV series *21 Jump Street*. I thought Grieco was at least a name that people might have heard of, and he was also a handsome guy which didn't hurt. Unfortunately, he was just terrible during the first rehearsals we held. He was so awful I literally couldn't bear to watch him. I knew he wasn't going to work out as our lead, so I quickly made the decision to fire him. When I informed Grieco of my decision, he couldn't believe it. He stared at me incredulously, and said, "But I *add* value. Don't you see? I make things better!" He couldn't understand why I would even consider letting him go, but I did just that. He had a pay-or-play deal, so we paid him his $50,000 and sent him on his way. After Grieco was gone I replaced him with Richard Edson, a well-known actor who had appeared in a lot of outstanding films such as *Platoon* and Jim Jarmusch's *Stranger Than Paradise*. I thought Edson was particularly wonderful in Jarmusch's movie and I'd always wanted to work with him.

When I first cast him in *Suspended Animation*, I remember Edson suddenly announced to me, "You know, I have to tell you something: I'm not a trained actor. The truth is I really can't act." Of course, on the strength of his previous work, I didn't believe him. But as we started working in rehearsals, I quickly discovered that what Edson couldn't do was effectively pretend to be afraid. He could not convincingly simulate the appropriate levels of fear and anxiety as these two crazy women were terrorizing him. That was a serious problem because this character was going to be in a state of profound terror for a considerable period of time. Frankly, I used to dread going to rehearsals because he was so boring and flat, no energy. Edson had gotten by on this strong natural quality he had. You couldn't take your eyes off him in certain supporting roles, but he had no technique, no facility to be able to carry an entire film. So, like Grieco before him, I had to let Edson go. It's hard enough firing one lead actor on a movie, but firing two lead actors on the same movie is *extremely* difficult. When I broke the bad news to Edson, he took it a lot better than Grieco had. He was a much cooler guy, far more gracious and accepting. He shrugged, and said, "Yeah, okay," then added, "but I *did* tell you I couldn't act."

With our start date looming and two male leads already dismissed, we had to find another actor very quickly. Now that I think about it, we had already begun shooting! In fact, we had shot a week of *Suspended Animation* without the role of Kempton being cast. Naturally, not having the pivotal actor secured placed considerable pressure on all of us. So, on the first weekend of the shoot, literally our first day off after wrapping a long day's shooting in the snow, Bob Hiler flew Dorothy and me in his jet—in the middle of the night—to L.A. where we hastily read several actors. Our plan was to find somebody, read him, and fly back with the guy the following night to continue filming. It was exhausting and I can remember feeling tense and nervous. Then we got hold of Alex McArthur, whom I had worked with on my first episode of *Hill Street Blues* sixteen years earlier. I thought he was wonderful in that show and we had got on great with each other. Back in 1985, I really believed that Alex would go on to be a big star as he had the looks, the charisma and the talent. He'd had an affair with Madonna and appeared in a music video with her for the song "Papa Don't Preach." Alex had also done *Rampage* with Billy Friedkin (a serial killer thriller that, like *Weeds*, was another casualty of DEG's bankruptcy), so I had always enjoyed his performances. For whatever reason Alex never did become a star, but I was delighted to see him again and immediately cast him as Tom. As soon as we snagged Alex, we flew back across the country with him and kept on shooting.

The rest of the cast came together fairly easily. We found Maria Cina, who plays Vanessa's natural daughter Clara Hansen, in Los Angeles. Rosemary brought her in and I liked the way Maria read. She is really good in *Suspended Animation* and has this strange, fragile quality. Clara is something of a red herring, as the audience is left to wonder for a while whether she is crazy or not. One of the interesting things that occurred during casting was when we were looking for somebody to play Clara's teenage son, Sandor, and came across Fred Meyers. It's revealed in the story that Sandor has inherited his grandmother's psychotic tendencies. Fred actually came to our meeting totally in character, which is one of those mistakes actors sometimes make. He literally walked into the room as this evil, scowling teenager and I almost didn't hire him. The first five minutes I spent in his company, I said to myself, "Jesus, this kid is so obnoxious and unpleasant. Let's move on to somebody else." Only at the last minute, when Rosemary came to me and said, "No, John, he isn't like that at all. Believe me, Fred is a nice kid." I trusted her judgment and found out that Fred was indeed a wonderful kid. I looked at some of his previous credits and saw that he'd co-starred with Shia LaBeouf in the successful Disney TV show *Even Stevens*, and was a talented actor. Fred deftly captured that disturbing sense of a burgeoning psychopath. What I find interesting is that with all the violence and morbidity in the film, fingers being chopped off and skulls sitting on platters, the moments when Sandor pops the zits on his neck are arguably the most excruciating and sickening for people to sit through. Weirdly enough, I find the more personal moments of disgust that relate to bodily secretions—shit, piss and pus—are usually the things that agitate an audience.

Other members of the cast were made up of people I'd worked with previously and wanted to work with again. Robert Breuler makes a cameo as the doctor whom Tom shows the sample of human skin that Sandor has squirreled away in a junkyard (which turns out to be the vaginal lips of a woman). I also cast Rebecca Harrell as Hilary Kempton, Tom's young pregnant wife. In order to be acceptable to the gaunt modern look of Hollywood actresses, Rebecca had recently lost a lot of weight. She was very thin and, in my opinion, wasn't as sexy as she'd been in *A Piece of Eden* when she had more meat on her bones. I also don't think she was particularly strong in *Suspended Animation* and I don't know why. I suspect it was our fault as the role may have been underwritten and too insubstantial for her to make a real dent with it. There was nothing much for her to do other than stare adoringly at Alex and appear frightened at the end. Tom's wife effectively functioned as a sounding board for him to relay certain anxious expository dialogue about how he was feeling or what he was doing. There was also the fact that her life, and the life of their unborn child, later comes under threat when Vanessa Boulette comes back from the dead and threatens to destroy Tom's world. Rebecca doesn't do much acting anymore and is now producing and directing documentaries on environmental issues with her husband. I believe they won an award at the Sundance Film Festival a couple of years ago.

We also needed a suitably scary-looking guy to play the last of the Boulette clan, Vanessa and Ann's convict brother Philip, who is locked away in prison. I had initially approached Andreas Katsulas for the role, but he wouldn't do it. Andreas did not want to play another villain (particularly following on from his positive role in *A Piece of Eden*), so we cast J.E. Freeman instead. Again, even though it wasn't a pre-requisite that the actor look like he could be her blood relative, Freeman had this scrawny physicality that seemed to resemble Laura somehow. He did a good job for me, but I do remember that Freeman was kind of creepy to be around. He was an actor who fully embraced the unnerving and threatening qualities of the guy he was playing. Some actors like to stay in character off-camera and that can be interesting—particularly when they are playing extreme or unsavory people—but it can also be fairly unsettling. We ended up expanding the part of Philip a little when we were shooting as he was originally there just to fill in some of the details of his family history. But we gave him a few more things to do and say. It wasn't so much that what Freeman was giving us was exceptionally good; rather Philip was a character that needed a little more fleshing out, as he was going to reappear again just before the end credits rolled. So, he had to make an impression on the audience during his time onscreen.

> *Awarded a generous shooting schedule of forty-eight days,* Suspended Animation *was the first film Hancock had lensed using High Definition digital cameras. After scouting locations in and around LaPorte, problems with the required weather conditions presented certain difficulties in maintaining a workable schedule. Thus, the company was forced to consider other places in order to complete several key early scenes in the narrative including the lengthy snowmobile chase. The production then moved on to Malibu, California, to shoot at half a dozen locations that depicted Tom Kempton's return to the "relative normalcy" of Hollywood.*

I had not worked with High Definition cameras before doing *Suspended Animation*, so they were all fairly new to me. I'm always open to investigating new technologies if I think they can benefit the filmmaking process and make it easier and better. I'm not the kind of director who will use a newfangled piece of equipment simply because it's available and fashionable. I want to know if it can help me tell the story that I want to tell more effectively. That's all, really. We used a Sony High Definition Digital Camera to shoot *Suspended Animation*, which we rented from Fletcher Camera in Chicago. Needless to say, the particular camera we deployed is now out-dated and the real benefits and technological advancements in the digital format occurred *after* we made our film, with George Lucas doing his *Star Wars* prequels and everything. I do understand why certain directors criticize digital cinema—some of the film purists out there— because like everything these days it really all comes down to money and economics. Those are the two most important considerations it seems. But as the technology keeps moving forward, I don't imagine there are quite as many glitches and mishaps these days as there once were.

You see, I had been assured that the digital cameras we acquired for our movie would detect enormous details in shadows and near darkness, and that the images would still be rich. As shadows and darkness are fairly prevalent in a scary movie, I was excited to hear this. We did some tests and I was pleased with what we got. For all that, when I look at the movie now I find it a little grainy and muddy in certain sections. I don't find the image to be particularly crisp and sharp, and the blacks to be very deep. Initially, after the tests we did, I felt the quality of the digital cameras was good enough and it was cheaper than going through the whole process of converting the film to digital in order to edit on the Avid, and then reconverting back to film for a theatrical release—all that kind of stuff. We felt we were saving money as it was cheaper and quicker than shooting on film; it was easier to light and there was no financial limit to the amount of takes we could do. As a result of those freedoms, I did a lot of takes and was able to experiment with some scenes a little more and steer the actors into trying different things. That was certainly one of the bonuses.

We always wanted to shoot *Suspended Animation* in Indiana, as we knew it was the ideal place to shoot a snow picture. Shooting *Prancer* there had been such an easy experience in terms of the amount and quality of the snow we had available to us. There was always a lot of snow all winter, without fail. On this particular year, the winter of 2001, we still had a lot of snow, but it gradually got dark, ugly and dirty. I didn't want to shoot it anymore because I didn't like the way the snow looked. It wasn't as photogenic as I'd hoped and imagined it would be. So, instead of continuing to shoot the snow in its present deteriorating state, I said, "Look, we'll always have snow here as this is a dependable location for it. But I don't want to shoot dirty snow. I want to go inside and shoot some of the interiors." Now, when you're making a movie, you try to shoot your exteriors when they are shoot-able and reserve your interiors for cover. Thus, I met with some opposition to this suggestion, but I was most insistent about it. "This snow is far too crummy. I want to go inside now and come back to the exteriors later." The production manager then pleaded with me: "Please, John, don't do that! Shoot the snow while we've got it." I said, "It's okay, we'll still have it. Just relax." As fortune would decree it, it then didn't snow again for that one year in ten! I couldn't believe it. We still had the snowmobile chase and the avalanche to shoot and we had no fucking snow. It then became necessary to find it someplace else. So, we were in effect chasing the snow and that resulted in us having to travel up to Canada to shoot there. We ended up going to Sault Ste. Marie, Ontario, which is located close to the border with the U.S., and finished the snowmobile sequences up there. It was an amazing experience, just moving back and forth from our camp where we were based to the set on a frozen lake. It was just me on a snowmobile traversing this area, soaking in all the majesty of nature.

After getting all our snow stuff, and having shot all our interiors in LaPorte, we then traveled to Southern California with our crew from Chicago to film at half a dozen locations there. We also shot some scenes where our house had burnt in Malibu as we still owned the area at this point. We were actually based out of where our house had once stood. We had the two mobile homes there that we were using as an office and a place to live, so it worked out fine for us. It was interesting to be based where our beloved house had burnt in '93. It was a very strange feeling to have everybody we knew from LaPorte come and see the place where we had once lived. It felt like visiting the distant grave of a family member or friend. We needed a beach house for several scenes where we see Tom at home with Hilary. Our neighbor, Tony DeVivo, generously allowed us access to his house, which, I'll remind you, was located down the road from where our house had stood, for free. He had leased the property for as much as $25,000 a day for previous film shoots and we only had the use of it for two days, but that was enough. We shot all the exteriors of the house in Malibu and shot the interiors of the house in a property here in LaPorte.

> *A pivotal and extended sequence in* Suspended Animation *details the Boulette Sisters systematically incapacitating, kidnapping, torturing and maiming Kempton in their*

> *isolated cabin after he is drugged and bound to a chair. In contempt of Hancock's aversion to portraying protracted acts of explicit physical violence onscreen, Tristan wanted the early portions of the film to disturb and confront the audience. At the same time these moments would also provide their stricken protagonist with an experience that would justify his all-consuming psychological obsession and malaise.*

Dorothy felt those scenes had to be tough, even cruel. I must confess that a part of me liked the idea of two women strapping a man to a chair and torturing him, as most horror movies are misogynistic. They often depict men torturing women and it rarely goes the other way, at least not back then. Dorothy and I felt it was high time that the roles were reversed and so we put a man in serious physical and emotional jeopardy. Alex came to the set so fast he didn't really have time to prepare in advance for those scenes. As I said, he was not present at the rehearsals, so I was relying on him to quickly grasp the terror his character was experiencing and project it. After witnessing Grieco and Edson fail to deliver, those first few moments on the set with Alex were pretty tense. Fortunately for us, he understood the full horror of what was happening to Kempton and it was all there for him to respond to. I mean, a sinister and disturbing thing that the women do to Tom is give him their "stamp of approval"—branding his head with the kind of blue stamp that's used on meat. They then use this mark as the very place where they intend to drill into his skull. That's just so creepy and weird to me, the sense of preparation. It's kind of like the Iraqi style of torture as I understand they are currently doing a little drilling into heads over there in Iraq. It's a truly hideous thing to contemplate. Alex got all that horror and played it just right.

I also like the touch where the sisters start blasting out Stravinsky's *The Rite of Spring* in the basement as they are about to kill Tom. Then Vanessa does this weird thing where she starts to whip herself as she advances. It's as if the self-flagellation is a means of purifying herself before they commit this terrible act. It echoes the moment in Bergman's *The Virgin Spring* when Max von Sydow whips himself with birch branches before he kills the three goatherds who have raped and murdered his daughter. It's been a long time since I've seen that film, but some of the images in it still live with me. I think Vanessa's self-flagellation has certain religious connotations that are absent from *Suspended Animation*. I mean, she is clearly a psychopath who is acting without remorse or conflict. She is not seeking forgiveness from God for what she is about to do and so this ritual is not designed to cleanse her in that sense. I don't think she cares about atoning for her evils and that gave her character an even more perverse quality. Again, whipping herself like that is more an act of preparation whereas in *The Virgin Spring* it's probably both an act of preparation and expurgation. I know that some cultures hold the belief that if you consume human flesh you can acquire all of the victim's power and knowledge. We obviously didn't go in that direction with *Suspended Animation*, but I still find that a fascinating idea.

Horror stories often play with the idea of an unavoidable and terrible destiny. Vanessa even says to Tom at one point: "Fate brought you here. Every road you took; each choice you made." Personally, I do not believe in the concept of fate. I believe in accident, and cause and effect, and bad timing, and coincidence. Those things I can accept. But I don't accept that there's a pre-destined outcome for each of us that is inevitable and is merely waiting to be fulfilled. It just doesn't make any sense to me unless you believe that time is like a circle in which you are forever going round and round, doomed to be repeating the same life. How can you change the course of events if everything is already determined and there are no other possibilities? If I ever found myself in Tom's predicament—being tortured by two crazed women—I would probably do just what he did. I would try to fake my way out of it somehow. I'd certainly offer them a part in my movie if it would save my life. I'm always amused by the way Tom feels compelled to defend his occupation when he is questioned about it by the sisters: "No, animation is not just cartoons! These are *real* films! I'm a *real* filmmaker! I'm an artist!" The moment when he lies to the sisters as a delaying tactic and announces that he directed *The Lion King* makes perfect sense to me; that he would name a film that these isolated women might actually have seen. I've never been tempted to tell a stranger that I directed *The Godfather* or *Chinatown*, or some other recognizable classic. I'm sure some filmmakers have lied like that. Of course, with immediate access to the Internet these days, such a lie could easily be exposed.

While I still watch a lot of horror movies, I don't enjoy them as much as I did at a certain point in my life. Nevertheless, I'm quite well-versed in the genre. Some of my favorites include *The Exorcist*, *Psycho*, *The Haunting* and *The Texas Chainsaw Massacre*. I've always thought that *Texas Chainsaw* is a masterpiece which goes right to the very center of the genre. It's such a beautifully made movie, so powerful, it feels much more violent than it actually is. I must admit that I'm not against the portrayal of violence in cinema. Am I against mindless splatter without conscience or consequences? Yes, very much so, but I'm not against the joy of violence. I do feel the kind of cartoon violence we sometimes see in movies is ridiculous and untrue. I think we must always be aware as viewers that the worst violence causes irreparable pain and damage. Violence *hurts*! So, in certain instances, it shouldn't be something that we treat too lightly or deny because it's very real and apparent. It's everywhere. Be that as it may, I don't want to suppress anything. I really believe in art and personal expression and creative freedom, and I believe in people understanding the truth of our world through those things. I don't think audiences are harmed by what they see in films, but, contrary to that view, maybe they are. Maybe they can be. I don't know anything for certain as I don't have all the answers. But I would not want to limit how we depict acts of violence onscreen when they are placed in a certain social, political and intellectual context that is honest and authentic.

I haven't seen any of the nasty "Torture Porn" horror films that have been made in the years following *Suspended Animation*. Whenever I am inadvertently exposed to one of these movies, I quickly turn them off. I feel the impact of emotional violence is far more potent than physical violence. For instance, there is a Michael Haneke picture called *Funny Games* that I found deeply disturbing and difficult to watch, but I couldn't deny there was a cinematic intelligence behind that film which was demanding certain things of me. It wasn't the typical approach; it wasn't just violence for the sake of violence. It was thoughtful and pointed and questioning. In *Suspended Animation*, there is a moment when the sisters brutally chop off Tom's finger and Ann quips, "Ooh, num-num! Finger McNuggets!" Now, admittedly, that comes awfully close to being Torture Porn. I don't deny it. This is what I meant earlier when I talked about Laura's performance taking the joy out of what it is the sisters are doing. Because Laura didn't play it as enticingly as Dorothy had in rehearsals, such moments threatened to change the tone of the picture and make it remorselessly grim. So, when you have a scene like that where fingers are being hacked off, it does verge on mindless gratuity. Thankfully, I think Sage Allen got the appropriate feeling in that instance, so it wasn't as nasty and depressing as it might have been.

There is something else I feel I should mention: there is a moment in the film where the Boulette sisters teasingly show Tom a preserved penis in a jar; a "pickled pecker" that evidently belonged to one of their previous male victims. Honestly, that was an effort to capture or illustrate that same kind of joy I'm speaking about. It's scary and horrific, but it's also deliciously funny. By the way, that's a real dick. We were extremely lucky to obtain an actual human penis for that scene. Our prop lady, Kathy Gleser, found it in Belgium in a store which sold certain exotic items. She was able to buy the penis, bring it through customs, and we used it in the movie. I was very happy to shoot that penis. As a matter of fact, I was proud to shoot it! One other curious fact I should add is that nobody outside of the production knew that was an actual severed penis. They thought it was a fake one. I guess now everybody will know. The rest of our special make-up effects on the picture were done by a make-up artist named Victor Cao, who had a business in nearby South Bend. He created things like the life-like hand we used to chop off Tom's finger and a prosthetic appliance for Laura Esterman's scarred face after she is shot. He also did a terrific blood-spurting effect for Sandor's death by stabbing. We were literally pumping torrents of the red stuff out of Fred Meyers' neck and it was exceedingly grim.

> *The most complicated and physically demanding passage to realize in* Suspended Animation *was the lengthy snowmobile chase, which takes place shortly after Kempton is liberated from certain death by his companions who have been diligently searching the hinterland for him. After killing Ann and wounding Vanessa, Tom's friends temporarily reattach his severed digit with tape moments before the three men flee the cabin on their snowmobiles. However, they soon realize they are being pursued across the dark and desolate wastes by a vengeful Vanessa. The sequence culminates rather spectacularly with a huge avalanche that threatens to consume both the hunter and her intended quarry.*

The thought of doing an elaborate chase sequence on snowmobiles was one of the first ideas that came to Dorothy and me, this aforementioned intention of doing "*Deliverance* on snowmobiles." For my part, the chase was an opportunity to do an action sequence in the film that was exciting and visually dramatic. Also, I really wanted to test myself as a director and create an action sequence that was purely mechanical in terms of its construction. It was like, okay, in order to see *this* we must have *that*, so we need to go *here* and then move over *there*. That was the kind of automated thinking that when into realizing it. It was interesting to work that way, but perhaps not as fulfilling as just coming up with something on the spot. The truth is we had to contend with too many variables—actors, stunts, coverage, weather conditions—to be able to just turn up with a camera and kind of wing it. On top of all that we were shooting a sequence where the characters were speeding along in snowmobiles and that presented its own unique problems and challenges.

The obvious thing about snowmobiling is it's a lot of fun. The fact you are moving so quickly through the snow is deeply exhilarating. I remember that when Dorothy and I were first researching *Suspended Animation*, we both got snowmobiles and took a trip up to Northern Michigan. Right from the beginning, while we were riding around up there, I quickly realized two things: first, that snowmobiles are fast and grotesquely overpowered vehicles. Second, they are also extremely dangerous. As if to illustrate this point, I crashed my snowmobile into the side of my barn here and put a hole in it. I hurt my leg during the crash and that wasn't fun at all. It was a painful reminder to me that these vehicles are not to be treated at all lightly. Snowmobiles are very much like motorcycles in that they are really powerful and compact and potentially lethal. So, with that thought very much at the forefront of our minds before we started shooting, we organized these sessions in which the actors were schooled in how to properly drive a snowmobile. They had to be shown how to do it, what the dangers were. We didn't want, nor could we afford, to have anybody get seriously hurt on the picture.

We shot some of the snowmobile chase here in Indiana, but, as I said, a lot of that sequence was realized up at a frozen lake in Canada. It was such a tremendous area, not only in terms of the visual look, but the fact it was so expansive we were able to go incredibly fast on the snowmobiles. We had the sequence play across a vast area, over fields of ice, through a forest, along a trail, etc, but that sequence was really built up in the editing. It was not difficult in itself to stage, but there were a number of stunts we shot that I didn't feel were well enough executed to be included in the finished film. For instance, at one point, Tom and his friend were almost hit by a passing train. I didn't feel we were able to bring that moment off technically as a stunt, certainly not at the level I thought was necessary. We did shoot the train stunt, but if you're working fast and everybody is freezing, and you're dealing with the limitations of your stuntmen, you have to weigh up how important the scene is to get; how much time and money you are wasting chasing something that might not look great anyway. More than that, you don't want to get anybody killed. When we were shooting it, the question became, okay, how close does the train actually come to hitting them? That was the problem we faced. Ultimately, I didn't think the stunt looked particularly convincing so I cut it. Another important thing we had to realize was the avalanche that brings the snowmobile chase to a dramatic end. The obvious choice was to do it either as a visual effect or incorporate some stock footage. We ended up doing both, its stock footage augmented with CGI. It was quite effective. I discovered there was a lot of stock footage of avalanches available—some of it very scary! We selected what was appropriate and, as always, then just matched that material to our stuff.

After Vanessa is supposedly killed during the avalanche, we cut to a scene where the Boulette sisters' cabin is being emptied of all its grisly contents by the police and forensic teams. It's worth remembering that when you make a picture, you can draw your imagery and inspiration from all kinds of places and sources: television, art, literature, other movies, even news events. Some of that imagery—like the big barrels containing human body parts being wheeled out and also the idea of drilling into a person's skull—has obvious echoes of the Jeffrey Dahmer case. I believe Dahmer, who let's not forget was a cannibalistic serial killer who murdered seventeen men and boys, is also name-checked in the movie at one point. He was very much in our minds when Dorothy and I were working on the script. I can vividly recall watching the news footage after Dahmer was arrested by the cops and his disturbing crimes were revealed. The authorities came walking out of his apartment carrying various boxes and bags, and steering barrels containing human remains. I was fascinated with that case, but it was some pretty grim stuff.

> *For Hancock, the underlying horror of* Suspended Animation *is that evil such as the Boulette sisters is entirely possible and contains the malevolent power to infect and destroy all those exposed to it. "It's what always fascinates us," he insists. "Knowing that kind of darkness lives in the world, and has a human face; we just can't let it go." This idea is given emphasis in the realization of Tom Kempton as a man tormented by nightmares and obsessed with his brush with death. It also recalls Hancock and Tristan's initial vision for the damaged Chief Brody in* Jaws 2.

The fact Tom is haunted by this traumatic event and becomes fixated on it was not a conscious holdover from *Jaws 2*. Actually, the whole thread was a painful expression of Dorothy's experiences with Bobby De Niro on *Weeds*. I can't emphasize how difficult she found Bob's problem with her playing Umstetter's girlfriend in the film to be. Dorothy just couldn't get over the fact she was unable to do that part and, as time passed, it continued to trouble her. Are you aware of that predicament where you can become obsessed with the person whom you feel has injured you? Over the years you think about them periodically—perhaps even incessantly—and the memory of them stings you each time it enters your head. That was what Dorothy was experiencing in regards to De Niro. She would have these recurring dreams in which Bob would appear and be nice to her. Then she would wake up, recall what had happened and be crazed by it. It was hard for Dorothy to come to terms with the situation on *Weeds*. Indeed, it took quite some time. She simply could not lose that nagging sense of rejection and injustice she was feeling. The fact that she was also beaten as a child (there was a lot of violence from her father and mother) made it difficult for Dorothy to get over things and move on. That was and remains important to her: how the memory of pain can linger and enslave you. I don't think De Niro ever knew the extent to which Dorothy was affected by his behavior on *Weeds*, and how strongly she felt about what had transpired. Well, Bob may have known about it, I don't know. Frankly, back then, we did not want to give him the satisfaction.

Suspended Animation was really an attempt to examine that idea: how difficult it is to shrug off memories of bad experiences, even when you know that dwelling and obsessing about them is doing you harm. Picking at psychic scabs is bad, but it's often a case of what you do with that negative stuff. Dorothy repurposed and redirected all of it into her writing and used it as inspiration. The character of Tom pretty much does the same. He is compelled to immerse himself in this dreadful experience he's had to the point where it dominates his every waking thought. He goes to the extremes of tracking down the daughter of one of his tormentors and including a representation of her in his animated film. In a way, he's turning personal tragedy and misfortune into art. I also think, in terms of what has happened to Dorothy as a child and everything, it's almost an effort to somehow understand evil and make sense of what has happened. More than once Dorothy has said to me, "I want to see the face of evil." That's what Tom is trying to do as well, although for most of us I would imagine that such a prospect—really looking upon evil up close and personal—would be the last thing we'd want to do. Still, Dorothy's curiosity is very strong.

When Dorothy and I talked about the various ways we could convey the depths of Tom's obsession, his work as an animator was one of the most obvious we had at our disposal. So, the animated sequences were written into the script and there was even a little more of it, too, that we didn't end up doing. There was some stuff detailing more of Tom's relationship to this evil female character in both the book and the screenplay, but that was pared back slightly as we felt it was a little too much. The animated sequences were done by some capable people in Chicago at a company called Calabash. There was a husband and wife team working there named Ed Newman and Monica Kendall. They had done a short film called *Stubble Trouble* that had been nominated for an Academy Award just as we started shooting *Suspended Animation*. I understand that Ed and Monica are no longer affiliated with the company, but they did some good work. They were also helpful when we were dressing the set for Tom's office space; Ed and Monica made it resemble more of an actual animator's workstation replete with an animation desk, lightbox, sketches, cels, that kind of thing.

Another thing Dorothy conceived with the intention of indicating Tom's deepening fascination with Vanessa Boulette was to write a scene where Kempton acquires a portrait of her as a beautiful young woman. We hired a local artist named Connie Kassal to do this lovely painting of a youthful Laura Esterman as a ballerina. I liked the idea of showing an image of Vanessa when she was a relatively sane person—a time in her life when she could possibly disguise her madness or it hadn't yet consumed her. I think the best portraits can often be powerful and evocative in detailing who a person is or was, and also what they aren't or never were. What I'm saying is the painting could be a lie or an idealized representation like the antiquated portraits of Kings and Queens that removed all the warts, wrinkles and bad teeth. If it's an old painting of a person that happens to be still alive, the subject may have changed their physical appearance and that adds poignancy, too. The portrait of Vanessa is rather haunting in that regard as it tells us how far she's fallen. Tom has to reconcile that image with the crazed harridan that was trying to kill and eat him.

> *In a sincere attempt at trying something different, Hancock and Tristan structured their screenplay as a series of distinct "chapters" which echoed the framework of the novel*

from which it was derived. Thus, the first forty minutes of Suspended Animation *consists of Kempton's brutal encounter with the Boulette sisters and the subsequent chase across the snow. The middle section is taken up with Tom's deepening psychological obsession: his pursuit of Clara Hansen and subsequent meeting with her troubled son, Sandor, leading to a violent passage in which the teenager is fatally stabbed in the neck and tasered after trying to rape and mutilate his own mother. The final section of the film details the drawn-out confrontation with the resurrected Vanessa in Tom's Malibu home and her eventual "re-destruction," as well as Clara's inadvertent death and a brief epilogue which reveals that the threat is far from over.*

Dorothy and I decided to structure the movie in this fashion as we thought it was a far more involving way to tell our story. A result of doing it, I think, is the audience received a lot more value for money as we gave them a movie and then pretty much integrated a sequel within that same movie. But I thought this approach also presented certain problems in that *Suspended Animation*—and the irony of the title was not lost on me—threatened to grind to a halt in the middle. I was aware of this during the writing stage, the fact that the narrative seemed to break in half at a certain point, but was more conscious of its implications during the editing phase. I honestly did not know what to do about it. I wished it didn't, but, during my early discussions with Dorothy, I wasn't sure exactly how to remedy the problem. We could have possibly reorganized the narrative as a series of flashbacks and started with the pursuit of the daughter and then gradually revealed Tom's reasons for doing it. But, for some reason, that didn't work for me and I never attempted to experiment with the idea while we were editing. Looking back, it might have worked better if we had tried it. Maybe it would have been profitable and given the story a little more resonance. Who knows?

When people see the movie for the first time, they may think after viewing the early sections that the entire story will be set in the snowy wilderness. But after Tom comes back to California, the audience doesn't know where the film is going. Perhaps that makes them feel a bit uneasy as they basically have to reset their motors and start over again. They are literally and figuratively in new terrain as all the characters they've been introduced to, with the exception of Tom, have been killed off. *Suspended*

Animation begins as a straight horror movie but then it develops into more of a thoughtful family drama and a thriller. Maybe some people were disappointed by that aspect of it. They may have felt that the picture changes tracks completely and never fully recovers. That was something I was concerned about, I must admit, but I felt there was still enough in there to compel the attention of the audience and keep them gripped. I also thought it was a brave and unusual way to go—killing off nearly the entire cast, getting the whole "city versus country" opposition out of the way and attempting to tell a different story. When she is writing, Dorothy occasionally has a tendency to follow the Ouija Board in terms of what she is doing and where she is going with a story. If her instincts and imagination are telling her *that* is the direction the narrative should go in, that is indeed where it goes. Granted, it later becomes much harder to fix some of these issues if you haven't addressed them early on.

It occurs to me now that something interesting we could have tried would have been to make Tom Kempton a more creepy character and not so much the wholesome, likable hero. We could have played with the notion that the disturbing events he has experienced with the Boulette sisters has possibly affected him more negatively, resulting in him having profound psychological problems, dark thoughts and urges. That might have been more intriguing, but we didn't go that way. I feel that Tom's growing fascination with Clara is already somewhat impure anyway. I mean, what he does with her—hiring Clara as a model for his new animated feature in order to get close to her—is a little suspect when you think about it. It shows you just how profound his morbid obsession with Vanessa Boulette has become; how it dominates his thoughts and actions during the day, and haunts his dreams at night. The audience still feels that unseemliness, but we could have pushed the idea even further and had Kempton possibly exhibiting or repeating the same psychopathic characteristics of Vanessa that he suspects also reside within her daughter.

I find the idea of hereditary evil, and the question of whether or not evil genes can be passed down from one generation to the other, fascinating. That's the question Tom is wrestling with throughout his relationship with Clara. It's also something that Clara begins to ask herself when she learns of her unfortunate lineage. So, it's that whole nature versus nurture argument: are monsters born or are they made? I do think that hereditary or genetic evil exists, but I also feel that monsters can be created. It's strongly hinted in the film that Vanessa was made a monster due to the childhood abuse she suffered at the hands of her father, and the fact her own child was taken away from her and adopted by somebody else. Of course, not every person who has suffered abuse as a child grows up to be a monster. Some do, but certainly not all. Dorothy didn't become a monster after experiencing the abuse she endured as a child and was fortunate enough to be saved by a woman named Mabel Nichols. The *Herald-Tribune*, which was the second or third most important paper in New York, had, every spring and summer, a fundraising program to send poor kids from the city to the country to get fresh air. It was known as The *Herald-Tribune* Fresh Air Fund. Dorothy qualified because of poverty, but also because she'd spent sixteen months in a TB asylum in the East River. She was sent to a family in the suburbs and then on to Cape Cod where Mabel became her foster mother. Mabel then wanted to adopt her and became an important influence and source of support for Dorothy. Without that woman, Dorothy's life would have gone in a much different direction. So, to clarify, I think that evil people are both born and made, but I think they are mainly born. I feel that's the case with Sandor, who has been born an irredeemable psychopath.

The demise of Sandor is a tense and disturbing passage in the film. It culminates with Clara's decision to allow her son to bleed to death in her arms after stabbing him rather than calling for help, as she now understands the truth of who—or what—he is. She feels it's better he should die. This entire sequence is unremittingly dark. First, the idea of Clara being tied to a chair by her own child, who then proceeds to expose his mother's breasts before threatening to cut off her nipples and rape her, is fairly sick and creepy. There is obviously a disturbingly sexual and incestuous aspect to that act, but that's my wife for you! That's exactly how Dorothy's twisted imagination works. She is utterly unafraid to delve into the darkness. I find it interesting that a scene like that was written by a woman. Dorothy is extremely bloody-minded, not only in the aforementioned sense of venturing forth into these dark places, but also in regards to her inventing moments of despicable violence. She's a little like the Marquis de Sade that way. Incidentally, in her mind, she firmly believes in amputation and other near-Medieval acts of torture as a form of punishment for certain criminal acts. For instance, Dorothy feels that child molesters should have their dicks cut off. I mean, she is quite a handful when you get her started on a particularly emotive subject. She is a formidable woman with very strong views on things. She isn't squeamish.

Clara's own death, where she is accidentally shot by Vanessa, seems a cruel end to a rather desperate life because Clara is a character that the audience have hopefully come to like. I believe I did have some initial reservations about killing her off, but Dorothy wanted to do it. She *wanted* Clara to die that way. At one point, we did have a different version of the climax—and this variation may have only existed in the book—where Tom and Clara actually ended up together and it was Tom's wife and unborn child who are in fact killed by Vanessa. After the terrible events of that night are over, Tom and Clara were going to eventually find each other again and live happily together. But I don't think it was something I ever really wanted to try with the movie because that ending would have been too stringy and uncomfortable. I mean, once the bad woman is dead, to have had a coda where Tom comes together with her daughter just wouldn't have worked. It seemed a little post-coital as it were, and possibly a disgrace to the memory of his recently deceased wife. I don't think the audience would have accepted it. They would have probably viewed it as a betrayal.

However, one scene I did shoot but later cut from the finished film (it was the only major scene I shot that was dropped during editing) featured Tom and Clara making love on the floor of his bungalow at the studio. This was going to occur shortly after the big emotional outburst Clara has when she learns that Vanessa Boulette is her mother. I lost that scene because I didn't stage it very well and it felt somewhat clumsy in the proceedings. Love scenes are surprisingly hard to do and they can often feel forced within the context of a story where two people meet and an emotional charge of some kind occurs between them. Clara was clearly vulnerable at this moment and it felt too coldly opportunistic on Tom's part to take advantage of her. There was also the small matter of Tom having a pregnant wife at home and the love scene potentially compromised both his character and his relationship to the audience. That was the thought I had at the time. Oddly enough, that betrayal was what was so interesting to me, the fact that he was deeply flawed and damaged. I now feel it would have been an intriguing development and was another opportunity we failed to seize in making Tom a much darker and more conflicted protagonist. Again, there is an inherent perversity about the way he vigorously and obsessively chases after Clara. She is also a beautiful woman, so it would be no surprise if his fascination would then develop into sexual areas as well. Tom wants to see if Clara is crazy or not and perhaps, in his thinking, fucking her might have been one way of finding out.

The final scene of *Suspended Animation*, our "blood feud" coda, reveals that Phillip Boulette has been released from prison. It's strongly implied that he will now come looking for Kempton and take his revenge. Admittedly, that ending hints at a sequel but I had no burning desire to do one. *Suspended Animation* is its own self-contained story and we had no wish to repeat ourselves. Also, because the picture wasn't enough of a financial hit, it frankly didn't generate enough interest to warrant a sequel. Our ending is very circular in that we know the horror and the evil will start all over again. We understand that it's only a matter of time before Tom's past catches up with him once more. The cycle of evil continues and Tom will have to fight for his life and the lives of his family as he did before. In that regard the climax of *Suspended Animation*—at least restricted to that final scene—is fairly traditional and conventional, but that's fine. I don't mind meeting certain expectations the audience may have of the genre, whether those expectations are high or low. It's okay, because I see that ending as once again illustrating what I said to you earlier regarding *Let's Scare Jessica to Death*: you can't ever defuse or defeat evil. It's eternal and impervious; it's always going to be there, patiently lurking and waiting. We simply have to learn how to fight it and resist it with integrity and love.

> *Shot in 2001,* Suspended Animation *was not sold until the summer of 2003 after First Run Features acquired the North American rights for an undisclosed sum. Founded in 1979 by a group of filmmakers determined "to advance the distribution of independent film," First Run was initially under the stewardship of Fran Spielman and, during its formative years, quickly earned a reputation for procuring a number of highly regarded documentaries. By 1984, the company was being run by Seymour Wishman who later distributed such acclaimed documentaries as Michael Apted's* Up Series *(1964-present) and Eugene Jarecki's* The Trials of Henry Kissinger *(2002), as well as fictional films like Kim Ki-duk's gruesome horror tale* The Isle *(2000) and Matteo Garrone's Italian noir-drama* The Embalmer *(2002).*

The reason for the delay in the release of *Suspended Animation* was down to the fact I take a long time in post-production. When I'm editing, mixing, doing all the sound work, and trying to get the score just right, I like to consider all these things carefully. This period is then followed by us submitting the film to various companies, before finding a distributor to release it. All of that took some time to accomplish on this particular movie. We'd had no producer's rep on *A Piece of Eden*, as I didn't think we needed one. By that time I'd been in the business for more than thirty years. I'd formed a lot of connections and relationships with some important people, so I didn't think I needed anybody to get me through the door. Subsequently, you wonder if that was the right decision or not. Maybe we could have used a strong advocate for the picture, but I had previously made several independent films that had secured good distribution and I didn't feel I needed a producer's rep. The thing about reps is they don't like to consider a movie without a name actor. It makes their job tougher. We had no stars in *Suspended Animation*, so some people didn't take us seriously. John Sloss, who is a successful lawyer and film agent, had *Suspended Animation* on his desk for three months without ever looking at it. We screened the movie for several distributors, but got the same response from each of them: "Sorry, I don't know how to sell this. Where are the names?" We had hired a Los Angeles attorney named Robert Marshall (who was Bert Fields' second in command) to represent the film and paid him a considerable fee. This didn't help us much in the grand scheme of things, as I ended up selling the movie to a guy I'd known for years in New York.

This gentleman was Seymour Wishman, who was the President of First Run Features when they bought *Suspended Animation*. He's enjoyed an interesting career. Seymour was involved in law and politics before entering the movie business and has written plays, screenplays and novels. So, he is an astute and articulate guy. Seymour is also an old friend, and Dorothy and I still stay in his wonderful townhouse whenever we go to New York. I recall that during our early discussions, one of the things First Run wanted was a new title for the movie. I never felt that *Suspended Animation* was a good title and John Lahr had suggested we call it *Mayhem*, which I thought was a more suitable label for a scary picture. Unfortunately, Seymour did not want his company to release a movie called *Mayhem*. No doubt this was because he does a lot of worthy documentaries and he didn't think that a film called *Mayhem* belonged in his esteemed catalogue. I disagreed, but Seymour refused to let me change the title. It simply had to be called *Suspended Animation*. I like and admire Seymour, but I must admit his decision bothered me. I felt like telling him, "Hey, you have only been involved in this project for a month but I've been toiling on it for more than two years!" For that reason alone it seemed only right to me that the title should be my call. Nevertheless, to keep him happy and maintain our good relations, I politely backed down on that. It's now my understanding that *Suspended Animation* was indeed released in parts of Europe as *Mayhem*. So, make of that what you will.

The whole process of selling and distributing a movie can be fraught. I have several horror stories I can tell concerning the ruthlessness of foreign sales agents and *Suspended Animation* is a case in point: after our upsetting experiences on *A Piece of Eden*, we intended to be much more cautious in our dealings with foreign sales agents. We did not want to get ripped off again and took our time in finding somebody to work with. We eventually found a couple of guys at the Paragon Film Group, namely Matt McCombs, who was the CEO, and Scott Bedno who was with the sales. We told them the story of what had happened to us; how Eric Louzil of Lions Share had fucked us and disappeared with our money. They listened sympathetically to us, and then said, "Oh, we would *never* do something like that." Those assurances made us feel a lot more secure, but then *they* kept the money, too! Can you believe that? It took a while for me to accept that the same thing had happened twice, although Louzil was far more ruthless than Bedno. But what happened to us was terrible. For someone to come in at the end of a long and arduous process, and just steal from filmmakers like that is utterly abhorrent. What these people then do is they dissolve the company and you can't find them anywhere. They simply vanish in the air like smoke and are gone. You might eventually track them down at some other company—it's my understanding that Bedno is now Vice President of International Sales for Voltage Pictures—but they won't return phone-calls and, somewhat conveniently, they are never in their office. It's always that kind of duplicity you are dealing with. There is just no way that you can get that money back. It's incredibly painful and depressing.

> *Rather fittingly for its grim subject matter,* Suspended Animation *was released on October 31, 2003, in New York, and then later in Los Angeles, Chicago, and other markets. The film engendered a diverse critical reaction that ran the gamut from wildly enthusiastic to outright hostility. Kevin Thomas of the* Los Angeles Times *hailed it as "a bold and unqualified triumph, [a] nifty trick and treat for Halloween that is arguably Hancock's best film ever." Although many welcomed the fact that Hancock had*

> "returned to his horror roots," this judgment proved to be at variance with most reviewers. Ronnie Scheib of Variety characterized Suspended Animation as "a psychological drama cum genteel shocker that's long on ambition and short on delivery." Writing for the Chicago Tribune, Ellen Fox felt the movie was hampered by several self-defeating structural problems: "This film should have clocked in at ninety minutes, rather than almost two hours. A good, healthy scissor-snipping might have allowed some of its quirkier aspects (like the use of a stun gun and a jaw-dropping lab result) to stand out more." These adverse opinions were positively subdued in comparison with Scott Brown's rant for Entertainment Weekly: "Describing what's bad about this movie is like describing what's orange about an orange, but suffice it to say that the best performance is given by a crucified raccoon."

Wow! I really have no response to that. I was unhappy with the critical reaction to *Suspended Animation*, but before I tackle that I want to talk about something else I was unhappy about: the way the film was sold. I felt it required a more traditional horror movie campaign. The poster and DVD cover featured the curious image of Alex McArthur's eye peering through a hole, which seemed too ambiguous and nebulous to me. I didn't quite know what we were saying with that. What did it mean? We needed to have something that caught your attention and let people know right off the bat that this was a horror movie. The ad campaign for *Let's Scare Jessica to Death* left no doubt in anybody's mind what kind of picture it was, and we should have followed that example. This is why I still feel *Suspended Animation* should have had a more traditional horror film title; something with a lot more bite. For instance, I was recently informed that the movie was released in Brazil under the title *Mutilated*. I wasn't aware of this, but *Mutilated* is a very strong title—probably too strong. I would have much preferred the film to have been called *Mayhem*, which is a comfortable step back from that but still has a little threat to it. For me, the title of *Suspended Animation*, other than being just a little too cute, is somewhat obscure. I mean, that could have been the title for anything from a science fiction movie to a sitcom.

Despite some of the violence that's depicted in the picture—shootings, stabbings, the severing of human parts—we didn't have any problems with the censors. They understood the context in which the violence existed and, as much as it was strong in one or two instances, it was neither unreasonable nor excessive. I believe that *Suspended Animation* was released unrated and I didn't see any disadvantages to that. I daresay it often adds a certain interest. In terms of the audience I was trying to reach with the film, it wasn't strictly the horror fanatics per se; I was making it for everyone. I was trying to reach as many people as possible. Was I making it for young people? No, not especially. I don't know to what extent I actually thought about the audience on this one. To be honest, my thoughts revolved more around just delivering a solid and scary picture that the general audience could enjoy. I do recall wanting to make *Suspended Animation* as scary as I could, but I don't believe it's as frightening or as emotionally affecting as *Let's Scare Jessica to Death*. Forgive my lack of modesty here, but I don't think there are too many horror movies around that are.

I also didn't make *Suspended Animation* for the critics. I think that fact is born out by some of the quotes you just read to me. I do recall us getting the positive review from Kevin Thomas, who much preferred *Suspended Animation* to *Bang the Drum Slowly*. I remember Thomas used his review as a kind of club to once again beat *Bang the Drum Slowly* with, as he had never liked that movie. I found some of his comments amusing, I must say, but Thomas is a peculiar guy. I've known him for many years and, if I'm not mistaken, he preferred *Baby Blue Marine* to *Bang the Drum Slowly* also. But I was happy and appreciative of the fact he liked *Suspended Animation*. He even described it as "scary, stylish and compelling," which was a quote we ended up using on the poster. Conversely, Dave Kehr's review in *The New York Times* was a little less enthusiastic ("a sturdy, well-made piece that never quite overcomes its structural flaws"), as were several other rather bluntly-worded notices. Nonetheless, as surely as oranges are orange, you expect that type of reaction and there were plenty of reviews that were fairly respectful.

Some critics did feel that the picture was too lopsided and long, and that it started out promisingly but then petered out. I guess they were responding to what I mentioned earlier: the fact that the movie almost comes to a halt following the tense and exciting early sections. That's the point where you are likely to feel that it's unbalanced or disjointed. I think the middle section, even with the obvious change of pace, is crowded with enough small incident and engaging character stuff to grab you. Admittedly, there is a trend in horror movies today which demands that you have a big scare or a moment of gore every few minutes in order to keep the audience excited and interested. I think that if you can do that it's a good thing, because people now have an emotional expectation of that happening. So, if you can gratify that expectation successfully without compromising your story and characters, or the tone and tenor of your picture, I say go ahead and do it. But I just couldn't see how to do that in *Suspended Animation* without turning it into something else completely, or by sacrificing some of the other things I wanted to do.

As the director of *Suspended Animation*, I naturally hoped to make a good picture that would provide the best possible return for my investors. I had a financial obligation to them that I wanted to satisfy. In the case of both *A Piece of Eden* and *Suspended Animation*, that desire for the film to be successful was felt all the more acutely as we would run into our investors at the local supermarket, or at the mall, or the movie theater. That brought its own attendant pressures as there was simply no way of getting away from them—other than to move away and that was never going to happen. So, I had all my fingers and toes crossed that these movies would do well. Sadly, *Suspended Animation* did poor business in Los Angeles and New York, better of course around here in Indiana, but not wildly so. I believe Seymour opened it in Portland or Seattle—and maybe in Boston, too—on the basis of the extremely positive review in the *L.A. Times*, but it didn't do much business up there either.

I suspect that some of the things I've spoken about may have colored my perceptions of the film over the years. When I finished *Suspended Animation*, I was not as happy with the picture as I imagined I would be when I first started shooting it. That was a strange feeling to have, but not an entirely unexpected one. I was aware there was a debilitating absence of humor in the movie as I was making it. Again, that problem could have been solved by Dorothy playing Laura's part. I don't want to go on about that but it's true. As weird as it may sound, I happen to believe that most of the film's problems stem from that one thing. It's fascinating how one decision you make on a movie can have a seismic effect on its overall success. Looking back, I did not enjoy the experience of shooting *Suspended Animation*. It was difficult, not only because of Laura's profoundly black depression, but because shooting in almost waist-deep snow is exhausting. I had learned on *Prancer* that simply walking around in the snow from the actors to the camera and back again was incredibly energy-sapping. As you get older and continue to direct movies, it's not your mental faculties that degenerate it's your physical stamina. It's your ability to stay on your feet and maintain your energy levels and concentration. By the time *Suspended Animation* rolled around I was that little bit older and it was occasionally very tough.

> *Ignoring their avowed desire never to make two films of the same genre consecutively, shortly after completing* Suspended Animation, *Hancock and Tristan began developing a follow-up horror project that once again tackled the themes of cannibalistic murder and homicidal men-killing women. The untitled film was to explore the morbid crimes of Norwegian émigré Belle Gunness, a notorious serial killer known as "The Black Widow" who (alongside Hancock himself) is among LaPorte's most famous residents. Born Brynhild Paulsdatter Størseth in Selbu, Norway, in 1859, Gunness was an unusually large woman who stood six feet tall and weighed more than 200 lbs. The total number of her victims varies between sources, but it is estimated that she murdered somewhere in the region of forty men and children between 1884 and 1908. Her apparent motives for these crimes were the collecting of life insurance and other cash and valuables, as well as the callous disposing of any witnesses to her atrocities. Gunness was declared dead in 1908 after her farmhouse burnt to the ground. Four human skeletons were discovered in the ruins, three of which were identified as Gunness' foster children. The fourth, believed to be that of Gunness herself, was inexplicably missing its skull.*

Since she is our very own serial killer here in LaPorte, Belle Gunness was a subject of fascination for Dorothy and me for a little while. In truth, Dorothy was more interested in her story than I ever was, but I agreed it could potentially make a good period horror movie. There was a lot grim stuff for us to play with, I guess. Belle was a decidedly big and imposing woman who had immigrated to America from Norway in the early 1880s. At some point she changed her name to the more pronounceable "Belle Gunness" as Brynhild Paulsdatter Størseth was too much of a mouthful for the locals. She then corresponded with a number of men, luring them to her home on the promise of romance and the sharing of her farm and the delicious Norwegian desserts she promised to make them. Usually

Belle would ask these poor guys to bring whatever money they had, as well as a warm fur coat and boots. Inevitably, these gentlemen would then disappear arousing some suspicion in the local community. Rumor has it that Belle was turning her victims into sausage which she later sold to various citizens around the town.

The suggestion that big Belle disappeared, and the headless corpse found in the smoldering ruins of her home did not belong to her, gives the case an added frisson. It means that—very much like the more famous case of Jack the Ripper—the story lives on in some ways, as she may never have answered for her crimes. It makes us ponder exactly what fate befell her (some think that shortly before burning down her own home, Belle skipped town after withdrawing a large amount of cash from her bank accounts and later assumed a new identity). Dorothy and I toyed with the idea of doing a picture that dramatized these events, but it eventually came to nothing and we dropped the project altogether. Was I put off by Belle's size? Maybe, but something made me not want to do it. Perhaps it was the lack of ambiguity. We ultimately felt the story had too many similarities with *Suspended Animation*, with Vanessa Boulette already being a contemporary rendering of Belle Gunness. That was part of the reason why we abandoned the project, the other part being the fact I did not want to make two horror movies in a row. I wanted to try something different, as is my way.

18 *The Looking Glass* (2015)

AFTER SUSPENDED ANIMATION, it would be more than a decade before Hancock shot his next film. In February 2013, several charming and revealing videos were uploaded on YouTube that detailed the director and his wife's efforts to make yet another feature in their home state of Indiana. This latest FilmAcres production—announced as Swan Song but eventually re-titled The Looking Glass— would be a family drama scripted by Tristan, one that exhibited the same sensitivity and feeling as their previous work in its delicate evocation of the commonplace. It would also be laced with a surfeit of intimate autobiographical elements, representing a further blurring of the real with the reel for its creators. Once again Hancock and Tristan called on the support, participation and cooperation of the local community in order to make the picture a reality. In one short video titled "The Town that Made a Movie," a visibly emotional Hancock declared to camera his heartfelt ambitions for the project: "You know, here Dorothy and I are coming to the end of our lives and we very much want to pass on all we know. I mean, that's part of this film, it's part of the content of this film, and it's part of our reason for doing this film."

The Looking Glass *concerns a troubled thirteen year-old girl named Julie, who arrives in a small Indiana town to live with her widowed grandmother, Karen. Julie's mother is recently deceased and her life with her father and stepmother in Pittsburgh has proved difficult in* recent months. Disturbed by the unpleasant atmosphere at home, Julie feels she has no alternative but to stay with her elderly relative—despite the fact they are nearly strangers. A former actress of stage and screen, and something of a local celebrity, Karen has her own hardships: she is battling the debilitating onset of Alzheimer's disease as well as resolving her own lingering grief at losing her daughter to cancer. Desperate to form a meaningful connection with her only grandchild and provide Julie with a loving and stable environment, their relationship gets off to a rocky start with the two butting heads at every turn. Julie is sullen and solitary, preferring to immerse herself in an iPad than engage in conversation; whereas Karen is impatient and set in her ways. Although she sees much of her stubborn self in Julie, Karen is at a loss as how to reach the teenager and seeks the advice of Terry, her caretaker, on how best to deal with her.

One afternoon as she potters about the garden, Karen overhears Julie singing in the kitchen and is struck by the purity and beauty of her voice. Recognizing her considerable talent, Karen encourages Julie to audition for a musical production of Alice's Adventures in Wonderland that the local theater is mounting. Julie is initially reluctant to be involved, but eventually agrees to try out for the play. After impressing the producers, she gets the part. Meanwhile, Julie begins dating Anthony, a handsome teenager she meets at the beach, who eventually betrays her with another girl. Utterly despondent, Julie attempts suicide by drinking iodine and has the poison flushed from her system at the hospital. Shortly after this incident, Karen suffers a heart attack. She survives but now begins exhibiting more obvious symptoms of Alzheimer's. The presence of Julie's father and stepmother, who have both traveled from Pittsburgh to be with her, exacerbates the already discernible tension. However, Julie recovers and resumes rehearsals for the forthcoming musical. As the bond between them continues to deepen, some of the terrible grief Karen and Julie feel at their mutual loss is lifted.

The reasons why Dorothy and I wanted to make *The Looking Glass* were very precise and sincere: yes, we wanted to pass on all we know, but we also wanted to express something about creativity, mortality and love. In order to achieve these aims, we kind of went for broke with this picture. I mean, one of the things we considered before we started the project was that *Suspended Animation*, and to a certain degree *A Piece of Eden*, were both like genre movies. With *The Looking Glass* we wanted to make a film that really represented *us* at this present stage of our lives, everything we felt about growing old and one's efforts to communicate to the younger generation the wisdoms one accumulates throughout a lifetime. It's only natural that when you get to the age that Dorothy and I are, you begin to reflect on your life and speculate about what kind of legacy you are leaving behind. There will come a day—sooner rather than later—when we will no longer be here and that eventuality fills me sorrow. But I take comfort from the thought that I've accomplished certain things as an artist and a man that have had meaning. I hope I've not only touched people's lives with my movies, but also touched those I've worked with and those I've taught. With that thought very much in mind, we wanted to make a picture that would inspire a new generation of filmmakers to make personal movies about personal subjects.

So, we conceived the story of a dying grandmother who is trying to inculcate her teenage granddaughter with all of her courage and life-force. In a sense, this woman's approaching demise effectively makes her mission a race against time. She has to galvanize this young girl and impart all her wisdom and hope before it's too late. In that regard and almost every other, *The Looking Glass* is a deeply personal film. Before we started writing it, Dorothy had been diagnosed with Alzheimer's disease and this became one of the motivating factors for her wanting to write the script. We both thought we better do this film quickly, while Dorothy could still do it, as Alzheimer's had already begun to impact on her life. It was not only getting harder for her to write in terms of Dorothy's ability to structure a story (though her gift for dialogue and detail was unaffected) it was going to be harder for her to remember the lines when she was acting. For all her personal struggles with the disease, Dorothy is still as determined and funny as she's always been. She remains wonderful company at dinner parties and still has a lot of the old fire inside her. Another important thing was the fact that our daughter, Alexandra, has terminal breast cancer and we actually thought she would be gone by the time the picture opened. Thankfully, she's still alive because she's on permanent chemotherapy. But the idea of an elderly woman with Alzheimer's who has lost her daughter and was a former actress makes *The Looking Glass* an extremely intimate film that touches on some sensitive nerves.

Now, it could be argued that all my films are autobiographical in a manner of speaking, but some films are more autobiographical than others. From the beginning of my moviemaking career I have invested details and memories of my life into a lot of my pictures, even projects that I didn't write. I may not have originated *Baby Blue Marine*, *California Dreaming* and *Prancer*, but they all have something of me in them—for better or for worse—as I made a lot of the big creative choices in those movies that made them what they are. That can be read as a form of autobiography, can it not? It seems perfectly feasible to me. *A Piece of Eden* and *The Looking Glass* are more resolutely autobiographical, as is *Suspended Animation* in a way, but there is an argument to be made that any film a director makes is autobiographical as it comes from you; your thoughts and feelings and observations, everything that you've learned and has made you the person and artist that you are. Dorothy is also committed to using autobiography in her writing. She understands that it's a way of accessing a truth that can be beneficial to the work. You are closer to it in so many ways as again it reflects your life. I admire Dorothy's bravery in doing that. I really do. Since the character of Karen is getting confused and is losing her memory, this is her last chance to fill her granddaughter with all of her spirit. There was a discernible poignancy in that element, which I think we could all feel. With Dorothy writing the script and playing Karen, *The Looking Glass* was very close to the bone but we are both hugely proud of that fact.

Once again, in order to get this picture off the ground, I asked for support from the local community. They were as enthusiastic as ever about providing it and the response was extremely good, wonderful even. The amount of cooperation we received was a result of the previous experiences the locals had had on *Prancer*, *A Piece of Eden* and *Suspended Animation*. Everybody in LaPorte was excited at the prospect of possibly doing another movie. We got twenty-five restaurants that fed us on a revolving basis, all on deferment; we got motels for cast and crew to stay at, all on deferment; we got cars for them to drive, again on deferment; and we got a high number of volunteers. I sold the project to the community in terms of what the film could offer them: money and experience, but it was not so much about the money. I was very open about that and told them, "Don't do it for the dough!" We pitched it to them as a chance to be a part of something that they could feel proud of—"the Town that Made a Movie"—and showed the area in a nice way. We felt those were worthy ambitions. I mean, it could be argued that both *The Looking Glass* and *A Piece of Eden* are effectively extended commercials for the Northern Indiana/Lower Michigan area. The place looks extremely pretty in both movies.

I said in an interview that *The Looking Glass* is the community's movie, but I don't really feel that way. I hope I don't sound unkind or ungrateful, I'm just being honest, but their assistance was invaluable. As I said, the movie was all about imparting wisdom, hope and courage from one generation to another and in keeping with that theme, we had seasoned professionals working with the next generation of filmmakers in the Midwest. My reasons for doing the film were not entirely altruistic, but it was certainly a massive part of why I wanted to make it. Thankfully, I was able to achieve everything I wanted and secure everything I needed within the budgetary constraints, as the script was written to be made within very close budgetary restraints. *The Looking Glass* didn't take a long time to get set up. We decided we were going to make a movie regardless of whether or not we could raise money. Dorothy and I felt that if we ended up making it for the $30,000 or $40,000 we had, we were fully prepared and committed to do just that. We doggedly set out to secure more financing and were able to with surprising speed. I think the fact we kept insisting that we were going to make a movie—again, even if we couldn't raise a penny we were still going to make a movie—was invigorating. That was it, I feel, simply our stated determination to make this picture a reality. I've learned that if people start thinking and believing that something is going to happen, they are able to get behind it.

Also, the long hiatus between *Suspended Animation* and *The Looking Glass* compelled me to get another picture off the ground. I simply *had* to make it and nothing was going to stand in my way. So, we wrote the picture for locations that we knew we could obtain and control like our own house and garden for instance, which doubled as Karen's residence. We used a variety of locations in LaPorte and other places: we shot the beach scenes where Julie and her new friends hang out on Lake Michigan; the scene where Karen and Julie visit a café was in shot in the American Café, a place I frequent in LaPorte; the fairground scene where Julie and Karen confront Julie's unfaithful beau was filmed at our LaPorte County Fair; and the hospital where Julie is taken after her suicide attempt was our local hospital. We received a lot of cooperation from the hospital's staff and administration, as we'd shot a scene there for *Suspended Animation* and they kindly allowed us to return. The sequences where Julie and the locals audition for the *Alice in Wonderland* musical were shot at two places: the Dune Summer Theatre, the community summer stock theater in Michigan City, and Indiana University in South Bend, which is where we shot the rehearsals for *Alice* as well as the opening night performance. The university has a big, deep stage—it's actually the deepest stage I've ever seen and is something like three times the depth of a Broadway stage. So, we were able to obtain permission to shoot there and I was ecstatic with that set. It really looked the way that a lot of theater productions look. It's a kind of Berliner Ensemble set, very real in terms of the placement of objects in space, particularly those two lines of real trees that Grace walks down. It was nice to have that depth to work with.

Of equal importance to the locations, I knew we could cast the film as we'd written certain parts for specific actors. Obviously, the role of Karen was reserved for Dorothy, but we also wrote the part of Terry the caretaker for Jeff Puckett who had previously appeared in *A Piece of Eden* and *Suspended Animation*. *The Looking Glass* was a non-Screen Actors Guild picture, so we didn't have to contend with issues and complications regarding union rules and what have you. I wanted enough time to be able to shoot the picture. I mean, you make low-budget movies by filming them in eighteen or twenty-five days which can be uncomfortably tight. Theoretically, I suppose I could still do that, but I didn't want to. I wanted the time to improvise and do another take and get the lighting nice. I didn't want to slop through a picture the way you slop through episodic television.

In order to do the film right, I required something close to forty or forty-one days and I traded a lot to secure that schedule. Principally, I traded SAG actors and a more experienced crew to make it happen, but it was worth it. I mean, we had grips from Columbia College where I was teaching, who were volunteers. Everybody worked for free on the movie. Nobody was paid. Well, the sound man was paid, and so was the assistant cameraman, because everything had to be in focus and with a dialogue picture you need to be able to understand what the actors are saying. But those were the only two individuals who received payment. Even Misha Suslov came in and shot the film with no salary. I was able to pull that feat off as I had given Misha a lot of work in the past (aside from the movies we'd done together, he had also shot all of my Kmart commercials). So, I called in a lot of favors from friends.

Auditions for The Looking Glass *were situated at the LaPorte County Library. Hancock had earlier convinced the library's officials to donate a conference room and scheduled the first pre-production meetings there in early 2013. The response to the announcement of his latest project was immediate and aroused much excitement in the surrounding communities. In a repeat of Rebecca Harrell's casting in* Prancer, *one of the people who tried out for the film was a thirteen year-old unknown named Grace Tarnow, whom Hancock would eventually cast in the crucial role of Julie. Once again working with a lively mix of professionals and amateurs, the shoot would require the filmmaker to demonstrate his renowned and sensitive handling of actors in order to ensure a dependably high level of performance.*

I basically broadcast it to everyone: "Okay, folks, we're going to make another picture and anybody who is interested in getting involved is more than welcome." I then deliberately chose a small room at the local library that would hold around seventy-five people and crossed my fingers. Much to my surprise and delight, somewhere in the region of 300 or 400 people turned up! That really helped to generate a lot of interest and excitement as there's nothing like a long line of people not being able to get in somewhere to make them think that something worthwhile and important is happening. We then organized a weekend where we auditioned possible actors. I brought in Susan Willett, my trusted casting director for many years, and together we saw something like 600 people. One of those people was a pretty young girl named Grace Tarnow. She came in and read a little bit and sang a song or two. Almost immediately we thought, "Oh, my God! Who is *this*?!" She was utterly captivating and the hairs on the back of my neck were standing on end. We then read her a couple more times, but I knew in my heart she was the one to play Julie.

It's worth noting that the actual genesis of *The Looking Glass* involved another pretty young blonde girl of considerable ability named Sophie Thatcher. There is a little theater up in Three Oaks, Michigan, which is about ten miles north of LaPorte, known as the Acorn Theatre. Dorothy and I had attended a production there that was fashioned like a tryout for a Broadway musical. It was about a young girl who adores the singer Ethel Merman and becomes her go-fer. Sophie played the youngster, and she had an incredible voice and could belt out songs just like Merman. After seeing her perform, I said to Dorothy, "Here is a young talent that nobody knows. Why don't we do a movie where this kid plays your granddaughter? You should try and come up with a good story for it." Dorothy then wrote a screenplay in which an aspiring teenage singer is being molested by her father. That idea worried me a little, as it seemed to be somewhat over-the-top and melodramatic. We then read Sophie for the role and discovered that while she had been wonderful in the musical tryout we'd seen, she was not an actress at the level we required. I realized we had to find somebody else to play Julie who could deliver a performance for us. So, we started to cast that weekend and found Grace Tarnow. We were just incredibly lucky. Truly, it was one of those magical occurrences where the right person walks in the room at exactly the right time.

What enraptured me most about Grace was that she seemed so real. She'd had no previous acting experience whatsoever, but she possessed this remarkable ability to find the camera. Wherever we put it, wherever we hid it away, she would find it. Everybody connected with the project felt we had discovered somebody special. For instance, when we were about two-thirds of the way through filming, I remember Misha being totally knocked out by Grace. He came to me one day and was shaking his head: "How does she know how to do all this stuff? How is it possible?" I mean, aside from her ability and instincts, Grace matched perfectly between different set-ups and takes. If she sat up on the couch, or did this or that, it always worked. She was simply a natural, just an astounding find. I'm not exaggerating when I say I had the same reaction to Grace as I did when Robert De Niro auditioned for *Bang the Drum Slowly*. I suddenly felt, *Oh boy! Here we go! This is it!* You see, I do love a good actor. What I prefer to do is just sit there and watch the actor do it without my having to direct them. In a perfect world I simply want to be a fan and gush: "Oh, that's awfully good!" I don't want to have to fix the performance, or struggle to draw it out of them.

With Grace that was never a problem. Even though she was completely new to film and acting, she had such maturity and flair. That's so rare. As a matter of fact, it wasn't difficult for her to improvise new material during shooting as she just fearlessly took to everything like the proverbial duck to water. For instance, when we first started rehearsals, it didn't look like Grace was going to be able to dance all those complex numbers for the *Alice in Wonderland* musical. Then we started to shoot and she pretty much featured in every scene, which meant we had to work out in the schedule when she could go and work with the choreographer, Irina Tsikurishvili, in order to perfect all the moves she needed to execute. Despite my having some nagging concerns about this, Grace simply went away and did it. No problem! She somehow managed to find the time and muster the stamina to shoot a long day and then go off to work with Irina. I was so impressed by her commitment to the role and Grace managed to end up dancing to a fairly reasonable level, all things considered.

Another important consideration was the relationship between Grace and Dorothy. It needed to be good if the film was going to succeed. Early on Dorothy rather shrewdly said to me, "Let's really spend a lot of time in advance with Grace and bond with her." So, we would pick Grace up after school around three times a week and go shopping for clothes, or have a bite to eat, or she'd come to our house and we'd read through the various scenes. Throughout this process Dorothy and Grace quickly fell in love, which was wonderful to see. They developed a real closeness, and it became a deep relationship and still is. One of the interesting things about Grace's performance is that certain things appear to be inadvertent. Those moments can be hard for an actor because they try to *act* them. But with Grace it really was unintentional.

Here's a good example: there's the scene where Karen and Julie are sitting down by the pond and Karen has been advising her on singing: "You mustn't gesture right on the word, you have to gesture before the word," and all that. Then, after they talk a little, Karen touches Julie's face and says softly, "You're a deep soul and we'll never forget each other." That was actually filmed on the first day of principal photography and Grace's look there of trying not to cry as she listens to Dorothy was entirely inadvertent. I remember they finished the lines for the scene, and I said, "Keep rolling." I then quietly said to Dorothy, "Tell her how you feel about her." And she did, Dorothy speaking to Grace in these hushed tones, almost like a whisper. So, that wonderful little moment there with Grace looking like she is about to burst listening to those words, not wanting to break down and cry, was improvised. Elsewhere in the film, there are scenes where it's kind of miraculous what Grace does. Whether it's a gesture, or a word, or a look, she really has an innate sense of truth as an actress.

Dorothy insists that one of my strengths as a director is I give actors freedom and don't impose my will on them. When I teach directing I try to communicate this approach to my students, but I'm continually frustrated about my inability to get through to them on that score. They all have the disease of wanting to talk too much and don't know when it's better for a director to simply listen or remain silent. There is a bullying aspect to directing that manifests most visibly in the relationship between a director and his or her actors. Admittedly, I contracted this disease myself as a novice. When I first started directing at Harvard, I *directed* a lot more. I'd be demonstrating everything and trying to control it more. Robert Chapman attended a rehearsal one day, saw what I was doing and quipped, "It's good, I'm just wondering when you're going to let the actors do their performance." That got through to me and I changed my ways. Dorothy often says that telling an actor how to do it before you've even seen what they can bring is insulting and self-defeating. Basically, you are communicating to them that save for the brilliance of *me* and what I'm telling you, you will fail. That's a terrible message to send to an actor. You are trying to empower them, get them to catch fire, not make them entirely dependent on you. So, your mantra should be: don't dictate, liberate! A lot of the best directors innately understand this. I mean, you have to be part psychologist and figure out exactly who an actor is and what they need. If you arrive on the set with the attitude of, "I'm going to do everything like The Actors Studio, or like Stanislavski, or like Laurence Olivier," and you come at an actor with a theory, you are making a big mistake. You need to bob and weave, and adapt to every individual situation you're confronted with.

When I was teaching directing at Columbia College, and we were preparing for the fall semester, I remember a decision was made to revise the curriculum. I'd noticed that in the first year of the directing course—which I didn't teach, I taught the second year—they had the students read Elia Kazan's notes that he'd composed before directing *A Streetcar Named Desire*. I was glad about that, because those notes are one of the principal ways in which I learned how to direct. With no directing courses and no practical theater courses at Harvard at all, I had to learn from books and I pored over Kazan's notes religiously. Just recently I've come to feel something interesting about his observations: one of the things Kazan talks about a lot is that Blanche Dubois' behavior should be based on pre-Raphaelite paintings. Well, that was probably sound advice to give Jessica Tandy, who played Blanche in the original Broadway production of *Streetcar* in 1948, because it would be stimulating to an American actress like her. But I imagine Vivien Leigh looked at those notes too much before she took on the same role when the production opened in London—and particularly when she appeared in Kazan's movie adaptation made a couple of years later. I despise Leigh's performance in that film by the way, as I think it's fake and mannered. I'd even suggest her performance was the result of Kazan showing her too many pre-Raphaelite paintings. It was perhaps a case of a brilliant director taking what was good direction for one actress and mistakenly imposing it on another.

I made no such mistakes on *The Looking Glass*. I was always conscious of who I was working with, and what I had to do (and not do) to get the best performance out of them. Take Jeff Puckett, for instance. This being the third movie we'd done together, I could see how much he'd grown over the years as an actor. So, I knew when to talk and when to shut up. I'm very happy with Jeff's performance. I particularly love the scene where Karen tells Terry he is Julie's father. Jeff plays that moment beautifully. The character of Terry is based on another real person from our world, our handyman, and Jeff has a lot of his same expressions and mannerisms down. He had the opportunity to meet the real Terry as he was working as the greens-man on the picture and was always around. Anthony Panzica, who plays Arthur, Julie's father, was another local actor. I had not seen him before he came in to read. I was less happy with him, but he was okay. Panzica seemed to lack a little humor and warmth, but in some ways that suited his character. It possibly made Arthur a less appealing choice for Julie—and for the audience—than Terry.

The auditions that Julie attends was a chance for me to work into the film some more of the faces of the local community, as I had done with the cherry pit spitting montage in *A Piece of Eden*. For instance, the guy awkwardly reciting *Richard III* is the main reporter for the local newspaper. So, he gave us at least four or five front page articles on the movie and that was a nice payback. The woman singing "Danny Boy" is the daughter of an investor; the tap dancer is Kelly Daisy's daughter, Kelly being one of the producers on *The Looking Glass*; and then there's Harry Musselwhite singing "Swing Low, Sweet Chariot." Harry, who has directed several short films, features as one of the two bassos in the musical that play ladies in drag. I like Harry a lot. He was one of the two guys who ran the Rome International Film Festival in Rome, Georgia. We went down there with *A Piece of Eden* and the movie received the award for Best Audience Favorite.

I had originally cast somebody else to play the part of Sybil, Julie's stepmother. This actress was very pretty and read well, but when it came time to rehearse she didn't seem real enough. She just wasn't convincing at all, so I fired her during that first day of rehearsal. It was one of my quickest ever firings, actually. I'm sure you've already gathered by now that I've fired a *lot* of actors throughout my career. Over the years I've become very good at it, but it's never easy to do. I usually approach a firing by telling the person, "Look, I've made a terrible mistake. It's not your fault, it's my fault. You're wonderful, but you are not how I see this character and I'm going to have to replace you." I've witnessed many emotional and difficult reactions during these kinds of encounters, but I repeatedly stress to them, "I'm so very sorry. Please don't feel badly. It's my mistake." I've often said things like that. I know it sounds totally insincere, but it's not. It really isn't. The most important thing for me is always the movie. My focus is fixed on making the best film I possibly can, so I like to get this regrettable business over and done with as quickly as possible. I don't linger over it. One important aspect of being a director is that *you* are the person who defends everybody else's work. A lot of people are giving a hundred percent and somebody needs to be there to protect their hopes and expectations for the project. It falls on the director to ultimately say, "No, I'm afraid you're not working out. You are hurting this whole endeavor and I have to make a change."

I'm sure that part of my willingness to fire people stems from my having been fired in the past. My bad experiences on *The Freaking Out of Stephanie Blake* and *Jaws 2* assisted in helping me to develop a somewhat ruthless edge when it comes to making the tough decisions. It's certainly not some twisted form of revenge I'm administering, nor is it something I ever enjoy doing. It's painful. Maybe it reveals a weakness in me, in terms of my indecision surfacing at certain times. I don't know. I don't analyze it too much. I don't want to. After firing my original choice for Sybil I replaced her with Faith Marie, an actress who had worked in the office on my last two pictures (she had been the production coordinator on *Suspended Animation* and had also done some of the make-up). In the time since those movies had come out Faith had become a successful singer around our area. She is very busy with her band, as they play all kinds of county fairs and one thing or another. I worried that she wouldn't have the time to do the film as we were shooting in the summer and that's when Faith fundamentally earns her living. But she managed to do it by driving all night and showing up whenever we needed her. We had to schedule around her to some degree, which I hate to do, but it was necessary. Aside from playing Sybil, Faith also plays the Queen of Hearts in the *Alice* musical Julie stars in. I didn't intend to have the same actress play those two parts. In a way it was too pointed to have Faith performing both. It seems like we were trying to say something and we really weren't.

> Hancock had always intended to shoot The Looking Glass with High Definition digital cameras and had discussed a "distinctive" visual style for the film with his cinematographer Misha Suslov. Before principal photography commenced in the summer of 2013, he visited Fletcher Camera, the rental house in Chicago he had plundered before shooting Suspended Animation in 2001. All other equipment utilized in the picture was appropriated from Columbia College and various other local sources.

When we were gearing up to do the film, we could have secured—for free—two Sony digital cameras and the entire set of lenses from Fletcher Camera. They had no use for them and Tom Fletcher had said, "You can have these if you want them." So, I took the two Sonys and the lenses, and carried them in the camera truck, thinking we could use them to shoot multiple cameras on certain scenes. Ultimately, we didn't do that and had the use of three different cameras (two REDS and a Canon) from Columbia College. We did some tests and noted how superior the RED was to the Sony in terms of sharpness and image quality, so we used the RED exclusively. Maybe there is one shot in the movie executed with the Sony, but I doubt even that. We originally intended to shoot The Looking Glass with extremely de saturated colors so that it would not look like a family picture. Misha and I really wanted to lose most of the color until the performance of Alice in Wonderland, when the images would suddenly explode into vivid life with all these intense hues. Unfortunately, people complained so much during screenings about the "dead look" of the photography we gradually introduced more and more color into the picture, until it finally became more conventional looking and our initial approach was discarded entirely. We also did several shots of Karen driving in her car against green screen exterior backgrounds that were filmed in a studio. Dorothy can drive, but I chose to shoot them that way due to sound issues. There were several lengthy dialogue scenes that took place inside the vehicle and I felt we would get better sound, and be able to control everything more, if we shot it that way. We could have shot those scenes using a flat-bed truck, but we didn't have the rig and it would have cost too much to rent.

When I'm shooting a movie I sometimes go into a mode in which I try to make a classical picture; a John Ford film where you don't move the camera a whole lot. I like to get the camera almost at eye-level so that it's merely observing the events and isn't so noticeable. It's a kind of filmmaking where you are relying on the actors to convey things and isn't so reliant on technical extravagance. You'll notice there's no show-off directing in *The Looking Glass*, with the possible exception of the opening shot of the film where the camera flies over the pond towards Karen's house, but even that isn't too much. We also did a flying overhead shot of Terry and Julie fishing in the boat near the end of the film. Both of those sequences utilized drones, little remote control helicopters that had a Go-Pro Camera attached to them. This equipment came courtesy of Thad Donavan, who did some second unit footage for me and executed all those flying shots. They look remarkably smooth, all things considered, and they aren't too flashy. Interestingly, as a theater director, I was fairly demonic about calling attention to myself. I was very outlandish and attention-grabbing in everything I did. I wanted people to know exactly who had directed the play they were watching. Somehow, throughout my movie career, the reverse has happened. I can remember even saying to myself at one point, "In terms of the theater I'm more like Ken Russell, but in terms of my movies I'm more like John Ford." I'm not comparing myself to Ford as a director; I'm just saying that somehow I've gotten into an entirely different mindset where my style is more restrained and anonymous. Like Ford, I'm more interested in simply telling a good story. *The Looking Glass* is very much like that. It's a classical film where I'm kind of standing back and just letting the actors do it.

Indeed, it may surprise you to know that a lot of *The Looking Glass* was improvised as that approach is in direct contrast to some of Dorothy's previous scripts where we often stuck closely to the lines as written during shooting. The experience on *The Looking Glass* reminded me how rewarding it was to improvise at certain key moments. There was one improvised moment we filmed in our living room where Karen and Julie are at odds about something. After we had finished shooting the lines in the script, I said to Dorothy, "Okay, we're going to keep rolling. Just really try to get through to her this time." Dorothy then said in character, "What can I do to help you, honey?" Grace replied, "Nothing. I was long gone, a long ago time. There's no helping me." That dialogue was entirely spontaneous and the camera was on Dorothy as Grace uttered it. So, as she had just inadvertently popped out with that dialogue, we had to go back and try to get a shot of Grace repeating those lines that was at the same level performance-wise it had been when she'd originally spoken them. We were never quite able to do that under slightly more rigorous conditions. The freshness of it, the sadness of it, was slightly dissipated, but we really needed to see Julie's face when she revealed something of that emotional and psychological significance.

Now, when the audience hears a line like that coming from the mouth of a thirteen year-old teenager they can be forgiven for insisting, "Oh, that doesn't sound like something a young girl would ever say. It sounds like a line that's been written for her by mature adults." Of course, as I've already mentioned, the truth is Grace did come out with those words all by herself. The fact she spoke such a line strongly anticipates a comment Karen makes to Julie in a later scene: "You are an old soul." Grace is like that in reality. There is something worldly about her, an intelligence and honesty that seem to transcend her youthfulness. Working with Grace and Dorothy in such moments, I learned how advantageous it was to shoot two ways with two cameras at the same time when you are improvising. The scene where Karen and Julie are having lunch in the café, and Julie complains that she "feels stuck here," was equally revealing for that same reason. This is because shooting in opposite directions can sometimes be difficult to light, meaning shooting both actors at the same time is harder for directors of photography to accomplish. But following the opportunities we'd missed in the earlier scene in Karen's house, I decided to do it in this particular instance and was pleased with the result.

> *After settling on* Alice in Wonderland *as the production Julie tries out for, Hancock and Tristan began developing ideas for musical numbers in collaboration with Orville Stoeber. The songwriter composed several tracks including the raunchy "Teach Me To Sin," which features in a lively sequence where Alice is confronted by the Cheshire Cat, and "The Promises We Make," a soulful duet performed by Alice and The Caterpillar (the latter played by a masked Stoeber at the head of a retinue of dancers who form its segmented body). Complimenting this material was "Final Alice: Acrostic Song," by Pulitzer Prize-winning composer David Del Tredici, taken from his acclaimed work* Final Alice *(1974-75). Famed for his persistent fascination with Lewis Carroll's books* Alice's Adventures in Wonderland

> *(1865) and its sequel* Through the Looking-Glass *(1871), as well as other works of literature, Tredici is considered by many to be a leading figure of the Neo-romantic movement. A long-time fan of the lyrical surrealism of Tredici's works, Hancock was delighted to obtain permission to use the American composer's music in his film. The choreography that features in the musical was supervised by Irina Tsikurishvili, the Georgian choreographer who co-founded the Synetic Theater in 2001 with her husband Paata. A non-profit physical theater company based in Arlington, Virginia, Hancock had enjoyed their performances of "Silent Shakespeare" and sought to secure Tsikurishvili's services for* The Looking Glass.

The musical was an integral part of the film. I needed music for it that was a clash between darkness and light, innocence and experience, good and evil, as all of those contrasting elements are present in *Alice in Wonderland*. I had remembered Orville's inability during the scoring of *Let's Scare Jessica to Death* to compose music that sounded evil and threatening. Back then, he just couldn't get a handle on it. By the time we were working on *The Looking Glass*, I happily discovered that Orville had learned how to bring the proper amount of malevolence into his work. The song "Teach me to Sin"—which features in the sequence where Alice dances with the Cheshire Cat—is evidence of that, and I really like it. It made sense to have Orville play the caterpillar. He's wearing the white mask and is singing and playing the song "The Promises We Make" to Julie, which is another track I adore. The melody has a sweet, haunting quality as does the music of David Del Tredici. David is an important composer who writes in a kind of retro Richard Strauss style. I've admired his work for a long time and was aware of *Final Alice*, which is a symphonic suite with a soprano voice. The literature of Lewis Carroll holds a strong enchantment for him, and he's written something like twenty works about *Alice in Wonderland* and *Alice Through the Looking Glass*. We sing pieces of David's beautiful melody, the "Acrostic Song," about four times throughout the picture. I love the whole piece to which it belongs and thought it would be marvelous to include more of it in the film. I understood it was music that could potentially work for a lot of different sections, but we finally ended up using much less than I thought as actual scoring.

Working with Irina Tsikurishvili was another wonderful experience.

The Synetic Theatre is an incredible company and I urge people to Google the words "Synetic Silent Shakespeare" so that they can see for themselves the fabulous YouTube videos that are online of four or five of their productions. They do wordless adaptations of Shakespeare principally and it's all terrific stuff—the movement, the drama, the emotion. While visiting our daughter in Washington, Dorothy and I would often go see their performances. I loved it so much that I introduced myself to Irina and we got to be friendly. I had initially wanted her to choreograph the musical of *Weeds* that I've been working on for several years, but she didn't think she could do it. Irina said, "I don't know how to do tap-dancing. I don't think I'm the right person for the job." Later, when the production we planned for *The Looking Glass* turned into a musical, I immediately thought how wonderful it would be to get Irina to choreograph those numbers.

In fact, Irina proved to be just as much an inspirational choice for the movie as Grace Tarnow, her contribution was that wonderful. Irina is extremely talented and I covered the dancing very basically using multiple cameras in an effort to try and find some interesting moments that I could integrate into the sequences. I shot the dancers performing the various pieces in their entirety, except in a few instances where I wanted to get some specific action or point-of-view that I felt we needed. I wanted to show even more of the musical in the finished film, but I think in *The Looking Glass* I probably showed it a little too much. Be that as it may, the Mad Hatter's Tea Party section of the production, which was a wonderful and elaborate piece of chorcography, is currently lying somewhere on the cutting room floor. So, I did show some restraint.

Our primary reason for selecting *Alice in Wonderland* as the production Julie appears in was it offered a thematic resonance in that she—like the character of Alice—is a girl who is hovering between childhood and adulthood, innocence and awareness. That can be a difficult transition in a person's life and can lead to confusion and pain. One of the prominent themes of our film is the conflict and lack of understanding that occurs between different generations. This is evidenced in small things like Karen going to bed early and Julie's refusal to avert her eyes from her iPad, to more philosophical differences. It does seem to me that each new generation sees the previous one almost as an irrelevance or a hindrance, despite the fact young people could learn a great deal from older people. I feel that conflict is often addressed in movies in a heavy-handed way, but I don't think that's the case with *The Looking Glass*.

Plainly, the grandmother and granddaughter are exactly alike: both are talented and stubborn. So, it's about these characters building a bridge between them. That's not always an easy thing to accomplish. I mean, *The Looking Glass* is partially based on mine and Dorothy's frustrating experiences with our grandson. No matter how hard we try, we can't seem to pry him away from his computer or his iPad. It's an addiction for him that is hard to deal with at times, as he sometimes prefers to be engaged with these pieces of technology than he does conversing with us.

The wall between Karen and Julie is overcome by their discovery of a mutual love of and innate talent for artistic expression. If *Suspended Animation* deals with the possibility of hereditary evil, *The Looking Glass* deals with the idea of hereditary creativity. A recurring theme that is present in the film is one that we also explored in *Weeds*: that creativity is essential to life and can have restorative and life-enhancing properties. As Karen says, it can bring you "freedom, success and happiness." I feel particularly passionate about this having grown up with a musician father who filled the house with classical music and gave me *Hamlet* to read when I was eight. Those were wonderful gifts, even if I didn't fully understand just how helpful and important they were at the time.

Contrary to this view, I appreciate that some viewers may read Dorothy's character as being some kind of "pushy parent" figure. Certainly, Karen's persistent efforts to steer Julie towards a career in show business could be viewed as potentially harmful to the girl psychologically considering her delicate emotional state. What are her chances of really making it? That said I do feel it's important that a person has dreams and ambitions, particularly a young person, never mind how unrealistic and improbable they seem. So many people have the life choked out of them at an early age it's vital that they retain the belief that their dreams are indeed obtainable. Without dreams, I feel life can lose so much of its magic.

Some of the imagery and symbolism in *The Looking Glass* is uncomplicated and direct. That was always my intention, to weave these things into the fabric of the film. Aside from the subtext of the *Alice* musical itself, there's also the moment where Julie releases the lightning bugs from the jar and watches them soar into the night sky like burning embers. That clearly signifies her growth and her desire to be free, as well as her luminous spirit. Then there is Oliver, the dog that is forever chained up in a neighbor's garden, which also represents Julie as she is something that is in a sense confined by her circumstances and her insecurities. They share a unique bond and I was always amused by the idea of Oliver wearily looking up whenever Julie passes by in the car, as if they were almost exchanging a knowing look. Oliver was originally based on a neighbor's dog and it made Dorothy crazy for a couple of years whenever we drove by and she saw this animal chained up in the garden—always chained up. Whatever the conditions, whether it was raining or the middle of winter or a hot summer's day, there it would unfailingly be, looking rather miserable. Dorothy actually went in there one day and tried to feed the dog. The neighbor saw her and yelled, so she complained to the Animal Welfare people. They said, "Five people have already called about this animal, but we can't do anything. The dog has a little kennel with water and straw, and we have no grounds to interfere."

As you can imagine, it then required a considerable amount of courage on my part to knock on our neighbor's door and say, "Can we use your dog in my film? I'd like to shoot where you have your dog chained up?" My neighbor rather coolly replied, "Well, that's interesting because your wife was here not so long ago and reported us to the authorities." Oh, man! So, that little encounter involved some very careful negotiation. At one point as we were discussing the dog, he said, "This is an Irish Coonhound and if you let him off the chain, he runs into the woods and is *gone*! It will then take around three days before I can get him back again, because all he instinctively wants to do is hunt coons. That's the reason why he is always chained up in the garden." I said, "Okay, but why don't you put him in the house?" He said, "No, we can't do that. Whenever he's in the house, he goes totally crazy." Anyway, our neighbor finally gave us permission to use his dog in the movie, and we then tried to work him with a trainer. Unfortunately, the animal stopped eating and shitting and the trainer said, "This is not going to work out." Luckily, one of the guys on the camera crew also owned an Irish Coonhound and so we used his dog instead. But it's true, that breed does run straight for the woods the moment you let them off the leash. By the way, I don't think our neighbors have seen *The Looking Glass*. I promised to put something in the end credits that stated their dog was well treated, but I didn't. I betrayed them.

> *As in* A Piece of Eden, *Hancock and Tristan depict characters in* The Looking Glass *that are reunited with loved ones either after or near the point of death. During an extended dream sequence that takes place in a sun-dappled forest, Karen encounters her deceased husband and their daughter, Belinda, who has recently succumbed to cancer.*

> *This touching scene is used as a pretext for Karen to later inform Terry on her deathbed that he is in fact Julie's natural father; a narrative device the director initially feared would be viewed as contrived, but now acknowledges as "eloquent."*

Karen's late husband, who embraces her in the dream, is also named John. I was tempted to play that part myself for obvious reasons, but I chose not to. So much of the picture is already based on our lives I felt there was the danger of going too far in blurring the lines between reality and fantasy. It might have possibly been a little too on the nose. So, I instead cast Allen Turner as John and he proved to be a better choice. Aside from being one of the producers on *The Looking Glass*, Allen is an important person in Chicago. He's the lawyer for The Pritzker Organization, and has been the President of the Board of the Goodman Theatre, which is one of the two big regional theaters in Chicago, and the Museum of Contemporary Art. He was also the President of Columbia College and happens to be a terrific guy. I think the scene where Karen meets John is another indication of Dorothy wanting to believe in some kind of afterlife. Of course, Karen's dream could also be just that—a dream. But I liked the idea that it reveals or reawakens Karen to the fact that Terry once had an affair with Belinda and is Julie's natural father. Dorothy thought it would be more interesting to disclose it that way, having it almost be drawn out of Karen's subconscious. Call it woman's intuition or whatever, but I suspect that Karen knew it all along. The dream merely shows the audience what she already knows. We could have gotten away with the suggestion that Julie is Terry's daughter without having the dream sequence in the film. Karen could have simply told Terry the truth on her deathbed, but the dream makes for a rather poignant and tender moment.

Sometimes I'm loathed to cut a scene that Dorothy loves, but if I feel strongly that it shouldn't be in there, she will often see things my way. However, Dorothy is not the reason why I left the dream sequence in the film. The truth is a lot of people wanted me to cut that scene entirely. I've thought about this a lot and I know exactly why I kept it: one of the difficult things when doing a story where you're going to reveal at the end what is supposed to be a surprise is that it has to be like an Agatha Christie mystery. When the reveal arrives you often say, "Oh, I should have seen that coming! Why didn't I guess?" You're not supposed to figure out the mystery early on, but you do feel you should have deduced what was going on sooner from the clues presented to you. In order for it to work, the reveal has to seem both surprising and inevitable. In the early screenings we had of *The Looking Glass*, the moment when Karen says to Terry, "You don't want to miss your daughter's opening, do you?" the audience would audibly *gasp*. On that basis alone, I figured that the movie was working and people were engaged with the narrative and the characters. Granted, there are a few people who do guess a little earlier and I have a small statistical grasp on this: I would say that at least twenty percent of the audience guesses when they see the dream sequence. Conversely, the other eighty percent do not guess. I felt that in spite of these kinds of reveals being tricky to pull off, there are several hints sprinkled throughout the film. There is the restrained hostility between Terry and Arthur, as if Arthur knows he's had a relationship with his first wife. There's the tension between Terry and his own wife, Marge, over his repeated mentioning of Belinda's name. Also, Julie tells Terry at one point that her mother liked him a lot and that look she gives him is telling; it's like Julie knows right there in some way.

Getting back for a moment to Karen's dream, it's almost like magic. I find it interesting that some directors find it difficult to reconcile moments of fantasy with their more realist impulses. They have a problem integrating fantasy within a realist structure, and a dream or a hallucination is a way out for them. Again, there were people who felt I should have cut the dream; that the film could have survived it, but I love it. There's a really touching line in the sequence that somehow feels very real and very powerful to me. It occurs when Karen looks up at the figures of Belinda and Terry on the bridge, and quietly says, "Did it go away?" Karen's deceased daughter is now hopefully in a place where there is no longer any pain or suffering for her. *That* is why I did not want to cut the dream. There's a reason I retained it and it's a deeply personal one: I don't want to break down and cry here, but you can imagine how devastatingly upset Dorothy is about the prospect of her daughter dying. It's truly a dreadful thing for us and Alexandra to deal with. I remember that when we were out in the woods shooting Karen's dream that line simply came out of Dorothy's mouth. It wasn't written or discussed previously; it was just Dorothy speaking from the heart in that moment. If you watch the scene again, that line doesn't feel scripted. It has so much truth and feeling, it's beautiful, and it gets me every time.

Another thing that certain people wanted me to cut was the lengthy story Karen relays to Julie in the garden about her troubled childhood; how as a young girl she got into the All City High School Choir after successfully auditioning against thousands of other kids from the five boroughs of New York. Karen heartbreakingly reveals what happened after she rushed excitedly over the two-and-a-half miles between Carnegie Hall and her home, eager to tell her parents all about it: when she gets there, she sees her mother is doing the dishes in the kitchen and her pro-Nazi father and his German pal, Gus, are playing chess. Karen tells them of her success and begins singing "Summertime," the song she performed at the audition. One by one, without as much as a word or a look, the three adults quietly leave the room. In the face of such crushing emotional cruelty, Karen defiantly keeps on singing the song at the top of her voice to the empty kitchen, refusing to be beaten. Now, as far as autobiography is concerned, that moving story is obviously something that happened to Dorothy as a child. It's an anecdote that also features in her memoir *Joy Street*, and is fairly long and detailed. In order to get through that monologue, Dorothy partly used cue cards that were placed just off-camera. Still, for most of the speech—at least two-thirds or more of it—she merely recounted those events from memory, improvising and just telling the story as herself. Evidently, it is something that has lived with Dorothy a long time and she had no trouble recalling those details as the pain of that day is always there.

John Lahr was one of those who wanted me to take Karen's speech out of the finished film. As a matter of fact, I seem to recall he was fairly determined that I remove it. Lahr felt the scene was almost "Odetsian," like something from Clifford Odets' *Awake and Sing*, and threatened to come across as a little corny and forced in its plaintiveness. Okay, that was a fair consideration, but in all the preview cards where we invited the audiences to comment on what scenes they liked best and what scenes they liked least, Karen's speech to her granddaughter was unanimously everybody's favorite passage. They loved it and really responded to the sincere emotion of the story. They felt Karen's pain and appreciated her fierce determination and dignity to pursue her dreams regardless of those who had belittled and abused her. There's no question about it, I would have been lynched in this area if I had cut that scene. I think it's wonderful and it's also important as it's the moment that Karen kind of accomplishes her objective with this young girl, or at least makes a sizable impact on her thinking. Lahr was the only dissenting voice about it, and as much as I value his opinion and friendship, I felt I had to keep it in the movie. So, I did.

The scene also represents some of Dorothy's best ever acting, which was another reason why I couldn't bring myself to cut it. It would have been quite impossible for me. I also love the look Dorothy has on her face when Karen is sitting alone on the bench at night and Julie arrives at the house and sees that she has wet her pants, and is just totally out of it. That is another strong moment for Dorothy, I feel. She has a vacant look in her eyes that is very spooky. Dorothy's performance is utterly fearless in terms of her having no make-up, not trying to look younger or anything. She wanted to look old and vulnerable and ill, something she hadn't wanted to do a decade earlier on *Suspended Animation*. But some time had passed and she was now ready and willing to embrace it. She was in no way reluctant or concerned at revealing such personal stories about herself. She remarked to me that playing such an elderly and physically and mentally impaired character was like playing herself. She said, "This is not acting, this is me." She said this in a positive way; it wasn't in any way self-pitying: "This is me and so I just do it." I was incredibly proud of her willingness to go to such painful places.

As in the case of her recent memoir, I think that scene was another means for Dorothy to exorcise some of the ghosts from her past. Writing and performing these things in a movie, revealing these painful and soul-scarring episodes in one's life, can be deeply cathartic. It's also a way of bringing your life to a conclusion. When you read *Joy Street*, you will understand more about Mabel Nichols and realize just how important this woman was to Dorothy. As I told you, Mabel became her foster mother and she really gave Dorothy a sense of worth. We actually had a couple of scenes with Aunt Mabel that we cut from the movie. Mabel would appear to Karen as a ghost and she would say, "I'm having such trouble with this girl. Was I like that?" In a way, the relationship between Julie and Karen—in Dorothy's mind—is like her own relationship with Aunt Mabel. She sees the film partly as a repaying of a debt to Mabel; gratefully acknowledging this woman's goodness and the passing on of love and knowledge. Dorothy accepted my decision to excise this material from the picture and we agreed the scenes simply didn't work. The truth is we were not able to cast the role of Aunt Mabel really well. She was played by Emily Bentley, a mentee I found at Harvard who worked on the picture as a production assistant. Emily still receives an actor's credit on the film, and is an excellent actress, but she was just too young for the part. I mean, she was just out of Harvard! What possessed me, casting her?

Gliding elegantly to a predictable but nonetheless powerful

> *and affecting conclusion,* The Looking Glass *cuts between scenes of the ailing Karen gradually succumbing in her bed to illness and those of Julie performing to acclaim in the musical. Karen informs Terry that Julie is his daughter, which comes as a considerable surprise to him. He then races off to the theater leaving Marge behind to tend to Karen, and catches the final triumphant moments of Julie's assured debut.*

The question of whether or not we should show Karen's death in the film was something we thought long and hard about. I had no interest in shooting Bruce Pearson's death in *Bang the Drum Slowly*, but I did shoot that same scene in *The Looking Glass* with Karen dying in her bed. Why did I think that scene belonged in this picture and not in the earlier one? Well, we initially thought that Karen would die off-camera during the musical performance. Julie would then come home later that night and discover that her grandma was dead. We were not going to show the two of them together at the moment of Karen's passing, but Dorothy ultimately felt that we should just go for it. Someone else who was influential in my decision to depict Karen's death—and was also involved in the creative work on the screenplay—was Faith Marie. She said, "No, John, you've got to show this. You've got to give Dorothy the chance to die onscreen and you also need to show the funeral." Faith was so adamant about it we reconsidered and wrote those things into the script. I now feel these moments really should be in the movie and I have no regrets about including them. Karen's funeral was shot at the same funeral parlor where we'd earlier filmed Robert Breuler's funeral in *A Piece of Eden* (the Carlisle Funeral Home in Michigan City). Like Breuler, Dorothy had to climb into a coffin and that was not her favorite moment of the shoot. It's an experience that can be disturbing for some actors and I wouldn't really want to do it myself. For all her apprehension, like every other challenge she meets, Dorothy just did it.

Although she was always up for everything, Dorothy did find the shoot very tiring. She was not particularly stable on uneven ground and I knew before we started shooting that we needed to have her walking on even ground, or have her sit down, in certain scenes as she found it hard to act and move around on rough surfaces. We originally had a scene that took place in a cemetery where Karen takes Julie to see the family graves. She is putting flowers around her late husband's resting place, and is talking a little bit about the family history, but Julie is not listening to her. A terse exchange follows, which begins with Karen saying, "Don't cry, Julie." Julie then replies, "I'm not." "Yeah, I see that you aren't. How can somebody so young be so cold?" "Well, what do I care about these people?" Then they both stomp off and clamber into the nearby car. Karen then angrily backs up the car while trying to get out of the cemetery, accidentally hitting over a tombstone and breaking it. They both get out of the vehicle and stare at the shattered monument. Julie says, "Oh, no! Oh my God, put it back up!" Karen simply shrugs and says, "Ah, fuck it. Let's get out of here." It was a good scene, very funny, but you could noticeably see that Dorothy was having terrible difficulty moving around the uneven ground of the cemetery. Her discomfort was just too obvious and distracting, so I cut it.

Another thing I cut was a number of the climactic scenes. One of the final shots of the movie is one I referred to earlier—Terry and Julie sitting in a rowing boat, fishing. I suppose that shot leaves the audience to presume that Terry has told Julie he is indeed her father, but there were in fact several scenes that were excised or not filmed which would have affirmed that Julie now knows the truth. We never filmed the scene where Terry told her because we didn't know how to have Julie's response be an entirely satisfying one. Clearly, it would not have been a satisfying one at first. We did have a scene that took place after Karen's funeral where Julie tells Arthur that she is not going home with him. We then saw Arthur and Sybil leave together and Julie says goodbye to them. So, there was a lot of stuff that was removed from the end and that was mostly at John Lahr's suggestion. Lahr basically said, "You are not wrapping this story up effectively and believably. The father would not go back to Pittsburgh right away, so just lose all that material. I think you should leave the resolution more mysterious, as if the girl doesn't know now she will someday." That was a wise observation on Lahr's part as I had initially felt we should say *all* of those things. I then realized that the important thing is Julie's expression in the final shot as she sits on the bench with Oliver the dog and we run the closing credits: we can see in this last moment that she has taken in all of her grandmother's spirit and courage and hopefulness and toughness, and can move forward with all these gifts she has absorbed. I love that final shot, actually.

A further consideration we had to make during editing involved the *Alice in Wonderland* musical. It had broken my heart to lose some of the stage performances in *Weeds*, but I was a little more ruthless in trimming down Julie's production in *The Looking Glass*. Again, the musical was an important element of the story, but it couldn't slow the narrative down or consume it entirely. You may notice that the number "Teach Me to Sin" is played in its entirety and that's always a tricky thing to do in a film as proceedings can grind to a halt. I like that sequence, but I might have done better shortening it a little more. My original cut, which contained some of the deleted material I've identified like the aforementioned Mad Hatter's Tea Party, the cemetery scene, and the stuff at the end that resolved Julie's future, came in at around fifteen minutes longer than the present cut. So, the film was initially over two hours long. In order to get the running time down I lost all of those scenes, some of which I really liked. We also lost a scene that featured Karen sitting up in her office writing her autobiography, what was in essence *Joy Street*. She is remembering her father's funeral and we filmed a speech that Dorothy details in her memoir in which she recalls how her father's hands had only ever hit her and had never touched her with love. It was another moving passage, beautifully played by Dorothy, but we eventually cut it. There were also a number of early scenes we dropped featuring Oliver the dog, and more scenes of Karen valiantly trying to get Julie off the iPad. At some of our early screenings there were people who said, "You are stating and re-stating all of that stuff too heavily." So, we took those scenes out.

What I find interesting is when you delve into the special features on a DVD or Blu-ray there can sometimes be as much as thirty minutes or so of deleted scenes that didn't make the final cut. On viewing this material one could be forgiven for asking, "Geez, couldn't you see that a lot of this stuff didn't work or wasn't necessary when you were writing and re-writing the script? Why take the trouble and money to shoot these scenes if they are destined to be excised from the finished film?" Of course, you can't always know beforehand what scenes are going to work and what scenes will not. There are a lot of factors involved in making a movie—budget, schedule, locations, weather, actors, technical problems—any of those things can ultimately affect the success of any given scene. But wouldn't it be great if you could identify all of those problems at the writing stage? Think of the money you would save. Also, it's difficult sometimes to be objective about a scene although it seems like you ought to be able to. It's just a shame to shoot so much material that doesn't make it into the picture. You could have spent that time and money on other things, possibly improving what you already have. Contrary to that, you definitely don't want to miss something important because you haven't got it in the can.

The fact that you can come into the middle of a movie and pretty much understand everything that is going on makes exposition all a waste of time. But people always have contrasting views about what you should keep in a movie and what you should lose.

We screened *The Looking Glass* for the locals, just as we had done with *A Piece of Eden* in 2000, and the reaction was equally as positive. There were some people who were disgruntled at being cut out of the film, but we simply had to do it. Those individuals didn't bitch beyond a certain point and eventually accepted my reasons for doing it. I told each of them, "Look, you were wonderful, but I had to leave that bit out. The movie was so long, we had to cut it for time." That was mostly the truth, too. Sometimes the performances just weren't strong enough, or there was some other technical problem. I now wonder if I should have been tougher and trimmed even more stuff. Several people did comment that the film was "slow starting" and I wanted to address that as much as I could. *The Looking Glass* probably remains slow starting in its present state, but I wanted the relationship between Karen and Julie to have a chance to breathe and deepen. I don't think it feels laborious in any way. You may notice that the film repeatedly fades to black throughout its running time as opposed to deploying a dissolve or a hard cut between scenes. I generally like fading to black rather than cutting back in to the next scene, but there was some concern that such an approach would make the movie feel even slower. *The Looking Glass* is an intimate story anyway, so the pacing feels appropriately steady. It has a confident pace to it, it's not rushing. I like that about the picture.

As always, I selected the music for the film carefully. For the opening titles, I used "The Moldau" by Bedrich Smetana, a beautiful piece he wrote about the Vltava River that is probably his most famous composition. I also got another chance to use my beloved *Nabucco* for the scene where Karen overhears Julie singing in the kitchen. Another favorite I used was Angelo Badalamenti's shimmering song "Mysteries of Love," which is heard when Karen delivers her long monologue to Julie. Needless to say, having used it previously in *Weeds* and *Prancer*, I adore "Mysteries of Love." It seems to me that the chord progressions convey a process of working towards something. It's an emotional and mental process pending to some insight, some deep revelation and understanding, and so I use it in that context in my films. Characters like Jessica and her father in *Prancer*, or Umstetter in *Weeds*, are coming to know something profound about themselves; something is about to change for them. The song is reprised during the end credits of *The Looking Glass*, this time with the lyrics sung by Grace. When I discussed this with Angelo, he said, "Make sure you mic her very close and have her sing like an angel." So, we did that and the result was wonderful. Angelo was happy about my using "Mysteries of Love" again, as he understands my profound love for it. He gave me a unique recording of the song. It turns out that Angelo had earlier received a prestigious award in Belgium and the Brussels Symphony had recorded an orchestral version for the ceremony. We were then able to use this as a backing track, and Grace sang over the accompaniment.

At a certain point in post-production, my old friend Garth Drabinsky became involved with *The Looking Glass*. In the years since he'd put up the money for *Prancer* and was running Cineplex Odeon, Garth had experienced mixed fortunes. After his disastrous decision to go up against Lew Wasserman and Sid Sheinberg, he had formed a theater production company called Livent and had mounted hugely successful Tony Award-winning productions of musicals like *Ragtime* and *Kiss of the Spider Woman*, and also had a production of *Phantom of the Opera* that ran forever up in Toronto. Garth was then charged with misappropriating millions of dollars, and he and his partner Myron Gottlieb were found guilty of fraud and sentenced to seven years imprisonment. When I was trying to get the musical of *Weeds* on, I re-established contact with Garth, and Dorothy and I visited him at the Beaver Creek Correctional Facility north of Toronto. I thought maybe being incarcerated would stimulate his interest in the prison subject matter, but I suspect it worked the other way. Still later, I had thought to myself, okay, here is a guy who is getting out of jail and *The Looking Glass* is a worthy project that will appeal to his sensibilities. More than that, it might help redeem him in the eyes of the public. Also, with Garth's brother, Cyril Drabinsky, running Deluxe, with its great sound facility in Toronto, I thought he might help me get a good price to do the mix there—which he did. Additionally, I anticipated that Garth would also be helpful with involving the Toronto Film Festival and in marketing the film.

So, taking all of this into consideration, I involved Garth in the project and that proved to be a wise decision. I visited him twice after his release from Beaver Creek, showing him various cuts of the movie, and he made some sound and insightful suggestions. In truth, he was especially helpful in boiling the picture down and strengthening it emotionally as well as structurally. Garth is somebody whom I'm very, very fond of and he's undoubtedly a unique character. He can be dangerous, but he's incredibly smart and alert. Incidentally, Garth was in no way insistent about receiving his credit as executive producer, but I thought it would be advantageous to award it to him. He wanted that credit, but more than anything he loved the picture and was delighted with it. He was a terrific proponent for *The Looking Glass*, and went all over Toronto telling people how wonderful it was. I suspect that my visiting Garth in prison also went a long way with him. I think he appreciated the fact I'd made that effort, even though it proved to be beneficial for me. Perhaps not everybody in the business would be as eager to do such a thing; they'd prefer to distance themselves from somebody who has been convicted of a crime, but not me. I'm proud to know Garth and I'm grateful to have worked with him more than once.

The Looking Glass was eventually released in New York and Los Angeles at the end of October 2015 through First Run Pictures, the company that had earlier distributed *Suspended Animation*. The circumstances that led me back to the company were simply the fact that we were encountering the same difficulty we'd had before with the majors: the studios might like the picture but they claim not to know how to sell it without any names. As you know, I find that encumbrance frustrating and restrictive. Each time I stress the fact that I've made pictures with no stars that were successful the message just seems to get lost in the ether. Anyway, I was moved by Seymour Wishman, who was still the CEO of First Run, as he adored the picture. He kept coming back to the screenings we held in New York, bringing people with him, and each time *The Looking Glass* ended he would come to me with wet eyes, bitter that the picture had got to him again. So, I thought Seymour would do a good job of releasing the film, and it's always nice to deal with an old friend. You feel there's less chance of their stealing from you.

We originally called the picture *Swan Song* and were going to release it under that title, but then we changed our minds. The thinking behind that decision was that *Swan Song* seemed like a bit of a downer and we didn't want to give the impression that the picture was a drag. So, we decided to carry out a little test at a local multiplex theater. We went in and set up a table in the lobby—this was on the very same night that Clint Eastwood's *American Sniper* opened, believe it or not. We had prepared five different posters with five different titles including *Swan Song*, *Lost and Found* and *The Looking Glass*, and polled people going in and out of the multiplex which movie they would most be inclined to see. Interestingly, *Swan Song* scored last of the five which confirmed our suspicions. I realize now that

Swan Song would have also been too revealing as a title, as the audience may have deduced beforehand that the movie dealt with an elderly character that is almost assuredly going to die. Since you pretty much know that outcome anyway, I wanted to change the title and we settled on *The Looking Glass*, which scored well. One of the things about the story is that it concerns two people who don't get along but who you know are eventually going to fall in love. Even if you suspect that the old lady is going to die, I think what's really interesting about the film is exactly how those inevitable things happen. Also, on top of everything, *The Looking Glass* obviously felt closer to Lewis Carroll and *Alice in Wonderland* as a title and it just felt right.

> *Whereas most notices welcomed Hancock and Tristan's return to filmmaking and recognized the ambitious handmade quality with which the picture had been crafted, the general critical consensus labeled it an inauspicious comeback. "If their homespun collaboration is any indication, time has not been kind to the talents of veteran director John Hancock and his wife, writer-star Dorothy Tristan," declared Gary Goldman in his spiky review for the* Los Angeles Times. *Blasting the movie for what he saw as its sluggish pacing, creaky script and episodic structure, Goldman did manage a grudging acknowledgment of Tristan's committed performance: "Despite her lived-in visage and uneven gait, her past beauty and strength—even her onetime acting chops—are clearly evident. But more all-around finesse, including sharper editing and smoother staging, would have greatly helped this obvious labor of love." In her notice for* Film Journal International, *Simi Horowitz was equally effusive in her praise for Tristan's "complex portrait" of an elderly lady as well as Tarnow's "impressively self-possessed and poised" performance as her granddaughter: "*The Looking Glass *is a lyrical, haunting film ... The movie as a whole is so well-acted—and so pleasing to look at—it hits all the right notes in portraying an evolving intergenerational relationship in a story centering on legacy and continuity."*
>
> *Writing for* The New York Times, *Glenn Kenny began his review promisingly by condemning Hollywood's past failure to favorably treat "the strikingly beautiful and very*

talented Ms. Tristan," an infraction he hints may have precipitated her thirty-year absence from the screen. All the same, Kenny did not feel *The Looking Glass* marked a triumphant return: "The film teems with over-familiar commonplaces (the looming debilitation inherent in aging, the metaphor of an unseen neighbor's sorely neglected dog, and so on) as it saunters to its climax. ... The strongest scenes in the picture are intimate exchanges, shot in close-up, between Ms. Tristan and the engaging Ms. Tarnow. ... But the fact the film's most resonant and likable portions are those in which nothing actually happens almost too nicely encapsulates why *The Looking Glass* falls sadly flat through much of its running time." In a post for the *Media Mikes* website in which he awarded the movie four stars out of five, Mike Smith was in contrast enchanted by the movie: "In his four-decade career, director Hancock has always excelled in smaller, personal films. From *Bang the Drum Slowly* to the Nick Nolte prison drama *Weeds*, Hancock manages to give the characters meaning, bringing them to the forefront of the story. He achieves that again here. The quiet scenes between Julie and Karen are deeply moving and heartfelt. You almost feel as if you are eavesdropping on a personal conversation. ... The storyline offers many opportunities to travel into "Movie of the Week" territory but Tristan refuses to take that easy route, instead giving the film real dialogue and situations."

The Looking Glass did receive some positive reactions, but *The New York Times* and *L.A. Times* absolutely killed us! They did not like the film at all. The latter paper thought the picture was too talky and had pacing problems. They also accused us of overreaching ourselves in tackling so many different themes and issues—family, mortality, grief, art, etc. I didn't understand that criticism, that it was too weighty. I thought it was unfair. We felt we'd given the audience something rich and substantial, and that all those topics interlaced quite nicely with each other. They thought differently. Frankly, some of their comments were painful to read. I mean, every film you make means something to you, but when you make such a thoroughly personal film as *The Looking Glass*, in which certain aspects of your life are laid bare, it can be especially hurtful. When you invest so much of yourself in a piece of work and expose your soul a little, it makes some shots all the more painful to absorb. There were others, like the critic for *The Village Voice* for instance, who gave us a review that was both positive and mixed. He thought the picture was too verbose and conventional for the first hour, but that it steadily got better as it progressed. He did allow that the final act was strong and that Grace's voice was wonderful; and also praised Dorothy and me for having apparently discovered a young star.

There was a comment by somebody else that accused me of having Faith Marie play Sybil as a typically unappealing stepparent; a grating "caricature" of a wicked stepmother. I refute that suggestion, as that character is not without warmth and sympathy. I don't want to use this conversation as a stick to hit back at the critics, but one does hope for a little civility. Among the positive notices I mentioned, there were those that commended us on the humanism and nuance of the film. Maybe *The Looking Glass* wasn't grand and loud enough for some people. It wasn't action-packed, discernibly, but that was not the movie we set out to make. I called *A Piece of Eden* subdued and intimate, but *The Looking Glass* is even more so. There are fewer characters, fewer locations, and the focus is mostly on two people: Karen and Julie and those that orbit their small world. The online review by The NYC Movie Guru was one of the few that pointed out the fact that dramas like *The Looking Glass*—films preoccupied with story and character, as opposed to blockbusters loaded with special effects and spectacle—were once the rule rather than the exception. But when I talk to people that have seen the movie, I feel a lot more secure about it. Maybe it does wear all my strengths and frailties as a director, but at least I know they've enjoyed those aspects of the movie that certain critics rejected.

> *As he approaches his seventy-ninth birthday, Hancock still feels a renewed sense of optimism and pride following the completion of his most recent feature. The Looking Glass may seem somewhat elegiac due to its tone and subject matter, and thus appear something of a swan song for its director, but Hancock insists it in no way marks a culmination of his work as a filmmaker. Indeed, the experience of making it has only refueled his desire to continue developing new projects for as long as he is physically and mentally able. Whether or not these artistic endeavors will be realized in*

> Indiana, he does not know, but with offerings like A Piece
> of Eden and The Looking Glass one could make a case that
> he is now a provincial filmmaker.

I don't reject that idea outright, but my province is not restricted to one location. Well, I guess it is really, as I've made nearly all my movies in America, and I'm an American, but I'm aiming wider than that. I hope it doesn't sound cloying, but my province is the province of the human heart and mind. That's a pretty big place to explore, right? I was discussing this with Dorothy just the other day: even if you had all the money and backing in the world, I don't think anyone has enough time to make the movies you want to make—not ones which are a reflection of who you are and what your life has been. It would probably take several lifetimes and careers to explore everything you are, everything you've felt and known as a human being. More than that, it might be boring to watch! I think you could get part of the way there by tapping into some universal truths that we all recognize and accept. Or you can focus on one particular theme or idea that interests you, and go with that. That's what I've tried, and sometimes failed, to do. I prefer to make films about our better natures, because I tend to believe that most people are inherently good. We don't always do the right thing, but we do *want* to. I think that truth is reflected in several of my films, and I enjoy that. I hope audiences do, too. So, in summation, I consider myself a filmmaker who is exploring the landscape of human emotions. Now, in saying that, I love the area where I live, I love the people, and I love living and working here. It's where I belong; where I'm meant to be. Taken from that standpoint, yes, I am totally a provincial filmmaker. I would love to make more movies about this place and its people, as over the years I've built up a lot of friendships and good will here.

Making *The Looking Glass* was an extremely positive experience, almost the best I've ever had. Some big emotions were involved on my and Dorothy's part in creating this movie, but that always feels good. It's what you're really in this business to do as a filmmaker: make deeply personal work that resonates with you and those who see it. That's the best you can aspire to. I can honestly say that I've felt more shooting this picture than I've ever felt doing anything else in all my years of directing. After making movies for forty-five years, it feels amazing to state such a thing but it's true. *The Looking Glass* is not my best film (it's probably my third or fourth best), but as a work of the heart I'm immensely proud of it.

I find it interesting that critics often argue that a director's creative powers decline as they get older, but I feel like I've done some of my best work with this latest offering. I don't consider myself a relic and I certainly don't want others to think of me that way. In fact, I feel a more accomplished director now than at any time during my career. It's wonderful to feel that level of satisfaction at this autumnal juncture of my working life, but it only leaves me with a hunger to do more. Right now, I can't foresee a time in which that hunger will go away and I'll willingly stop. My body may fail me, but I would happily drop dead on a set as making motion pictures has given me so much pleasure. So, although *The Looking Glass* may look like it's a good picture to go out on, I have no intentions of making it such. I go on.

19 *Future Projects*

The Klansman • Fire Music • Bohemian Nights • Hood • Fugitive Days • Radical • American Steel • Putzi

AS A DIRECTOR I'm always juggling a number of projects, feverishly trying to get them made. For every movie you make there can be as many as six or seven movies you never get to make. Do the math: over a career that can amount to a multitude of broken promises, shattered dreams, dead ends, lost time and wasted potential. It's tremendously painful if you are in love with a piece of material that goes nowhere. It's awful! Throughout my career there have been pictures I didn't get to do—*Ruby Red* and *Regiment of Women* being two particularly devastating examples—that haunt me to this day. Well, maybe *haunt* is too strong a word as the disappointment has lessened appreciably over the years, but thinking about these lost movies can feel like picking at a scab. I do occasionally imagine how those films might have turned out in an alternate universe, what they could have been, how they would have played, what my career would now be if they had been successful. I try not to obsess about these things as it's not healthy, but one does wonder. As I told you, back when I finally did *Weeds* in '87, I felt its time had passed in a way. I still had the burning desire to make that picture; I just happen to believe that *Weeds* would have been far more successful had it come out back in 1982. Now, there are certain unmade movies I've been involved with over the years that have never left me, projects that are not so firmly tied to the zeitgeist, or to current tastes, trends and politics. Some of these projects have never quite died for me. They are still very much alive in my heart.

> *One of several projects Hancock has preserved for decades is* The Klansman. *Back in 1982, following a strong recom-*

> *mendation from John Lahr, he was alerted to a chapter of Studs Terkel's acclaimed book of oral history* American Dreams: Lost and Found *(1980). The chapter in question was titled "Why I Quit the Klan," and featured an interview with the former segregationist Claiborne Paul Ellis. Born in 1927, Ellis had at one time been Exalted Grand Cyclops of the Ku Klux Klan in Durham, North Carolina, the city he lived all his life. Due to his position as a high-ranking Klansman, Ellis was pressed to join a committee consisting of local people from diverse backgrounds and occupations to formulate suggestions on how to resolve the racial problems in the school system. He reluctantly accepted the invitation and—to his surprise—was elected to co-chair the meetings alongside Ann Atwater, an African-American activist and welfare mother he despised (three years earlier, in 1968, Atwater had attempted to stab Ellis during a city council meeting after he'd mouthed several racial obscenities in her presence). The discussion on desegregation lasted for ten days, with Ellis and Atwater spending twelve hours of each meeting arguing. Nevertheless, during this process Ellis and Atwater formed an unlikely friendship, which inspired Ellis to experience what Terkel terms "many small epiphanies" about their commonalities as human beings. This led Ellis to leave the KKK shortly afterwards, where he made a public gesture of tearing up his membership card.*

The Klansman has lived with me a long time. When I first read Studs Terkel's interview with C.P. Ellis at John Lahr's urging, I was deeply moved by it. I agreed with Lahr that it would indeed make a wonderful movie. It's probably one of the best interviews Terkel ever did, and is the standout chapter in *American Dreams*. Ellis talked about how he had come from a poor family and his father, who worked at a local mill, was a ferocious racist who hated Blacks with a passion and felt the Ku Klux Klan was the only thing that could save the White race. C.P. had joined the Klan when he was a young man and had steadily risen through the ranks to become a local leader. He had also been instrumental in creating a Youth Corps in the KKK, designed to indoctrinate children into the system of beliefs they held sacred. So, C.P. was deeply immersed in everything that the organization stood for. Through the economic and personal hardships he had endured throughout his life, C.P. had surmised that all of the misery and financial difficulties he, his wife and children were experiencing was the fault of Durham's Black population. He was a hardworking guy surviving on a low salary, toiling every day of his life but barely having enough to feed his loved ones. For that reason, he probably wanted to find something to blame for his misfortune, something to hate. Considering his early exposure to his father's bigoted views, Black people were the obvious target for this hatred.

In the early 1970s, a series of meetings were called in order to address several problems the local community was facing. As a result of this, C.P. had been thrown together—much against his will—with Ann Atwater, "a fat, Black lady agitator" whom he'd always hated. It goes without saying that, as a civil rights activist, Atwater hated Ellis right back. Since they had both been voted in to co-chair these discussions, they spent many afternoons together in a local high school trying to get the community involved. C.P. couldn't get any White people to attend, nor could Atwater get any Black people to come, as both sides knew the other was going to be there. In being forced to spend all this time together, and despite the first few meetings being tense, C.P. began to undergo a seismic change. One afternoon, he unexpectedly broke down crying and apologized to Atwater about his behavior. C.P. had suddenly realized that Black people were human and that both the Whites and Blacks in Durham faced a lot of the same problems; they were both victims of poverty and exploitation, and their mutual outlooks appeared somewhat bleak. Shortly after this epiphany, C.P. resigned from the KKK and disbanded the Youth Corps. Inevitably, following this decision, nobody in the White community would talk to him. C.P.'s friends began to ignore and ostracize him, and he suffered insults and threats. He then became a drunk and was at a low ebb, but remained a changed man. Things did start gradually picking up for C.P., and he was finally elected the head of the Janitors Union with the help of the people in the Civil Rights Movement. C.P. worked there until he retired and his friendship with Ann Atwater continued until his death in 2005 at the age of seventy-eight. She even attended his funeral.

This powerful story was not only potentially a fascinating peek inside the Ku Klux Klan and the racist attitudes festering in America, it was an irresistible tale of friendship, courage and redemption. With those thoughts in mind I passed the idea, which I first called *C.P. Ellis* and then later *The Klansman*, on to Bob Chartoff as he was involved with *Weeds* at this point in time. Bob loved it and immediately wanted to produce it. He then set the project up as a development deal at MGM and we got some front money. They paid for the option as well as a number of wonderful research trips that Dorothy and I undertook to Durham over the course of the next few years. While in Durham, we talked extensively to not only Ellis and Atwater, but various members of the Ku Klux Klan and the kids in the Klan Youth Group. I enjoyed these trips and I learned a lot about what it is to live with prejudice, both in your heart as a racist and in your everyday world as a victim. I remember Ellis was an extremely hospitable host during our visits, and was understandably proud of himself for having made that difficult change. We went back there five or six times, staying for maybe a week each visit, interviewing him, his wife and his children.

Throughout our time together, I felt C.P. liked Dorothy and me. He certainly liked us more than the first screenwriter he'd dealt with previously. Highgate Productions had initially optioned the property and had sent a guy down to Durham to talk with Ellis. C.P. had hated him and felt the writer was judging him, as who wouldn't, right? Naturally, the problem—or trap—of judging was one that Dorothy and I had to be careful to avoid if we were going to get C.P. to open up to us. We didn't agree with the views of the KKK, but I guess we didn't always feel we had to point out our disagreements. Dorothy and I weren't there to argue, we were there to learn, specifically how someone could hold those views in the first place. That, coupled with the fact we genuinely liked C.P. on a human level, enabled us to empathize with him. Of course, one must remember that he was no longer a racist. Personally, I took him to be an unconscious Marxist as, to me, it was about class rather than race. You have no idea how far down these Klansmen come from. Again, it is worth repeating, a big part of the recognition that led to Ellis' conversion was that Ann Atwater was every bit as poor as he was. I remember Ann taking Dorothy and I to a service at her church on one occasion (I believe she had earlier introduced C.P. to the delights of Gospel Music after he had reformed). It was full-on Black Church ecstasy! It was thrilling, actually—the music, the motion, everything. I told C.P. what a great time we'd had and he replied, "Not for me, Bub. Too emotional!"

Dorothy and I also talked to other members of the community. One of the prominent Black leaders in Durham at that point was an insurance man. This individual had been helpful to C.P. when he'd run for the head of the Janitors Union, which mostly consisted of African-American members. I do recall this gentleman telling us that he still had an eye on

C.P.—"my one good eye." He then added cautiously, "Sure, the man has changed, but you know, he *might* change back." I then began to appreciate the suspicion that C.P. had faced at various times from both sides. In effect, he had been rejected and made an outcast by his former White associates, but he was still being regarded with distrust by one or two Black people in Durham who may not have entirely bought his transition. But C.P. was for real and the majority of people knew this, Atwater being one of them. When I talked to the kids in the Klan Youth Group, I principally spoke with a brilliant, charismatic young man named George Andrews. At that point, George was still strong in the faith and had felt terribly let down by C.P.'s conversion: "I don't know what happened to him," he once remarked to me with sadness and incredulity. George was quite open about his racism and his desire for violence. Later, though, on subsequent trips, and as the years passed, he changed. George mellowed and made a lot of money—for him—investing in pharmaceutical stocks. Was he still a white supremacist? Not so you'd notice, but I'm pretty sure that he voted for Donald Trump!

After gathering all this terrific research material, Dorothy and I went home and wrote *The Klansman*. The early drafts proved to be sensational, and we were both excited and proud of the work. Many of the scenes carried an emotional charge, particularly the scene that takes place one afternoon in the high school offices when Ellis and Atwater are talking to each other, and he breaks down. It was a rare piece of writing from Dorothy, as she was able to deftly put herself in that situation and write it so that you believed this racist had experienced a realization. The script was full of strong moments like that, and I knew we had something good. I gave it to Nick Nolte while we were shooting *Weeds* in North Carolina. Nick was quickly taken with the role of C.P. and he really wanted to do the film. I then had him meet C.P. while we were filming the theater scenes in Durham. We did it sitting on the steps outside the theater building where we were shooting. C.P. and Nick both got along. I think they liked each other as they were both straightforward guys. The thing about C.P. is he was not afraid of anyone, which is interesting now that I think of it. I remember he called Nick "Bud."

Next we thought of Whoopi Goldberg to play Ann Atwater, as she was fast becoming a big star following her Academy Award-nominated performance in *The Color Purple*. So, we made an approach to her and she responded positively to the material. I then went to meet Whoopi to discuss the project in more detail. Before I went, Sam Elliot—who was

Whoopi's next door neighbor and had recently done a picture with her called *Fatal Beauty*—told me that I would like her very much and I did. I remember the delight with which Whoopi showed me her collection of KKK memorabilia, which included slave bills of sale. I also remember that at the time she had a seemingly lowlife White biker boyfriend, a stunt man perhaps that she'd met on some film. She took great pleasure, I guess, in shocking. Even with Nick and Whoopi firmly onboard, coupled with the added attraction of a very strong script, we could not get *The Klansman* set up. Somehow, that pairing simply did not have enough voltage to get the movie on. I guess we needed to have Kevin Costner and Whitney Houston—just to throw two names out there—as Ellis and Atwater in order to get the project approved.

When MGM eventually decided not to move forward with *The Klansman*, I optioned the rights myself. I maintained them for a number of years, through several renewals, finally relinquishing them when I couldn't get the project financed with Nick and Whoopi. Then, after several years and with the project still greatly occupying my thoughts, I tried to reactivate it once again. By this time, Nick had gotten too old to play C.P. and so I decided that I was going to have to recast the film. As I was in the process of considering various possibilities, I discovered that the rights situation had become all fucked-up. It turned out that the guy that had produced and financed *Fried Green Tomatoes at the Whistle Stop Café* had also fallen in love with the same story. I've looked for the name of this individual in subsequent years, but I can't find it nor do I remember it. He's not listed on IMDb, but he was a nice old gentleman from Texas whom I think is deceased now (at least I believe I read an obituary). Anyway, he was not involved in the project back when Dorothy and I were. His interest arose more than a decade later, after a well-received book about the case by Osha Gray Davidson called *The Best of Enemies* was published in 1996. I do know that this Texan producer wanted his version, much like Davidson's book, to divide its focus equally between Ellis and Atwater. Needless to say, in our screenplay, Dorothy and I had Ann in there big-time, as she was a pivotal ingredient of the story. However, since she so firmly resided on the right side, we found it more dramatically interesting to award more screen time to the guy on the wrong side.

Once I had let the option lapse—again, after optioning it year after year—and the gentleman from Texas had eagerly moved in, he then made a considerable mistake: he only bought the Klansman's rights but did *not* buy the Black activist's rights! That error has effectively put Ann Atwater in a more dominant and demanding position. You see, Ann has all these grandchildren and she is determined to send each of them to graduate school. This means she is flat-out asking for half a million dollars for the rights and that's a game-changing figure for anybody to contend with. Basically, it means that the budget for *The Klansman* would now have to be huge and, regrettably, that's become a major obstacle in our efforts to get this movie made. I still hope to do the film one day, but I guess it will only happen when Ann Atwater dies. I know that sounds rather droll and distasteful, but it's probably true. Coincidentally, I was only thinking about *The Klansman* this morning. I thought I would try to get that project going yet again because it's one of the best pieces of material I've ever had. It was bitterly frustrating not seeing that picture get made, and to this day it remains one of the screenplays I'm proudest of—truly one of the greatest things Dorothy and I have ever done. When you have something that significant in your hands, it's always immensely difficult to just let it rot away in obscurity. You desperately want to keep fighting for it. I still wish I'd kept the rights after the Nick and Whoopi version failed to ignite, as I'd dearly love to make that movie a reality. In all respects, *The Klansman* is not a project I ever think of as being in my past. For more than thirty years, it's always been in my present; it's always in my future. It just hasn't happened yet.

> *In 1986, shortly before he succeeded in securing the greenlight for his long-gestating passion project* Weeds, *Hancock conceived a screenplay that explored Adolf Hitler's early life. Entitled* Fire Music, *it chronicled the future Fuehrer's time as a young man in Vienna and his failed attempts to gain admittance into the Academy of Fine Arts. Inspired by a chapter he had read in Erik Erikson's landmark book* Childhood and Society, *this project bears the stamp of Hancock's authorship in its vigorous examination of the aspiring artist's struggle for creative expression. Despite plowing the same thematic furrow as some of his earlier works,* Fire Music *is an altogether different beast. It not only makes daringly effective and complex use of its central premise, but presents an uncomfortably human portrait of Hitler while posing some difficult questions on the problem of evil. This powerful script has undergone several revisions in the thirty years since its inception, and has come*

> *exceedingly close to being made on at least one occasion. Like* The Klansman, *Hancock considers* Fire Music *to be among the most accomplished of his unrealized projects; a work rich in authentic detail and psychological truth.*

Fire Music is like Weeds stood on its head, in that it concerns a thwarted artist who becomes a criminal rather than a thwarted criminal who becomes an artist. So, it's the antithesis of Weeds in some ways, but that's initially what was so interesting to me. The idea for the film first struck me around the time I was trying hard to get Weeds on, after I'd been thinking so positively for so long about the redemptive power of art and creativity. I realized that Umstetter's wonderful quote—"Could it be that even in the least of us, there are crumbs of all abilities and potentials"—potentially took on a different and sinister meaning when transposed to Adolf Hitler's ambitions. Thus, Fire Music explores the souring of creativity and the impeding of the artistic urge; how such a thing might lead to bitterness and frustration, and assist in giving birth to the most terrible hatred. The Hitler story is more complex than just the fact he was a failed artist, but that was something the script broached. Of course, a movie about Hitler's early life is not an easy subject to get on because it's about the making of a real-life monster. It traces the beginnings of how a man transforms into something irredeemably evil and destructive, and how do you do that? When I first started writing and thinking about the script, I tried to figure out in my own mind how a person could become that heinous. How can somebody with ambitions to be an artist, and fulfill the role of a creator, instead become one of history's most notorious destroyers? What happened to him? What, if anything specific, caused it?

The screenplay is based in part on the memoirs of Hitler's Vienna roommate, August Kubizek, which were first published in 1953 as The Young Hitler I Knew. The book offers some fascinating glimpses into Hitler's formative years and is deeply revealing, although some historians do question its worth and veracity. A friend from their hometown of Linz (they had first met each other in 1904), Kubizek was a violist and composition student at the musical wing of the state run Academy of Fine Arts, to which Hitler was twice denied entry—the first time in 1907 and then again in 1908. Hitler took a long time in telling Kubizek that he didn't get in, pretended to go to classes and spent his days wandering around Vienna. When the truth finally came out, Hitler and Kubizek unsuccessfully tried to write an opera together. It was derived from a draft of a libretto by Richard Wagner called *Wieland der Schmied*, which was based on the Germanic myth of Wayland the Smith. It was about a jewelry maker who becomes the smith of the gods. The work includes a fiery climax in which Wieland ends up destroying the world: he tips over his forge and burns everything, laying it all to waste. It's like an eerie forecasting of later events in a strange way. The friendship between Kubizek and Hitler continued for the next four years, but after Hitler suddenly moved out of the small room they shared, the pair would not see each other again until 1939 when the Fuehrer invited his friend to the Bayreuth Festival. They would meet just one more time before Hitler's death in 1945.

Another chunk of *Fire Music* has to do with the death of Hitler's mother, Klara, when he was eighteen years-old. There was a respected Jewish doctor in Linz named Eduard Bloch who visited Klara every day to pack the wound of her unsuccessful mastectomy with a caustic substance known as iodoform. This was done in an effort to burn out her breast cancer, but it was a painful and smelly procedure. Hitler didn't blame Bloch when Klara eventually died in December 1907. Indeed, he sent a note thanking him effusively for all the house calls he'd made, offered the doctor his "everlasting gratitude," and even presented him with one of his watercolors. Then, more than thirty years later, Hitler protected Bloch during the holocaust by allowing him and his wife to emigrate from Austria to America in 1940. Eerie! Did the un-experienced fury at Bloch transfer to the entire Jewish race? Maybe, but that wasn't the whole story. One has to be careful about explaining Hitler—in fact, about explaining anything. I believe strongly in plural causes, but there *are* causes. You can't just abdicate trying to understand, especially something like Hitler. Take away the First World War and I don't think it would have happened. Is the same true of his mother's death? I'm not sure, possibly. What about the Academy of Fine Arts, if they had let him in? Or was his unfortunate destiny so baked in that he would never have been satisfied with the life of an artist? I do know one thing: I consider it a sin to think that Hitler wasn't human. The terrible thing is he was.

Like a lot of these unmade projects, *Fire Music* is something I've lived with for many years. I've worked on it, off and on, for a long time and made it an even stronger and more affecting piece of material. It's a wonderful script, the most important of all the unrealized movies I've ever been involved with. We've come fairly close once or twice to making it. Back in 2002, we almost did *Fire Music* as the next picture after

Suspended Animation. Bob Hiler was seriously interested in producing it, as he loved the script and thought the concept was impressive. When we had some preliminary discussions about casting the lead, our choices were limited because the actor had to be young and have a name. At this point, I wanted John Cusack for the role of Hitler as I've always been an admirer of his. Before Cusack, I did offer the role to Richard Gere, even though he was too mature, but Richard passed. None of this mattered anyway, as at the last minute Bob suddenly had some reservations about doing the picture. He felt it would be too difficult to pull off as the budget was prohibitively high; it was a period piece with elaborate costumes, sets, props, etc, and would also have required some shooting in Germany. Bob remained a big fan of the project and still really wanted to get it going. That was until his unfortunate death from pancreatic cancer in February 2003. Bob's passing effectively put an end to this iteration of *Fire Music*, but I still harbor hopes of one day making it. Like *The Klansman*, the script is just too damn good to rot away.

When you sit on a project for as long as I have, somewhere down the line you can expect another filmmaker to come out with a movie that tackles the same subject. Around the time Bob and I were trying to get *Fire Music* activated, I learned about a new movie called *Max*, which similarly dealt with Hitler's life as an aspiring artist. It was written and directed by Menno Meyjes, who had previously written *The Color Purple* for Spielberg. *Max* was about a fictional art dealer in Munich (played by John Cusack no less), who meets Hitler in the years following World War I. So, this Adolf was a veteran, older and bitter about Germany's devastating loss and the humiliating reparations the nation was forced to pay in the wake of the Treaty of Versailles. To some degree Meyjes was addressing some of the things I was interested in exploring in *Fire Music*, and for that reason I was anxious to see *Max*. As a historical drama I found his film more philosophical than factual, but it did contain an unpleasantly negative view of Hitler. Plainly, you have to form a negative view of Hitler due to the sheer vastness of the carnage and chaos he inspired, but I tried to avoid easy shots in *Fire Music*. Again, to me, the most terrifying thing about Hitler was that he was a human being. What he did was not unusual, only the appalling scale of it was. If you say, "Only crazy people are capable of such deplorable evil," that view is too easy, simplistic and dismissive. It definitely doesn't explain why the German nation got so behind Hitler's ideology and willingly marched into the mouth of Hell with him.

During the enforced eleven-year hiatus Hancock endured between Prancer *and* A Piece of Eden *which produced no features, he and Tristan began developing "a brave and bawdy romp" they christened* Bohemian Nights. *This screenplay concerns a Chicago wife who indulges her husband's all-consuming fetish by allowing him to covertly observe her having sex with other men as a perverse means of preserving the romance in their lives. After struggling for more than a decade to secure financing for this provocative project—a journey that at one point attracted the interest of South African investors—Hancock and Tristan finally reworked* Bohemian Nights *as a play at the invitation of Kim Clark. A screenwriting professor at DePaul University and co-owner of the Acorn Theatre in Three Oaks, Michigan, Clark had admiringly described the script as resembling "[The Adventures of] Ozzie and Harriet on crack!" The production received its world premier at the Acorn on June 9, 2006, where it played for two consecutive weekends to considerable acclaim.*

Early the following year the show moved to Chicago, where it played at the Chopin Theatre for twelve weeks in the face of a predominantly negative critical reception. Chris Jones, chief theater critic of the Chicago Tribune, *labeled the play "truly bizarre," asserting that "it feels mostly like an ill-conceived try for creative freedom [that is] tough to watch." Kris Vire of* Time Out Chicago *was equally damning in his evaluation: "The worst thing about* Bohemian Nights— *and there are many, many bad things—is the nagging sense that most everyone involved should know better. It's mind-boggling that the husband-and-wife team of Hancock and Tristan, not to mention the cast, crew and producers, could not step back and look at this absolute fiasco and think it was a good idea." An unrepentant Hancock, convinced of the project's virtues after witnessing the unanimously positive reactions of audiences as well as receiving favorable feedback from all those who've perused the screenplay, still retains ambitions of one day realizing* Bohemian Nights *as a movie.*

Back in the early 1990s, I was knocking the brains out of my skull trying to set-up various films with little success. One of these projects, *Bohemian Nights*, was a comedy about voyeurism that I thought—and still do—was a winner. It was inspired by something I had read in *Penthouse*. I don't know if they even have them anymore as there are porn websites devoted to the same subject, but back then there were all these White guys exchanging anecdotes about how much joy and excitement they felt watching Black guys fuck their wives. I thought that was an uncommonly funny and original subject to deal with on film, particularly if you had a husband that was constantly getting caught while peeping on these unsuspecting Black gentlemen. The magazine had a section called "*Penthouse* Forum" (another, if I remember correctly, was called "*Penthouse* Letters"). The stories were no doubt partly written by in-house wags, but augmented by real guys that wrote in about how they had screwed two stewardesses over the Atlantic, or had their nude wife serve drinks at a late-night convention cocktail party where she ended up having sex with everybody in attendance. These articles would have rather sordid titles like "Take My Wife Please," and there was a whole batch of letters on the aforementioned theme of Ebony and Ivory: White guys observing their spouses fucking massively endowed Black fellows.

In keeping with the tenor of these sleazy escapades we had read, *Bohemian Nights* was scripted by Dorothy to be both shocking and hilarious in equal measure. The story concerns Donald Cervanka and his wife Cathy who are musicians living in Cicero in a conservative Bohemian enclave—Bohemian as in Czech, not Left Bank. He conducts the orchestra at the same high school where I was once concertmaster; she plays the violin, but not professionally, and feels somewhat thwarted artistically. Because of this, perhaps, and because he's a pervert and loves it, the couple get into the regular pattern of Donald sharing Cathy with other men. Mainly he secretly watches the copulation from the armoire in some hotel room. She picks the guy up, brings him to the room, screws him, and nobody is the wiser. Everybody ends up happy and satisfied. In the opening scene, however, the Black guy Cathy has picked up sees the mirrored door of the armoire move slightly. This is our first hint that anybody is in there. They're busted! Tumult and humiliation ensues, followed by amusingly desperate attempts at explaining why Donald likes it and heartfelt apologies from Cathy.

After this embarrassing incident, Cathy is unexpectedly left with feelings for the guy this time, something she really hasn't experienced for any of their previous conquests. She wants to see him again and, at her husband's urging, she tracks this man down to the place where he works. Cathy then arranges to have the guy come to a nice Bohemian dinner at the house in Cicero—lily-white Cicero at this point in time, where they have to bring out the tanks whenever Black people attempt to move into the neighborhood. Cathy tells him that Donald is in Toronto, but he still arrives rather warily. He tells Cathy, "A voyeur is a voyeur; I just wonder if he isn't hiding in the bushes somewhere." The pair have dinner, and it's all very funny with Donald trying to spy on them through a hole he's bored in the ceiling over the dining room table. He is making suspicious noises in the attic, eager to see everything that is going on below him. Things between Cathy and her lover then move to the bedroom where Donald has tricked out the closet so that he can watch from there without getting caught. Suffice it to say, in the middle of the lovemaking, he does indeed get caught again and the story progresses from there.

I had several actors in mind for the role of Cathy: Jamie Lee Curtis, Goldie Hawn, and a whole string of others. I tried to get *Bohemian Nights* on over a long period of time with Julie Hagerty, who had earlier starred in *Airplane!* and *Lost in America*, and she really wanted to do it. At one point, Kirstie Alley tried to get Wesley Snipes to do the picture with her, but he passed. Robert Evans wanted to produce the film (it figures!) but he asked that the guy Cathy pursues be Italian, not African-American. We did a version of the screenplay that way for Bob, but it never happened and that draft wasn't quite as strong and spicy as the original version. John Daly also loved the script (again, it figures, as the project appealed to all horn dogs) and empowered me on behalf of his company Hemdale to make a firm offer to some star or other whose name I now forget. I do remember meeting with Paula Wagner at CCA about *Bohemian Nights* for one of her stars—maybe that was Goldie Hawn. Paula liked the script but did not trust Daly, and that avenue eventually petered out.

Later, I remember having a reading of the screenplay at our house in Malibu, which was very successful. Dorothy read the part of the wife; Ned Wynn, the writer of *California Dreaming*, read the part of the husband and was hilarious; an actor from around Los Angeles named Richard Lawson, who had previously appeared in *Poltergeist* and *Streets of Fire*, read the Black lover; Felton Perry was also involved in it, as was the English actress and singer Georgia Brown who read the role of Cathy and Donald's neighbor. Georgia had famously played the role of Nancy in the original 1960 production of *Oliver* in London, and was a good friend of ours at the time. Others present that evening were the agent Larry Mirisch, and Bill Badalato, and a lot of other people. Our big living room was full and the reading was really funny. Undeniably funny! Honestly, *Bohemian Nights* was something that would often make people burst out laughing whenever they read it aloud. Glynnis O'Connor was also there that evening and decided she would play Cathy in the film, but then got cold feet about doing the nudity.

Years passed. I had enjoyed working with Yoram Ben-Ami on *Steal the Sky* and we liked each other, and wanted to find another project to do together. I gave him the script for *Bohemian Nights* and he loved it. Yoram took it to some South African investors he knew, who also liked it. In the early 1990s, they flew Dorothy, Yoram, my lawyer and me to South Africa and it was a nice trip. Then we discovered that they wanted to set the movie *in* South Africa! Now that was a truly shocking idea, but I guess they understand their own country. Actually, it was a pretty good notion: an Afrikaner woman living with her musician husband in Cape Town, which is a beautiful place, both get involved with a Xhosa guy—Nelson Mandela's tribe. This was, I might add, during the time of the embargo and disinvestment from South Africa due to the nation's politics of apartheid. We didn't see how we could hold our heads up in the business if we violated the international injunction against working there. It would be one thing to take their money and do it in Cicero, or in an American studio, but we could not do the picture in South Africa, which was where there was real interest. Again, it was frustrating, but there was nothing to be done about it.

We did, though, shoot a promo for *Bohemian Nights*. This was after Yoram and I had visited his South African investors. They thought, and we agreed with them, that if we could do something that demonstrated how funny and sexy the project could be, it would enable them to finance it from South Africa, but produce it here. So, they put up $25,000 to pay for it. We then hired casting people and looked for the leads in New York and Los Angeles. We wanted full body nudity, so that cuts down somewhat on candidates who can act. It's not easy to act well with your clothes off even if you're willing. The result was I don't think we filled the role of Cathy as well as we could have. There was a Czech actress in New York who could have done it, but Dorothy was determined to find an American actress for this American wife. She felt it was a cop-out to cast a European, where such kinkiness perhaps, at least in the minds of some people, comes easier. I think, in retrospect, Dorothy was wrong. She would have been wonderful. Incidentally, this actress had previously had some kind of strange relationship like that with a famous Czech director (Sally Kirkland had starred in the film *Anna*, which was based on them).

The finished promo came in at around ten or twelve minutes. The shoot was only for three or four days and we filmed two scenes, really: the first detailed Donald and Cathy preparing for the lover to arrive; then we staged a second scene where Donald is hidden, watching them making love. For the role of Cathy's lover, we used John Toles-Bey; for the part of her husband we cast Mark Rolston. Misha Suslov shot it in a studio in Burbank. The shoot went well, but I wasn't happy with the way the promo turned out, nor was Yoram. The girl we eventually used for Cathy just didn't have the sexy gravitas, or the masochism, or some kind of quality that would have made it funny. In short, she just wasn't right, and her lightness and chipper attitude made it seem cheap and exploitative rather than real. It was the same problem with the look that Misha and I decided on: we went for a lush jewel box look, when what was needed was something drier and more rooted in the real world, like what Sven Nykvist gave *The Unbearable Lightness of Being*. Predictably, the South African investors did not like the footage any better than we did, and the project died, at least for the moment.

Around this time, Mariel Hemingway wanted to do the film, but I couldn't get the money together with her attached either. I knew that *Bohemian Nights* was difficult material because it was so outrageous, but I believed in it. So, I thought if I couldn't get it on as a movie, maybe I could as a play. And we did. When we first performed it in 2006 at the Acorn Theatre, close to where I live, we had Cary Cronholm playing Cathy and Jim Moehl playing Donald. We also had great support from Jeff Puckett, Kevin Giese and others. Now, Three Oaks was "The Home of *Prancer*" and it was quite an unsettling shift moving from *Prancer* to *Bohemian Nights*! But the play was sufficiently successful—and got such huge laughs from the audience—people wanted to take it to Chicago, which I agreed was the next logical step. I was proud of the Chicago production we did at the Chopin in February 2007 and it had some wonderful actors in it. We kept Cary and Jeff in their roles, but we recast it with the husband now played by B.H. Ward and the Black lover by Kenn E. Head. We got some big laughs all during the previews and I had high hopes for the play.

Unfortunately, we were then killed by the two main daily papers, the *Chicago Tribune* and the *Chicago Sun-Times*. I think mainly in the case of the *Trib* it was because Dorothy and I were from Hollywood. It was like,

"If you think you can come here and exploit our wonderful actors in your filth, you're sadly mistaken!" The lady critic at the *Sun-Times*, Hedy Weiss, was a little more favorable, as were a number of the critics for the smaller papers, but she was also shocked by the material. Weiss went as far as commenting that on the night she saw the show, it appeared that much of the audience was made up of "outpatients from a psychiatric hospital or inmates from a minimum security prison who were being rewarded for good behavior." I do remember that remark, as it was hardly a ringing endorsement of the quality of Chicago theater-goers. The critics just dismissed the play as weird and nasty—beneath our talents and a waste of their time. Well, I say fuck 'em if they can't take a joke! Their adverse opinions never made me lose confidence in *Bohemian Nights*, quite the opposite. If you were to ask me if I would still like to make it as a movie, my response would be an emphatic: "Yes! Let's get it *on!*"

> *Shortly before the release of* Suspended Animation *in late 2003, and with Bob Hiler's premature death inflicting a significant setback in his efforts to acquire financing for* Fire Music, *Hancock began researching a contemporary film that was to be located a lot closer to home. Based on the documented case of a sizable undercover drugs operation that had been carried out in two Indiana high schools in 1982, this unnamed project required fewer period trappings (and by extension called for a more modest budget) than a historical drama set in pre-First World War Austria. Unusually for the writer/director, Hancock decided that neither he nor Tristan would assume writing duties this time around and instead assigned a young writer named Joe Weisberg to the task of delivering a script. Like other tentative projects of the period, this police procedural/teen drama never materialized, and would be superceded by alternative projects that Hancock and Tristan were developing.*

How this one came about was interesting: one day, I went to the local sheriff here in LaPorte, and politely said, "I'm looking for a good subject to write a screenplay about. Can I look through your files and see if anything inspires me?" The sheriff then kindly recommended a case file to me that immediately captured my attention. It turns out that the authorities had once sent two undercover police officers into two high schools here in Indiana: New Prairie High School and Westville High School. One cop was a man and the other was a woman. Their investigations meant they were undercover for most of a school year, but their efforts eventually resulted in a major bust that involved around twenty or thirty students. So, it was a pretty big deal. When I looked into the details of the case—the arrests had been made more than twenty years earlier—and examined the stories of those involved, I realized it was something that could potentially make a movie.

Joe Weisberg is a Chicago-born writer who in recent years has enjoyed huge success with *The Americans*, the wonderful TV series he created for the FX network. Back in 2003, when he was unknown in the business, I contacted Joe and got him to write a draft for me. I don't often farm out script assignments to another writer, but on this particular project I did. I wanted to work with Weisberg and I thought he would be a sound choice for it. Although he had not written a screenplay at this point in time, I believed in Joe, as I had previously read a coming-of-age novel he had written called *10th Grade*. It was about a kid at a high school, who gets good grades and is also a jock. This teenager is dealing with the familiar problems that most teenagers face—chasing after girls, trying to find one's identity and purpose, dealing with parents, teachers and other kids—but the first-person stream-of-conscious narrative Joe had adopted made it funny and engaging. *10th Grade* clearly demonstrated that he could write and had a real insight into the mindset of an adolescent. So, for those two very good reasons, I thought he would be a good fit for my project.

Joe and I then spent time with the two undercover officers involved in the bust in an attempt to gather up some more first-hand information. Actually, I spent much more time with the male officer than I did with the female officer. Blunderingly, I made the mistake at our first meeting of asking her if the rumor I heard was true, that she'd had an affair with the detective in charge of the investigation. She clammed right up after that, and didn't want to meet anymore. At the time, I didn't know if there had been any repercussions or reprisals for either of the two cops involved in the case, or for the criminals that had been arrested. Neither was I certain of exactly how many people went to jail and for how long. Thus, the research we did was important. Weisberg's draft, which I don't believe ever had a title and was known simply as *The High School Undercover Story*, was not liked by the people around me. There was concern that it was too much like *21 Jump Street*, the TV series from the 1980s that had starred Johnny Depp and Richard Grieco as young undercover police officers who were going into high schools and colleges to investigate various crimes. So, we eventually decided not to proceed with the project. That was a shame, as I still think it's a compelling and commercial idea.

You know, I've had lots of different dealings with screenwriters, both good and bad dealings. I've had the typical experience you suffer with a Hollywood writer—I had it with Howard Sackler on *Jaws 2* and Ernest Tidyman on *Forfeit*, as well as on most of the development deals I've had. What happens is you get lumbered with a name writer who's tasted some success and he eventually types up a steaming piece of shit, hands it in, and collects his fee. In essence this person has merely done it for the money, and can see no better reason to be involved with the project than that. The money a screenwriter receives is generally so good they are tempted to take deals that they have no personal feeling or affinity for. Now, to me, that's fucking infuriating! It's mercenary! If it hasn't already become clear from your initial meetings with the writer, it certainly becomes evident from the first draft that they have insufficient passion for the subject. So, then he or she is owed a polish for another sum and, in a way, what's the point of having the writer do the polish? It's not going to get any better, that's for damn sure. All the same, the writer does the polish, turns it in, and the script is easily no better. Sometimes it's even *worse*! Dorothy is not like that, she doesn't do it just for the money. We are often working on the script together, so I feel that I'm creating it, too. This is very valuable to me, because I know in this instance the writer has the same intensity of feeling for the project that I have.

Joe wasn't in it for the money either. In fact there was *no* money for him, he was doing the script on spec, but he did his best to do an excellent job. On this occasion it didn't turn out well, but he is a talented writer and during our association there was good will on all sides. I don't know, sometimes things just don't happen for you. I felt at a certain point he was looking for more guidance from me, but I wasn't certain what to tell him to make the script better. Maybe the problem was social class. Joe is a scion of an important Chicago family: his father, Bernard Weisberg, was a brilliant lawyer, and his mother, Lois Weisberg was simply a phenomenon. She was Mayor Richard Daley's cultural czar for decades, and knew everybody from Lenny Bruce to Ann Roosevelt. On the other end of the spectrum she was actually a friend of my mother's. (I was also amused to read in Billy Friedkin's recent autobiography that it was in Lois's living room where he met Sidney Korshak, who is universally thought to be the Chicago Mob's guy in Hollywood). Joe's brother, Jacob, runs *Slate Magazine*, and Joe himself is a former CIA officer. He went to Francis Parker, a prestigious Chicago prep school filled with budding artists. New Prairie High School was an entirely different world. I think neither Joe nor I had any real idea how the kids there talked and thought. I mean, the reason Joe's work on *The Americans* is so brilliant is because he *knows* that world. Maybe Joe and I were just rushing and needed to keep at it longer, soak in the world, and do another draft. I bet he could have licked it.

> *Considering the regret he still carries at his decision to turn down* Glory *in 1988, it should come as no surprise that Hancock has long sought to locate or originate another film project set amid the tumultuous milieu of the American Civil War. In the spring of 2008, following a busy period in which the previous fall he'd already adapted his screenplay* The Brother *into a play and was rehearsing both it and* 'night Mother *in The Theatre Building Chicago, Hancock somehow found time to extensively research and complete a 162-page screenplay entitled* Hood. *A sprawling historical drama cum love story, it chronicles the ignominious fall of the legendary Confederate general John Bell Hood. Born in Owingsville, Kentucky in 1831, Hood attended the United States Military Academy against the wishes of his father. After graduating at the age of twenty-two, he was stationed as a junior Army officer in both California and Texas, before resigning his commission and joining the Confederate Army of the 4th Texas Infantry at the start of the Civil War where he was rapidly promoted to the rank of colonel. After distinguishing himself on a dozen fields of combat, Hood came to prominence for his aggressive leadership as a brigade commander in the army of Robert E. Lee during the Seven Days Battle in 1862.*
>
> *Hood was also a significant participant in the Battle of Gettysburg in 1863, a skirmish in which he was severely wounded. Just two months later, he led a daring assault into a gap in the Union line at the Battle of Chickamauga, where he was again critically wounded. After recuperating from his terrible injuries, Hood returned to field service during the Atlanta Campaign of 1864 with the Army of Tennessee. He*

> was temporarily promoted to the rank of general at the age of thirty-three, making him the youngest Army commander of the war. However, Hood's forces were decisively defeated during the Franklin-Nashville Campaign, and he was relieved of his rank—at his own request—in January 1865. After the war ended that same year, Hood moved to Louisiana, where he married Anna Marie Hennen and had eleven children. He worked as a cotton broker and later became President of the Life Assurance of America, earning a prosperous living until suffering a financial crisis in 1878. He died in August 1879 of yellow fever just days after the epidemic had claimed the lives of his wife and eldest child, leaving his remaining ten children destitute.

John Bell Hood earned a reputation both for his unflinching bravery in battle and for a series of crushing defeats he suffered during the Civil War (there's such a thing as being *too* brave!) The screenplay of *Hood* is partly based on a very famous and very wonderful diary written by Mary Boykin Chesnut, a Confederate wife who was married to an aide of the Confederate President, Jefferson Davis. Her memoirs offer an inside view of the goings-on in Richmond and Charleston, South Carolina during the conflict; who all the major players were and exactly what went down. It's such a remarkable and important piece of writing, perhaps the most important of its time, as Chesnut was witness to so much of these turbulent events and documented them over the course of four years between 1861 and 1865. You get a sense when you're reading her diary of these significant and defining events unfolding, and it's gripping stuff. It's also a love story, glimpsed in pieces between the lines of the diary, between Hood and the most beautiful Southern belle of her time, Sally "Buck" Preston. Their love is tested when Hood keeps coming back from combat with pieces of him missing. First he lost the use of an arm at the Battle of Gettysburg, and then an entire leg at the Battle of Chickamauga. This put pressure on his love affair with this fabulously beautiful woman.

I would characterize *Hood* as the story of a loser; it's the story of a losing cause, and the sacrifices and setbacks a man is willing to endure in the name of doing what he believes is right and just. Hood was unstoppable, in love and in war, and he was eventually stopped big-time in both. Okay, so what happens to a man in those circumstances? That is what interested me. And, happily, the film potentially presented me with the chance to do a big battle scene since the screenplay climaxes with the Battle of Franklin, which commenced on November 30, 1864. Hood has marched his army north after being forced to evacuate Atlanta, and he concocts the plan to capture Nashville, and then perhaps even Chicago. He hoped to end the war, but the truth is Hood was a classic over-reacher. He is met by the Union Army at Franklin, south of Nashville, which was under the command of Major General George H. Thomas (who had been Hood's former instructor during his formative years at West Point). General Hood then makes a tragic mistake that costs him his reputation: he charges a fortified position. Eleven generals under him are either killed or wounded and his army is destroyed, but he *still* keeps going! He besieges Nashville in the winter with diminished forces, which ends as badly as you might imagine. So, *Hood* is about the limits of unstopability—to coin a new word—and of sheer dumb go-ahead. Did I identify with the general for that reason? Sure.

I wrote the screenplay with Dorothy's help, and I'm very proud of it. This is more my script than others we've collaborated on together, but she made some important contributions. I researched the life and times of John Bell Hood in fastidious detail, as when I research something I really do it. I look at my bookcase and I see two shelves full of Civil War books which I devoured for this project, as well as a further two shelves of books about Hitler which I devoured while researching *Fire Music*. Now, those are merely the volumes I purchased; I also spent a lot of time in libraries. For *Hood*, I went to the Library of Congress and read every issue of the Richmond newspapers from 1860 to 1865. My research process tends to start by reading, and then writing while I'm reading some more, and then I start to think about visiting places where things happened. I drove south in the early spring of 2008 to visit the battlefields at Franklin and Chickamauga, as well as stopping by Buck Preston's grave in Columbia, South Carolina. Looking at this research material and the script, I think *Hood* is a wonderful story that would make a terrific movie. At the moment, I'm trying to get Scarlet Johansson to play Buck the rapturous Southern belle. My lawyer is presently trying to get the script to her. I also thought of Ryan Gosling for the part of Hood as I like him a lot. I think Gosling is a brave actor, who makes a lot of interesting choices in the kinds of roles he takes on. We'll just have to wait and see what happens with it.

> *During the summer of 2008, immediately following their exhaustive efforts on* Hood, *Hancock and Tristan completed a screenplay adaptation of the controversial*

2001 book Fugitive Days: A Memoir *written by former activist-turned-educator Bill Ayers. Once the leader of the Weather Underground Organization, or "Weathermen," the latter title derived from a line in Bob Dylan's 1965 song "Subterranean Homesick Blues" ("You don't need a weatherman to know which way the wind blows"), Ayers had co-founded the radical left-wing group in 1969 as a militant outgrowth of Students for a Democratic Society. Shortly after their formation, the Weathermen issued a "Declaration of a state of war" against the United States Government, commencing a campaign of bombings that targeted a number of official buildings. This included the 1970 bombing of the New York City Police Department headquarters, the 1971 bombing of the U.S. Capitol, the 1972 bombing of the Pentagon, and the 1975 bombing of the U.S. State Department building. Following these attacks, Ayers and his wife, Bernadine Dohrn, would spend the next decade on the run from the Government as fugitives from justice before eventually surrendering themselves to authorities in 1980.*

Prior to Hancock optioning Ayers' memoir in 2006, the subject of the Weather Underground had already inspired two movies as well as a feature-length documentary. The first film, Jeremy Kagan's TV movie Katherine *(1975), starred Sissy Spacek as a wealthy debutante who undergoes a transformation from delicate hippie activist to fervent radical extremist after being confronted with the various social and political injustices of the world. Spacek's character was loosely based on the real-life figure of Ayers' girlfriend, Diane Oughton. The privileged daughter of a middle-class Illinois family, Oughton was killed on March 6, 1970, after the nail bomb she was constructing (a device intended to detonate at a Fort Dix military dance event) exploded prematurely in the basement of a Greenwich Village townhouse, reducing the four-storey building to rubble. Two members of the group, Terry Robbins and Ted Gold, were also killed, whereas a further two affiliates, Kathy Boudin and Cathy Wilkerson, survived the blast. The second film,* Running on Empty *(1988), directed by*

> *Sidney Lumet, concerns a couple (played by Judd Hirsch and Christine Lahti) that have been on the run since the 1970s following their involvement in the anti-war protest bombing of a napalm factory. Some have presumed it to be loosely based on Ayers and Dohrn, but Hancock questions this: "I liked* Running on Empty, *but it didn't seem to me that the movie was based on Bill and Bernadine. There were other couples."* Fugitive Days *promises to be the definitive version of their story.*

The Weathermen have always fascinated me, how they came about, what they did, what the consequences of their actions were. It plays like a movie anyway, only it really happened. *Fugitive Days* recounts Bill Ayers' days as an activist opposing the war in Vietnam and then as a fugitive from justice—he and Bernadine spent ten years on the run, changing jobs and identities, moving from place to place. Can you imagine the stress of having to do that? Oh, man! But he and others felt it was a price worth paying. Despite setting bombs off in the Pentagon and the Capitol building, Bill did not consider himself and his fellow Weathermen to be terrorists. They had made the bomb that exploded in the Pentagon for a couple of hundred bucks, but it didn't do nearly as much damage as they'd hoped. Bill thought the Weathermen were involved in an important common struggle: waging war on the systematic brutality, dishonesty, and oppression of the U.S. Government. He saw the authorities as preserving and enforcing racism and imperialism, and they were killing innocent people in Vietnam. Bill wanted to do something about this—I mean, *really* do something—in a way that brandishing a placard and marching down a street could never achieve. I had protested the war myself. I was deeply troubled by America's involvement in Vietnam, the terrible things we were doing over there—the intensive bombings, the atrocities—but I wasn't affiliated with the Weathermen or any other radical movements or groups.

Those years were some turbulent times in America. There was a lot of parochialism and duplicity from the U.S. Government, and I found that I shared Ayers' views. I believed that the Weathermen were right to do what they did, that it was important to resort to violence to try to end the war in Vietnam. There are many who considered Bill to be a traitor to his country, and the actions of his group to be sedition, but there were others in high office who could be accused of the same crime. What about the terrible cost of Vietnam to our country? Who do we hold to account for that conflict? I abhor violence, but sometimes it's the only option available when your voice isn't being heard. It's easy to dismiss what they tried to do, or paste over the facts and rewrite history. So much was going on. Bill wanted America to be defeated and for Vietnam to triumph. I've recently learned that a quote has been attributed to Bill that he supposedly made back in 1970, which explained what the Weathermen was all about: "Kill all rich people. Break up their cars and apartments. Bring the revolution home. Kill your parents. That's where it's really at." Well, did he in fact say that? It's not in the book, I don't think. There's a lot of distortion and, frankly, a lot of craziness too on their part. Again, it was a *bad* time. I'm sure Bill would totally disown that quote today, except for the "Bring the revolution home" part. I mean, c'mon, "*Kill your parents*"!? The fact is Bill nursed his Alzheimer-afflicted father for years. His father lived with Bill and Bernadine in their Hyde Park home.

When *Fugitive Days* was first announced as a film back in October 2008, it was shortly before the presidential nominees Barrack Obama and John McCain were going head-to-head for the Oval Office hot seat. The Republicans had attacked Obama for his tenuous dealings with Ayers as, apparently, Bill and Bernadine had organized a fundraiser for Obama several years earlier. During the third of the three televised presidential debates between the candidates, McCain rather dismissively said, "I don't care about some old washed-up terrorist, but we do need to know the extent of the relationship between Mr. Obama and Mr. Ayers." Obviously, McCain *did* care and he knew what he was doing—allying his political rival with a known former radical. So, why mention it in the first place? It was a bullshit move, really. There was some feeling that as all this was going on with McCain and Sarah Palin talking on the news about Ayers' links to Obama, interest in a film about the Weathermen could potentially be substantial. At the very least we thought it would remind people of these events, and expose those who weren't familiar with what happened to the history. It seemed to be the right time to get the project financed, but, in actual fact, that wasn't the case at all. Entertainment executives on the Left were anxious not to hurt Obama by reminding them of his connection to Ayers.

Interestingly, in December 2008, a second edition of *Fugitive Days* was published. This was possibly done to capitalize on the publicity drummed up during the presidential elections. The revised volume came with a new afterword by Bill in which he discussed the hate mail he'd received after the publication of the first edition in 2001 from those who still considered him a terrorist. I've read the afterword and most of Bill's other books, including his 2013 book *Public Enemy: Confessions of an American Dissident*, in which he addresses the whole Obama thing at length. Bill can be quite funny about the death threats he has received, and there were a *lot* of them. The University of Illinois at Chicago, where Bill was teaching at that point in time, actually assigned him a bodyguard. This individual was a rather colorful guy, according to Bill. You see, there were two especially credible threats to his continued existence: one was from a man who enclosed photographs of Bill's front door, saying that he was coming to Chicago to stake him with a sniper rifle. The other was from someone who intended to come to Chicago to kidnap Bill and water-board him before executing him. The bodyguard told Bill, "Just pray the sniper gets here first!"

Upon first reading *Fugitive Days* I thought there was a plain-speaking economy and wit to Bill's writing, but I felt the book also had a force and directness to it. Others feel differently and there are some who've called the memoir "self-serving." Me, I felt it was a story worth telling. When it originally came out, certain claims were made by critics and analysts that the book was "morally clueless." I happened to glance at the Wikipedia entry on *Fugitive Days* one afternoon, and saw that Cathy Wilkerson, a former member of the Weathermen, called it "inaccurate" and "a cynical, superficial romp," as well as accusing Bill of making their struggle seem like "a glorious carnival." Those were her exact words. Really, it's like members of any group chewing around at each other after the fact. People did fall out over this and that. After the Greenwich Village townhouse bomb went off, Bill and Bernadine quarreled with another leader of the group named Mark Rudd. He now attacks Bill from the Right, saying they were all crazy, but then Rudd qualified as a full-on (to use Communist jargon) Left-Wing Deviationist. Mark wanted to continue the violence against people even in the wake of the townhouse explosion. He thought *not* killing people was a cop-out, an abnegation of the necessity for revolutionary violence by what were in essence White middle-class kids. I've read Wilkerson's book, and I don't remember where she came down on that serious split in the organization, but I suspect she sided with Bill and Bernadine. As far as Bill's inaccuracies, yes, I feel that the entire story is not always being told because there are people to protect. But I have no doubt as to his essential truthfulness.

The reason why I wanted to make *Fugitive Days* into a movie was because it had action, it had heart, it was a wonderful love story, and I thought it had relevance to our time. I conceived the film during George

W. Bush's invasion of Iraq. I thought young people would rise up against that, like they did in the 1960s. Sadly, that didn't happen, perhaps because there was no draft. Thus, my hope of riding a wave of popular protest failed to materialize. Then I thought it might get renewed heat from the Obama connection, but that too fizzled out for the reasons I mentioned: people were desperate not to hurt Obama by dragging up the past. There's a tremendous role of timing in what gets on and what succeeds, and what doesn't. It's usually not within your control. In preparing the adaptation of *Fugitive Days*, I spent forty hours interviewing Bill and Bernadine, gathering as much additional information as I could. You see, there is a lot to their story that has never been told.

During this time, I grew to be fond of the both of them. Truly, these are exceptional people. Dorothy and I shared a lot of happy dinners with Bill and Bernadine. So, it wasn't just our working on the project, we became good friends. When he reflected on his time in the Weathermen, Bill regretted some of his actions but not others. I think Bernadine, who is very smart and eloquent, is more embarrassed by some of the extremes they went to. There's a certain rueful humor in Bill, but we also discussed some very personal and painful experiences he suffered. For instance, we talked about Diane Oughton, Bill's girlfriend who perished in the townhouse explosion at the age of twenty-eight. She was somebody whom he spoke of a lot during our conversations and Diane is an important character in the first half of the screenplay. As Bill and I once said to each other, "This film is really *two* love stories, separated by an explosion."

After Dorothy and I finished the screenplay, my agent duly sent it out to various producers. There were a few little nibbles but nobody bit. I sent it to Mike Medavoy who turned it down. I then tried Craig Baumgarten, who had co-produced *Hook* for Steven Spielberg, and Gary Lucchesi, who is the President of Lakeshore Entertainment and has produced pictures like *Million Dollar Baby*. It didn't work out with either of them. We did get a positive reaction at one point from HBO, but that too finally came to nothing. I remember Dorothy sent it to her friend Jon Voight, who was totally aghast. Voight exclaimed, "My God, Dorothy! Don't you know that I'm a *patriot*?!" I worked very hard at getting *Fugitive Days* on as a movie, but, ultimately, I wasn't able to. That was disappointing, as I had considerable confidence in the film. Just the same, there have been some recent developments with another project that treads similar territory. My old friend, Steve Scheffer, who was second in command at HBO for thirty years, and another guy who was Co-President at the network, have an idea to make a television series about the Weathermen and the Black Liberation Army.

It's called *Radical*, and is set in New York during the 1970s. The project will hopefully be a high-end, quality show like *Homeland*—only transposed to a period setting—that will be intricately plotted and have a discernible emotional and visceral punch. It's about radical groups, and bombers bombing places, and FBI guys working undercover, and all kinds of compelling things. Basically, it involves domestic terrorists with high ideals and anti-war beliefs, who are trying to end the conflict in Vietnam by blowing things up in America. So, again, it's the use of violence in order to prevent further violence—a contrariety I find interesting. Since I have written a screenplay about the Weathermen, this subject matter is right up my alley. I know a great deal about the history and the people and the politics involved. I've been working on some ideas for it and the next time I go to New York, I'm going to be meeting with Steve and others to discuss the project, and see if we can get some traction on it. I'm really excited about it, and if *Radical* does happen it will be of some consolation to me now that *Fugitive Days* has possibly died a death.

> *Two of the most intriguing projects Hancock has recently been laboring on are* American Steel, *a gritty drama about spirited steelworkers in an Indiana plant, and* Putzi, *a partially fictionalized account of Ernst "Putzi" Hanfstaengl (1887-1975), a Bavarian businessman and trusted confidante of Adolf Hitler who later defected to the United States from Nazi Germany after falling out of favor with the Fuehrer. As of this writing,* American Steel *is still very much a work in progress as Hancock sifts through the plenitude of research and interview materials he has amassed. Happily, an impressive first draft of* Putzi *was completed in just ten days by Hancock and Tristan in late January 2016. Based on the strength of this screenplay, the filmmaker hopes to secure a starry cast for the production.*

A number of years ago I wanted to make a film about steelworkers and gave a series of interviews to local newspapers in the steelworker area around Gary and Michigan City. Basically, I let it be known that I was looking for a story. Following this, a whole bunch of guys who had worked at Bethlehem Steel, which was at one time America's second-largest steel producer before the plant closed, came to me with stories about their experiences. So, I began conducting lengthy interviews with all of them. Many of the stories they told me were profoundly sad and tragic. Somebody would say, "I worked at the plant my whole life, but now I don't have a pension. My wife and I are dying of cancer and we don't have medical insurance. We don't know what to do." At least five or six different guys came to me recounting that same terrible situation. What happened was Bethlehem declared bankruptcy in order to get out of paying all of the workers' pensions, medical plans, and what have you, or they simply cut them way, way back. It was tough hearing such devastating personal stories, very emotional. In truth, it seemed to me like it was just too sad and too awful a story. It was an important story, but not one I wanted to make a movie of.

A little time passed. Now, let me say that when he isn't appearing in my movies, Jeff Puckett is a steelworker. While we were on the set of *The Looking Glass*, I got talking to him about the situation at the mill, which is open again under another name (he works in the furnace area). I asked Jeff how the workers feel about the work they do, and each other, and their lives and families. The guys, he told me, now all have this unique camaraderie, this kind of elite esprit. They say, "Yeah, we make the best steel in the world! We're friends, and we stick up and fight for each other. We all drink beer and some of us guys cheat on our wives, and we lie for each other. We do *everything* together!" It then suddenly struck me that maybe there was a film about American workers with high morale. I mean, the current plight of the steelworker in Indiana is this: it's the best industrial job in the area. These guys earn big salaries, drive Lexus cars, and enjoy the local casinos (of course, you have to be able to pass the drug tests at the mills, which not everybody can). Anyway, I interested a bunch of Jeff's friends at the mill in speaking to me and later transcribed the interviews. Presently, I'm still trying to devise a story out of this material that has enough plot; something that isn't just about cheating on your wife and perhaps involves the stealing of precious metals from the mill, and so on and so forth.

The truth is I'm stuck on it at the moment. Jeff is actually taking a crack at it too, parallel to my efforts. So, we're trying to forge something powerful out of what I think is a wonderful subject. But that's not quite enough, as the story has to be *right*. It has to be rich, and absorbing, and entertaining; it has to be saying something too, possibly about male relationships, and responsibility, and family, and tragedy. At this point in time, I haven't convinced myself that I've got the right story yet. I've got a lot of great stuff, but I need to select and shape it. Sometimes, when you do a lot of research, you can get lost. If you conduct a lot of interviews with people connected to a particular occupation or event, or read about it, you can be trapped in the minutiae of the information you've gathered when you should be trying to find a good story. That process can be difficult and distressing. It's the same problem Hal Ashby had on *8 Million Ways to Die*: you fall in love with the side-trips. It's hard to control documentary material because it's *all* so interesting. That's always the danger. I thought of involving Robert Ward, and we emailed ideas back and forth, but it came to nothing: he didn't seem to have any better idea than I did about how to crack the story. Then too, there's something troubling to me here about my whole involvement in this subject. How can I tell an important story about American working men when I've never had a job? Really, am I the right guy for this? I think probably not. To start with, I don't know how they talk. But it's still a good idea with another writer.

Like *American Steel*, I feel *Putzi* is another project with strong potential. I've only just finished the script—I wrote it very quickly, which was nice. Ernst "Putzi" Hanfstaengl was Hitler's piano player among other things. I wanted to write a script about him after I came upon his 1957 memoir *Unheard Witness* while researching *Fire Music,* and I was intrigued by his story. An inside view of Hitler's rise to power, the book helped me to understand how such a thing could have happened, and what people liked about Hitler since he seems so repellent and crazy when you look at his public speeches. Some of the script is historically authentic in its details, but a great deal of it is invented. One example: *Putzi* is primarily an action picture about Hanfstaengl's attempt to get out of Germany, when in reality he had little trouble in escaping. He simply got on a train to Zurich, spending some months there before going to England. He was later interned as an enemy alien when the Second World War broke out and was transferred from England to a prison camp in Canada. He was finally released to what eventually became Camp David in Maryland, so Putzi was close enough to Washington to advise President Roosevelt on the inner workings and potential weaknesses of the Nazi power elite.

In my screenplay, we have an exciting and extended sequence that details Putzi's rescuing of his Hitler Youth daughter. Now, as I've readily admitted, I do adopt a certain poetic license with the truth in some sections of the story. For instance, the dramatization of Hanfstaengl's involvement in Kristallnacht, and Dachau and so forth, are all made up (also, there's a scene where Putzi quite literally shits his pants while riding on a plane, which he didn't do in reality as far as I know!) I recently showed the script to John Lahr and he feels it's important that the character of Hanfstaengl have more charm and wit. I agree with him, and I'm trying to figure out how best to achieve that aim. I talked to Arthur Kopit about perhaps providing some additional lines of dialogue, but we decided together that he wasn't the right guy. I wished and hoped that Lahr could do it, but he's got a wonderful play that Scott Rudin is producing (it concerns the Stork Club in New York and is a two-hander with Walter Winchell and Sherman Billingsley), and he's far too busy.

With *Fire Music* I am dramatizing the young, invisible Hitler who is drifting around pre-First World War Vienna. The Hitler in *Putzi* is much older and is now the all-powerful Fuehrer. At this juncture of his life and career, I thought it was important to see Hitler's charm as well as how dangerous he is in the process of becoming. Hanfstaengl was a close witness to the change in him, and ran seriously afoul by trying to tell his ex-friend what he saw happening. One of the things I like about Putzi's exchanges with Hitler in the script is that Hanfstaengl doesn't come across as some fawning ass-kisser trying to curry favor, as no doubt so many others were. He spoke to Hitler as somebody who had known him before his rise to total power. Putzi felt they were close enough that there was a chance that Hitler would actually listen to him. He was hopelessly mistaken about that.

The script also features an appearance by the groundbreaking German filmmaker Leni Riefenstahl in two scenes, one in which she "dances seductively" for Hitler. Riefenstahl appears in the screenplay exactly as Hanfstaengl describes her in his memoir—this part of it is not made up at all—a sexy woman trying to see how far Hitler would go. I do not buy Riefenstahl's subsequent claims that she was not a Nazi. The fact is they were *all* Nazis. Consider this: what did it mean in that world to not be a Nazi? I imagine there were things she didn't approve of, but people merely think "nothing's perfect." That doesn't make you not a Nazi! Clearly, from looking at her work, particularly *Triumph of the Will* which spectacularly documented the 1934 Nazi Party Congress in Nuremberg, one can see that Riefenstahl adored Hitler and what he was doing for Germany. Incidentally, it's interesting to look at the range of these unmade projects we've discussed and what they have in common. They're mostly about guys on the wrong side: the KKK, Hitler, Hood, the Weathermen, Hanfstaengl. This undoubtedly says something about me.

In regard to the question of financing *Putzi*, it's possible to get quite a bit of money from the German and Bavarian film funds, but Hollywood money has to come in first. It's one of those chicken or egg things that delay so many enterprises. I have a partner on this project in Munich, Uli Limmer, who has done a number of pictures for the German market, and we're trying to get *Putzi* on. At this early stage, what *Putzi* needs is a big star attached to it in order to secure the money. Bill Badalato and I have been talking about various Hollywood actors who can play the titular role: Russell Crowe, Christian Bale, possibly even Tom Hardy or Michael Fassbender—although Hardy may be a little too young (but is *so* good) and Fassbender a little too tough. Whoever plays Hanfstaengl needs to have a certain aristocratic Bavarian charm, mixed with an ability to be a bit of a clown. The actor must also possess the strength to become what Putzi eventually becomes—he toughens under duress and confinement in the Dachau concentration camp. The clown becomes a man. The screenplay has a big important character arc: we see Hanfstaengl transform from a Nazi sympathizer to someone determined to do everything in his power, short of giving his life, to bring them down. We need a strong lead to convey that process.

Mark Ruffalo has some of the right characteristics for the part, but is too American. The Jeremy Irons we saw as Claus von Bülow in *Reversal of Fortune* would be delicious, but Badalato says we could not raise the money based on him anymore. Besides, Irons turned it down when we offered it to him. Somebody recently suggested Michael Shannon as Putzi to me, and he's an actor I like, but I bet Badalato will say the same thing: we can't raise money on him—at least not yet. Let's see how his career progresses. It's the same predicament with John C. Reilly and Vincent D'Onofrio, two other actors I've considered in my head for the role, who aren't fundable at that budget level. Aiming exceedingly high, Daniel Day Lewis is another one I'd love to play Putzi, but I now understand that he's semi-retired, or is about to retire. Sure, he's very choosy about the roles he takes on, but I'm hoping that the right picture would lure him out. Based on the strength of my script, *Putzi* could possibly be that picture.

As I've been working on all these projects, I've also been teaching directing. I started teaching at Columbia College Chicago, which in terms of the number of students is the biggest film school in the United States, about ten years ago. I still teach there, one day a week, as well as at Second City's Harold Ramis Film School. Teaching is not something I ever consciously planned to do, it just happened. Allen Turner, who was still President of the Board at that time, approached me to teach at Columbia, and I said, "Sure, okay." He then put me in touch with the dean there, Doreen Bartoni, and the chair of the Cinema Department, Bruce Sheridan, and they hired me. Last year, when I got the offer from Second City to help organize their new film school, I worked with Trevor Albert (he produced *Groundhog Day* for Harold Ramis as well as several other pictures) and Jack Newell to devise the curriculum. I teach there now, very happily, and we focus on comedy. As a matter of fact, it's the only film school in the country that does that, and we have big hopes for its future.

Sometimes as a director, or as a writer, when you take a teaching job or decide to go out on the lecture circuit, you can get the terrible sensation that your career has stalled. I've not allowed that to happen to me. I'm never entirely standing still. I'm always working on something, as our discussion of all these prospective projects evidently shows. For all that, I can say that teaching has proved to be a valuable experience for me. What I've found interesting about it is my constant attempts at trying to tell people in words what it is I do intuitively, which, in some ways I guess, is exactly what our conversations in this book have been. What teaching has done for me is it's helped me to understand what it is I do to some degree. What I mean is a lot of the things you do as a director you almost communicate them in a verbal shorthand of some kind. So, you don't think them in a way that you can explain to someone as a succinct methodology. I'm constantly being struck by this fact when I'm teaching. Indeed, I think about it all the time, but I've never expressed this dilemma to my students. You see, just because you know how to do something doesn't mean you know how to convey that process to another person so that they can do it, too. You have to learn how to articulate the knowledge if you want to be a teacher and I've found that experience revealing.

When I started out as a director there were very few film schools in America that taught you the craft of making movies: how to light, shoot, edit, produce and direct. Today, film schools are everywhere and it's now become a bit of a racket. Perhaps the question we should confront is this: are we empowering students to have a career in this highly competitive field, or are we teaching creativity, teaching somebody how to have a nice life? There's a lot to be said for having a nice life, so I don't feel the effort is wasted with those who decide not to go into the business. For those who do, I always stress that they leave no stone unturned. I try to talk to them about how to raise money; how to conduct themselves as professionals, and how to be resolute and determined. I try to teach them how to work with actors without bullying them and killing their spirit (again, the disease of directing is talking too much) and how they must always be open and accessible.

To be a good director, one must possess the patience and willingness to listen to a good idea when it's offered by a cast or crew-member, and the humility to use it. That's really one of the keys of directing: developing the ability to successfully balance the amount of power you exhibit with a healthy dose of deference. It's very hard to get students to want to do that. Too many have this hunger to be heard and obeyed. Naturally, a lot of what I say to my students is colored by my own experiences in filmmaking. If another director was teaching my class, he or she would probably be doing the same thing: drawing on their own lives and careers, their own mistakes and triumphs, in telling these kids what they should and perhaps shouldn't do. That is what makes the job of teaching so interesting and personal in some ways, because you do these things both consciously and unconsciously. As you know, a lot of what I've done in my movies has contained autobiographical content—both intentionally and unintentionally—and is filtered through my own perceptions and history. I can't imagine that teaching is any different.

When one considers how much the movie business has changed in recent years, maybe we should adjust our curriculum to compensate for it. I'm not just talking about the problems of distribution nowadays, or the way technology has impacted on how we make movies, and project them, and consume them. No, it's more than that. I'm teaching these young people how to have a career, but maybe I should also be teaching them what they should be doing if they *don't* have a career; or what they should be doing between jobs. To clarify, I must say that I don't believe in the recommendation that a person should pursue a career in the arts as long as they have something to fall back on—like plumbing or carpentry or computers. I believe you need to go for it; commit yourself totally and absolutely to your goal. Do not entertain failure until it's quite apparent.

Another thing I say to my students is, "What's the worst that can happen? You'll probably end up addicted to something—narcotics or alcohol, or both—and be living with a producer. Why not go for it? You won't die if you don't have a career in movies, as long as you keep your head. But don't stay in Chicago. Go to Los Angeles and try to make your way in whatever capacity you can. Just give it your best shot. Nothing ventured, nothing gained." I mean, yes, it's a tough business, but it always has been. Of course, with the plethora of film schools in America, a lot of these students are preparing, or have consigned themselves, to a career in teaching anyway. Many of them don't have the necessary fight and the fire in their bellies to begin with. Too many are timid and square. They don't possess enough bravery and buccaneering spirit to positively try something. They certainly don't need to be encouraged to be conservative. Again, it's like all these unmade projects—I won't give up on them. I'll keep fighting, because I believe in them and I believe in myself.

I'll ask my students, "Okay, if you want to be a screenwriter would you do better taking a course in Shakespeare or a course in screenwriting?" Too many say: "A course in screenwriting." That's the wrong answer. There are much better and more fulfilling courses in Shakespeare than there are in screenwriting, and you can learn a great deal about writing. When you look at Shakespeare's plays, the language, the drama, the interplay, the humanity, all the intoxicating things in there, you can discover so much. Also, in my opinion, I don't think you can necessarily teach writing. You can appreciate writing and be exposed to it, and perhaps acquire knowledge of the mechanics involved, but that spark of true creativity and originality is either in you or it isn't. You can spend years honing your craft as a writer, but not move very far forward in terms of developing your skills. You either have an innate ability to tell a good story or you don't. You sometimes encounter writers with great narrative and structural sense, but who can't write dialogue or characters; or you encounter great dialogue and character writers who can't structure a story. It's the same thing with acting: these things almost have to be God-given. Now, the flipside of what I implied earlier, having the guts to fight for something, can also make people somewhat delusional; the talent simply isn't there, but the belief and the commitment is.

When I look back on my own career, from the very beginning I realize that belief and commitment were two of my biggest attributes. I never questioned my choice of career. Granted, I do wish that I had made more pictures—that those long gaps between projects were filled—but I do feel satisfied with the movies I did get to make. I feel a profound sense of accomplishment and pride, and I look forward to the films I'm yet to make. I don't preserve too many regrets and embittered feelings; quite the reverse, actually. I think you'll agree that I'm rather philosophical and accepting of nearly all that has happened to me in the business over the years. You have to be or you wouldn't be able to get a wink of sleep at night. I've come to realize that there are a lot of directors out there who may have made more movies than I have, but few have done it with as much feeling and commitment as me. I've fought for everything I've made (and everything I haven't made). I may not have always enjoyed the fight, but I've always hung in there. That's why I'm proud of the work I've done. When I consider where I've come from, and who I am, I can honestly say that I tried my best. I've kept going. I wasn't kidding when I told you I'll happily keep on trying until I drop. I can't think of a better way to go, can you?

Credits

THEATER

Plays directed while a student at Harvard University, Cambridge, Massachusetts:
Georg Büchner's *Woyzeck* (1958)
Cervantes' *The Judge of the Divorce Court* (1958)
Ludvig Holberg's *The Healing Spring* (1958)
Tennessee Williams' *The Glass Menagerie* (1959)
Sean O'Casey's *The Plough and the Stars* (1960)
Bertolt Brecht's *The Caucasian Chalk Circle* (1961)
Shakespeare's *As You Like It* (1961)
Jean Anouilh's *Antigone* (1961)
Bertolt Brecht's *A Man's a Man* (1961)

Plays directed while Artistic Director of the New Repertory Theatre Company, New York:
Alexander Ostrovsky's *The Storm* (1962)
A Man's a Man (1962)

Bertolt Brecht's *Life of Galileo* (1963), Rice University, Houston, Texas

Plays directed while Artistic Director of the San Francisco Actor's Workshop:
Bertolt Brecht's *The Life of Edward II of England* (1965)
Saul Bellow's *The Last Analysis* (1965)

Tennessee Williams' *The Milk Train Doesn't Stop Here Anymore* (1965)
August Strindberg's *The Father* (1966)
William Shakespeare's *A Midsummer Night's Dream* (1966)

Plays directed while Artistic Director of the Pittsburgh Playhouse:
A Midsummer Night's Dream (1967)
A Man's a Man (1967)

A Midsummer Night's Dream (1967), Theatre De Lys, New York

Robert Lowell's *Endicott and the Red Cross* (1968), the American Place Theatre, New York

Plays directed while teaching at Hunter College, New York:
Arthur Miller's *A Memory of Two Mondays* (1968)
Walter Ferris and Alberto Cassella's *Death Takes a Holiday* (1969)
Anton Chekhov's *Three Sisters* (1969)

Tennessee Williams' *The Two-Character Play* (1977), Callboard Theatre, Los Angeles

Jonathan Falla's *Topakana Martyrs' Day* (1984), Los Angeles Actors Theatre, Los Angeles

Elaine May's *Adult Entertainment* (2005), Dunes Summer Theater, Michigan City

Dorothy Tristan's *Bohemian Nights* (2006), the Acorn Theatre, Three Oaks, Michigan

Bohemian Nights (2007), the Chopin Theatre, Chicago

John Hancock's *The Brother* (2007), Theatre Building, Chicago

Marsha Norman's *'night Mother* (2007), Theatre Building, Chicago

Michael Frayn's *Noises Off* (2009), Wellfleet Harbor Arts Theatre Julie Harris Stage, Cape Cod, Massachusetts

Productions begun by Hancock which were cancelled or taken over by others:

Tennessee Williams' *The Milk Train Doesn't Stop Here Anymore* (1964), the Royal Court, London, England (co-director: George Devine)

Richard Chandler's *The Freaking Out of Stephanie Blake* (1967), Eugene O'Neill Theatre, Broadway, New York (replaced by Michael Kahn)

Roland Tavel's *Boy on the Straight-Back Chair* (1969), the American Place Theatre, New York (replaced by Lee Von Rhau)

FILM

STICKY MY FINGERS, FLEET MY FEET (1970)
Production Company: American Film Institute
Director: John Hancock
Producers: Kit Clarke and Sanford Evans
Executive Producer: William P. Wilson
Associate Producer: Lance Bird
Screenwriters: John Lahr and John Hancock
Based on the short story by Gene Williams
Cinematography: Robert Elfstrom
Additional Photography: Joseph Consentino
Editors: Toni Mendell and John Hancock
Associate Director: Jeff Strickler
Music: Orville Stoeber
Costumes: Claire Copley
Cast: Gene Williams (Norm), Val Bisoglio (Marv), Charles Durning (Gratzwald), Marshall Efron (Big Marshall), Havelock Hewes (Wesley), John Lahr (Johnny), Tom Meehan (George), Al Leberfeld (Dr. Lieberman), Carolee Campbell (Marian), Don Koehler (Bruno), Layton McCartney (Harvard LaCrosse), Rhoda Gemignani (Mother).

LET'S SCARE JESSICA TO DEATH (1971)
Release Date: August 27, 1971
Production Company: Paramount Pictures, The Jessica Company

Director: John Hancock
Producer: Charles B. Moss, Jr.
Co-Producer: Bill Badalato (as William Badalato)
Screenwriters: Norman Jonas (Lee Kalcheim) and Ralph Rose (John Hancock)
Cinematography: Bob Baldwin
Editor: Murray Solomon
Set Decoration: Norman Kenneson
Music: Orville Stoeber and Walter Sear
Costume Designer: Mariette Pinchart
Make-up: Irvin Carlton
Cast: Zohra Lampert (Jessica), Barton Heyman (Duncan), Kevin O'Connor (Woody), Mariclare Costello (Emily/Abigail Bishop), Gretchen Corbett (The Girl), Alan Manson (Sam Dorker), Charles Moss, Sr. (Bandaged Old Man, uncredited).

BANG THE DRUM SLOWLY (1973)

Release Date: August 26, 1973
Production Company: Paramount Pictures, Dibs Partnership, ANJS
Director: John Hancock
Producers: Maurice Rosenfield and Lois Rosenfield
Screenwriter: Mark Harris, based on his novel
Cinematography: Richard Shore
Editor: Richard Marks
Production Designer: Robert Gundlach
Music: Stephen Lawrence and Orville Stoeber
Costume Designer: Domingo A. Rodriguez
Cast: Robert De Niro (Bruce Pearson), Michael Moriarty (Henry 'Arthur' Wiggen), Vincent Gardenia (Dutch Schnell), Phil Foster (Joe Jaros), Ann Wedgeworth (Katie), Patrick McVey (Bruce's Father), Heather MacRae (Holly Wiggen), Selma Diamond (Tootsie), Tom Ligon (Piney Woods), Barbara Babcock (Team Owner), Maurice Rosenfield (Team Owner), Andy Jarrell (Ugly), Marshall Efron (Bradley), Danny Burks (Perry), Tom Signorelli (Goose Williams), James Donahue (Canada), Hector Elias (Dego), Nicolas Surovy (Aleck Olson), Danny Aiello (Horse), Tony Major (Jonah), Barton Heyman (Red Traphagen), Alan Manson (Doc Loftus).

BABY BLUE MARINE (1976)
Release Date: May 5, 1976
Production Company: Columbia Pictures, Spelling-Goldberg Productions
Director: John Hancock
Producers: Leonard Goldberg and Aaron Spelling
Associate Producer: Robert LaVigne
Screenwriter: Stanford Whitmore
Cinematography: Laszlo Kovacs
Editor: Marion Rothman
Production Designer: Walter Scott Herndon
Music: Fred Karlin
Wardrobe Supervisor: Richard La Motte
Make-up: Garrett Morris
Cast: Jan-Michael Vincent (Marion Hedgepeth), Glynnis O'Connor (Rose Hudkins), Katherine Helmond, (Mrs. Hudkins) Bert Remsen (Mr. Hudkins), Art Lund (Mr. Elmore), Bruno Kirby (Pop Mosley), Richard Gere (Marine Raider), Dana Elcar (Sheriff Wenzel), Michael Conrad (Drill Instructor), Allan Miller (Capt. Bittman), Michael LeClair (Barney Hudkins), Will Seltzer (Pvt. Phelps), Kenneth Tobey (Buick Driver), Lelia Goldoni (Mrs. Townsley), Marshall Efron (Cook), Barton Heyman (Barber), Adam Arkin (Rupe), Damon Douglas (Dobbs), John Calvin (Paratrooper), Richard Narita (Masamura), Evan Kim (Harakawa), Keone Young (Katsu).

CALIFORNIA DREAMING (1979)
Release Date: April 1, 1979
Production Company: American International Pictures
Director: John Hancock
Producer: Christian Whittaker
Executive Producer: Samuel Z. Arkoff
Executive in Charge of Production: Lou Arkoff
Associate Producer: Mike Moder
Screenwriter: Ned Wynn
Cinematography: Bobby Byrne
Editors: Herb Dow and Roy Peterson
Production Designer: William M. Hiney

Music: Fred Karlin
Costumer: Ernie Misko
Make-up: Tom Ellingwood and Beverly Turner
Cast: Glynnis O'Connor (Corky), Seymour Cassel (Duke Slusarski), Dorothy Tristan (Fay), Dennis Christopher (Tony "T.T." Thompson), John Calvin (Rick), Tanya Roberts (Stephanie), Alice Playten (Corrine), Todd Susman (Jordy Banks), Ned Wynn (Earl Fescue), James Van Patten (Mike), Stacey Nelkin (Marsha), Johnny Fain (Tenner), Tom McFadden (Dan), Tom Rosqui (George Booke), Marshall Efron (Ruben), Barton Heyman (Jerry), Kirsten Baker (Karen), Shannon Terhune (Missy), Vivian Bonnell (Alma), Bonnie Bartlett (Melinda Booke), James Staley (Airline Officer), Carol O'Leary (Lynn Neighbors), Ernie Misko (Geezer).

WOLFEN (1981)
Release Date: July 24, 1981
Production Company: Orion Pictures, King-Hitzig Productions
Director: Michael Wadleigh
Additional direction: John Hancock (uncredited)
Executive in Charge of Production: Mike Medavoy
Producers: Rupert Hitzig and Alan King
Screenwriters: Michael Wadleigh and David Eyre
Based on the novel by Whitley Strieber
Cinematography: Gerry Fisher
Additional photography: Jan de Bont (uncredited)
Editors: Chris Lebenzon, Marshall M. Borden, Martin J. Bram, Dennis Dolan, Stuart H. Pappé (uncredited) and John Hancock (uncredited)
Production Designer: Paul Sylbert
Music: James Horner
Costume Designer: John Boxer
Special Make-up: Carl Fullerton
Cast: Albert Finney (Dewey Wilson), Diane Venora (Rebecca Neff), Gregory Hines (Whittington), Edward James Olmos (Eddie Holt), Tom Noonan (Ferguson), Dick O'Neill (Warren), Dehl Berti (Old Indian), Peter Michael Goetz (Ross), Sam Gray (Mayor), Ralph Bell (Commissioner), Max

M. Brown (Christopher van der Veer), Anne Marie Pohtamo (Pauline van der Veer), Sarah Felder (Cicely Rensselaer), Reginald Vel Johnson (Morgue Attendant), James Tolkan (Baldy), John McCurry (Sayed Alve), Chris Manor (Janitor) Donald Symington (Lawyer), Jeffrey Ware (Interrogation Operator), E. Brian Dean (Fouchek), Jeffrey Thompson (Harrison).

8 MILLION WAYS TO DIE (1986)
Release Date: April 25, 1986
Production Company: Tri-Star Pictures
Director: Hal Ashby
Additional direction: John Hancock (uncredited)
Producer: Stephen J. Roth
Screenwriters: Oliver Stone and David Lee Henry, and Robert Towne (uncredited)
Based on the novel by Lawrence Block
Cinematography: Stephen H. Burum
Editors: Robert Lawrence and Stuart H. Pappé
Production Designer: Michael D. Haller
Music: James Newton Howard
Costume Designer: Gloria Gresham
Special Make-up: Rick Stratton (uncredited)
Cast: Jeff Bridges (Matthew Scudder), Rosanna Arquette (Sarah), Andy Garcia (Angel Maldonada), Alexandra Paul (Sunny), Randy Brooks (Chance), Lisa Sloan (Linda Scudder), Christa Denton (Laurie Scudder), Vance Valencia (Quintero), Vyto Ruginis (Joe Durkin), Wilfredo Hernandez (Hector Lopez), Luisa Leschin (Hector's Wife), Tommy "Tiny" Lister (Nose Guard), Henry O. Arnold (Chip Duncan), James Avery (Deputy D.A.), Jack Younger (Drunk), Zoaunne LeRoy (Nurse), Abigail Shelton (AA Member), Don Edmonds (Elderly Man), Phil Peters (Rugged Man), Elva Garcia (Daughter), Pete Galindo (Son #1), Michael Galindo (Son #2).

WEEDS (1987)
Release Date: October 16, 1987
Production Company: De Laurentiis Entertainment Group (DEG), Kingsgate Films
Director: John Hancock
Producer: Bill Badalato
Associate Producers: Fred Baron, Patricia Carr and Ken Kitch
Executive Producer: Mel Pearl
Screenwriters: Dorothy Tristan and John Hancock
Cinematography: Jan Weincke
Editors: Dennis O'Connor, Chris Lebenzon, Jon Poll and William Anderson (uncredited)
Production Designer: Joseph T. Garrity
Music: Angelo Badalamenti, Melissa Etheridge, Richard Peaslee and Orville Stoeber
Costume Designer: Mary Kay Stolz
Make-up: Edouard F. Henriques
Cast: Nick Nolte (Lee Umstetter), Ernie Hudson (Baghdad Everhardt), Rita Taggart (Lillian Bingington), Lane Smith (Claude Mullins), John Toles-Bey (Navarro), William Forsythe (Burt), Mark Rolston (Dave), Joe Mantegna (Carmine), Nick Wyman (Associate Warden San Quentin), Essex Smith (Vocalist), Sam L. Waymon (Vocalist), Orville Stoeber (Lead Guitar), Cyro Baptista (Bass Guitar), J.J. Johnson (Lazarus), Anne Ramsey (Mom Umstetter), Ray Reinhardt (Pop Umstetter), Amanda Gronich (Baghdad's Girlfriend), Felton Perry (Associate Warden Dannemora), Barton Heyman (Godot Player), Walter Charles (Godot Player), Richard K. Olsen (Derrick Mann), Drew Elliot (Fisher Cobb), Charlie Rich (himself).

STEAL THE SKY (1988)
Release Date: August 26, 1988
Production Company: Home Box Office and Paramount Pictures
Director: John Hancock
Producer: Yoram Ben-Ami
Screenwriters: Christopher Wood and Dorothy Tristan
Cinematography: Misha Suslov

Editors: Dennis O'Connor and Jon Poll
Production Designer: Keith Wilson
Music: Yanni
Costume Designer: Monique Long
Make-up: Zivit Yakir
Cast: Mariel Hemingway (Helen Mason), Ben Cross (Munir Redfa), Sasson Gabai (Kamel Djem), Nicolas Surovy (David Mason), Ronald Guttman (Mohammed), Mark Rolston (Colonel Bukharin), Sam Gray (General Guri), Andreas Katsulas (Colonel Gemayel), Etti Ankri (Fara Redfa), Richard Libertini (Uncredited), Michael Shillo (General Tal), Tamara Triffez (Chantal), Yossi Shiloa (Aziz), Reuven Bar Yotam (Dr. Taupe), Faim Saadi (Amwar), Maria Cavaiani (Nadi), Ilan Zahavi (Marcel), Tikva Aziz (Lila), Victor Ken (Yusef), Uri Gavriel (Akmed), Ted Kasanov (President Arif), Rivka Bachar (Servant), Motti Levy (Ticket Collector), Gabi Amrani (Station Owner).

PRANCER (1989)
Release Date: November 17, 1989
Production Company: Cineplex-Odeon Films, Nelson Entertainment and Raffaella Productions
Director: John Hancock
Producer: Raffaella De Laurentiis
Associate Producer: Hester Hargett
Co-Producers: Mike Petzold and Greg Taylor
Screenwriters: Greg Taylor and Dorothy Tristan (uncredited)
Cinematography: Misha Suslov
Editor: Dennis O'Connor and John Rosenberg
Production Designer: Chester Kaczenski
Music: Maurice Jarre
Costume Designer: Denny Burt
Special Make-up: Lance Anderson
Cast: Sam Elliott (John Riggs), Cloris Leachman (Mrs. McFarland), Rebecca Harrell (Jessica Riggs), Rutanya Alda (Aunt Sarah), Abe Vigoda (Orel Benton), Michael Constantine (Mr. Stewart), John Joseph Duda (Steve Riggs), Ariana Richards (Carol Wetherby), Mark Rolston (Herb Drier), Johnny Galecki (Billy Quinn), Walter Charles (Minister), Victor Truro (Mr. Young), Marcia

Porter (Mrs. Fairburn), Michael Luciano (Bert), Loren James (Mr. Soot), Shirley Starnes (Mrs. Hofsetter), Robert Zimmerman (Wagnall), Belinda Bremner (Miss Bedelia), Jesse Bradford (Boy #1), Eric Sardeson (Boy #2), Joseph Morano (Boy with Santa), Steven Pressler (Hank).

A PIECE OF EDEN (2000)
Release Date: September 15, 2000
Production Company: FilmAcres
Director: John Hancock
Producers: John Hancock and Ken Kitch
Executive Producer: Robert J. Hiler
Associate Producers: Dean Jacobson and Susan Willett
Screenwriter: Dorothy Tristan
Cinematography: Misha Suslov
Editors: Dennis O'Connor, Christopher S. Baird and John Hancock (uncredited)
Art Direction: Wendy Jo Martin
Music: Angelo Badalamenti, Orville Stoeber, Alan Barkus and Tim Tobias
Costume Designer: Rochelle Zaltzman
Make-up: Jeni Zaharian
Cast: Marc Grapey (Bob Tredici), Rebecca Harrell (Happy Buchanan), Tyne Daly (Aunt Aurelia), Frederic Forrest (Paulo Tredici), Andreas Katsulas (Giuseppe Tredici), Robert Breuler (Franco Tredici), Jeff Puckett (Gregory Tredici), Tristan Rogers (Victor Hardwick), Irma St. Paule (Maria at 90), Marshall Efron (Andres), Julia Swart (Claire Tredici), Rengin Altay (Maria at 30), Lara Phillips (TV Reporter), Jeannette Washluske (Nurse), James Ferguson (Teenage Franco), Tracy Lopresto (Bob's Mother), Jesse Giuliani (Young Franco), Kevin Hundt (Young Paulo), Annastecia Spano (Young Aurelia), Matthew T. Mender (Bob at 9), Kiva Wenig (Bob at 4).

SUSPENDED ANIMATION (2003)
Release Date: October 31, 2003
Production Company: FilmAcres, First Run Features

Director: John Hancock
Producers: John Hancock and Robert. J. Hiler
Co-Producers: Dean Jacobson and Ken Kitch
Executive Producer: Carey Westberg
Screenwriter: Dorothy Tristan, based on her novel
Cinematography: Misha Suslov
Editors: Dennis O'Connor and Christopher J. Brown
Production Designer: Don Jacobson
Music: Angelo Badalamenti and Chris Ussery
Costume Designer: Richard Donnelly
Special Make-up: Victor Cao
Cast: Alex McArthur (Tom Kempton), Rebecca Harrell (Hilary Kempton), Laura Esterman (Vanessa Boulette), Sage Allen (Ann Boulette), Maria Cina (Clara Hansen), Fred Meyers (Sandor Hansen), Dan Riordon (Jack Starr), Jeff Puckett (Cliff Modjeska), J.E. Freeman (Philip Boulette), Sean Patrick Murphy (Fred Phelps), Daniel Mooney (Arnold Mann), Gary J. Mion (Sheriff Montaigne), Joe Forbrich (Coroner), Robert Breuler (Dr. Leo Sagan), Mike McCalmet (Joe Moss), Glenn Hutchinson (Bar Customer), David P. Matevia (Minister), Denise Bohn (Correspondent #1), Faith Marie (Correspondent #2).

THE LOOKING GLASS (2015)
Release Date: October 23, 2015
Production Company: FilmAcres, First Run Features
Director: John Hancock
Producers: Allen Turner, Andrew Tallackson, Doreen Bartoni and Kelly Daisy
Executive Producer: Garth Drabinsky
Associate Producers: Dean Jacobson, Margaret Clifford and Thad Donovan
Line Producer: Kevin McGrail
Screenwriter: Dorothy Tristan
Additional Dialogue: Robert Ward (uncredited)
Cinematography: Misha Suslov
Editor: Dennis O'Connor
Production Designer: Victor LaPorte
Music: Orville Stoeber, David Del Tredici, Koki Lortkipanidze,

Chris Ussery, Angelo Badalamenti and David Lynch
Choreography: Irina Tsikurishvili
Costume Designer: Richard Donnelly
Make-Up: Dora F. Kwak, Kristen Ludwig, Ebony Rogers and Amy Paprocki
Cast: Dorothy Tristan (Karen), Grace Tarnow (Julie), Jeff Puckett (Terry), Anthony Panzica (Arthur), Faith Marie (Sybil/Queen of Hearts), Elizabeth Stenholt (Mallory), Griffin Carlson (Anthony), Allen Turner (John), Trish Basinger (ER Nurse), Ed Ernstes (Café Customer), Cian Deegan (Harvey), Jace Casey (Cheshire Cat), Harry Musselwhite (White Queen), Dallas Tolentino (The Mad Hatter), Jason Noone (The White Rabbit), Adair Washington (Queen of Clubs), Tim Tobin (Red Queen), Casey James Moore (Stage Manager), Andrew Tallackson (Alice Pianist), Alex Ludwig (Boy on Beach), Mariah Daisy-Sharp (Auditioning Dancer), Emily Bentley (Mabel).

TELEVISION

Episodes listed chronologically in order of broadcast:

COVER UP: "Adams' Ribs"
Airdate: March 23, 1985
Network: CBS
Created by Glen A. Larson
Director: John Hancock
Executive Producer: Glen A. Larson
Producers: Chris Larson, Jim O'Keefe and Bob Shayne
Supervising Producer: Don Carlos Dunaway
Associate Producers: Scott Levitta and Dave Fisher
Writer: Robert Hamilton
Story Editor: Doug Heyes, Jr.
Cinematography: Edward Rio Rotunno
Editor: Edwin F. England
Set Decoration: Martin Price
Music: Ken Harrison
Theme Music: "Holding Out for a Hero" by Jim Steinman and Dean Pitchford

Cast: Jennifer O'Neill (Danielle Reynolds), Anthony Hamilton (Jack Striker), Richard Anderson (Henry Towler), Cindy Fisher (Sally Benson), Ray Girardin (Paul Adams), Gavan O'Herlihy (Drew Simpson), Mykel T. Williamson (Rick), Ingrid Anderson (Gretchen), Irena Ferris (Billie), Dana Sparks (Ashley), Teri Hafford (Model), Billy Beck (Marce), Renos Mandis (Pierre), Ted Roter (Andre), Clint Young (Security Guard).

I HAD THREE WIVES: "You and I Know"
Airdate: August 15, 1985
Network: CBS
Director: John Hancock
Executive Producers: Carla Singer, Nick Thiel, Peter Lefcourt and Marc Merson
Producers: Michael McLean, Stephen Hattman, Donald A. Baer and Tom Chehak
Associate Producer: Skip Schoolnick
Writer: Tom Chehak
Script Supervisor: Nancy Greene
Cinematography: Robert Seaman
Editor: Dennis Mosher
Art Direction: Patricia Van Ryker
Music: Sylvester Levay
Theme Music: Bill Conti
Cast: Victor Garber (Jackson Beaudine), Mary Parker (Maggie Cooper), Samantha Collins (Teri Copley), Elizabeth Bailey (Shanna Reed), David Faustino (Andrew Beaudine), Luis Avalos (Lt. Gomez), John Calvin (Baines), Keri Houlihan (Lucy Baines), Walter Olkewicz (Johnny Shore), Armin Shimerman (Herb), Cynthia Sikes (Dr. Harris), Beau Billingslea (Announcer), Caroline Seymour (Susan), Nicholas Shaffer (Toy Store Owner), Melissa Etheridge (Singer).

THE TWILIGHT ZONE: "Kentucky Rye"
Airdate: October 11, 1985
Network: CBS
Created by Rod Serling

Director: John Hancock
Executive Producer: Philip DeGuere
Supervising Producer: James Crocker
Producer: Harvey Frand
Writers: Richard Krzemien and Chip Duncan
Story Editor: Rockne S. O'Bannon
Executive Story Consultant: Alan Brennert
Creative Consultant: Harlan Ellison
Cinematography: Bradford May
Editor: Tom Pryor
Art Direction: Ward Preston
Music: The Grateful Dead & Merl Saunders
Theme Music: The Grateful Dead & Merl Saunders
Cast: Jeffrey DeMunn (Bob Spindler), Michael Greene (Irving Schlesser), Philip Bruns (Old Man), Arliss Howard (Stranger), Clarence Felder (Randy), Scott Jaeck (Pete), John DeMita (George), Brad Burlingame (Larry), Rosemarie Thomas (Nancy), Gloria Rusch (Laura), Lisa Long (Debbie), John Davey (Officer #1), Tim Russ (Officer #2).

THE TWILIGHT ZONE: "If She Dies"
Airdate: October 25, 1985
Network: CBS
Created by Rod Serling
Director: John Hancock
Executive Producer: Philip DeGuere
Supervising Producer: James Crocker
Producer: Harvey Frand
Writer: David Bennett Carren
Story Editor: Rockne S. O'Bannon
Executive Story Consultant: Alan Brennert
Creative Consultant: Harlan Ellison
Cinematography: Bradford May
Editor: Tom Pryor
Art Direction: Ward Preston
Music: Jerrold Immel
Theme Music: The Grateful Dead & Merl Saunders
Cast: Tony Lo Bianco (Paul Marano), Nan Martin (Sister Agnes),

Jenny Lewis (Sarah), Andrea Barber (Cathy Marano), John Gowans (Dr. Brice), Donna-Jean Lansing (Nun), Adele Miller (Nurse).

HILL STREET BLUES: "Oh, You Kid"
Airdate: November 7, 1985
Network: NBC
Created by Steven Bochco and Michael Kozoll
Director: John Hancock
Executive Producers: Jeffrey Lewis and David Milch
Producers: Walon Green, Michael Vittes and Ellen S. Pressman
Supervising Producer: Scott Brazil
Writer: Robert Ward
Executive Story Editor: Jacob Epstein
Cinematography: Jack Whitman
Editor: David Handman
Art Direction: Ned Parsons
Music: Mike Post
Cast: Daniel J. Travanti (Capt. Frank Furillo), Charles Haid (Officer Andy Renko), Bruce Weitz (Det. Mick Belker), Veronica Hamel (Joyce Davenport), Michael Warren (Officer Bobby Hill), Betty Thomas (Sgt. Lucy Bates), Joe Spano (Lt. Henry Goldblume), James B. Sikking (Lt. Howard Hunter), Dennis Franz (Lt. Norman Buntz), Robert Prosky (Sgt. Stan Jablonski), Ed Marinaro (Officer Joe Coffey), Taurean Blacque (Det. Neal Washington), Kiel Martin (Officer J.D. LaRue), Felton Perry (Bobby Castro), Alex McArthur (Brent), Shirley Jo Finney (Lynnetta), Paul Drake (Wendell Morrison), George Wyner (Irwin Bernstein), Tegan West (Teddy).

HILL STREET BLUES: "The Virgin and the Turkey"
Airdate: December 12, 1985
Network: NBC
Created by Steven Bochco and Michael Kozoll
Director: John Hancock
Executive Producers: Jeffrey Lewis and David Milch
Producers: Walon Green, Michael Vittes and Ellen S. Pressman

Supervising Producer: Scott Brazil
Co-ordinating Producer: Penny Adams
Writers: David Milch, Walon Green and Robert Ward
Story: Jeffrey Lewis, Walon Green and Robert Ward
Executive Story Editor: Jacob Epstein
Cinematography: Jack Whitman
Editor: David Handman
Art Direction: Ned Parsons
Music: Mike Post
Cast: Daniel J. Travanti (Capt. Frank Furillo), Charles Haid (Officer Andy Renko), Bruce Weitz (Det. Mick Belker), Veronica Hamel (Joyce Davenport), Michael Warren (Officer Bobby Hill), Betty Thomas (Sgt. Lucy Bates), Joe Spano (Lt. Henry Goldblume), James B. Sikking (Lt. Howard Hunter), Dennis Franz (Lt. Norman Buntz), Robert Prosky (Sgt. Stan Jablonski), Ed Marinaro (Officer Joe Coffey), Taurean Blacque (Det. Neal Washington), Kiel Martin (Officer J.D. LaRue), Daniel Faraldo (Pinzon), Val Bisoglio (Landlord), Penny Santon (Barbara Furillo), Michael Durrell (Joe Furillo), Richard Bull (Mr. Furillo), Eric Pierpoint (Tom Hopper).

LADY BLUE: "Scorpio's Sting"
Airdate: January 11, 1986
Network: ABC
Director: John Hancock
Executive Producer: David Gerber
Supervising Producer: Christopher N. Seiter
Producers: Anthony Lawrence and Nancy Lawrence
Co-Producers: Robert Vincent O'Neill and Mark Rodgers
Writer: Robert Vincent O'Neill
Story: Robert Vincent O'Neill and David Barry
Cinematography: Paul F. Vombrack
Editor: Jack Harnish
Music: John Cacavas
Cast: Jamie Rose (Katy Mahoney), Danny Aiello (Lt. Terry McNichols), Ron Dean (Sgt. Gino Gianelli), Bruce A. Young (Cassidy), Ralph Foody (Capt. Flynn), Richard Fire (Scooter), Jerome Landfield (Douglas Kirby), Steve Sandor (Caleb Holbrook), Shelley Smith (Tish Stahlman).

THE TWILIGHT ZONE: "Profile in Silver"
Airdate: March 7, 1986
Network: CBS
Created by Rod Serling
Director: John Hancock
Executive Producer: Philip DeGuere
Supervising Producer: James Crocker
Producer: Harvey Frand
Writer: J. Neil Schulman
Story Editor: Rockne S. O'Bannon
Executive Story Consultant: Alan Brennert
Creative Consultant: James Crocker
Cinematography: Chuck Arnold
Editor: Noel Rogers
Art Direction: Ward Preston
Music: Basil Poledouris
Theme Music: The Grateful Dead & Merl Saunders
Cast: Lane Smith (Professor Joseph Fitzgerald), Andrew Robinson (President John F. Kennedy), Louis Giambalvo (Raymond Livingstone), Barbara Baxley (Dr. Kate Wang), Jerry Hardin (Lyndon B. Johnson), Mark Taylor (Inspector), Charles Lanyer (Anchorman), David Sage (Professor), Ken Hill (Aide), Huck Liggett (Texan), Gerard Bocaccio (Student).

THE TWILIGHT ZONE: "The Library"
Airdate: March 28, 1986
Network: CBS
Created by Rod Serling
Director: John Hancock
Executive Producer: Philip DeGuere
Supervising Producer: James Crocker
Producer: Harvey Frand
Writer: Anne Collins
Story Editor: Rockne S. O'Bannon
Executive Story Consultant: Alan Brennert
Creative Consultant: James Crocker
Cinematography: Robert Seaman
Editor: Greg Wong

Production Designer: Joseph Altadonna
Music: Dennis McCarthy
Theme Music: The Grateful Dead & Merl Saunders
Cast: Uta Hagen (Gloria), Frances Conroy (Ellie Pendleton), Lori Petty (Lori Pendleton), Joe Santos (Doug Kelleher), Candy Azzara (Carla Mollencami), Alan Blumenfeld (Edwin Dewett), Jay Gerber (Man), Mimi Monaco (Woman).

THE TWILIGHT ZONE: "The Saucer of Loneliness"
Airdate: September 27, 1986
Network: CBS
Created by Rod Serling
Director: John Hancock
Executive Producer: Philip DeGuere
Supervising Producers: Anthony Lawrence and Nancy Lawrence
Producer: Harvey Frand
Writer: David Gerrold
Based on the story "A Saucer of Loneliness" by Theodore Sturgeon
Story Editors: George R. R. Martin, Martin Pasko and Rebecca Parr
Executive Story Consultant: Alan Brennert
Story Consultant: Rockne S. O'Bannon
Creative Consultant: James Crocker
Cinematography: Bradford May
Editor: Greg Wong
Production Designer: John Mansbridge
Music: Robert Folk
Theme Music: The Grateful Dead & Merl Saunders
Cast: Shelley Duvall (Margaret), Richard Libertini (Lonely Man), Nan Martin (Margaret's Mother), Edith Diaz (Religious Woman), Andrew Masset (Margaret's Date), Mari Gorman (Jill), Myrna White (Psychiatrist), Michael Zand (Clerk), Brick Karnes (Boyfriend), James Edward Thomas (Hank Charles), Bruno Aclin (Officer), Laura Harlan (Waitress), Geoff Witcher (Anchorman), Mary Ingersoll (Reporter #1), David Grant Hayward (Reporter #2), Shannon Lee Avnsoe (Reporter #3), J. Omar Hansen (Reporter #4).

CRACKER: "Madwoman"
Airdate: October 2, 1997
Network: ABC
Created by Jimmy McGovern
Director: John Hancock
Executive Producers: James Sadwith, Gub Neal and Donald Kushner
Co-Executive Producers: Scott Brazil and Jim Leonard, Jr.
Producer: Natalie Chaidez
Consulting Producer: Ilene Amy Berg
Writer: Jim Leonard, Jr.
Adapted from the Original Teleplay by Jimmy McGovern
Cinematography: Roy H. Wagner
Editors: John Duffy and Michael Ripps
Set Decoration: Susan Mina Eschelbach
Music: Stanley A. Smith
Cast: Robert Pastorelli (Gerry 'Fitz' Fitzgerald), Angela Featherstone (Det. Hannah Tyler), Carolyn McCormick (Judith Fitzgerald), Josh Hartnett (Michael Fitzgerald), R. Lee Ermey (Lt. Fry), Robert Wisdom (Det. Danny Watlington), Adewale Akinnuoye-Agbaje (John Doe), Don McManus (Garson Shepherd), Matt Malloy (Richard Wheeler), Keene Curtis (John Wheeler), Scott Sowers (Det. Allen Parker), Gay Thomas (Sally), Paul Perri (Waldron), Ming Lo (Dr. Chong), Lionel Mark Smith (Train Porter), Christopher Michael (Policeman), Frankie Jay Allison (Dealer), Jack Wallace (Gambler #1), Clement E. Blake (Gambler #2), Roxanne Reese (Gambler #3).

DELLAVENTURA: "Dreamers"
Airdate: December 11, 1997
Network: CBS
Created by Julian Neil, Bernard L. Nussbaumer and Richard Di Lello
Director: John Hancock
Executive Producer: Danny Aiello
Co-Executive Producers: Frank Abatemarco, Michael Dinner and Jonathan Estrin
Producers: Danny Aiello III and Sascha Schneider

Co-Producers: Sharon Boyle, Scott Citron, Julian Neil and Bernard L. Nussbaumer
Associate Producer: David DeClerque
Writer: David Assael
Story: Georgina Lindsey
Cinematography: Anthony Jannelli
Editor: Marc Laub
Production Designer: Dean Taucher
Music: Joe Delia
Cast: Danny Aiello (Anthony Dellaventura), Ricky Aiello (Teddy Naples), Byron Keith Minns (Jonas Deeds), Anne Ramsay (Geri Zarias), Melanie Norris (Christina Bradley), Tony Darrow (Victor), Rebecca Harrell (Nina), John Christopher Jones (Doctor Benson), Olinda Turturro (Celia), Sandor Tecsy (Leeka), Frank Bongiorno (Frankie), Willie Peterkin (Process Server), Aaron Gryder (Aaron the Jockey), Dave Johnson (The Announcer).

CRACKER: "Best Boys"
Airdate: March 5, 1999
Network: ABC
Created by Jimmy McGovern
Director: John Hancock
Executive Producers: James Sadwith, Gub Neal and Donald Kushner
Co-Executive Producers: Scott Brazil and Jim Leonard, Jr.
Producer: Natalie Chaidez
Supervising Producer: Ilene Amy Berg
Writer: Jim Leonard, Jr.
Adapted from the Original Teleplay by Paul Abbott
Cinematography: Roy H. Wagner
Editors: Stan Salfas
Production Designer: Jeffrey L. Goldstein
Set Decoration: Susan Mina Eschelbach
Music: Roy Hay
Cast: Robert Pastorelli (Gerry 'Fitz' Fitzgerald), Angela Featherstone (Det. Hannah Tyler), Carolyn McCormick (Judith Fitzgerald), Josh Hartnett (Michael Fitzgerald), R. Lee Ermey

(Lt. Fry), Robert Wisdom (Det. Danny Watlington), Peter Firth (Mitchell Grady), Jared Rushton (Bill Lane), Ashley Crow (Linda Benson), Micole Mercurio (Mrs. Franklin), Ramon Bieri (Witness), Geoffrey Rivas (Alvarez), Christopher Stanley (Dale), Scott Sowers (Det. Allen Parker), Sally Livingstone (Hope Fitzgerald), Paul Perri (Waldron), Andrew Ducote (Steven).

Bibliography

Select interviews, articles and reviews:

Bernstein, Abbie. "*Suspended Animation*: Cannibal Hang-up," *Fangoria* #228, November 2003.

Bonfiglio, Jeremy D. "A Life Less Ordinary," *SouthBendTribune.com*, Friday, June 9, 2006.

Bozung, Justin. *TV Store Online Blog*: "Director John Hancock on his criminally-underrated ode to absurdist theatre *Weeds* (1987)," Thursday, June 18, 2015.

Burns, James H. "Michael Wadleigh and The *Wolfen*," *Fangoria* #13, June 1981.

Canby, Vincent. "*Wolfen* with Finney," *The New York Times*, July 24, 1981.

Dare, Michael. "How to Kill a Movie," *L.A. Weekly*, May 16, 1986.

Dawson, Nick. *Being Hal Ashby: Life of a Hollywood Rebel*, The University Press of Kentucky (2011)

Doyle, Michael. "*Wolfen*: A Political Animal—Part One," *Fangoria* #301, March 2011.

Doyle, Michael. "*Wolfen*: A Political Animal—Part Two," *Fangoria* #302, April 2011.

Doyle, Michael. "The Woman in the Water," *Rue Morgue* #173, December 2016.

Doyle, Michael. "Hell and Cold Water," *Rue Morgue* #173, December 2016.

Doyle, Michael. "Let's Scare Jessica to Death," *Rue Morgue's 200 Alternate Horror Films to See Before You Die*, MARRS Media, 2012.

Dretzka, Gary. "Shooting a Thriller on a Tight Budget," *Chicago Tribune*, April 20, 2001.

Ebert, Roger. "*Bang the Drum Slowly,*" *Chicago Sun-Times*, August 26, 1973.
Ebert, Roger. "*Baby Blue Marine,*" *Chicago Sun-Times*, June 15, 1976.
Ebert, Roger. "*Wolfen,*" *Chicago Sun-Times*, July 24, 1981.
Ebert, Roger. "*Weeds,*" *Chicago Sun-Times*, October 16, 1987.
Ebert, Roger. "*Prancer,*" *Chicago Sun-Times*, November 17, 1989.
Ebert, Roger. "*A Piece of Eden,*" *Chicago Sun-Times*, April 21, 2000.
Emmerman, Lynn. "Hollywood Does Time in Stateville," *Chicago Tribune*, February 24, 1987.
Fake, Douglass. Liner Notes to *Prancer* Soundtrack: Intrada Special Collection, Volume 259 (2013)
Floyd, David. *Small Town Film Rambler*: "John Hancock and *Jaws 2* (1978)", Wednesday, October 1, 2014.
Geller, Doron. "Israel Military Intelligence: Stealing a Soviet MiG," *Jewish Virtual Library*.
Glaessner, Verina. "*Baby Blue Marine,*" *Monthly Film Bulletin*, Vol. 43, No. 512, September 1976.
Gow, Gordon. "John Hancock: A Feeling in the Throat," *Films and Filming*, Vol.25, No.1, issue No.289, October 1978.
Greenspun, Roger. "Hippie Vampire: *Let's Scare Jessica to Death* Arrives," *The New York Times*, August 28, 1971.
Harmetz, Aljean. "*Wolfen*: A Case of Director's Rights," *The New York Times*, August 4, 1981.
Jankeweiz, Patrick A. *Just When You Thought It Was Safe: A Jaws Companion*, BearManor Media (2009)
Kaltenheuser, Skip. "The Prison Playwright," *Gadfly* #21, September/October, 1999.
Katz, Allan. "*The Caucasian Chalk Circle* at the Loeb Drama Center, through December 17," *The Harvard Crimson*, December 10, 1960.
Kehr, Dave. "*Prancer*: A Contradictory Christmas Card," *Chicago Tribune*, November 17, 1989.
Konow, David. "Let's Scare Audiences to Death," *Fangoria* #241, March 2005.
Koziarski, Ed M. "Hancock's Horror Story Goes Beyond his New Feature," *Ruth Ratny's Chicago Reel*, Thursday, April 24, 2003.
Koziarski, Ed M. "Legacy Theme of New John Hancock Film and in His Life," *Ruth Ratny's Chicago Reel*, Tuesday, May 28, 2013.
Lahr, John. *Tennessee Williams: Mad Pilgrimage of the Flesh*, W.W. Norton & Company (2014).

Lofficier, Jean-Marc & Lofficier, Randy. *Into The Twilight Zone: The Rod Serling Programme Guide*, Virgin Books, 1995.

Loynd, Ray. *The Jaws 2 Log*. W.H. Allen, London, (1978).

MacPherson, Les. "Syrian Pilot's Defection in MiG-21 Stirs Cold War Memories," *The Star Phoenix*, June 30, 2012.

Maslin, Janet. "Nolte in *Weeds*," *The New York Times*, October 16, 1987.

Pisano, Louis R. & Smith, Michael A. *Jaws 2: The Making of a Hollywood Sequel*, BearManor Media (2015)

Rayns, Tony. "*Let's Scare Jessica to Death*," *Monthly Film Bulletin*, February 1972.

Rick. *Rick on Theater*: "Dueling Brechts—Part 1," Friday, January 24, 2014.

Rick. *Rick on Theater*: "Dueling Brechts—Part 2," Monday, January 27, 2014.

Rosenberg, Howard. "Some Shows Prove You Can't Go Home Again," *Los Angeles Times*, August 21, 1985.

Rosenberg, Howard. "*Steal the Sky* Leaves All Suspense Up in the Air," *Los Angeles Times*, August 26, 1988.

Saddik, Annette. J. *Tennessee Williams and the Theatre of Excess*, Cambridge University Press, Cambridge, (2015)

Sayre, Nora. "*Sticky My Fingers* and Four Other Early Works: The Program," *The New York Times*, January 15, 1974.

Schulman, J. Neil. *Profile in Silver and Other Screenwritings*, Pulpless (1996)

Smith, Sally Bedell. "*Hill Street* to Trim its Cast and Plots," *The New York Times*, March 28, 1985.

Stone, Judith. "Making a Small Miracle," *The New York Times*, January 2, 1966.

Tanner, Louise. "John Hancock and Dorothy Tristan," *Films in Review*, Vol. XXXIX, No. 1, January 1988.

Tristan, Dorothy. *Joy Street*, CreateSpace Independent Publishing Platform (2014)

Thomas, Kevin. "*Prancer*: An Unapologetic Christmas Heart-Tugger," *Los Angeles Times*, November 17, 1989.

Waddell, Calum. "Still Scary After All These Years: John Hancock on *Jessica*," *Videoscope* #60, Fall 2006.

Williams, Tennessee. *Memoirs*, New Directions (1975)

About the Author

MICHAEL DOYLE is a journalist and author whose words have appeared in such publications as *Rue Morgue*, *Fangoria* and *Scream*. He has interviewed many celebrated filmmakers including William Friedkin, John Carpenter, Philip Kaufman, David Cronenberg, Roger Corman, Guillermo Del Toro, Ivan Reitman, Joe Dante, Paul Verhoeven, Wes Craven, Larry Cohen, Sydney J. Furie, Michael Wadleigh, Peter Medak, Mick Garris, Brad Anderson, Lewis Teague and Stuart Gordon. His first book, *Larry Cohen: The Stuff of Gods and Monsters*, was published by BearManor Media in 2015. He currently lives in Wales with his wife and two children.

Michael Doyle. Photo courtesy of Siân Doyle.

Index

Numbers in **bold** indicate photographs

10th Grade 699
11/22/63 407
21 Jump Street 623, 699
8 Million Ways to Die 417, 423-437, 439, 459, 711, 725

"Adams' Ribs" 348-352, 730-731
Adler, Stella 48
Adult Entertainment 80, 82, 720
Aiello III, Danny 373, 737
Aiello, Danny 366, 367, 369, 370, 371, 372, 373, 374, 375, 453, 722, 734, 737, 738
Aiello, Ricky 373, 738
Akinnuoye-Agbaje, Adewale 378, 737
Albert, Trevor 714
Alda, Rutanya 551, 552, 727
Aldrich, Robert 268
Alexander, Jane 26, 85
Allen, Dede 171
Allen, Jr., Herbert 181-182, 189, 195, 349
Allen, John 20
Allen, Sage **503**, 621, 622, 631, 729
Allen, Woody xii, 103, 160, 187, 295
Alley, Kirstie 695
Alonzo, John 205
Altman, Robert 151, 174, 294, 413
Alves, Joe 160, 242, 244, 245, 260, 261-262, 263, 268-269, 275
American Dreams: Lost and Found 684
American Steel 364, 709-711
Americans, The 382, 699, 701
Anderson, Lance 565, 727
Anderson, Richard 348, 731
Andrews, George 687
Ankri, Etti 520, 727
Ann-Margret 188
Anspach, Susan 41, 62, 63, 278
Antigone 26, 719
Arachnophobia 541, 542-543

Arbus, Allan 126-127
Arbus, Diane 127
Archer, Anne 518, 537
Arensberg, Ann xi, 51, 63, 104, 153, 174, 179, 189-191, 197
Arkin, Adam 199, 723
Arkoff, Louis **228**, 299-301, 302, 305, 723
Arkoff, Samuel Z. 288, 299-300, 302, 305, 723
Arnold, Chuck 387, 405, 735
Arquette, Rosanna 424, 434, 725
Arrangement, The 38
Arthur, Jean 65, 66-68, 85, 117
As You Like It 26, 719
Ashby, Hal 234, 417, 423-437, 711, 725
Ashley, Ted 106
Atherton, William 153
Atkins, Eileen 85
Atkinson, Brooks 611
Aubrey, Jim 512
Autograph Hound, The xii, xiv, 91
Avakian, Aram 50-51, 172, 372, 617-618
Ayers, Bill 704-705, 706

Baby Blue Marine 81, 128, 169, 179-216, **223**, **224**, 229, 232, 288, 291, 294, 296, 359, 459, 476, 515, 604, 645, 652, 723
Bad Seed, The 574
Badalamenti, Angelo 463, 464-465, 569, 612, 675-676, 726, 728, 729, 730
Badalato, Bill 109, 118, 123, 126, 159, 167, 261, 262, 268, 455-456, 457, 460, 461, 468, 477, 512, 590-591, 696, 713, 722, 726
Bailin, Bob 122-123, 160
Balaban, Bob 153
Balanchine, George 617
Baldwin, Robert 122-123, 244, 722
Bale, Christian 549, 713
Bananas xii, 103, 104

Bang the Drum Slowly xii, 42, 44, 63, 89, 91, 123, 143-177, 179, 180, 181, 184, 186, 189, 198, 203, 214, **220, 221, 222**, 229, 232, 244, 249, 282, 290, 296, 298, 316, 354, 360, 367, 371, 372, 394, 403, 433, 446, 447, 448, 449, 512, 519, 571, 574, 604, 606, 611, 645, 656, 672, 679, 722
Banham, Reyner 293
Barber, Andrea 393, 396, 733
Barnes, Bill 73, 77
Barnes, Clive 64, 442, 484
Barr, Tony 399
Bart, Peter 65, 187
Barth, John 48-49
Baumgarten, Craig 708
Beach Blanket Bingo 288, 305
Beatty, Warren 175, 285-286, 287, 424
"Bech Takes Pot Luck" 90
Beck, Julian 29, 30, 31, 32
Beckett, Samuel 27, 51, 84, 208, 439, 440, 442, 455, 467
Bedno, Scott 643
Begelman, David 182, 195, 542
Behler, Beth 622
Bellow, Saul 42, 56, 90
Ben-Ami, Yoram 511-512, 513, 514, 515-516, 520, 524-525, 535, 696, 697, 726
Benjamin, Bob 311
Bentley, Eric 24, 26, 27, 29, 37, 45, 197, 410, 471, 671
Bergen, Candice 47
Berger, Thomas 283
Bergman, Ingmar 18, 203
Bernstein, Bill 311, 326
Bernstein, Leonard 10, 172
Berridge, Elizabeth 263
"Best Boys" 375, 380, 738-739
Best of Enemies, The 688
Bethel, Del 162
Beyond the Valley of the Dolls 612
Big Wednesday 291
Billy Budd 17
Bisoglio, Val 92, 93, 95, 361, 721, 734
Bixby, Bill 353
Black, John 261
Black, Karen 450
Bladen, Barbara 443
Blalack, Robert 322
Blau, Herbert 51, 52, 53, 439, 440, 441
Block, Lawrence 424, 432, 725
Bochco, Steve 354, 355, 356-359, 733
Bogdanovich, Peter 83, 306
Bohemian Nights 368, 693-698, 720
Bounty, The 455

Boy on the Straight-Back Chair 68, 70-71, 117, 127, 721
Brazil, Scott 355, 357, 359, 376, 377, 733, 734, 737, 738
Brecht, Bertolt 22-23, 24, 25, 29, 30, 32, 37, 39, 40, 45, 46, 54, 55, 72, 208, 307, 470, 471
Brecht, Stefan 30, 69
Brenner, Marie 188
Brennert, Alan 386, 399, 732, 735, 736
Breuler, Robert 83, 595, 597, 598, 606, 625, 672, 728, 729
Bridges, James 277
Bridges, Jeff 425, 425, 428, 434, 436, 437, 725
Brodsky, Jack 187-189, 203, 286
Brother, The 80-83, 701, 720
Brown, Blair 77, 78
Brown, Bruce 291
Brown, David 106, 229, 231-232, 235, 236, 243, 246, 249, 252, 263, 266, 267
Brown, Georgia 695
Brown, Pat 440, 441
Brubaker, Jim 466-467
Brzezinski, Zbigniew 17
Bush, George W. 539, 540
Butler, Bill 243, 244
Butler, Michael 244-245, 259, 261, 264, 265, 266-268
Byrne, Bobby 206, **227**, 296-298, 723

Caan, James 153, 185
Caen, Herb 54
Cage, The 53, 440, 441, 442, 471-472, 475
Cagney, James 61, 107
California Dreaming 206, **227, 228**, 277-307, 314, 348, 416, 442, 545, 604, 652, 695, 723-724
Calvin, John 290, 294-295, 301, 303, 723, 724, 731
Cammell, Donald 517
Campbell, Carolee 93, 721
Cao, Victor 632, 729
Capra, Frank 106-107, 572
Caridi, Carmine 153
Carnival of Souls 114, 115
Carpenter, John 103, 105, 325
Carradine, Robert 293-294
Carren, David Bennett 393, 732
Casey, John 16, 138-139, 143
Cassel, Seymour 294, 295, 305, 724
Cather, Willa 131
Caucasian Chalk Circle, The 23-27, 719
Chaikin, Joseph 31, 36, 278
Chaikin, Judy 278
Chandler, Richard 65-66, 67-68

Chapman, Michael 242, 243
Chapman, Robert 17, 24, 25-26, 250, 658
Charles, Walter 467, 552, 726, 727
Charterhouse of Parma, The 179, 180-181
Chartoff, Robert 447, 450, 452-453, 466, 685
Chesnut, Mary Boykin 702
Chew, Richard 312, 319, 320, 344, 345
Childhood and Society 17-18, 689
China Syndrome, The 277, 278-279, 280, 281, 542
Christie, Julie 515, 516-517, 518, 524
Christopher, Dennis **227**, 294, 304, 724
Chulak, Christopher 368
Cimino, Michael 160, 449
Cina, Maria 624, 729
Clarke, Kit 93, 98, 189, 721
Clayburgh, Jill 42
Cluchey, Rick **227**, 439-443, 455, 461, 465, 466, 467, 470, 471-473, 475, 482, 483, 488
Clurman, Harold 27, 29, 48, 49, 52, 65, 66, 68, 172
Coburn, Arthur 319, 320, 323
Collins, Anne 411, 735
Coltrane, Robbie 375, 376, 377, 382
Comer, Anjanette 88
Conrad, Joseph 143-144
Conrad, Michael 33-34, 35, 200, 201, 359, 723
Conroy, Frances 408, 410, 414, 736
Constantine, Michael **499**, 551, 552, 727
Conte, Dino 453
Conti, Bill 353, 731
Conway, Kevin 153
Cooper, Gary 197
Copland, Aaron 172, 173
Corbett, Gretchen 116, 722
Corboy, Karen 263
Corman, Cis 456, 458, 459
Costello, Mariclare 117, 125, 126-127, 139, **218**, 722
Cover Up 347, 348, 349-352, 356, 366, 367, 369, 387, 418, 730-731
Cox, Nell 41-42, 44
Cracker 356, 374, 375-382, 468, 577, 589, 737, 738
Crawford, Cheryl 49, 64, 65
"Cried the Fox" 76
Cristofer, Michael 459
Crocker, James 386, 387, 732, 735, 736
Cronholm, Cary 697
Cross, Ben **495**, 516, 526, 537, 596, 727
Crowe, Russell 713
Cruise, Tom 152, 198, 515
Curtis, Jamie Lee 425, 695

Cusack, John 692
Cyrano de Bergerac 10

Daisy, Kelly 729
Daly, John 695
Daly, Tyne 595, 597, 600, 728
Damon, Mark 426, 429, 430, 431, 432, 453
Darrow, Tony 370, 373, 738
David, Saul 188
Davidson, Osha Gray 688
Davis, Jefferson 702
Day the Sun Fell, The 179, 191-193, 195
De Bont, Jan 335, 724
De Laurentiis, Dino 452, 455-456, 461, 482, 486, 487, 543, 547, 726
De Laurentiis, Federico 547
De Laurentiis, Raffaella 543-544, 545-548, 549-550, 561, 566, 570, 573, 574, 727
De Palma, Brian 41-42, 90, 107, 153, 435, 459
De Sica, Vittorio 207
Dead of Winter 468
Deason, Paul 387
Death Takes a Holiday 720
Deathwatch 441, 471-472
Deeley, Michael 453
Deer Hunter, The 16, 245-246, 247, 448, 449, 452, 453, 456, 552
DeGuere, Phil 385-386, 387, 388, 390, 414, 417, 418, 419, 420, 732, 735, 736
DeHaven, Carter 192, 193
Del Toro, Guillermo 544
Del Tredici, David 663-664, 729
Deliverance 173, 243, 615, 616, 632
Dellaventura 367, 370-375, 376, 378, 418, 577, 596, 737-738
Demon Seed 398, 516-517
DeMunn, Jeffrey 389, 390, 732
De Niro, Robert xii, 153-157, 158, 165, 166-167, 169, 171, 173, 174, 177, 186, 198, **220**, **222**, 246, 249, 265-266, 348-349, 364, 382, 429, 446, 447-453, 456, 459, 465-467, 486, 488, 515, 519, 552, 588, 635, 656, 722
Devine, George 43, 721
DeVivo, Tony 628
DeVore, Gary 455
Diller, Barry 106-107
Dillon, Melinda 450
Dine, Jim 49, 60
Doll's House, A 203, 621
Donavan, Thad 662
D'Onofrio, Vincent 713
Douglas, Michael 88, 278, 280, 518
Dowd, Nancy 233-234, 235

Drabinsky, Garth 546, 573, 676, 729
"Dreamers" 370-375, 737-738
Dreyfuss, Richard 246, 252, 265
Duane, Daniel 480-481
Duda, John 549, 727
Dukakis, Olympia 34, 36
Dunaway, Don Carlos 349-350, 730
Dunaway, Faye 26
Duncan, Chip 389, 390, 732
Duncan, Robert L. 179, 192
Durning, Charles xii, 57-58, 85, 92, 95, 159, 721
Duvall, Robert 151,
Duvall, Shelley 412, 413-414, 415, 416, 417, 736
Dwan, Allan 11
Dylan, Bob 42, 704

Eastwood, Clint 233, 268, 403, 426, 677
Ebert, Roger 174, 213-214, 215, 340, 485-486, 571, 609-612
Edson, Richard 623-624, 629
Edward II 23, 51, 54, 55, 56, 61, 719
Efron, Marshall xii, 92, 97, 101, 200, 248, 269, 595, 721, 722, 723, 724, 728
Elcar, Dana 269, 723
Elfstrom, Robert 93-94, 96, 721
Elliott, Sam **497**, **498**, 550-551, 557-558, 571, 687-688, 727
Ellis, C.P. 684-688
Ellison, Harlan 386, 387, 732
Emigrants, The 202
End of the Road, The 47-48, 49-50, 51, 60, 189, 202
Endgame 27, 159, 440, 442
Endicott and the Red Cross 48, 68-69, 70, 463, 720
Endless Summer, The 291
Erikson, Erik 7, 17
Ermey, R. Lee 377, 737, 738
Esterman, Laura **503**, 621-623, 626, 631, 632, 636, 729
Eternal Husband, The 48
Etheridge, Melissa 354, 462-463, 464, 488-489, 726, 731
Evans, Robert 140, 153, 187, 695
Evans, Sanford 97-98, 721

Fain, Johnny 290, 724
Falla, Jonathan 81
Fantastic Seven, The **226**
Fassbender, Michael 713
Father, The 56-57, 720
"Faustian Fitz" 382
Faustino, David 353, 731

Featherstone, Angela 377, 379-380, 737, 738
Feldman, Eli 577-578
Fields, Bert 642
Fields, Freddie 542
Fields, Verna 239-240, 252, 258, 260, 263-265, 268-269, 275, 316
Fine, Mark 87-88, 160, 278
Finney, Albert 316, 317, 328-329, 336, 343, 724
Fioramonti, Glory 368
Fire Academy 343
Fire Music 18, 429, 689-692, 698, 703, 711, 712
Fireman's Ball, The 343
Fisher, Carrie 191
Fisher, Gerry 335, 724
Fleckenstein, John 260, 261
Fletcher, Tom 661
Fonda, Jane 198, 278, 280, 364, 424
Ford, John 11, 107, 192, 196, 197, 609, 662
Foreman, Carl 88
Forfeit 179, 182-183, 185, 187, 195, 196, 700
Forman, Milos 263, 343
Forrest, Frederic 595, 597, 728
Forsythe, William 458-459
Foster, David 191
Foster, Phil 159, **221**, 722
Fournier, John 489
Fox, William Price 179, 183, 184
Fraker, William 160, 243, 296
Francis, Dick 47, 179, 182
Frand, Harvey 386, 387, 732, 735, 736
Franz, Dennis 354, 358, 361, 362, 733, 734
Freaking Out of Stephanie Blake, The 64-68, 70, 71, 117, 660, 721
Freeman, J.E. 626, 729
Friedkin, William 106, 182, 183, 245, 386, 388, 405, 420, 624, 700
Fuchs, Michael J. 512
Fugitive Days 704-709
Fulfillment, The 443
Full Metal Jacket 208, 377, 390
Funny Games 631

Gabai, Sasson 520, 727
Galecki, Johnny 549, 727
Galileo 23, 38, 39-40, 719
Gandolfini, James 382
Garber, Victor 352, 353, 731
Garcia, Andy 424, 434-435, 437, 459, 725
Gardenia, Vincent 158-159, 174, 177, **221**, 722
Garrity, Joseph 356, 726
Gary, Lorraine 237, 238, 239, 245, 248, 252, 275
Gavin, James 532, 534
Geffen, David 286

Index • 751

Gemignani, Paul 54, 100
Gemignani, Rhoda 100, 721
Generale Della Rovere 207
Genet, Jean 51, 441, 444, 455, 471, 472, 477
Gerber, David 366-367, 368, 734
Gere, Richard 201-202, **223**, 692, 723
Gerrold, David 414-415, 736
Giese, Kevin 697
Gilpen, Marc 269
Giorgio, Luis San 282
Glaessner, Verina 214, 215
Glass Menagerie, The 21, 53, 76, 79, 80, 719
Gleser, Kathy 632
Glory 279, 541-542, 701
Goldberg, Leonard 193, 198, 199, 205, 723
Goldberg, Whoopi 687-688
Golden, Dave 88, 160, 161
Goldstein, Jeffrey L. 356, 738
Goldwyn, Jr., Sam 588
Good Woman of Szechwan, The 23, 410
Goodbye Girl, The 157, 265
Gordon, Ruth 43-44
Gosling, Ryan 703
Gottlieb, Carl 230, 249, 262-263, 270-271
Graham, Donald E. 58-59, 89, 143, 181, 293
Grant, Cary 107, 453
Grapey, Marc 596, 597, 600, 602, 609, 728
Greenspun, Roger 135, 174
Grieco, Richard 623, 624, 629, 700
Grosbard, Ulu 41
Grossman, Dick 190
Grossman, Teddy 255
Guber, Peter 203-204
Guetti, Jim 89
Guillermin, John 455
Gunness, Belle 647-648
Guttenberg, Steve 270

Hackman, Gene 30, 449, 482
Hagen, Uta 408, 410, 736
Hagerty, Julie 695
Haid, Charles 354, 360, 363, 733, 734
Haigh, Kenneth 68, 69
Hail the Conquering Hero 207
Hall, Conrad 160, 243, 296
Hamel, Veronica 354, 363, 733, 734
Hamerow, Eleanor 97-98, 101
Hamill, Brian 372
Hamill, Pete 372
Hamilton, Anthony 350, 351-352, 367, 731
Hamilton, Murray 245, 248
Hamlin, Harry 77
Hancock, Ella Mae xiv, 1-3, 5, 6, 7, 8, 13, 15, 24, 138-139, 202, 307, 367, 452, 467, 546, 593, 604, 605

Hancock, Ralph 1, 2-3, 4, 5, 6-7, 8, 10, 12, 13, 15-16, 17, 21, 113-114, 136, 138, 368, 471, 546, 554, 592-593, 604, 605, 606, 666
Haneke, Michael 631
Hanfstaengl, Ernst 709, 711-713
Hanley, Barbara 456
Harbison, John 16
Hardy, Tom 713
Harrell, Rebecca 373, 454, **497**, **498**, **500**, **504**, 548, 549-550, 555-559, 564-565, 566, 571, 574, 596-597, 602, 608, 609, 612, 625, 655, 727, 728, 729, 738
Harris, Barbara 450, 467
Harris, Mark 144, 145, 146, 167, 722
Harrison, Linda 237, 238-239
Hartnett, Josh 377, 737, 738
Haunting, The 115, 630
Hausman, Howard 180
Hawn, Goldie 185, 695
Head, Kenn E. 697
Healing Spring, The 19, 719
Hecker, Scott 339
Heinz, John 57, 59
Heller, Joseph 281-282
Heller, Liz 441
Heller, Rosilyn 192
Helmond, Katherine 202, 723
Hemingway, Mariel **495**, **496**, 518-519, 522, 523, 537, 697, 727
Henderson, Cathy 456
Hendler, Gary 453
Henning, Joel 16
Henry V 18
Hepburn, Audrey 532
Heston, Charlton 104, 106
Hewes, Havelock 92-93, 721
Hewes, Henry 92
Hexum, Jon-Erik 348, 350-351, 352
Heyman, Barton 54, 62, 63-64, 92, 117, 137, 159, 200, **218**, 467-468, 722, 723, 724, 726
High School Undercover Story, The 699-700
Hiler, Robert J. 594, 618, 622, 624, 692, 698, 728, 729
Hill Street Blues 41, 81, 354-365, 369, 376, 378, 387, 389, 418, 543, 578, 624, 733-734
Hill, R. Lance 425
Hill, Walter 425, 429, 430
Hilton, Conrad 144
Hines, Gregory 317, 327, 724
Hitchcock, Alfred 115-116, 133
Hitzig, Rupert 309-310, 311, 312, 313, 315, 328, 329, 330, 332, 336, 341, 345, 724
Hoffman, Dustin 280, 286-287, 365

Holcomb, Sarah 263
Hood 701-703, 712
Horner, James 339, 724
How Green Was My Valley 11, 196, 197
Howard, Arliss 389, 390, 397, 732
Hudecek, Robert 368
Hudson, Ernie 457, 458, 484, 726
Hudson, Garth 464
Hutton, Lauren 189

I Had Three Wives 352-354, 418, 463, 731
"If She Dies" 393-398, 405, 406, 413, 414, 604, 732-733
Irons, Jeremy 713
Irving, Jules 51, 52, 441
It Drinks Hippie Blood 109, 111
It's a Wonderful Life 544

Jacobson, Buddy 371-372
Jaffe, Robert 399
Jagger, Mick 287
James, Clifton 37
Jannelli, Tony 372, 738
Janni, Joseph 234-235, 267
Jarre, Kevin 542
Jarre, Maurice 542, 568-569, 570-571, 727
Jaws 2 ix, xiii, 72, 106, 123, 126, 130, 160, 229-276, 277, 278, 279, 281, 299, 305, 306, 307, 315, 316, 343, 348, 427, 445, 451, 512, 543, 616, 634-635, 660, 700
Joe Hill 206
Johansson, Scarlet 703
John, Elton 294
Johnson, J.J. 460, 463, 726
Jonas, Norman see Kalcheim, Lee
Jones, Tommy Lee 153
Jonovich, Charemon 378
Jordan, Richard 77, 293
Joyce, James 13-14, 16-17, 22
Joyner, Tom 260
Judge of the Divorce Court, The 19, 719
Jungle, The 2
Juszkiewicz, Ryan 599

Kagan, Jeremy 704
Kahn, Michael 65, 721
Kalcheim, Lee 109, 111-112, 722
Kapnick, Arnold 360
Karlin, Fred 81-82, 128, 216, 300, 305, 724
Kassal, Connie 636
Katherine 704
Katsulas, Andreas **501**, 520, 595, 598, 601, 626, 727, 728
Katzenberg, Jeffrey 106, 542
Kaufman, Boris 161

Kaufman, Philip 268
Kazan, Elia 37-38, 41, 52, 161, 172, 658-659
Kazanoff, Ted 26
Kelly, Gene 12
Kendall, Monica 636
Kennedy, John F. 26, 30, 42, 47, 99, 153, 174, 291, 399-407, 483, 735
Kent, Allegra 617-618
"Kentucky Rye" 389-393, 394, 396, 397, 405, 406, 412, 416, 420, 731-732
Kiner, Ralph 164-165
King Kong 455
King Lear 157
King of Comedy, The 450
King, Alan 315, 724
King, Stephen 139, 386, 407
Kirby, Bruno 200, 201, **223**, 476, 723
Kirkland, Sally 450, 697
Kitch, Ken 52, 72, 74, 441, 442, 475, 479, 608, 726, 728, 729
Klansman, The 683-689, 690, 692
Klute 50, 202, 246, 278
Kmart 451, 577-578, 580, 590, 654
Kopit, Arthur 16, 92, 712
Kovacs, Laszlo 160, 205-206, 244, 296, 723
Kozoll, Michael 354, 357, 733
Kramer, Jeffrey 248-249
Krapp's Last Tape 440, 442, 467, 472
Kratina, Dick 160
Krim, Arthur 311, 326, 327, 333, 341
Kropf, Robert 83
Krzemien,, Richard 389, 390, 391, 732
Kubizek, August 690-691
Kubrick, Stanley 50, 208, 390, 413
Kuehn, Andrew J. 272

Lady Blue 365-369, 418, 734
Lahr, John xi-xiv, 63-64, 72, 76, 91, 92, 156, 516, 642, 670, 673, 684, 712, 721
Lampack, Peter 180
Lampert, Zohra 116-117, 127, 130, 132, **218**, 722
Landau, Nina 20-21, 24
Lansing, Robert 201
Lansing, Sherry 517, 607-608
Larson, Glen A. 347-348, 350, 730
Last Analysis, The 51, 55-56, 719
Last Picture Show, The 239, 289, 300, 305, 306, 553
Laub, Mark 372, 738
Lavigne, Bob 70, 119, 205, 723
Lavin, Linda 93
Lawrence, Bob 425-426, 427
Lawrence, Stephen 171, 172-173, 722
Lawson, Richard 695

Le Mat, Paul 550
Lea, Timothy see Wood, Christopher
Leachman, Cloris **500**, 552, 553, 727
Lean, David 12, 568, 570
Lebenzon, Chris 319, 320, 323, 724, 726
Leberfeld, Al 92, 721
Lee, Spike 265
Leigh, Vivien 658-659
Lemmon, Jack 278-279
Lenya, Lotte 40
Leonard, Jim 381, 737, 738
LeRoy, Mervyn 106, 574
Let's Scare Jessica to Death ix, 63, 71, 109-141, 143, 146, 159, 160, 164, 166, 169, 172, 174-175, 198, **218, 219, 220**, 258, 323, 342, 419, 546, 574, 604, 606, 611, 615, 616, 641, 644, 645, 664, 721-722
Leval, Pierre 189
Levin, Harry 16-17
Levin, Sid 301
Levine, Joseph E. 111
Levinson, Barry 515
Lewis, Daniel Day 597, 713
Lewis, Jeffrey 355, 733, 734
Lewis, Jenny 394, 396, 397, 733
Libertini, Richard 413, 414, 416, 419, 727, 736
Libin, Paul 59
"Library, The" 408-412, 416, 735-736
Liebman, Ron 153
Lithgow, John 153
Littman, Robert 192
Lo Bianco, Tony 393, 397, 398, 413, 414, 732
Logan, John 191
Long Voyage Home, The 11
Lookabaugh, Len 206
Looking Glass, The xiii, 80, 82, 164, 270, 364, 464, **504, 505, 506**, 512, 571, 589, 599, 604, 607, 649-682, 710, 729-730
Los Angeles: The Architecture of Four Ecologies 293
Louzil, Eric 608, 643
Lowell, Robert 48, 68, 69, 463, 720
Luciano, Michael 555, 728
Luck 365
Lumet, Sidney 705
Lund, Art 200-201, 212, 723

Mack, The 443, 472
MacMillan, Michael 418
MacRae, Heather 176, **222**, 722
"Madwoman" 375, 377, 378-380, 737
Malina, Judith 30, 31, 32
Malle, Louis 47
Mamet, David 365
Man Is Man 29, 31, 36

Man's a Man, A 23, 27, 29-39, 40, 42, 45, 48, 52, 57-59, 150, 173, 200, 286, 359, 719, 720
Mandell, Alan 441
Manhunter 456, 468, 486
Mann ist Mann 29
Mann, Michael 365
Mann, Ted 59, 60
Manson, Alan 62, 63, 65, 117, 159, 722
Manson, Charles 184
Mantegna, Joe 460, 463, 484, 726
Marie, Faith 660-661, 672, 680, 729, 730
Marinaro, Ed 358, 361, 733, 734
Marks, Richie 171-172
Marshall, Robert 642
Martin, Nan 393, 412, 414, 732, 736
Martin, Wendy Jo 599, 728
Mascolo, Joseph 269
Mattey, Robert 256-258
Matthaei, Gay 29, 30, 32, 49
Matthaei, Konrad 29, 30, 49
Max 692
May, Bradford 387, 397, 405, 732, 736
May, Elaine 80, 82, 720
McArthur, Alex 360, **502**, 624, 729, 733
McCain, John 706
McCombs, Matt 643
McCormick, Carolyn 377, 737, 738
McGovern, Jimmy 375, 376, 737, 738
Medavoy, Mike 309, 310, 311, 313-314, 315, 316, 318, 324-326, 332, 333, 339, 341, 343, 708, 724
Meehan, Thomas xii, 92, 721
Mellon, R.K. 58, 88
Melnick, Daniel 517
Memoirs xi, 53
Memory of Two Mondays, A 720
Mendell, Toni 101, 721
Mendes, Sam 620
Mengers, Sue 455
Meyers, Fred 624-625, 632, 729
Meyjes, Menno 692
Midsummer Night's Dream, A xi, 23, 54, 57, 59, 61, 64, 65, 92, 208, 278, 720
Milch, David 355, 357, 358, 362, 365, 543, 733, 734
Milius, John 291, 386
Milk Train Doesn't Stop Here Anymore, The xi, 39, 42-44, 52, 53, 69, 720, 721
Mingalone, Dick 160
Minkler, Mike 339
Minnelli, Liza 185, 448, 452
Miracle on 34th Street 106, 545
Mirisch, Larry 696
Misalliance 26

Modor, Mike 297
Moehl, Jim 697
Molina, Alfred 514, 516, 531
Moriarty, Michael 153, 154-155, 156-158, 161-162, 169, 177, 198, **220**, **222**, 722
Morrow, Vic 534
Mosk, Edward 312-313, 339
Moss, Jr., Charlie 109, 111, 112, 118, 123, 124, 126, 135, 166, 258, 722
Mother Courage 23, 37, 46, 54-55, 117, 317
Motherkill 234-235
Mulvehill, Charles 426
Musselwhite, Harry 659, 730
My Ántonia 131

Naïves hirondelles 46, 47
Nasitar, Marcia 184
Nathan, Vivian 34, 35
Neil, Julian 370, 737, 738
Nelkin, Stacey 295, 724
Nerve 47, 93, 182
Newman, Ed 636
Newman, Paul 149, 620
Nichols, Mabel 639, 671
Nichols, Mike 265
'night Mother 80, 82, 83, 701, 720
Night of the Iguana 76
Night of the Living Dead 114-115
"Nightcrawlers" 388, 394
Noises Off 80, 83-84, 720
Nolte, Nick xiii, 251, 365, 367, 425, 452, 453-456, 458-459, 460, 461, 462, 470, 480, 484, 485-486, 488, **490**, 555, 584, 586, 593, 679, 687, 688, 689, 726
Noonan, Tom 317, 456, 724
Noone, Peter 81
Norris, Melanie 372, 374, 738
Notkoff, Bobby 10

O'Bannon, Rockne S. 386, 732, 735, 736
O'Casey, Sean 22, 719
O'Connor, Dennis 535, 726, 727, 728, 729
O'Connor, Glynnis 200, 206, 216, **225**, 294, 295, 304, 306, 696, 723, 724
O'Connor, Kevin 70, 117, **218**, 722
O'Neill, Dick 333-334, 724
O'Neill, Eugene 11, 60, 65, 67, 79, 721
O'Neill, Jennifer 348, 349, 731
Obama, Barrack 706, 707, 708
Obst, Lynda 286
Oh! What a Lovely War 49, 65, 81
"Oh, You Kid" 357-361, 363, 364, 733
Olivier, Laurence 18, 328, 658
Olmos, Edward James 317, 327-328, 332, 459, 724

Omen, The 235, 331
On the Waterfront 161, 172
Ornitz, Arthur 160-161
Otto, Linda 202
Outlaw Josey Wales, The 268

Pacino, Al 176, 447
Palitzsch, Peter 27
Palmer, Linda 453
Panzica, Anthony **507**, 659, 730
Pappé, Stuart 320, 323, 426, 432, 724, 725
Parks, Larry 197
Pastorelli, Robert 374, 377, 378-380, 381-382, 737, 738
Patinkin, Mandy 456
Peaslee, Richard 463, 726
Peck, Gregory 88-89, 104, 331, 532
Penn, Arthur 184-185, 188, 244, 468
Perry, Alex Ross 140
Perry, Eleanor 354
Perry, Felton 377-378, 477, 695, 726, 733
Perry, Frank 354
Pesci, Joe 382, 514, 519
Peterson, Lenka 200
Peterson, Roy 301, 723
Petty, Lori 408, 410, 414, 736
Pickren, Stacey 287
Piece of Eden, A xiii, 164, 382, 453, **501**, 520, 546, 577-613, 615, 618, 619, 625, 626, 642, 643, 646, 651, 652, 653, 654, 659, 667, 672, 675, 680, 681, 693, 728
Pinter, Harold 35, 51, 84
Playten, Alice 295-296, 724
Pleskow, Eric 326
Plough and the Stars, The 22, 719
Polanski, Roman 147, 184
Poledouris, Basil 407, 735
Police Academy 343
Poll, Martin **226**, 279-280
Pollack, Sydney 147, 286
Pollock, Tom 232
Poole, Bobby 443, 444, 446, 459, 460, 472, 476
Porter, Bobby 564-565
Potter, Marcia 555
Prancer 123, 126, 337, 369, 373, 395, 464, **497**, **498**, 541-575, 577, 590, 594, 596, 599, 602, 604, 610, 611, 618, 619, 627, 646, 652, 655, 675, 676, 693, 697, 727-728
Price, Arthur 357
"Profile in Silver" 398-408, 409, 414, 416, 418, 420, 457, 604, 735
Prosky, Robert 359, 360, 361, 733, 734
Puckett, Jeff 82, 600, 654, 659, 697, 710, 728, 729, 730
Putzi 709, 711-713

Index • 755

Queen of Earth 140

Radical 708-709
Raggedy Man 191
Raging Bull 155, 186, 243, 446, 447, 449, 451, 456, 519
Rampling, Charlotte 514, 518
Ramsey, Anne 373, 460-461, 474, 736
Ramsey, Logan 460
Ransohoff, Marty 151
Raposo, Joe 37, 173
Redford, Robert 151
Reed, Carol 12
Regiment of Women 283, 284-287, 683
Reilly, John C. 713
Remsen, Bert 202, 723
Resistible Rise of Arturo Ui, The 27, 37, 45
Resurrection of Broncho Billy, The 103, 105
Rhames, Ving 457-458
Rhodes, Shari 246, 249
Richards, Ariana 549, 727
Richardson, Tony 39, 42, 43, 88
Richter, W.D. "Rick" 185, 187, 188, 192-193
Riefenstahl, Leni 712
Rimbaud, Arthur 71-72, 75, 76, 109
Rise and Fall of the City of Mahagonny 40
Ritchie, Michael 30-31, 175, 184
Rivkin, Elaine 83
Road to Perdition, The 620
Robbins, Jerome 35, 37, 117, 317
Roberts, Julia 515
Roberts, Tanya 295, 724
Robinson, Andrew 153, 400, 403, 735
Rockwell, Norman 211, 212
Rodriguez, Domingo 163, 722
Rogers, Tristan 596, 598, 728
Roisman, Owen 243
Rolston, Mark 460, 519-520, 531, 551, 552, 697, 726, 727
Roman Holiday 532
Rose, Jamie 365, 367, 368, 369, 734
Rosenberg, Howard 353, 536-537
Rosenfield, Lois 147, 159, 167, 722
Rosenfield, Maurice 144-149, 152, 153, 157, 159, 163, 165-170, 171, 172, 173, 175, 722
Ross, Ted 456
Rossellini, Roberto 18, 207
Roth, Steve 425, 429-430
Rourke, Mickey 453
Ruby Red 176, 179, 183, 184-188, 189, 193, 195, 196, 447, 683
Rudd, Mark 707
Rudin, Scott 712
Ruffalo, Mark 713

Ruginis, Vyto 434, 725
Running on Empty 704-705
Running the Wild Red 191
Rydell, Mark 91

Sackler, Howard 230, 231, 233, 235, 236, 237, 239, 240, 270, 271, 272, 700
Sadwith, James Steven 376-378, 381, 737, 738
Safan, Craig 338-339
Saint Joan 66
Salmi, Albert 149, 150
Sands of Iwo Jima 11, 208
Sarandon, Susan 450
"Saucer of Loneliness, The" 412-418, 736
Sawyer, Nancy 268, 269
Scarfiotti, Ferdinando 205
Scenes from a Marriage 281
Schaffer, Peter 180-181
Scheider, Roy 245-247
Schickel, Richard 42, 174, 175
Schneider, Alan 27, 29, 35-36
Schroeder, Ricky 249, 268, 269-270
Schulman, J. Neil 149, 398-399, 400, 401, 404, 406-408, 735
Schwartz, Alan 68, 179, 281, 282, 452-453, 586
"Scorpio's Sting" 366-369, 734
Scorsese, Martin 107, 158, 243, 315, 447, 449, 450, 464
Scott, George C. 181
Scott, Tony 512, 533
Sear, Walter 128-129, 722
Searls, Hank 270
Seaton, George 106
Selznick, Daniel 191
Serling, Rod 262, 385, 386, 392, 393, 419, 420, 421, 731, 732, 735, 736
Serpent's Egg, The 203
Shannon, Michael 713
"Shatterday" 394
Shayne, Alan 354
Sheinberg, Sidney 236-238, 239, 240, 256, 257, 258, 264-265, 266, 267-268, 274, 275-276, 307, 573, 676
Shelmerdine, Mark 418
Sherman, Bob 313-314, 324, 335, 339, 341
Shiloa, Yossi 519, 727
Shiloach, Joseph see Shiloa, Yossi
Shining, The 413
Shmuger, Marc 468
Shore, Richard 159-160, 161, 244, 722
Short, Bobby 172
Shut Up...I'm Crying 103, 105
Sikking, James B. 354, 361, 733, 734
Simon, John 51
Simon, Neil 67, 157

Sinclair, Upton 2
Singer, Carla 353-354, 399, 731
Slap Shot 233-234
Sloss, John 642
Smith, Arthur "Guitar Boogie" 173
Smith, Lane 399, 403, 404, 457, 457, 726, 735
Snipes, Wesley 695
Solin, Harvey 34-35
Somerville, Geraldine 377
Something Happened 281, 282
Spacek, Sissy 185, 191, 704
Spano, Joe 361, 733, 734
Spelling, Aaron 193, 198, 199, 205, 352, 723
Spielberg, Steven 229, 230, 232, 233, 236, 238, 239, 241-242, 243, 244, 245, 246, 249, 252, 253, 254, 256, 257, 261, 262, 272, 333, 542, 543, 549, 557, 570, 572, 692, 708
Spikings, Barry 452, 453, 546
Spinotti, Dante 468
Springer, Gary 270
Springer, John 175, 180
St. Paule, Irma 595-596, 598, 728
Stark, Ray 180, 184, 185, 187
Starr, Mike 555
Steal the Sky 337, **495, 496**, 509-540, 541, 545, 560, 563, 577, 596, 612, 696, 726-727
Stern, Bert 617
Stevens, George 66, 67, 89, 104, 105, 106, 282
Stevens, Liz 104, 105, 282
Sticky My Fingers, Fleet My Feet xii, 71, 87-108, 109, 110, 111, 117, 121, 127, 143, 146, 161, 162, 164, 169, 174, 181, 282, 361, 462, 512
Stock, Alan 250, 269
Stoeber, Orville 70, 96, 127, 164, 172, 447, 462, 463, **507**, 569, 612, 663, 721, 722, 726, 728, 729
Stone, Oliver 309, 339, 424, 432, 725
Stopped Rocking 53, 75-77, 78
Storm, The 29, 30, 719
Strasberg, Lee 49
Streep, Meryl 448
Streetcar Named Desire, A 79, 80, 287, 658
Streisand, Barbra 180, 187, 456
Strieber, Whitley 309, 310, 317, 319, 331, 724
Strindberg, August 56, 720
Stubble Trouble 636
Sturgeon, Theodore 386, 412, 413, 414, 415, 417, 736
Sturges, Preston 207
Subotnick, Morton 128
"Subterranean Homesick Blues" 704
Suchet, David 514, 516, 531
Surovy, Nicolas 519, 722, 727

Suslov, Misha **498, 499**, 560, 599, 654, 661, 697, 726, 727, 728, 729
Suspended Animation xiii, 80, 82, 301, 360, 368, **502, 503**, 589, 604, 607, 612, 615-648, 649, 651, 652, 653, 654, 660, 661, 666, 671, 677, 692, 698
Svec, Lillian 14, 15, 19
Sylbert, Paul 312, 326-327, 724
Sylbert, Richard 327
Szwarc, Jeannot 248, 249, 254, 256, 262, 267, 269, 272-274, 386

Taggart, Rita 251, 460, **492**, 726
Tandy, Jessica 658
Tanen, Ned 252, 263
Tarnow, Grace **504, 505, 507**, 654, 655, 656-657, 662-663, 665, 676, 678, 679, 680, 730
Tate, Sharon 184
Tavel, Ronald 70-71, 721
Taylor, Greg 543, 544, 546, 571, 573, 727
Tennant, Bill 184
Terkel, Studs 684
Thaler, Todd 372
Thatcher, Sophie 655-656
Third Man, The 12
Thirty Years of Treason 197
Thomas, Betty 354, 362-363, 733, 734
Thomas, Kevin 485, 571, 643, 645
Thomas, Richard 198
Thompson, Hunter S. 387
Thornton, Jim 599
Three Sisters 19, 720
Tidyman, Ernest 182-183, 185, 700
Toles-Bey, John 459-460, 606, 697, 726
Tolland, Gregg 11
Tootsie 286-287
Top Gun 123, 456, 512, 521
Topakana Martyrs' Day 80-82, 720
Toth, George 329, 334, 335
Towne, Robert 425, 432, 433, 725
Travanti, Daniel J. 354, 363-364, 365, 733, 734
Travis, Neil 264
Tristan, Dorothy xiii, 50-51, 71, 73-74, 81, 83, 85, 127, 144, 176, 180, 190, 202, 203, 210, 231, 234, 235, 236, 237-238, 239, 247, 250-251, 252, 253, 254, 263, 266, 267, 268, 270, 271-272, 273, 277, 278, 283, 284, 287, 293, 294, 295, 296, 305-306, 347, 354, 355, 395, 439, 442, 443, 444, 445, 446, 447, 448, 449-450, 452, 453, 458, 460, 461, 466, 467, 472, 473, 474, 475, **504, 506, 507**, 513, 514, 517, 523, 524, 525-526, 528, 532, 545, 546, 573, 575, 579-580, 581, 582, 584, 585,

Index • 757

586, 587, 588, 589, 590, 591, 594, 597, 605, 606, 607, 611, 612, 616, 617-618, 621, 622, 624, 629, 631, 632, 633, 634, 635-636, 637, 638, 639, 640, 642, 646, 647, 648, 649, 651, 652, 653, 654, 655, 656, 657, 658, 661, 662, 663, 665, 666, 667, 668, 669, 670-671, 672, 673, 674, 676, 678, 680, 681, 686, 687, 688, 689, 694, 695, 696-697, 698, 700, 703, 708, 720, 724, 726, 727, 728, 729, 730
Truitt, Stephen 16
Tsikurishvili, Irina 657, 664, 730
Turman, Lawrence 191
Turn of the Screw, The 115
Turner, Allen **506**, 668, 713-714, 729, 730
Tweed, Shannon 517-518
Twilight Zone, The 81, 153, 353, 365, 369, 385-421, 457, 519, 534
Twilight Zone: The Movie 385, 534
Two-Character Play, The

Ufland, Harry 450
Ullmann, Liv 202-203
Ulysses 13-14
Under Western Eyes 143-144
Unheard Witness 711
Updike, John 90

Valenti, Jack 104
Van Patten, Jimmy 290, 295, 299, 724
Van Zandt, Billy 271
Veitch, John 192
Venora, Diane 316, 317, 320, 323, 325, 327, 336, 338, 724
Vigoda, Abe 56, 61, 552, 727
Vincent, Jan-Michael 198-199, 204, 213, **223**, 294, 295, 723
"Virgin and the Turkey, The" 361-364, 733-734
Virgin Spring, The 629-630
Voight, Jon 269, 287, 424, 708
Von Rhau, Lee 70, 721
Von Sydow, Max 202, 629
Vorisek, Richard 128, 171, 172

Wadleigh, Michael 309-319, 320-322, 323, 324-325, 326-327, 328, 329-330, 331, 332, 333, 334, 335, 336, 338, 339, 340, 341, 342, 343-345, 430, 724
Wagner, Paula 695
Wagner, Lindsay 189-191, 193, 200
Wagner, Roy H. 468, 737, 738
Waiting for Godot 439-441, 444, 467-468, 472
Walton, Ortiz Montaigne 4
Waltons, The 197, 198

Ward, B.H. 697
Ward, Robert 364, 711, 729, 733, 734
Wardlow, David 252, 277, 286, 287, 366
Warhol, Andy 70
Warren, Michael 354, 361, 733, 734
Washbourne, Deric 16
Waterston, Sam 203
Wedgeworth, Ann 165, **222**, 722
Weeds xiii, 81, 123, 155, 164, **227**, 251, 320, 347, 348-349, 354, 356, 365, 367, 368, 378, 387, 417, 429, 435, 437, 439-489, **490**, **493**, **494**, 511, 512, 515, 519, 533, 541, 542, 543, 544, 545, 552, 555, 560, 563, 571, 574, 577, 590, 599, 604, 606, 607, 611, 619, 624, 635, 665, 666, 673, 675, 676, 679, 683, 685, 687, 689, 690
Weigel, Helene Helli 22, 30, 45-46
Weill, Kurt 40
Weincke, Jan 468, 726
Weisberg, Joe 698-701
Weitz, Bruce 354, 360-361, 733, 734
Welch, Raquel 450
Welden, Rosemary 514, 619, 620
Whalen, Kenneth 443
Whitehead, Robert 52
Whitmore, Stanford 154, 193, 194, 195, 209, 214, **224**, 723
Whittaker, Chris 302, 723
Widerberg, Bo 206
Wild Duck, The 30, 40, 449
Wilkerson, Cathy 704, 707
Willett, Susan 549, 552, 578, 589, 619, 620, 655, 728
Williams, Gene xii, 90, 91, 92, 95, 96, 99, 721
Williams, John 570
Williams, Rose 72, 76
Williams, Tennessee xi, xiv, 21, 39, 42, 43, 52-54, 67, 69, 71-80, 89, 148, 460, 611, 719, 720, 721
Williams, Treat 153
Willis, Bruce 361
Willis, Gordon 50, 160, 243, 261
Wilson, Bill 93, 97, 721
Wilson, Keith 521, 727
Winkler, Irwin 186, 447, 448, 449, 450, 451, 452, 453, 466
Wise, Robert 115
Wishman, Seymour 641, 642, 677
Wizan, Joe 91
Wizard of Lies, The 515
Wolfen 309-345, 426-427, 429, 430, 431, 456, 459, 604, 616
Women Speak 278
Wood, Christopher 513, 529, 726
Woods, James 153

Woodstock 310, 315, 324
Woodward, Bob 365
Words and Music 12
Woyzeck 19, 719
"Wrecker, The" 42,, 90
Wyler, Catherine 111, 190
Wyler, William 11, 111, 190
Wynn, Ned 288, 289-290, 291, 296, 298, 306, 695, 723, 724

Yablans, Frank 134, 176, 185, 187, 189
Yanni 535-536, 727
York, Michael 598
"You and I Know" 353, 731
Young Hitler I Knew, The 690

Zanuck, Richard D. 105, 130, 229, 231, 232, 235, 236, 237, 238, 239, 240, 243, 246, 249, 251, 252, 255, 256, 258, 263, 266, 267, 274, 275, 293
Zarlengo, Dan 599
Zieff, Howard 296
Ziskind, Margery 20, 24, 26, 41
Zonis, Marvin 521
Zsigmond, Vilmos 160, 243, 261
Zwick, Edward 542

www.ingramcontent.com/pod-product-compliance
Lightning Source LLC
Chambersburg PA
CBHW071428300426
44114CB00013B/1350